THE ENGLISH RUGBY

WHO'S WHO

NEIL FISSLER & ADAM HATHAWAY

First published in Great Britain in 2024
Copyright © Victor Publishing 2024
Neil Fissler and Adam Hathaway have asserted their right under the Copyright, Designs and Patents Act 1988
to be identified as the author of this work.
All rights reserved. No part of this publication may be reproduced, distributed, or transmitted in any form or by any means, including photocopying, recording, or other electronic or mechanical methods, without the prior written permission of the authors.
All information in this publication correct as at 1st January 2024. Whilst every effort has been made to ensure all information contained in this publication is accurate and correct, the author or publishers can not be held responsible for any errors or ommisions which, if found, they will endeavour to update/rectify.

www.victorpublishing.co.uk

ISBN: 9798869593436

THE ENGLISH RUGBY

WHO'S WHO

ACKNOWLEDGEMENTS

A book like this would not be impossible without the help of a great many people who have gone above and beyond to give their time to answer queries, offer information, and expertise.

We would especially like to thank John Griffiths for his unwavering encouragement and for allowing us to pillage his records collated over many years. JG, we would never have got this far without your help.

Our thanks also go to Steve Bale, Huw Richards, Stephen Jones (Jack), Jon Newcombe, The Staff of the British Newspaper Library, Dave Swanton, Alan Joseph, Graham McKechnie, Michael Turner, Andy Wilson, Mark Stevens, Mike Bulpitt, Hilda Jackson, Mark Smith, Rob Kitson, Stuart Barnes, Phil Mitchell, Brendan Gallagher, Matt and Sam Emery, Nick Greenstock of ERIC (England Rugby Internationals Club), Hugh Godwin and Lawrence Dallaglio.

We would also like to give a special mention Merv Payne, and his team at Victor Publishing for their expertise in finally getting this project into print.

PLAYERS IN CAP ORDER

For an alphabetical index of players, please see page 230

#	Name	#	Name	#	Name
1	John Bentley	71	Mark Bulteel	141	Wilfred Bolton
2	Reginald Birkett	72	Charles Clark	142	Herbert Fuller
3	Benjamin Burns	73	John Graham	143	James Hunt
4	John Clayton	74	Walter Greg	144	Bernard Middleton
5	Charles Crompton	75	Charles Gunner	145	Aubrey Spurling
6	Alfred Davenport	76	Spencer Login	146	Philip Newton
7	John Dugdale	77	Ernest Marriott	147	John Payne
8	Arthur Gibson	78	Edward Turner	148	William Tatham
9	Joseph Green	79	Courteney Verelst	149	Arthur Evanson
10	Arthur Guillemard	80	Arthur Heath	150	Robert Henderson
11	Alfred Hamersley	81	William Hunt	151	Richard Kindersley
12	Harry Luscombe	82	William Hutchinson	152	Alan Rotherham
13	Arthur Lyon	83	Frederic Lee	153	Graham Standing
14	William MacLaren	84	William Rawlinson	154	Arthur Taylor
15	Richard Osborne	85	Thomas Tetley	155	Greg Wade
16	Charles Sherrard	86	George Turner	156	Charles Wooldridge
17	Frederic Stokes	87	Henry Fowler	157	Edward Moore
18	Frank Tobin	88	Gillie Harrison	158	Richard Pattisson
19	Dawson Turner	89	Monkey Hornby	159	Henry Tristram
20	Henry Turner	90	Petley Price	160	Charles Chapman
21	Thomas Batson	91	Charles Touzel	161	Charles Marriott
22	James Body	92	Harry Garnett	162	Edmund Strong
23	James Bush	93	Archibald Law	163	Henry Bell
24	Fred Currey	94	Robert Todd	164	Herbert Fallas
25	Francis d'Aguilar	95	John Biggs	165	Charles Sample
26	Stephen Finney	96	Frank Fowler	166	Alfred Teggin
27	Harold Freeman	97	Howard Fowler	167	Henry Wigglesworth
28	Francis Isherwood	98	Temple Gurdon	168	Albert Wood
29	Frank Luscombe	99	Henry Kayll	169	Edward Court
30	James Mackinlay	100	George Thomson	170	John Hawcridge
31	Frederick Mills	101	George Vernon	171	Arthur Kemble
32	William Moberly	102	John Bell	172	Henry Ryalls
33	Nipper Pinching	103	Thomas Blatherwick	173	Frank Moss
34	Percy Wilkinson	104	Jimmy Budd	174	Drewy Stoddart
35	Cecil Boyle	105	Ernest Dawson	175	Charles Horley
36	Ernest Cheston	106	Henry Enthoven	176	Fred Bonson
37	William Fletcher	107	Herbert Gardner	177	William Clibborn
38	Henry Lawrence	108	Allan Jackson	178	Charles Elliot
39	Henry Marsh	109	William Penny	179	Froude Hancock
40	Murray Marshall	110	George Burton	180	Rupert Inglis
41	Sydney Morse	111	Harry Huth	181	George Jeffery
42	Cyril Rickards	112	Norman McLeod	182	Rawson Robertshaw
43	Ernest Still	113	Stuart Neame	183	Edgar Wilkinson
44	Charles Vanderspar	114	Hugh Rowley	184	Norman Spurling
45	John Batten	115	Henry Springmann	185	Rev Brutton
46	Marshall Brooks	116	Henry Taylor	186	Hiatt Baker
47	Henry Bryden	117	Harold Bateson	187	Charles Cleveland
48	William Collins	118	William Openshaw	188	John Dewhurst
49	Charles Crosse	119	Henry Twynam	189	John Hickson
50	Foster Cunliffe	120	Sidney Ellis	190	John le Fleming
51	James Genth	121	Thomas Fry	191	Dicky Lockwood
52	Edward Kewley	122	Charles Gurdon	192	Sam Roberts
53	William Milton	123	Robert Hunt	193	Bob Seddon
54	Sidney Parker	124	Barron Kilner	194	Arthur Fagan
55	William Stafford	125	Ellis Markendale	195	Frank Pease
56	Roger Walker	126	John Schofield	196	Mason Scott
57	Frank Adams	127	Ernie Woodhead	197	Charles Anderton
58	Edward Fraser	128	Charles Coates	198	Harry Bedford
59	Harry Graham	129	Richard Finch	199	John Cave
60	William Hutchinson	130	Charles Phillips	200	Frank Evershed
61	Arthur Michell	131	Charles Sawyer	201	Donald Jowett
62	Edward Nash	132	Charles Fernandes	202	Fred Lowrie
63	Alec Pearson	133	Walter Hewitt	203	Arthur Robinson
64	Edward Perrott	134	John Ravenscroft	204	Arty Royle
65	Lennard Stokes	135	Ryder Richardson	205	William Scott
66	Louis Birkett	136	James Ward	206	John Sutcliffe
67	Wyndham Evanson	137	Harry Vassall	207	Harry Wilkinson
68	Josiah Paul	138	Charles Wilson	208	William Yiend
69	Jeaffreson Brewer	139	Frank Wright	209	Richard Budworth
70	Charles Bryden	140	Teddy Beswick	210	Francis Fox

#	Name	#	Name	#	Name
211	Willie Mitchell	291	George Hughes	371	Bernard Oughtred
212	Dolly Morrison	292	Edward Knowles	372	Henry Weston
213	John Rogers	293	Bob Poole	373	Denys Dobson
214	Jim Valentine	294	William Ashford	374	George Fraser
215	Samuel Woods	295	Francis Byrne	375	John Jewitt
216	James Wright	296	Percy Ebdon	376	Philip Nicholas
217	Randolph Aston	297	Tom Fletcher	377	John Raphael
218	Jack Dyson	298	Frederick Jacob	378	Leonard Tosswill
219	Edgar Holmes	299	Roland Mangles	379	Thomas Willcocks
220	Jack Toothill	300	Robert Oakes	380	Samuel Williams
221	William Spence	301	Wilfred Stoddart	381	Peter Hardwick
222	Frederic Alderson	302	Frank Stout	382	Thomas Simpson
223	John Berry	303	William Bunting	383	Robert Bradley
224	William Bromet	304	Samuel Northmore	384	Vincent Cartwright
225	Percy Christopherson	305	Tot Robinson	385	James Duthie
226	Tom Kent	306	John Taylor	386	Frankie Hulme
227	William Leake	307	James Davidson	387	Jack Miles
228	Eustace North	308	Herbert Dudgeon	388	Reginald Spooner
229	James Richards	309	Osbert Mackie	389	Walter Heppel
230	Roger Wilson	310	Joseph Blacklock	390	Basil Hill
231	Launcelot Percival	311	Philip Jacob	391	Edward Barrett
232	Edgar Bonham-Carter	312	Harry Myers	392	Walter Butcher
233	Alfred Allport	313	Richard Pierce	393	Edward Dillon
234	Arthur Briggs	314	Fred Shaw	394	Patrick Hancock
235	Ned Bullough	315	Charles Wilson	395	George Keeton
236	Charles Emmott	316	William Pilkington	396	Jumbo Milton
237	George Hubbard	317	Harold Ramsden	397	Norman Moore
238	William Nicholl	318	Arthur Rotherham	398	Charles Newbold
239	James Pyke	319	Percy Royds	399	William Cave
240	Wardlaw Thomson	320	James Shaw	400	Thomas Gibson
241	Abel Ashworth	321	Percy Stout	401	Sam Irvin
242	Samuel Houghton	322	Geoffrey Unwin	402	John Mathias
243	James Marsh	323	Robert Livesay	403	Francis Palmer
244	Ernest Taylor	324	John Daniell	404	Walter Rogers
245	Harry Bradshaw	325	Joseph Davidson	405	John Green
246	Thomas Coop	326	Reggie Forrest	406	William Grylls
247	Harry Varley	327	Herbert Gamlin	407	Harry Shewring
248	Tom Broadley	328	George Gibson	408	Christopher Stanger-Leathes
249	Robert de Winton	329	Charles Harper	409	George Vickery
250	Edwin Field	330	William Mortimer	410	Curly Hammond
251	John Greenwell	331	Stanley Anderson	411	Sidney Osborne
252	Frederick Lohden	332	Arthur Darby	412	Adrian Stoop
253	Howard Marshall	333	John Shooter	413	Jacky Braithwaite
254	Philip Maud	334	Aubrey Dowson	414	Dai Gent
255	Horace Duckett	335	Reginald Hobbs	415	Reginald Godfray
256	Thomas Nicholson	336	John Matters	416	Alfred Hind
257	Frederic Jones	337	Reginald Schwarz	417	Henry Imrie
258	John Robinson	338	Bim Baxter	418	John Jackett
259	Buster Soane	339	Fred Bell	419	Richard Russell
260	Cyril Wells	340	Robert Bell	420	George Summerscale
261	Fred Byrne	341	Arthur Brettargh	421	George Dobbs
262	Frederick Firth	342	William Cobby	422	Harold Hodges
263	John Hall	343	Arthur Cockerham	423	Arthur Hudson
264	Charles Hooper	344	Sydney Coopper	424	Raphael Jago
265	Samuel Morfitt	345	Gerald Gordon-Smith	425	Thomas Kelly
266	Harry Speed	346	Wallace Jarman	426	Alf Kewney
267	William Tucker	347	George Marsden	427	William Mills
268	Bob Wood	348	Elliot Nicholson	428	James Hutchinson
269	Albert Elliott	349	Shirley Reynolds	429	Cecil Milton
270	Walter Jackson	350	Charles Scott	430	Joseph Sandford
271	William Walton	351	Harry Alexander	431	John Birkett
272	Edward Baker	352	John Marquis	432	Robert Dibble
273	Godfrey Carey	353	Alexander Todd	433	Jimmy Peters
274	Dick Cattell	354	Arthur Luxmoore	434	Cecil Shaw
275	John Fegan	355	Edgar Elliot	435	Thomas Hogarth
276	Horace Finlinson	356	Nigel Fletcher	436	Arnold Alcock
277	Frederick Leslie-Jones	357	Charles Gibson	437	Freddie Brooks
278	Frank Mitchell	358	David Graham	438	Tremlett Batchelor
279	Francis Poole	359	Arthur O'Neill	439	John Hopley
280	Charles Thomas	360	Ernest Roberts	440	Danny Lambert
281	Herbert Ward	361	John Sagar	441	Harry Lee
282	Thomas Dobson	362	Whacker Smith	442	Billy Nanson
283	Ernest Fookes	363	Elliott Vivyan	443	Andrew Slocock
284	Lyndhurst Giblin	364	Katie Walton	444	Thomas Wedge
285	John Pinch	365	Charley Hall	445	Frank Scott
286	John Rhodes	366	Robert Wood	446	Jumbo Leather
287	Anthony Starks	367	Norman Cox	447	Arthur Pickering
288	John Ward	368	Charles Edgar	448	Walter Wilson
289	Willie Whiteley	369	Jock Hartley	449	Andrew Newton
290	James Baron	370	Toggie Kendall	450	Khaki Roberts

451	Sydney Start	530	Francis Steinthal	609	John Worton
452	Patsy Boylen	531	George Ward	610	Thomas Devitt
453	Ernest Chambers	532	Arthur Dingle	611	Leslie Haslett
454	Harry Havelock	533	Alfred Kitching	612	Bill Tucker
455	Walter Lapage	534	Francis Oakeley	613	James Webb
456	Garnet Portus	535	Joseph Brunton	614	Thomas Colston
457	Herbert Sibree	536	Arthur Bull	615	Jerry Hanley
458	Alf Wood	537	Alfred Maynard	616	Colin Laird
459	Dick Gilbert	538	Tim Taylor	617	Monkey Sellar
460	Rupert Williamson	539	Bungy Watson	618	Kendrick Stark
461	Jumbo Vassall	540	Pedlar Wood	619	Harry Davies
462	Fischer Burges-Watson	541	Arthur Harrison	620	Wallace Eyres
463	Maffer Davey	542	Robert Pillman	621	Douglas Law
464	George Lyon	543	Francis Stone	622	William Pratten
465	William Oldham	544	Alexander Sykes	623	William Alexander
466	Tommy Woods	545	Barry Cumberlege	624	Colin Bishop
467	Alec Ashcroft	546	Harold Day	625	Ralph Buckingham
468	Eric Assinder	547	George Halford	626	Jack Wallens
469	Barrie Bennetts	548	Ernest Hammett	627	Carl Aarvold
470	John Cooper	549	Cecil Kershaw	628	William Kirwan-Taylor
471	Percy Down	550	Jannie Krige	629	Thomas Lawson
472	Frederick Knight	551	Frank Mellish	630	James Richardson
473	Edgar Mobbs	552	Laurence Merriam	631	David Turquand-Young
474	Alfred Morris	553	James Morgan	632	Godfrey Palmer
475	Sid Penny	554	Wavell Wakefield	633	Doug Prentice
476	Frank Tarr	555	Jock Wright	634	Robert Sparks
477	Herbert Archer	556	Geoffrey Conway	635	Tom Brown
478	Frank Handford	557	Wilfrid Lowry	636	Roy Foulds
479	Ernest Ibbitson	558	Harry Millett	637	Geoffrey Sladen
480	William Johns	559	Alastair Smallwood	638	Robert Smeddle
481	Charles Bolton	560	Sos Taylor	639	Jack Swayne
482	Frank Hutchinson	561	Stan Harris	640	Herbert Whitley
483	Ronald Poulton-Palmer	562	Edward Myers	641	Harry Wilkinson
484	Harold Morton	563	Tom Voyce	642	Guy Wilson
485	Alick Palmer	564	Freddie Blakiston	643	Thomas Harris
486	Arthur Wilson	565	Tom Woods	644	Stephen Meikle
487	Cyril Wright	566	Reg Edwards	645	Tony Novis
488	Harold Harrison	567	Ernest Gardner	646	Henry Rew
489	Lancelot Barrington-Ward	568	Ron Cove-Smith	647	Edward Richards
490	Harry Berry	569	Quentin King	648	Eric Coley
491	Fred Chapman	570	Len Corbett	649	Charles Gummer
492	Leonard Haigh	571	Vivian Davies	650	Sam Martindale
493	Billy Johnston	572	Sam Tucker	651	Jim Reeve
494	Cherry Pillman	573	Matthew Bradby	652	Roger Spong
495	Fenton Smith	574	Robert Duncan	653	John Askew
496	Bert Solomon	575	John Maxwell-Hyslop	654	Alfred Bateson
497	Leslie Hayward	576	Reg Pickles	655	Brian Black
498	Alan Adams	577	Leo Price	656	Jeff Forrest
499	Harry Coverdale	578	John Middleton	657	Peter Howard
500	Reginald Hands	579	James Pitman	658	Joe Kendrew
501	Anthony Henniker-Gotley	580	Peveril William-Powlett	659	Frank Malir
502	John Ritson	581	Frederick Gilbert	660	Matthew Robson
503	Edward Scorfield	582	William Luddington	661	Wilf Sobey
504	Cyril Williams	583	Frank Sanders	662	Alan Key
505	Norman Wodehouse	584	Toff Holliday	663	Peter Brook
506	Guy Hind	585	Harold Locke	664	John Hubbard
507	Percy Lawrie	586	Carston Catcheside	665	Christopher Tanner
508	Tim Stoop	587	Bunny Chantrill	666	Jimmy Barrington
509	Bruno Brown	588	Jake Jacob	667	Lawrence Bedford
510	John King	589	Alan Robson	668	Maurice Bonaventura
511	William Mann	590	Arthur Young	669	Don Burland
512	Alan Roberts	591	Chubby Faithfull	670	Richard Davey
513	John Scholfield	592	Richard Hamilton-Wickes	671	Maurice McCanlis
514	Stanley Williams	593	Jim Brough	672	Brian Pope
515	Ronald Lagden	594	John Gibbs	673	Deneys Swayne
516	Henry Brougham	595	Ronald Hillard	674	Tinny Dean
517	John Eddison	596	Harold Kittermaster	675	Pop Dunkley
518	Dave Holland	597	Rex Armstrong	676	Gordon Gregory
519	Alfred MacIlwaine	598	Edward Massey	677	Ernest Harding
520	John Pym	599	Joe Periton	678	Cliff Harrison
521	Dick Stafford	600	Richard Lawson	679	Peter Hordern
522	John Greenwood	601	Roderick MacLennan	680	Tom Knowles
523	William Hynes	602	Duncan Cumming	681	John Tallent
524	Maurice Neale	603	Stanley Considine	682	Eric Whiteley
525	William Cheesman	604	Alfred Aslett	683	Bobby Barr
526	Vincent Coates	605	Hyde Burton	684	Alfred Carpenter
527	Dave Davies	606	Tim Francis	685	Ronald Gerrard
528	Cyril Lowe	607	Bob Hanvey	686	Reginald Hobbs
529	Sidney Smart	608	Edward Stanbury	687	John Hodgson

#	Name	#	Name	#	Name
688	Doug Norman	767	Squib Donnelly	846	Vic Leadbetter
689	Arthur Rowley	768	James George	847	Ernie Robinson
690	Les Saxby	769	Cyril Holmes	848	Johnny Williams
691	Charles Webb	770	Ossie Newton-Thompson	849	Doug Baker
692	Barney Evans	771	Bob Weighill	850	William Hancock
693	Walter Elliot	772	George Gibbs	851	George Hastings
694	Bernard Gadney	773	Syd Newman	852	David Hazell
695	Reginald Roberts	774	Vic Roberts	853	Peter Ryan
696	Arthur Vaughan-Jones	775	Eric Evans	854	Noddy Taylor
697	Ray Longland	776	John Keeling	855	Ian Beer
698	Reggie Bolton	777	Richard Madge	856	Harry Scott
699	Lewis Booth	778	Douglas Vaughan	857	Frank Sykes
700	Anthony Roncoroni	779	Humphrey Luya	858	Noel Estcourt
701	Ted Sadler	780	Ivor Preece	859	Fenwick Allison
702	Carlton Troop	781	Dick Uren	860	Ned Ashcroft
703	William Weston	782	Tom Price	861	John Currie
704	Peter Cranmer	783	Martin Turner	862	Peter Jackson
705	John Dicks	784	Lewis Cannell	863	Ron Jacobs
706	Henry Fry	785	Patrick Sykes	864	Dickie Jeeps
707	Graham Meikle	786	Allan Towell	865	David Marques
708	Tuppy Owen-Smith	787	Mike Berridge	866	Peter Robbins
709	Tim Warr	788	Bryan Braithwaite-Exley	867	Mike Smith
710	John Wright	789	Tom Danby	868	Peter Thompson
711	Charlie Slow	790	Jack Gregory	869	Ricky Bartlett
712	Harold Boughton	791	Barry Holmes	870	Bob Challis
713	Peter Candler	792	Edward Horsfall	871	Phil Horrocks-Taylor
714	Allan Clarke	793	Geoffrey Hosking	872	Ron Syrett
715	Arthur Cridlan	794	Gordon Rimmer	873	Jim Hetherington
716	Jimmy Giles	795	Clive van Ryneveld	874	Malcolm Phillips
717	Jack Heaton	796	John Kendall-Carpenter	875	John Young
718	Dudley Kemp	797	Robert Kennedy	876	Alfred Herbert
719	Roy Leyland	798	John Matthews	877	John Scott
720	Ernie Nicholson	799	John Steeds	878	Gordon Bendon
721	Arthur Payne	800	Brian Boobbyer	879	Bev Risman
722	Dick Auty	801	Ian Botting	880	Stephen Smith
723	Edward Hamilton-Hill	802	John Cain	881	John Wackett
724	Alexander Obolensky	803	Murray Hofmeyr	882	Larry Webb
725	Hal Sever	804	Wally Holmes	883	Brian Wightman
726	Harold Wheatley	805	Herbert Jones	884	Jeff Clements
727	Herbert Toft	806	Harry Small	885	Herbert Godwin
728	Arthur Butler	807	John Smith	886	Stan Hodgson
729	David Campbell	808	Akker Adkins	887	Derek Morgan
730	Thomas Huskisson	809	John Hyde	888	Jim Roberts
731	Tommy Kemp	810	John Baume	889	Don Rutherford
732	Dermot Milman	811	Jasper Bartlett	890	Richard Sharp
733	Robin Prescott	812	Ted Hewitt	891	Mike Weston
734	Arthur Wheatley	813	Philip Moore	892	Peter Wright
735	John Cook	814	Lionel Oakley	893	Bill Patterson
736	Jeff Reynolds	815	George Rittson-Thomas	894	Laurie Rimmer
737	Jimmy Unwin	816	Trevor Smith	895	Ray French
738	Hubert Freakes	817	Bob Stirling	896	Mike Gavins
739	Basil Nicholson	818	Vic Tindall	897	John Price
740	Mike Marshall	819	Squire Wilkins	898	Budge Rogers
741	Grahame Parker	820	Peter Woodruff	899	John Willcox
742	Alan Brown	821	Evan Hardy	900	Victor Harding
743	Tom Berry	822	Bruce Neale	901	Phil Judd
744	Robert Carr	823	John Williams	902	Martin Underwood
745	Paul Cooke	824	William Hook	903	Mike Wade
746	Dickie Guest	825	Dennis Shuttleworth	904	John Dee
747	George Hancock	826	Albert Agar	905	Andy Hurst
748	Derek Teden	827	Alec Lewis	906	Thomas Pargetter
749	Gus Walker	828	Chris Winn	907	Stanley Purdy
750	John Watkins	829	Ted Woodward	908	Simon Clarke
751	Jack Ellis	830	Elliott Woodgate	909	Mike Davis
752	Ernest Parsons	831	Philip Collins	910	Beverley Dovey
753	Billy Bennett	832	Reginald Bazley	911	Nick Drake-Lee
754	Arthur Gray	833	Nick Labuschagne	912	Dick Manley
755	Nim Hall	834	Martin Regan	913	John Owen
756	Alan Henderson	835	Jeff Butterfield	914	John Thorne
757	Geoffrey Kelly	836	Tug Wilson	915	David Perry
758	Bill Moore	837	Phil Davies	916	Tug Wilson
759	Joe Mycock	838	Reg Higgins	917	Roger Hosen
760	Sam Perry	839	Ian King	918	Victor Marriott
761	Edward Scott	840	Pat Quinn	919	John Ranson
762	Micky Steele-Bodger	841	Sandy Sanders	920	Roger Sangwin
763	David Swarbrick	842	Peter Yarranton	921	Peter Ford
764	Jika Travers	843	Peter Young	922	Bob Rowell
765	Harry Walker	844	John Bance	923	Tom Brophy
766	Don White	845	Nigel Gibbs	924	Colin Payne

925	Thomas Peart	1004	Mike Burton	1083	Bryan Barley
926	David Wrench	1005	Alan Old	1084	Rory Underwood
927	Geoff Frankcom	1006	Andy Ripley	1085	Steve Redfern
928	Tony Horton	1007	Jan Webster	1086	Andy Dun
929	Stephen Richards	1008	Peter Knight	1087	Paul Rendall
930	David Rosser	1009	Lionel Weston	1088	Mark Bailey
931	Ted Rudd	1010	Nick Martin	1089	Chris Butcher
932	Nicholas Silk	1011	Geoff Evans	1090	Richard Hill
933	Colin Simpson	1012	Sam Doble	1091	John Palmer
934	Peter Cook	1013	Alan Morley	1092	Malcolm Preedy
935	Andy Hancock	1014	Peter Preece	1093	Steve Brain
936	Terry Arthur	1015	John Watkins	1094	Gary Rees
937	Piggy Powell	1016	Frank Anderson	1095	Stuart Barnes
938	John Pullin	1017	Peter Warfield	1096	Gareth Chilcott
939	Keith Savage	1018	Steve Smith	1097	Rob Lozowski
940	John Spencer	1019	Roger Uttley	1098	Nigel Melville
941	Bob Taylor	1020	Martin Cooper	1099	Nigel Redman
942	Clive Ashby	1021	Peter Squires	1100	Rob Andrew
943	Dick Greenwood	1022	David Roughley	1101	Wade Dooley
944	Colin McFadyean	1023	Keith Smith	1102	Richard Harding
945	Bill Treadwell	1024	Dusty Hare	1103	John Orwin
946	Bob Hearn	1025	Bill Beaumont	1104	Kevin Simms
947	George Sherriff	1026	Peter Wheeler	1105	Simon Smith
948	Trevor Wintle	1027	Neil Bennett	1106	Chris Martin
949	Mike Coulman	1028	Peter Butler	1107	Mike Teague
950	Peter Glover	1029	Peter Kingston	1108	Mike Harrison
951	Christopher Jennins	1030	Neil Mantell	1109	Paul Huntsman
952	Peter Larter	1031	Andy Maxwell	1110	Jamie Salmon
953	John Barton	1032	Barry Nelmes	1111	Simon Halliday
954	John Finlan	1033	Alan Wordsworth	1112	Graham Robbins
955	John Pallant	1034	Alastair Hignell	1113	Fran Clough
956	Roger Pickering	1035	Bob Wilkinson	1114	Dean Richards
957	Dave Rollitt	1036	Barry Corless	1115	David Cusani
958	Dave Watt	1037	Mark Keyworth	1116	Graham Dawe
959	Rod Webb	1038	Mike Lampkowski	1117	Brian Moore
960	Bill Gittings	1039	David Cooke	1118	Peter Williams
961	Bob Lloyd	1040	Derek Wyatt	1119	Jon Webb
962	Peter Bell	1041	Garry Adey	1120	Will Carling
963	David Gay	1042	Mike Slemen	1121	Jeff Probyn
964	Bob Hiller	1043	Chris Williams	1122	Mickey Skinner
965	Brian Keen	1044	Robin Cowling	1123	Chris Oti
966	Jim Parsons	1045	Charles Kent	1124	John Bentley
967	Derek Prout	1046	Mike Rafter	1125	Dave Egerton
968	Bill Redwood	1047	Malcolm Young	1126	Barry Evans
969	Bryan West	1048	John Scott	1127	Andy Robinson
970	Terence Brooke	1049	Paul Dodge	1128	Paul Ackford
971	David Duckham	1050	John Horton	1129	Andy Harriman
972	Keith Fairbrother	1051	Bob Mordell	1130	Dewi Morris
973	Keith Fielding	1052	David Caplan	1131	John Buckton
974	Nigel Horton	1053	Maurice Colclough	1132	Steve Bates
975	John Southern Spencer	1054	Tony Bond	1133	Jerry Guscott
976	Timothy Dalton	1055	Gary Pearce	1134	Simon Hodgkinson
977	Ken Plummer	1056	Richard Cardus	1135	Mark Linnett
978	Tony Bucknall	1057	Colin Smart	1136	Andy Mullins
979	Peter Hale	1058	John Carleton	1137	Nigel Heslop
980	Roger Shackleton	1059	Les Cusworth	1138	Jason Leonard
981	Nigel Starmer-Smith	1060	Nick Preston	1139	David Pears
982	Stack Stevens	1061	Phil Blakeway	1140	Dean Ryan
983	Chris Wardlow	1062	Clive Woodward	1141	John Olver
984	John Novak	1063	David Cooke	1142	Martin Bayfield
985	Mike Bulpitt	1064	Austin Sheppard	1143	Tim Rodber
986	Barry Jackson	1065	Huw Davies	1144	Ian Hunter
987	Tony Jorden	1066	Nick Jeavons	1145	Victor Ubogu
988	Mike Leadbetter	1067	Bob Hesford	1146	Tony Underwood
989	Gerry Redmond	1068	Marcus Rose	1147	Ben Clarke
990	Charlie Hannaford	1069	Gordon Sargent	1148	Phil de Glanville
991	Jeremy Janion	1070	John Fidler	1149	Martin Johnson
992	Tony Neary	1071	Steve Mills	1150	Kyran Bracken
993	Barry Ninnes	1072	Tony Swift	1151	Jon Callard
994	Jacko Page	1073	Peter Winterbottom	1152	Neil Back
995	Peter Rossborough	1074	Nick Stringer	1153	Steve Ojomoh
996	Ian Wright	1075	Jim Syddall	1154	Mike Catt
997	Fran Cotton	1076	Steve Bainbridge	1155	Paul Hull
998	Dick Cowman	1077	Steve Boyle	1156	Graham Rowntree
999	Chris Ralston	1078	David Trick	1157	Richard West
1000	Roger Creed	1079	Nick Youngs	1158	Damian Hopley
1001	Peter Dixon	1080	Paul Simpson	1159	John Mallett
1002	Mike Beese	1081	Colin White	1160	Mark Regan
1003	Alan Brinn	1082	Jon Hall	1161	Lawrence Dallaglio

#	Name	#	Name	#	Name
1162	Matt Dawson	1241	Alex Codling	1320	Dan Cole
1163	Paul Grayson	1242	Michael Horak	1321	Matt Mullan
1164	Jon Sleightholme	1243	Ben Johnston	1322	Ben Youngs
1165	Garath Archer	1244	James Simpson-Daniel	1323	Chris Ashton
1166	Adedayo Adebayo	1245	Robbie Morris	1324	Shontayne Hape
1167	Andy Gomarsall	1246	Ollie Smith	1325	Dave Attwood
1168	Simon Shaw	1247	Mike Worsley	1326	Hendre Fourie
1169	Chris Sheasby	1248	Stuart Abbott	1327	Tom Wood
1170	Tim Stimpson	1249	Dan Scarbrough	1328	Alex Corbisiero
1171	Phil Greening	1250	Chris Jones	1329	Manu Tuilagi
1172	Rob Hardwick	1251	Matt Stevens	1330	Mouritz Botha
1173	Nick Beal	1252	Michael Lipman	1331	Charlie Sharples
1174	Richard Hill	1253	Andy Titterrell	1332	Joe Simpson
1175	Austin Healey	1254	Tim Payne	1333	Brad Barritt
1176	Darren Garforth	1255	Mark Cueto	1334	Phil Dowson
1177	Martin Corry	1256	Andy Hazell	1335	Owen Farrell
1178	Tony Diprose	1257	Andrew Sheridan	1336	Lee Dickson
1179	Nick Greenstock	1258	Hugh Vyvyan	1337	Ben Morgan
1180	Martin Haag	1259	Harry Ellis	1338	Geoff Parling
1181	Jim Mallinder	1260	Mathew Tait	1339	Jordan Turner-Hall
1182	Kevin Yates	1261	James Forrester	1340	Rob Webber
1183	Richard Cockerill	1262	Duncan Bell	1341	Tom Johnson
1184	Danny Grewcock	1263	Andy Goode	1342	Joe Marler
1185	Mark Mapletoft	1264	Mark van Gisbergen	1343	Jonathan Joseph
1186	Alex King	1265	Louis Deacon	1344	Alex Goode
1187	Will Green	1266	Perry Freshwater	1345	Thomas Waldrom
1188	Will Greenwood	1267	Lee Mears	1346	Tom Youngs
1189	Andy Long	1268	Tom Varndell	1347	Joe Launchbury
1190	Matt Perry	1269	Alex Brown	1348	Mako Vunipola
1191	David Rees	1270	Magnus Lund	1349	Freddie Burns
1192	Dorian West	1271	Peter Richards	1350	Billy Twelvetrees
1193	Phil Vickery	1272	George Chuter	1351	Matt Kvesic
1194	Jonny Wilkinson	1273	Nick Walshe	1352	Christian Wade
1195	Scott Benton	1274	Anthony Allen	1353	Kyle Eastmond
1196	Spencer Brown	1275	Shaun Perry	1354	Henry Thomas
1197	Richard Pool-Jones	1276	Paul Sackey	1355	Billy Vunipola
1198	Steve Ravenscroft	1277	Toby Flood	1356	Jonny May
1199	Ben Sturnham	1278	Andy Farrell	1357	Marland Yarde
1200	Dominic Chapman	1279	Olly Morgan	1358	Stephen Myler
1201	Stuart Potter	1280	Tom Rees	1359	Joel Tomkins
1202	Josh Lewsey	1281	Nick Easter	1360	Luther Burrell
1203	Pat Sanderson	1282	David Strettle	1361	Jack Nowell
1204	Tom Beim	1283	Shane Geraghty	1362	George Ford
1205	Dave Sims	1284	James Haskell	1363	Joe Gray
1206	Jos Baxendell	1285	Stuart Turner	1364	Chris Pennell
1207	Rob Fidler	1286	Mike Brown	1365	Kieran Brookes
1208	Paul Sampson	1287	Dean Schofield	1366	Semesa Rokoduguni
1209	Dan Luger	1288	Matt Cairns	1367	George Kruis
1210	Neil McCarthy	1289	Darren Crompton	1368	Anthony Watson
1211	Steve Hanley	1290	Roy Winters	1369	Sam Burgess
1212	Barrie-Jon Mather	1291	Ben Skirving	1370	Calum Clark
1213	Trevor Woodman	1292	Nick Abendanon	1371	Henry Slade
1214	Joe Worsley	1293	Dan Hipkiss	1372	Luke Cowan-Dickie
1215	Ben Cohen	1294	Luke Narraway	1373	Jamie George
1216	Mike Tindall	1295	Danny Cipriani	1374	Jack Clifford
1217	Iain Balshaw	1296	Lesley Vainikolo	1375	Paul Hill
1218	Julian White	1297	Richard Wigglesworth	1376	Maro Itoje
1219	David Flatman	1298	Tom Croft	1377	Elliot Daly
1220	Leon Lloyd	1299	Paul Hodgson	1378	Teimana Harrison
1221	Jason Robinson	1300	Topsy Ojo	1379	Ollie Devoto
1222	Steve Borthwick	1301	Danny Care	1380	Ellis Genge
1223	Ben Kay	1302	David Paice	1381	Tommy Taylor
1224	Lewis Moody	1303	Jason Hobson	1382	Nathan Hughes
1225	Jamie Noon	1304	Delon Armitage	1383	Kyle Sinckler
1226	Michael Stephenson	1305	Riki Flutey	1384	Ben Te'o
1227	Dave Walder	1306	Nick Kennedy	1385	Charlie Ewels
1228	Steve White-Cooper	1307	Ugo Monye	1386	Tom Curry
1229	Martyn Wood	1308	Dylan Hartley	1387	Alex Lozowski
1230	Fraser Waters	1309	Jordan Crane	1388	Harry Williams
1231	Olly Barkley	1310	Steffon Armitage	1389	Mark Wilson
1232	Tom Palmer	1311	Ben Foden	1390	Don Armand
1233	Tom Voyce	1312	Matt Banahan	1391	Will Collier
1234	Charlie Hodgson	1313	Tom May	1392	Piers Francis
1235	Alex Sanderson	1314	David Wilson	1393	Nick Isiekwe
1236	Steve Thompson	1315	Sam Vesty	1394	Jack Maunder
1237	Nick Duncombe	1316	Chris Robshaw	1395	Denny Solomona
1238	Henry Paul	1317	Ayoola Erinle	1396	Sam Underhill
1239	Geoff Appleford	1318	Courtney Lawes	1397	Sam Simmonds
1240	Phil Christophers	1319	Paul Doran Jones	1398	Alec Hepburn

1399	Brad Shields	1418	Jack Willis	1437	Harry Wells
1400	Ben Spencer	1419	Max Malins	1438	Mark Atkinson
1401	Zach Mercer	1420	Beno Obano	1439	Alex Mitchell
1402	Ben Moon	1421	George Martin	1440	Bevan Rodd
1403	Joe Cokanasiga	1422	Callum Chick	1441	Raffi Quirke
1404	Ted Hill	1423	Joe Heyes	1442	Nic Dolly
1405	Dan Robson	1424	Curtis Langdon	1443	Ollie Chessum
1406	Willi Heinz	1425	Lewis Ludlow	1444	Henry Arundell
1407	Lewis Ludlam	1426	Josh McNally	1445	Jack van Poortvliet
1408	Joe Marchant	1427	Harry Randall	1446	Tommy Freeman
1409	Jack Singleton	1428	Marcus Smith	1447	Guy Porter
1410	Ruaridh McConnochie	1429	Freddie Steward	1448	Will Joseph
1411	George Furbank	1430	Jamie Blamire	1449	Alex Coles
1412	Will Stuart	1431	Ben Curry	1450	Dave Ribbans
1413	Ben Earl	1432	Trevor Davison	1451	Ollie Hassell-Collins
1414	Jonny Hill	1433	Jacob Umaga	1452	Jack Walker
1415	Tom Dunn	1434	Alex Dombrandt	1453	Tom Pearson
1416	Ollie Lawrence	1435	Dan Kelly	1454	Theo Dan
1417	Ollie Thorley	1436	Adam Radwan	1455	Tom Willis

PLAYER PROFILES

1. BENTLEY, John Edmund
Half-back 2 caps 1871-1872
Born: Calver, Derbyshire, 17 January 1847
Died: West Hampstead, London, 12 December 1913
Career: Gipsies
Debut: v Scotland, Raeburn Place Edinburgh, March 1871

Bentley was a half-back who played in England's first-ever international. He was the son of an industrialist educated at Merchant Taylors' School in Middlesex and was said to be very fast, with great weight and strength. He played for Peckham-based Gipsies Rugby Club, a founding member of the Rugby Football Union. One was one of only six survivors from the defeat in Scotland to play in England's first home international in the return match at The Oval a year later. Bentley spent his working life in the civil service and was a clerk in the General Office of the Supreme Court of Judicature.

2. BIRKETT, Reginald Halsey
Forward 1 cap 1871
Born: City of London, 28 March 1849
Died: Wimbledon, London, 30 June 1898
Career: Clapton Rovers
Debut: v Scotland, Raeburn Place, Edinburgh, March 1871

Birkett was one of the thirteen original committee members of the Rugby Football Union, having attended the meeting at the Pall Mall Restaurant, which saw the union formed on 26th January 1871. He scored England's first try in their first inaugural international against Scotland. He also played association football for England, winning one cap as a goalkeeper, and was an FA Cup winner with Clapton Rovers in 1880. His brother Louis and son John also played rugby for England. A commercial clerk, a hide brokers clerk, and a skin and fur broker. Birkett died while delirious from diphtheria. He jumped through a window, falling 20 feet.

3. BURNS, Benjamin Henry
Forward 1 cap 1871
Born: Perth, Scotland 28 May 1848
Died: Christchurch, New Zealand, 3 June 1932
Career: Edinburgh Academical, Blackheath
Debut: v Scotland, Raeburn Place, Edinburgh, March 1871

Burns was born in Scotland when his father was the General Manager of the Royal Bank of Scotland. Burns was club secretary of Blackheath when leading Scottish clubs wrote and issued the challenge for a match between England and Scotland and wrote back accepting. Burns wasn't due to play in the game but was drafted following Francis Isherwood's withdrawal. He followed his father into banking, taking him to India and Christchurch, New Zealand, where he settled, founding a share brokers Henderson and Burns and was also on the board of directors of bookshop chain Whitcombe & Tombs at the time of his death.

4. CLAYTON, John Henry
Forward 1 cap 1871
Born: Liverpool, Lancashire, 24 August 1848
Died: London 21 March 1924
Career: Rugby School, Liverpool, Lancashire
Debut: v Scotland, Raeburn Place, Edinburgh, March 1871

Clayton was one of ten Old Rugbeians to play in England's first-ever international against Scotland in March 1871. He is credited with popularising the game in Lancashire, where he was a Cotton Broker in Liverpool. Clayton was a member of the London Stock Exchange, chairman of the London and Lancashire Insurance Company, and director of several other insurance companies. At the time of his death, Clayton was also a director of Lloyds Bank, dying in the back of a taxi cab following a board meeting in London. John also played golf and was captain of Wallasey Golf Club.

5. CROMPTON, Charles Arthur
Forward 1 cap 1871
Born: Cork, Ireland, 21 October 1848
Died: Cherat, Bengal, India, 6 July 1875
Career: Blackheath
Debut: v Scotland, Raeburn Place, Edinburgh, March 1871

Crompton was a professional soldier who, along with Charles Sherrard, were the first members of the armed forces to play for England when they played in the first international against Scotland in March 1871. Crompton was born in Ireland but went to boarding school in Congleton, Cheshire and then moved to London before joining the army. A lieutenant with the Royal Engineers, he was doing duty with the Bengal Sappers and Miners. The inscription on his grave reads, "Strong, brave and straight-forward, faithful, honourable & true."

6. DAVENPORT, Alfred
Forward 1 cap 1871
Born: Oxford, Oxfordshire, 5 May 1849
Died: Bagley Wood, Oxfordshire, 2 April 1932
Career: Oxford University, Ravenscourt Park
Debut: v Scotland, Raeburn Place, Edinburgh, March 1871

Oxford-born Davenport was appointed the first captain of Oxford University when the club was founded in November 1869 but had graduated by the time of the first Varsity match three years later. He played in England's first international against Scotland at Raeburn Place, Edinburgh, in March 1871. A solicitor like his father, Davenport was a member of the London-based law firm Cunliffe & Davenport until his retirement in 1919. A son, Frank, was a Captain in the 52nd Battalion of the Oxfordshire & Buckinghamshire Light Infantry but was killed in action in Clesiphon in Mesopotamia in November 1915.

7. DUGDALE, John Marshall JP
Forward 1 cap 1871
Born: Salford, Lancashire 15 October 1852
Died: Llanfyllin, Wales, 30 October 1918
Career: Rugby School, Oxford University, Ravenscourt Park,
Debut: v Scotland, Raeburn Place, Edinburgh, March 1871

Dugdale was a member of Ravenscourt Park Rugby Club, which was a stronghold of Old Rugbeians. Dugdale was one of nine players educated at Rugby School who played in England's first international against Scotland at Raeburn Place, Edinburgh, in March 1871. He ttended Brasenose College, Oxford and trained as a barrister, being called to the bar in 1875. After moving to Montgomeryshire, he became a member of the Northern Circuit as a justice of the peace. Dugdale also held several political offices, including the Mayor of Llanfyllin and High Sheriff of Montgomeryshire, and sat on the board of Bangor University College.

8. GIBSON, Arthur Sumner
Forward 1 cap 1871
Born: New Forest, Hampshire, 14 July 1844
Died: Binfield, Berkshire, 23 January 1927
Career: Manchester, Lancashire
Debut: v Scotland, Raeburn Place, Edinburgh, March 1871

Gibson was one of four Manchester players selected to play in England's first international against Scotland in Edinburgh in March 1871, but none managed to keep their places in the side for England's first home international in the return game 12 months later. Gibson was educated at Marlborough College and Trinity College, Oxford, but never won his blue despite his international recognition. Gibson became a civil engineer working for Bateman & Hill Civil Engineers and was elected to join the Institute of Civil Engineers.

9. GREEN, Joseph Fletcher
Half-back 1 cap 1871
Born: West Ham, Essex, 28 April 1847
Died: Leeds, Yorkshire, 28 August 1923
Career: Rugby School, West Kent
Debut: v Scotland, Raeburn Place, Edinburgh, March 1871

Rugby School-educated Green, who was the brother-in-law of captain Fred Stokes suffered a knee injury early during England's first international against Scotland in March 1971 and was forced from the field, leaving his side a man short. Sadly, he never played again. He was said to have been one of the best half-backs of his time. Green had also played cricket for the MCC and the Gentleman of the South, while another brother-in-law, Frank Penn, played cricket for Kent and England. He sat on the board of Ship repairers R.H. Green & Silley Weir of Blackwall, London.

10. GUILLEMARD, Arthur George
Full-back 2 caps 1871-1872
Born: Eltham, Kent, 18 December 1846
Died: Eltham, Kent, 7 August 1909
Career: Rugby School, West Kent, Blackheath, Richmond
Debut: v Scotland, Raeburn Place, Edinburgh, March 1871

Guillemard, the son of French Protestant refugees who was educated at Rugby School, was one of the founding members of the Rugby Football Union, and he played in both of England's first two internationals against Scotland in Edinburgh in March 1871 and then at The Oval a year later. Guillemard became an international referee and the first of two men to hold all five chief RFU offices, serving four terms as president. He was president when they accepted the Calcutta Cup. A solicitor by profession, he practised in London and, later in life, Eltham, Kent.

11. HAMERSLEY, Alfred St George
Forward 4 caps 1 try 1871-1874
Born: Great Haseley, Oxfordshire, 8 October 1848
Died: Bournemouth, Dorset, 25 February 1929
Career: Marlborough College, Marlborough Nomads, Canterbury (NZ)
Debut: v Scotland, Raeburn Place, Edinburgh, March 1871

Hamersley was a Barrister-at-law in Middle Temple who played in England's first four internationals against Scotland and became the second-ever England captain. Hamersley is credited with fathering the game in New Zealand and Canada, where he was the first president of the British Columbia Rugby Union. He helped found Oxfordshire Nomads Rugby Union Football Club upon returning to England. Hamersley was 68 when he went to France as Commanding Officer of the Heavy Artillery and served as Conservative MP for Woodstock between 1910 and 1918. He spent his final years living in Bournemouth.

12. LUSCOMBE, Sir John Henry
Forward 1 cap 1871
Born: Forest Hill, London 1848
Died: Worth, Sussex, 3 April 1937
Career: Gipsies
Debut: v Scotland, Raeburn Place, Edinburgh, March 1871

Luscombe was from a family with considerable shipping interests, leading him to Lloyds of London when he was 21, starting as an underwriter and retiring as chairman 61 years later. But being away at sea probably played a part in him only being capped once. His brother Francis played in England's first home international. Luscombe was also a director of Prudential Assurance and was knighted in 1902 for his services to underwriting. He was the last surviving member of England's first-ever international side.

13. LYON, Arthur
Back 1 cap 1891
Born: West Derby, Lancashire, 4 August 1852
Died: Woodbury, South Canterbury, 4 December 1905
Career: Rugby School, Liverpool
Debut: v Scotland, Raeburn Place, Edinburgh, March 1871

Lyon was one of ten players who played in England's first-ever international against Scotland at Raeburn Place, Edinburgh, in Match 1971 who had attended Rugby School. And is likely to have been hugely influential along with J H Clayton in recommending other players from the North to the selection committee. A Member of Chester Rowing and Chester Athletics clubs, Lyon was also a captain in the 1st Battalion Cheshire Volunteer Rifles with his England team-mate Frank Tobin. He emigrated to New Zealand, where he was an agent and promotor in Christchurch before styling himself as a farmer and retiring to Woodbury, a small farming community near Geraldine.

14. MACLAREN, William
Back 1 cap 1871
Born: Chorlton, Lancashire, 1844
Died: Witham, Essex, June 1916
Career: Manchester
Debut: v Scotland, Raeburn Place, Edinburgh, March 1871

MacLaren was one of four players from Manchester to play in England's first-ever international against Scotland in Edinburgh in March 1871. He captained Manchester in 1868 and was the brother of James MacLaren, the sixth president of the RFU, serving between 1882 and 1884. He was also the uncle of AC MacLaren, the Lancashire and England cricketer. A noted runner from 100 yards to 440 yards, MacLaren won many prizes and was also a Cumberland Wrestler and noted breeder of magpie pigeons and was a merchant for all his adult life, mainly in Home Goods.

15. OSBORNE, Richard Robinson
Back 1 cap 1871
Born: Ashgill, Yorkshire, 20 May 1848
Died: Rochdale, Lancashire, 4 November 1926
Career: Hurstpierpoint College, Manchester, Rochdale Hornets
Debut: v Scotland, Raeburn Place, Edinburgh, March 1871

Hurstpierpoint College-educated Osborne was the first Yorkshireman to play for England when he became one of four players from the Manchester Club to play in England's first international against Scotland in Edinburgh in March 1971. Osborne became the first captain of Rochdale Hornets in August 1871 and would become a founder member of the Northern Union. He was a solicitor with Hartley, Son & Osborne before setting up a practice and was Rochdale's oldest solicitor when he died. Osborne's brother was a jockey and racehorse trainer, John "the Pusher" Osborne, and his father was also a trainer.

16. SHERRARD, Charles William
Forward 2 caps 1871-1872
Born: Paddington, Middlesex, 25 December 1849
Died: Beckenham, Kent, 11 December 1938
Career: Rugby School, Blackheath, Royal Engineers, The Army
Debut: v Scotland, Raeburn Place, Edinburgh, March 1871

Sherrard was educated at Rugby School and joined Blackheath. He played in England's first international against Scotland in March 1871 and was then one of a handful of players to retain their place for the return at The Oval 12 months later. Along with fellow Royal Engineer Charles Crompton, were the first members of the army forces to play for England. He served in the South African War and rose to become a colonel. Sherrard later commanded the Chatham sub district before retiring to Beckenham, where he lived until his death aged 89.

17. STOKES, Frederic
Forward 3 caps 1871-1873
Born: Greenwich, Kent, 12 July 1850
Died: Inhurst Ho, Berkshire, 7 February 1929
Career: Rugby School, Blackheath, Kent
Debut: v Scotland, Raeburn Place, Edinburgh, March 1871

Stokes represented Blackheath at the Pall Mall Restaurant in January 1871 when the Rugby Football Union was formed. He captained England in their first-ever international match against Scotland 13 months later and was named captain for their next two matches. One of only three players to have played in all three games. He effectively retired from international rugby after his last match and, in 1874, became the RFU's youngest-ever president. Stokes played cricket for Kent alongside his brother Lennard, who also captained the England Rugby team. A solicitor like his father and the brother-in-law of Joseph Green.

18. TOBIN, Frank CBE
Half-back 1 cap 1871
Born: Liverpool, Lancashire, 23 September 1849
Died: Liverpool, Lancashire, 6 February 1927
Career: Rugby School, Cambridge University, Liverpool, Lancashire
Debut: v Scotland, Raeburn Place, Edinburgh, March 1871

Tobin was a merchant in business in Peru who played in England's first international against Scotland in Edinburgh in 1871, one of a handful of players from outside London to be selected and 'played splendidly behind the scrum'. He played cricket for Rugby School and captained Liverpool between 1970 and 1872, later serving the club twice as president. After returning from South America, he became a well-known stockbroker in Liverpool and, among his other appointments, was chairman of the Liverpool Nitrate Company. During the First World War, Tobin organised the Avenue Auxiliary Hospital and was Corps Superintendent of the St. Johns Ambulance.

19. TURNER, Dawson Palgrave
Forward 6 caps 1871-1875
Born: Calcutta, India, 15 December 1846
Died: Tunbridge Wells, Kent, 25 February 1909
Career: Rugby School, Richmond
Debut: v Scotland, Raeburn Place, Edinburgh, March 1871

Turner played in England's first international against Scotland in 1871 and was the only man to play in England's first six internationals. He was described as "desperately hardworking forward, always keen and untiring regardless of risk or danger." At one time, he trained to be a doctor and, in 1871, was a student Obstetrician at University College Hospital before joining The Army. Turner was widely travelled until his health suffered after being kicked by a horse in the base of the spine, and he was staying with friends at the time of his death.

20. TURNER, Henry John Cecil
Forward 1 cap 1871
Born: Wartling, Sussex, 23 January 1850
Died: Rattery, South Devon, 27 September 1887
Career: Manchester, Lancashire
Debut: v Scotland, Raeburn Place, Edinburgh, March 1871

Turner was educated at Lancing College along with Reg Birkett, and they played together in England's first international against Scotland at Raeburn Place in March 1871. Henry was one of four Manchester players selected for the game, which England narrowly lost. It proved to be the only cap he won, but he didn't retain his place for their first home international game a year later. Turner was a banker's clerk and entered the cotton trade in Rochdale, Lancashire, before returning to the South and living in Rattery, a Village just outside Totnes aged 37.

21. BATSON, Thomas
Forward 3 caps 1872-1875
Born: Ross-On-Wye, Herefordshire, 18 May 1846
Died: Battersea, London 5 February 1933
Career: Sidney College Bath, Oxford University, Blackheath
Debut: v Scotland, Kennington Oval, London February 1872

Batson was educated at Sidney College Bath and Oxford University, where he won a blue in athletics for the hammer and shot but narrowly missed out on rowing and cricket. Batson was a cousin of Frederick and Lennard Stokes, who both captained England, which could have helped his selection for England's first-ever home test against Scotland at The Oval in February 1872. He was an assistant master at Blackheath Proprietary School and later a vice-master and housemaster at Rossall until he retired to Devon, where he won many prizes for growing daffodils.

22. BODY, James Alfred
Forward 2 caps 1872-1873
Born: Tenterden, Kent, 3 September 1846
Died: East Malling, Kent, 9 September 1929
Career: Tonbridge School, Gipsies, Brighton Wasps
Debut: v Scotland, Kennington Oval, London, February 1872

Body was the founder of Gipsies Rugby Club with two friends, including Francis Luscombe from Tonbridge School, and the club was one of the founding members of the Rugby Football Union. Body made his international debut against Scotland at The Oval, and his second and final appearance came at the West of Scotland club in Glasgow a year later. He formed The College Brewery in Brighton and owned the Hare and Hounds in Rye before emigrating to Canada, opening a flax-crushing firm in Winnipeg, and was the proprietor of an oil mill before retiring.

23. BUSH, James Arthur
Forward 5 caps 1872-1876
Born: Cawnpore, India 28 July 1850
Died: Clevedon, Somerset, 21 September 1924
Career: Bedminster, Blackheath, Clifton, Gloucestershire
Debut: v Scotland, Kennington Oval, London, February 1872

Bush was an all-round sportsman who was a wicket-keeper for Gloucestershire for 20 years, and the best man at his wedding was WG Grace. He was one of four brothers to play for Clifton, seen as the strongest club in the South outside London. He toured Australia with WG Grace's XI in 1873/74, which caused him to miss an international against Scotland. He had made his international debut against Scotland at The Oval in February 1872. A merchant and then, in 1905, took over the family business, a Public Bonded Warehouse in Bristol.

24. CURREY, Frederick Innes
Forward 1 cap 1872
Born: Blackheath Park, Kent, 3 May 1849
Died: St John's Wood, London, 18 December 1896
Career: Marlborough College, Marlborough Nomads
Debut: v Scotland, Kennington Oval, London, February 1872

Currey was one of the founders of the Rugby Football Union and was a member of the committee that drafted the first rugby laws. Currey helped make Marlborough Nomads one of the best clubs in the country in the early 1870s. A solicitor in Gray's Inn, he served the union as president and on the committee and was a member of the International Board. He refereed Scotland vs Wales in 1886 and attended the South vs North match a week before his death, and ironically, he put together the first team that represented the South against the North.

25. D'AGUILAR, Francis Burton Grant
Forward 1 cap (1t) 1872
Born: Meerut, Bengal, 11 December 1849
Died: Bath, Somerset, 24 July 1896
Career: Royal Engineers, The Army, Bath, Somerset
Debut: v Scotland, Kennington Oval, London, February 1872

D'Aguilar followed Charles Sherrard in attending the Royal Military Academy, Woolwich and playing for England, scoring a try on his only international appearance against Scotland at The Oval in February 1872. A major in the Royal Engineers, he was posted to India, where he spent the whole of his military career. D'Aguilar played for Bath and Somerset like his son John. He " had a splendid physique and great strength, making him a most valuable forward." Francis had fallen ill after returning home on leave four months before his unexpected death aged 46.

26. FINNEY, Sir Stephen CIE
Half-back 2 caps 1 try
Born: Marylebone, London, 8 September 1852
Died: Kensington, London, 1 March 1924
Career: Clifton College, Royal Indian Engineering College
Debut: v Scotland, Kennington Oval, London, February 1872

Finney was a crack half-back of his era who played for Coopers Hill, one of England's strongest teams. He scored a debut try against Scotland at the Oval in February 1972, one of three England scored before winning his second and last cap in the return game in Glasgow twelve months later. Finney worked for the Indian Public Works Department, East Bengal State Railways and, Indian North West Railways and the Indian Railway Board. He was knighted in 1913 and died at his home in Evelyn Gardens, Kensington, 11 years later, aged 71.

27. FREEMAN, Harold Back
Three-quarter 3 caps (2dgs) 1872-1874
Born: Dursley, Gloucestershire, 15 January 1850
Died: Pancras, London, 15 July 1916
Career: Marlborough Nomads,
Debut: v Scotland, Kennington Oval, London, February 1872

Freeman debuted in England's first-ever home match against Scotland at The Oval and scored their first-ever drop goal. He was the only three-quarter back named in a side of 20 and on the winning England side twice in his three matches. The other ended scoreless. While at Oxford University, Freeman assisted in forming the original rules of the Rugby Union and was one of the original Rugby Union committee. He settled in Malvern Wells but died in London following an operation just months after his son Edward, a major with 10th Welsh Fusiliers, lost his life at Flanders.

28. ISHERWOOD, Francis William Ramsbottom
Forward 1 cap (1c) 1872
Born: Reading, Berkshire, 16 October 1852
Died: Southsea, Hampshire, 30 April 1888
Career: Rugby School, Oxford University, Ravenscourt Park
Debut: v Scotland, Kennington Oval, London, February 1872

Isherwood was educated at Rugby School and was the scorer of England's first-ever converted try on his only test appearance in the inaugural home game against Scotland at The Oval in February 1872. He won his university colours in rugby and cricket and scored the winning try in the first varsity match against Cambridge University in 1872. He also played first-class cricket for the MCC and Essex. Isherwood was an oil prospector who worked in the Carpathian Mountains in Central and Eastern Europe. His nephew was Lionel Ramsbottom-Isherwood, who played cricket for the MCC, Hampshire and Sussex.

29. LUSCOMBE, Francis
Forward 6 caps 1872-1876
Born: Norwood, Surrey 23 November 1849
Died: Crawley, Sussex, 17 July 1926
Career: Tonbridge School, Gipsies, The Football Company
Debut: v Scotland, Kennington Oval, London, February 1872

Luscombe founded Peckham-based Gipsies Rugby Club with two friends, including fellow international James Body from Tonbridge School. He was present at the Pall Mall Restaurant when the Rugby Football Union was formed and was one of 13 original members of the RFU committee, later serving as vice president. "Spoiling for a fight,' he urged B H Burns to accept the Scottish club's challenge. The brother of Sir John Luscombe, who played in England's first international, he made his debut in England's first home game. An insurance broker before becoming a celebrated racehorse owner and breeder and sat on the Council of the Racehorse Owners' Association.

30. MACKINLAY, James Egan Harrison M.R.S.S.L.R.C.P. JP
Forward 3 caps 1872-1875
Born: Merrow, Surrey, March 1851
Died: Coatham, Redcar, Yorkshire 1 July 1917
Career: Rugby School, St George's Hospital
Debut: v Scotland, Kennington Oval, London February 1872

Educated at Kensington and Rugby, MacKinlay won the first of his three caps in England's first-ever home game against Scotland at The Oval in February 1872. He was never on the losing team for England, winning twice and drawing the other. A surgeon like his father, he undertook his medical training at St George's Hospital and practised in Redcar for almost all of his career. Interested in education, MacKinlay was chairman at the time of his death of Redcar School Managers. A familiar figure at local race meetings and for a long time was a director of the racecourse.

31. MILLS, Frederick William
Full-back 2 caps 1872-1873
Born: Walton on Thames, Surrey, 5 May 1850
Died: Paddington, London, 2 February 1904
Career: Marlborough College, Marlborough Nomads, Bradford, Yorkshire
Debut: v Scotland, Kennington Oval, London, February 1872

Mills was educated at Marlborough College, where he learnt the game and was a full-back who made the first of his two appearances for England in the first home international against Scotland at The Oval in February 1872. Mills then played in the return game in Scotland a year later, when he had been admitted as a solicitor. He also played for Bradford and Yorkshire, became the solicitor for the Great Western Railway at Paddington Station, and was still employed by the GWR at the time of his death.

32. MOBERLY, William Octavius
Back 1 cap 1872
Born: Shoreham, Sussex, 14 November 1851
Died: Mullion, Cornwall, 2 February 1914
Career: Oxford University, Ravenscourt Park, Clifton, Gloucestershire
Debut: v Scotland, Kennington Oval, London, February 1872

Moberly was a clever three-quarter who played in England's first-ever home international against Scotland at The Oval. He had already won an Oxford University blue when he was capped and was Oxford's captain in the very first Varsity Match, whose rules stated: "that the captain be always a Rugbeian." Moberly also played cricket as a top-order batsman and occasional wicketkeeper for his University and Gloucestershire CCC along with Clifton and England team-mates James Bush. He was a schoolmaster teaching at Clifton College between 1874 and 1913. He died a few months later after suffering from failing health.

33. PINCHING, William Wyatt
Forward 1 cap 1872
Born: Gravesend, Kent 24 March 1851
Died: At Sea 16 August 1878
Career: King's College School, Cheltenham College, Guy's Hospital
Debut: v Scotland, Kennington Oval, London, February 1872

'Nipper' Pinching learnt the game at Kings College School and then Gloucestershire College. He was the first player supplied by Guy's Hospital, where he was undertaking his medical training when he made his only appearance for England in their first-ever home international match against Scotland at The Oval in February 1872. He would never get the opportunity to play for England again, and like his father, he was a surgeon. Pinching went into practice before serving aboard the steamship Eldorado. Tragically, but was lost overboard a day out from Columbo, Ceylon, aged just 27.

34. WILKINSON, Percival
Half-back 1 cap 1872
Born: Hampstead, London, 16 December 1847
Died: Bahia, Brazil, 9 May 1885
Career: The Hampstead Football Club, Law Club, Harlequins
Debut: v Scotland, Kennington Oval, London, February 1872

Wilkinson was a half-back whose family was deeply rooted in the legal profession. His father, grandfather, two brothers and two sons all worked in the law. The family firm had an office at Lincoln's Inn Field, and he was listed as a member of the Law Club, a club that exclusively drew their players from members of the legal profession when he made his England debut against Scotland at Kennington Oval in February 1872. Perceval would also later turn out for Harlequins. Perceval died a fortnight after reaching Bahia, Brazil, of yellow fever, aged 37.

35. BOYLE, Cecil William
Half-back 1 cap 1873
Born: Westminster, London 16 March 1853
Died: KIA Boshof, Orange Free State, South Africa, 5 April 1900
Career: Oxford University
Debut: v Scotland, West of Scotland Club, Glasgow, March 1873

Boyle was the first player from Oxford University to be capped for the England rugby team when he played his only test against Scotland at the West of Scotland Club in March 1873. Cecil won a cricketing blue the same year and took a first-class hat trick for Oxford University against Middlesex. Boyce, a member of the Stock Exchange, served in the Boer War as a captain in the Queen's Own Oxfordshire Hussars regiment of the Imperial Yeomanry. He took 30 horses to South Africa and became the first member of the Imperial Yeomanry to be killed in action.

36. CHESTON, Ernest Constantine
Forward 5 caps 1 try 1873-1876
Born: Hackney, Middlesex, 24 October 1848
Died: Deal, Kent, 9 July 1913
Career: Haileybury and Imperial Service College, Oxford University, Law Club, Richmond
Debut: v Scotland, West of Scotland Club, Glasgow, March 1873

Cheston was the captain of Haileybury and Imperial Service College and then captain of the Boat Club while attending Merton College, Oxford. He was registered to the Law Club, a club only open to members of the legal profession, when he made his England debut against Scotland at the West of Scotland Club in March 1873. He moved to Richmond, where he won his other caps and scored his only try in England's first international against Ireland at The Oval in February 1875. Cheston became a solicitor like his father, operating from Great Winchester Street, London.

37. FLETCHER, William Robert Badger
Forward 2 caps 1873-1875
Born: Darjeeling, West Bengal, 10 December 1851
Died: Kensington, London, 20 April 1895
Career: Marlborough College, Oxford University, Blackheath, Marlborough Nomads, South
Debut: v Scotland, West of Scotland Club, Glasgow March 1873

Fletcher was born in West Bengal when his father, John, served in the Army but returned to England to be schooled at Marlborough College and Oxford University, where he won his colours in 1872, in the first-ever Varsity meeting, 1873 and 1874. He made international appearances in Scotland in 1873, the third meeting between the two nations and then in 1875. Fletcher played his cub rugby for Blackheath and Marlborough Nomads, with whom he was registered when he made his debut. Fletcher, a merchant, died suddenly at the home of a sister due to rapid consumption.

38. LAWRENCE, Hon Henry Arnold
Forward 4 caps 1873-1875
Born: Lahore, India, 13 March 1848
Died: Minchinhampton, Gloucestershire, 16 April 1902
Career: Wellington College, Richmond
Debut: v Scotland, West of Scotland Club, Glasgow March 1873

Lawrence was the son of the first Baron Lawrence and was educated at Wellington College, whom he captained in 1864. He made his international debut against Scotland at the West of Scotland Club in March 1873. Lawrence captained England in their first-ever international against Ireland at The Oval in February 1875 and was only the third man after Fred Stokes and Alf Hamersley to do so. Later, serving as vice president of the union but did not seek election as president because of business commitments. He was a director of the London office of the Ottoman Bank.

39. MARSH, Henry CIB
Forward 1 cap 1873
Born: Mountrath, County Laois, 8 September 1850
Died: Chalfont St Peter, Buckinghamshire, 25 April 1939
Career. Royal Indian Engineering College
Debut: v Scotland, West of Scotland Club, Glasgow, March 1873

Marsh went to the Royal Indian Engineering College in Cooper's Hill with Sir Stephen Finney, a team-mate, when he made his only international appearance against Scotland at the West of Scotland Club in March 1873. Marsh would have been unavailable the following year as he was by then working as a Civil Engineer in India in the employment of the India Public Works Department. He later served the Government of India as a Consulting Engineer for Irrigation in Central India and then worked in Mexico and Argentina before returning home to London for his retirement.

40. MARSHALL, Murray Wyatt
Forward 10 caps 1873-1878
Born: Guildford, Surrey, 7 October 1852
Died: Godalming, Surrey, 28 July 1930
Career: Blackheath, Surrey
Debut: v Scotland, West of Scotland Club, Glasgow, March 1873

Wyatt debuted against Scotland at the West of Scotland Club in March 1873 and became England's most-capped player, making his tenth and final appearance when he captained the first visit to Lansdowne Road in March 1878. His record was to stand for 36 years. He was said to be "in every respect one of the best forwards England ever turned out. Possessed of great height and strength, he was invaluable in a scrummage, used his feet well when the ball got loose, and was a very clever tackle." Wyatt was a Timber merchant and served on the Surrey CCC committee.

41. MORSE, Sydney
Back 3 caps 1873-1875
Born: Birmingham, Warwickshire, 1 June 1854
Died: Campden Hill, London, 27 January 1929
Career: Marlborough College, Law Club, Marlborough Nomads
Debut: v Scotland, West of Scotland Club, Glasgow, March 1873

Morse was a solicitor registered with the Law Club whose membership was only open to members of the legal profession when he made his England debut against Scotland at the West of Scotland Club in March 1873. Described as "a dashing runner and good drop with either foot," his only two appearances were when he joined Marlborough Nomads, his former school's old boys club. He established a law firm, Sydney Morse & Co, in the City of London, while his brother, Edward St John Morse, played for Cambridge University in the first varsity match.

42. RICKARDS, Cyril Henry
Forward 1 cap 1873
Born: Jeypore, India, 11 January 1854
Died: Thanet, Kent, 25 February 1920
Career: Rugby School, Cheltenham College, Royal Military Academy Woolwich, Gipsies
Debut: v Scotland, West of Scotland Club, Glasgow, March 1873

Rickards, born in India into a military family, was educated at Rugby School, Cheltenham College and the RMA Woolwich. He played for Peckham-based Gipsies and made his only international appearance against Scotland at the West of Scotland Club in March 1873 in a match which produced England's first 0-0 draw. He was probably restricted from making more international by following his father, a colonel serving in the Army. Serving in the Royal Artillery in Woolwich, Ratcliff Gardens, Southsea, and Bengal. After retiring as a major, he moved to Lingfield, Sussex.

43. STILL, Ernest Robert
Forward 1 cap 1873
Born: Epsom, Surrey, 14 July 1852
Died: Windfield, Surrey, 30 November 1931
Career: Rugby School, Oxford University, Ravenscourt Park
Debut: v Scotland, West of Scotland Club, Glasgow, March 1873

Old Rugbeian Still captained Oxford University before becoming the fifth and last player from Ravenscourt Park to play for England. He was selected to make his only international appearance in a scoreless draw against Scotland at the West of Scotland Club in March 1873. He became a solicitor with Trower, Still, Kelling & Parkin at Winfield Leatherhead. He played a key role in forming Imperial Tobacco. Still became the company solicitor and was later appointed to the board of directors. He was also a director of the Guardian Assurance Company and several other companies before his death.

44. VANDERSPAR, Charles Henry Richard
Full-back 1 cap 1873
Born: Kandy, Ceylon, 1 July 1852
Died: Columbo, Ceylon, 9 April 1877
Career: Wellington College, Richmond
Debut: v Scotland, West of Scotland Club, Glasgow, March 1873

Vanderspar was born in Ceylon, now Sri Lanka, but was sent to England to be educated at Wellington College, where he first played the game. After leaving, he applied to join Richmond and was only 19 when he won his only international cap against Scotland at the West of Scotland Club in March 1873 in a game that ended in a scoreless draw. Vanderspar wasn't selected again because he left the country and returned to Ceylon soon afterwards to start a career as a merchant in Singapore and Australia. Tragically, he was dead four years later, aged just 23.

45. BATTEN, John Maxwell
Full-back 1 cap 1874
Born: Almora, Kumaon 28 February 1853
Died: St Albans, Hertfordshire, 15 October 1917
Career: Oxford University, Kelly College.
Debut: v Scotland, Kennington Oval, London February 1874

Batten won a Cambridge University blue between 1871 and 1874 and was the captain for his last two seasons. He also played rackets for the university. Batten, who played in the first encounter between the great establishments, scored one of three tries in Cambridge's first Varsity success. A schoolmaster who taught at his old school, Haileybury College, then Kelly College, where he also played for and coached the rugby team, Newton Abbott School, was headmaster at Plymouth College between 1884 and 1889. Batten became Secretary of the British Branch of the Equitable Life Assurance Society.

46. BROOKS, Hon Marshall Jones
Full-back 1 cap 1874
Born: Crawshawbooth, Lancashire, 30 May 1855
Died: Tarporley, Cheshire, 5 January 1944
Career: Rugby School, Oxford University
Debut: v Scotland, Kennington Oval, London February 1874

Brooks was the son of the 1st baron Crawshaw and won his Oxford University blue in 1873, which led to his only England appearance against Scotland at The Oval in February 1874. Brooks was more noted for his achievements in Athletics, winning a blue between 1874 and 1976. He also held the world record for the High Jump on three occasions, one standing for over half a century. A land and mineral owner and a director of the Manchester and County Bank. Brooks was a Justice of the peace for Cheshire and, at one point, for Lancashire.

47. BRYDEN, Henry Anderson
Forward 1 cap 1874
Born: Banbury, Oxfordshire, 3 May 1854
Died: Parkstone, Dorset, 23 September 1939
Career: Clapton Rovers
Debut: v Scotland, Kennington Oval, London, February 1874

Bryden was already an acclaimed long-distance runner, the English amateur mile record holder when he came second to Walter Slade, the RFU treasurer when he set the world best of 4m 24.5s at Stamford Bridge in 1875. He played his club rugby for the dual code side Clapham Rovers alongside older brother and fellow international Charles and made his only international appearance against Scotland at The Oval in February 1874. Although Bryden was trained as a solicitor, he became an author of books on African sport and natural history after moving to Africa in the 1890s.

48. COLLINS, William Edward
Half-back 5 caps (1t) 1874-1876
Born: Monghyr, India 14 October 1853
Died: Wellington, New Zealand, 11 August 1934
Career: Old Cheltonians, St George's Hospital, Oxford University
Debut: v Scotland, Kennington Oval, London, February 1874

Collins was a half-back who debuted against Scotland at The Oval in February 1874 and scored his only try against the same opposition two years later. William also played in the first Hospital's Cup Final between St George's and Guy's in 1875. He worked at the Brompton Hospital for Consumptives before emigrating to New Zealand three years later. In New Zealand, Collins kept wicket for Wellington in first-class cricket and was an Honorary physician and then Honorary surgeon at Wellington Hospital. He served in the NZ Medical Corps during World War One, having entered politics as a member of the Legislative Council of New Zealand from 1907 until his death.

49. CROSSE, Charles William
Forward 2 caps 1874-1875
Born: Bushey, Middlesex 13 June 1854
Died: Paris, France, 28 May 1905
Career: Rugby School, Oxford University, Royal Military Academy Sandhurst
Debut: v Scotland, Kennington Oval, London, February 1874

Crosse won his university colours in 1874, the year he was selected to win his first game for England. He retained his place for the first-ever international with Ireland but, along with Edward Nash, was refused permission by Oxford University to play against Scotland in Edinburgh in March 1875. He played cricket for his university and then Scotland. Crosse joined the 1st Dragoon Guards in 1876, served in the Transvaal campaign in 1881, and was Adjutant in the North Devon Yeomanry Cavalry before taking retirement pay as a major in 1894. He then appears to have died in Paris 11 years later.

50. CUNLIFFE, Foster Lionel
Forward 1 cap 1874
Born: Llanfyllin, Wales, 20 April 1854
Died: Cuckfield, Sussex, 15 April 1927
Career: Rugby School, RMA Woolwich
Debut: v Scotland, Kennington Oval, London February 1874

Rugby School-educated Cunliffe won his only international cap against Scotland at The Oval in February 1874, while at the Royal Military Academy Woolwich. It is almost certain that his military career ended any further chance of international caps. A career soldier, he had been gazetted to the Academy before winning his cap and rose through the ranks fighting in the Second Anglo-Afghan War and the North West Frontier India and Tirah Expedition. Cunliffe later became a lieutenant colonel in the Royal Horse Artillery and was commander of the Artillery Territorial Forces between 1908 and 1911.

51. GENTH, James Scherer
Forward 2 caps 1874-1875
Born: Ardwick Lancashire, 17 July 1849
Died: Fulham, London, 2 April 1926
Career: Manchester
Debut: v Scotland, Kennington Oval, London, February 1874

Born Jacob Genth, he was picked alongside Manchester team-mate Roger Walker to make his England debut for England at The Oval in a game that they won by one drop goal to a try. Then after missing the first-ever game against Ireland a year later, he was recalled to the side for the return game with the Scots in Edinburgh in a game that ended 0-0. Sometime later in life, he changed his name to James and was a yarn buyer and then a shipping merchant. And moved to South-West London and lived in Fulham until his death.

52. KEWLEY, Edward
Forward 7 caps 1874-1878
Born: Eton, Buckinghamshire, 20 June 1852
Died: Winchester, Hampshire, 17 April 1940
Career: Liverpool, Lancashire
Debut: v Scotland, Kennington Oval, London, February 1874

Kewley was educated at Marlborough College but moved to Lancashire to work in the cotton industry as a cotton broker and joined Liverpool. He captained England three times and was the first captain to be drawn from The North, whom he also represented on the RFU committee. Kewley's first game as captain was against Ireland in February 1877, the first game when teams were reduced to 15-a-side. He also played first-class cricket for Lancashire. He served Liverpool as honorary secretary, treasurer and president and Lancashire Football Club as a president and committee member.

53. MILTON, Sir William Henry
Three-quarter 2 caps 1874-1875
Born: Great Marlow, Buckinghamshire, 3 December 1854
Died: Cannes, France, 6 March 1930
Career: Marlborough Nomads, Villagers (Cape Town)
Debut: v Scotland, Kennington Oval, London, February 1874

Milton was a half-back who debuted for England against Scotland at The Oval in February 1874 and won his second and final cap a year later against Ireland at the same venue. After emigrating to South Africa, he played test cricket and became the second-ever skipper of his adoptive country. England also capped his sons Cecil Milton and Jumbo Milton. Worked in colonial service as Mashonaland's 3rd Administrator and then Administrator of Southern Rhodesia. Milton retired in September 1914, aged 60, for health reasons and has a school in Bulawayo named after him.

54. PARKER, Hon Sidney
Forward 2 caps 1874-1875
Born: Shirburn Castle, Oxfordshire, 3 October 1853
Died: Knightsbridge, Middlesex, 21 May 1897
Career: Rugby School, Liverpool, Lancashire
Debut: v Scotland, Kennington Oval, London, February 1874

Parker was one of 15 children born to Thomas Augustus Wolstenholme Parker, the 6th Earl of Macclesfield, and was educated at Rugby School. He made his international debut against Scotland at The Oval in February 1874. He missed their next game, the first-ever international against Ireland, a year later. But was recalled to the side for the trip to Scotland in March 1875. Parker, the nephew of the Duke of Westminster, owned a freehold tea plantation, The Oaklands, in Dibrugarh, Assam, India but returned to London before his death when he was aged 44.

55. STAFFORD, William Francis Howard CB
Forward 1 cap 1874
Born: Hansi, India, 19 December 1854
Died: Wokingham, Berkshire, 8 August 1942
Career: Royal Engineers, The Army
Debut: v Scotland, Kennington Oval, London, February 1874

Stafford was born into a military family. His father was Major-General WJF Stafford, so it was always likely he would make a career in The Army. He served in the Royal Engineers in the Afgan War and South Africa. He reached the rank of brigadier general, and his career choice is almost certainly why he only won one England cap against Scotland at The Oval in February 1874. Despite retiring in 1911, he re-enlisted for World War One aged 60 and was mentioned in dispatches after commanding the South Irish Defences in the North-West Frontier of India.

56. WALKER, Roger
Forward 5 caps 1874-1880
Born: Bury, Lancashire, 18 September 1846
Died: Reading, Berkshire, 11 November 1919
Career: Manchester
Debut: v Scotland, Kennington Oval, London, February 1874

Walker was a "sterling and useful forward" and used his weight and strength well in the scrum. He debuted against Scotland at The Oval in February 1874 after joining the RFU committee to give The North a say in international selection. Also served on the international board, was RFU President, managed the British team, which toured South Africa in 1896 and helped found Reading Rugby Club. Roger also played first-class cricket for Lancashire and turned out for the MCC. Walker was an iron founder who became an engineer but had retired by the time he was 44.

57. ADAMS, Frank Reginald
Forward 7 caps (2t) 1875-1879
Born: Newcastle-upon-Tyne 14 September 1852
Died: Vancouver, British Columbia, 10 October 1932
Career: Wellington College, Richmond, Middlesex
Debut: v Ireland, Kennington Oval, London February 1875

Adams was educated at Wellington College like many of England's earliest internationals and was one of nine new caps when he debuted in England's first-ever international against Ireland at The Oval in February 1875. He won his caps over four years and was captain for the first Calcutta Cup match against Scotland in 1879. He captained Middlesex and was a shipping insurer in business in Australia, New Zealand and the United States, and it was a career which ended his rugby playing days because of his extensive travelling. Adams lived in Canada until his death.

58. FRASER, Sir Edward Cleather CMG
Forward 1 cap 1875
Born: Mauritius, 2 April 1853
Died: Sheringham, Norfolk, 15 October 1927
Career: Merton College, Oxford University, Blackheath
Debut: v Ireland, Kennington Oval, London, February 1875

Mauritius-born Fraser played for Merton College in 1872 and played for Oxford University from 1873 to 1875, appearing in the second varsity game. He was educated at Blackheath Prep School, whose old boys club founded Blackheath, where he played his club rugby. Fraser made his only international appearance in England's first-ever fixture against Ireland at The Oval, and following his graduation, he returned to Mauritius to work in his father's business, Fraser & Co, becoming a partner. He was the island's consul for Sweden, a director of the Bank of Mauritius, and a member of the Council of Government of Mauritius until 1923, when he was knighted.

59. GRAHAM, Henry James
Forward 4 caps 1875-1876
Born: Wimbledon, Surrey, 12 August 1853
Died: Remenham, Surrey, 22 December 1911
Career: Wimbledon Hornets, Surrey
Debut: v Ireland, Kennington Oval, London, February 1875

Graham made his international debut against Ireland at The Oval in February 1875 but then played alongside his younger brother John for the first game in Ireland at Leinster Cricket Club a year later. Graham was treasurer of the RFU between 1876 and 1878. He was also the person that the donors of the Calcutta Cup corresponded with when they offered the trophy to the Union for the annual competition against Scotland. Graham won two of his caps against Scotland. A wine merchant who was then described as living by private means.

60. HUTCHINSON, William Henry Heap
Forward 2 caps 1875
Born: Cottingham, Yorkshire, 31 October 1850
Died: Elloughton, Yorkshire, 4 July 1929
Career: Rugby School, Hull, Yorkshire
Debut: v Ireland, Kennington Oval, London, February 1875

Hutchinson was a "fine strapping forward known as The Baron" who made both international appearances against Ireland at The Oval and then was a member of the first side to cross the Irish Sea in December 1875. Yorkshire's first-ever captain was the first county player to play for England, but Richard Osborn was the first Yorkshireman to win an international cap. Hutchinson was a founding member of Hull, a club which helped form the Northern Union in 1895. He was a stone mason and became a steamship owner like his father until he retired.

61. MICHELL, Rev Arthur Tompson
Half-back 3 caps (1t) 1875
Born: Headington, Oxford, 19 September 1853
Died: Headington, Oxford, 13 August 1923
Career: Rugby School, Oxford University, Ravenscourt Park
Debut: v Ireland, Kennington Oval, London, February 1875

Michell won an Oxford University blue between 1871 and 1874, while during his time at Oxford, he also won the university sculls. Arthur made his England debut in the first-ever international against Ireland at The Oval in February 1875, scoring a debut try and winning two more caps against Scotland and then the return match with the Irish at the Leinster Cricket Ground in December 1875. Michell edited three volumes of the Rugby School Register and was a clergyman ordained in 1879, spending 31 years in Shifnal, Shropshire before returning to his native Oxford.

62. NASH, Edward Henry
Half-back 1 cap (1dg) 1875
Born: Upton-cum-Chalvey, Buckinghamshire, 20 December 1854
Died: Gerrards Cross, Buckinghamshire, 18 September 1932
Career: Rugby School, Oxford University, Richmond
Debut: v Ireland, Kennington Oval, London, February 1875

Nash won his rugby blue and Cricket blue at Oxford in 1874 and 1875. He won one England cap against Ireland at The Oval in February 1875, scoring a drop goal, but was denied another cap after, along with Charles Crosse, was refused permission by the Dean of Trinity College to play against Scotland in Raeburn Place the following month. Nash was a founding member of the Hockey Association in 1885, later serving as vice president and president. He was with Wood, Nash and Co. solicitors of Grays Inn Field until his retirement in 1925 and was a landowner in Slough.

63. PEARSON, Alexander William
Full-back 7 caps (4c) 1875-1878
Born: Kalkallo, Australia, 30 September 1853
Died: Charlton, Victoria, 1908 January 27, 1930
Career: Guy's Hospital, Blackheath
Debut: v Ireland, Kennington Oval, London, February 1875

Pearson was the son of a Liverpool sea captain who became the first Australian-born rugby international but was educated in London. He was a member of the Guy's Hospital team, which won the first-ever Hospitals' Cup in 1875. Although Lennard Stokes, the full-back that also won his first international cap against Ireland at The Oval in February 1875, said Alec "never did any work at Guy's and only entered to play in the cup ties." Pearson returned to Australia to run the family's Mount Ridley and Wheatlands properties with a brother who played for Blackheath.

64. PERROTT, Edward Simcocks
Forward 1 cap 1875
Born: Llanfyllin, Montgomeryshire, 16 September 1852
Died: Llansantffraid, Montgomeryshire, 22 April 1915
Career: Cheltenham College, Old Cheltonians
Debut: v Ireland, Kennington Oval, London, February 1875

Perrott was educated at Cheltenham College, where he first played the game and went on to play for his school's Old Boys side, Old Cheltonians. He made his only international appearance in England's first-ever test against Ireland at The Oval in February 1875. He was a businessman in China with interests including a tea plantation before retiring back to his native Montgomeryshire, where he became a farmer while also taking an interest in county-wide and local affairs, serving as a justice of the peace and a county councillor. Edward was also a regular follower of Border Counties Otter Hounds.

65. STOKES, Dr Lennard
Full-back 12 caps (17c,2dgs) 1875-1881
Born: Greenwich, Kent, 12 February 1856
Died: Alton, Hampshire, 3 May 1933
Career: Guy's Hospital, Blackheath, Kent
Debut: v Ireland, Kennington Oval, London, February 1875

Stokes, the most scientific player of his age, was the brother of Frederick Stokes and the brother-in-law of Joseph Green. He captained Blackheath for five seasons and England in five of his 12 caps, including their first test against Wales on his home ground, Richardson's Field (a ground he acquired for Blackheath), in February 1881 when he kicked six conversions. Elected to the RFU committee in 1876 and served for over 50 years. Also played county cricket for Kent. Stokes became a GP in Blackheath and later in Hampshire and was an honorary surgeon at St John's Hospital, Lewisham.

66. BIRKETT, Louis
Full-back 3 caps 1875-1877
Born: Southwark, London, 1 January 1853
Died: Barnstaple, Devon, 11 April 1943
Career: Clapton Rovers, Middlesex
Debut: v Scotland, Raeburn Place, Edinburgh March 1875

Birkett was educated at Haileybury and played two of his three international games with elder brother Reginald, including his debut against Scotland at Raeburn Place, Edinburgh, in March 1875. A commercial clerk who then spent many years working as a wool brokers manager for Ducroz, Doxat, and Company living in Chislehurst, Kent. He then moved to Barnstaple, Devon, during the Second World War and was one of England's longest-living internationals when he died. Birkett was also the uncle of John, the third member of the Birkett family to win international caps.

67. EVANSON, Wyndham Alleyn Daubeny
Half-back 5 caps (1t) 1875-1879
Born: Llansoy, Monmouthshire, June 1851
Died: Crowborough, Sussex, 30 October 1934
Career: Owls, Civil Service, Richmond, Middlesex
Debut: v Scotland, Raeburn Place, Edinburgh March 1875

Evanson was a half-back who spent the later stages of his debut against Scotland at Raeburn Place, Edinburgh, in March 1975 as a three-quarter after switching with Arthur Michell. A distinguished oarsman and sculler, a member of the London Rowling Club and won the Grand Challenge Cup at Henley. A brother, Arthur, also wore the red rose. A surveyor in the General Post Office working in Ireland, Scotland, the Home Counties and then the South Eastern district before moving to Crowborough to retire, where he became a scratch golfer aged 60. During World War Two, Wyndham moved to Barnstaple, Devon, where he died.

68. PAUL, Josiah Edward
Forward 1 cap 1875
Born: Tetbury, Gloucestershire, 24 April 1853
Died: Malvern, Worcestershire, 5 August 1928
Career: Rugby School, Royal Indian College
Debut: v Scotland, Raeburn Place, Edinburgh, March 1875

Paul started playing rugby football at Rugby School and continued to play the game after joining Cooper's Hill College, which had one of the leading teams of the time. He was registered to Cooper's Hill when he won his only international cap against Scotland at Raeburn Place, Edinburgh, in March 1975. He joined the Madras Public Works Department six months after finishing his training. This was almost certainly why Paul didn't win at further caps, remaining with them all his working life and working his way up to become an executive engineer, retiring in December 1900.

69. BREWER, Jeaffreson Vennor
Forward 1 cap 1875
Born: Ebbw Vale, Monmouthshire, October 1853
Died: Islington, London, 25 May 1924
Career: The Royal Medical Benevolent College, Gipsies, Middlesex
Debut: v Ireland, Leinster Cricket Ground, Rathmines, December 1875

Brewer captained his school, The Royal Medical Benevolent College, along with his brother Frederick. He joined Gipsies Football Club and was elected to the club committee aged 15 in 1868 and was the only member who didn't attend Tonbridge School. Brewer won his only international cap against Ireland at Leinster Cricket Ground in December 1875. A leading figure in 1878, he was one of seven men asked by the RFU to review and revise the laws of rugby. Brewer left school to become a spice broker and a market clerk for Dalton & Young General Labourer Brokers.

70. BRYDEN, Charles Cowper
Forward 2 caps 1875-1877
Born: Banbury, Oxfordshire, 16 June 1852
Died: Parkstone, Dorset, 20 February 1941
Career: Cheltenham College, Clapham Rovers
Debut: v Ireland, Leinster Cricket Ground, Rathmines, December 1875

Bryden was the elder brother of Henry, who also played for their local team, Clapham Rovers, whom he later served as a vice president. He had learnt to play the game during his education at Cheltenham College and won the first of his two caps against Ireland at Leinster Cricket Ground in December 1875 but had to wait until March 1877 and the defeat to Scotland to win his second and last cap at the expense of Eric Kewley. Bryden became a City of London freeman, working as a hide broker before becoming a colonial broker.

71. BULTEEL, Andrew Marcus
Forward 1 cap 1875
Born: Liverpool, Lancashire 29 September 1849
Died: Melbourne, Australia, 3 June 1888
Career: Manchester
Debut: v Ireland, Leinster Cricket Ground, Rathmines, December 1875

Bulteel was born in Liverpool but grew up in Manchester after his family moved when he was a child. After leaving school, he worked as a clerk and played rugby for Manchester. He did enough to catch the eye of selectors and was selected for his only England cap against Ireland at the Leinster Cricket Ground, Rathmines, in December 1875, which England won by one try and goal to nil. Bulteel joined the 40th Lancashire Rifle Volunteer Corps, becoming a lieutenant. After resigning from his commission in 1879, he lived in India before dying in Melbourne, Australia, aged 38.

72. CLARK, Charles William Henry
Half Back 1 cap (1t) 1875
Born: Everton, Lancashire, 19 March 1856
Died: Aughton, Lancashire, 17 October 1943
Career: Rugby School, Liverpool, Lancashire
Debut: v Ireland, Leinster Cricket Ground, Rathmines, December 1875

Clerk was a half-back who attended Rugby School, where he first played rugby football. After playing his club rugby for Liverpool, he made his only England appearance against Ireland at Leinster Cricket Ground, Rathmines, in December 1875. He scored a try, but it wasn't counted in the scoring after Alec Pearson failed to convert. Despite his try-scoring performance, he wasn't retained for the next game when the selectors called up W C Hutchinson. A commercial clerk who became a partner in spice millers and general merchants. A keen golfer, Clerk became captain of Ormskirk Golf Club in 1914.

73. GRAHAM, John Duncan George
Forward 1 cap 1875
Born: Wimbledon, Surrey 1856
Died: Ryde, Isle of Wight, 6 March 1931
Career: Wellington College, Wimbledon Hornets, Surrey
Debut: v Ireland, Leinster Cricket Ground, Rathmines, December 1875

Wellington College-educated Graham won his only international cap against Ireland at Leinster Cricket Ground, Rathmines, in December 1875 alongside brother Henry. The Wimbledon Hornets pair were the first brothers to be capped in the same game. But Graham couldn't retain his place for the next match against Scotland at Kennington Oval three months later. A member of the Stock Exchange and in the First World War was the Minister of Munitions. He then took up journalism and was on the staff of The African World. Graham was also the owner of the African Industries, which he later sold and retired to the Isle of Wight.

74. GREG, Walter
Forward 2 caps 1875-1876
Born: Bollington, Cheshire, 4 February 1851
Died: Assouan, Egypt, 5 February 1906
Career: Marlborough College, Marlborough Nomads, Manchester, Lancashire
Debut: v Ireland, Leinster Cricket Ground, Rathmines December 1875

Greg went to Marlborough College and then played for Marlborough Nomads, but when winning his two England caps, he was registered with Manchester, whom he captained and played alongside a cousin. Greg won his first England cap against Ireland at Leinster Cricket Ground, Rathmines, in December 1875 and then retained his place for the fixture against Scotland three months later, but it proved to be his final cap. A solicitor who was a partner in Cuncliffe Greg in Manchester, he twice served as under-sheriff of Lancashire and Cheshire. He died in the Cataract Hotel in Assouan, Egypt.

75. GUNNER, Charles Richards
Three-quarter 1 cap 1875
Born: Bishops Waltham, Hampshire, 7 January 1853
Died: Bishops Waltham, Hampshire, 4 February 1924
Career: Marlborough College, Marlborough Nomads
Debut: v Ireland, Leinster Cricket Ground, Rathmines December 1875

Marlborough College-educated Charles Gunner played for Marlborough Nomads and won his only England cap against Ireland at Leinster Cricket Ground, Rathmines, in December 1875 but lost his place for the game against Scotland three months later. He also made a single first-class appearance for Hampshire CCC against Derbyshire. His son John also played for Hampshire before being killed in World War One, one of three sons Gunner lost during the First World War. He was a solicitor and banker and served as a clerk to Droxford magistrates for 40 years until his death.

76. LOGIN, Spencer Henry Metcalfe CVO
Full-back 1 cap 1875
Born: Futleghur, Punjab, 24 September 1851
Died: Claygate, Surrey, 22 January 1909
Career: Wellington College, Royal Naval College (Dartmouth)
Debut: v Ireland, Leinster Cricket Ground, Rathmines December 1875

Login was one of two full-backs selected for the win over Ireland at Leinster Cricket Ground, Rathmines, in December 1875, playing alongside Alex Pearson. But for England's next international against Scotland three months later, he lost his place to Arthur Heath and never played again, more than likely because of his navy duties. Login joined the Navy as a cadet and later commanded battleships, rising through the ranks to become a Rear Admiral in 1906, the year he became a founder member of the Royal Navy RFU and served as their first president.

77. MARRIOTT, Ernest Edward
Forward 1 cap 1875
Born: Salford, Lancashire, 15 January 1857
Died: Tottenham, London, October 1914
Career: Rugby School, Manchester, Lancashire
Debut: v Ireland, Leinster Cricket Ground, Rathmines, December 1875

Marriott was educated at Rugby School and played for Manchester, the club that his father Henry founded in 1860 and who served as their first president. He won his only England cap against Ireland at Leinster Cricket Ground, Rathmines, in December 1875 alongside Manchester club-mates Walter Greg and Andrew Bulteel. Interestingly, despite ending up on the winning side, none of the trio kept their places for the next game against Scotland three months later. Marriott was a businessman who was a commission agent before becoming a paint manufacturer based in London.

78. TURNER, Edward Beadon
Forward 3 caps (1t) 1875-1878
Born: Chigwell, Essex, September 1854
Died: Hype Park, London, 30 June 1931
Career: Uppingham School, Old Uppinghamians, St George's Hospital, Middlesex
Debut: v Ireland, Leinster Cricket Ground, Rathmines December 1875

Turner, the brother of Sir George, made his debut against Ireland at Leinster Cricket Ground, Rathmines, in December 1875. He scored his only try against Ireland in the first-ever international played at Lansdowne Road in March 1878. He was a talented sportsman with several tricycle world records from two to 25 miles. Like his brother, Turner went into medicine and was in private practice near Hyde Park before joining the British Medical Association Council. During his lifetime, he served on numerous committees and medical bodies and was president of the Old Uppinghamians Rugby Club.

79. VERELST, Courteney Lee
Forward 2 caps 1875-1878
Born: Claughton, Wirral, 16 November 1855
Died: Pembrokeshire, Wales, 1 January 1890
Career: Charterhouse School, Liverpool, Lancashire
Debut: v Ireland, Leinster Cricket Ground, Rathmines, December 1875

Verelst was educated at Charterhouse School and played his club rugby for Liverpool, where he was a team-mate of Eric

Kewley. Courteney won his first international cap against Ireland at Leinster Cricket Ground, Rathmines, in December 1875. He was a coffee planter in Ceylon, which is probably why he had to wait until the first visit to Lansdowne Road in March 1878 to win his second and final cap. His life ended in tragic circumstances when he entered Priory Lunatic Asylum in Pembrokeshire, Wales, in February 1889, where he would remain until his death on New Year's Day 1890, aged 34.

80. HEATH, Arthur Howard JP MP
Full Back 1 cap 1876
Born: Titterton, Staffordshire, 29 May 1856
Died: Portman Square, London, 21 April 1930
Career: Clifton College, Oxford University, Blackheath
Debut: v Scotland, Kennington Oval, London, March 1876

Heath was the son of Robert Heath, who was the MP for Stoke. He went to Oxford University and won a blue in rugby and cricket. Heath made his only international appearance against Scotland at Kennington Oval, London, in March 1876. He also played county cricket for Gloucestershire, Middlesex and Staffordshire and was a playing member of the MCC. An industrialist, his business interests included newspapers, a colliery proprietor, iron master and Conservative MP for Hanley and then Leek and Staffordshire County Council. During the First World War, Heath was mentioned in dispatches as a lieutenant colonel on the Staff of the Royal Field Artillery.

81. HUNT, William Henry
Forward 4 caps 1876-1878
Born: Preston Lancashire, 11 May 1854
Died: Chorlton, Lancashire, 13 May 1904
Career: Preston Grasshoppers, Manchester, Lancashire
Debut: v Scotland, Kennington Oval, London, March 1876

Hunt was the eldest of three brothers to play for England. Younger siblings John and Robert followed him into the national team. He won his first cap against Scotland at Kennington Oval, London, in March 1876, playing three of the following four games. Initially in the Army, he commanded the 5th Lancs Artillery Volunteers. A talented horseman, he won the Royal Military Tournament Lance v Sword (mounted) competition in 1889. After leaving the Army, he became a wine and spirit merchant while living in Ansdell nr Lytham St Annes until he retired just before his death on a visit to Manchester.

82. HUTCHINSON, William Charles
Half-back 2 Caps (2t) 1876-1877
Born: Charlton, Kent Q2 1855
Died: At sea, Aden, 26 March 1880
Career: Royal Indian Engineering College,
Debut: v Scotland, Kennington Oval, London, March 1876

Hutchinson ran the 100 yards before taking up rugby. Hutchinson was one of a handful of players to play in both the 20 and 15 a-side eras. He made his debut against Scotland at Kennington Oval, London, in March 1876 in the last 20 a-side game and then his last in the first 15 a-side contest against Ireland at The Oval in February 1877 when he scored two tries. His job with the Indian Public Works department curtailed his rugby career, but he was on his way home on sick leave when he died on board the Peninsular and Oriental steamship Nepaul.

83. LEE, Frederic Hugh
Forward 2 caps (1t) 1876-1877
Born: Chelsea, London, 14 September 1855
Died: Aberdeen, Scotland, 6 February 1924
Career: Marlborough College, Oxford University, Marlborough Nomads
Debut: v Scotland, Kennington Oval, London, March 1876

Lee was educated at Marlborough College and won a blue in each of his four years at Oxford University. He then scored a try on his international debut against Scotland at Kennington Oval, London, in March 1876, which Lennard Stokes converted. He then retained his place for the first 15-a-side contest against Ireland the following year. Lee also played first-class cricket for the Gentleman of Worcestershire and Suffolk. He followed his father, John, into the law, becoming a solicitor, and was appointed Registrar of the Court of Arches (ecclesiastical court of the Church of England) in 1899.

84. RAWLINSON, William Cecil Welsh
Forward 1 cap 1876
Born: Chedburgh, Suffolk, 17 December 1855
Died: Northampton, Northamptonshire, 14 February 1898
Career: Blackheath
Debut: v Scotland, Kennington Oval, London, March 1876

Rawlinson was educated at Clifton College and the Royal Military Academy (Sandhurst) and was one of three Blackheath players in the England side when he debuted against Scotland at Kennington Oval, London, in March 1876. The other two were Lennard Stokes and Murray Marshall. His career was in the military, which almost certainly ended any hopes he had of winning more international caps. Rawlinson was an instructor in fortifications at the Royal Military College and became a major in the 1st Battalion Lincolnshire Regiment before his death when he was 42.

85. TETLEY, Thomas Spence
Three-Quarter 1 cap 1876
Born: Bradford, Yorkshire, 12 April 1856
Died: Ben Rhydding, Yorkshire, 15 August 1924
Career: Bradford, Yorkshire
Debut: v Scotland, Kennington Oval, London, March 1876

Tetley was one of the first members of Bradford FC, which was formed as a rugby union side before joining the Northern Union and finally becoming an association football side, Bradford Park Avenue. He played for Bradford when they played at Apperley Bridge before moving to Park Avenue. An accomplished 100-yard sprinter, he retired from playing just before Bradford won the Yorkshire Cup in 1884, eight years after winning his only England cap against Scotland at The Oval. Tetley, a worsted spinner, was a director of TS Tetley in Bradford and Halifax.

86. TURNER, Sir George Robertson CB, KBE
Forward 1 cap 1876
Born: Chigwell, Essex, 22 October 1855
Died: Hove, Sussex, 7 April 1941
Career: St George's Hospital, United Hospitals XV, South, Middlesex
Debut: v Scotland, Kennington Oval, London, March 1876

Educated at Uppingham School, Turner made his single England appearance against Scotland at Kennington Oval, London, in Match 1876. His elder brother Edward Beadon played for England against Ireland three months earlier. He played for the South against the North in 1875. After serving as a house surgeon at St George's, he moved to the Seaman's Hospital, Greenwich, before returning to St George's for 20 years until retiring. During the First World War, which claimed the lives of two of his three sons, Turner was a surgeon rear-admiral in Plymouth and Chatham, eventually retiring to Hove.

87. FOWLER, Robert Henry
Forward 1 cap 1877
Born: Melksham, Wiltshire, February 1851
Died: Regent's Park, London, 4 May 1919
Career: Leeds, Yorkshire Wanderers, Yorkshire
Debut: v Ireland, Kennington Oval, London, February 1877

Fowler was a powerful heavy forward who was the first player from Leeds to win international honours when he gained his cap in England's first ever 15-a-side international against Ireland at The Oval in February 1877. Even though England won, he wasn't selected again, as selectors wanted a fast and lightweight pack. He went to work for his uncle John Fowler, a well-known agricultural engineer who pioneered the steam plough setting up a factory in Leeds. Fowler, who travelled extensively, became the chairman of J Fowler & Co, Hunslet, Leeds, in 1888 and ran the company for many years.

88. HARRISON, Gilbert
Forward 7 caps 1877-1885
Born: Cottingham, East Riding of Yorkshire 13 June 1858
Died: Sculcoates, East Riding of Yorkshire, 9 November 1894
Career: Hull, Yorkshire Free Wanderers, Yorkshire, The North
Debut: v Ireland, Kennington Oval, London, February 1877

Cheltenham College-educated Harrison, who captained Hull, Yorkshire and the North. He won the first of his seven England caps against Ireland at the Kennington Oval, London, in February 1877, in the first 15-a-side international. Harrison led Hull to the Yorkshire Cup Final in 1884, where they lost to Bradford Park Avenue. After retiring as Hull captain in 1888, he served the club as president and sat on the Yorkshire committee. A merchant's clerk, Gilbert was an avid stamp collector and, long after his death from cancer of the spine, was described as one of the "Fathers of Philately."

89. HORNBY, Albert Neilson
Three Quarter 9 caps (1t) 1877-1882
Born: Blackburn, Lancashire, 10 February 1847
Died: Nantwich, Cheshire, 17 December 1925
Career: Preston Grasshoppers, Manchester, Lancashire, The North
Debut: v Ireland, Kennington Oval, London, February 1877

'Monkey' Hornby was the first man to captain England in rugby and cricket. He won his first cap against Ireland at Kennington Oval, London, in February 1877, five days before his 30th birthday and scored a try. Hornby would have won another cap against Scotland in 1883 but refused to play in the game as it interfered with his plans for a weekend's shooting. He served Lancashire CCC for over 30 years and was later president of the county and sat on the MCC committee. Educated at Harrow School, he played football for Blackburn Rovers. Landowner who was Captain in the 1st Royal Cheshire Militia.

90. PRICE, Petley Lloyd Augustus
Half-back 3 caps 1877-1878
Born: Poonah, India, 25 April 1856
Died: Salt Spring Island, Canada, 30 December 1910
Career: Royal Indian Engineering College
Debut: v Ireland, Kennington Oval, London, February 1877

Price was one of nine players who attended the Royal Indian Engineering College in the 1870s and who were a leading club side at the time. Price debuted internationally against Ireland at Kennington Oval, London, in February 1877 he retained his place for the next two games, but then, like so many players of his time. His career ended when he travelled to India to work as an Assistant Engineer in the Bengal Civil Service. After marrying, Price emigrated to Canada to become a farmer in Mereside Ganges, Salt Spring Island, British Columbia, where he lived until his death.

91. TOUZEL, Charles John Cliff
Forward 2 caps 1877
Born: Birkenhead, Cheshire, 7 June 1855
Died: Stroud, Gloucestershire, 24 August 1899
Career: Wellington College, Cambridge University, Liverpool, Blackheath
Debut: v Ireland, Kennington Oval, London, February 1877

Touzel was a 'brilliant forward' who first played Rugby Football at Wellington College and then won three blues at Cambridge University. He won the first of his two caps against Ireland at Kennington Oval, London, in February 1877, the first international which saw teams reduced from 20 a-side to 15 a-side. He was ordained as a deacon in 1878 but disclaimed his orders in 1886 to study the law, then became a captain in the 3rd Royal Welsh Fusiliers. Touzel was only 44 when he died in the Cotswold Sanatorium, where author George Orwell famously corrected proofs of his book 1984.

92. GARNETT, Harry Wharfedale Tennant
Forward 1 cap 1877
Born: Otley, Yorkshire, 16 September 1851
Died: Otley, Yorkshire, 27 April 1928
Career: Bradford, Yorkshire
Debut: v Scotland, Raeburn Place, Edinburgh, March 1877

Garnett's "fine physique made him one of the notable players of his day", and he won his only international cap against Scotland at Raeburn Place, Edinburgh, in March 1877. Harry often played without stockings and was joint captain of Yorkshire with William Henderson before resuming the role on his own. Later served Yorkshire as its first president, a role he also held with the RFU. He also sat on the Yorkshire committee. Chairman of the Wharfedale and Otley Conservative Association and was a magistrate. Garnett was the fifth generation to run the family paper mill, P Garrett and Sons.

93. LAW, Sir Archibald Fitzgerald KB
Forward 1 cap 1877
Born: Nice, France, 2 February 1853
Died: Staybridge, Dorset, 26 June 1921
Career: Wellington College, Oxford University, Richmond, Middlesex
Debut: v Scotland, Raeburn Place, Edinburgh, March 1877

Wellington College-educated Law was born in the South of France. He won an Oxford University blue in 1875 and then made his only international appearance against Scotland at Raeburn Place, Edinburgh, in March 1877. Law was called to the bar two years later and almost immediately was appointed assistant commissioner of Cyprus. He held several high-profile legal posts, becoming Judicial Commissioner for the Federated Malay Sattes and a judge of the Puisne Supreme Court in the Straits Settlement. A son, Edward, was killed in action during the First World War.

94. TODD, Robert
Forward 1 cap 1877
Born: Holcombe, Lancashire, March 1847
Died: Stockport, Cheshire, 9 February 1927
Career: Manchester, Lancashire
Debut: v Scotland, Raeburn Place, Edinburgh, March 1877

Todd is credited with introducing tall goalposts into rugby, although the laws permit the upright to be as little as a foot higher than the crossbar. He made his only international appearance against Scotland in March 1877 in the first 15-a-side encounter between the two countries. He was one of three new caps in the team that was defeated by a drop goal to nil, but he was never selected again. Todd worked as a cotton cloth and an oil agent before becoming the director of a cotton mill company in the Stockport area.

95. BIGGS, Dr John Maundy
Forward 2 caps 1878-1879
Born: Reading, Berkshire, 25 October 1855
Died: Barnstaple, Devon, 3 June 1935
Career: University College Hospital, United Hospitals, Wasps, South, Middlesex
Debut: v Scotland, Kennington Oval, London, March 1878

Biggs made his international debut against Scotland at Kennington Oval in March 1878. Interestingly, he was registered to University College Hospital and then United Hospitals when he won his two international caps despite being Wasps captain between 1877 and 1880 when he succeeded Jack Angle. Wasps claimed he was their first international despite not being registered with them when he played for England. Biggs worked as a GP in Hendon, North London, for 20 years before becoming a surgeon in London and Spalding, Lincolnshire. He retired to Barnstaple, Devon, where he died in June 1935.

96. FOWLER, Frank Dashwood
Forward 2 caps 1878-1879
Born: Brimpton, Berkshire, 16 August 1855
Died: Brimpton, Berkshire, 14 November 1940
Career: Cheltenham College, Royal Engineering College, Manchester, Lancashire
Debut: v Scotland, Kennington Oval, London, March 1878

Fowler was educated at Cheltenham College and then went to Royal Indian Engineering College, one of the leading teams of the time. During his time at Cooper's Hill, he won the first of his England caps against Scotland at Kennington Oval in March 1878. He was registered to Manchester when he played in Scotland a year later after moving north of the border to work. Fowler was a college oarsman before joining the Public Works Department of India. He later served as undersecretary to the Indian Government before retiring and returning to live in his native Berkshire.

97. FOWLER, Howard
Forward 3 caps 1878-1881
Born: Tottenham, Middlesex, 20 October 1857
Died: Burnham on Sea, Somerset, 6 May 1934
Career: Clifton College, Oxford University, Walthamstow, Blackheath, Middlesex
Debut: v Scotland, Kennington Oval, London, March 1878

Fowler was captain of Clifton before going to New College, Oxford, where he won blues for both Rugby and Cricket. He captained Oxford in 1878, the year he made his international debut against Scotland at The Oval. His three caps were spread out over three years, and after Oxford, he played for Blackheath and was also captain of Middlesex. Fowler also played for Walthamstow and cricket for Essex. He followed his father into the law and was called to the bar of Inner Temple in 1883, then became a ship owner and broker before reverting to being a barrister until retiring.

98. GURDON, Edward Temple
Forward 16 caps 1878-1886
Born: Barnham Broom, Norfolk 25 January 1854
Died: London 12 June 1929
Career: Haileybury & ISC, Old Haileyburians, Cambridge University, Richmond, Middlesex
Debut: v Scotland, Kennington Oval, London, March 1878

Gurdon was educated at Haileybury College, studied at Trinity College Cambridge, and won his blue in 1874. He captained the University in the last two of his three years. It was written, "Despite his comparatively slight physique, one of the greatest forwards that ever played for England." While the 16 caps he won don't reflect his influence. Gurdon joined Richmond, captaining them for several seasons, including 1886-87, when they didn't lose a game. He served on the RFU committee and was president of the Union. He worked in the Public Records Office before becoming a solicitor in Lincoln's Inn Fields.

99. KAYLL, Henry Edward
Full-back 1 cap 1878
Born: Sunderland, Tyne & Wear, 16 July 1855
Died: Vancouver, British Columbia, 14 February 1910
Career: The North, Sunderland, County Durham
Debut: v Scotland, Kennington Oval, London, March 1878

Kayll was one of six brothers who played for Sunderland. He was also honorary secretary for six seasons and one of the best backs in the whole country. He was the first man from the North East to play for England after picking up the ball on his own line and running the whole length of the field in a trial match. A cricketer, cyclist and runner, he set a world best for the pole vault at 11ft 1 in 1877. Kayll emigrated to Canada in 1880, which is almost certainly why he only won one cap. He was a glassworker and then became a farmer in Canada.

100. THOMSON, George Thomas
Forward 9 caps (1t) 1878-1885
Born: Skircoat, Yorkshire, 26 November 1856
Died: Sydney, Australia, 31 October 1899
Career: Halifax, Yorkshire
Debut: v Scotland, Kennington Oval, London, March 1878

Thomson became the first player from Halifax to win international honours when he won his first cap against Scotland at Kennington Oval in March 1878. He captained Yorkshire between 1880 and 1884 and represented his club on the Yorkshire committee. He was a vice president of the Rugby Football Union between 1884 and 1887 while still playing the game. Thomson, who made 170 appearances for Halifax in his decade with the club, scored 60 tries and kicked 16 goals was a Merchant as well as a manufacturer of sheeting. He died in Australia in October 1899, aged just 42.

101. VERNON, George Frederick
Forward 5 caps 1878-1881
Born: Marylebone, Middlesex, 20 June 1856
Died: Elmina, Gold Coast, Africa, 10 August 1902
Career: Rugby School, Blackheath, Middlesex
Debut: v Scotland, Kennington Oval, London, March 1878

Vernon was educated at Rugby School and was credited with being one of rugby's first line-out experts with Blackheath and Middlesex winning the first of his five caps against Scotland at Kennington Oval in March 1878 but was probably better known as a cricketer for Middlesex and won one test cap against Australia in 1882 on the first ever Ashes tour. Vernon was a barrister and was called to the bar at Middle Temple in 1880. He died of malarial fever during a trip to the Gold Coast, Africa, in what is now Ghana, aged just 46.

102. BELL, John Lowthian
Half-back 1 cap 1878
Born: North Elsewick, Newcastle on Tyne, 19 April 1853
Died: Bournemouth, Dorset, 17 December 1916
Career: Merchiston Castle School, Darlington, County Durham, Northumberland, The North
Debut: v Ireland, Lansdowne Road, Dublin March 1878

Bell was one of three brothers who learnt the game at Merchiston Castle School, Edinburgh and who went on to become one of the most outstanding half-backs of his time. He won his only England cap against Ireland in Lansdowne Road in March 1878, two weeks after Henry Kayll became the first player from County Durham to win international recognition. He twice captained his native county against Durham and Cumberland. His father, Thomas, was an iron master, and Bell was a merchant and steel manufacturer. He died at the Royal Exeter Hotel, Bournemouth.

103. BLATHERWICK, Thomas
Forward 1 cap 1878
Born: Quebec, Canada, 25 December 1855
Died: Bucklow, Cheshire, 29 January 1940
Career: Epsom College, Manchester, Lancashire
Debut: v Ireland, Lansdowne Road, Dublin March 1878

Blatherwick was born in Canada, where his father, also named Thomas, was a staff surgeon in the British Army and was educated at Epsom College, captaining the rugby team. Blatherwick played in the same Manchester and Lancashire teams as 'Monkey' Hornby and made his international debut against Ireland in the first-ever international played at Lansdowne Road in March 1878 alongside another Manchester player William Hunt. Blatherwick spent 53 years working for cotton merchants Robert Pullar and Sons in Manchester and was sitting on the board when he retired in 1929.

104. BUDD, Arthur James
Forward 5 caps (1t) 1878-1881
Born: Bristol, 14 October 1853
Died: St. Bartholomew's Hospital, London, 27 August 1899
Career: Clifton College, Clifton RFC, Ravenscourt Park, Edinburgh Wanderers, Blackheath, Kent
Debut: v Ireland, Lansdowne Road, Dublin March 1878

Budd remains the only person to have been President of the RFU while still playing. He won the first of his caps against Ireland at Lansdowne Road in March 1878. His opposition to player payments started the events, leading to the formation of the Rugby League. He later became an international touch judge, secretary of the London Society of Referees, and a member of the International Board. He first studied for the bar before changing his mind and entering medicine like his famous father, William. A brother, George, was in partnership with Sir Arthur Conan Doyle for a short time.

105. DAWSON, Ernest Frederick
Forward 1 cap 1878
Born: Charlottetown, Prince Edward Island, 10 May 1858
Died: Hampstead, London, 7 April 1904
Career: Royal Indian Engineering College, Richmond, Surrey
Debut: v Ireland, Lansdowne Road, Dublin March 1878

Dawson was a Canadian-born forward who came to London to complete his studies and, in 1875, entered the Royal Indian Engineering College at Coopers Hill. Three years later, in March 1878, he won his only England cap against Ireland in the first-ever international match that was played at Lansdowne Road, Dublin. He joined the Bombay Works Department as an assistant engineer within a year. Later appointed undersecretary of Public Works to the Bombay Government and was acting superintending engineer. Dawson had suffered poor health for some time and died a month after being ordered home to London.

106. ENTHOVEN, Henry John
Three-quarter 1 cap 1878
Born: Liverpool, Lancashire, 16 March 1855
Died: Moreton-in-Marsh, Gloucestershire, 11 December 1925
Career: Ravenscourt Park, Richmond, Middlesex
Debut: v Ireland, Lansdowne Road, Dublin March 1878

Enthoven played his club rugby for Ravenscourt Park before joining Richmond, and he made his England debut alongside his Middlesex half-back partner Allan Jackson but was played in the Three-quarter. A successful businessman who was a director of H. J. Enthoven and Sons, Ltd., led merchants and manufacturers and was a director of several other companies. Enthoven died when he was thrown from his horse while hunting with the Heythrop Hounds. His nephew, Tom, was a distinguished cricketer playing for Harrow, Cambridge, Middlesex and the Gentlemen.

107. GARDNER, Herbert Prescott
Forward 1 cap (1t) 1878
Born: Delhi, India, 4 December 1855
Died: Toogoolawah, Queensland, 7 December 1938
Career: Wellington College, Richmond, Middlesex, The South
Debut: v Ireland, Lansdowne Road, Dublin, March 1878

Gardner was a commercial clerk born in India during the Delhi troubles where his father, also named Herbert, who was commissioned in the British Army. He won his only cap against Ireland at Lansdowne Road in March 1878 and scored the first-ever international try on the famous Dublin ground. Also, a talented cricketer representing his school, Wellington College, Gardner played for Richmond until emigrating to Australia, settling in Queensland, where he ran a dairy farmer until his death. He also served the community as a justice of the peace and sat on the town council.

108. JACKSON, Allan Heslop
Half-back 2 caps 1878-1880
Born: Spanish Town, Jamaica, 12 August 1858
Died: Douglas, Manitoba, Canada, 15 July 1912
Career: Guy's Hospital, Blackheath Middlesex
Debut: v Ireland, Lansdowne Road, Dublin March 1878

Jackson, whose father was a barrister, was born in Jamaica and made his England debut alongside his Middlesex half-back partner Henry Enthoven against Ireland at Lansdowne Road in March 1878. But despite being a prolific try scorer for Blackheath, 22 in 37 appearances between 1877 and 1881, he had to wait until the return visit to Dublin two years later for his second and final cap. Jackson was registered with Guy's Hospital when he won his first cap and then Richmond with his second, becoming a GP in Lowestoft, Suffolk, before emigrating to Canada.

109. PENNY, William John
Full-back 3 caps (1t) 1878-1879
Born: Kingsbury Episcopi, Somerset, 15 November 1856
Died: Mombasa, British East Africa, 25 December 1904
Career: United Hospitals, Kings College Hospital, The South, Clifton Middlesex, Somerset
Debut: v Ireland, Lansdowne Road, Dublin March 1878

Penny was the 'most brilliant full-back of his day' and made his international debut against Ireland at Lansdowne Road in March 1878 and became the first full-back to score in an international. One of the ten founding members of the Middlesex Rugby Union while playing for United Hospitals. Penny captained United's Hospitals and played for Clifton in the Bristol area when he went into medicine. He was a Demonstrator of Anatomy at Bristol Medical School and was later elected House Surgeon at Bristol General Hospital for eight years until ill health forced his retirement.

110. BURTON, George William
Forward 6 caps (6t) 1879-1881
Born: Wakefield, Yorkshire, 29 August 1855
Died: West Hampstead, Middlesex, 17 September 1890
Career: Winchester College, Blackheath, Kent, The South
Debut: v Scotland Raeburn Place, Edinburgh March 1878

Burton was a brilliant forward in open play and scored the first ever try in a Calcutta Cup match in March 1879, a year after making his first international appearance at Raeburn Place, Edinburgh. Burton scored four tries in England's first international with Wales at Blackheath in February 1881. A close friend of Arthur Budd later captained Blackheath and served as secretary. A solicitor who sat on the Kent County committee, he died aged 35, three weeks after being taken ill when rapid consumption set in.

111. HUTH, Henry
Full-back 1 cap 1879
Born: Huddersfield, Yorkshire, 14 February 1856
Died: Kensington, London, 31 December 1929
Career: Huddersfield, Yorkshire
Debut: v Scotland, Raeburn Place, Edinburgh March 1879

Huth had a German father and a London-born mother and was one of three brothers who played for Huddersfield and Yorkshire. Huth captained his club and won his only international cap against Scotland at Raeburn Place,

Joe Green

Alfred Hammersley

Fred Currey

Murray Marshall

William Collins

Edward Kewley

Sir William Milton

William Hutchinson

Edward Turner

'Monkey' Hornby

Edward Gurdon

Henry Kayll

George Vernon

Jimmy Budd

William Penny

Edinburgh, in March 1879, becoming the first Huddersfield player to play for his country. He also represented his club on the Yorkshire committee and played cricket for Huddersfield and one-first class match for Gentlemen of the North against Players of the North in 1877. A woollen merchant like his father, Frederick, who was also a justice of the peace. After moving to London, Huth became a financial agent.

112. McLEOD, Norman Frederick
Forward 2 caps 1879
Born: Madras, India, 30 June 1856
Died: South Kensington, London, 20 April 1921
Career: Clifton College, Royal Indian Engineering College
Debut: v Scotland, Raeburn Place, Edinburgh March 1879

McLeod was a student at the Royal Indian Engineering College, Cooper's Hill, which had one of the strongest teams of the time. McLeod played both games in March 1879, making his debut against Scotland in Edinburgh and then playing against Ireland at the Kennington Oval two weeks later. His choice of occupation would have stopped him from playing any further games because he worked as a civil engineer for the Indian Public Works Department, which he joined in September 1878. McLeod was posted to NW Province and Oudh and rose through the ranks, becoming a superintending engineer before retiring.

113. NEAME, Stuart
Forward 4 caps 1879-1880
Born: Preston, Kent, 15 June 1856
Died: Bromley, Kent, 16 November 1936
Career: Cheltenham College, Old Cheltonians, Blackheath, Kent
Debut: v Scotland, Raeburn Place, Edinburgh March 1879

Neame, the son of a Kent landowner, was educated at Cheltenham College and made his international debut against Scotland at Raeburn Place in March 1879 and kept his place for the following three games. All his England caps were won when he played for Old Cheltonians, but he later represented Blackheath and Kent. A hop farmer who became a senior partner of Hop Agents Wild Neame & Co in Borough High Street, London, Neame was president of the Cheltonian Society between 1921 and 1922 and lived in Bromley, Kent, until his death.

114. ROWLEY, Hugh Campbell
Forward 9 caps (3t) 1979-1882
Born: Chorlton-upon-Medlock, Lancashire, 27 April 1858
Died: Canada between 1910-1920
Career: Manchester Grammar School, Bowdon & Lymm, Manchester, Cheshire, Lancashire
Debut: v Scotland, Raeburn Place, Edinburgh March 1879

Manchester Grammar School-educated Campbell was described as 'One of the most useful of football players, very strong and fast, was never done with, could play any position in the field equally well, and had his whole heart in the game'. His brother Alexander, who also played for Manchester and Lancashire, was one of the founders of Lancashire CCC and Old Trafford. Campbell, a solicitor, emigrated to Winnipeg, Canada, in 1883 and later lived in Alaska. The exact date of his death is unknown, but his wife appears as a widow on Canada's 1920 census.

115. SPRINGMANN, Herman Heinrich
Forward 2 caps 1879-1887
Born: Liverpool, Lancashire AMJ 1859
Died: Trefnant, Denbighshire, 17 October 1936
Career: Craigmount School, Liverpool, Lancashire, The North
Debut: v Scotland, Raeburn Place, Edinburgh, March 1879

Springmann, born to German parents, later changed his name to Springman and emigrated to the US after winning his first cap against Scotland at Raeburn Place in March 1879. He had been educated in Edinburgh, going to the Craigmount School. After returning from the United States seven years later, he immediately picked up his rugby career from where it left off and won his second and final cap against Scotland in Manchester in March 1887. Springmann, a cotton broker, became a justice of the peace in North Wales, and his brother Paul won an Oxford blue in 1887 and 1888.

116. TAYLOR, Henry Herbert
Half-back 5 caps (6t)
Born: Lewisham, Kent, 21 September 1858
Died: Steyning, Sussex, 25 May 1942
Career: Merchant Taylors' School, St George's Hospital, Blackheath, Kent
Debut: v Scotland, Raeburn Place, Edinburgh March 1879

Taylor was the first England player to score a hat-trick, against Ireland at Whalley Range, Manchester, in February 1881. He would have won another cap against Scotland two months later but missed the train to Glasgow, and Frank Wright took his place. Taylor was a house surgeon and physician at the West London Hospital before moving to Sussex, where he was a surgeon at the Sussex Eye Hospital and then the Royal Alexandra Hospital for Children. He served as a justice of the peace and alderman to Hove Town Council. Henry's brother Arthur also played for Blackheath and England.

117. BATESON, Harold Dingwell
Forward 1 cap 1879
Born: Liverpool, Lancashire, 2 May 1856
Died: Liverpool, Lancashire, 20 October 1927
Career: Rugby School, Oxford University, Blackheath, Liverpool, Lancashire
Debut: v Ireland, Kennington Oval, London March 1879

Liverpool-born Bateson who was educated at Rugby School before going to Trinity College, Oxford, he won a blue three times and captained them at a time when the captain and the secretary had to be an Old Rugbeian. Bateson made his only international appearance against Ireland at Kennington Oval in March 1879. A solicitor partner in the firm Bateson and Co. and a Liverpool justice of the peace read the Riot Act during a Police strike in 1911 when soldiers opened fire on strikers, killing two people. Bateson was also chairman of the Council of the Liverpool Chamber of Commerce.

118. OPENSHAW, William Edward
Half-back 1 cap 1879
Born: Cape Town, South Africa, 5 February 1851
Died: Newton-le-Willows, Lancashire, 15 February 1915
Career: Harrow School, Manchester, Lancashire
Debut: v Ireland, Kennington Oval, London March 1879

South African-born merchant Openshaw traded with Africa and later became a cotton-spinning merchant. He was based in Manchester and played in the second-ever Roses match between Yorkshire and Lancashire. Openshaw made his only test appearance against Ireland at Kennington Oval in March 1879. He was later described as a 'wonderful dribbler'. A fine all-round sportsman who played cricket for Harrow against Eton in 1870. A right-handed batsman, he also made four first-class appearances for Lancashire. While at Harrow, Openshaw won half-mile and one-mile races. Before his death, he was the vice president of Lancashire CCC.

119. TWYNAM, Henry Thomas
Half-back 8 caps (4t) 1879-1884
Born: Bishopstoke, Hampshire, 14 February 1853
Died: Kensington, London, 19 May 1899
Career: Sherborne School, St Andrew's Rovers, Richmond, Middlesex, London, The South
Debut: v Ireland, Kennington Oval, London March 1879

Twynam was one of the best half-backs of his time, described as "a fine runner with a very difficult dodge, but was a trifle uncertain, and had no powers of dropping." He first played rugby football at Sherborne School, then for St Andrew's Rovers before joining Richmond. He immediately impacted the international stage after scoring a try on his debut against Ireland at Kennington Oval in March 1879. Twynam was a fine cricketer playing for Sherborne School, Ealing, the Gentleman of Worcestershire, Shirburhians and the MCC. He was a solicitor at Staple Inn Chambers in Holborn.

120. ELLIS, Sidney JP
Forward 1 cap (1t) 1880
Born: Blackheath, Kent, 13 March 1859
Died: Croydon, Surrey, December 1937
Career: Dulwich College, Faversham, Queen's House, Blackheath, Kent
Debut: v Ireland Lansdowne Road, Dublin February 1880

Ellis was educated at Dulwich College and scored a try on his only international appearance against Ireland at Lansdowne Road in February 1880 alongside Thomas Fry, who also played for Queen's House. He continued to play for them until they disbanded in 1884 when he joined Blackheath. Ellis spent all his adult life working as a stockbroker and was a member of the Stock Exchange from 1882 until 1937. He was the father of the Stock Exchange at his death and served as a justice of the peace in Croydon.

121. FRY, Thomas William
Full-back 3 caps (1t) 1880-1881
Born: Greenwich, Kent, 15 September 1858
Died: Chislehurst, Kent, May 1944
Career: Queens House
Debut: v Ireland Lansdowne Road, Dublin February 1880

Fry was a full-back who debuted against Ireland at Lansdowne Road in February 1880 alongside his club-mate Sidney Ellis. Tom became England's first sole full-back against Scotland in Whalley Range, Manchester, a month later and scored his only international try. He made his final appearance against Wales the following season, after which 'Monkey' Hornby became the regular full-back. Fry's retirement in 1884, together with the emigration to Canada of his brothers Fred and Sidney, led to the Queen's House club disbanding. A mercantile clerk before becoming a grain merchant and grain broker.

122. GURDON, Charles
Forward 14 caps 1880-1886
Born: Forehoe, Norfolk, 3 December 1855
Died: Westminster, London, 26 June 1931
Career: Haileybury & ISC, Cambridge University, Richmond, Middlesex
Debut: v Ireland Lansdowne Road, Dublin February 1880

Gurdon, the younger brother of Edward, captained Haileybury at both rugby and cricket, won a blue at Cambridge University in 1877 and a rowing blue between 1876 and 1988. He made his international debut against Ireland at Lansdowne Road in February 1880 and played alongside his brother ten times until a knee injury ended his rugby career. Gurdon was called to the Bar in November 1881 and specialised as an equity draughtsman and conveyancer. In 1913, he became a bencher of the Inner Temple, and in January 1923, he was appointed as a County Court Judge on the Plymouth and Cornwall circuit.

123. HUNT, Robert
Three quarter, 4 caps (2t 1c 1d) 1880-1882
Born: Preston, Lancashire 21 January 1856
Died: Blackburn, Lancashire, 19 March 1913
Career: Preston GS, Owen's College, Preston Grasshoppers, Manchester, Blackheath, Lancashire
Debut: v Ireland Lansdowne Road, Dublin February 1880

Hunt was one of the best backs of his day and the second of three brothers to play for England. He made his international debut against Ireland at Lansdowne Road in February 1880. Scored a try, kicked a goal and dropped a goal in the rout of Wales at Blackheath in February 1881. Hunt scored a try on his last appearance against Ireland a year later in a game when youngest brother James made his debut. A one-time house surgeon at Manchester Royal Infirmary, he became a well-known GP in Blackburn. Hunt died suddenly of pneumonia the day after playing golf at Pleasington Links.

124. KILNER, Barron JP
Forward 1 cap 1880
Born: Thornhill Lees, Yorkshire 11 October 1852
Died: Wakefield, Yorkshire, 28 December 1922
Career: Wakefield Trinity, Yorkshire
Debut: v Ireland Lansdowne Road, Dublin February 1880

Kilner won his only international cap against Ireland at Lansdowne Road, Dublin, in February 1880. He is said to have made his debut for Wakefield wearing ordinary clothes. After his playing days finished, he became a leading referees administrator, served Yorkshire as president, and sat on the RFU committee. A glass bottle manufacturer, Kilner ran his grandfather's company, J Kilner & Sons. He was the Mayor of Wakefield and a magistrate. One of the most vigorous opponents of the Northern Union, which led to his exposition from Wakefield Trinity in February 1897 and his name being struck off the vice president's list.

125. MARKENDALE, Ellis
Forward 1 cap (1t) 1880
Born: Salford, Lancashire, 11 November 1856
Died: Ashbourne, Derbyshire, 9 May 1938
Career: Uppingham School, Manchester Rangers, Lancashire
Debut: v Ireland Lansdowne Road, Dublin February 1880

Markendale was a fine dribbler who scored a try on his only international appearance against Ireland at Lansdowne Road in February 1880. He was a forward who captained his club Manchester Rangers. Ellis was a hide dealer from a prominent butchering family. But in 1888, he decided to emigrate to the New World and, over the next 23 years, became a stock raiser, a rancher in Texas and Mexico. After returning to England in 1911, Markendale settled in Derbyshire, running a farm. He suffered from a long spell of ill health before his death in May 1938, aged 38.

126. SCHOFIELD, John Wood
Forward 1 cap 1880
Born: Stretford, Lancashire, 10 March 1858
Died: Knutsford, Cheshire, 4 May 1931
Career: Uppingham School, Manchester Rangers, Manchester, Lancashire
Debut: v Ireland Lansdowne Road, Dublin February 1880

Schofield, the son of Alderman Schofield of Manchester, was a good all-round athlete and made his only international appearance against Ireland Lansdowne Road in February 1880 alongside his Manchester Rangers and Lancashire club mate Ellis Markendale, who also won his only England cap in the same game, who incidentally also attended Uppingham School. Schofield was a long-standing captain of the Manchester club after switching from Manchester Rangers. He worked his way up from stock broker's clerk to become a partner in the firm of Whitehead and Co., stock and share brokers in Manchester and was principal at the time of his death.

127. WOODHEAD, Ernest
Forward 1 cap 1880
Born: Huddersfield, Yorkshire, 2 February 1857
Died: Huddersfield, Yorkshire, 10 June 1944
Career: Huddersfield College, Edinburgh University, Dublin University, Huddersfield, Yorkshire
Debut: v Ireland Lansdowne Road, Dublin January 1880

Woodhead and Barron Kilner were seen as one of the finest forwards in Yorkshire of his time. He was said to be a 'fine dribbler and follower-up. Great try-getter.' He played for Edinburgh University for four seasons, including one as a three-quarter back. His father, Joseph, founded the Huddersfield Examiner newspaper and edited the paper for many years before becoming chairman of Joseph Woodhead & Sons Ltd, the paper's publisher. Woodhead served on Huddersfield Town Council for over 30 years, was mayor in 1902, and sat as a borough and West Riding magistrate.

128. COATES, The Rev Charles Hutton
Forward 3 caps 1880-1882
Born: Yorkshire Clapham Rise, London 5 April 1857
Died: Christchurch, Dorset 14 February 1922
Career: Christ College Finchley, Cambridge University, Leeds, Yorkshire Wanderers, Bishop Auckland, Surrey, Yorkshire
Debut: v Scotland, Whalley Range Manchester February 1880

Coates was educated at Christ College Finchley and won his Cambridge University blue between 1877 and 1879, making his England debut against Scotland at Whalley Range, Manchester, in February 1880. All three of his caps were to come against the Scots. An all-round sportsman who excelled as an oarsman and archer competing in the 1908 London Olympics. Coates was ordained as a clergyman in 1881 and served as Royal Navy chaplain between 1885 and 1991, then Vicar Hutton Sands, Yorkshire and Rector at Burton Argus, Yorkshire, before becoming Rural Dean of Bridlington until retiring in 1922.

129. FINCH, Richard Tanner
Half-back 1 cap 1880
Born: Kensington, Middlesex Q3 1857
Died: Seaton, Devon, 12 January 1921
Career: Sherborne School, Cambridge University, St George's Hospital, Richmond, Surrey, Kent
Debut: v Scotland, Whalley Range, Manchester, February 1880

Cambridge University half-back Finch won his only test cap against Scotland at Whalley Range Manchester in February 1880 when he was one of four new caps for his country. Richard had won his first blue in 1876, and in his last season, 1879, he was appointed captain. A Surgeon at St George's Hospital before becoming surgeon and asylum manager at Old Manor Hospital, Salisbury, which the Finch family ran. Finch would later become medical superintendent. A talented cricketer, he played for Sherborne School, Sidmouth and Seaton.

130. PHILLIPS, Charles
Forward 3 caps 1880-1881
Born: Rugby, Warwickshire, 14 August 1856
Died: Westminster, London 11 September 1940
Career: Rugby School, Exeter College, Oxford University, Birkenhead Park, Cheshire
Debut: v Scotland, Whalley Range, Manchester, February 1880

Rugby School-educated Phillips captained Oxford University in 1880, the year along with club mate John Ravenscroft, they became the first players from Birkenhead Park to be capped by England after being selected to play against Scotland at Whalley Range, Manchester. Phillips won his first blue in 1876 and played twice more for his country against Ireland and Scotland the following season. He was admitted as a solicitor for Layton & Jacques in Manchester, then Ingledew Sons & Philips in Swansea before returning to Manchester with W.H & C Phillips. Phillips later became a director of Richard Thomas (Tinplate).

131. SAWYER, Charles Montague
Three-quarter 2 caps (1t) 1880-1881
Born: Rusholme, Manchester, 20 March 1856
Died: Southport, Lancashire, 30 March 1921
Career: Broughton Wasps, Broughton, Lancashire
Debut: v Scotland, Whalley Range Manchester February 1880

Sawyer debuted against Scotland at Whalley Range, Manchester, in February 1880 and retained his place for their next match 12 months later against Ireland at the same ground when he scored a try on what became his last international appearance. A fine cricketer who was a member of Broughton CC for many years and played two first-class matches for Lancashire CCC in August 1884 against Surrey and Somerset. Sawyer was a clerk to his father, a cotton merchant, eventually taking over the business and running it for the rest of his working life.

132. FERNANDES, Charles Walker Luis
Forward 3 caps (1t) 1881
Born: Wakefield, Yorkshire, 3 April 1857
Died: Thirsk, North Yorkshire, 12 August 1944
Career: Rossell School, Wakefield, Leeds, Yorkshire Wanderers, The North, Yorkshire
Debut: v Ireland, Whalley Range Manchester February 1881

Rossell-educated Fernandes made all three of his England appearances in the 1881 campaign, with his debut against Ireland at Whalley Range, Manchester. He was then a try scorer in the rout of Wales at Blackheath in the first meeting between the two countries. A popular captain of the Wakefield club before moving on to play for Leeds. Fernandes was a solicitor before becoming a partner in the Fernandes Brewery. He also played first-class cricket for Yorkshire Gentleman and played for the Bagby Club until his 70th birthday, scoring a half-century in his last innings.

133. HEWITT, Walter William
Forward 4 caps 1881-1882
Born: New Cross, Kent, October 1854
Died: Greenwich, Kent, 6 January 1910
Career: Queen's House
Debut: v Ireland, Whalley Range Manchester February 1881

Hewitt was a powerhouse of the Queen's House scrum along with brother Malcolm but was probably better known for being a renowned international oarsman than for his rugby. Walter debuted against Ireland at Whalley Range Manchester in February 1881 and was already an amateur middle-weight champion wrestler but excelled on the water. London Rowing Club member Hewitt, who worked for the Inland Revenue, was in the winning crew for the Grand Challenge Trophy at Henley three times and won more than 160 trophies. He was also an early naval volunteer and became a captain in the Fife Royal Garrison Artillery.

134. RAVENSCROFT, John
Forward 1 cap 1881
Born: Oxton, Cheshire, 11 June 1857
Died: Buenos Aires, Argentina, 18 August 1902
Career: Rugby School, Oxford University, Birkenhead Park, Cheshire
Debut: v Ireland, Whalley Range Manchester February 1881

Ravenscroft and his former Oxford University team-mate Charles Phillips were capped from the Birkenhead Park club when they debuted against Ireland at Whalley Range in February 1881. Ravenscroft was a banker, the son of a South American merchant, who went to live in Puan, Buenos Aires, to work for a railway company and wanted the British community of Argentina to practise sports in the same place, so he formed the Hurlingham Club (Argentina) taking inspiration from the club of the same name in West London. Ravenscroft was also a polo player who started the Buenos Aires Polo Club in 1882.

135. RICHARDSON, William Ryder
Half-back 1 cap 1881
Born: Chorlton, Lancashire, 13 September 1861
Died: Dover, Kent, 29 July 1930
Career: Manchester GS, Oxford University, Manchester, Lancashire
Debut: v Ireland, Whalley Range Manchester February 1881

Richardson was educated at Manchester Grammar School and became the first schoolboy to be selected to play for England, winning his only cap against Ireland at Whalley

Range Manchester in February 1881. Richardson won his blue later the same year before moving to Walmer, Kent, in 1900 to become secretary of Royal St George's Golf Club and was also secretary to the Amateur Golf Championship committee. During the First World War, he served as a lieutenant in the West Yorkshire Regiment. Richardson served on the Walmer Urban District Council and was a district commissioner in the Boy Scout movement. He died suddenly after addressing a scout meeting in Dover.

136. WARD, James Ibotson
Forward 2 caps 1881-1882
Born: Staines, Middlesex, 24 April 1858
Died: Marylebone, Middlesex, 28 September 1924
Career: Tonbridge School, Gipsies, Richmond, Middlesex
Debut: v Ireland, Whalley Range Manchester February 1881

Farmer's son Ward was educated at Tonbridge School, and his first club was Gipsies, a club set up for former pupils of his school. But after disbanding in 1880, James moved to Richmond, and they were the club he was registered to when he made his England debut against Ireland in Whalley Range, Manchester, in February 1881. It would be another year before he won his last cap, also against Ireland at Lansdowne Road. A commission agent's clerk and stock jotter, Ward rowed for the London Rowing Club at Henley between 1879 and 1981 and was a Royal Marine lieutenant for the City of London.

137. VASSALL, Henry
Forward 5 caps (3t) 1881-1882
Born: Barwick-in-Elmet, Yorkshire, 22 October 1860
Died: Repton, Derbyshire, 5 January 1926
Career: Marlborough College, Yeovil, Oxford University, Marlborough Nomads, Blackheath, Somerset
Debut: v Wales, Richardson's Field, Blackheath, February 1881

Vassall was educated at Marlborough College, where he first played rugby, moving on to Oxford, where he won a blue in 1880 and was appointed secretary of the University's team in the same season. Vassall scored three tries on his international debut in the rout of Wales at Richardson's Field, Blackheath, in February 1881, the first-ever scorer of a hat-trick in international rugby. Vassall was RFU treasurer between 1884 and 1894. His nephew Jumbo Vassall played for England. He was a master at Repton School and had been bursar for 21 years until his death.

138. WILSON, Charles Plumpton
Forward 1 cap 1881
Born: Roydon, Norfolk, 12 May 1859
Died: East Dareham, Norfolk, 9 March 1938
Career: Uppingham School, Marlborough College, Cambridge University
Debut: v Wales, Richardson's Field, Blackheath February 1881

Wilson was educated at Marlborough College, where he first played rugby football. After moving to Cambridge, he won blues in rugby and cricket. At Cambridge, he won his only international cap against Wales at Richardson's Field, Blackheath, in February 1881. He also played association football for Hendon, Casuals and Corinthians, winning him two international caps, making him one of three people to play rugby and football for England. Wilson also played cricket for Norfolk and Lincolnshire and was an assistant master at Elstree School before becoming headmaster of Sandroyd School, Cobham, Surrey, until retiring in 1920.

139. WRIGHT, Frank Thurlow
Half-back 1 cap 1881
Born: Leigh, Lancashire, 2 July 1862
Died: Marseilles, France, 30 April 1934
Career: Edinburgh Academicals, Scottish Academicals, Manchester, Lancashire
Debut: v Scotland, Raeburn Place, Edinburgh, March 1881

Wright won his only England cap against Scotland at Raeburn Place, Edinburgh, in March 1881 in quite bizarre circumstances. Blackheath's Henry Taylor was due to play in the game but missed his train to the Scottish capital. It is likely that Monkey Hornby pointed out that Wright was studying at Edinburgh Academy when he was called up. A talented cricketer, he captained Edinburgh Academy and played for Liverpool. Wright trained as a solicitor in Leigh before becoming resident Chairman of Galphele Tea and Rubber Estates Limited in Wattegama, Ceylon.

140. BESWICK, Edmund
Three-quarter 2 caps 1882
Born: Penrith, Northumberland, Q3 1860
Died: Salford, Lancashire, 22 January 1911
Career: Weaste, Irlams-o'th'-Height, Stratford, Swinton, Lancashire, The North
Debut: v Ireland, Lansdowne Road Dublin February 1882

Beswick captained the famous Swinton team of 1881 when they supplied most of the Lancashire side and made his international debut against Ireland at Lansdowne Road Dublin in February 1882. He then retained his place for the next game against Scotland in Manchester a month later. But by the following game against Wales in Swansea in December 1882, he lost his place to the Cambridge University duo Arthur Evanson and Charles Wade. Beswick, who also captained the Red Rose County, was a mechanical engineer's draughtsman who took up refereeing. He lost a battle with cancer, leaving a wife and ten children.

141. BOLTON, Wilfred Nash OBE
Three-quarter 11 caps (6t, 2c) 1882-1887
Born: Worthing, Sussex, 14 September 1862
Died: Comtrexeville, France, 12 August 1930
Career: RMC Sandhurst, Gosport, Blackheath, Kent
Debut: v Ireland, Lansdowne Road, Dublin February 1882

Sandhurst-educated Bolton, nicked named Baby, was an army athletics champion and a high-class gymnast. He made a try-scoring debut against Ireland at Lansdowne Road in February 1882. Bolton formed a deadly partnership with Gregory Wade when England in 1883 became the first team to claim the Triple Crown. A major in the Wiltshire Regiment, Bolton served in the Boer War, and despite being wounded three times, he was mentioned in dispatches twice. He stayed in South Africa after the war, becoming Resident Magistrate in Transvaal. He was later Provost Marshall & Food Controller of Cyprus and was awarded an OBE.

142. FULLER, Herbert George
Forward 6 caps 1882-1884
Born: Finchley, Middlesex, 4 October 1856
Died: Streatham, London 2 January 1896
Career: Christ's College, Finchley, Cambridge University, Bath, Somerset
Debut: v Ireland, Lansdowne Road Dublin February 1882

Fuller was a forward who captained his school, Christ's College Finchley, before winning a record six blues between 1878 and 1883, but this forced the rules of Cambridge University Rugby Club rules to be altered, preventing fifth-year students from appearing in the varsity match. During his time at Cambridge, he won the first of his caps against Ireland at Lansdowne Road in February 1882. Fuller was a popular coach working in university administration at Peterhouse, Cambridge, becoming a member of the RFU committee until his death of a cereal tumour following a lengthy illness.

143. HUNT, James Thomas
Forward 3 caps 1882-1884
Born: Longton, Preston, 14 February 1858
Died: Wye, South Australia, 5 October 1924
Career: Preston Grasshoppers, Manchester, Lancashire
Debut: v Ireland, Lansdowne Road Dublin February 1882

The youngest of the three Preston Grammar School-educated Hunt brothers, the others being William and

Robert, with whom he played against Ireland on his England debut at Lansdowne Road in February 1882. He and William had strong links to the Manchester team, which was needed at the time to play for Lancashire as a stepping stone to the North vs South trial match. A wine and spirit merchant like his eldest brother William and father Robert, he was also a prominent cricketer, playing for the Preston club. After emigrating to Australia in 1886, Hunt became a reliable and effective stock station estate manager.

144. MIDDLETON, Bernard Boswell
Forward 2 caps 1882-1883
Born: Whitehaven, Cumberland, 25 December 1858
Died: Bridge, Kent, 22 October 1947
Career: Marlborough College, Marlborough Nomads, Birkenhead Park, Cheshire
Debut: v Ireland, Lansdowne Road Dublin February 1882

Educated at Marlborough College, Middleton played for Marlborough Nomads, but when he won the first of his England caps against Ireland at Lansdowne Road in February 1882, he was registered to Birkenhead Park. It was almost a year until he won his second and last cap against Ireland at Whalley Range, Manchester. While living in Liverpool, he was a cotton brokers salesman's merchant, Employing four clerks & four apprentices. Middleton then moved his family south to become a paving contractor in Hackney and then an Artificial Stone Manufacturer, retiring to Kent, where he lived until his death.

145. SPURLING, Aubrey
Forward 1 cap 1882
Born: Peckham, Surrey, 19 July 1856
Died: Sevenoaks, Kent, 26 March 1945
Career: Blackheath Proprietary School, Blackheath, Kent
Debut: v Ireland, Lansdowne Road Dublin February 1882

Spurling played for Blackheath Proprietary School, Kent and England like his younger brother Norman. Spurling was a Blackheath 'club patriot' and made his only international appearance against Ireland at Lansdowne Road in February 1882 alongside clubmate Baby Bolton. He was treasurer of Blackheath until resigning in 1899, a year after being appointed auditor to the Kent Rugby Union, the first club historian, and a member of Blackheath Cricket, Rugby and Lawn Tennis Company. Spurling was a member of the Stock Exchange. He was awarded the freedom of the City of London and lived in Sevenoaks, Kent, until his death.

146. NEWTON, Philip Arthur
Forward 1 cap 1882
Born: Brentford, Middlesex, 11 April 1860
Died: Dictoin Parlieu, Hampshire, 25 December 1946
Career: Blackheath Proprietary School, Oxford University, Blackheath, Kent
Debut: v Scotland, Whalley Range Manchester March 1882

Newton was a forward who captained both Blackheath Proprietary School and Oxford University, where he won a blue in 1879 and 1880 and then appeared in his only test match against Scotland at Whalley Range, Manchester, in March 1882. He was due to win another cap against Wales in Swansea in their first home test the following December, but after getting lost on his way to the ground travelling reserve Charles Wade took his place, and he never won another cap. Newton was the senior partner in the London-based patent agents Newton & Son until his retirement.

147. PAYNE, John Henry
Half-back 7 caps (1c) 1882-1885
Born: Broughton, Lancashire, 19 March 1858
Died: Victoria Park, Manchester, 24 January 1942
Career: Manchester GS, Cambridge University, Broughton Rangers, Lancashire
Debut: v Scotland, Whalley Range Manchester March 1882

Payne was a half-back who won his Cambridge University blue in 1879 before winning seven international caps over four seasons, making his debut against Scotland at Whalley Range, Manchester, in March 1882. His only points came in his penultimate match against Wales in 1885, converting a Richard Kindersley try. John also served as secretary to the Lancashire Rugby Football Union. A right-handed batsman, he played first-class cricket for Cambridge University and Lancashire, while his father played for Manchester and the North of England. Payne, a solicitor, in partnership with his father-in-law in the Manchester law firm Payne, Galloway & Payne.

148. TATHAM, The Rev William Meaburn
Forward 7 cap (1t) 1882-1884
Born: Ryburgh, Norfolk, 30 July 1862
Died: Cantley, Doncaster, 18 October 1938
Career: Marlborough College, Marlborough Nomads, Oxford University
Debut: v Scotland, Whalley Range Manchester, March 1882

Marlborough College-educated Tatham, the son of a clergyman, won his first cap against Scotland at Whalley Range, Manchester, in March 1882 while at Oxford University, whom he captained in 1883. The following year, he scored his only try in his third test against Ireland. Tatham was ordained in 1885, working in Folkestone and Kennington before becoming vicar at Cantley nr Doncaster for 46 years between 1892 and his death. He was also acting chaplain to the Armed Forces in the 1902 South African War. Tatham captained the Cantley Village cricket team for many years and served on the Cantley Parish Council.

149. EVANSON, Arthur McDonnell JP
Three-quarter 4 caps (4c) 1882-1884
Born: Llansoy, Monmouthshire, 15 September 1851
Died: Dover, Kent, 31 December 1934
Career: Oundle School, Oxford University, Richmond, Middlesex
Debut: v Wales, St Helen's, Swansea, December 1882

Evanson was eight years younger than his England international brother Wyndham. He gained his Oxford University blue in 1880 and 1881 and was the captain in 1882 but didn't play. He also won his athletic blue in the shot put. Evanson debuted against Wales at St Helen's in December 1882 and kicked two conversions. He lived in Chilverton Elms near Dover, where he was headmaster of Chilverton Elms Preparatory School. Evanson also reared pedigree cattle, served as a Justice of the peace for Kent and commanded a detachment of Dover Volunteers, and he lost one of his two sons during the First World War.

150. HENDERSON, Sir Robert Samuel Findlay KCMG CB
Forward 5 caps (1t) 1882-1885
Born: Calcutta, India, 11 December 1858
Died: Milbank, London, 5 October 1924
Career: Bedford GS, Fettes College, Edinburgh University, Blackheath, St Mary's Hospital
Debut: v Wales, St Helens Swansea December 1882

Henderson, the son of a Bengal chaplain, learnt the game at Fettes College and Edinburgh University and scored a try on his England debut against Wales at St Helen's Swansea in December 1882. He studied medicine at Edinburgh University and St Mary's Hospital before entering the Army in August 1884. His army doctor's exam cost him another cap against Ireland earlier that year. He served in the South African War in 1901-02 and then the First World War when he was mentioned in dispatches. Henderson was also an honorary physician to The King and retired from the Army in December 1917 with the rank of major general.

151. KINDERSLEY, Richard Stephen
Forward 3 caps (2t) 1882-1885
Born: Exeter, Devon, 27 September 1858
Died: Beaminster, Dorset, 26 September 1932
Career: Clifton College, Oxford University, Exeter, Devon
Debut: v Wales, St Helen's, Swansea, December 1882

Kindersley was educated at Clifton College before going to Oxford, where he won a rowing blue in his first two years and then his rugby blue in his second two years. The first Devonian to win an international cap and his first international try against Scotland in March 1884 was one of the most controversial in the early history of the game and led to a break from international fixtures between the two counties and, ultimately, the formation of the International Board. Kindersley, a schoolmaster, taught at Radley College and then at Eton from 1888 until his retirement in 1920.

152. ROTHERHAM, Alan
Half-back 12 caps (2t) 1882-1887
Born: Coventry, Warwickshire, 31 July 1862
Died: Portman Squad, London, 30 August 1898
Career: Uppingham School, Oxford University, Coventry, Richmond, Middlesex
Debut: v Wales, St Helens Swansea December 1882

Rotherham was the cousin of Arthur, also an England international who went to Oxford University, where he won a blue between 1882 and 1884 as a member of Harry Vassell's Famous Oxford Fifteen. Rotherham captained his country in his last three caps before a dispute between the Union and the IRB ended his international career. He was called to the bar in 1888 and later became the secretary of Brewers Watneys. Tragically, Alan shot himself in the head at his residence in Portman Squad, and a verdict of returned of 'Suicide while of unsound mind'. Rotherham is a member of the World Rugby Hall of Fame.

153. STANDING, Graham
Forward 2 caps 1882-1883
Born: Clapham, London, 20 December 1860
Died: Fernhurst, Sussex, 23 October 1909
Career: Blackheath, Hastings, Colchester, Essex, Kent, The South
Debut: v Wales, St Helen's Swansea December 1882

Standing was probably one of the most versatile players in the game's early history. He started as a back at Blackheath and Hastings and appeared as a three-quarter for Kent. But made his two England appearances as a forward. After moving to Colchester, he helped founded Essex Rugby Football Club and played in their "missionary" county matches with Suffolk in 1885. Standing over Christmas 1884, turned out for Colchester in association football against Romford. A brewer, he moved to Fernhurst, Sussex, where he died after a long illness.

154. TAYLOR, Arthur Sneyd
Half-back 4 caps 1882-1886
Born: Greenwich, Kent, 7 December 1859
Died: Surbiton, Surrey, 7 April 1921
Career: Merchant Taylors School, Cambridge University, Guy's Hospital, Blackheath, Kent
Debut: v Wales, St Helens Swansea December 1882

Taylor, the brother of Henry and one of three brothers who played rugby for Blackheath. Arthur went to Cambridge University, where he won a blue between 1879 and 1881. The following December, he made his international debut against Wales at St Helen's Swansea. After finishing his medical studies at Guy's Hospital, he was a surgeon at Surbiton Cottage Hospital, then practised at Richmond House, Eliot Park, Blackheath, later becoming a GP in Lovelace Lodge, Surbiton. Taylor was a medical officer to the Hearts of Oak and a medical referee to various assurance companies until his sudden death following an operation.

155. WADE, Sir Charles Gregory
Three-quarter 8 caps (7t) 1882-1886
Born: Singleton, New South Wales, 26 January 1863
Died: Sydney, New South Wales, 26 September 1923
Career: All Saints' College Bathurst NSW, King's School Parramatta, Oxford University, Middlesex, New South Wales
Debut: v Wales, St Helen's, Swansea, December 1882

Wade was the first overseas player to play for England when he scored a hat-trick on his debut against Wales at St Helen's in December 1882. He scored on every one of his four appearances against Wales. A barrister who was called to the bar in 1886 and was appointed a QC in 1891. After returning to Australia, he played for New South Wales against the British Team. After entering politics, Wade served as Attorney General of New South Wales, Minister for Justice, Premier for New South Wales, and then a judge in the Supreme Court of New South Wales.

156. WOOLDRIDGE, Charles Sylvester
Forward 7 caps 1882-1885
Born: Winchester, Hampshire, 31 December 1858
Died: Winchester, Hampshire, 19 February 1941
Career: Winchester College, Oxford University, Blackheath, Hampshire
Debut: v Wales, St Helen's, Swansea, December 1882

A product of a football-playing school, Winchester College, after going to Oxford University, Wooldridge won a blue in 1882, the year he won his first international cap against Wales at St Helen's. He captained a Hampshire side that included his brother A T. After returning to Winchester, which had no rugby club, he played football for Winchester City and Hampshire. He was president of Winchester Rugby Club and of the Hampshire FA. He joined his father Chas' law firm, C Woolridge and Son, Solicitors and a major in the 1st Volunteer Battalion, Hampshire Regiment for 28 years and was a city councillor for three years.

157. MOORE, Edward James CB VD
Forward 2 caps 1883
Born: Dudley, West Midlands, 25 May 1862
Died: Lewisham, London, 7 March 1925
Career: Epsom College, Oxford University, Bart's Hospital, Blackheath, Kent
Debut: v Ireland, Whalley Range, Manchester, February 1883

Moore was head prefect at Epsom College, representing them in rugby and cricket. He won his Oxford blue in 1882 and 1883, also captaining the university and was still only 20 years old when he made his England debut against Ireland at Whalley Range, Manchester, in February 1883 and won his second and last cap a month against Scotland in Edinburgh. After completing his medical training at St Bartholomew's Hospital, he became a GP in Blackheath. Then, during the First World War, he was a Lt Col in the Royal Army Medical Corps Commanding the 3rd Battalion, Royal West Kent Regiment.

158. PATTISSON, Richard Murrills
Forward 2 caps 1883
Born: Tonbridge, Kent, 5 August 1860
Died: Cambridge, Cambridgeshire, 28 November 1948
Career: Tonbridge School, Cambridge University, Gipsies, Blackheath
Debut: v Ireland Whalley Range, Manchester February 1883

Richard Pattisson was an Old Tonbridgian who furthered his education at Cambridge University, where he won his blue in 1881 and 1882. He was one of seven (five from Oxford) varsity players in the side when he won the first of his two international caps against Ireland at Whalley Range, Manchester, in February 1883 and retained his place for his last cap in Scotland a month later. Pattisson was an examiner in law & modern history at Cambridge before being called to the Bar in 1888 and practised as an equity draftsman and conveyancer in London until retiring to Cambridge.

159. TRISTRAM, Henry Barrington
Full-back 5 caps 1883-1887
Born: Greatham, County Durham, 5 September 1861
Died: St Helier, Jersey, 1 October 1946
Career: Winchester College, Loretto School, Oxford University, Durham City, Fettesian-Lorettonians, Newton Abbott, Durham University, Devon
Debut: v Scotland, Raeburn Place, Edinburgh February 1883

Tristram was universally known as Tim and was described by Billy Bancroft as the 'best ever' full-back winning a blue between 1882 and 1884. He debuted in the final game of the inaugural Home Nations Championship against Scotland at Raeburn Place, Edinburgh, in February 1883. He later played two more trial matches without winning a further cap. Tristram also played first-class cricket for Oxford University and Durham CCC. He was a classics master at Newton College and then headmaster of Loretto School for five years until 1908, moving south to teach at St. Paul's School for four years until retiring to Jersey.

160. CHAPMAN, Charles Edward
Three-quarter 1 cap 1884
Born: Bourn, Lincolnshire, 26 August 1860
Died: Scrivelsby, Lincolnshire, 23 August 1901
Career: Oxford University, Edinburgh Wanderers, Trojans, Hampshire
Debut: v Wales, Cardigan Field, Leeds January 1884

Chapman was educated at Oxford University, winning a blue in 1881 and 1884, when he made his only international appearance against Wales at Cardigan Field, Leeds. He was an assistant master at Carlisle Grammar School and spent five years in Australia at the Church of England Grammar School in Melbourne. Chapman returned to England and went to Cambridge before being ordained as a clergyman. For the last four years of his life, he was Reverend of Scrivelshy with Palderby when he took his own life after shooting himself in the head, and a verdict was returned of suicide while temporarily insane.

161. MARRIOTT, Charles John Bruce JP
Forward 7 caps 1884-1887
Born: Rensham, Suffolk, 15 July 1861
Died: Ipswich, Suffolk, 25 December 1936
Career: Blackheath Proprietary School, Tonbridge School, Cambridge University, Gipsies, Blackheath, Middlesex
Debut: v Wales, Cardigan Field, Leeds January 1884

Marriott was a Cambridge University blue between 1881 and 1883, wing the first of his England caps against Wales at Cardigan Field, Leeds, in January 1884. He represented Cambridge on the RFU committee between 1897 and 1907 and was an International Board Member. Marriott was a housemaster at Highgate School and a landowner before becoming Secretary of the RFU from 1907 to 1924, overseeing making Twickenham its headquarters. He was also secretary of the Queen's Club for a short time. During the First World War, he was a captain in the Royal Army Service Corps and Justice of the peace for Suffolk.

162. STRONG, Edmund Linwood
Forward 3 caps 1884
Born: Burnham, Somerset, 27 December 1862
Died: Barisal, East Bengal, 19 March 1945
Career: Edinburgh Academy, Oxford University, Bath, Somerset
Debut: v Wales, Cardigan Field, Leeds January 1884

Strong was educated at Edinburgh Academy before attending Oxford, where he won his blue in 1881 and 1883. He seemed set for an England cap in 1883 but injured his knee, and he had to wait until the following January. He also played cricket for Scotland against G F Grace's XI. After being Ordained in 1887, he was the curate at St John the Divine, Kennington, until moving to Calcutta to serve with Oxford University Mission between 1894 and 1900. Strong then transferred to Barisal, and for the next 45 years, he was a priest of the Oxford Mission Brotherhood of the Epiphany.

163. BELL, Henry
Forward 1 cap 1884
Born: Liverpool, Lancashire Q1 1860
Died: Marylebone, London, 20 September 1935
Career: Liverpool Institute, Liverpool Old Boys, New Brighton, Cheshire
Debut: v Ireland, Lansdowne Road, Dublin, February 1884

Bell was registered with New Brighton on his native Wirral when he won his only England cap against Ireland at Lansdowne Road Dublin in February 1884 after being called up as several players were unavailable. He spent all of his working life in the banking industry, firstly as a junior with Liverpool Union, working his way up to become a senior manager, and when Lloyds took them over, he was appointed General Manager. Bell founded Lloyds Bank Rugby Club in 1913 and, during the First World War, was a member of The Committee of War Savings, becoming a director of Lloyds until his death.

164. FALLAS, Herbert
Three-quarter 1 cap 1884
Born: Wakefield, Yorkshire, 1 November 1861
Died: Unknown
Career: Wakefield Trinity, Yorkshire
Debut: v Ireland, Lansdowne Road Dublin February 1884

Fallas won his only international cap against Ireland at Lansdowne Road after England got badly hit by players pulling out of the game. In 1890, he was Wakefield Trinity's captain when they lost the Yorkshire Cup Final to Huddersfield and retired at the end of that season. He later became a referee, served on the Yorkshire committee, and was a member of the Ossett Club. Fallas was the Town Clerk of the Borough of Ossett, then an auctioneer, valuer, and accountant. He also attended the foundation meeting of the Northern Union at the George Hotel, Huddersfield, in August 1895.

165. SAMPLE, Charles Hubert OBE
Full-back 3 caps 1884-1886
Born: Matfen, Northumberland, 22 November 1862
Died: Matinee, Northumberland, 2 June 1938
Career: Edinburgh Academy, Cambridge University, Durham County, Northumberland
Debut: v Ireland Lansdowne Road Dublin February 1884

Sample was an Edinburgh schoolboy when he saw Lennard Stokes almost kick a goal from his own half, and it inspired him. Sample went to Cambridge University, where he won blues between 1882 and 1884. A full-back with an intuitive knowledge of how the play was developing, a sureness of tackle and above all else, the length of his drop kicks made him a useful player. He also played cricket for Northumberland, where he was an estate agent and farmer. During the First World War, Sample served as District Commissioner for Northern Counties for the Board of Agriculture & Fisheries, which saw him granted an OBE.

166. TEGGIN, Alfred
Forward 6 caps (1t) 1884-1887
Born: Broughton, Manchester, 22 October 1860
Died: Cleveleys, Blackpool, 23 July 1941
Career: Broughton Rangers, Lancashire
Debut: v Ireland, Lansdowne Road, Dublin, February 1884

Teggin was one of several changes England made for their trip across the Irish Sea to face Ireland at Lansdowne Road in

February 1884. He had to wait until the following January for his second cap against Wales in Swansea and scored his only international try. A leg-break bowler who played six first-class matches for Lancashire under 'Monkey' Hornby, taking 16 wickets at an average of 11 each and then Longsight. Teggin was described as an artistic engineer, becoming a copper plate engraver in Manchester and then a pictorial copper plate engraver on the Fylde Coast.

167. WIGGLESWORTH, Henry John
Three-quarter 1 cap 1884
Born: Stainton, South Yorkshire, Q3 1861
Died: Beeston, Leeds, 3 March 1925
Career: Thornes, Yorkshire
Debut: v Ireland, Lansdowne Road Dublin February 1884

Wigglesworth kicked the winning goal as Wakefield-based Thornes pulled off one of the earliest shocks in rugby history in the 1882 Yorkshire Cup Final win over neighbours Wakefield Trinity. After impressing in the North vs South in December 1883, he won his only England cap against Ireland at Lansdowne Road, Dublin, in February 1884 when several players pulled out of the game. Wigglesworth would later serve the game as Thornes' captain and as a referee. A warehouseman and was then a fish dealer in Hunslet. He was ill at his home in Beeston, Leeds, for some time before his death.

168. WOOD, Albert
Forward 1 cap 1884
Born: Netherholme, Upper Thong nr Holmfirth 31 March 1862
Died: Unknown
Career: Halifax, Yorkshire
Debut: v Ireland, Lansdowne Road Dublin, February 1884

Wood formed a half-back combination with his younger brother Tyas for Halifax in the early 1880s. But Albert was picked for Yorkshire as a forward in county games, and it was as a forward that he was selected to play for England against Ireland at Lansdowne Road in February 1884. He travelled across the Irish Sea along with his Halifax club mate George Thomson in a strong Yorkshire contingent. Despite helping England win by one goal to nil, it proved to be Wood's only cap as he emigrated to Australia later in 1884.

169. COURT, Edward Darlington
Forward 1 cap 1885
Born: Middlewich, Cheshire, 22 June 1862
Died: Cheltenham, Gloucestershire, 3 April 1935
Career: Rugby School, Oxford University, Blackheath, Kent
Debut: v Wales St Helens, Swansea January 1885

Educated at Rugby School, Court went to Oxford, where he won his blue in 1882 and 1883. Five players from his first Varsity match became team-mates when he won his only England cap against Wales at St Helen's in January 1885, just a month after being called up as a late replacement for the South vs North trial match. Court was a career civil servant holding several posts, including Local Government Board Inspector, Assistant Commissioner with the Boundary Commission and an Inspector for the Ministry of Health in the South-West.

170. HAWCRIDGE, John Joseph
Three-quarter 2 caps (2t) 1885
Born: Macclesfield, Cheshire, 28 September 1863
Died: San Francisco, USA 1 January 1905
Career: Manningham Albion, Manningham, Bradford
Debut: v Wales St Helen's, Swansea January 1885

Hawcridge was one of the most talked about players of his time. A deceptive swerve and sidestep saw him nicknamed the 'Artful Dodger'. John debuted against Wales at St Helens, Swansea, in January 1885, scoring a try. He then scored another try against Ireland a month later but then picked up an injury in a club match against Hull saw him lose form for two seasons. A hatter who then manufactured sports goods. He retired in 1892 to emigrate to the United States, where he became an attorney in Chicago but died of typhoid fever on a trip to San Francisco.

171. KEMBLE, Arthur Twiss
Forward 3 caps 1885-1887
Born: Sebergham, Carlisle, 3 February 1862
Died: Crawley Down, Sussex, 13 March 1925
Career: Appleby GS, Liverpool, Leicestershire, Lancashire
Debut: v Wales St Helen's, Swansea January 1885

Twiss was a Liverpool solicitor who made his England debut against Wales at St Helen's in January 1885 but was far better known as one of the best amateur wicketkeepers in England for 20 seasons. He captained both Lancashire and Liverpool CC. Was president of Liverpool Rugby Football Club and chairman of Lancashire committees for cricket and rugby while also serving on the committee of Sussex CCC. Twiss was elected to Garston District, Liverpool City Councils, and several local committees after moving to Crawley Down in 1904, where he died of septic pneumonia following influenza.

172. RYALLS, Henry John
Forward 2 caps 1885
Born: Claughton, Cheshire, 12 December 1858
Died: Birkenhead, Cheshire, 17 October 1949
Career: Birkenhead School, New Brighton, Cheshire
Debut: v Wales St Helen's, Swansea January 1885

Ryalls was called into the December 1884 North vs South trial match when Charles Horley was ruled out through illness, and he impressed enough to make his against Wales at St Helen's the following month and retained his place for his last cap for the visit of Ireland to Whalley Range in February 1885. He followed his father, William, selling pianos and music and became the managing director of the music business Ryalls and Jones in Birkenhead. Ryalls served the Disablement Commission during the First World War and was President of the Music Industry Association of GB and Birkenhead Park Rugby Club.

173. MOSS, Frank Jacob Slazenger
Forward 3 caps 1885-1886
Born: Cheetham, Manchester Q1 1860
Died: Bellgrande, United States, 9 August 1938
Career: Broughton, Lancashire
Debut: v Wales, St Helen's, Swansea, January 1885

Moss hailed from the prominent Manchester side Broughton and won his only international cap alongside club-mate John Payne. He became one of three brothers who set up the sporting goods firm Slazenger. Two of them, Albert and Ralph, headed the London operation, and Frank moved to New York, where he changed his name to Frank Leigh Slazenger. Leigh was the Manchester Street the brothers lived in before setting out to make their fortunes. Moss patented several golf club heads and maintained an interest in rugby, acting as an honorary secretary to a club in New York. He died while visiting friends in Maine.

174. STODDART, Andrew Ernest
Three-quarter, 10 caps (2t,1c,1gm) 1885-1893
Born: South Shields, Tyne and Wear, 11 March 1863
Died: St John's Wood, London, 3 April 1915
Career: Rev G.W Oliver's St John's Wood School, Harlequins, Blackheath, Barbarians, Middlesex
Debut: v Wales St Helen's, Swansea, January 1885

A household name in the late 19th century, Stoddart is the only man who captained England and the British Team in rugby and the England cricket team. He won the first of his rugby caps against Wales at St Helen's in January 1885. Five years later, he captained his country against Wales. In 1888, he stayed in Australia after a cricket tour to play for the British Team and was named captain after Robert Seddon drowned. Stoddart played for Middlesex CCC, working as a stockbroker, and was club secretary of Queens Club before committing suicide after being hit by financial problems.

175. HORLEY, Charles Henry
Forward 1 cap 1885
Born: Pendlebury, Greater Manchester, 1861
Died: Birkdale, Lancashire, 10 May 1924
Career: Pendlebury Rangers, Swinton, Lancashire
Debut: v Ireland, Whalley Range, Manchester February 1885

A native of Pendlebury, Horley was full-back for Pendlebury Rangers in 1877 for two years before leaving for Swinton and, after four trials with the reserves, progressed to the first team. Horley was soon moved into the forwards, staying for the next fourteen seasons. Described as a capable exponent in the art of dribbling. 'His displays were always of the honest and hard-working sort.' His international debut was delayed after he missed the December 1884 trial through illness. A civil engineer for the Lancashire and Yorkshire Railway for 40 years and was a familiar figure at Hunts Bank Manchester.

176. BONSON, Frederick Fernand DCM QVM
Half-back 6 caps 1886-1889
Born: France, 1862
Died: Lewisham, London, 14 April 1932
Career: Bradford, Yorkshire
Debut: v Wales, Rectory Field, Blackheath January 1886

Bonson was born in France to English parents who moved to Shipley, Yorkshire, before his tenth birthday. He was part of the Bradford side that won the Yorkshire Cup in 1884, making his test debut against Wales two years later. The first Yorkshireman to captain England against the New Zealand Natives at Blackheath in 1889. Bonson studied for the Civil Service examination but went into industry, becoming a wholesale bottler and agent. Serving in the Boer War, he won a DCM and QVM (three clasps). He later farmed in Alberta, Canada, for 12 years and then at Grubbs Farm, Staffhurst Wood, Eden Bridge, Kent.

177. CLIBBORN, William Goff
Forward 6 caps 1886-1887
Born: Clonmel, Co Tipperary 28 September 1859
Died: Epsom, Surrey, November 15, 1939
Career: Richmond, Middlesex, London
Debut: v Wales Rectory Field, Blackheath January 1886

Clibborn was born in Clonmel, Co Tipperary and played rugby for Richmond. He made six successive international appearances after debuting against Wales at Rectory Field, Blackheath, in January 1886. His England career ended following the 1888 clash with Scotland in a game in which caps weren't awarded. The 1888-1889 season saw him elected Richmond captain. Clibborn was one of the leading oarsmen of his day. He was a merchant in the tea-buying trade, living in Datchet until moving to Epsom shortly after his marriage in April 1901. He spent the rest of his days in Surrey.

178. ELLIOT, Charles Henry
Forward 1 cap 1886
Born: Sunderland, Tyne & Wear, 31 May 1861
Died: Chard, Somerset, 1 April 1934
Career: Repton School, Sunderland, Blackheath, Durham
Debut: v Wales, Rectory Field, Blackheath January 1886

Elliot was educated at association football, playing Repton School and made just one international appearance against Wales at Rectory Field, Blackheath, in January 1886. Elliott was one of seven players from the host club to play in the game after benefitting from having a good trial match. He made the mark which allowed Andrew Stoddart to take the match-winning goal. He was a Good "dribbler", earning himself a reputation as one of the earliest "winging" forwards. Elliot's elder brother William played for Sunderland and Durham, and England capped his nephew, Edgar. A timber merchant who was Treasurer of Durham County Union.

179. HANCOCK, Philip Froude
Forward 3 caps 1886-1980
Born: Wellington, Somerset, 23 August 1865
Died: Clifton, Somerset, 16 October 1933
Career: Cavendish College, Cambridge University, Wiveliscombe, Blackheath, Barbarians, Somerset, British Team
Debut: v Wales Rectory Field, Blackheath January 1886

Hancock was known as Baby. Standing 6ft 6in tall and weighing 17 stone, he was one of England's biggest early players. He was one of five brothers who played for Wiveliscombe and Somerset. His brother Frank played for Cardiff and Wales, and they originated the four-Three-quarter system in 1886. Hancock played against Scotland in 1888, but caps were not awarded. He and Johnny Hammond toured South Africa with the British Team in 1891 and 1896. He travelled from Somerset to play for Blackheath, walking the last ten miles home, and was a director of the family brewery.

180. INGLIS, Rev Rupert Edward
Forward 3 caps 1886
Born: Hanover Square 17 May 1864
Died: KIA nr Ginschy, France 18 September 1916
Career: Rugby School, Oxford University, Blackheath, Middlesex
Debut: v Wales Rectory Field, Blackheath January 1886

Inglis was the son of Sir John Inglis, the Defender of Lucknow, and was educated at Rugby School, playing rugby and cricket before going to Oxford University, where he won a blue in 1883 and 1884. He won the first of his England caps against Wales at Rectory Field, the home of his club, Blackheath, in January 1886 while studying at Ely Theological College. Inglis was ordained in 1890, volunteered for service during the First World War, and was commissioned as a Chaplain to the Forces. He was killed during the Battle of Ginchy during the Battle of the Somme.

181. JEFFERY, George Luxton
Forward 6 caps (1t) 1886-1887
Born: St George's, London, 26 December 1861
Died: Mount Eccleshall, Staffordshire, 4 November 1937
Career: St John's Wood School, Cambridge University, Harlequins, Blackheath, Barbarians, Middlesex
Debut: v Wales Rectory Field, Blackheath January 1886

Jeffery won a Cambridge University blue in 1884 and 1885 and was one of four Blackheath players in the pack and seven in the team when he made his debut when his club side hosted Wales at Rectory Field in January 1886. He scored his only try on what turned out to be his last appearance against Ireland but did play in the 1888 game against Scotland, where caps were not awarded. It was the last time he was selected. Jeffery started his working life as a clerk before going to Cambridge. He then became a member of the Stock Exchange.

182. ROBERTSHAW, Albert Rawson
Three-quarter 5 caps 1886-1887
Born: Bradford, Yorkshire, Q4 1861
Died: Bradford, Yorkshire, 17 November 1920
Career: Bradford, Barbarians, Yorkshire
Debut: v Wales Rectory Field, Blackheath January 1886

Robertshaw was one of four brothers, Jeremiah, Herbert and Percy, who played in the 1888 game against Scotland, where caps weren't awarded. The quartet all played for Bradford and Yorkshire. He introduced the three-quarter centre theory to England after debuting against Wales at Rectory Field, Blackheath, in January 1886. Two years earlier, he was part of the Bradford team that won the Yorkshire Cup. He had joined Bradford as a forward but became the greatest centre of his generation. Robertshaw was a worsted manufacturer. He died at his home in Bradford after an attack of pneumonia.

183. WILKINSON, Edgar
Forward 4 caps (2t)
Born: Bradford, Yorkshire, 27 October 1863
Died: Bradford, Yorkshire, 27 August 1896
Career: Bradford, Yorkshire
Debut: v Wales, Rectory Field, Blackheath, January 1886

Wilkinson was a prominent member of the Bradford side whose social standing saw them dubbed the 'Shirt Necked Team." A member of their Yorkshire Cup-winning side of 1884 and was described as "one of the finest exponents of the dribbling art in the country. Prominent in the line-out and could pass as well as many of the three-quarter backs." Wilkinson scored a try on his international debut against Wales at Rectory Field, Blackheath, in January 1886. He served the club as treasurer and sat on the committee until his premature death from rheumatic fever when he was only 32.

184. SPURLING, Norman
Forward 3 caps 1886-1887
Born: Blackheath, London 15 February 1864
Died: Stratton, Cornwall, 20 July 1920
Career: Blackheath Proprietary School, Blackheath, Kent
Debut: v Ireland Lansdowne Road, Dublin, February 1886

Spurling was eight years younger than his brother Aubrey, an England international who debuted against Ireland at Lansdowne Road, Dublin, in February 1886. He also played in the 1888 game against Scotland, which caps were not awarded after missing the previous two matches. But by the time they played again, England selected nine new forwards, and he didn't play again. Spurling was a member of the Stock Exchange like his father Percival and brother, but he took early retirement leaving London and spending the rest of his life living in various parts of Cornwall until his death aged 56.

185. BRUTTON, Ernest Bartholomew
Three-quarter 1 cap 1886
Born: Tynemouth, Tyne & Wear 29 July 1863
Died: Aylesbeare, Devon, 19 April 1922
Career: Durham College, Cambridge University, Lichfield Theological College, Northumberland, County Durham
Debut: v Scotland Raeburn Place, Edinburgh March 1886

Durham College-educated Brutton won his first Oxford University blue in 1883, aged 19. He won his Athletic blue the following year before returning to rugby in 1885 and 1886 when he was captain. He made his only international appearance against Scotland at Raeburn Place in March 1886, but after being outpaced by Scotland three-quarter Reginald Morrison, he was never picked again. Brutton played cricket for Northumberland in 1891 and Devon between 1901 and 1904. A one-time Assistant master at Lancing College, he was vicar of Aylesbeare, Devon, from 1893 until his death.

186. BAKER, Hiatt Cowles
Forward 1 cap 1887
Born: Westbury-on-Trym, Gloucestershire, 30 July 1863
Died: Almondsbury, Bristol 19 September 1934
Career: Rugby School, Clifton, Bristol, Gloucester
Debut: v Wales, Stradey Park, Llanelli January 1887

Rugby school-educated Baker joined Clifton in 1883 and was captain from 1886 to 1889. He made his only England appearance against Wales at Stradey Park, Llanelli, in appalling conditions. His father, William Baker, ran Baker & Co., Warehousemen and Drapers, later changing the name to Baker & Baker Co. Baker became pro-chancellor of Bristol University, his former house, The Holmes, forms part of the university and was the base for General Bradley and the other US generals in their preparations for the D-Day invasion of Normandy. The Hiatt Baker Hall of Residence is named after him.

187. CLEVELAND, Sir Charles Raitt KCIE, KBE
Forward 2 caps 1887
Born: Bombay, India, 2 November 1866
Died: London, 18 January 1929
Career: Christ's College Finchley, Oxford University, Blackheath, Kent
Debut: v Wales, Stradey Park, Llanelli January 1887

Raitt was a Cambridge University blue in 1885 and 1886 and an Athletic blue in the Hammer. He made his international debut against Wales at Stradey Park, Llanelli, in January 1887 in appalling snowy conditions. Even though he missed the next game against Ireland in Dublin, he returned for the last international of the season against Scotland at Whalley Range, Manchester. Raitt was a member of the Indian Civil Service from 1885 and was appointed director of intelligence from 1910 until retiring in 1917. Returning home, he became secretary of an omnibus company and sat on the London transport committee.

188. DEWHURST, John Henry MBE
Forward 4 caps 1887-1890
Born: Skipton, Yorkshire, 27 December 1863
Died: Bedhampton, Hampshire, 22 April 1947
Career: Mill Hill School, Cambridge University, Richmond, St Thomas Hospital, Surrey
Debut: v Wales, Stradey Park, Llanelli January 1887

Dewhurst was educated at Mill Hill School before attending Cambridge University, where he won a blue in 1885 and 1886. His first England cap came in the scoreless draw against Wales at a snowbound Stradey Park in January 1887. He played in the 1888 game against Scotland that never was after Scottish protests but returned to the side to win his final cap against Wales in Dewsbury in February 1890. After graduating, Dewhurst became a house surgeon at St Thomas' Hospital and then at the General Hospital, Tunbridge Wells, before spending many years in practice in Chipping Campden in the Cotswolds.

189. HICKSON, John Lawrence
Forward 6 caps 1887-1890
Born: Clapham Common, Surrey, 18 July 1862
Died: Bradford, West Yorkshire, 4 August 1920
Career: Bingley, Bradford, Barbarians, Yorkshire
Debut: v Wales, Stradey Park, Llanelli January 1887

Hickson was said to be one of the finest forwards in the game's early history. A Yorkshire Cup winner with Bradford in 1884, he should have won more England caps, and was a member of the 1888 side that played Scotland where caps weren't awarded and then missed the 1889 game against the New Zealand Natives because he was abroad on business. He was chairman of brewers Joseph, Spink & Son and connected to oil and chemical companies. Hickson was also a Colonel in the Athlete Battalion during the First World War, served as a magistrate and was president of the Yorkshire Rugby Football Union.

190. LE FLEMING, John
Three-quarter 1 cap 1887
Born: Tonbridge, Kent, 23 October 1865
Died: Montreux, Switzerland, 9 October 1942
Career: Tonbridge School, Cambridge University, Blackheath, Barbarians, Kent
Debut: v Wales, Stradey Park, Llanelli January 1887

Tonbridge School-educated Le Fleming went to Cambridge University, where he won a Rugby blue between 1884 and 1886. He was also an athletics blue and was the Amateur Athletics Association 120-yard hurdles champion in 1887. He also played for Kent CCC between 1889 and 1899, making one first-class century and won the Davos Bowl for ice skating in 1893. During the First World War, he served in the Queen's Own Regiment and was a master at the Eton House School founded by his father, Rev John. Le Fleming died in Montreux after being stranded in Switzerland by the outbreak of the Second World War.

191. LOCKWOOD, Richard Evison
Three-quarter 14 caps (31 - 5t 8c) 1887-1894
Born: Crigglestone, Yorkshire, 11 November 1867
Died: Leeds, Yorkshire, 10 November 1915
Career: Dewsbury, Heckmondwike, Wakefield Trinity, Yorkshire
Debut: v Wales, Stradey Park, Llanelli January 1887

Universally known as Dicky Lockwood but dubbed 'Little Marvel' made his debut in a scoreless draw against Wales. Two of his caps were won as captain, including the last one against Ireland seven years later. After losing the captaincy, he turned down the chance to play, blaming business commitments and was never selected again. Lockwood was a woollen printer and wire rope engineer and was the landlord of the Queen Hotel, Heckmondwike when he died the day before his 48th birthday after having an operation for mouth cancer, which resulted in him losing his tongue and a large part of his lower jaw.

192. ROBERTS, Samuel
Full-back 2 caps 1887
Born: Bury, Lancashire, 5 July 1860
Died: Bury, Lancashire, 4 September 1927
Career: Swinton, Rochdale Hornets, Lancashire
Debut: v Wales, Stradey Park, Llanelli January 1887

Roberts was Swinton's regular full-back between 1885 and 1890 and won his first England cap after impressing in the North vs South trial at Blackheath in December 1886. He won back-to-back caps before being replaced by Henry Tristram and was never selected again. An amateur in the Lancashire Cricket leagues with both Ramsbottom CC and Bury CC. Roberts became a surveyor and was a successful businessman as a partner in his father's land-owning and coal merchant business, while at the time of his death, he had interests in a mill, iron founders, and weighing machine makers.

193. SEDDON, Robert Lionel
Forward 3 caps 1887
Born: Salford, Lancashire Q4 1860
Died: West Maitland, NSW 15 August 1888
Career: Broughton Rangers, Swinton, Lancashire
Debut: v Wales, Stradey Park, Llanelli January 1887

Seddon was an original member of the Broughton Rangers club and was widely seen as the country's best forward. He only managed to play three internationals for England. A warehouse tallyman, Seddon was captain of the first touring British Team to Australia in 1888, a private venture by cricketers Alfred Shaw and Arthur Shrewsbury. But tragedy struck 20 matches into the 35-game tour when he drowned while sculling on River Hunter in West Maitland, New South Wales, trying to reach a boat carrying other players after staying at the hotel to write letters home.

194. FAGAN, Arthur Rupert St Legar
Three-quarter 1 cap 1887
Born: Calcutta, India, 24 November 1862
Died: Highgate, London, 15 March 1930
Career: Guy's Hospital, United Hospitals, Richmond, Tiverton, Devon, Middlesex
Debut: v Ireland Lansdowne Road, Dublin February 1887

Fagan was one of many players born in India, and his performances for Guy's Hospital helped him win a trial place. In February 1887, he won his only cap against Ireland at Lansdowne Road, Dublin, after other players pulled out of the game. He remained in the thoughts of selectors, and in 1888, he played in the game against Scotland that had been wiped from the records because of a Scottish protest. Fagan was a doctor in Tiverton, Devon, before moving back to London, where he had a practice in Islington and then lived in Highgate at the time of his death.

195. PEASE, Frank Ernest
Forward 1 cap 1887
Born: Darlington, County Durham, 17 January 1864
Died: Croft, County Durham, 27 June 1957
Career: Harrow School, Darlington, Hartlepool Rovers, Barbarians, Durham
Debut: v Ireland Lansdowne Road, Dublin February 1887

Pease played for Hartlepool Rovers between 1886 and 1891 and was the first player from the club to win an England cap when he made his only international appearance against Ireland at Lansdowne Road, Dublin, in February 1887. He was also an original member of the Barbarians Football Club. Pease followed his father Edward into the wine and spirits industry and took over the running of the family business T Pease, Son and Co of Darlington. At the time of his death in June 1957, aged 93, he was one of the longest-living internationals.

196. SCOTT, Mason Thompson
Half-back 3 caps 1887-1890
Born: Newcastle Upon Tyne, Tyne and Wear 20 December 1865
Died: Carlisle, Cumberland, 1 June 1916
Career: Craig Mount School, Cambridge University, Northern Football Club, Blackheath, Barbarians, Northumberland
Debut: v Ireland Lansdowne Road, Dublin February 1887

Scott was the older brother of Martin and went to Cambridge University, where he won his blue between 1885 and 1887. He was described as "One of the most resourceful and best-tempered exponents of the game, whoever entered the arena on behalf of his county." He won the first international caps against Ireland at Lansdowne Road in February 1887. Scott was well known on Tyneside for construction and as a colliery owner and steel manufacturer as director of Walter Scott Limited, living in Cumberland for many years until his death due to pneumonia.

197. ANDERTON Charles
Forward 1 cap 1889
Born: Ardwick Manchester 30 September 1862
Died: Hale, Cheshire, 9 April 1953
Career: Manchester Free Wanderers, The Rest of England, Lancashire, The North
Debut: v New Zealand Natives, Rectory Field, Blackheath, February 1889

Anderton was one of the unlucky players who played against Scotland in 1888, which doesn't appear in the records after Scottish protests. Therefore, his only appearance was against New Zealand Natives at Rectory Field Blackheath in February 1889, but he kept his place for the Rest of England vs County Champions Yorkshire a month later. He did captain the North in the trial match against the South the following season but didn't catch the selectors' eye. Anderton was a hemp and cotton twine dealer like his father and brother before becoming a paper and hessian merchant in Hale, Bucklow.

198. BEDFORD, Harry
Forward 3 caps 1889-1890
Born: Gildersome, Yorkshire, Q1 1866
Died: Leeds, Yorkshire, 15 January 1929
Career: Batley, Morley, Yorkshire
Debut: v New Zealand Natives, Rectory Field Blackheath February 1889

Bedford started his career with Batley, winning the first Yorkshire Cup Final in 1886 before joining Morley and becoming their first international when he scored two tires on his international debut against New Zealand Natives at Rectory Field, Blackheath, in February 1889. Bedford was described as "a player of fine physique, a hard scrummager and very useful with both hands and feet." After returning from playing, he went into the licensed trade in Cudworth before retiring to Roundhay, Leeds and was a director of Leeds Football Club and had been ill for three or four years before his death.

199. CAVE, John Watkins
Forward 1 cap 1889
Born: Surbiton, Surrey, 5 February 1867
Died: Wokingham, Berkshire, 4 December 1949
Career: Wellington College, Cambridge University, Richmond, The South, Surrey, The Rest of England, London & The Midlands
Debut: v New Zealand Natives, Rectory Field Blackheath February 1889

Cave was the eldest son of High Court Judge Hon. Mr Justice Cave. He was educated at Wellington College and went to Cambridge University, where he won a blue in 1887 and 1888. John was one of 13 new caps when New Zealand Natives visited Rectory Field, Blackheath, in February 1889. He kept his place for the Rest of England clash with County Champions Yorkshire later in the same month but wasn't again selected for another trial match. After leaving Cambridge, Cave returned to his former school, Wellington and was a schoolmaster at the college between 1893 and his retirement in 1923.

200. EVERSHED, Frank
Forward 10 caps (3t) 1889-1893
Born: Stapenhill, Burton-on-Trent, 6 September 1866,
Died: Burton-on-Trent, Staffordshire, 29 June 1954
Career: Reading, Burton, East Sheen, Blackheath, Barbarian FC, Midland Counties, Rest of England, London
Debut: v New Zealand Natives, Rectory Field Blackheath February 1889

Evershed, the son of Sydney Evershed, a brewer and MP for Burton, failed to win a blue while at Oxford University but still made his international debut against New Zealand Natives at Rectory Field, Blackheath, in February 1889 after John Hickson declared he wasn't available. Evershed was one of four brothers and a cousin to play cricket for Derbyshire CCC and was one of the founders of Burton Hockey Club. A founding member of the Barbarian FC, he was a solicitor in his native Burton-Upon-Trent for many years. His only son Raymond became Baron Evershed, the Master of the Rolls.

201. JOWETT, Donald
Forward 6 caps
Born: Bradford, Yorkshire, 4 December 1866
Died: Heckmondwike, Yorkshire, 27 August 1908
Career: Heckmondwike, Yorkshire,
Debut: v New Zealand Natives, Rectory Field Blackheath February 1889

Jowett was nicknamed the 'Heckmondwike Infant' standing at 6' 1", he was a prominent forward of his time and is said to have been a useful long-range kicker who was able to get the full force of his 20-stone weight behind the ball. He won the first of his international caps against New Zealand Natives at Rectory Field Blackheath in February 1889. He remained with Heckmondwike after they joined the Northern Union. Jowett worked as a warehouseman and was a brewer's traveller before running the Crown Hotel and the Sir Robert Peel Inn in Heckmondwike, where he died of a burst blood vessel.

202. LOWRIE, Frederick William
Forward 2 caps 1889-1890
Born: Wakefield, Yorkshire, 1 March 1868
Died: Leeds, Yorkshire, 9 August 1902
Career: Wakefield Collegiate School, Wakefield Trinity, Batley, The North, Yorkshire
Debut: v New Zealand Natives, Rectory Field Blackheath February 1889

Lowrie broke into the Wakefield Trinity side at age 18. He won the first of his two international caps against New Zealand Natives at Rectory Field Blackheath in February 1889 but he had moved onto Batley when he won his last cap against Wales in Dewsbury 13 months later. He remained a Batley player when they switched to the Northern Union following the great split. He worked as a hatter's assistant to his hatter father, John and then worked in a wine and spirits warehouse. Lowrie fell victim to consumption and died at home in Leeds aged 34.

203. ROBINSON, Arthur
Forward 4 caps 1889-1890
Born: Brittanby Manor, Yorkshire, 8 November 1865
Died: Scone, Perth, 9 April 1948
Career: Cheltenham College, Cambridge University, Hartlepool Rovers, Blackheath, Middlesex
Debut: v New Zealand Natives, Rectory Field Blackheath February 1889

Robinson was educated at Cheltenham College before attending Cambridge University, where he won a blue in 1886 and 1887. He debuted against Scotland in 1889, but the match has been scrubbed from the record books after a Scotland protest. Instead, he was one of 13 new players when the New Zealand Natives visited Rectory Field, the home of his club side Blackheath, in February 1889. A barrister who was called to the bar in 1890 and who worked the North-Eastern circuit. Robinson played first-class cricket for Durham before they entered the Minor Counties.

204. ROYLE, Arthur
Full-back 1 cap 1889
Born: Salford, Lancashire 28th January 1862
Died: Ilsington, Devon, 17 March 1942
Career: Broughton Rangers, Wilmslow, New Brighton, Ye Olde Sports, The Rest of England, The North, Lancashire
Debut: v New Zealand Natives, Rectory Field Blackheath February 1889

Royle was a three-quarter and then a full-back for Broughton Rangers between 1882 and 1890. He also appeared for Wilmslow as a forward, winning his only cap against New Zealand Natives at Rectory Field Blackheath in February 1889. He played cricket for Eccles and Broughton until 1904, alongside his brothers James and Herbert. Royle worked as a clerk, merchant's cashier, shipping merchant's cashier, and later a secretary to Thomas G Hill & Co, a limited company in the cotton trade, before retiring to Ilsington, Devon, where he died in March 1942.

Henry Springmann

Henry Twynam

Chris Sawyer

Alan Rotherham

Charles Wade

Charles Marriott

Arthur Kemble

Andrew Stoddart

Froude Hancock

Rupert Inglis

Hiatt Baker

John Hickson

Richard Lockwood

Bob Seddon

Arthur Royle

205. SCOTT, William Martyn
Half-back 1 cap 1889
Born: Gateshead, Tyne and Wear, 27 March 1870
Died: Horsham, Sussex, 26 February 1944
Career: Craigmount School, Cambridge University, Blackheath, Northern, Barbarians, Northumberland, The Rest of England
Debut: v New Zealand Natives, Rectory Field Blackheath February 1889

Scott was the brother of Mason and won a Cambridge University blue in 1888, but injuries prevented further appearances, including in 1889, when he was captain. He is credited with being among the first players to employ a dummy pass. He won his only cap against New Zealand Natives at Rectory Field Blackheath in February 1889, partnering Fred Bonsor at half-back, but was never selected again. One of the founding members of the Barbarian FC, he played cricket for Cambridge University Cricket Club and football for Corinthians. Scott was a major in the Royal Engineers during the First World War.

206. SUTCLIFFE, John William
Three-quarter 1 cap (1t 1c) 1889
Born: Shibden, Yorkshire, 14 April 1869
Died: Bradford, Yorkshire, 7 July 1947
Career: Kirkstall, Bradford, Heckmondwike, Yorkshire
Debut: v New Zealand Natives, Rectory Field Blackheath February 1889

Sutcliffe played rugby for three seasons, making his England debut against New Zealand Natives at Rectory Field Blackheath in February 1889, scoring a try and kicking a conversion. After being suspended for professionalism, he switched to association football. He played in goal for Bolton Wanderers, where he won five England caps. Later, with Millwall Athletic, Manchester United, Plymouth Argyle and Southend United, he served Rochester City (USA) and Vitesse Arnhem (Holland) as a coach and Bradford City trainer. Sutcliffe was chairman of Bradford Northern RL and was on the Committee of Bradford CC and Bradford Fish Market.

207. WILKINSON, Harry James
Forward 1 cap 1889
Born: Halifax, Yorkshire, 16 April 1864
Died: Halifax, Yorkshire, 7 June 1942
Career: Halifax, Yorkshire, The North
Debut: v New Zealand Natives, Rectory Field Blackheath February 1889

After making his debut for his home town club, Halifax, in 1886, Wilkinson quickly became known as one of the speediest forwards in English rugby. It was a reputation that was enough to see him make his only international appearance against New Zealand Natives at Rectory Field Blackheath in February 1889. He captained Halifax in 1889 and 1890 and retired from playing three years later. A pattern dryer who later became a licensee in the town, running the West Hill Hotel for many years until retiring in 1925. His son, also named Harry, won four caps.

208. YIEND, William
Forward 6 caps 1889-1893
Born: Winchcombe, Gloucestershire, 29 September 1861
Died: Cheltenham, Gloucestershire, 22 January 1939
Career: Leicester Victoria, Hartlepool Rovers, Gloucester, Peterborough, Keithley, Barbarians, Durham, The North, The South, The Rest of England
Debut: v New Zealand Natives, Rectory Field, Blackheath, February 1889

Yiend was known as 'Pusher' and became one of the original members of the Barbarians Football Club, who started playing rugby and football on alternate weekends with Leicester Victoria. One of the few players to play trial matches for the South and the North. He played all three games in England's 1892 Triple Crown-winning side. A talented cricketer who won the Yorkshire Cup with Hull. He spent the whole of his working life working around the country with Midland Railway, starting as a junior clerk and retiring in 1925 as a Traffic Agent. Yiend died three weeks after a fall.

209. BUDWORTH, Canon Richard Thomas Dutton
Forward 3 caps (1t) 1890-1891
Born: Greensted, Essex 17 October 1867
Died: St James's, London, 7 December 1937
Career: Oxford University, Blackheath, London Welsh, Clifton, Barbarian, Kent, Sussex
Debut: v Wales Crown Flatt, Dewsbury, February 1890

Oxford University-educated Budworth won his blue between 1887 to 1889. He scored his only international try against Wales in 1891, but the forward's poor performance against Scotland in the following year saw him never selected again. An original member of the Barbarians, Budworth taught at Lancing College and entered the priesthood in was ordained in 1902 at Clifton College. He was headmaster at Durham School for 25 years before becoming canon at Durham Cathedral and then Vicar in Horspath, Oxfordshire. Budworth died at the New University Club on the morning of the 37th Varsity match with the ticket for the match in his pocket.

210. FOX, Francis Hugh JP
Half-back 2 caps 1890
Born: Wellington, Somerset 12 June 1863
Died: Taunton, Somerset, 28 May 1952
Career: Marlborough College, Marlborough Nomads, Wellington, Somerset, Barbarians
Debut: v Wales Crown Flatt Dewsbury February 1890

Fox could be forgiven for thinking that his England cap might never come after playing in the 1888 game against Scotland when caps weren't awarded. He had to wait two years for another chance. Fox won his first cap alongside Bradford's James Fox and Mason Scott for his second a final game against Scotland a month later. He offered long service to the game as Somerset secretary, treasurer, and member of the International Board and RFU President. Fox was Chairman of Fox Brothers Woollen Manufacturers, a partner in Fox, Fowler and Co Bankers, Wellington and a member of Somerset County Council.

211. MITCHELL, William Grant
Full-back 7 caps 1890-1893
Born: Quebec, Canada, 23 May 1865
Died: Victoria, British Columbia, 13 January 1905
Career: Bromsgrove School, Cambridge University, Guy's Hospital, Richmond, Barbarians, Middlesex, British Team
Debut: v Wales Crown Flat Dewsbury February 1890

Canadian Mitchell was educated at Bromsgrove School before going to Cambridge University, where he won a rugby blue in 1886 and then an Athletics blue in the shot a year later. He played all 19 games on the 1891 British team tour to South Africa. His goal from the mark won the Second test in Kimberley. An original member of the Barbarian Football Club, he trained to be a doctor before returning to his homeland. Mitchell later joined the Gold Rush in Alaska but appeared to have returned to medicine when he died from pneumonia.

212. MORRISON, Piercy Henderson
Three-quarter 4 caps (1t) 1890-1891
Born: Brotton, North Yorkshire, 30 July 1868
Died: Jesmond, Newcastle Upon Tyne, 12 July 1936
Career: Loretto School, Cambridge University, Northern, Barbarians, Northumberland
Debut: v Wales Crown Flatt Dewsbury February 1890

Morrison was educated at Cambridge University, where he won his blue between 1888 and 1890, captaining them in 1889. Despite reading medicine at Caius College, he did not take his finals. He debuted against Wales at Crown Flatt, Dewsbury, in February 1890 after the international dispute was settled and scored one of three tries against Ireland two weeks later. His international appearance under the captaincy of his old Cambridge team-mate Frederic Alderson. A founding member of the Barbarians and company director, he served in the First World War as a special constable and motor driver.

213. ROGERS, John Henry OBE
Forward 4 caps (1t) 1890-1891
Born: Aston, Warwickshire 15 February 1867
Died: Birmingham, Warwickshire, 30 March 1922
Career: Bromsgrove School, Moseley Woodstock, Moseley, Barbarians, Midland Counties, London
Debut: v Wales, Crown Flatt, Dewsbury February 1890

Rogers was described as 'strong, sturdy forward, always to be found in the thick of the fight." He started playing for Moseley Woodstock, whom he captained before becoming the first Moseley player to win an international cap. Rogers, an original member of the Barbarians, was succeeded as Moseley captain by his brother Alfred. He also captained and was treasurer of Midland Counties. Rogers was a chartered accountant and the St. Johns Ambulance Association secretary for 30 years. He was awarded an OBE for his work as secretary and treasurer of the Joint V.A.D committee.

214. VALENTINE, James
Three quarters 4 caps (2-1c) 1890-1896
Born: Pendlebury, Lancashire, 29 July 1866
Died: Barmouth, Merionethshire, 25 July 1904
Career: Brindley Heath, Pendlebury, Swinton, Lancashire
Debut: v Wales Crown Flatt Dewsbury February 1890

Valentine turned out alongside Charles Horley at Three-quarter for Pendlebury Rangers as Swinton didn't have a game, and within two months, he took his place in the Swinton team. Unluckily, he played in the 1888 game against Scotland, but no caps were awarded, and after winning his first cap against Wales in February 1890, he had to wait six years to win his second. Valentine was barred from playing when Swinton joined the Northern Union in 1896 and helped the club win the first Challenge Cup in 1900. A soap boiler and then a publican he was killed by lightning while on holiday in Wales.

215. WOODS, Samuel Moses James
Forward 13 caps (1t-1c) 1890-1895
Born: Ashfield, New South Wales, 14 April 1868
Died: Taunton, Somerset, 30 April 1931
Career: Sydney GS NSW, Brighton College, Cambridge University, Wivelscombe, Wellington, Blackheath, Bridgewater, Somerset, Barbarians
Debut: v Wales, Crown Flatt, Dewsbury, February 1890

Woods, known as 'Smudgy', was born in Australia before moving to the mother country to complete his education and won Cambridge University blues in rugby and cricket. He was one of nine players from Blackheath when he captained England against Scotland in March 1895. A Cricketer of the Year in 1889, he played test cricket for both Australia and England and was Somerset's captain for 12 summers. A fine all-round sportsman, he played association football for Sussex and hockey for Somerset. Woods studied brewing at Philip Hancock's Taunton Brewery, entered the brewing industry, and acted as Somerset CCC secretary for two years.

216. WRIGHT, James Frost
Half-back 1 cap 1890
Born: Bramham, Yorkshire, 1 April 1863
Died: Blackpool, Lancashire, 4 October 1932
Career: Bowling Old Lane, Idle, Bradford, Yorkshire
Debut: v Wales, Crown Flatt, Dewsbury, February 1890

Wright learnt the game at Bowling Old Lane and Idle to become one of the most outstanding players in the history of Bradford, whom he helped win the 1894 Yorkshire Cup working in half-back tandem with Fred Bonsor. Ironically, Bonsor was stood down to give him his only international cap after he was initially named as a reserve. Wright, a wool sorter, became a Licensee at the Royal Oak Kirkgate and then a rep for Halifax brewers T Ramsden and Son. He died while on holiday in Blackpool, collapsing in Boots after being told his wallet that contained £90 had been found.

217. ASTON, Randolph Littleton
Three-quarter 2 caps 1890-1891
Born: Kensington, London, 6 September 1869
Died: Tonbridge, Kent, 3 November 1930
Career: Cheltenham College, Westminster School, Berkhamsted School, Tunbridge School, Cambridge University, Blackheath, Barbarians, Kent, British Team
Debut: v Scotland Raeburn Place, Edinburgh, March 1890

Aston, standing at 6 feet 3 and weighing 15 stone, went to Cambridge University, where he won a blue in 1889 and 1890. He made both his international appearances alongside his Varsity team-mate Piercy Morrison. His brother Ferdy captained South Africa against the British team in 1896 and was himself a tourist in 1891 when he scored 30 tries in 19 appearances. Aston was an assistant master at Blair Lodge School in Perthshire and then at Tonbridge School between 1892 before his retirement in 1923 because of ill health. He served as a Rugby Football Union Committee member between 1906 and 1910.

218. DYSON, John William
Three-quarter 4 caps (1t) 1890-1893
Born: Skelmanthorpe, West Yorkshire, 6 September 1866
Died: Huddersfield, West Yorkshire, 3 January 1909
Career: Skelmanthorpe, Huddersfield, Yorkshire
Debut: v Scotland, Raeburn Place, Edinburgh, March 1890

Dyson was an all-round athlete and noted sprinter who scored a try on his international debut against Scotland at Raeburn Place, Edinburgh, in March 1890. He was said to have been one of the greats of Yorkshire rugby after scoring 105 tries in four seasons helping Huddersfield win the Yorkshire Cup in 1890, and stayed with the club when they helped form the Northern Union. Dyson was a licensee running the Royal Oak Inn in Huddersfield and the Warren House Inn in Milnesbridge, then the Slubbers Arms Inn in Hillhouse at the time of his death from liver cancer.

219. HOLMES, Edward
Forward 2 caps 1890
Born: Girlington, Bradford, 20 April 1862
Died: Morecambe, Lancashire, 19 May 1932
Career: Manningham, Yorkshire
Debut: v Scotland Raeburn Place, Edinburgh March 1890

Holmes caught the eye of the selectors with an impressive display playing for the North in the December 1889 trial against the South. It was enough to earn him the first of his two caps against Scotland at Raeburn Place, Edinburgh, the following March, the first time both nations had met since the infamous 1888 clash where Scotland objected to an England try. Holmes captained Yorkshire and earned a living as a cabinet maker and upholsterer running his own company, Holmes & Wood. After losing a son during the First World War, the family went to live in Morecambe for health reasons.

220. TOOTHILL, John Thomas
Forward 12 caps (1t) 1890-1894
Born: Thornton, Yorkshire, March 1866
Died: Bradford, Yorkshire, 29 June 1947
Career: Bradford, Yorkshire
Debut: v Scotland, Raeburn Place, Edinburgh, March 1890

Toothill began his rugby career with Manningham Rugby Club, playing alongside Eddie Holmes before joining Bradford. He won the first of his 12 caps against Scotland at Raeburn Place Edinburgh in March 1890 and made 50 county appearances for Yorkshire between 1888 and 1894. A Bradford stalwart who continued to play for the club when they switched to the Northern Union, Toothill was a worsted spinner aged 15 and then a labourer in a wool dye factory. In common with many former Yorkshire players, he became a licensee and a hotelier in Bradford, but in his retirement, he returned to Thornton.

221. SPENCE, Frederick William
Half-back 1 cap 1890
Born: Claughton, Cheshire, May 1867
Died: Kalgoorlie, Western Australia 25 July 1937
Career: Fettes College, Birkenhead Park
Debut: v Ireland, Rectory Field, Blackheath, March 1890

Edinburgh-educated Spence won his only cap against Ireland, at Rectory Field, Blackheath, in March 1890 while playing for Birkenhead Park, partnering with Mason Scott. He was living in Liverpool and working as a stockbroker at the time. Later, he emigrated to Australia, living in New South Wales, where he saved a woman from drowning in Sydney Harbour before moving to Western Australia. Spence then went to work for the Western Australia Mines Department and acted as mines registrar at various mining centres until retiring in 1921. He lived in Kalgoorlie, where he died after a long illness.

222. ALDERSON Frederic Hodgson Rudd JP
Three-quarter 6 caps (1t 4c) 1891-1893
Born: Hartford, Northumberland, 27 June 1867
Died: Hartlepool, Durham, 18 February 1925
Career: Durham School, Cambridge University, Tyndale, Hartlepool Rovers, Blackheath, Northumberland, County Durham, Barbarians, Rest of England
Debut: v Wales Rodney Parade Newport January 1891

Alderson won an Oxford University blue in 1887 and 1888 and captained England on his debut against Wales at Rodney Parade Newport in January 1891, kicking two conversions in a 7-3 victory. He captained the side in his other five appearances and led England to the 1892 Triple Crown without conceding a point. Frederic played for Hartlepool Rovers in the Barbarians' first-ever match and refereed Scotland vs Ireland in 1903. Settling in Hartlepool, Alderson became an assistant master at Henry Smith School and then headmaster from 1892 until his sudden death aged 57.

223. BERRY, John
Half-back 3 caps 1891
Born: Kendal, Westmorland 25 September 1866
Died: Manchester, Lancashire 10 May 1930
Career: Kendal Hornets, Tyldesley, Lancaster, Westmorland, Lancashire
Debut: v Wales Rodney Parade Newport January 1891

'Buff' Berry was one of the best half-backs of his day, a wonderfully skilful player who spent the early part of his career learning the game with his home town club, Kendal Hornets. But it was after joining Tyldesley that his career really took off. John soon won county honours and impressed England selectors enough that he was partnered with William Martin-Leake in all three 1891 tests but lost his place the following season. Berry, a licensee and then a builder's labourer, stayed with Tyldesley when they helped form the Northern Union in 1895. His younger brothers Robert and William played for Swindon.

224. BROMET, William Ernest
Forward 12 caps (2-1t) 1891-1896
Born: Tadcaster, Yorkshire, 17 May 1868
Died: Winchester, Hampshire, 23 January 1949
Career: Richmond School (Yorkshire), Oxford University, Richmond, Tadcaster, Yorkshire, Middlesex
Debut: v Wales Rodney Parade Newport January 1891

Bromet was the youngest of six brothers who played for Tadcaster. He won his Oxford University blue in 1889. William captained Yorkshire to the 1891 County Championship, and the same year, along with one of his brothers, Edward became the first siblings to play for the British Team when they toured South Africa. He then moved to London, playing for Richmond and Middlesex. After leaving university, Bromet followed his father, John, into the law and qualified as a solicitor in his native Yorkshire before returning to London and later living in Birmingham, where he became a director of the Royal Mint.

225. CHRISTOPHERSON, Percy JP
Three-quarter 2 caps (2t) 1891
Born: Blackheath, Kent, 31 March 1866
Died: Folkestone, Kent, 4 May 1921
Career: Marlborough Collage, Bedford School, Oxford University, Blackheath, Barbarians, Kent
Debut: v Wales, Rodney Parade, Newport, January 1891

Christopherson was an Oxford University blue between 1886 and 1888. He captained his University, Blackheath and Kent and scored two tries on his international debut against Wales at Rodney Parade Newport in January 1891. But was then dropped in favour of Piercy Morrison for the following game in Ireland. Even though he returned for the final match of the campaign against Scotland, he was never selected again. Christopherson was a talented cricketer who played for Oxford, Berkshire CCC and Kent CCC. A brother, Stanley, was a Kent fast bowler. He was a master at Wellington College and principal of Lockers Park in Hemel Hempstead.

226. KENT, Thomas
Forward 6 caps 1891-1892
Born: Nottingham, Nottinghamshire 19 June 1864
Died: Bury, Lancashire, 2 June 1930
Career: Radcliffe, Salford, Lancashire
Debut: v Wales Rodney Parade Newport January 1891

Kent learnt the game at Radcliffe Rugby Club and then joined Salford, where he "distinguished himself" and was selected as a member of the 1888 British Team tour to Australia and New Zealand, the first overseas tour before he won the first of his England caps against Wales at Rodney Parade in January 1891. The following year, he helped England win the Triple Crown without conceding a point, but he was out in the cold the following season and was never picked again. Kent was a builder and contractor who captained Salford before re-joining Radcliffe, later serving on the club committee.

227. MARTIN-LEAKE, William Ralph
Half-back 3 caps 1891
Born: Ceylon 31 December 1865
Died: Godalming, Surrey 14 November 1942
Career: Clifton Collage, Dulwich College, Cambridge University, Old Alleynians, Harlequins, Barbarians; Surrey
Debut: v Wales, Rodney Parade, Newport, January 1891

Martin-Leake was the first player directly capped from Harlequins when he won his international caps in 1891. He had captained Dulwich at rugby and cricket, won his Cambridge University blue between 1885 and 1887, and was an original member of the Barbarians. A clergyman, he taught at Dulwich College, where he coached rugby, and his charges included England international Cyril Lowe and John Greenwood between 1889 and 1937 when he was Assistant Chaplain of the College and head of Dulwich Prep London. Martin-Leake is briefly mentioned in Hugh de Selincourt's novel Realms of Day.

228. NORTH, Eustace Herbert Guest
Forward 3 caps 1891
Born: Lewisham, London 4 November 1868
Died: Wokingham, Berkshire, 17 March 1942
Career: St Paul's School, Blackheath Proprietary School, Oxford University, Blackheath, Barbarians, Sussex, Kent
Debut: v Wales Rodney Parade Newport January 1891

North won three successive Oxford University blues between 1888 and 1890 and played cricket for Oxford Authentics. He made all three of his international appearances in the 1891 season, making his debut against Wales at Rodney Parade, but a defeat to Scotland at the Athletic Ground Richmond spelt the end of his England career. A Blackheath team-mate of Barbarians founder William Percy Carpmael which led to an invitation. Eustace was an assistant master at Wellington College and then a master at Farnborough School until 1927. North served the Prep Schools Association as chair and treasurer until his death in March 1942.

229. RICHARDS, James Joseph
Forward 3 caps 1891
Born: Bedworth, Warwickshire, 31 August 1867
Died: Unknown
Career: Bradford, Yorkshire
Debut: v Wales, Rodney Parade, Newport, January 1891

Richards was the son of a butcher and was born in Warwickshire, but his family moved to Manningham, Yorkshire, when he was still at school. He joined Bradford, one of the strongest clubs in the country, and made his international debut alongside Jack Toothill, his club and county team-mate. He retained his place for the remaining two games but was out of the picture by the start of the following season and was never selected again. Richards was a wool comber and then a publican in Bradford. But after losing his license after betting on the premises, he mined diamonds in South Africa and served in the Kalahari Horse regiment.

230. WILSON, lieutenant Colonel Roger Parker CIE
Forward 3 caps (2t) 1891
Born: West Derby, Lancashire, 15 March 1870
Died: Birkdale, Lancashire, 12 December 1943
Career: Liverpool Collage, Liverpool Old Boys, Liverpool University, Bart's Hospital, Lancashire
Debut: v Wales Rodney Parade Newport January 1891

Wilson was registered to Liverpool Old Boys when he made three successive England appearances in the 1890-1891 season. He scored two tries on his second appearance against Ireland, although one source credited one of them to Donald Jowett. After qualifying as a doctor, Wilson worked in India as a surgeon to the Indian Medical Service, Superintendent of Distract and Central Jails in India from 1903-1910 and was surgeon-general in Bengal Province when he retired after 33 years of service in 1924. Wilson then joined the board of Twiss & Robinson textile manufacturers in Manchester.

231. PERCIVAL, The Rev Launcelot Jefferson KCVO
Forward 3 caps (1t) 1891-1893
Born: Clifton, Gloucestershire 22 May 1869
Died: Woking, Surrey, 22 June 1941
Career: Oxford University, Rugby, Barbarians, Midlands
Debut: v Ireland, Lansdowne Road, Dublin, January 1891

Percival was an Oxford University friend of Eustace North and won his blue between 1889 and 1891. He won his three England caps in three successive seasons. After leaving University, he played for Rugby, whom he captained in 1892/93 and was an original member of the Barbarians. He also played cricket for the MCC and Hertfordshire CCC. Percival took holy orders and served the Ecclesiastical Household of Queen Victoria, King Edward VII, King George V, King Edward VII and King George VI, and in 1937, was appointed Knight Commander of the Royal Victorian Order.

232. BONHAM-CARTER, Sir Edgar KCMG CIE
Forward 1 cap 1891
Born: Paddington, Middlesex, 2 April 1870
Died: Alton, Hampshire, 24 April 1956
Career: Clifton College, Oxford University, Blackheath, Barbarians
Debut: v Scotland, Athletic Ground, Richmond, March 1891

Bonham-Carter was an Oxford University blue between 1890 and 1891. He won his only cap against Scotland at Athletic Ground Richmond in March 1891 after Ernest Bromet withdrew from the game through injury. A defeat ended England's hopes of a Triple Crown and his international career. Bonham-Carter was called to the bar in 1895 and undertook serious overseas postings. Later, he was elected to London County Council, was chairman of First Garden City Ltd and sat on the board of the National Trust. His great-niece is the actress Helena Bonham-Carter.

233. ALLPORT, Alfred
Forward 5 caps 1892-1894
Born: Brixton, London, 12 September 1867
Died: Maidenhead, Berkshire, 2 May 1949
Career: London International Collage, West of Scotland, Sutton, Guy's Hospital, Clapham Rovers, Blackheath, Barbarians, Surrey
Debut: v Wales, Rectory Field, Blackheath, January 1892

Allport captained the London International Collage in Isleworth before spending a year in Scotland, where he played for West of Scotland. He then returned to London to study medicine at Guy's Hospital, but they could not win the Hospitals Cup under his captaincy. Allport played in several North vs South trial matches before winning his first cap against Wales at the home of his club, Blackheath. He played in the Barbarians' first-ever match against Hartlepool Rovers. After serving in the Royal Army Medical Corps, Allport became a consultant surgeon at St Paul's Hospital and a general practitioner.

234. BRIGGS, Arthur
Half-back 3 caps 1892
Born: Dewsbury, West Yorkshire, 30 November 1867
Died: Bradford, West Yorkshire, 18 August 1943
Career: Otley, Bradford, Yorkshire
Debut: v Wales, Rectory Field, Blackheath, January 1892

'Spafty' Briggs started his career with Otley, but only after moving on to Bradford did his career take off. He made his England debut alongside Charles Emmott against Wales in January 1892 in a match that saw the host nation win easily 17-0. He retained his place for the remaining three matches that season, which saw England win the Triple Crown without conceding a point. But he was out in the cold by the start of the following international season and wasn't selected again. Briggs was an iron moulder who was a noted swimmer and breeder of Sealyham terriers.

235. BULLOUGH, Edward
Forward 3 caps 1892
Born: Nerquis, Flintshire, 17 December 1866
Died: Manchester, Lancashire, 6 July 1934
Career: Haigh School, Aspull, Wigan, Oldham, Swinton, Lancashire
Debut: v Wales, Rectory Field Blackheath January 1892

Bullough played for Haigh School and Aspull before joining Wigan in 1889 as a three-quarter but soon found a place in the pack. Just months later, he played for Lancashire against Yorkshire. Ned was the first player from Wigan to win international honours when he made all three international appearances in 1892, helping England win the Triple Crown without conceding a point. His career was cut short in September 1892 after breaking an ankle against Wakefield Trinity. Bullough was a bookkeeper before spending 29 years on staff at Haigh Brewery, then had cotton concerns in Chorley and Atherton.

236. EMMOTT, Charles
Half-back 1 cap 1892
Born: Shipley, West Yorkshire Q1 1868
Died: Saltaire, West Yorkshire, 10 March 1927
Career: Saltaire, Bradford, Yorkshire
Debut: v Wales, Rectory Field, Blackheath, January 1892

Emmott was an attacking half-back who arrived at Bradford via Saltaire and Shipley. An impressive showing against The Barbarians brought him county and international honours. There is little doubt that he owed his England selection to Frederic Alderson. He won his only cap alongside club-mate Arthur Briggs, the first time two half-backs from the same club side were picked in an international. A millhand and then a cabinet maker for over 20 years, he then became a furniture broker. During the First World War, Emmott lost two of his three sons, James and Lawrence.

237. HUBBARD, George Cairns
Three-quarter 2 caps (2-1t)
Born: Benares, India 23 November 1867
Died: Eltham, Kent, 18 December 1931
Career: Tonbridge School, Blackheath, Barbarians, Kent
Debut: v Wales, Rectory Field, Blackheath, January 1892

Hubbard was known as 'Scatter' and played in the 1888 game against Scotland when caps weren't awarded. But he forced his way back into the reckoning four years later due to a prolific try-scoring record with Blackheath. He scored a try on his England debut against Wales at Rectory Field, the home of his club side, but after failing to score in his next game against Ireland, he was never seen again. A member of the London Stock Exchange played for Kent CCC and was caught and bowled by WG Grace on his debut. A son, John, won one England cap.

238. NICHOLL, William
Forward 2 caps (1t) 1892
Born: Raistrick, West Yorkshire, 30 October 1868
Died: Brighouse, West Yorkshire, 10 April 1922
Career: Brighouse Rangers, Yorkshire
Debut: v Wales, Rectory Field, Blackheath, January 1892

Nicholl was the best forward his club, Brighouse Rangers ever possessed. 'A robust and vigorous player who was always prominent in open play.' He scored a try on his debut against Wales at Rectory Field, Blackheath and played in every position for the Yorkshire. He stayed with Brighouse when they helped form the Northern Union in 1895 and took up bowls after retiring from rugby. Nicholl was a publican in Brighouse, running The Stagg and Pheasant Inn for four years and then the Round House Inn for 11 years until he was forced to stop working because of ill health.

239. PYKE, James
Forward 1 cap 1892
Born: St. Helens, Lancashire, 8 February 1866
Died: St. Helens, Lancashire, 17 May 1941
Career: St. Helens Recreation, Lancashire
Debut: v Wales, Rectory Field, Blackheath, January 1892

Pyke only needed two games for St Helens Recreation's A team before being drafted into the first team. James was called up by England selectors to face Wales in January 1892, only to break his nose in a club match, but he did not disclose the injury to selectors for fear of losing his place. A glass-cutter examiner and sorter then became the manager of the grinding department of Pilkington Brothers. He was also a sprinter and had an outstanding record at athletics meetings in Lancashire. Pyke's son, James, went on to play for St Helens Recreation after the First World War.

240. THOMSON, Wardlaw Brown
Full-back 4 caps (3-1t) 1892-1895
Born: Inyati, Matabeleland, 27 June 1871
Died: Wynberg, Cape Town, 25 April 1921
Career: Bedford Modern School, Lewisham Park, Blackheath, West of Scotland, Crusaders Club (Port Elizabeth)
Debut: v Wales, Rectory Field, Blackheath, January 1892

Thomson was sent to England to be educated. He was the first Southern African-born player to represent England when he won the first of his caps against Wales at Rectory Field, the home of his club, Blackheath. Even though he later moved to Glasgow and played for the West of Scotland, he would return to London and play important games for Blackheath. Thomson was regarded as the finest three-quarter in the United Kingdom in his prime, and after returning to South Africa, he worked for a paper-making firm for many years and lived in Wynberg near Cape Town until his death.

241. ASHWORTH, Abel
Forward 1 cap 1892
Born: Ashton-under-Lyne, Lancashire, Q2 1864
Died: Shaw, Lancashire, 10 January 1938
Career: Oldham, Mossley, Rochdale Hornets, Lancashire
Debut: v Ireland, Whalley Range, Manchester February 1892

Oldham's Ashworth was the only new cap in the England pack when Ireland visited Whalley Range in 1892. England won the game, and he remained in the selectors' thoughts, playing for the Rest of England against Yorkshire a fortnight later. Ashworth didn't impress enough, as he wasn't picked to face Scotland in Edinburgh the following month. He joined Mossley the following season and then Rochdale Hornets staying with them when they joined the Northern Union, where he also saw service with Crompton and Werneth. Ashworth was a typical working man. His jobs included cotton operative, cloth finisher, coke finisher and engineer's labourer.

242. HOUGHTON, Samuel
Full-back 2 caps
Born: Runcorn, Cheshire, 16 August 1870
Died: Runcorn, Cheshire, 17 August 1920
Career: Runcorn, Birkenhead Wanderers, Cheshire
Debut: v Ireland, Whalley Range, Manchester, February 1892

Houghton was only 22 when he won his first international but then found out of the international reckoning for four years. But following the formation of the Northern Union in

1895 and with the pool of available players vastly depleted, now playing for Birkenhead Wanderers, he won himself a recall to the international stage. But it wasn't long before he switched codes, returning to play for Runcorn despite being selected for a third cap. Houghton was a carpenter before becoming the licensee of the Egerton Arms in Runcorn, which he ran for almost 20 years before his sudden death following a seizure.

243. MARSH, James
Three-quarter 1 cap 1892
Born: Bolton, Lancashire 31 October 1865
Died: Boothstown, Greater Manchester, 1 August 1928
Career: Edinburgh Institute, Edinburgh Institute FP, Edinburgh, Swinton, Lancashire
Debut: v Ireland, Whalley Range, Manchester, February 1892

Marsh had already played twice for Scotland against Wales and Ireland in 1889 with England in international exile. But three years later, after he crossed the border to practice medicine and joined Swinton. After impressing in a trial, he was selected to play for the Red Rose against Ireland at Whalley Range, Manchester, making him the only player to play an international rugby match for Scotland and England. Marsh was never picked for England again but served as the medical officer for Atherton for 28 years. His brother John was on the board of Bolton Wanderers.

244. TAYLOR, Ernest William
Half-back 14 caps (16 pts, 2t, 3c, 1gm) 1892-1899
Born: Newcastle upon Tyne, Tyne & Wear, 20 February 1869
Died: Whitley Bay, Northumberland, 16 March 1936
Career: Rockcliff, Barbarians, Northumberland
Debut: v Ireland Whalley Range, Manchester February 1892

Taylor was better known as Little Billy and, when he died, was described as the Prince of Half-Backs, one of the best scrum halves of his generation. He was part of the Northumberland side that beat The Midlands in Coventry to win the 1898 County Championship. A talented all-round sportsman, his rugby career was ended by injury. He played cricket for Northumberland and was captain of Whitley Bay Golf Club. Taylor was a good enough golfer to turn professional. He has previously worked as a cashier and then as a footwear retailer.

245. BRADSHAW, Harry
Forward 7 caps (6-2t) 1892-1894
Born: Bramley, Yorkshire, 17 March 1868
Died: Halifax, Yorkshire, 31 December 1910
Career: Bramley, Yorkshire
Debut: v Scotland, Raeburn Place, Edinburgh, March 1892

Bradshaw was the only new cap in the pack for the game against Scotland that saw England clinch the 1892 Triple Crown without conceding a point. And he was an ever-present in the side over the next two seasons, playing all six games. But like so many other Northern players of his generation, he was lost to the game when he joined Leeds when the Northern Union was formed in 1895. Bradshaw, a horse teamster, cloth dresser, and licensee, moved to Halifax after his retirement and worked as a presser at Armitage Dyers until his death due to pneumonia.

246. COOP, Thomas
Full-back 1 cap 1892
Born: Tottington, Lancashire, 10 March 1863
Died: Bucklow, Cheshire, 16 April 1929
Career: Tottington, Leigh, Lancashire
Debut: v Scotland, Raeburn Place, Edinburgh, March 1892

Coop was the first Leigh player to play for Lancashire and then England. He played nearly 300 games for Leigh in rugby union and then in the Northern Union when he earned £1 a game, but he never scored a try for the club. Sadly, his rugby career ended prematurely after he was the victim of rough play in a game at Widnes in 1898. Coop was an engineering printer, then a hatter and hosier, commercial traveller and shipping clerk. His life ended in tragedy when he committed suicide less than a month after his wife Annie had taken her own life.

247. VARLEY, Harry
Scrum-half 1 cap 1892
Born: Cleckheaton, West Riding of Yorkshire, 25 November 1868
Died: Oldham, Greater Manchester, 21 November 1915
Career: Liversedge, Oldham, Yorkshire, Lancashire
Debut: v Scotland, Raeburn Place, Edinburgh, March 1892

Varley learnt the game at Liversedge before joining Oldham in 1880, playing outside half-half back. His partnership with fellow England international Arthur Lees was among the finest of the era. Varley won his only England cap against Scotland in Edinburgh. He stayed with Oldham after they joined the Northern Union and later for Leeds and Dewsbury. He later returned to Oldham, was the A-Team's trainer, and kept a public house in the local area. But when Varley retired, the former collier was employed at Hartford Old Works until his death.

248. BROADLEY, Thomas
Half-back 6 caps 1893-1896
Born: Bingley, West Yorkshire, 18 August 1871
Died: Bradford, West Yorkshire, 26 November 1950
Career: Bingley, West Riding, Yorkshire
Debut: v Wales, Arms Park, Cardiff, January 1893

Broadley won all six of his international caps while playing for Bingley. He had a two-year gap between his fifth cap and his final international appearance against Scotland at Hampden Park in March 1896. Despite being captain of Yorkshire at the time and less than six months after his final international, he had accepted an approach to turn professional with Bradford in the Northern Union. He stayed with the club until retiring at the end of the 1902-03 season and, even then, had few equals. Broadley was a maltster and then a licensee in Bingley, running the Fleere Inn.

249. DE WINTON, Robert Francis Chippini
Half-back 1 cap 1893
Born: Newport, Gwent, 9 September 1868
Died: Porterville, California, 14 March 1923
Career: Summer Fields School, Marlborough College, Marlborough Nomads, Oxford University, Blackheath
Debut: v Wales, Arms Park, Cardiff, January 1893

de Winton won his Oxford University blue between 1880 and 1890. He turned down the chance to play for the country of his birth, Wales, preferring to play for England, and he won his only international cap at the Arms Park, Cardiff, which ended in defeat for his adopted country by one point. He was headmaster at Gore Court, Sittingbourne, while during the First World War, he was a Temporary lieutenant, Lancashire Fusiliers and commanded a company in the Graduated Battalion, Leicestershire Regiment, de Winton then emigrated to California and was engaged in vine culture, he died falling from a window of his house.

250. FIELD, Edwin
Full-back 2 caps 1893
Born: Hampstead, Middlesex, 18 December 1871
Died: Bromley, Kent, 9 January 1947
Career: Clifton College, Cambridge University, Middlesex Wanderers, Richmond, Barbarians, Middlesex
Debut: v Wales, Arms Park, Cardiff, January 1893

Field was a double Cambridge University blue in both rugby and cricket. He was registered to the University and

Middlesex Wanderers when he made both of his England appearances in 1893 against Wales and Ireland. He was then dropped in favour of William Mitchell and never appeared again. Then, after Middlesex Wanderers folded, he joined Richmond alongside his team-mate Charles Hooper. Field was a talented cricketer who captained Clifton College and later played first-class matches for Berkshire and Middlesex. He was a solicitor in London and then Bromley in Kent for over 30 years until retiring.

251. GREENWELL, John Henry
Forward 2 caps 1893
Born: Cullercoats, Northumberland, 10 August 1864
Died: Whitley Bay, Northumberland, 22 November 1943
Career: Eastcliffe, Rockcliffe, Tynemouth, Barbarians, Northumberland
Debut: v Wales, Arms Park, Cardiff, January 1893

Greenwell didn't need a second invitation to join his local side in Cullercoats when Rockcliffe Rugby Club was formed, and he became known as the club's father for many years after he stopped playing. He won both international caps in 1893, his final one coming alongside his club-mate Tom Nicholson. Greenwell was said to have a remarkable physique and stamina and helped Northumberland to County Championship honours. During the First World War, he received a special long service medal as a special constable. Greenwell was a bricklayer by trade and became a builder and a public works contractor.

252. LOHDEN, Frederick Charles OBE JP
Forward 1 cap (2-1t) 1893
Born: West Hartlepool, County Durham, 13 July 1871
Died: Sutton, Surrey, 13 April 1954
Career: Durham School, Hartlepool Rovers, Blackheath, Barbarians, Durham County, Surrey
Debut: v Wales, Arms Park Cardiff January 1893

Frederick Lohden played for the Durham School XV when he was 15, and after completing his education in mainland Europe, he returned to England and joined Hartlepool Rovers. After moving to Blackheath, he came to selectors' attention and won his only international cap against Wales in January 1893, scoring a try. A steamship broker during the First World War, he worked for the Ministry of Shipping and was awarded an OBE in 1919. Lohden became chairman of the Council of the Lawn Tennis Association and then represented Great Britain on the International Lawn Tennis Federation. He later served Sutton & Cheam as a councillor, mayor and Justice of the peace.

253. MARSHALL, Howard OBE
Half-back 1 cap (6-3t) 1893
Born: Sunderland, Tyne & Wear, 20 December 1870
Died: Westminster, London, 9 October 1923
Career: Elham School, Cambridge University, Bernard Castle, Sunderland, Bart's Hospital, Blackheath, Barbarians, London, Kent
Debut: v Wales, Arms Park, Cardiff, January 1893

Marshall toured South Africa with the British team in 1891 while he was uncapped and made two test match appearances. He scored a hat-trick against Wales at Arms Park, Cardiff, in January 1893 on his only England appearance and was also the first Barbarian to score points in Wales with a try against Cardiff. Despite his achievements, a Cambridge University blue eluded him. Marshall was a house surgeon at St Bart's and an assistant house surgeon at Nottingham General Hospital before becoming a GP in Bexhill-on-Sea and Cirencester, where he then became a surgeon at a local Hospital and a medical officer at the Royal Agricultural College.

254. MAUD, Philip CMG OBE
Forward 2 caps 1893
Born: Assington, Suffolk, 8 August 1870
Died: Chelsea, London, 28 February 1947
Career: Leamington Collage, RAM Woolwich, Royal Engineers, Blackheath, Barbarians, Kent
Debut: v Wales, Arms Park, Cardiff, January 1893

Maud was a career soldier and is notable for setting the Maud Line, an imaginary border in Kenya, which set the original position of the disputed Ilemi Triangle. One of the first players asked by William Percy Carpmael to form the first-ever Barbarians squad, and only four men have played more times for them than Maud. He captained Blackheath and played in England's first two games of their 1893 campaign against Wales and Ireland but lost his place for the final game against Scotland. After leaving the Army, Maud was Chief Officer for London County Council's Park Department.

255. DUCKETT, Horace
Half-back 2 caps 1893
Born: Thornton, West Yorkshire, 11 October 1867
Died: Cornholme, West Yorkshire, 3 March 1939
Career: Bradford, Yorkshire
Debut: v Ireland, Lansdowne Road, Dublin, February 1893

Duckett played for Bradford when they had one of the strongest teams in the country and was one of the pluckiest half-backs to have ever played the game at the time. He was seen as safe in catching and purposeful in passing. Horace made his Yorkshire debut in 1892 and won both England caps a year later. When Bradford joined the Northern Union, he became professional and played for Heckmondwike before retiring. Duckett was a member of Todmorden CC who lived in Cornholm for 30 years and worked as a shuttle maker at Calvervale Mill until retiring.

256. NICHOLSON, Thomas
Three-quarter 1 cap 1893
Born: Cullercoats, Northumberland 1872
Died: Unknown
Career: Rockcliff, Northumberland
Debut: v Ireland, Lansdowne Road, Dublin, February 1893

Nicholson joined Rockcliff as a 16-year-old just a year after their formation in 1887 and helped them win the Northumberland Cup four years in succession between 1889 and 1893. Tommy won his only England cap against Ireland in February 1893 after impressing in a trial match for the Rest of England and was a regular in the Rockcliff side until switching codes in 1899 when he joined Wigan Rugby League Club. A fruit retailer by trade, Nicholson was a talented sprinter and won the pro sprinting championships at Powderhill and the Booth Hall Plate.

257. JONES, Frederic Phelp
Three-quarter 1 cap 1893
Born: Liscard, Cheshire, June 1871
Died: Hooton, Cheshire, 14 August 1944
Career: Wallasey GS, New Brighton, Birkenhead Park
Debut: v Scotland, Headingley, Leeds, March 1893

Jones played in a trial match for The Rest against the Champion County Yorkshire in February 1893, but the selectors decided to retain Richard Lockwood, and Jones would probably have thought his chance was gone. But Lockwood then failed a fitness test on the day of the Scotland game, and Jones was called upon as his replacement for his only game. The manager of Seacombe Pressed Brik & Tile Works Limited brickworks before becoming a manufacturer running Buckley Junction Metallic Brick Company. He also patented many improvements that related to the manufacturing of bricks.

258. ROBINSON, John James
Forward 4 caps (3-1t)
Born: Burton-on-Trent, Staffordshire, 28 June 1872
Died: Headingley, West Yorkshire, 3 January 1959
Career: Appleby GS, Cambridge University, Headingley, Burton, Barbarians, Midlands, Yorkshire
Debut: v Scotland, Headingley, Leeds, March 1893

Robinson won blues for rugby and cricket while at Cambridge University. He made his international debut against Scotland in 1893 when he was still a teenager but then made to wait until 1902 for his second. The gap of nine years was the longest in international history. A try on his return against Wales won him further caps against Ireland and Scotland. The son of a Burton-on-Trent brewer, Robinson opted to go into the law and was a solicitor in Nottingham and then in Leeds with firm Marklands for over 40 years until his retirement just before his death.

259. SOANE, Frank
Forward 4 caps 1893-1894
Born: Bath, Somerset, 12 September 1866
Died: Bath Somerset, 1 April 1932
Career: Clifton House Eastbourne, Oldfield Park, Bath, Barbarians, Somerset, The South, Western Counties, Rest of England
Debut: v Scotland, Headingley, Leeds, March 1893

Soane earned the nickname Buster because of his vigorous style of play. He first played for Bath when he was 15 after turning up to watch a game and discovering they were one man short. He became a fixture in the side for 16 years and captained the club from 1890 to 1898. He was also Somerset captain and secretary between 1896 and 1899 and president in 1900 before serving as an executive committee member for another 25 years. Soane was still a teenager when he set up a family music business, Soane and Sons, which he ran until retiring.

260. WELLS, Cyril Mowbray
Half-back 6 caps 1893-1897
Born: St Pancras, London, 21 March 1871
Died: St. Johns Wood, London, 22 August 1963
Career: Dulwich Collage, Old Alleynian Football Club, Cambridge University, Harlequins, Barbarians, Surrey
Debut: v Scotland, Headingley, Leeds, March 1893

Wells was educated at Dulwich College before winning Cambridge University blues in Rugby and Cricket. He was registered with his university when he made his debut and was a Harlequins player for his next five appearances. Cyril also played first-class cricket for Surrey and Middlesex and played for the Gentleman against the Players three times during the school holidays. A master and housemaster at Eton between 1893 and 1926. He was also Eton's cricket coach, taking influential cricket administrator Gubby Allen to the college and is credited as the mentor of England cricket captain Lionel Tennyson.

261. BYRNE, James Frederick
Full-back 13 caps (24–2c2d4p) 1894-1899
Born: Birmingham, Warwickshire, 19 June 1871
Died: Birmingham, Warwickshire, 10 May 1954
Career: Moseley, Barbarians, Midland Counties
Debut: v Wales, Birkenhead Park, January 1894

Byrne was 'a vigorous player even for his period.' He played in 21 matches and scored 100 points on the British Team 1896 tour to South Africa while appearing alongside brother Francis against Wales in 1897, later captaining the side three times. His international career is likely to have been cut short by his decision to fight in the Boer War. Fred also played cricket for Warwickshire between 1897 and 1912. Byrne was an industrialist running Byrne Brothers India Rubber Co. and became managing director of Howes and Burley and chairman of Smith-Clayton Forge and Smith's Stamping Works, both of Coventry. He was also the first President of the North Midlands Union.

262. FIRTH, Frederick
Wing 3 caps 1894
Born: Cleckheaton, West Riding of Yorkshire, 1870
Died: Olneyville, USA February 1936
Career: Brighouse Rangers, Halifax
Debut: v Wales, Birkenhead Park, January 1894

Firth was a member of England's first four-man three-quarter line against Wales in January 1894. He was an ever-present in the England line-up that season, winning all three of his caps. He was a sprinter of some note in the North of England, but his international career ended when he decided to remain with Halifax when they helped form the Northern Union. Firth, who retired from playing in 1902, was a machine shop foreman in Yorkshire before emigrating to the United States seven years later, where he worked as a machinist foreman at Victoria Mills, Johnson, for many years.

263. HALL, John
Forward 3 caps
Born: Gateshead, Tyne & Wear 20 June 1869
Died: Chiswick, Middlesex, 13 January 1945
Career: Gateshead Institute, North Durham, Hartlepool Rovers, Blackheath, Durham
Debut: v Wales, Birkenhead Park January 1894

Hall started his rugby career with Gateshead Institute, where he won his first county honours for Durham in 1887, but he would have to wait until seven years after moving to North Durham to win his international caps, two of which would end in defeat with the only win coming on his debut against Wales. Hall's county appearances were restricted to 16 because he spent long periods working in the South. A steam engine engineer and then a foreman engineer, he would go on to settle in Chiswick, Middlesex, after living in the Birmingham area.

264. HOOPER, Charles Alexander
Centre 3 caps 1894
Born: Eastington, Gloucestershire, 6 June 1869
Died: Taplow, Berkshire, 16 September 1950
Career: Clifton College, Cambridge University, Richmond, Middlesex, West Gloucester, Gloucestershire, Barbarians
Debut: v Wales, Birkenhead Park, January 1894

Hooper was educated at Clifton College before attending Cambridge University, where he won a blue in 1890. After leaving, he became a member of Middlesex Wanderers and was part of England's first four-man three-quarter line against Wales in January 1894 and won his last two caps against Scotland and Ireland that same season. He joined Richmond after Middlesex Wanderers folded a year later but was never selected to play for his country again. Hooper was a solicitor who emigrated to Hong Kong in 1914, where during the First World War, he served in the Hong Kong Police Force.

265. MORFITT, Samuel
Back/Wing 6 caps (9-3t) 1894-1896
Born: Hull, East Riding of Yorkshire, December 1868
Died: Hull, East Riding of Yorkshire, 16 January 1954
Career: Holderness Free Wanderers, Hull Southcoates, West Hartlepool, Hull Kingston Rovers, Durham Counties, Yorkshire
Debut: v Wales, Birkenhead Park, January 1894

Shipyard riveter Morfitt started his career with Holderness Free Wanderers before moving to Hull Southcoates. He was the first player from West Hartlepool to be capped when he scored a try on his international debut against

Wales at Birkenhead Park in January 1894. He played at West Hartlepool alongside his brother John until joining Hull Kingston Rovers in 1895 and switched codes when they joined the Northern Union in 1897. Morfitt, a crack marksman and boxer, drove a Hackney carriage and was a boiler maker, fruiter, and licensee in his hometown.

266. SPEED, Harry
Forward 4 caps
Born: Glasshoughton, West Yorkshire, 19 August 1871
Died: Castleford, West Yorkshire, 3 July 1937
Career: Castleford
Debut: v Wales, Birkenhead Park, January 1894

Speed started his career at Glasshoughton before he was invited to join Castleford in 1891, where he became one of the finest forwards in the country. He captained Castleford to 1896 Yorkshire Cup success with a pack that contained his fellow internationals Anthony Starks, James Ward and Jack Rhodes. Harry's International career ended when they joined the Northern Union the following season when he retained the captaincy. Speed was a surface worker at Glasshoughton Colliery before becoming a licensee in Castleford and Airedale. He served on Castleford Urban Council for six years near the end of the First World War.

267. TUCKER, Dr William Eldon
Forward 5 caps 1894-1895
Born: Hamilton, Bermuda, 8 August 1872
Died: Paget Bermuda, 18 October 1953
Career: Trinity Collage Port Hope Canada, Cambridge University, St George's Hospital, Blackheath, Barbarians, Kent
Debut: v Wales, Birkenhead Park, January 1894

Tucker was a Bermudan who was educated in Canada before arriving to study at Cambridge University, where he won a rugby blue and a half blue for billiards. On his debut against Wales in January 1894, he was one of seven new caps and retained his place for their next game against Ireland. Despite playing all three games the following season, he was never picked again. Tucker was a house surgeon at St George's Hospital before returning home to work at King Edward VII Memorial Hospital. His son Bill Tucker also played for England.

268. WOOD, Robert
Half-back 1 cap 1894
Born: Pontefract, West Yorkshire, 14 November 1872
Died: Knottingley, West Yorkshire, 1 March 1928
Career: Liversedge, Yorkshire
Debut: v Ireland, Rectory Field, Blackheath, February 1894

Wood replaced Cyril Wells to win his only cap against Ireland at Blackheath in February 1894 in nothing short of dramatic circumstances. The Harlequins man was injured playing for Eton and ignoring a serious finger injury when he was telegraphed calling him up the evening before the game. Unbeknown to Wood, the Union had pencilled in Bob de Winton to play if he didn't turn up. Two months later, Wood, a licensee, tried to join Bradford, but the Liversedge committee blocked the move. He also remained with the Hightowners when they helped form the Northern Union in 1895.

269. ELLIOTT, Albert Ernest M.R.C.S., L.R.C.P.
Forward 1 cap 1894
Born: Basset Mount, Hampshire, 5 March 1869
Died: Middelburg, South Africa, 1 December 1900
Career: Cheltenham College, Cambridge University, St Thomas's Hospital, Barbarians, Middlesex
Debut: v Scotland Raeburn Place, Edinburgh, March 1894

Elliott was educated at Cheltenham College before attending Cambridge University, where he won his blue in 1891. He continued his medical studies at St Thomas's Hospital and was registered to them when he won his only England cap against Scotland in Match 1894. The resident medical officer at Queen Charlotte's Hospital volunteered for service after the outbreak of the Boer War. Elliott was attached to the No 4 Field Hospital as a civil surgeon and then with the 4th Brigade Division Royal Artillery and was present at the battles of Spion Kop and Vaal Kranz. He died of enteric fever.

270. JACKSON, Walter Jesse
Wing 1 cap 1894
Born: Gloucester, Gloucestershire, 16 March 1870
Died: Halifax, West Yorkshire, 1 December 1958
Career: Gloucester, Halifax, Rest of England, Yorkshire
Debut: v Scotland, Raeburn Place, Edinburgh, March 1894

Jackson was the first Gloucester-born player to be capped by England, although he played for Halifax when he won his only international cap against Scotland in March 1894. However, he was a Gloucester player when he toured South Africa with the British Team toured to South Africa in 1891. Jackson joined Halifax on his return and stayed with them when they helped form the Northern Union in 1895. He was a boilermaker in Gloucester, and then Halifax was forced to retire soon after joining the professional ranks due to a serious injury he sustained at work.

271. WALTON, William
Forward 1 cap 1894
Born: Castleford, West Yorkshire, 23 September 1874
Died: Wakefield, West Yorkshire, 1 July 1940
Career: Castleford, Yorkshire
Debut: v Scotland, Raeburn Place, Edinburgh, March 1894

Walton was only 19 and had only been in Castleford's first XV for a few months when he made his only England appearance against Scotland in March 1894 in the pack alongside his club-mate Harry Speed. He switched codes with Wakefield Trinity when the Northern Union was formed in 1895, as Castleford didn't make the switch until the following season. Walton also scored Castleford's first try under Northern Union rules. He won county honours in union and league and worked as a coal miner and a labourer in America before entering the licensed trade.

272. BAKER, Edward Morgan
Wing 7 caps 1895-1897
Born: New Jersey, United States, 12 August 1874
Died: Winchester, Hampshire, 25 November 1940
Career: Denstone Collage; Oxford University; Moseley; Blackheath; Wolverhampton; Burton; Barbarians; Midland Counties
Debut: v Wales, St Helen's, Swansea, January 1895

Baker made seven successive appearances during his time at Oxford University. He was ever-present in 1895 and 1896 but lost his place after a defeat to Wales in 1897 and was never selected again. Baker was ordained in 1897 and held various curacies before resigning in 1911 and at the invitation of the Archbishop of Brisbane, he moved to Australia, where he continued as a clergyman until 1919. He then became headmaster of King's School in Parramatta until 1932. When Baker retired, he returned to the United Kingdom to live in Andover, Hampshire.

273. CAREY, Godfrey Mohan
Forward 5 caps (3-1t)
Born: St Peter Port, Guernsey, 17 August 1872
Died: Sherborne, Dorset, 18 December 1927
Career: Sherborne School, Oxford University, Blackheath, Barbarians, Somerset
Debut: v Wales St Helens Swansea January 1895

Carey was the son of Sir Godfrey Carey, the Bailiff of Guernsey and first played rugby at Sherborne School before

The English Rugby Who's Who

John Willie Sutcliffe

Richard Budworth

Jack Toothill

Frederic Alderson

Launcelot Percival

Dr Alfred Allport

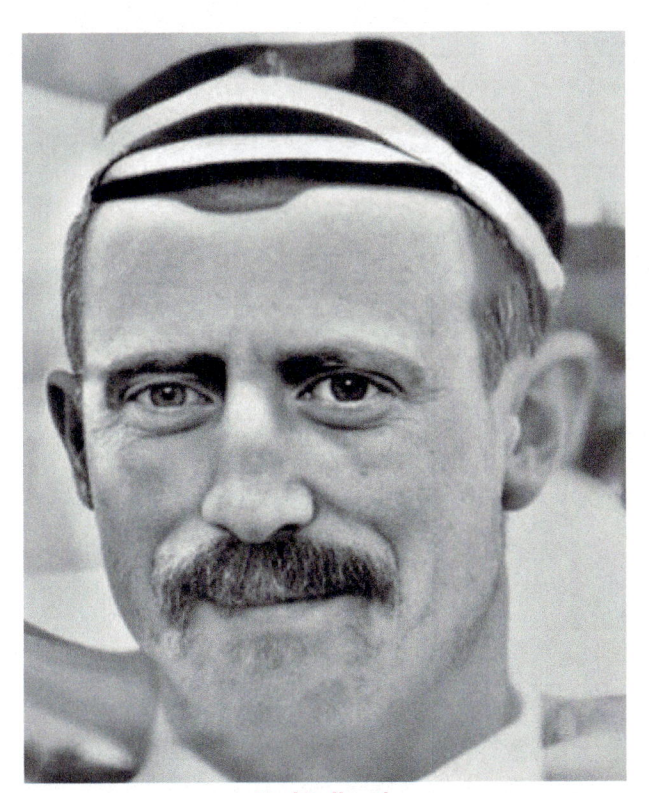

Ned Bullough

Abel Ashworth

Harry Varley

Tom Broadley

Edwin Field

Cyril Wells

The English Rugby Who's Who

Fred Byrne

John Hall

Dr William Tucker

attending Oxford University. He soon won his blue and was appointed captain in 1894. He scored a try on his England debut against Wales in January 1895 and was a member of the Barbarians committee. After completing his education in 1897, he returned to his former school as an assistant master and continued to teach at Sherborne until his death. Carey was supposedly the model for the housemaster known as 'The Bull' in Alec Waugh's autobiographical novel, The Loom of Youth.

274. CATTELL, Richard Henry Burdon
Fly-half 7 caps (6-2t) 1895-1900
Born: Birmingham, Warwickshire, 23 March 1871
Died: Fakenham, Norfolk, 19 July 1948
Career: Trinity Collage Stratford-upon-Avon, Oxford University, Blackheath, Moseley, Barbarians, Midland Counties
Debut: v Wales, St Helen's, Swansea, January 1895

Cattell was educated at Oxford University, where he won a blue in 1893. He was a regular in the England team for two seasons, but after being ordained in 1897, he was never selected again. He became vicar of St Michael's, Berkhamsted and switched to football in 1898, playing for Welwyn AFC until 1903, then Tring for three more seasons. Cattell did play for the Barbarians until 1900. During the First World War, he served as Chaplain to the Armed Forces. When peacetime returned, he was rector at Watlington, Norfolk and then Warham, Norfolk, until his death.

275. FEGAN, John Herbert Craugle L.S.A, M.R.C.S., L.R.C.P.
Wing 3 caps (3-1t) 1895
Born: Old Charlton, Kent, 29 January 1872
Died: Leverstock Green, Hertfordshire, 26 July 1949
Career: Blackheath Proprietary School, Cambridge University, Blackheath, Barbarians, Kent
Debut: v Wales St Helen's, Swansea, January 1895

Fegan failed to win a much-coveted blue during his time at Cambridge University, but it didn't stop him from going on to play for his country. He made his appearances in 1895, making his debut against Wales at St Helen's and scoring his only try on his second appearance against Ireland at his home ground, Rectory Field, Blackheath. After leaving Cambridge, Fegan went into medicine and became a surgeon. At the outbreak of the First World War joined the Royal Army Medical Corps and later went to work for the Ministry of Pensions.

276. FINLINSON, Horace William
Forward 3 cap 1895
Born: Bedford, Bedfordshire, 9 June 1871
Died: Bedford, Bedfordshire, 31 October 1956
Career: Bedford Modern School, Blair Lodge, Blackheath, Newport, Bedford, Barbarians, Kent, Eastern Counties
Debut: v Wales, St Helen's, Swansea, January 1895

Finlinson was educated at Bedford School, where his father Wilkinson was headmaster. He was a robust forward who won his caps in 1895. But after losing their final match to concede the Triple Crown to Scotland, he was never selected again. Finlinson became the first captain of East Midlands when they were formed in 1897 and later served as president. He went into teaching and was a master at Lancing School. Returning to Bedford on retirement, becoming Chairman at Goldington Road, and in later years crippled by arthritis, he would watch a game from a bath chair behind the touchline.

277. LESLIE-JONES, Frederick Archibald OBE
Centre 2 caps (2-1t) 1895
Born: Fylde, Lancashire, 9 July 1874
Died: Upton, Worcestershire, 24 January 1946
Career: Hereford Cathedral School, Bromsgrove School, Cambridge University, Blackheath, Richmond, Barbarians
Debut: v Wales, St Helen's, Swansea, January 1895

Leslie-Jones captained Oxford University in his final year, 1896, by which time he had already scored a try on his England debut against Wales and won his second and last cap against Ireland. He was a clergyman and schoolmaster at Marlborough College, Principal of Aitchison College Lahore and Mayo College, Ajmer, India, and then was an assistant master at Malvern Collage until 1931. During the First World War, he served the Indian Defence Force and became a lieutenant Colonel 1st Punjab Rifles. He was the author of "A View of English History" and a special constable in the Second World War.

278. MITCHELL, Frank
Forward, 6 caps (5-1t,1c)
Born: Market Weighton, East Riding of Yorkshire, 13 August 1872
Died: Blackheath, London, 11 October 1935
Career: St Peter's School York, Cambridge University, Blackheath, Yorkshire, Kent, Barbarians, Sussex
Debut: v Wales St Helen's Swansea January 1895

Mitchell was a sporting all-rounder at Cambridge University, winning blues in rugby, cricket and athletics. He also played cricket test matches for England and first-class cricket for Yorkshire, MCC, London County and Transvaal. A Cricketer of the year in 1902, he served in the Boer War and the First World War when he reached the rank of lieutenant colonel. Mitchell also played in goal for Sussex in association football. He was a stockbroker by profession who also taught before going to University and then wrote for The Cricketer until his sudden death.

279. POOLE, Francis Oswald
Forward 3 caps 1895
Born: West Rainton, County Durham, 17 December 1870
Died: Newcastle under Lyme, Staffordshire, 22 May 1949
Career: Cheltenham College, Oxford University, Gloucester, Sunderland, Barbarians, Gloucestershire, County Durham
Debut: v Wales, St Helen's, Swansea, January 1895

Francis Poole captained Cheltenham College at rugby and in the boats, and when he went to Oxford University, he won his blue in rugby and water polo. He was a regular of Sunderland's first XV while still in his teens but was registered at Cambridge University when he won his caps in 1895. Following his ordination, he was the curate at Herrington near Sunderland. Over the next 54 years, Poole worked in various parts of the North of England, and his last post was rector in Mucklestone, near Market Drayton, where he lived until his death.

280. THOMAS, Charles James
Forward 3 caps (3-1t) 1895
Born: Barnstaple, Devon, 6 September 1874
Died: Barnstaple, Devon, 12 May 1936
Career: Barnstaple Oaks, Barnstaple, Devon
Debut: v Wales, St Helen's, Swansea, January 1895

Thomas had already helped Barnstaple to two Devon Cups when he caught the eye of selectors by scoring a try in the South versus North trial match. He was one of the lightest forwards at 11st 3lb to be capped when he won his first cap against Wales in January 1895. A month later, he scored a try on his second appearance against Ireland, and a defeat to Scotland ended his international career. Thomas, who worked cabinet maker's Shapland & Petter all his life, captained Devon to success in the 1899 County Championship before a knee injury ended his career five years later.

281. WARD, Herbert
Full-back 1 cap 1895
Born: Bradford, West Yorkshire, 15 September 1873
Died: Baildon, West Yorkshire, 18 February 1955
Career: Bradford, Yorkshire
Debut: v Wales, St Helen's, Swansea, January 1895

Ward was noted for his quickness and kicking into touch, making his name for Bradford. He made his only England appearance as the first reserve when regular full-back Fred Byrne was ill. Then injury and being outplayed by Byrne in a trial match between Midlands against the Rest of England ended his brief international career. Ward stayed with Bradford when they switched codes and remained in their team, losing his place to Welshman Gomer Gunn in 1903. An apprentice mechanic, he ran the Greenhouse Inn, Bradford, until becoming a maintenance mechanic at a mill in Baildon.

282. DOBSON, Thomas Hyde
Centre 1 cap 1895
Born: Bradford, West Yorkshire, February 1872
Died: Bradford, West Yorkshire, 12 November 1902
Career: Bowling FC, Bradford, Yorkshire
Debut: v Scotland, Athletic Ground, Richmond, March 1895

Tom Dobson was a clever and fast three-quarter who earned himself the nickname "Le Fleche" (French for arrow). He won many events at Yorkshire athletics meetings and made his only England appearance just before his club side, Bradford helped form the Northern Union, and he moved with them. His father, Harry, well known in athletic circles, trained the Bradford team he played in when they won the Yorkshire Cup a year earlier. Dobson was employed as a journeyman tailor at the time of his death from organic poisoning due to eating raw mussels aged 30.

283. FOOKES, Ernest Faber
Wing 10 caps (15 -5t)
Born: Wairoa, New Zealand, 31 May 1874
Died: New Plymouth, New Zealand, 3 March 1948
Career: New Plymouth Boys HS (NZ) Heath Grammar School, Owen's Collage Manchester, Manchester University, Halifax, Sowerby Bridge, Yorkshire, Taranaki, Tukapa, Taranaki-Wanganui-Manawatu
Debut: v Wales, Rectory Field, Blackheath, January 1896

Fookes learnt the game at New Plymouth Boys High School but was capped after coming to England from his native New Zealand to complete his education. He played for Halifax but left to join Sowerby Bridge after the Northern Union was formed in 1895. The scorer of two tries on his debut against Wales at Blackheath, he was selected to tour the British Isles with New Zealand in 1905 but could not travel. Fookes was the president of the Taranaki Union and gained his medical qualifications before returning to New Zealand in 1900, living in New Plymouth. He was a physician and surgeon.

284. GIBLIN, Lyndhurst Falkiner DSO MC
Forward 3 caps
Born: Hobart, Tasmania, 29 November 1872
Died: Hobart, Tasmania, 2 March 1951
Career: Hutchins School Hobart, London University, Cambridge University, Blackheath, Barbarians, Middlesex
Debut: v Wales, Rectory Field, Blackheath, January 1896

Hobart-born Giblin travelled across the globe to complete his education at London University and then Cambridge University, where he was a double blue in Rugby and Rowing before winning three caps for England. During the First World War, he became a major with the 40th Battalion and was awarded an MSC and DSO. Giblin was a gold miner in the Klondyke and Canada's NW Territories and a Fruit Grower in Tasmania. Later in life, he was the Australian Government's Official Statistician, a Professor of Economics at Melbourne University, and a director of the Commonwealth Bank.

285. PINCH, John
Forward 3 caps 1896-1897
Born: Lancaster, Lancashire, 2 December 1870
Died: Lancaster, Lancashire, 3 March 1946
Career: Lancaster
Debut: v Wales, Rectory Field, Blackheath, January 1896

Pinch was the lynchpin of the Lancaster side for almost 20 seasons and was the first man from North Lancashire to win international honours. John made his debut against Wales in their first match after the formation of the Northern Union in 1896 and retained his place for the next match against Ireland. But he had to wait until March 1897 for a recall to win the last cap against Scotland. His father, John, was manager of Storey Mills, and he served them for 47 years and was the foreman when he retired in 1937.

286. RHODES, John
Forward 3 caps 1896
Born: Castleford, West Yorkshire, 6 September 1869
Died: Anlaby, East Riding of Yorkshire, 22 May 1925
Career: Idle Boys, Castleford, Yorkshire
Debut: v Wales, Rectory Field, Blackheath, January 1896

Rhodes was a brilliant scrummager who was one of the heaviest of his era at 14 stone. He spent one season at Idle Boys before joining Castleford, where he was to play in a pack that contained Anthony Starks and John Ward, who also made their international debut on the same day. He and Starks joined Hull Kingston Rovers in October 1896 after winning the Yorkshire Cup. The pair worked with glass bottle manufacturers John Lumb & Co. at the time. Rhodes became the landlord of the St Leger Hotel in Hull and was a director of the Kingston Rovers until his death.

287. STARKS, Anthony
Forward 2 caps 1896
Born: Castleford, Yorkshire, 11 August 1874
Died: Kingston-Upon-Hull, East Riding of Yorkshire, 23 January 1952
Career: Castleford Victoria, Castleford
Debut: v Wales, Rectory Field, Blackheath, January 1896

Starks was described as 'a splendid dribbler' who learnt the game during three years with Castleford Victoria before moving across town to join Castleford. He worked as a glassblower at Lumb and Company along with Jack Rhodes before switching codes in October 1896 and joining Hull KR in Northern Union. In April 1904, he became the first dual code international with John Rhapps when he played for England against Other Nationalities and eventually called him on his 16-season career a year later. Starks later became a licensee, running the Rugby Hotel and then the Black Swan Hotel in Hull.

288. WARD, John William
Forward 3 caps 1896
Born: Castleford, West Yorkshire, 29 January 1873
Died: Harmsworth, West Yorkshire, 30 April 1939
Career: Castleford, Yorkshire
Debut: v Wales, Rectory Field, Blackheath, January 1896

Ward was one of a trio of Castleford forwards with Jack Rhodes and Anthony Starks, who made their international debuts against Wales at Blackheath in the first international following the formation of the Northern Union. He kept his place for all three games that season and made his last appearance alongside another Castleford player, Harry Speed. A glassblower with Rylands Glassworks, he was dismissed after joining Pudsey in the Northern Union the following season. Ward remained in the West Riding of Yorkshire as a licensee running the King William Cutsyke, Castleford and The Victoria Hemsworth until his death.

289. WHITELEY, William
Forward 1 cap 1896
Born: Bury, Lancashire, 31 May 1870
Died: Dearnley, Lancashire, 28 October 1938
Career: Littleborough, Bramley, Lancashire, Yorkshire
Debut: v Wales, Rectory Field, Blackheath, January 1896

A fast and energetic forward, Whiteley was a wool warper and then a labourer and started playing rugby at Littleborough, where he won county honours for Lancashire. In 1893, he joined Leeds City Police and moved to Bramley, which gave him the residential qualification for Yorkshire. He won his only England cap against Wales in 1896. After spending 26 years in the police, reaching the rank of sergeant, he retired in 1919. Whiteley later did an occasional relief duty in the Littleborough District and worked as a part-time night watchman for Henry Whittle Ltd, Featherstall, but was confined to bed for 18 months before his death.

290. BARON, John Henry
Forward 3 caps 1896-1897
Born: Micklethwaite, West Yorkshire, 28 August 1874
Died: Eldwick, West Yorkshire, 2 December 1942
Career: Bingley, Bradford, Yorkshire
Debut: v Scotland, Old Hampden Park, Glasgow, March 1896

Baron was educated at Bingley Grammar School and joined the local rugby club when he was 18. But it wasn't until he moved to Yorkshire's leading club at the time, Bradford, that he gained county honours. In 1896, he won the first of his international caps against Scotland. Then the following season, he played against Wales and Ireland until suffering a knee injury, ending hopes of more international caps and forcing his retirement. He spent 40 years working as a coal merchant at John Baron and Sons, a business his father started and was also a property owner.

291. HUGHES, George Edgar
Forward 1 cap 1896
Born: Otley, West Yorkshire, 24 February 1870
Died: Walney-in-Barrow, Cumbria, 6 September 1947
Career: West Hartlepool, Otley, Yorkshire, Barrow, Lancashire
Debut: v Scotland Old Hampden Park, Glasgow, March 1896

Hughes started his career with West Hartlepool when he was working as a steam engine fitter but then returned to his native Otley in February 1892, where he continued playing after moving to Barrow to work as a ship fitter. He won his only England cap against Scotland months later, Salford announced in July 1896 that he had signed crossed codes to the Northern Union and was among the second batch of players they registered. Hughes appears to have changed his mind but later played rugby league for Barrow with a younger brother, Herbert while continuing to work in the shipyards.

292. KNOWLES, Edward
Forward 2 caps 1896-1897
Born: Waberthwaite, Cumberland, 3 April 1868
Died: Millom, Cumberland, 17 March 1945
Career: Millom, Cumberland
Debut: v Scotland, Old Hampden Park, Glasgow, March 1896

Knowles was the first player from Millom to be capped by England when he made his international debut against Scotland in March 1896. His club and county team-mate Sam Northmore wasn't capped until the following season. Knowles' only other international cap also came against Scotland in March 1897, but any hopes of further caps ended after he stayed with Millom when they joined the Northern Union following the collapse of the North-West Rugby League in July 1897. Knowles was appointed captain a year later and earned his living as an iron ore miner for the Hodbarrow Mining Company.

293. POOLE, Robert Watkins
Full-back 1 cap 1896
Born: Hartlepool, Durham, 4 November 1874
Died: Southampton, Hampshire, 26 December 1933
Career: Hartlepool OB, Hartlepool Rovers, Barbarians, Durham Counties
Debut: v Scotland Old Hampden Park, Glasgow, March 1896

Poole, like Robert Oakes, was born in Hartlepool Militia Barracks, the son of a sergeant. He played rugby with Hartlepool Old Boys and then Hartlepool Rovers, winning a single international cap against Scotland in 1896. In 1903, he switched codes, joining Broughton Rovers Rugby League club, and two years later won a single England league cap. A shipyard rivetter in the North-East, he became a boilermaker in the North-West and then on the South Coast working for Harland and Wolff in Southampton until just before his death after a long illness.

294. ASHFORD William OBE JP
Forward 4 caps 1897-1898
Born: Woodbury, Devon, 18 December 1871
Died: Topsham, Devon, 1 January 1954
Career: St Thomas's Hospital, Richmond, Exeter, Barbarians, Surrey, Devon
Debut: v Wales, Rodney Parade, Newport, January 1897

Ashford was educated at Exeter School but underwent medical training at St Thomas' Hospital. During his time in London, he played for Richmond and was registered with them when he won his first two caps. But by the time of his final two caps a year later, he was back with Exeter. William also played cricket for Devon. A civil surgeon in the Boer War and during the First World War, he was the Commanding Officer of the Topsham Volunteer Auxilary Division Hospital. A member of Topsham Parish Council and St Thomas' Rural Council, Ashford was president of Exeter Rugby Club until his death.

295. BYRNE, Francis Alban
Wing 1 cap 1897
Born: Aston, Warwickshire, May 1873
Died: Nairobi, Kenya 23 July 1949
Career: Moseley, Midland Counties
Debut: v Wales, Rodney Parade, Newport, January 1897

Byrne was educated at St. Joseph's College, Rugby and won his only cap alongside brother Fred and partnering future Moseley team-mate Edward Baker in the centres. The Byrne brothers were the first catholic boys to play for England. But after being outwitted by Jim Pearson, he never got selected again. Byrne, however, later did represent Warwickshire in golf. He was the manager of the family rubber mill and then became the director of several companies like his brother Fred. Byrne was living in Epsom, Surrey, when he travelled to Kenya in late 1948, and it was there that he died six months later.

296. EBDON, Percy John
Forward 2 caps 1897
Born: Milverton, Somerset, 16 March 1874
Died: Wellington, Somerset, 16 February 1943
Career: Wellington, Somerset
Debut: v Wales, Rodney Parade, Newport, January 1897

Ebdon made two international appearances in 1897 against Wales and Ireland, but they both ended in defeat, and he was never selected again. He played in the same Wellington team as Hugh Fox and later served the club as secretary. Ebdon succeeded his father, John, as secretary of Fox's textile manufacturing business, Fox Brothers and Company, in 1896 and held the post until his retirement in March 1939. Before his death, Ebdon was a fuel overseer for Wellington and was a director of the Wellington Building Society. In his younger days, he played for Somerset CCC like his brothers Edward and John.

297. FLETCHER, Thomas
Centre 1 cap 1897
Born: Seaton, Cumberland, 11 April 1874
Died: Barugh, Cumbria 28 August 1950
Career: Northside Council School, Seaton
Debut: v Wales Rodney Parade Newport January 1897

Tobacconist Fletcher started playing for his hometown, Seaton, and was the first Cumbrian to be capped by England when he played against Wales at Rodney Parade in January 1897. He was a member of the Cumbria side that lost the 1897 County Championship Final, but his performances attracted the attention of Northern Union clubs, and he signed for Oldham. Shortly afterwards, Fletcher returned to Cumbria to run Moorhouse Guards Colliery, re-joining Seaton, and he did not finish playing for his village until after his 45th birthday. Fletcher sat on the Harrington Urban Borough Council and ran Barugh Quarries until his death.

298. JACOB, Fredrick
Forward 8 caps 1897-1899
Born: Northbourne Kent 4 January 1873
Died: Srinagar, Kashmir, 1 September 1945
Career: Sandwich School, Thanet Wanderers, Cambridge University, London University, Blackheath, Richmond, Cheltenham, Barbarians, Gloucestershire, Kent
Debut: v Wales, Rodney Parade, Newport, January 1897

Jacob was a talented all-round sportsman at Cambridge University. He won a double blue for Rugby in 1895 and 1896, as well as water polo. He won the first of his England caps in January 1897 and, just two months later, helped Kent win the County Championship against Cumberland. Jacob made eight successive appearances, but after back-to-back defeats against Wales and Ireland in 1899 was never selected again. Jacob was an assistant master at Bradfield College and Cheltenham College before becoming a housemaster at Felsted Prep School. He then moved to India and was a master at C.M.S. Schools in Srinagar, Kashmir.

299. MANGLES, Roland Henry DSO CMG CB
Forward 2 caps 1897
Born: Losely Park, Surrey, 9 February 1874
Died: Dedham, Essex, 29 September 1948
Career: Marlborough College, Richmond, The Army, Barbarians, Surrey
Debut: v Wales, Rodney Parade, Newport, January 1897

Mangles was educated at Marlborough College and was commissioned into The Queen's Royal Regiment in December 1894. A career in the Army didn't stop him from enjoying rugby at the very highest level. He saw service in West and South Africa and later in France at Flanders. Mangles commanded the Cairo Infancy Brigade before retiring in 1927. In the Second World War, he served in the Home Guard. His father, Ross Mangles, is one of only five civilians to have been awarded the Victoria Cross, carrying an injured fellow soldier for several miles during the Indian Mutiny despite being wounded.

300. OAKES, Robert Frederick
Forward 8 caps 1897-1899
Born: Hartlepool, County Durham, 20 December 1872
Died: Adel, West Yorkshire, 23 October 1952
Career: Hartlepool Trinity, Hartlepool Rovers, Headingley, Durham Counties
Debut: v Wales, Rodney Parade, Newport, January 1897

Oakes, like Bob Poole, was born in Hartlepool Militia Barracks and was the son of an army sergeant. Under his captaincy, Hartlepool became one of the best sides in the North-East, winning the County Cup three times in six years at the helm. As a representative and much later a director for George Horsley and Co, Timber Merchants, he moved to Sheffield and then Leeds on business, where he joined Headingley. Oakes became one of the most influential figures in the game, serving as club treasurer before becoming Yorkshire secretary for 40 years, an England selector, and sat on the RFU committee for 25 years.

301. STODDART, Wilfred Browning JP
Forward 3 caps 1897
Born: West Derby, Liverpool, 27 April 1871
Died: Grassendale, Liverpool, 8 January 1935
Career: Royal Liverpool Institute, Liverpool, Barbarians, Lancashire
Debut: v Wales, Rodney Parade, Newport, January 1897

Stoddard played in the early Liverpool Schools boy team and won all three caps in 1897, while his cousin George Leather also played for England. A talented sportsman, he captained Lancashire CCC, played for the MCC, and was the Captain of the Royal Liverpool GC and President of the English Golf Union. His brother, Lawrence, won the first US Amateur Golf Championship. Stoddard ran the family shipping business and was an Alderman and Liberal councillor in his native Liverpool. He was a wise counsellor on the administrative side of rugby and was President of Liverpool Rugby Club until his death.

302. STOUT, Frank Moxham MC
Forward 14 caps (5–1t,1c) 1897–1905
Born: Liverpool, Lancashire, 21 February 1877
Died: Abbey Storrington, Sussex, 30 May 1926
Career: Gloucester, Richmond, Gloucestershire, Barbarians
Debut: v Wales Rodney Parade Newport January 1897

Stout was a latecomer to rugby as he started playing association football with Gloucester before switching codes. The captain of his club side Richmond for three years, he played for England four times with his elder brother Percy. They became the first brothers to score in the same international against Wales in 1898. He also toured Australia and New Zealand in 1899 and South Africa in 1903 with British Team. At the start of the First World War, Stout joined the 20th Hussars and reached the rank of lieutenant but was badly wounded and remained an invalid for the rest of his life.

303. BUNTING, William Louis
Centre 9 caps 1891-1901
Born: Daventry, Northamptonshire, 9 August 1873
Died: Odiham, Hampshire, 15 October 1947
Career: Bromsgrove School, Cambridge University, Bromsgrove, Richmond, Moseley, Kent, Barbarians, Midlands
Debut: v Ireland, Lansdowne Road, Dublin, February 1897

Bunting was widely acknowledged as the best attacking centre of his day. Educated at Cambridge University, he won his blue in 1894 and 1895 and helped Kent win the County Championship two years later. Bunting succeeded John Taylor as England captain in 1901 against Ireland and Scotland, but both games ended in defeat, and he never asked to captain his country again, nor was he ever selected.

He was an assistant master at the Royal Naval School, Eltham, Bromsgrove School and then at the Royal Naval College, Osborne, until spending the rest of his career at Royal Naval College, Dartmouth.

304. NORTHMORE, Samuel
Fly-half 1 cap 1897
Born: Millom, Cumberland, 2 March 1872
Died: Askern, South Yorkshire, 18 March 1946
Career: Millom, Cumberland
Debut: v Ireland Lansdowne Road Dublin February 1897

As a youth, Northmore had captained Millom's 'A' team and led them through a season without a single defeat. He helped his hometown club become one of the strongest teams in the north and was rewarded when he made his only international appearance against Ireland in Dublin in February 1897. Unsurprisingly, he and his brother-in-law Joe Young stayed with Millom when they joined the Northern Union after the North-West Rugby League folded in July 1897. Northmore was an Iron ore miner working at Purtmans Colliery before spending 19 years living in Askern near Doncaster.

305. ROBINSON, George Carmichael JP
Wing 8 caps (24-8t) 1897-1901
Born: Gateshead, Tyne and Wear, 4 May 1876
Died: Penrith, Cumberland, 29 May 1940
Career: Dame Allan's School Newcastle, Gosforth, Percy Park, Northumberland, Blackheath, Barbarians
Debut: v Ireland Lansdowne Road Dublin February 1897

'Tot' Robinson was seen as one of the best Three-quarter of the 1890's scored a try in all but one of the eight matches he played for England. The only game he failed to score was a 0-0 draw against Scotland in March 1900 despite being played in excellent conditions. Robinson was the Northumberland Representative on the RFU council for 17 years, served as an England selector for eight and was President at the time of his death. A coal exporter running the Widdrington Colliery Company, he also served as a Justice of the peace between 1932 and 1940.

306. TAYLOR, John Thomas
Centre 11 caps (5 1t, 1c) 1897-1905
Born: Castleford, Yorkshire, 26 May 1876
Died: Ashington, Northumberland, 3 September 1951
Career: Castleford, West Hartlepool, Durham County, Yorkshire
Debut: v Ireland, Lansdowne Road, Dublin, February 1897

'Jacky' Taylor was renowned as a drop kicker in club and county rugby and played for Castleford aged 17 and captained Yorkshire before moving to West Hartlepool in 1896. He would go on to help Durham win the County Championship eight times and captained England against Wales at Arms Park in 1901. A tobacconist, he was touted for a move to Oldham in the Northern Union in 1902. He stayed with West Hartlepool but caused fury when he helped Castleford win the Yorkshire Cup. Taylor retired in 1907 and was a stone works manager for the Ashington Coal Company and then a licensee.

307. DAVIDSON, James
Forward 5 caps 1897-1899
Born: Chester-Le-Street, County Durham, 28 December 1868
Died: Aspatria, Cumbria, 23 December 1945
Career: Aspatria, Cumberland
Debut: v Scotland Whalley Range Manchester March 1897

Davidson learnt the rudiments of rugby during his education at Aspatria Agricultural College, and from there, he went on to become one of Cumberland's most noted players, captaining both Aspatria and Cumberland. He impressed selectors with his scrummaging ability, which won him his first international cap against Scotland at Whalley Range, Manchester, in March 1897 and was seen as an early specialist in that area. Davidson played alongside brother Joe against Scotland at Blackheath in 1899. Davidson was a stonemason before becoming a well-known building contractor. He was the Cumberland representative on the RFU committee.

308. DUDGEON, Herbert William
Forward 7 caps 1897-1899
Born: Wallsend, Tynemouth, 4 September 1872
Died: Cairo, Egypt, 4 October 1935
Career: Croydon, Durham University, Guy's Hospital, Northern, Richmond, Barbarians, Northumberland, Surrey
Debut: v Scotland Fallowfield Manchester March 1897

Dudgeon was the son of naval architect Andrew and completed his early education in Switzerland. He started playing rugby with Croydon, where he first won county honours in 1896. A year later, when he first played for England, he moved on to Richmond. His last appearance came just as his first had done against Scotland in 1899. Dudgeon was under his medical training at Guy's Hospital and became a doctor in London. Then, after joining the government, he was posted to Egypt and was appointed director of the lunatic asylum in Khanka near Cairo, where he worked until his death.

309. MACKIE, Osbert Gadesden
Centre 2 caps 1897-1898
Born: Wakefield 23 August 1869
Died: Redcar 25 January 1927
Career: Haileybury & SIC, Cambridge University, Wakefield Trinity, Barbarians, Yorkshire
Debut: v Scotland, Whalley Range, Manchester, March 1897

Mackie was captain of Wakefield Trinity before resigning when the club announced they were joining the Northern Union. Instead, he went to Cambridge University, winning a blue and being appointed captain. While at Cambridge, he toured South Africa with Johnny Hammond's British Team in 1896. After returning, he won his two England caps in successive seasons. Mackie was a businessman in Hamburg, Hull, and Wakefield before going to Cambridge and was ordained in 1899, becoming a curate in Leeds, then was the Vicar of St Paul's in Middlesbrough and the Rector of Guisborough until his death.

310. BLACKLOCK, Joseph
Forward 2 caps 1898-1899
Born: South Shields, Tyne and Wear, 20 October 1878
Died: Fletchertown, Cumbria, 28 June 1945
Debut: v Ireland, Athletic Ground, Richmond, February 1898
Career: Mayport, Aspatria, Cumberland

Blacklock made his name, helping Mayport win back-to-back County Cups in 1893 and 1894. He was a deputy foreman in a coal mine and joined Aspatria after moving to the town for work. And it was with Aspatria that he won his two England caps against Ireland in 1898 and then again the following season. He was a member of the Cumberland County Championship-winning sides of 1895, 1896 and 1899 when he was captain. Blacklock also had a short spell as an amateur at Broughton Rangers, then Workington before retirement and was a deputy at Allhallows Colliery for many years.

311. JACOB, Philip Gordon
Scrum-half 1 cap 1898
Born: Sundi, India 14 May 1875
Died: Tooting Bec, London, 10 November 1953
Career: Bedford Grammar School, Cambridge University, Blackheath, Kent
Debut: v Ireland, Athletic Ground, Richmond, February 1898

India-born Jacob finished his education at Cambridge University, where he won a blue between 1894 and 1896. As a member of the Blackheath club, he won his only cap against Ireland in February 1898 in partnership with Harry Myers. 1898 was the year that he joined the Indian Civil Service, which is likely to have contributed to him not playing again. He held several financial posts in various parts of India. Jacob retired in August 1927 after serving as accountant-general in Burma. Jacob returned to London, living in Brook Green until he died in Tooting Bec Hospital.

312. MYERS, Harry
Fly-half 1 cap 1898
Born: Horsforth, West Yorkshire, 3 February 1875
Died: Keighley, West Yorkshire, 19 December 1906
Career: Bramley, Keighley, Yorkshire
Debut: v Ireland Athletic Ground Richmond February 1898

After being spotted when he turned up as a spectator, Myers quickly made the grade for Bramley but filled in at half-back. He helped Yorkshire win the county championship, but after Bramley joined the Northern Union, he furthered his union career at Keighley until they switched codes in 1900. The decision ultimately cost him his life due to a spinal injury sustained match following a collision with Dewsbury's Fred Richardson. Before his death, Myers ran a billiard hall and became an innkeeper at the Brunswick Arms, the Fleece Tap and the Worth Valley, Ingrow.

313. PIERCE, Richard
Forward 2 caps 1898-1903
Born: West Derby, Lancashire 30 May 1874
Died: Unknown 7 December 1906
Career: Charterhouse School, Liverpool, Barbarians, Lancashire
Debut: v Ireland Athletic, Ground, Richmond, February 1898

Pierce was the son of William, who helped found Price & Pierce timber merchants and was sent to be educated at Charterhouse School. He joined Liverpool Rugby Club in 1891, had two spells as captain, and represented Lancashire for six seasons between 1893 and 1899. A timber merchant himself, he won his first cap against Ireland in 1898 and his second five years later after impressing in a trial match. Richard's life then appeared to take a bizarre twist. His name appears on probate records in 1926, stating he died on or around 7th December 1906 but offering no explanation why probate was applied for 20 years later.

314. SHAW, Frederick
Forward 1 cap 1898
Born: Huddersfield, Yorkshire 1879
Died: East Bierley, Yorkshire, 27 October 1938
Career: Cleckheaton, West Riding, Yorkshire
Debut: v Ireland, Athletic Ground, Richmond, February 1898

Shaw was a forward of exceptional calibre, and his height and smartness made him particularly useful in the line out. He started his career with Cleckheaton before moving to West Riding. After returning to Cleck in 1895, his career took off, making his county debut a year later. He won his only England cap against Ireland in February 1898, but his rugby career was ended not long afterwards by injury. Shaw was an apprentice at Samuel Haley and Sons, Pyenot Hall. He became a stonemason employed by West Riding County Council, working on highway repairs and attending matches at Moorland until the weekend before his sudden death.

315. WILSON, Charles Edward
Forward 1 cap 1898
Born: Fermoy County, Cork, 2 June 1871
Died: KIA, Aisne France 17 August 1914
Career: Dover College, Blackheath, The Army, Surrey
Debut: v Ireland Athletic Ground Richmond February 1898

Ireland-born Wilson had to be patient to win his only international cap. He was a long-standing member of the Blackheath side and had played for the Barbarians by the time he was one of six new caps and four in the pack against Ireland. England were no match for Ireland, and he wasn't picked again. A career soldier like his major general father, he also played rugby for the Army and served in the Boer War, seeing action at the Relief of Ladysmith. Wilson made the ultimate sacrifice during the Battle of the Aisne in the First World War and was awarded the Legion d'Honneur.

316. PILKINGTON, William Norman DSO JP
Wing 1 cap 1898
Born: Prescot, Lancashire, 26 July 1877
Died: Prescot, Lancashire, 8 February 1935
Career: Clifton College, Cambridge University, St Helens Recreation, Blackheath, Barbarians, Lancashire
Debut: v Scotland Powderhall Edinburgh March 1898

Pilkington learnt the game at Clifton College and was a member of the St Helens Rec before winning double blue in rugby and athletics in his first year at Cambridge University and was due to be captain in 1898 until he suffered an injury. Norman played three trial matches but only won one cap. He joined the family glass manufacturers Pilkington Brothers at Cowley Hill and Sheet Glassworks. He was a colonel in the Volunteer and Territorial Forces until his retirement in 1928. Pilkington was also on the St Helens and District Reporter board and was president of St Helens Recs at his death.

317. RAMSDEN, Harold Edward
Forward 2 caps 1898
Born: Harden, Bingley September 6, 1873
Died: Ilkley, Yorkshire, 6 March 1938
Career: Bingley
Debut: v Scotland, Powderhall, Edinburgh, March 1898

Ramsden was a product of Binley Grammar School and Bradford Grammar School. And was one of the most sought-after forwards in Yorkshire when he ignored Bradford's attempt to lure him to the Northern Union in 1898 and was rewarded with two England caps. The managing director of Harold E Ramsden and Son, top makers, was a well-known wool buyer in various parts of the country. Ramsden was a major in the Ilkley Volunteers during the First World War and served on the Wool Control Board. Then, he spent 10 years as vice-president of the British Wool Federation.

318. ROTHERHAM, Arthur
Scrum-half 5 caps 1898-1899
Born: Coventry, Warwickshire, 27 May 1869
Died: Hambledon, Hampshire, 3 March 1946
Career: Uppingham School, Cambridge University, St Thomas's Hospital, Middlesex West, Richmond, Coventry, Barbarians, Surrey, Midland Counties
Debut: v Scotland, Powderhall, Edinburgh, March 1898

Rotherham was the cousin of Alan Rotherham, and he won a Cambridge University blue in 1890 and 1891, the year he was selected for Bill MacLagan's British Team tour to South Africa. But it would be another seven years before he was selected for his country. Rotherham succeeded Fred Bryne as captain, but three of his five tests in charge ended in defeat, and he was never picked again following the disastrous 1899 campaign. A house surgeon at Nottingham General Hospital before becoming Assistant Medical Officer at several asylums in London and Home Counties then worked as Senior Commissioner at Darenth Mental Home.

319. ROYDS, Admiral Sir Percy Molyneux Rawson CMG CB MP
Centre 3 caps (3-1t) 1898-1899
Born: Rochdale, Lancashire, 5 April 1874
Died: Marylebone, London, 25 March 1955
Career: Eastmans Naval School Southsea, Royal Navel College Greenwich, US Portsmouth, Royal Navy, Blackheath, Barbarians, Kent
Debut: v Scotland, Powderhall, Edinburgh, March 1898

Royds scored a try on his international debut to earn England a 3-3 draw against Scotland at Powderhall, Edinburgh. He didn't score again, and a heavy 1899 defeat ended his international career in Wales, but later in life, he refereed two internationals. Royds made the Royal Navy his career, and during the First World War, he commanded HMS Canterbury in Zeebrugge and Jutland. He represented the Navy on the RFU board, was a selector, a member of the International Board and RFU President. Royds also wrote the first book on the history of rugby laws and was a Conservative MP for Kingston-on-Thames.

320. SHAW, James Fraser
Forward 2 caps 1898
Born: Barton upon Irwell, Lancashire, 2 January 1878
Died: Bromley, Kent, 23 July 1941
Career: King William School Isle of Man, RNEC Keyham, Barbarians, Devon
Debut: v Scotland, Powderhall, Edinburgh, March 1898

Shaw played in the same Royal Naval Engineering College and Devon team as 'Pongo' Matters, who was capped a season later. Shaw won back-to-back caps against Scotland and Ireland, but by the time of the next international in 1899 was out of the picture. An amateur boxing champion, he served as an engineer commander on HMS Invincible, HMS Suffolk and HMS Cordelia during the First World War before transferring to the Ministry of Munitions. After leaving the Navy in 1922, Shaw stayed in the civil service, working as Chief Engineer for the Fuel Research Station of the Department of Scientific and Industrial Research.

321. STOUT, Percy Wyfold DSO OBE
Wing 5 caps (3-1t) 1898-1899
Born: Barnwood, Gloucester, 20 November 1875
Died: Marylebone London, 9 October 1937
Career: Crypt Grammar School, Gloucester, Richmond, Bristol, Barbarians, Gloucester
Debut: v Scotland, Powderhall, Edinburgh, March 1898

Stout won four of his five caps alongside his younger brother Frank. The brothers both scored against Wales in 1898, and it wasn't until 1993 that Rory and Tony Underwood scored in the same game. Percy played association football for Corinthian-Casuals and Gloucester City and was also on the books of Bristol City. He was a stockbroker in Cairo, then during the First World War, became an acting captain in the Machine Gun Corps and was mentioned in dispatches five times. Stout was later a director of the Egyptian Delta Land Co and the Anglo-American Nile.

322. UNWIN, Geoffrey Thomas
Fly-half 1 cap 1898
Born: Sheffield, Yorkshire, 1 June 1874
Died: Hemel Hempstead, Hertfordshire, 12 February 1948
Career: Marlborough College, Oxford University, Moseley, Blackheath, Cheltenham, Derby, Barbarians, Midlands
Debut: v Scotland, Powderhall, Edinburgh, March 1898

Unwin learnt rugby at Marlborough College and won his Oxford University blue between 1894 and 1896. During his career he captained both his University and Cheltenham. Despite being one of the most brilliant half-backs of his time, he only won one international cap, against Scotland at Powderhall, Edinburgh, in a new half-back pairing with Alan Rotherham. He spent his working life in the brewing industry and was a director of Rawson's Brewery. Unwin married Edwardian stage actress Dora Langham, and while living in the North of England, he was Joint Master of Stainton Hounds before retiring to Hemel Hempstead.

323. LIVESAY, Robert O'Hara DSO CMG
Fly-half 2 caps 1898-1899
Born: Gillingham, Kent, 27 June 1876
Died: Magham Down, Sussex, 23 March 1946
Career: Wellington College, RMC Sandhurst, Blackheath, The Army, Barbarians, Kent
Debut: v Wales Rectory Field Blackheath April 1898

Livesay made his England debut against Wales on familiar soil at Rectory Field, the home of his club side Blackheath, in 1898, and he retained his place for the return fixture in January 1899. But then served for the Queen's (Royal West Surrey) Regiment in the Boer War, winning a DSO. Even though Livesay never played international rugby again, he did continue to play first-class cricket for Kent, who awarded him his cap in 1897. Robert stayed in the Army until his retirement in 1920 and saw action during the First World War at the Battle of the Somme, Messines, and Passchendaele.

324. DANIELL, John
Forward 7 caps 1899-1904
Born: Bath, Somerset 12 December 1878
Died: Holway, Somerset, 24 January 1963
Career: Clifton College, Cambridge University, Richmond, Barbarians, Middlesex, Somerset
Debut: v Wales St Helen's Swansea January 1899

Daniell, dubbed The Prophet, was a double blue in rugby and cricket. Aged just 21, he was handed the England captaincy after winning just one cap, and even though injury interrupted his international career, he captained England six times. Daniell was then a selector for 26 years and the last seven as chairman and sat on the International Board. He played first-class cricket for Somerset and was also an England cricket selector. During the First World War, he served as a captain in the Royal Army Service Corps. Daniell was also a master at Stanmore Park Preparatory School and a tea planter in India.

325. DAVIDSON, Joseph
Forward 2 caps 1899
Born: Aspatria, Cumberland, 5 October 1878
Died: Wigton, Cumbria, 8 October 1910
Career: Aspatria, Cumberland
Debut: v Wales St Helen's, Swansea, January 1899

Davidson was a regular for Aspatria and Cumberland long before he caught the eye of England selectors after a North vs South trial. When he debuted against Wales in January 1899 alongside brother Jim, it was the first-time siblings had played for England in the same game. He helped Aspatria win the Cumberland Cup ten years apart. Davidson, a stonemason and builder by trade and an outstanding all-round sportsman at cricket, boxing, and athletics, was tragically killed when he was buried alive in the family sand quarry. Another rugby-playing brother, George, was rescued and survived.

326. FORREST, Reginald
Wing 6 caps (3-1t) 1899-1903
Born: Montpelier, Bristol, 12 May 1878
Died: Minehead, Somerset, 11 April 1903
Career: Christ's College Blackheath, Blackheath, Wellington, Taunton, Barbarians, Somerset
Debut: v Wales, St Helen's Swansea January 1899

Forrest was a three-quarter of great speed and brilliant scoring powers who made his name with Taunton. He caught the eye of selectors in his first trial match and was named reserve against Scotland in 1898 before making his debut against Wales at St Helen's a year later. Forrest contracted typhoid fever, which eventually killed him after eating oysters during England's visit to Ireland in February 1903, and went down to the illness two days after scoring his only international try against Scotland a month later. He played association football for Minehead and was an electrical engineer at Newton Electrical Works, Taunton.

327. GAMLIN, Herbert Temlett
Full-back 15 caps (3-1p) 1899-1904
Born: Wellington, Somerset 12 February 1878
Died: Cheam, Surrey 12 July 1937
Career: Wellington School, Wellington, Devonport Albion, Blackheath, Somerset, Western Counties, London, The South
Debut: v Wales, St Helen's, Swansea, January 1899

Gamlin was educated at Wellington School and played rugby and cricket for Somerset, aged 16. After briefly playing association football, he turned to rugby with his hometown club Wellington. He was described as 'probably the most powerful and effective tackler on record.' Indeed, his tackling style earned him the nickname 'The Octopus' which stuck for the rest of his life. During his cricket career, he dismissed AC MacLaren when he made the highest individual score of 424 by an Englishman in first-class cricket. Gamlin was a Civil Service clerk who worked in the department of the Director of Dockyards to the Admiralty.

328. GIBSON, George Ralph
Forward 2 caps 1899-1901
Born: Gateshead, Tyne and Wear, 14 March 1878
Died: Newcastle-upon-Tyne, Tyne and Wear 1 October 1939
Career: Uppingham School, Northern, Barbarians, Northumberland
Debut: v Wales, St Helen's, Swansea, January 1899

Gibson was the middle of three brothers who played for England and also made his name with Northern. A hard-working forward, he won his first cap against Wales at St Helen's in January 1899 in what was an inexperienced pack. The same year, he was selected to go on the British Team's tour of Australia when he made seven appearances, scoring one try. Gibson was a timber merchant with his brother Thomas, who toured South Wales with the Barbarians in 1900. It would be another two years before he won his second cap against Scotland, ending in defeat.

329. HARPER, Sir Charles Henry KBE CMG
Forward 1 cap 1899
Born: Barnstable, Devon, 24 February 1876
Died: Christow, Devon, 13 May 1950
Career: Blundell's School, Oxford University, Blackheath, Exeter, Devon
Debut: v Wales, St Helen's Swansea January 1899

Harper won an Oxford University blue in 1897 and 1898 before, a year later, becoming one of only three internationals from Barnstaple when he won his only international cap as one of five new boys in the pack against Wales at St Helen's. A year later, he joined the Colonial Service as a cadet and was posted to the Gold Coast Civil Service. Harper was called to the bar at Inner Temple in 1909 and remained with the Colonial Office until 1941, when he worked for the Ministry of Food after serving as governor of St Helena.

330. MORTIMER, William
Forward 1 cap 1899
Born: Warrington, Cheshire, 2 May 1874
Died: Crowborough, Sussex, 31 October 1916
Career: Marlborough College, Cambridge University, Marlborough Nomads, Blackheath, Barbarians, Kent, Lancashire.
Debut: v Wales, St Helen's, Swansea, January 1899

Mortimer won a double Cambridge University blue in rugby and hockey and toured America with the University cricket team in 1895. A year later, despite being uncapped, he was selected for the British team tour to South Africa in 1896, making 16 appearances, including three test matches. When he was finally given a chance by England selectors as one of five new caps in an experienced pack, after a heavy defeat, he was never selected again. Mortimer was a member of the London Stock Exchange and had interests in the tanning trade and agriculture in Flintshire and Cheshire.

331. ANDERSON Stanley Watson
Winger 1 cap 1899
Born: Wallsend, Tynemouth, 5 August 1871,
Died: Alnwick, Northumberland, 12 February 1942
Career: Rockcliff, Northumberland
Debut: v Ireland Lansdowne Road Dublin February 1899

Anderson was one of several England internationals who played for Whitley Bay-based Rockcliff. He won his only international cap against Ireland at Lansdowne Road in February 1899. But he was better known in the North-East of England for being a cricketer. A brilliant batsman, he served Northumberland County Cricket Club for 25 years, retiring in 1915. He moved to Alnwick in 1921 and captained the local team until 1932. An iron ship plater on the Tyne for almost 30 years, Anderson became the licensee at the Plough Hotel, Alnwick, until his death.

332. DARBY, Arthur John Lovett
Forward 1 cap 1899
Born: Chester, Cheshire, 9 January 1876
Died: Dartmouth, Devon, 16 January 1960
Career: Cheltenham College, Cambridge University, Sorbonne, Birkenhead Park, Richmond, Moseley Wanderers, Barbarians, Surrey
Debut: v Ireland Lansdowne Road Dublin February 1899

Darby was the son of John Lionel Lovett, the Dean of Chester. He was educated at Cambridge University, where he won his blue between 1896 and 1898. Despite only playing for England once, he was a silver medallist for Great Britain at the 1900 Paris Olympic Games. Darby became an assistant master at Elizabeth College, Guernsey, and then an interpreter and instructor in Modern Languages to the Atlantic Fleet before joining the Royal Naval College Royal Naval, Dartmouth, in 1906 until retiring in 1935. During the First World War, Darby was a lieutenant in the Royal Naval Volunteer.

333. SHOOTER, John Henry
Forward 4 caps 1899-1900
Born: Selston, Nottinghamshire, 25 March 1874
Died: Leeds, Yorkshire, 13 August 1922
Career: Morley, Yorkshire
Debut: v Ireland, Lansdowne Road, Dublin, February 1899

Shooter had a reputation as a relentless attacker and as a renowned scrummager. A coal miner for the Howley Park Colliery Company, he lived in Morley while in his teens and played for the local rugby club. An ever-present in the Yorkshire side for four seasons, he won his first two caps in 1899, and then, after missing the first game of the 1900 campaign against Wales, he was recalled for the final two. Shooter's international career ended when he joined Hunslet in the professional ranks, becoming a pillar in a pack that gained a reputation as the 'Terrible Six.'

334. DOWSON, Aubrey Osler MC
Forward 1 cap 1899
Born: Gee Cross. Cheshire 10 November 1875
Died: Hanging Langford, Wiltshire, 5 October 1940
Career: Rugby School, Oxford University, Moseley, Manchester, London and the South, The Rest, Midlands
Debut: v Scotland, Rectory Field, Blackheath, March 1899

Rugby School-educated Dowson completed his education at Oxford and won a rugby blue in 1896, alongside Edward Baker and Geoffrey Unwin, who would go on to play alongside him at Moseley. His only rugby blue was sandwiched between athletics blues for the shot and hammer. England lost all three games in 1899, including the only game he played in. Dowson, a glass manufacturer and then a farmer, served during the First World War as a captain in the 12th Rifle Brigade and was awarded a Military Cross in January 1918 after being mentioned in dispatches. His wife Phillis was a well-known suffragette.

335. HOBBS, Reginald Francis Arthur CB CMG DSO
Forward 2 caps 1899-1903
Born: Tyldesley, Lancashire, 30 January 1878
Died: Sutton Veny, Wiltshire, 10 July 1953
Career: Wellington College, RMA Woolwich, Royal Engineers, The Army, Blackheath, Barbarians, Kent
Debut: v Scotland, Rectory Field, Blackheath, March 1899

Wellington College-educated Hobbs, who was the best athlete produced by the Royal Military Academy Woolwich. He won his first cap against Scotland at his club's home, Blackheath. But because he served in the Boer War, his second and last cap against Wales had to wait four years. Hobbs stayed in the Army until he retired in 1931. He served on the Sutton Veny Parish Council and then the Rural District Council. A son, Reg, also played for England, while two of his sons, William and Peter, were killed during World War Two.

336. MATTERS, John Charles
Wing 1 cap 1899
Born: Stoke Damerel, Devon 11 December 1878
Died: Limpsfield, Surrey, 24 April 1949
Career: RNEC Keyham, Devonport Albion, Barbarians, Devon
Debut: v Scotland Rectory Field Blackheath March 1899

'Pongo' Matters was the son of John Matters, who was chief constable of Devonport and was widely seen as the greatest all-round sportsman RNEC Keyham produced. He won his only international cap against Scotland at Blackheath in March 1899 and helped Devon win the County Championship just a month later. His international career ended when the Royal Navy posted him to the Pacific Station on HMS Warspite, and he later became an engineer commander and then Engineer Rear-Admiral. Following the First World War, Matters was first assistant to the engineer manager of Devonport and then Malta Dockyards before retiring to Surrey.

337. SCHWARZ, Reginald Oscar MC
Fly-half 3 caps 1899-1901
Born: Lee, Kent, 4 May 1875
Died: Étaples, France, 18 November 1918
Career: St Paul's School, Cambridge University, Richmond, Barbarians, Middlesex.
Debut: v Scotland, Rectory Field, Blackheath, March 1899

Schwarz was better known as a cricketer but won his blue in 1893. He won the first international cap in 1899 and had to wait until 1901 for his final two. He played cricket for Oxfordshire and Middlesex, before emigrating to South Africa, for whom he played test cricket 20 times. During the First World War he served as a major in King's Royal Rifle Corps. He served in the conflict only to die of Spanish flu a week after the Armistice. Schwarz was a member of the Stock Exchange before joining South African Railways. He was then a stockbroker in South Africa and again in London.

338. BAXTER, James
Forward 3 caps 1900
Born: Rock Ferry, Cheshire, 8 June 1870
Died: Rock Ferry, Cheshire, 5 July 1940
Career: Liverpool Institute, Birkenhead Park, Barbarians, Cheshire
Debut: v Wales, Kingsholm, Gloucester, January 1900

'Bim' Baxter had a remarkable record as captain of Birkenhead Park, who only lost 10 of the 85 games he skippered. He won three of his international caps in 1900, and then, between 1920 and 1925, he refereed six internationals, also serving the RFU as selector and president and sitting on the International Board. A manager with the North British and Mercantile Insurance Company, he was the tour manager for England's 1927 tour to Argentina and the British Isles to New Zealand three years later. Baxter also won a sailing silver medal in the 1908 Olympic Games and was Birkenhead president between 1903 and his death.

339. BELL, Frederick James
Forward 1 cap 1900
Born: Cullercoates, North Tyneside, 3 August 1876
Died: Whitley Bay, Northumberland, 7 September 1947
Career: Rockcliff, Northumberland
Debut: v Wales, Kingsholm, Gloucester, January 1900

Bell first played for Rockcliff in 1893, aged 17 and soon won himself county honours with Northumberland, whom he helped win the County Championship in 1898 for the first time. One of the best forwards in Rockcliff's history, he was called up to face Wales at Kingsholm in January 1900 when Lancashire's Charles Allen decided to play for Ireland. It proved to be only cap as Bell joined Hunslet in the Northern Union within a week and would later play for Hull. He worked as a nurseryman and market gardener and displayed at the prestigious Chelsea and Edinburgh Flower shows.

340. BELL, Robert William
Forward 3 caps 1900
Born: Newcastle-Upon-Tyne, Tyne & Wear, 19 December 1875
Died: Newcastle-Upon-Tyne, Tyne & Wear, 9 July 1940
Career: Durham School, Leeds Clergy School, Cambridge University, Northern, Blackheath, Barbarians, Northumberland
Debut: v Wales, Kingsholm, Gloucester, January 1900

Bell won his Cambridge University blue between 1897 and 1899, winning all three England caps a year later while completing his education representing his University and Northern. Robert was ordained in 1901 and held several posts in Newcastle, Benwell, Northumberland, Alnwick, Whittingham, and Gateshead. Bell, who also rowed for Jesus College, became Perpetual Curate of St Hilda's, Darlington, from 1915 until 1931. His last post before retiring was Vicar of Stamfordham, Northumberland, between 1931 and 1939. He returned to his native Newcastle, where he died a year later, aged 64.

341. BRETTARGH, Arthur
Centre 8 caps (3-1t) 1900-1905
Born: Egremont, Cheshire, 22 December 1877
Died: Thornton Heath, Surrey, 12 May 1954
Career: Liverpool OB, Barbarians, Lancashire
Debut: v Wales Kingsholm, Gloucester January 1900

Brettargh was one of 13 new caps when he was selected to make his international debut against Wales at Kingsholm in January 1900, but it would be a further three years until he was given another chance to play on the biggest stage. Brettargh's only international try helped secure a draw with Wales at Richmond the following January. Two months later, he played the first Barbarians fixture against Swansea on Easter Sunday at St Helen's. Brettargh spent all his working life working for Lloyd's Bank on Merseyside, Skipton, West Yorkshire and finally in London, where he lived until his death.

342. COBBY, William
Forward 1 cap 1900
Born: Swine, East Riding of Yorkshire, 5 July 1877
Died: Cottingham, East Riding of Yorkshire, 15 January 1957
Career: Uppingham School, Cambridge University, Hull, Castleford, Hull & East Riding, Barbarians, Yorkshire
Debut: v Wales, Kingsholm, Gloucester, January 1900

Cobby had the unusual distinction in the early rugby history of winning an international cap before a blue when he

Dick Cattell

John Fegan

Frank Mitchell

Charlie Thomas

Tom Dobson

John Ward

Tom Fletcher

Bob Oakes

The English Rugby Who's Who

Frank Stout

James Davidson

Harry Myers

Sir Percy Royds

Percy Stout

Joseph Davidson

Reg Hobbs

was called up to face Wales at Kingsholm in January 1900. It would be 11 months before he played in the Varsity Match. Cobby played for Castleford between 1899 and 1904 before founding Hull and East Riding RFC and serving as vice-president and on the committee of Yorkshire Schools RFC. Cobby was an assistant Master at Southcliffe School, Filey, Yorkshire, Dunchurch Hall School, Rugby and Hymers College, Hull, where he taught sport, Latin, and rugby from 1902 until retiring in 1945.

343. COCKERHAM, Arthur
Forward 1 cap 1900
Born: Little Horton, Bradford, 7 January 1876
Died: Carnforth, Lancashire, 28 May 1923
Career: Bradford Olicana, Yorkshire
Debut: v Wales Kingsholm, Gloucester January 1900

Cockerham made his only England appearance as one of 13 new caps out of 15, and part of an entirely changed pack against Wales in January 1900. He was called up for an unsuccessful trial a month later in place of James Baxter but wasn't. In June 1900, he moved to the Northern Union to play for Manningham, where he was a Joiner and builder. Arthur fought in the Boer War and was a captain in the West Yorkshire Regiment during the First World War and then Ireland, where he was wounded. Later, moving to Carnforth and became the licensee of the Queens Hotel for two years.

344. COOPPER, Sydney Frank
Wing 7 caps (6-2t) 1900-1907
Born: Hoo, Kent 8 October 1878
Died: St Mawes, Cornwall, 16 January 1961
Career: RNEC Keyham, Blackheath, Barbarians, Devon
Debut: v Wales, Kingsholm, Gloucester, January 1900

Coopper would become known as the father of the modern Twickenham. He won his first international cap with his Blackheath team-mate Gerald Gordon-Smith playing on the outside of him. Sydney made a career in the Royal Navy, serving as an engineering officer in the First World War and even survived the HMS Sparrowhawk sinking in the Battle of Jutland. He was stationed on the East Indies Station when offered the chance to succeed C J B Marriott as RFU Secretary in August 1924. He held a post until retiring in July 1947 when he retired to Cornwall.

345. GORDON-SMITH, Gerald Walter
Centre 3 caps (7-1t,1d) 1900
Born: Southampton, Hampshire, February 1877,
Died: Carbis Bay, Cornwall, 23 January 1911
Career: Camborne Students, Redruth, Blackheath, Barbarians, Cornwall, Kent
Debut: v Wales Kingsholm, Gloucester January 1900

Gordon-Smith was born in Southampton on the south coast but moved to Camborne to study at the School of Mines, and during his time in Cornwall, he excelled at rugby and association football. But despite his links with Cornwall, he was registered with Blackheath when he won all three of his international caps in 1900, scoring all of his points in a win over Ireland. After completing his course at Camborne, Gordon-Smith moved to Transvaal but returned to Cornwall a year before his death when his health started to fail, and he died at his father-in-law's home.

346. JARMAN, John Wallace
Forward 1 cap 1900
Born: Towcester, Northamptonshire, 17 July 1872
Died: Vancouver, Canada, 15 September 1950
Career: Knowle Bristol, Gloucestershire, British Team
Debut: v Wales, Kingsholm, Gloucester, January 1900

'Wally' Jarman was uncapped by England when he was selected to tour Australia with the British Team in 1899, and it wasn't until the following January that he won his only international cap against Wales. The Bristol captain was the first player to be capped from the club he joined from Knowle. A representative for the chocolate company J S Fry and Son, he moved to Canada in 1920 and then became a manager of Cadbury-Fry in Alberta for many years until his retirement in 1939. After this, Jarman moved to Vancouver, where he lived until his death.

347. MARSDEN, George Herbert
Fly-half 3 caps 1900
Born: Morley, Yorkshire, 16 October 1880
Died: Lytham-St-Annes, Lancashire, 7 July 1948
Career: Morley, Yorkshire
Debut: v Wales, Kingsholm, Gloucester, January 1900

Marsden started his career with his hometown club Morley in Yorkshire and captained the county, winning all three England caps in 1900 when they finished second to Wales. But like many other players, he chose to join the Northern Union, signing for Bradford Northern, which ended his England career. The clerk of electrical works injury ended his career in 1907. Working for Marsden, Drury, and Whitehead Solicitors in Preston. Marsden was a founding member of Fylde Rugby Club in 1919. He spent 35 years in Lytham-St-Annes as a cashier with Herbert Joyce and Sons.

348. NICHOLSON, Elliot Tennant
Wing 2 caps (3-1t) 1900
Born: Wavertree, Lancashire, 13 December 1871
Died: Hoylake, Wirral, 1 December 1953
Career: Liverpool College, Liverpool, Birkenhead Park, Cheshire
Debut: v Wales, Kingsholm, Gloucester, January 1900

Nicholson was described as a 'very fast wing' when the British Isles selected him for their 1899 tour of Australia despite not being capped by his country. He played in the final two tests and appeared out of the selector's plans the following season. But when George Robinson pulled out of the opening game against Wales, he was called up and scored a try on his debut. Nicholson was a chartered accountant like his father. He spent the whole of his professional life working for Harmond, Banner and Son and was a senior partner on his retirement in 1945.

349. REYNOLDS, Shirley
Forward 4 caps 1900-1901
Born: Lahore, India, 3 March 1873
Died: Epsom, Surrey, 9 January 1946
Career: Christ's Hospital, Richmond, Barbarians
Debut: v Wales Kingsholm, Gloucester January 1900

Reynolds was born in India but educated at Christ's Hospital and remained their only England international for well over a century until Wasps second row Joe Launchbury was capped in 2012. After leaving school, he joined Richmond, where he was eventually named captain and made his international debut against Wales in January 1900 after impressing in a trial a month earlier. Reynolds was ever-present in the first season of his international career following a defeat in Ireland a year later after another trial appearance. A stockbroker's clerk, he lived in New Malden until his death at a hospital in Epsom.

350. SCOTT, Charles Tillard
Forward, 4 caps 1900-1901
Born: Wimbledon, London, 26 August 1877
Died: Market Harborough, Leicestershire, 6 November 1965
Career: Tonbridge School, Cheltenham College, Cambridge University, The London Hospital, Blackheath, Barbarians, Kent
Debut: v Wales Kingsholm, Gloucester January 1900

Educated at Tonbridge and Cheltenham, Scott won his Cambridge University blue in 1899 and played for

Cambridgeshire CCC before finishing his medical studies at the London Hospital, where he was a house physician and helped win the Hospitals' Cup and was also a member of the Kent team that won the County Championship before moving to Market Harborough to join a private medical practice from which he retired in 1956. Scott also served as Deputy Medical Officer of Heath to Market Harborough Urban Council and then for Oxenden Rural Council.

351. ALEXANDER Harry
Forward 7 caps (7-2c,1p) 1900-1902
Born: Oxton, Cheshire, 6 January 1879
Died: Hulluch, France, 17 October 1915
Career: Bromborough School, Uppingham School, Oxford University, Birkenhead Park, Cheshire, Richmond, Barbarians, Middlesex
Debut: v Ireland Athletic Ground Richmond February 1900

Cambridge University blue Alexander won his caps representing Birkenhead Park and captained England against Wales at Blackheath in January 1902 in his penultimate international. After moving to Middlesex, he played for Richmond and was captain at the time of his retirement in 1906. He was also a county standard hockey player, a scratch golfer, a high-class ice skater and a professional singer. A schoolmaster at Stanmore Park Preparatory School, he joined the Grenadier Guards after the outbreak of the First World War, making the ultimate sacrifice on his 13th day of active service and was killed in action aged 36.

352. MARQUIS, John Campbell
Scrum-half 2 caps 1900
Born: Woodchurch, Cheshire, 15 February 1876
Died: Birkenhead, Cheshire, 28 January 1928
Career: Birkenhead Park, Barbarians, Cheshire
Debut: v Ireland, Athletic Ground, Richmond, February 1900

Marquis was the son of a Scottish corn merchant who was educated at Birkenhead School and Cambridge University. Marquis was described as a great half-back who was fierce in attack and dour in defence'. He played for Birkenhead, who formed the backbone of the Cheshire County side, playing alongside fellow internationals Bim Baxter and Harry Alexander. He was a solicitor with Alsop, Stevens and Co in Liverpool, then assistant to the Liverpool Registrar, High Court, Chancery and Admiralty Division. Marquis then joined the Lancashire and Yorkshire Railway and was Divisional Solicitor for the L.M.S Railway Company in Manchester.

353. TODD, Alexander Findlater
Forward 2 caps 1900
Born: Forest Hill, London 20 September 1873
Died: Ypres, Belgium, 20 April 1915
Career: Mill Hill School, Cambridge University, Blackheath, Barbarians, Kent
Debut: v Ireland, Athletic Ground, Richmond, February 1900

Todd captained his school, Mill Hill, at both rugby and association football and won a blue between 1893 and 1895 when attending Cambridge University. After leaving, he played for Blackheath, The Barbarians and captained Kent. He was a member of the British Team that toured South Africa in 1896, and it was four years later that he won both of his England caps. After serving in the Second Boer War, Todd married Alice Crean, the brother of Ireland international Tom. A wine merchant but, in 1914, joined the Reserve Battalion of the Norfolk Regiment and died of injuries at the Battle of Hill 60, Gallipoli.

354. LUXMOORE, RT Hon Arthur Fairfax Charles Croyndon KC PC Kt JP
Forward 2 caps 1900-1901
Born: Hendon, London, 27 February 1876
Died: Hammersmith, London, 25 September 1944
Career: King's School Canterbury, Cambridge University, Richmond, Barbarians, Kent
Debut: v Scotland, Inverleith, Edinburgh, March 1900

Luxmoore won a double blue in Rugby and Cricket. He joined Richmond in 1900, a year after being called to the bar. A year later, he won the first of his two international caps, and after winning his second in 1901, he set about building a successful legal practice. He took silk in 1919 and was a Liberal candidate for the Isle of Thanet in the 1924 General Election. A year earlier, Luxmoore became a judge and, in 1938, became the Lord Justice of Appeal and Privy Councilor. Luxmore liked knitting socks after a hard day in court.

355. ELLIOT, Edgar William
Wing 4 caps (6-2t) 1901-1904
Born: Sunderland, Tyne & Wear 9 July 1878
Died: Vancouver, British Columbia, 3 February 1931
Career: Wellington College, Sunderland, Barbarians, Durham Counties
Debut: v Wales Arms Park Cardiff January 1901

Elliot was Charles Henry's nephew and represented Sunderland and Durham, just as his uncle had done before him. Edgar made three appearances in 1901 before serving in his country in the Boer War. He would have to wait until January 1904 to win his last cap, scoring two tries against Wales at Leicester after replacing Rockcliffe's Tom Simpson. Elliot was also a top-class cricketer, spending a decade playing for Durham in the Minor Counties Championship. A soda mine manager in California, then manager for the British Columbia Rock Gas Company when he died.

356. FLETCHER, Nigel Corbet OBE
Forward 4 caps 1901-1903
Born: Pancras London, 3 August 1877
Died: Hampstead, Middlesex, 21 December 1951
Career: Merchant Taylors' School, Cambridge University, OMT, University College Hospital, Barbarians, Middlesex
Debut: v Wales, Arms Park, Cardiff, January 1901

Merchant Taylors' School-educated Fletcher won a classical scholarship to study at Cambridge, and won his blue between 1897 and 1899. He completed his medical studies at University College Hospital but was registered to Old Merchant Taylors' when he won his caps. An ever-present in 1901, he had to wait until March 1903 to win his first cap against Scotland. Fletcher was a house physician and senior obstetric assistant at UCH, London and in 1906, he started practice in Hampstead, where he worked until within a few days of his death. Fletcher was also Surgeon-in-Chief of the St John Ambulance Brigade.

357. GIBSON, Charles Osborne Provis MC DL
Forward 1 cap 1901
Born: Gateshead, Tyne & Wear 27 October 1876
Died: Stocksfield, Northumberland, 9 November 1931
Career: Uppingham School, Oxford University, Northern, Barbarians, Northumberland
Debut: v Wales Arms Park Cardiff January 1901

Gibson was the middle of three brothers to play for England, but despite attending Oxford University, he never won a blue. When he won his only cap against Wales in Cardiff, Gibson was one of ten new boys but was never selected again after England got soundly beaten. During the First World War he served in the Northumberland Fusiliers (TA), winning a Military Cross in June 1916 and being Mentioned in Despatches in 1915 and 1918. After the War, he was a lieutenant-Colonel in the Territorial Army. Gibson was a solicitor and a partner of the Newcastle law firm Clayton and Gibson.

358. GRAHAM, David
Forward 1 cap 1901
Born: Aspatria, Cumbria June 1875
Died: Carlisle, Cumbria, 28 January 1962
Career: Aspatria Hornets, Aspatria, Keswick, Rochdale, New Brighton, Cumberland
Debut: v Wales Arms Park Cardiff January 1901

Graham was from an Aspatria farming family and, at the time, it was one of the best rugby areas in the country, boasting half a dozen teams. Graham won his only cap against Wales in January 1901 while playing in two further trial games didn't produce any further caps. His last county appearance was for Cumberland against South Africans at Carlisle United's Devonshire Park. Graham was a teacher and left Aspatria in 1896 to take up an appointment in Lancashire, eventually becoming headmaster at Royton Central Council School. And was a member of the Lancashire Rugby Union selection committee for two decades.

359. O'NEILL, Arthur
Forward 3 caps 1901
Born: Teignmouth Devon, 14 April 1878
Died: Brighton, East Sussex, 12 May 1954
Career: Torquay Athletic, Bart's Hospital, Devon
Debut: v Wales, Arms Park, Cardiff, January 1901

O'Neill started his rugby career at Torquay Athletic and was called into the England side in January 1901 in place of the injured John Daniell. He retained his place for the following two games but wasn't ever selected again. O'Neill captained Devon before moving to London to study medicine at Bart's Hospital. O'Neill returned to Teignmouth after qualifying as a doctor in 1907 but then spent the rest of his career working at the Napsbury Psychiatric Hospital in St Albans, which was also known as the Middlesex County Asylum, until retiring to Devon before moving to Sussex just before his death.

360. ROBERTS, Ernest William OBE
Forward 6 caps 1901-1907
Born: Lowestoft, Suffolk, 14 November 1878
Died: Manchester, Lancashire, 19 November 1933
Career: Framlingham School, Merchant Taylors School Crosby, RNEC Keyham, RNC Dartmouth, Royal Navy, Barbarians, Devon
Debut: v Wales, Arms Park, Cardiff, January 1901

Roberts made his career out of the Royal Navy and was the first member of the services to captain an international team when, in March 1907, he replaced John Green in a bid to end a dismal home record of one win in 23 years against Scotland. The Calcutta Cup returned to Edinburgh, and Ernest was never selected again. He stayed in the Navy and reached the rank of Rear Admiral. During the First World War, Roberts served on Grand Fleet destroyers. He was a member of the RFU committee and died in his sleep following a selection meeting.

361. SAGAR, John Warburton
Full-back 2 caps 1901
Born: Trimdon, County Durham, 6 December 1878
Died: Bournemouth, Dorset, 10 January 1941
Career: Durham School, Cambridge University, Castleford, Wakefield, Barbarians, Yorkshire, Durham Counties.
Debut: v Wales, Arms Park, Cardiff, January 1901

Sagar was a brilliant full-back, educated at Durham School and then Cambridge University, where he won a blue in 1899 and 1900. And was still at the university when he made both international appearances in 1901 before losing his place to Herbert Gamlin. The former captain of Wakefield, he was a private tutor and then taught at Loretto School before joining the Sedan Civil Service. Sagar was promoted several times during his 21 years of service and acted as Governor of Kordofan province between 1917 and 1922, then Wadi, Halfa, Sudan between 1922 and 1924, when he retired to Bournemouth, where he died from heart trouble.

362. SMITH, Charles Albert
Wing 1 cap 1901
Born: Westgate, Gloucestershire, 18 July 1878
Died: Gloucester, Gloucestershire, 20 January 1940
Career: Gloucester, Gloucestershire
Debut: v Wales Arms Park Cardiff January 1901

'Whacker' Smith was one of 10 new caps when he made his only international appearance against Wales in Cardiff in January 1901. England were hammered as they were in their other two games that season, and he was never selected again. The following season, he broke the Gloucester club record after scoring eight tries against Clifton. After winning his cap, Smith turned down a £50 approach from Wigan, who offered a three-year contract to switch codes. He was a docker who, for many years, was employed by local timber merchants J Romans & Co Ltd until his death from influenza.

363. VIVYAN, Elliott John
Centre 4 caps (13 -3t, 2c) 1901-1904
Born: Stoke Damerel, Devon, 6 January 1879
Died: Bedlington, Cheshire, 3 December 1935
Career: Stoke School Devonport, Devonport Albion, RNE College, Liverpool, Waterloo, Devon
Debut: v Wales Arms Park Cardiff January 1901

The astonishing speed of Vivyan made him one of the best wingers of his time. After winning his first England cap, he helped Devon win the County Championship in 1901. Despite being ignored by the selectors for the next three years, he became the first player to score ten points in an international when England beat Ireland with two tries and two conversions. He turned down a Lancashire Northern Union club, who offered him £800, and later became a leading referee. Vivyan was an engineer fitter's apprentice who became a dockyard draughtsman before moving to Birkenhead to work for Cammell, Laird, and Co. as an assistant to the Admiralty Overseer.

364. WALTON, Ernest John
Scrum-half 4 caps 1901-1902
Born: York, North Yorkshire, 23 November 1879
Died: Waterford, Ireland, 8 April 1947
Career: St Peter's School York, Old Dewsburians, Oxford University, Castleford, Barbarians, Yorkshire
Debut: v Wales, Arms Park, Cardiff, January 1901

Walton was already playing for Castleford and Yorkshire when he won his university colours in 1900. And was still at Oxford when he made his England debut partnering Reggie Schwarz against Wales at Cardiff in January 1901. After retaining his place, he missed the following two games but was called up alongside Bernard Oughtred for two more caps a season later. After leaving university, he returned to play for Castleford and was captain when they retained the Yorkshire Cup in 1902. Walton then left the country and moved to Far East to work for the Bombay-Burmah Trading Company in Bangkok and later in Cork.

365. HALL, Charles John
Forward 2 caps 1901
Born: Gloucester, Gloucestershire, September 1874
Died: Oxford, Oxfordshire, 14 November 1944
Career: Gloucester
Debut: v Ireland, Lansdowne Road, Dublin, February 1901

Hall was one of seven brothers who played for Gloucester. They even formed their own sevens team and were unbeaten. Known as 'Nobby', he was a courageous forward who won his two caps in 1901, and despite trialling a year later, he didn't win any more. He worked as a lighterman at Gloucester docks and became a licensee running the Railway Inn and then the Market House. Hall moved to Sharpness, where he was mine host at the Sharpness Hotel for over 30 years and then the Plough Inn, Sutton Courtney, Abingdon, when he died.

366. WOOD, Robert Dudley
Forward 3 caps 1901-1903
Born: Liverpool, 3 January 1873
Died: Bidston, Cheshire, 23 May 1950
Career: Liverpool Old Boys, Barbarians, Lancashire
Debut: v Ireland, Lansdowne Road, February 1901

Liverpool-born Wood won his first cap against Ireland in February 1901 while the nation was still in mourning following the death of Queen Victoria. With England making wholesale changes in almost every game, it would be another two years before he got another chance. But successive defeats against Wales and Ireland saw his international career come to an end. Wood decided on a career as a mechanical engineer and later became a consulting engineer who advised many of the largest firms in the country about the erection of oil and spirit tanks.

367. COX, Norman Simpson
Centre 1 cap 1901
Born: Sunderland, Tyne & Wear, 3 September 1877
Died: Sunderland, Tyne & Wear, 29 March 1930
Career: Repton School, Sunderland, Barbarians, Durham Counties
Debut: v Scotland, Rectory Field, Blackheath, March 1901

Cox was the lynchpin of the Sunderland back division, captaining the club in 1901 when he won his only international cap and helping them win back-to-back Durham County Cup titles in 1903 and 1904. He was a director and company secretary of the Sunderland Gas Company for sixteen years, taking over from his father, who had run the firm for 60 years. Cox was also secretary of the North of England Gas Managers' Association and a Sunderland and South Shields Water Company director until his death and was captain of Wearmouth Golf Club.

368. EDGAR, Charles Stuart
Forward 1 cap 1901
Born: West Derby, Cheshire 1876
Died: Chester, Cheshire, 26 May 1949
Career: Birkenhead Park, Barbarians, Cheshire
Debut: v Scotland, Rectory Field, Blackheath, March 1901

Edgar, the son of a Scottish shipbroker, was already a member of the Barbarians club when he won his only England cap against Scotland at Blackheath in March 1901. Along with Birkenhead Park team-mates 'Toggie' Kendall and Harry Alexander, they couldn't prevent England from losing a third successive match. Edgar was Honorary Treasurer of the Cheshire Rugby Union and a Second lieutenant in the Liverpool Regiment during the First World War. Edgar worked in the shipping industry for 40 years as an owner and director of the Isle of Man Steam Packet Company and died in a car crash after having a heart attack.

369. HARTLEY, Major Bernard Charles CB OBE
Forward 2 caps 1901-1902
Born: Woodford, Essex, 16 March 1879
Died: Chichester, West Sussex, 24 April 1960
Career: Dulwich College, Cambridge University, Blackheath, Barbarians, Sussex, Kent
Debut: v Scotland, Rectory Field, Blackheath, March 1901

'Jock' Hartley first made name his name at Cambridge University, where he won a double blue in rugby and athletics in the hammer, and he twice rowed for Jesus College at Henley. He also represented Cambridge University and The Army on the RFU committee. Hartley was an England selector who managed the British Isles in South Africa in 1937. He was also RFU President and sat on the International Board. A stockbroker during the First World War, he served in the Hertfordshire Regiment and was gassed and wounded. Later, Hartley became secretary of the Army Sports Council Board and the National Playing Fields Association.

370. KENDALL, Percy Dale
Scrum-half 3 caps 1901-1903
Born: Prescot Lancashire 21 August 1878
Died: KIA Ypres 25 January 1915
Career: Tonbridge School, Cambridge University, Blackheath, Birkenhead Park, Cheshire
Debut: v Scotland, Rectory Field, Blackheath, March 1901

'Toggie' Kendall developed into a useful scrum-half at Tonbridge School before completing his education at Cambridge but never won a blue. After returning to his native Merseyside, he became a solicitor with Banks, Kendall, and Taylor, then started playing for Birkenhead Park. Kendall captained England against Scotland at Richmond in March 1903, winning the last of his three caps, although he would captain Cheshire against New Zealand in 1905. At the outbreak of the First World War, he enlisted in King's Liverpool Regiment and was posted to the 1/10th Battalion and commissioned as a lieutenant but was killed by a sniper.

371. OUGHTRED, Bernard
Fly-half 6 caps
Born: West Hartlepool, County Durham, 22 August 1888
Died: Barrow-in-Furness, Cumbria, 12 November 1949
Career: West Hartlepool GS, King Edward VI School Birmingham, Old Edwardians, Hartlepool Rovers, Hull & East Riding, Furness, Barrow, Barbarians, Westmorland, Durham Counties, Yorkshire.
Debut: v Scotland, Rectory Field, Blackheath, March 1901

Oughtred was the only one of three players and officials to survive after contracting typhoid fever during England's visit to Dublin in February 1903. Reggie Forrest and ex-RFU President RS Whalley weren't quite as lucky, it claimed their lives. Bernard's career took him all over the north of England and enabled him to be capped by three counties. After serving at Irving's Shipbuilding Yard, Oughtred was a naval architect and was attached to the Royal Navy during the First World War. He was present at the Battle of Jutland and later became a ship broker in Barrow.

372. WESTON, Henry Thomas Franklin JP
Forward 1 cap 1901
Born: Yardley Gobion, Northamptonshire, 9 July 1869
Died: Yardley Gobion, Northamptonshire, 5 April 1955
Career: Northampton, East Midlands
Debut: v Scotland, Rectory Field, Blackheath, March 1901

Weston was a stalwart member of the Northampton club and, at 31, was the first Northampton player to be capped when he played against Scotland at Blackheath in March 1901 and captained his club the following year. Weston also played cricket for Northamptonshire in the Minor Counties Championship in 1904. A farmer at the Elms, Yardley Gobion, where he was born and had been in the family since 1497. Weston served on 42 different authorities and committees during nearly 70 years of public service. A county magistrate from 1917 sitting at Towcester and Stony Stratford, his son Billy also played for England.

373. DOBSON, Denys Douglas
Forward 6 caps (9-3t)
Born: Douglas, Isle of Man, 28 October 1880
Died: Ngama, Nyasaland, 10 July 1916
Career: Newton College, Cheltenham College, Oxford University, Newton Abbot, Devonport Albion, Barbarians, London Welsh, Devon
Debut: v Wales, Rectory Field, Blackheath, January 1902

Dobson won an Oxford University blue between 1899 and 1901 and played for Newton Abbott when he scored a try on his England debut against Wales at Blackheath in January 1902. He toured Australia and New Zealand with the British Team in 1904, playing in all four tests and was sent off against Northern District in Newcastle, New South Wales, for using 'obscene language' although he was later cleared. Dobson was a member of the Colonial Civil Service and was killed by a charging rhinoceros while working as a colonial officer in Ngama.

374. FRASER, George William Frederick
Forward 5 caps 1902-1903
Born: Fulham, London, 15 September 1878
Died: Clewer Within, Berkshire, 20 August 1950
Career: Godolphin School Hammersmith, Richmond, Barbarians, Surrey, Middlesex
Debut: v Wales, Rectory Field, Blackheath, January 1902

Fraser was one of six new caps in the forward pack when he made his England debut against Wales in January 1902 and retained his place in the side for the next four games. Fraser also rowed for the London Rowing Club, serving them as vice captain and president. He was also the President of the Marlow Regatta and steward at the Henley Royal Regatta. Fraser was a Member of the Stock Exchange between 1904 and 1949. During the First World War, he served with the Royal Naval Volunteer Reserve and Royal Naval Air Service and was awarded an OBE and French Legion d'honneur.

375. JEWITT, John Henry
Lock 1 cap 1902
Born: Stockton-on-Tees, County Durham, 5 October 1878
Died: Vancouver, British Columbia, 8 June 1930
Career: Swansea, Hartlepool Rovers, Durham County
Debut: v Wales, Rectory Field, Blackheath, January 1902

Jewitt was reckoned to be one of the fastest forwards of his time and was given his chance for a trial at late notice. He took his opportunity and was selected against Wales at Rectory Field, Blackheath. It has been claimed that his selection was a case of mistaken identity, but Jewitt became the first reserve for the next two games against Scotland and Ireland. Something of a man of mystery, he switched codes by the start of the following season and played for South Shields, then Broughton Rangers and Durham in the Northern Union. John became an inspector of detectives.

376. NICHOLAS, Philip Leach
Wing 1 cap 1902
Born: Monmouth, Wales, 30 May 1876
Died: Barnstaple, Devon, 31 January 1952
Career: Monmouth School, Oxford University, Honiton Exeter, Barbarians, Devon, Gloucestershire
Debut: v Wales, Rectory Field, Blackheath, January 1902

Nicholas played for Monmouth School's XV aged 15 and was captain for two years before attending Oxford University, where he won his blue between 1897 and 1899. He was a versatile player who played everywhere, from full-back to the pack. Nicholas was an Exeter player when he won his only cap against Wales in January 1902 and helped Devon win the County Championship. A schoolmaster at All Hallows, Honiton, for 14 years, was also assistant chaplain after being ordained in 1908. Then, in 1915, he became Vicar of Bishops Tawton until his retirement in October 1948.

377. RAPHAEL, John Edward
Centre 9 caps (3-1t) 1902-1906
Born: Brussels, Belgium, 30 April 1882
Died: Remy, Belgium, 11 June 1917
Career: Merchant Taylors' School, OMT, Oxford University, Surrey
Debut: v Wales, Rectory Field, Blackheath, January 1902

Raphael was the son of Jewish multi-millionaire financier Albert Raphael and excelled at rugby, cricket, and water polo while at Oxford University. A lawyer who was the captain of the British Isles's 1910 tour to Argentina, his dream was to enter Parliament but he was an unsuccessful Liberal candidate for Croydon. During the First World War, Raphael returned to his native Belgium as a lieutenant in the King's Royal Rifle Corps but died of wounds after being hit by a German shell during the Battle of Messines. A highly-rated batsman who played cricket for London County, Surrey, Oxford University, and MCC.

378. TOSSWILL, Major Leonard Robert OBE
Forward 3 caps 1902
Born: Exeter, Devon, 12 January 1880
Died: Roehampton, Surrey, 3 October 1932
Career: Marlborough College, Marlborough Nomads, Bart's Hospital, Exeter, Barbarians, Devon
Debut: v Wales, Rectory Field, Blackheath, January 1902

Exeter's Tosswill made all three of his international appearances in 1902, and after qualifying from Bartholemew's Hospital in 1903, he continued his studies in Berlin and Vienna which may explain his not playing again. He became an assistant medical officer for the Public Health Department of London County Council and then a school medical officer for Devon County Council. During the First World War, Tosswill was a major in the Royal Army Medical Corps and was twice mentioned in dispatches before joining the Ministry of Pensions. He was one of the early BBC broadcasters on rugby before his death at St Mary's Hospital, Roehampton following an operation.

379. WILLCOCKS, Thomas Henry
Forward 1 cap 1902
Born: Buckfastleigh, Devon, Q2 1877
Died: Plymouth, Devon, 20 April 1958
Career: Buckfastleigh, Plymouth Albion, Devon
Debut: v Wales Rectory Field Blackheath January 1902

Willcocks started his rugby career in his home town, Buckfastleigh, before moving to Devon's first city, where he became the first player capped from Plymouth Albion to be capped as one of six new caps in the forwards when England entertained Wales at Rectory Field, Blackheath, in January 1902. A narrow defeat for England saw him dropped after just one game in favour of John Daniell, who was made captain after just one cap, and was never selected again. Willcocks, a tan yard labourer, became a blacksmith in Devonport Dockyard and lived in St Budeaux, Plymouth, until his death.

380. WILLIAMS, Samuel George
Forward 7 caps (6-2ts)
Born: Stoke Damerel, Devon, 14 May 1880
Died: Devonport, Devon, 19 March 1955
Career: Devonport Albion, Plymouth Albion, Devon
Debut: v Wales, Rectory Field, Blackheath, January 1902

Williams started his rugby career with Devonport Albion in 1900 and quickly made a name for himself, coming to the attention of representative selectors. He won his first cap two years later as one of three players drawn from clubs in his home city in the side which lost to Wales, and he scored tries in his next two appearances in wins over Ireland and Scotland. He was a member of the Devon side who beat Durham to win the 1906 County Championship, drawing with the same opposition a year to jointly retain their crown. Samuel worked as a master decorator.

381. HARDWICK, Peter Fenton
Forward 8 caps 1902-1904
Born: Tynemouth, Tyne & Wear, 15 May 15, 1877
Died: North Shields, Tyne & Wear, 13 February 1924
Career: North Shields West End, Rockcliff, Percy Park, Northumberland
Debut: v Ireland, Welford Road, Leicester, February 1902

Hardwick started his rugby career with North Shields West End Rugby Club in 1897. After they were disbanded a year later, he had a short spell with Rockcliff before joining Percy Park and playing for them until 1908. He became one of the best all-round forwards of his day. A life member of Percy Park he sat on the selection committee until the Smith's Dock Rugby Club was formed. Hardwick was employed as a foreman caulker at the Bull Ring department of Smith's Dock Compan, and during the First World War, he served as superintendent of repair of damaged warships.

382. SIMPSON, Thomas
Wing 11 caps (9-3t) 1902-1909
Born: Newcastle-upon-Tyne, Northumberland, 8 August 1881
Died: Whitley Bay, Northumberland, 25 June 1956
Career: Rockcliff, Northumberland, Barbarians
Debut: v Scotland, Inverleith, Edinburgh, March 1902

Simpson was a speedy winger in the balmy days of Rockcliff. He was born in Newcastle-upon-Tyne but lived in Whitley Bay for 72 years. During his younger days, he was The North's amateur sprinting champion. Simpson won his England caps over seven years and scored a try on his final appearance against France at Welford Road in January 1909. An accountant with North East Railway Company until he retired, he was Northumberland secretary between 1925 and 1932 until Sir Laurie Edwards, patron of Rockcliff, took over. Simpson was a life member of Rockcliff until his sudden death.

383. BRADLEY, Robert
Forward 1 cap 1903
Born: Crossgate, Durham 15 March 1873
Died: Seaton Carew, County Durham, 3 August 1952
Career: West Hartlepool, Durham Counties
Debut: v Wales, St Helen's, Swansea, January 1903

After catching the eye playing for Durham in a trial game against the Rest of England, Bradley was the first policeman to play for England and was selected to win his only cap against Wales in Swansea. He spent nearly 30 years in the Force, 12 in West Hartlepool and Seaton Carew. After being promoted to sergeant, Bradley was transferred to Middleton-in-Teesdale and Felling-on-Tyne and then Darlington, where he lived for some time in retirement. Bradley also played cricket for Thornaby, Stockton, West Hartlepool, and Season Carew, where he died at the home of his niece.

384. CARTWRIGHT, Vincent Henry
Forward 14 caps (8-4c) 1903-1906
Born: Nottingham, Nottinghamshire, 10 September 1882
Died: Loughborough, Leicestershire, 25 November 1965
Career: Rugby School, Nottingham, Oxford University, Harlequins, Barbarians, East Midlands
Debut: v Wales, St Helen's, Swansea, January 1903

'Lump' Cartwright captained Rugby School and then Oxford University four years later after playing in each of the previous three Varsity matches. He won his first caps at Oxford before becoming the first Nottingham player capped. Cartwright was appointed captain for the 1905 defeat to the All Blacks and led England throughout the following season. He served in the Royal Marines during the First World War, winning a DSO and Croix de Guerre. A solicitor with Freeth, Rawson and Cartwright, he played cricket for Notts and later served as a clerk to Nottingham City magistrates. He was also the 30th president of the RFU.

385. DUTHIE, James
Forward 1 cap 1903
Born: Hartlepool, County Durham, March 1881
Died: West Hartlepool, County Durham, 29 March 1946
Career: West Hartlepool, Winlaton Vulcans, Durham
Debut: v Wales, St Helen's, Swansea January 1903

Duthie played for Hartlepool at a time when they were able to field no less than seven internationals. He won his only cap against Wales in Swansea in January 1903, but a heavy defeat saw him never selected again, although he did have a trial for The North against the South in December 1908. Duthie continued to play for Durham until 1910 and club rugby until just before the outbreak of the First World War. He was a shipyard worker for Irvins Ship Buildings Company in Haverton Hill on the Tees until 1945, when he had to retire because of heart trouble, which caused his death.

386. HULME, Frank Croft
Fly-half 4 caps 1903-1905
Born: Oxton, Cheshire, 31 August 1881
Died: Birkenhead, Cheshire, 5 September 1935
Career: Birkenhead School, Birkenhead Park, Blackheath, Liverpool, Barbarians, Cheshire
Debut: v Wales St Helen's, Swansea, January 1903

Hulme learnt his rugby at Birkenhead School before joining Birkenhead Park in 1898, where he would form a dangerous half-back combination with fellow international 'Toggie' Kendall. He made his debut for Cheshire when he was 19 and would later captain the North in a trial match. Hulme was selected for the 1904 British Team tour to Australia and New Zealand. After retiring in 1910, he was a Cheshire selector for 17 years and served Birkenhead as honorary secretary and Vice President while working for P J H Rayner and Co. produce brokers and then wine merchants Bushall, Maples and Co.

387. MILES, John Henry
Wing 1 cap 1903
Born: Grimsby, Lincolnshire, 19 January 1880
Died: Sheffield, Yorkshire, 23 January 1953
Career: Medway Street School Leicester, Medway Athletic, Stoneygate, Leicester, Northampton, Midlands
Debut: v Wales, St Helen's Swansea, January 1903

Miles played for Medway Athletic and Stoneygate before joining Leicester, announcing himself with a hat-trick against Wandsworth in September 1899. He became the first in a long line of Leicester players to be capped when he replaced flu victim Reggie Forrest, who was to tragically die just two months later, for the trip to Swansea to face Wales in January 1903. Miles won the Midland Counties Cup in 1902, 1904 and 1904 before leaving the club because of business commitments. A farmer and later a chemist's valuer who became a referee, taking charge of three internationals between 1913 and 1914.

388. SPOONER, Reginald Herbert
Centre 1 cap 1903
Born: Litherland, Lancashire, 21 October 1880
Died: Lincoln, Lincolnshire, 2 October 1961
Career: Marlborough College, Marlborough Nomads, Liverpool, Lancashire
Debut: v Wales, St Helen's, Swansea, January 1903

Spooner made his name at Marlborough College as a brilliant schoolboy sportsman excelling at rugby and cricket. He won his only international cap against Wales in January 1903 after playing for the North against the South in a trial match a month earlier. He was better known as one of the best cricketers of the Edwardian era, playing for Lancashire and England, winning ten test caps. Spooner was a cricketer of the year in 1905. He served in the Manchester Regiment in the Boer War, became a captain in the Lincolnshire Regiment during the First World War, and was a land agent for the Earl of Londesborough.

389. HEPPEL, Walter George
Prop 1 cap 1903
Born: Weston-Super-Mare, Somerset, 2 January 1877
Died: Reading, Berkshire, 4 October 1939
Career: Devonport Albion, Devon
Debut: v Ireland, Lansdowne Road, Dublin, February 1903

Heppel took part in his only international trial, the South against the North, in December 1902. He must have done enough to impress because he was called up to win his only international cap against Ireland at Lansdowne Road in February 1903, partnering with Devonport Services teammate Sam Williams in the front row. Heppel was selected for a trial in December 1903 but was posted abroad by the Royal Navy, whom he joined as an assistant engineer in June 1896. A noted golfer, he served in the Royal Navy until retiring with the rank of Engineer Rear-Admiral in June 1928.

390. HILL, Sir Basil Alexander KBE CB DSO JP
Forward 9 caps (10-5c) 1903-1907
Born: Broughty Ferry, Cheshire, 23 April 1880
Died: Coupar Angus, Perth, 31 July 1960
Career: RNEC Keyham, The Army, United Services Portsmouth, Blackheath, Barbarians, Kent
Debut: v Ireland Lansdowne Road, Dublin February 1903

Hill was the most famous Royal Marine to have been capped by England. He captained England in their first-ever game on home soil in January 1907 when he kicked five conversations. He also helped Kent win the County Championship. He enlisted in the Royal Marine Artillery in 1897 and then the Army Ordnance Department in 1908, eventually becoming a Major General. During the First World War, he saw action at the Siege of Tsingtao and Gallipoli. Hill represented the Army on the RFU board and was RFU President. He was Colonel Commandant of the Royal Electrical and Mechanical Engineers during the World War.

391. BARRETT, Edward Ivo Medhurst CIE
Centre 1 cap 1903
Born: Churt, Surrey, 22 June 1879
Died: Boscombe, Dorset, 10 July 1950
Career: Cheltenham College, Lennox, RMC Sandhurst, The Army, Surrey
Debut: v Scotland, Athletic Ground, Richmond, March 1903

Barrett was wounded while serving with the 2nd Lancashire Fusiliers in the Boer War, but he returned and won his only cap against Scotland at The Athletic Ground Richmond in March 1903. But he was best known as a cricketer playing for Hampshire between 1895 and 1925. He also excelled at golf and hockey. Barrett was Deputy Commissioner of Police in Shanghai between 1907 and 1926 and commissioner between 1926 and 1929. He then worked for the Ministry of Aircraft Production. During the Second World War, he was second in command of an internment camp in Norfolk and died following an accident in Boscombe.

392. BUTCHER, Walter Vincent
Fly-half 7 caps 1903-1905
Born: Tooting Graveney, Surrey 2 February 1878
Died: Bexhill, East Sussex, 26 August 1957
Career: Carlisle Grammar School, Bristol, Streatham and Croydon, Royal Engineers, Barbarians, Gloucestershire
Debut: v Scotland, Athletic Ground, Richmond, March 1903

Butcher learnt to play rugby at Carlisle Grammar School but was an unknown when he arrived at Bristol in 1902 after going to work in Chipping Sodbury. Within months, he played for Gloucester. He returned to London almost immediately, joining Streatham and Croydon, partnering Pat Hancock at half-back, and winning his first international cap in March 1903. He played cricket for Surrey CCC seconds and was a railway engineer all his adult life at home and for Indian State Railways. Butcher joined the Royal Engineers during the First World War and reached the rank of major.

393. DILLON, Edward Wentworth
Centre 4 caps 1904-1905
Born: Penge, Kent, 15 February 1881
Died: Totteridge, Hertfordshire, 20 April 1941
Career: Rugby School, Oxford University, Blackheath, Harlequins, Barbarians, Kent
Debut: v Wales, Welford Road, Leicester, January 1904

Dillon was educated at Rugby School, but during his time at Blackheath, he developed into a classy three-quarter. During his time at Oxford, he only won a Cricket blue and scored 110 on his first-class debut for London against Worcestershire in 1900. Dillon made three international appearances in 1904, and his last came against Wales in January 1905. He played for Kent between 1900 and 1914 and was captained for the last six seasons. A ship and insurance broker during the First World War, Dillon was a captain in the West Kent Regiment and was wounded and mentioned in dispatches.

394. HANCOCK, Patrick Sortain
Fly-half 3 caps 1904
Born: Assam, India, 8 July 1883
Died: Manitoba, Canada, 22 December 1940
Career: Dulwich College, Leytonstone, Streatham, Richmond, Eastern Counties, Surrey
Debut: v Wales Welford Road, Leicester, January 1904

Hancock started his rugby career with Leytonstone and Streatham before moving to Richmond in 1902 to further his international ambitions. At the end of his first season was selected despite being uncapped for the British Team tour to South Africa, playing in three test matches. He won the first of his two caps against Wales in January 1903 after impressing in a trial match a month earlier. Hancock, a farmer and then a notary public, emigrated to Canada to serve in the First World War as a lieutenant in the Canadian Expeditionary Force, losing a leg after being wounded.

395. KEETON, George Haydn
Hooker 3 caps 1904
Born: Peterborough, Cambridgeshire, 13 October 1878
Died: Menton, France, 7 January 1949
Career: Oakham School, Cambridge University, Richmond, Leicester, Midland Counties
Debut: v Wales, Welford Road, Leicester, January 1904

Oakham School-educated Keeton attended Cambridge University, won a blue in 1899 and 1900, then joined Richmond and made all three international appearances in 1904. George taught at Fettes College in Edinburgh, became headmaster at Pocklington School in Yorkshire, and then Reading Royal Grammar School, where he started his career as an assistant master between 1914 and his retirement in 1939. After he died in the South of France, he was buried in the same cemetery in Menton as William Webb Ellis and Percy Carpmael, the founder of the Barbarians. His daughter Diana represented Oxford in lacrosse, lawn tennis and squash.

396. MILTON, John Griffith
Forward 5 caps 1904-1907
Born: Wynberg, Cape Province, 1 May 1885
Died: Boksburg Transvaal Province, 15 June 1915
Career: Bedford, Camborne School of Mines, Barbarian, East Midlands, Cornwall
Debut: v Wales, Welford Road, Leicester, January 1904

'Jumbo' Milton was born and raised in South Africa but was sent to Bedford School to complete his education. It was at Bedford that he first excelled at both rugby and cricket. He was 18 and still at school when he was selected to win his first three international caps but had moved on to the Camborne School of Mines, where he won his final two caps and helped Cornwall win the County Championship. After finishing his course at Camborne, he returned to South Africa, where he mined and played first-class cricket until his death from pneumonia aged 30.

397. MOORE, Norman John Neville Houghton
Forward 3 caps (6-2t) 1901
Born: Blackheath, London Q2 1877
Died: Bristol, 8 May 1939
Career: Bath, Bristol, Gloucestershire, Somerset
Debut: v Wales Welford Road, Leicester January 1904

Moore started his rugby career in the Bath second team in 1899 before progressing into the first team a season later. But in 1901, he moved to Bristol, spending the next nine years making 231 appearances. Moore, who had studied farming, made all three international appearances in 1904, scoring two tries against Ireland in his second game. He was selected for the British Isles tour to Australia later that year but turned down the invitation because of business commitments. Moore, an engineer, stayed in the Bristol area, where he ran a plumbing & sanitary business.

398. NEWBOLD, Charles Joseph DSO
Forward 6 caps 1904-1905
Born: Tunbridge Wells, Kent, 12 January 1881
Died: Chiswick, London, 26 October 1946
Career: Uppingham School, Cambridge University, Wanderers, Blackheath, Barbarians, Kent
Debut: v Wales, Welford Road, Leicester, January 1904

Newbold represented Cambridge University in the Varsity Match in 1902 and 1903 and was still studying when he won the first of his England caps in January 1904. An ever-present for two seasons, he represented Blackheath in 1905, by which time he joined brewers Guinness as a junior brewer in Dublin. He later joined the board as a managing director, taking charge of building the new brewery at Park Royal and then all the company's activities in the Republic of Ireland, Great Britain and abroad. Newbold was a lieutenant colonel in the Royal Engineers during the First World War, winning the Distinguished Service Order.

399. CAVE, William Thomas Charles
Forward 1 cap 1905
Born: Croydon, London 24 November 1882
Died: Deben, Suffolk, 2 February 1970
Career: Tonbridge School, Cambridge University, Blackheath, Barbarians, Kent
Debut: v Wales, Arms Park, Cardiff, January 1905

Tonbridge-educated Cave went up to Cambridge, where he won a blue between 1902 and 1904. In 1903, while still at university, he toured South Africa with the British Team, playing all three test matches. And it wasn't until January 1905 that he won his only England cap against Wales in Cardiff, but following a heavy 25-0, he wasn't selected again. Cave was a solicitor with the City of London law firm E. F. Turner & Sons, and during the First World War, he became a captain in the Inns of Court Officers Training Regiment and was taken Prisoner of War.

400. GIBSON, Thomas Alexander
Forward 2 caps
Born: Gateshead, Tyne & Wear, 30 January 1880
Died: Haydon Bridge, Northumberland, 27 April 1937
Career: Uppingham School, Cambridge University, Northern, Barbarians, Northumberland
Debut: v Wales, Arms Park, Cardiff, January 1905

Gibson was the youngest of the three Gibson brothers to play for England. He won a Cambridge University blue in 1901 and 1902 and toured South Africa with the British Team in 1903, playing in all tests. Gibson had to wait until January 1905 to win the first of his two England caps against Wales, with his last coming against Scotland two months later. He was a timber merchant with William Wear and Co in Hexham, then a partner in Hexham Saw Mills for many years, and served a brief term on Haydon Parish Council.

401. IRVIN, Samuel Howell
Full-back 1 cap 1905
Born: Hartlepool, County Durham, August 1880
Died: Oldham, Lancashire, 22 January 1939
Career: Hartlepool Old Boys, Devonport Albion, Devon
Debut: v Wales, Arms Park, Cardiff January 1905

Irvin first played in an international trial in 1903 but had to wait two years to become one of four full-backs to be capped by England in the 1905 Home Championship, making his only international appearance against Wales in Cardiff. But was generally thought not to be up to international standard, he switched codes and joined Oldham the same year after employment opportunities at Devonport Dockyard became limited. Irvin's career ended in 1909 after he fell over some wire while collecting a ball. He settled in the Lancashire town, where he worked as a publican and an engineer's iron turner.

402. MATHIAS, John Lloyd
Lock 4 caps 1905
Born: Cardigan, Wales, 23 August 1878
Died: Hale, Cheshire, 21 November 1940
Career: Bristol, Clifton, Gloucestershire
Debut: v Wales, Arms Park, Cardiff, January 1905

Wales-born Mathias appeared 186 times for Bristol, whom he captained between 1901 and 1903. He was first reserve for England in their three games in 1904, but by the time of their first international against Wales in January 1905, he became the first choice. Mathias made all four international appearances in the same season, his last game against New Zealand. Following a season with Clifton, he was made a life member of Bristol Rugby Club in 1912. Mathias was the senior representative in Manchester for E. S. & A. Robinson, a Bristol paper, printing, and packaging company.

403. PALMER, Francis Hubert MC
Wing 1 cap 1905
Born: Hereford, Herefordshire, 6 August 1877
Died: Exmoor, Devon, 7 December 1951
Career: Bedford Grammar School, Richmond, Barbarians, Middlesex
Debut: v Wales Arms Park, Cardiff January 1905

Bedford School-educated Palmer, the son of an army Major, Herrick Palmer, joined Richmond after completing his education. He won his only cap against Wales at the Arms Park, Cardiff, in January 1905. But after an under-strength England got routed he was never selected again. Palmer followed his father into the military during the First World War when he became a temporary captain in the service of the Cheshire Regiment. After being wounded twice and mentioned in despatches, he was decorated with the Military Cross in 1918. Palmer was a commercial clerk who became an insurance broker in Surrey.

404. ROGERS, Walter Lacy Yea DSO
Forward 2 caps 1905
Born: Pewsey, Wiltshire, 20 September 1878
Died: Kensington, Surrey, 10 February 1948
Career: Rugby School, Oxford University, The Army, Blackheath, Barbarians, Kent
Debut: v Wales, Arms Park, Cardiff, January 1905

Rogers was educated at Rugby School and Oxford University, where he won a blue between 1898 and 1900. Unfortunately, his international appearances in successive games against Wales and Ireland ended in heavy defeats, and he was never selected again. Rogers made the Army his career and was commissioned as a lieutenant to the Royal Field Artillery in 1900 before switching to the Royal Horse Artillery a year later. During the First World War he was mentioned in dispatches three times and, in 1918, awarded a Distinguished Service Order. Rogers was a lieutenant colonel when he retired in 1935.

405. GREEN, John
Forward 8 caps 1905-1907
Born: Silsden, Yorkshire, 17 September 1881
Died: Wharfedale, Yorkshire, 27 December 1968
Career: Giggleswick School, Skipton, Yorkshire
Debut: v Ireland, Mardyke, Cork, February 1905

Green joined Skipton Rugby Club soon after completing his education at Giggleswick School. He went on to make his England debut in a heavy defeat against Ireland in Cork and, in the following season, helped his country win the first international encounter with the French. In 1907, Green was appointed captain of Skipton, Yorkshire, and amid much controversy, England in succession to Basil Hill for his last cap, a defeat against Ireland in Dublin. Green was a timber merchant who retired from the game before the start of the following campaign and was Ilkley RUFC's president for many years.

406. GRYLLS, William Michell
Lock 1 cap 1905
Born: Redruth, Cornwall, 9 January 1885
Died: Wokingham, Berkshire 2 December 1962
Career: Haileybury & ISC, RMC Sandhurst, Redruth, The Army, Cornwall
Debut: v Ireland, Mardyke, Cork, February 1905

'Tiny' Grylls was a big, fast, and stylish forward who had already made a name for himself as captain of Haileybury School, whom he also represented in cricket and hockey. He became the first player from Redruth, the club his banker father Henry founded in 1875, to play for England when he won his only cap against Ireland in February 1905. His career with The Indian Army ended his rugby career. Grylls, a captain with the 52nd Sikhs Frontier Force, reached the rank of lieutenant Colonel and commanded the 2nd Sikhs, 12th Frontier Force Regiment, from 1930 until his retirement in 1934.

407. SHEWRING, Henry Edward
Centre 10 caps (3-1t) 1905-1907
Born: Keynsham, Somerset, 26 April 1882
Died: Keynsham, Somerset, 27 November 1960
Career: Colston's School, Bristol, Bath, Somerset
Debut: v Ireland, Mardyke, Cork, February 1905

Shewring started his rugby career at Colston's School before joining Bristol, where he would make 250 appearances and score 67 tries. He was a full-back before developing into one of the best centres in the country and was one of three Bristol players in the England side when he debuted against Ireland in Cork in February 1905. Matt Mathias and Wally Butcher were the others. Shewring captained Bristol and Somerset and played for his county against South Africa in 1912, five years after making his final international appearance. He was on the staff of the Bristol Waterworks.

408. STANGER-LEATHES, Christopher Francis
Full-back 1 cap 1905
Born: Kensington, Middlesex, 9 May 1881
Died: Gosforth, Northumberland, 27 February 1966
Career: Sherborne School, Northern, Northumberland
Debut: v Ireland, Mardyke, Cork, February 1905

Stanger-Leathes was uncapped when he toured Australia and New Zealand with the 1904 British Team and won his first test cap against Australia in Sydney. But he had to wait until the following February to win his only England cap, replacing Sam Irvin as one of four players tried at full-back that season. Stanger-Leathes was the Managing Director of ship ventilation manufacturers and sheet iron engineers Brown and Hood, Wallsend, North Tyneside. He played cricket for Newcastle between 1900 and 1925 and then Northumberland between 1926 and 1934, and he also captained the county golf side.

409. VICKERY, George
Forward 1 cap 1905
Born: Chard, Somerset, 29 May 1879
Died: Port Talbot, Wales, 30 June 1970
Career: Aberavon, Bath, Somerset
Debut: v Ireland, Mardyke, Cork, February 1905

Vickery was born in Chard, Somerset, but moved to Wales after becoming a police constable, making his debut for Aberavon in 1900. He played his first trial match three years later and was also a reserve for the Principality before winning his only international cap for England against Ireland in Cork in February 1905. A year earlier, he had been made Aberavon captain and was also captain of the Glamorgan County Police team. After leaving the police, Vickery became a coal trimmer on Port Talbot Docks until his retirement. His son Walter played for Wales, making them unique in England-Wales rugby history.

410. HAMMOND, Charles Edward Lucas
Forward 8 caps 1905-1908
Born: Pontefract, Yorkshire, 3 October 1879
Died: Ross-on-Wye, Herefordshire, 15 April 1963
Career: Oxford University, Harlequins, Barbarians, Middlesex
Debut: v Scotland, Athletic Ground, Richmond, March 1905

'Curly' Hammond captained the Hertford college XV during his time at Oxford University that saw him play in the Varsity match at the Queen's Club in 1899 and 1900. A keen oarsman, he was in the Bedford School eight and the College crew. He then captained Harlequins and Middlesex between 1902 and 1906. Hammond became an assistant master at Stanmore Park Preparatory School and Wellington College, then became a master at the Royal Naval College, Dartmouth, for 32 years, retiring in 1943, following for a further three at Felsted. His nephew Robin Prescott was RFU secretary between 1963 and 1971.

411. OSBORNE, Sidney Herbert
Forward 1 cap 1905
Born: Camberwell, London, 26 February 1880
Died: Hemel Hempstead, Hertfordshire, 15 July 1939
Career: Fettes College, Oxford University, Harlequins, St Bees, Middlesex, Cumberland
Debut: v Scotland, Athletic Ground, Richmond, March 1905

Osborne was educated at Fettes College, Edinburgh, and then Oxford University, winning a blue between 1900 and 1902. Ironically, he won his only international cap against Scotland, where he spent much of his adult life in March 1905. But he failed to impress in a struggling England side that lost all three games in the Home Championship, as he was never selected again. He was a master at St Bee's, then Edinburgh Academy, before becoming headmaster at Winchester House, Brackley and Dreyhorn Castle Edinburgh. Then, two years before his death, Osborne became a partner at Lockers Park School, Hemel Hempstead.

412. STOOP, Adrian Dura MC
Fly-half 15 caps (6-2t) 1905-1912
Born: Kensington, London, 27 March 1883
Died: Aldershot Hampshire, 27 November 1957
Career: Rugby School, Oxford University, Harlequins, Surrey, Barbarians
Debut: v Scotland Athletic Ground, Richmond, March 1905

Stoop was still at Rugby School when he joined Harlequins before completing his education at Oxford, whom he captained in the 1904 Varsity match. He also captained

England against Ireland in the first game played at Twickenham in February 1910. The captain of Quins between 1906 and 1914 turned out for the club aged 55 and was club secretary, then president and president of the RFU and Surrey. Stoop was a barrister. His brother Fred played for England, and his name still lives on today, with the Twickenham Stoop named in his memory. Stoop was awarded a Military Cross in 1919 after serving the Queen's Regiment in the First World War.

413. BRAITHWAITE, John
Scrum-half 1 cap 1905
Born: Leeds, Yorkshire, 21 April 1873
Died: West Humberstone, Leicester, 14 November 1915
Career: Holbeck, Leicester, Nottingham, Midland Counties
Debut: v New Zealand Crystal Palace London December 1905

'Jacky' Braithwaite was a hard-working scrum-half who won his only cap in England's first-ever game against New Zealand at Crystal Palace in December 1905 in place of Wally Butcher, who had been an ever-present for two seasons. He was a member of the Leicester side for several seasons, where he was best remembered for his partnership at Welford Road with W J Foreman. Braithwaite, an engineer, almost lost a leg in an accident at work but fully recovered and maintained an interest in Leicester after he retired. He sadly died from a bout of pneumonia.

414. GENT, David Robert
Fly-half 5 caps 1905-1910
Born: Llandovery, Wales, 9 January 1883
Died: Hollingley Sussex 16 January 1964
Career: St Paul's College Cheltenham, Gloucester, Gloucestershire, Glamorgan
Debut: v New Zealand, Crystal Palace, London, December 1905

Gent was dubbed the 'Tiny Giant'. Born in Wales, he moved to Gloucester to train as a teacher and was discovered by Cherry and Whites captain George Romans. In 1905, he had a Welsh trial and was a reserve in all three matches. A County Cup winner with Gloucestershire, he won five England caps, two of which were gained against Wales in 1906 and then after a four-year wait in 1910. Gent later became a headmaster of Saltash School and then another school in Eastbourne, Sussex, where for 30 years, he combined teaching with writing a rugby column for The Sunday Times.

415. GODFRAY, Reginald Edmond
Centre 1 cap 1905
Born: St Helier, Jersey, 10 May 1880
Died: Merton, London, 4 February 1967
Career: Victoria College Jersey, Park House (Blackheath), Richmond, Middlesex
Debut: v New Zealand, Crystal Palace, London, December 1905

Channel Islander Godfray had already suffered one defeat at the hands of New Zealand in 1905 when Middlesex got beaten 34-0 at Stamford Bridge. Godfray did enough to impress the England selectors when they picked their side for the only test match. The one-time Richmond captain was one of four new caps in England's back five. But he failed to impress in a five-try defeat as he was never picked again. Gibson was a stockbroker who was a Member of the Stock Exchange from 1914 until his death. Reg was also President of Chiswick Park Lawn Tennis Club.

416. HIND, Alfred Ernest
Wing 2 caps 1905-1906
Born: Preston, Lancashire, 7 April 1878
Died: Oadby, Leicestershire, 21 March 1947
Career: Uppingham School, Cambridge University, Leicester, Nottingham
Debut: v New Zealand, Crystal Palace, London, December 1905

Uppingham School-educated Hind was a double-triple blue at Cambridge University, where he only played in a Varsity match in 1900, an Athletics blue twice, running 100 yards in 9.8 seconds and cricket playing three times against Oxford at Lords. He was uncapped when he toured Australia and New Zealand in 1903 with the British Team. Hind also played for the Midland Counties against New Zealand in 1905, which helped him win his first cap. He also played cricket for Nottinghamshire CCC between 1900 and 1901 and, after leaving university, became a solicitor with Leicester firm Bray and Bray.

417. IMRIE, Henry Marshall
Wing 2 caps (3-1t) 1905-1907
Born: Durham, County Durham, Q3 1877
Died: Middleton St George, County Durham, 16 October 1938
Career: Durham YMCA, Durham City, Durham Counties
Debut: v New Zealand, Crystal Palace, London, December 1905

When he died, Imrie was described as a resourceful exponent and a prolific try scorer. He made his debut against New Zealand at Crystal Palace in December 1905 as one of eight new caps and then had to wait until February 1907 to score a try on his second and last appearance against Ireland in Dublin. Imrie made 26 appearances for Durham between 1904 and 1910, and he worked as a manager of an Iron Company and colliery manager of Chopwell Colliery, where he introduced Rugby. Imrie died at his Durham home following a long illness.

418. JACKETT, Edward John
Full-back 13 caps (4-2c) 1905-1909
Born: Falmouth, Cornwall, 4 July 1882
Died: Middlesbrough, Cleveland 11 November 1935
Career: Falmouth, Leicester, Cornwall, Plymouth Albion, Devonport Albion, Transvaal (SA), De Beers, Kimberley
Debut: v New Zealand, Crystal Palace, London, December 1905

As a youth, Jackett ran off to South Africa and joined the Cape Mounted Police in Kimberley and played for Transvaal against the British Team in 1903 until his mother bought him out, and he returned home. He saved a man from drowning while touring Australia and New Zealand in 1908, just months after becoming an Olympic silver medallist with brother Dick when Cornwall as County Champions represented Great Britain at the Olympic Games. Jackett turned to rugby league after moving to Dewsbury to manage the Empire Theatre in 1911. He later managed greyhound stadiums in Norwich and Middlesbrough until his death.

419. RUSSELL, Richard Forbes
Forward 1 cap 1905
Born: Shelton, Nottinghamshire, 5 April 1879
Died: Lezayre, Isle of Man, 30 May 1960
Career: St Peter's School York, Cambridge University, Leicester, Castleford, Cork, Yorkshire, Midlands
Debut: v New Zealand, Crystal Palace, London, December 1905

Russell was the son-in-law of England and Middlesex cricketer Sir Timothy Carew O'Brien, the first Irishman to captain the English cricket team. But he failed to win a blue during his time at Cambridge. He won his only cap in the first home test against New Zealand. During the First World War, he served as a special constable on Ramsey on the Isle of Man. He was an assistant master at Yorkshire, then Bilton Grange School, Rugby, before becoming headmaster of The Manor School, Fermoy, County Cork. Russell was a founding member of the Isle of Man Cricket Club and secretary of Ramsey CC.

420. SUMMERSCALE, George Edward
Forward 1 cap 1905
Born: Durham, County Durham, 3 September 1879
Died: Durham, County Durham, 31 December 1936
Career: Durham City, Durham Counties
Debut: v New Zealand, Crystal Palace, London, December 1905

Summerscale served Durham City for over 40 years in various capacities, with 19 of them as a player. He had trials for the North in 1903 and 1906 and won his only cap against New Zealand at Crystal Palace in December 1905. He appeared in eight County Championship Finals and a replay in a dominant period for Durham. A Durham selector and committee member in retirement and played against Northumberland as a 41-year-old when a player failed to arrive. Like his father, he spent the whole of his adult life working for Durham organ builders Harrison & Harrison.

421. DOBBS, George Eric Burroughs
Flanker 2 caps 1906
Born: Castlecomer, Kildare, 21 July 1884
Died: Poperinghe, Belgium, 17 June 1917
Career: St Stephen's Green School Dublin, Shrewsbury School, RMA Woolwich, Plymouth Albion, Devonport Albion, Llanelli, Royal Engineers, The Army, Barbarians, Devon
Debut: v Wales, Athletic Ground, Richmond, January 1906

Dobbs captained Shrewsbury School at association football, but by the time he joined the Royal Military Academy at Woolwich, he was playing rugby union. But despite his Irish heritage, he was picked to play for England against Wales at Richmond in January 1906. Dobbs kept his place for the following game for another heavy defeat against Ireland and was never selected again. He served in the United Kingdom and Singapore and saw action with the Royal Engineers Signal Service during the First World War. Dobbs was made a Chevalier of the Legion of Honour and died from wounds after being hit by a shell.

422. HODGES, Harold Augustus
Prop 2 caps 1906
Born: Mansfield Woodhouse, Nottinghamshire, 22 January 1886
Died: Ham, France 22 March 1918
Career: Roclareston House Nottingham, Sedbergh School, Oxford University, Sorbonne University, Nottingham, Blackheath, Midland Counties
Debut: v Wales, Athletic Ground, Richmond, January 1906

Hodges had already won his two England caps while representing Nottingham before captaining Oxford University in 1908, having first won his blue three years earlier. After leaving, he became a schoolmaster and taught at Tonbridge School between 1909 and 1914. A talented sportsman, Hodges played cricket for Nottinghamshire in 1911 and lacrosse for Oxford. In the First World War, he joined the 3rd Battalion, The Monmouthshire Regiment and was twice mentioned in dispatches. Having already been wounded by shelling, he was shot dead in a small factory on the road between Ham and Eppeville.

423. HUDSON, Arthur
Wing 8 caps (27-9t) 1906-1910
Born: Gloucester, Gloucestershire, 27 October 1882
Died: Gloucester, Gloucestershire, 27 July 1973
Career: Gloucester, Devonport, Harwich Naval Forces, Royal Navy, Combined Services, Gloucestershire
Debut: v Wales, Athletic Ground, Richmond, January 1906

Hudson was a railway clerk who switched to Rugby Union in 1902 and developed into one of his era's most prolific try scorers. And it was no surprise that he came to the attention of England's selectors and then scored a try on his debut against Wales in January 1906 and four more times against France in the same season. Hudson captained Gloucester for five seasons and served in the Royal Navy during the First World War, then became a sports outfitter and spent 42 years as club secretary, relinquishing the post in 1962, aged 80. He was also treasurer and fixture secretary.

424. JAGO, Raphael Anthony
Scrum-half 5 caps (3-1t) 1906-1907
Born: Chidcock, Dorset, 20 January 1882
Died: Plymouth, Devon, 1 March 1941
Career: Devonport Albion, Devon
Debut: v Wales Athletic Ground Richmond January 1906

Jago was a strongly-built scrum half that served Devonport Albion between 1899 and 1919, making 320 appearances and another 59 for Devon. He only missed one game for England in 1906, replaced by Plymouth Albion's Jimmy Peters against France after scoring his only try on his second appearance against Ireland. Raphael was employed by Devonport Corporation as a blacksmith and captained Devon to back-to-back County Championship successes in 1911 and 1912 when they beat Yorkshire at Headingley and Northumberland at Devonport, respectively. At the time of his death, he helped train the St Boniface College rugby team.

425. KELLY, Thomas Stanley
Lock 12 caps 1906-1908
Born: Tiverton, Devon, 15 August 1882
Died: Bolney, Sussex, 28 November 1959
Career: Blundell's School, Tiverton, Exeter, London Devonians, London Civil Service, Liverpool Old Boys, Harlequins, Devon, Lancashire
Debut: v Wales Athletic Ground Richmond January 1906

Old Blundellian Kelly came to the attention of Exeter while playing for his home club, Tiverton. Such was his influence on the side that he was elected captain in only his second season and was seen as one of the early line-out experts. Capped 12 times in total, one of which was as captain against France at Stade Colombes on New Year's Day 1908, he is the only Exeter player to captain England. Kelly worked for Customs and Excise, which enabled him to win 10 Lancashire caps while working in Liverpool. he was also secretary to the Devon RFU for 26 years.

426. KEWNEY, Alfred Lionel OBE
Forward 16 caps (6-2t) 1906-1913
Born: Tynemouth, Tyne & Wear, 13 September 1882,
Died: Barmby Moor, Yorkshire, 16 December 1959
Career: Rockcliff, Leicester, Barbarians, Northumberland
Debut: v Wales Athletic Ground Richmond January 1906

Kewney started his rugby career with Rockcliff, making his debut against Wales in January 1906 after his four initial appearances. It wouldn't be until 1909 that he would fight his way back into the international reckoning, by which time he made sporadic appearances for Leicester and was to make his last England appearance against South Africa in 1913. Kewney was a marine engineer with Hawthorn, Leslie and Co. in Whitley Bay, then Amos and Smith Ltd, in Hull, Palmer's in Hebburn on Tyne before returning to Amos and Smith as a director and was awarded an OBE in 1943.

427. MILLS, William Alonzo
No 8 11 caps (12-4t) 1906-1908
Born: Stoke Damerel, Plymouth, 2 February 1879
Died: Camels Head, Plymouth, 9 October 1953
Career: Devonport Albion, Plymouth Albion, Devon
Debut: v Wales, Athletic Ground, Richmond, January 1906

Mills was a fast and clever forward, one of the finest to play for Devon Albion in the golden period for the club. He was an England regular for three seasons after debuting against Wales in January 1906. Mills was connected to Plymouth Albion during the early days at Beacon Park. He was an inspector of Shipwrights Devonport Dockyard for many years. The last match he saw was Devon against the Springboks when he was wheeled onto the Home Park pitch in a wheelchair two years before his death after a long battle against illness.

428. HUTCHINSON, James Ernest
Wing 1 cap 1906
Born: Stockton-on-Tees, County Durham, 8 March 1884
Died: Bamburgh, Northumberland, 20 October 1961
Career: Bernard Castle School, Durham City, Northumberland
Debut: v Ireland Welford Road, Leicester February 1906

Hutchinson was one of the finest sprinters in the north of England during his youth and won an England cap against

Ireland in February 1906 despite the deformity of the hand following a childhood accident with a harvesting machine. His rugby career ended when he was forced to retire at 22 because of an ankle injury not long after winning his cap. Hutchinson was a farmer in New Zealand before the Great War and then ran Home Bank in Coldstream before becoming the third generation of his family to run Bamburgh Hall Farm.

429. MILTON, Henry Cecil
Centre 1 cap (3-1t) 1906
Born: Cape Colony, South Africa, 7 January 1884
Died: Boscombe, Dorset, 29 December 1961
Career: Bedford Grammar School, Camborne School of Mines, Barbarians, Cornwall
Debut: v Ireland, Welford Road, Leicester, February 1906

Milton was the son of Sir William and followed in the footsteps of his younger brother, 'Jumbo'. Cecil was sent to Bedford to complete his education, and he also went on to the Camborne School of Mines, where he won his only international cap by scoring a try in a defeat to Ireland at Welford Road, Leicester. During the First World War, Milton became a captain in the Royal Engineers, and for many years, he worked as a mining engineer in Southern Rhodesia before retiring to live on the Dorset coast. A second brother, Noel, was an Oxford University blue.

430. SANDFORD, Joseph Ruscombe Poole
Centre 1 cap 1906
Born: Landkey, Devon, 5 March 1881
Died: Khartoum, Sudan, 29 July 1916
Career: Allhallows School, Marlborough College, Oxford University, Exeter, Marlborough Nomads, Devon
Debut: v Ireland, Welford Road, Leicester, February 1906

Sandford was one of three sporting brothers, and his father, Ernest, was the Archdeacon of Exeter. He won a double blue in Rugby in 1902 and 1903, the year he won a Hockey blue. He made his first trial the following November but had to wait until February 1906 to win his only cap against Ireland at Welford Road, Leicester. An all-round sportsman, when in Devon, he played cricket for Exeter, Exmouth and Torquay. Sandford spent eight years in the Sudan Civil Service and became Acting Governor of Omdurman in 1916, shortly before his death following a brief illness.

431. BIRKETT, John Guy Giberne
Centre 21 caps (34-10t, 1dg) 1906-1912
Born: Richmond, Surrey, 27 December 1884
Died: Cuckfield, Sussex, 16 October 1967
Career: Haileybury College, Brighton, Harlequins, Barbarians, Surrey
Debut: v Scotland, Inverleith, Edinburgh, March 1906

Birkett followed in the footsteps of his father Reg and Uncle Louis in playing for England. He joined Harlequins after trials on Wandsworth Common in 1905. He became a centre under Adrian Stoop and, within a year, was capped for the first time by England. He captained England in 1908 and, two years later, helped England become the first-ever Five Nations Champions. He scored the first try at Twickenham for Quins against Richmond. Birkett served in the Royal Field Artillery during the First World War, becoming a brigadier in the Second World War, and was a land agent for Sussex County Council.

432. DIBBLE, Robert
Forward 19 caps 1906-1912
Born: Bridgwater, Somerset, 29 October 1882
Died: Bournemouth, Hampshire, 6 March 1963
Career: Bridgewater, Bridgewater Albion, Newport, Somerset
Debut: v Scotland, Inverleith, Edinburgh, March 1906

Dibble started his career with hometown clubs Bridgwater and Bridgwater Albion, where he won 16 of his 19 England caps. The three others came after he moved to Newport. He captained his club and England seven times and was a member of 'Boxer' Harding's 1908 British Isles side that toured New Zealand and Australia, playing in three test matches. Dibble served in the Army during the Boer War, made a record 73 appearances for Somerset between 1901 and 1921 and is one of the county's greatest forwards. He was publican of The George Inn, Maindee and the Lion Hotel Wiveliscombe.

433. PETERS, James
Fly-half 5 caps (6-2t) 1906-1908
Born: Salford, Lancashire, 7 August 1879
Died: Plymouth, Devon, 26 March 1954
Career: Bristol, Plymouth, Devon, Somerset
Debut: v Scotland, Inverleith Edinburgh, March 1906

Peters was the son of a lion tamer and a trained circus acrobat. He became the first black man to play for England and helped Devon win a County Championship. A printer and then a carpenter lost three fingers on his left hand. Then, in 1912, clubs in the South West of England attempted to join the Northern Union with Peters and several other players were banned for accepting payments. Despite being 34, he returned to his native North West, joining Barrow in 1913 and then St Helens in 1914 until his retirement when he returned to Plymouth working at the Royal Naval Hospital, Stonehouse.

434. SHAW, Major Cecil Hamilton
Forward 6 caps 1906-1907
Born: Wolverhampton, West Midlands, August 1, 1879
Died: Wolverhampton, West Midlands, 13 November 1964
Career: Sedbergh School, Wolverhampton, Moseley, Midland Counties
Debut: v Scotland, Inverleith, Edinburgh, March 1906

Shaw was educated at Sedbergh School in Yorkshire before returning to his home town, Wolverhampton, where he won gold in the local swimming championships in 1900, but it was in Rugby Union that he would make his name after making his debut against Scotland at Inverleith and captaining the Midland Counties. Shaw was a director of John Shaw and Sons, the Wolverhampton tool-making firm his grandfather founded and served in Royal Engineers during the First World War. Shaw later bought Horobin, a casting firm, and he became managing director. His cousin, Lord Rowllan, was a former chief scout.

435. HOGARTH, Thomas Bradley
Forward 1 cap (3-1t) 1906
Born: Hartlepool, County Durham, 16 February 1878,
Died: Middlesbrough, Cleveland, 12 July 1961
Career: Hartlepool Creelers, Hartlepool Rovers, West Hartlepool, Leicester, Grays, Durham City, Durham Counties
Debut: v France, Parc des Princes, Paris, March 1906

Hogarth helped Durham reach the County Championship Final in March 1906 and a week later was a late call-up to win his only international cap against France as a replacement for Sidney Osborne, scoring a try. By the start of the 1906-07 season, despite living in West Hartlepool helped by only working a three-day week, he joined Leicester and helped them to win three Midland Counties Cups before leaving in 1914. Hogarth was a blacksmith at Gray's Shipyard in West Hartlepool until retiring, even turning down a job in a Boston, Massachusetts, shipyard to continue playing rugby.

436. ALCOCK, Arnold
Hooker 1 cap 1906
Born: Woolstanton, Staffordshire, 18 August 1882
Died: Gloucester, Gloucestershire, 7 November 1973
Career: Newcastle-under-Lyme High School, Manchester University, Guy's Hospital, Richmond, Blackheath, Surrey
Debut: v South Africa, Crystal Palace, London, December 1906

Alcock was known as commonly known in rugby circles as 'The Doc'. He won his only cap due to a clerical error when he, a medical student at Guy's Hospital, was picked instead of Lancelot Slocock. The Doc was a good club player but not quite an international and wasn't ever picked again. He lived and worked as an ophthalmic surgeon in Gloucester for 66 years and became an administrator at the club and then President from 1924 for the next 45 years. Alcock was the last survivor of that England team, which had played the first South African team on home soil.

437. BROOKS, Frederick George
Wing 1 cap (3-1t) 1906
Born: Bombay, India, 1 May 1883
Died: Hermanus, Cape Province, South Africa, 5 September 1947
Career: Bedford Grammar School, Bedford, East Midlands, Rhodesia
Debut: v South Africa, Crystal Palace, London, December 1906

Brooks was almost certainly the finest schoolboy sportsman in the land, excelling in cricket, rugby and athletics and developing into a brilliant three-quarter. After scoring a try on his England debut, Rhodesia administrator William Milton, a fellow international, was tipped off by his sons Cecil and 'Jumbo' Milton about Brooks, with whom they had gone to school. Brooks was offered a position in the Rhodesian civil service and was Rhodesia's leading cricketer, athlete, footballer, rugby and tennis player for many years. He also served as Master of the High Court and then Chairman of the Public Service.

438. BATCHELOR, Tremlett Brewer
Wing 1 cap 1907
Born: Wirral, Cheshire 22 June 1884
Died: Liverpool, Lancashire, 21 December 1966
Career: Rugby School, Oxford University, Richmond, London Hospital, United Hospitals, Eastern Counties
Debut: v France, Athletic Ground, Richmond, January 1907

Rugby School-educated Batchelor won his university colours in 1906 and was still at Oxford when he won his only cap in the opening game of the 1907 Home Championship. He was a late replacement playing on the opposite wing to Danny Lambert, who scored five tries on his debut. Batchelor helped London Hospital win the Hospitals Cup 1912, and during the First World War, he served in the Royal Army Medical Corps and Fifth Cavalry Field Ambulance. He was a clinical assistant at Great Ormond Street Children's Hospital and worked as a physician and surgeon until his retirement.

439. HOPLEY, Frederick John Vanderbyl
Flanker 3 caps 1907-1908
Born: Grahamstown, South Africa, 27 August 1883
Died: Marandellas, Rhodesia, 16 August 1951
Career: Harrow, Cambridge University, Blackheath, Villagers (South Africa), Barbarians, Kent
Debut: v France, Athletic Ground, Richmond, January 1907

Harrow School-educated Hopley was British Public School's Heavyweight Boxing Champion in 1901 and 1902. He won a blue in boxing, cricket and athletics after attending Cambridge University, but surprisingly not in rugby. He won his first two England caps in 1907, and then after playing in his last international in 1908, he returned to southern Africa and established a farm in Marandellas in Rhodesia. Hopley was a reserve for South Africa during the British Isles 1912-1913 tour of South Africa and, was a lieutenant in the Grenadier Guards during the First World War and was twice mentioned in dispatches.

440. LAMBERT, Douglas
Wing 7 caps (46 -8t, 8c, 2p) 1907-1911
Born: Cranbrook, Kent, 4 October 1883
Died: Loos, France, 13 October 1915
Career: St Edwards Oxford, Eastbourne College, Harlequins, Middlesex
Debut: v France, Athletic Ground, Richmond, January 1907

Lambert arrived at Harlequins as a forward, but Adrian Stoop converted him into a winger. He made his international debut against France after Northumberland's Tom Simpson pulled out of the match, went on to score five tries and was rewarded by being dropped. He played in the first match at Twickenham against Wales in 1909, and then two years later, the 22 points he scored against France at the former cabbage patch would remain a record until 1990. Lambert, an assistant manager with Imperial Tobacco, became a second lieutenant with The Buffs Kent Regiment and was killed during the Battle of Loos.

441. LEE, Harry
Full-back 1 cap 1907
Born: Dewsbury, Yorkshire 8 December 1882
Died: Leeds, Yorkshire, 11 January 1933
Career: Tettenhall College, Cambridge University, Guy's Hospital, Blackheath, Barbarians, Kent
Debut: v France, Athletic Ground, Richmond, January 1907

Lee was educated at Cambridge University, winning a blue in 1904 before completing his medical training at Guy's Hospital. After John Jackett was ruled out of the game, he won his only England cap in the first home international against France. During the First World War, he saw action as a Captain in the Royal Army Medical Corps. Lee became one of the foremost ophthalmic surgeons of his day and a lecturer in ophthalmology at the School of Medicine in Leeds until he died after crashing his car into a wall after suffering a seizure and collapsing at the wheel.

442. NANSON, William Moore Bell
Forward 2 caps (3-1t) 1907
Born: Carlisle, Cumberland, 12 December 1880
Died: El Krithia, Gallipoli, 4 June 1915
Career: Loather Street School, Carlisle, Carlisle, Cumberland
Debut: v France, Athletic Ground, Richmond, January 1907

Nanson made his name with his home town club, Carlisle, but went away and served in the Border Regiment during the Boer War. Despite being invalided home, he went on to play for his country. He scored a try on his debut in the rout of France at Richmond in January 1907 and retained his place to face Wales. A year later, he switched codes with Oldham and turned professional. Nanson was a Slater and joined the Manchester Regiment during the First World War, losing his life at El Krithia. It was 13 months before he was declared dead, and his body was never recovered.

443. SLOCOCK, Lancelot Andrew Noel
Forward 8 caps (9-3t) 1907-1908
Born: Wooton Warren, Warwickshire, 25 December 1886
Died: Guillemont, France, 9 August 1916
Career: Marlborough College, Liverpool, Lancashire
Debut: v France, Athletic Ground, Richmond, January 1907

Slocock was originally chosen to play for England against South Africa in December 1906 but was omitted due to a clerical error by RFU, and Arnold Alcock played instead. He scored the match-winning try on his debut against France in January 1907 and was ever-present over the next two seasons, scoring a try and captaining his country on his last international appearance against Scotland. Secretary of the Liverpool Rugby Club, he worked in the cotton trade. During the First World War, Slocock was a second lieutenant in The King's Liverpool Regiment, fighting and dying alongside another England player, Jack King.

444. WEDGE, Thomas Grenfell
Scrum-half 2 caps 1907-1909
Born: Penzance, Cornwall, 15 September 1881
Died: St. Ives, Cornwall, 11 December 1964
Career: St Ives, Cornwall
Debut: v France, Athletic Ground, Richmond, January 1907

'Chicky' Wedge is the only player from St Ives to win international caps after impressing with Adrian Stoop's South XV against the North. He was selected to face France in January 1907 and Wales two years later. He played scrum-half for Cornwall when they won the County Championship in 1908 and was a member of the Cornish side that played Australia in the 1908 Olympic rugby final. Wedge won the draw when the team drew straws to see who would take the silver medal home. A fisherman, he served in the Royal Navy during the First World War and the Coastguard in the Second World War.

445. SCOTT, Frank Sholl
Wing 1 cap 1907
Born: Perth, Western Australia, 9 January 1886
Died: Ruanhighlanes, Cornwall, 4 February 1952
Career: Epsom College, Bristol, Gloucestershire, Devon
Debut: v Wales, St Helen's, Swansea, January 1907

Western Australian Scott was educated at Epsom College and then at Bristol University and played for Bristol, which led him to win his only cap against Wales at St Helen's in January 1907. After qualifying as a doctor, he returned home to Australia for three years, returning to the UK and following a short spell in Penzance he went into practice in Roseland for 36 years until retiring in 1952. His son Keith, England's captain just after the Second World War, assisted him. Scott served with the Royal Army Medical Corps during the First World War.

446. LEATHER, George
Forward 1 cap 1907
Born: West Derby, Lancashire, 22 February 1881
Died: Liverpool, Lancashire, 2 January 1957
Career: Liverpool College, Liverpool, Lancashire
Debut: v Ireland, Lansdowne Road, Dublin, February 1907

'Jumbo' Leather was the cousin of fellow England international Wilfred Stoddart, while his sons Arthur and William won rugby blues during their time at Cambridge University. Leather joined Liverpool in 1903, and four years later, he won his only cap alongside his club-mate Lancelot Slocock as the only new boy in the pack against Ireland. But a heavy defeat for England never saw him selected again. Leather, a chartered accountant with W.H. and W.J. Leather, continued to serve Liverpool Rugby Club as president between 1924 and 1928 and then as honorary treasurer until his death.

447. PICKERING, Arthur Stanley
Centre 1 cap (3-1p) 1907
Born: Dewsbury, Yorkshire, 24 March 1885
Died: York, Yorkshire, 17 February 1969
Career: Sedbergh School, Harrogate, Old Dewsburians, Headingley, Barbarians, Yorkshire
Debut: v Ireland, Lansdowne Road, Dublin, February 1907

Pickering became Harrogate's first international when he won his only cap against Ireland at Lansdowne Road in February 1907. He was selected in place of John Birkett after playing in both trial games, and despite kicking a penalty in the heavy defeat, the Harlequins man returned for the following game against Scotland. A move to Headingley in September 1908 failed to bring any further caps. A wool and waste merchant, Pickering was a past president and life member of Harrogate, where he lived until his death, played golf for Yorkshire, and was captain of Harrogate Golf Club.

448. WILSON, Walter Carandini
Wing 2 caps 1907
Born: Brisbane, Queensland, 22 June 1885
Died: Brighton, Sussex, 12 April 1968
Career: Tonbridge School, United Services Portsmouth, The Army, Richmond, Barbarians
Debut: v Ireland, Lansdowne Road, Dublin February 1907

Wilson was drafted into the England team after a heavy defeat against Wales in Swansea. But both of the games he played against Ireland and Scotland ended in losses. Walter made the military his career. During the First World War, he served in the Leicestershire Regiment and was awarded the Military Cross after being wounded and mentioned in dispatches three times, eventually retiring in 1932. He was then the administrative director of the Greyhound Racing Association. In the Second World War, he was a group captain in the RAF and later joined the board of the British Overseas Airways Corporation.

449. NEWTON, Andrew Winstanley
Wing 1 cap 1907
Born: Partaferry, Co Down, 12 September 1879
Died: Victoria, Australia, 14 September 1945
Career: Blackheath, The Army, Barbarians
Debut: v Scotland, Rectory Field, Blackheath, March 1907

Newton was commissioned in the Royal Dublin Fusiliers in May 1900 and promoted to lieutenant in August 1902. He played in the first two games between the Army and Navy in February and December 1907. His only England cap won against Scotland was sandwiched in between. He later served in the Indian Army and returned to the Royal Dublin Fusiliers during the First World War. Settling in Australia, Newton was appointed private secretary to Lord Chelmsford, the Governor of Queensland and later worked as a clerk before he died in St Kilda, Melbourne.

450. ROBERTS, Geoffrey Dorling OBE QC
Forward 3 caps (6-3c) 1907-1908
Born: Exeter, Devon, 27 August 1886
Died: Southwark, London, 7 March 1967
Career: Rugby School, Oxford University, Harlequins, Exeter, Barbarians, Devon
Debut: v Scotland Rectory Field, Blackheath March 1907

Exeter-born 'Khaki' Roberts got his nickname as a schoolboy because of his brick-dust complexion. At Oxford, he won a double blue in rugby and tennis. He won three successive England caps against Scotland, France, and Wales. Roberts was called to the bar in 1912 and was a major in the Devonshire Regiment during the First World War. He was a recorder at Exeter between 1932 and 1946 and then at Bristol from 1946 to 1950. A criminal barrister who served as Senior Treasury Counsel at the Old Bailey, he was also the British Prosecutor at the ßNuremberg War Trials.

451. START, Sydney Philip
Scrum-half 1 cap 1907
Born: Broughton, Manchester 17 May 1879
Died: Harrietsham, Kent 14 December 1954
Career: Manchester Grammar School, RNEC Keyham, United Services Portsmouth, Royal Navy, Devon, Surrey
Debut: v Scotland Rectory Field, Blackheath, March 1907

Start spent the whole of his working life in the Royal Navy after first signing up in 1894, and he was at the forefront of developing the game in the Services. He played in the first Navy vs Army match at Queens Club in February 1907 after the formation of the Army Rugby Union and Royal Navy Rugby Union a year earlier and won his only England cap against Scotland at Blackheath a month later. Start was a talented cricketer who played for Cambridgeshire CCC. He became a Rear Admiral and, in 1931, was appointed aide-de-camp to King George V.

452. BOYLEN, Francis
Forward 4 caps 1908
Born: East Hartlepool, Durham, December 1880
Died: Kingston-upon-Hull, East Riding of Yorkshire, 3 February 1938
Career: Hartlepool Excelsior, Hartlepool Rovers, Durham County
Debut: v France, Stade Colombes, Paris, January 1908

'Patsy' Boylan's rugby career in both codes spanned some 23 years. He won the County Championship with Durham in 1905 and 1907 and had already had one unsuccessful trial before enjoying better success a year later. He played four games for England in 1908. His international was brought to an end in September 1908 when he switched codes to play for Hull. Later playing for York and Hull Kingston Rovers, he also won England and Great Britain honours. Boylan was a driller and plater during his amateur days before working for the British Oxygen Company in Hull.

453. CHAMBERS, Ernest Leonard MC
Forward 3 caps 1908-1910
Born: Hackney, Middlesex, 24 July 1882
Died: Cheam, Surrey, 23 November 1946
Career: Bedford Grammar School, Cambridge University, Blackheath, Bedford, Kent, East Midlands
Debut: v France, Stade Colombes, Paris, January 1908

Chambers won a double blue at Oxford University in rugby and the Hammer in Athletics. But surprisingly, it wasn't until he was playing for Bedford that he won his England caps. He won the first on New Year's Day 1908, but he had to wait until 1910 to win his last two in the first games to be played at Twickenham. Chambers became a schoolmaster at his former school, Bedford Grammar, until July 1913, when he joined the Egyptian Civil Service Education Department. During the First World War, he served the Bedfordshire Regiment, the Northumberland Fusiliers and the King's Own Yorkshire Light Infantry.

454. HAVELOCK, Harold
Flanker 3 caps 1908
Born: Hartlepool, Durham, December 1880
Died: Hull, East Riding of Yorkshire, 12 May 1923
Career: Hartlepool Excelsior, Hartlepool Rovers, Hartlepool Old Boys, West Hartlepool, Durham Counties
Debut: v France, Stade Colombes, Paris, January 1908

Havelock's career was almost identical to that of his team-mate and fellow cross-code convert Patsy Boylen. He started his career with Hartlepool Excelsior in 1898, joining Hartlepool Rovers, playing full-back and centre and eventually in the forwards. He then captained Hartlepool Old Boys for three seasons and, in 1906, helped Durham win the County Championship. Like Boylen, his international career ended when he switched codes to join Hull in September 1908. Havelock served in the Royal Garrison Artillery during the First World War. He was a joiner with the North-Eastern Railway Company before a grazed leg became infected, and he died from blood poisoning.

455. LAPAGE, Walter Nevill OBE
Centre 4 caps (6-2t) 1908
Born: Nantwich, Cheshire, 5 February 1883
Died: New Milton, Hampshire, 17 May 1939
Career: Royal Naval College Greenwich, United Services Portsmouth, Royal Navy, Surrey
Debut: v France, Stade Colombes, Paris, January 1908

Lapage enrolled in the Royal Navy in January 1898, allowing him to play rugby. He debuted against France in January 1908 and was retained when 'Jumbo' Vassall was injured. He made all of his international appearances in one season. During the First World War, he was promoted and appointed to the staff of Rear Admiral Sir Roger Keyes. Lapage later commanded an anti-submarine station at Portland and retired as a Captain in 1929 after serving on HMS Hood. Lapage was seen as a good, solid all-round sportsman cricket for Hampshire, played golf, was a very useful shot and was a keen fisherman.

456. PORTUS, Garnet Vere
Fly-half 2 caps (3-1t) 1908
Born: Morpeth, New South Wales, 7 June 1883
Died: North Adelaide, South Australia, 15 June 1954
Career: Maitland High School (Australia), Sydney University, Oxford University, Blackheath, Barbarians
Debut: v France, Stade Colombes, Paris, January 1908

Portus won his England caps after coming over from Australia, where he played the game at school and university to complete his studies as a Rhodes Scholar and scored a try on his debut against France in Paris in 1908. Portus attended the theological college at Hereford and was ordained in 1911 after returning to Australia and serving the Church working as an assistant military censor in Sydney. He became a university professor and a successful author of many books on politics and economics. Portus later followed rugby as a journalist, New South Wales, and Australian selector.

457. SIBREE, Herbert John Hyde MC
Scrum-half 3 caps 1908-1909
Born: Antananarivo, Madagascar, 9 May 1885
Died: Ticehurst, Sussex, 20 August 1962
Career: Eltham College, Court Hill, Kensington, Harlequins, Barbarians, London Counties, Middlesex
Debut: v France, Stade Colombes, Paris, January 1908

Sibree joined Harlequins as a full-back after his previous club folded and was immediately converted into a half-back. He made his England debut in France in January 1909 but had to wait until the following February when he was recalled in place of Rupert Williamson to face Ireland in Dublin. Sibree won his final cap against Scotland a month later and played a trial alongside his Harlequins team-mate Adrian Stoop in 1911 but wasn't selected. During the First World War, he was an acting captain in the Royal Engineers and was a ship broker on the Baltic Exchange for 55 years.

458. WOOD, Alfred Ernest
Full-back 3 caps (8-4c)
Born: Wolverhampton, Staffordshire, 27 November 1883
Died: Oldham, Lancashire, 15 February 1963
Career: Bristol, Gloucester
Debut: v France, Stade Colombes, Paris, January 1908

Wood was a locomotive engine fitter who started playing rugby at Bristol before joining Gloucester in 1905 as a half-back before switching to full-back, which proved successful. He made his international debut against France on New Year's Day 1908. A week after his final international appearance switched codes after being recognised by a member of the Oldham committee when he was a spectator at the England against All Golds clash played at Athletic Ground Cheltenham. Wood went on to win England and

Great Britain honours before hanging up his boots in 1921 and was employed by AV Roe (Aircraft) until retirement.

459. GILBERT, Richard
Forward 3 caps 1908
Born: Dartmouth, Devon, 28 August 1878
Died: Plymouth, Devon, 5 April 1945
Career: Devon Albion, Royal Navy
Debut: v Wales, Ashton Gate, Bristol, January 1908

Gilbert spent his early teenage years in a Totnes workhouse before joining the Royal Navy. He became the first non-commissioned Navy rating to be selected by England four years after temporally losing his sight. Richard won his first cap against Wales at Ashton Gate, Bristol, as a last-minute replacement when captain Tom Kelly cried off. He was still playing rugby in 1918 for the Barbarians against Royal Artillery Cadets based at Topsham Barracks and reached the rank of petty officer before leaving the services and becoming a public house manager in Devonport, Plymouth and an office attendant at Mount Wise.

460. WILLIAMSON, Rupert Henry
Scrum-half 5 caps (6-2t)
Born: Transvaal, South Africa, 22 November 1886
Died: Sabie, Transvaal, 16 March 1946
Career: St Andrew's College (Grahamstown SA), Oxford University, Blackheath, Barbarians
Debut: v France, Stade Colombes, Paris, January 1908

Williamson learnt his rugby at St Andrew's College in Grahamstown, South Africa, before winning a Rhodes Scholarship to Oxford University, where he was a blue between 1906 and 1908. While still at Oxford, Williamson won all five England caps, scoring tries in his first two test appearances against Wales and Ireland. Even though he had returned to Transvaal to become a mining manager and was working for Glynns Lydenburg at his death. The British Team wanted to include him in their 1910 touring side to South Africa, but the South African Rugby Board strongly opposed the idea.

461. VASSALL, Henry Holland
Centre 1 cap 1908
Born: Torrington, Devon, 23 March 1887
Died: Over Storey, Somerset, 8 October 1949
Career: Oxford University, Yeovil, East Midlands, Somerset, Barbarians
Debut: v Ireland, Athletic Ground, Richmond, February 1908

Bedford School-educated 'Jumbo' Vassall followed his uncle Henry Vassal in representing his country when he won his only international cap against Ireland at the Athletic Ground, Richmond, in 1908. Vassall completed his education at Oxford University, where he won his blues between 1906 and 1908, when he was also selected to tour Australia and New Zealand with the British team, playing three test matches. His international career is likely to have been cut short by going into colonial service, working in the Kenyan Civil Service for many years. Vassall suffered from ill health in his later years and committed suicide.

462. WATSON, Rear-Admiral Fischer Burges
Forward 2 caps (3-1t) 1908-1909
Born: Portsea, Hampshire, 3 September 1884
Died: Chichester, West Sussex, 14 August 1960
Career: Ashdown House Forest Row, HMS Britannia, United Services Portsmouth, Royal Navy, Barbarians, Surrey.
Debut: v Scotland, Inverleith, Edinburgh, March 1908

The son of Rear Admiral Burges, Watson joined fellow Royal Navy officers Walter Lapage and George Lyon on the side for his debut against Scotland in March 1908. But it wasn't until the return match a year later that he won his second and final cap, scoring one of England's two tries. Watson joined the Royal Navy as a midshipman in 1900 and retired in 1935. He was recalled for convoy service at the start of the Second World War and saw service until retiring again in 1945 after becoming Flag Officer-in-Charge at Harwich.

463. DAVEY, James
Fly-half 2 caps 1908-1909
Born: Redruth, Cornwall, 25 December 1880
Died: Redruth, Cornwall, 18 October 1951
Career: Redruth, Transvaal, Cornwall, England, British Isles
Debut: v Scotland, Inverleith, Edinburgh, March 1908

'Maffer' Davey made his debut for Redruth aged 16 and for Cornwall a year later, but in 1902, he went to South Africa to work the gold mines of the Witwatersrand, captaining Transvaal in the Currie Cup and was under consideration to tour England with the Springboks but hadn't completed the three-year residency. After returning home, Davey scored a try in the 1908 County Championship Final, was a member of the Great Britain side that won Olympic silver and also toured with the first British Team to travel to New Zealand and Australia. Davey had his own shoe and boot making and repairer business in Tuckingmill for many years.

464. LYON, Admiral Sir George Hamilton D'Oyly KCB
Full-back 2 caps 1908-1909
Born: Bankipore, East India, 3 October 1883
Died: Midhurst, Sussex, 19 August 1947
Career: HMS Britannia, United Services Portsmouth, Royal Navy, Barbarians, Surrey, Hampshire
Debut: v Scotland, Inverleith, Edinburgh, March 1908

Lyon was one of three players from US Portsmouth and the Royal Navy in the England side when he made his debut against Scotland in March 1908, but unlike Walter Lapage and Fischer Watson, the others in the side, he kept his place for the next game against Australia in January 1909. Lyon was already a founding member of the Royal Navy RU in 1906 and played cricket for the Navy and Hampshire. He spent the First World War on board HMS Monarch as gunnery officer and rose steadily through the ranks until his retirement in August 1943.

465. OLDHAM, William Leonard
Forward 2 caps 1908-1909
Born: Coventry, Warwickshire, 15 June 1887
Died: Poole, Dorset, 27 April 1965
Career: Coventry, Midland Counties
Debut: v Scotland, Inverleith, Edinburgh, March 1908

Oldham was one of three brothers, with Tom and Percy, to play for Coventry, captaining the club between 1909 and 1913. He became the first home international produced by Coventry, winning his first cap against Scotland in 1908 and his second Australia the following year. He served in the 16th Lancers Leicestershire Yeomanry during the First World War. Oldham was a workhouse master from 1917 to 1924, then moved to Hornchurch, Essex, as a superintendent of a children's home. After retiring in 1951, he moved to Parkstone, Poole, where he died. His wife, Annie Dunn Kemp, was a well-known Coventry singer.

466. WOODS, Thomas
Forward 1 cap 1908
Born: Bridgwater, Somerset, 9 February 1883
Died: Rochdale, Greater Manchester, 12 April 1955
Career: Bridgewater Albion, Somerset
Debut: v Scotland, Inverleith, Edinburgh, March 1908

Woods won a single England cap against Scotland in March 1908 and was captain of Somerset when he switched codes in 1909 to join Rochdale Hornets. His switch to Rugby League brought him much success, winning the Lancashire League, Cup and Challenge Cup honours, and he also played for England and Great Britain. Woods joined the Guards regiment at the outbreak of the First World War, while his son Leslie later played rugby league for Swinton. Tommy was a licensee and the Hornets A team trainer for a spell before becoming a groundsman for the greyhound racing company until retiring.

467. ASHCROFT, Dr Alec Hutchinson DSO
Fly-half 1 cap 1909
Born: West Derby, Lancashire 18 October 1887
Died: Bath, Somerset 18 April 1963
Career: Birkenhead School, Cambridge University, Birkenhead Park, Blackheath, Edinburgh Wanderers, Cheshire
Debut: v Australia, Rectory Field, Blackheath, January 1909

Cambridge University-educated Ashcroft won a blue in 1908 and 1909, the year he won his only England cap. He went into teaching at Fettes College and was an assistant master between 1910 and 1914, when he was appointed headmaster. During the First World War, Ashcroft was a temporary major in the South Staffordshire Regiment and saw action in Gallipoli, Egypt and France, winning a DSO in 1919 before returning to Fettes, staying until he retired to Bath in 1945. He became a governor of several schools, a co-opted member of the Education Committee and a Bathavon Rural District Councillor.

468. ASSINDER, Eric Walter
Centre 2 caps 1909
Born: Kings Norton, Worcestershire, 29 August 1888,
Died: Snitterfield, Stratford-upon-Avon, 11 October 1974
Career: King Edward's School Birmingham, Old Edwardians, Midland Counties
Debut: v Australia, Rectory Field, Blackheath, January 1909

Assinder was one of 11 new caps selected to face Australia at Blackheath in January 1909, and he kept his place for the following game against Wales a week later. He then lost his place to Ronald Poulton and was never selected again. Assinder spent many years acting as a consultant physician at Birmingham General Hospital and Birmingham Midland Eye Hospital. He moved to Snitterfield when he retired but continued to work part-time locally. In his younger days, he was said to have been a good cross-country runner and then a good golfer in his later days.

469. BENNETTS, Barzillai Beckerleg
Wing 2 caps 1909
Born: Penzance, Cornwall, 14 July 1883
Died: Alverton, Cornwall, 26 July 1958
Career: Bridgend College, Penzance, Devonport Albion, Redruth, Richmond, Barbarians, Cornwall
Debut: v Australia Rectory Field Blackheath January 1909

Bennetts is one of the finest sportsmen Penzance and Cornwall have produced. A member of the Cornwall side that won the 1908 County Championship. He played football for Penzance FC and represented the duchy in cricket, golf and hockey. He was also President of the Cornwall Rugby Union. Bennetts was a solicitor and, for 25 years, was deputy coroner of West Cornwall and then Registrar of Penzance and Helston County courts until his death. He served in the Argyll and Sutherland Highlanders in the First World War, then in World War Two in the Local Defence Volunteer Force and later the Home Guard.

470. COOPER, John Graham
Forward 2 caps 1909
Born: Birmingham 3 June 1881
Died: Canada 26 October 1965
Career: Aston Grammer School, Aston Old Edwardians, Moseley, Midlands
Debut: v Australia, Rectory Field, Blackheath, January 1909

Cooper started playing rugby for Aston Old Edwardians 2nd XI before joining Moseley and playing as a forward and full-back. He had two spells as captain from 1905 to 1910 and then again from 1911-12. During his time as captain, he won his only two England caps against Australia in January 1909 and Wales in Cardiff a week later, but after two defeats, he was never selected again. Cooper was a captain in the Royal Warwickshire Regiment during the First World War. He was a solicitor and worked for Britannic Assurance before retiring to Canada.

471. DOWN, Percy John
Prop 1 cap 1909
Born: Clifton, Gloucestershire, 14 October 1882
Died: West Town, Gloucestershire, 29 June 1954
Career: Cotham, Bristol, Somerset
Debut: v Australia, Rectory Field, Blackheath, January 1909

Down was educated at Long Ashton School, where he played rugby and cricket, then joined Cotham in 1900. But searching for a higher standard, he moved to Bristol, where he spent the next 11 years. He toured New Zealand and Australia with the British Team in 1908 and survived falling overboard as the ship departed for Australia and won his only England cap the following January. He spent 15 years on the Bristol committee, the last seven as chairman, taking over from Billy Holden. Down was managing director of the potato merchants that carry his name in Bristol.

472. KNIGHT, Frederick Frank
Flanker 1 cap 1909
Born: Stoke Damerel, Devon, 22 March 1885
Died: Plymouth, Devon, 3 August 1965
Career: Devonport Albion, Plymouth Albion, Devon
Debut: v Australia Rectory Field Blackheath January 1909

Plymouth-born Knight served Devonport and Plymouth Albion, where he was captain when he helped Devon retain their County Championship crown in 1907. He won his only England cap against Australia at Blackheath in January 1909, and his union career ended in controversy three years later. The Rugby Union suspended him for breaching the rules on professionalism, and he immediately joined Plymouth's Northern Union side in December 1912 and was immediately elected captain. Fred served as a private in the Royal Army Service Corps during the First World War and was a draughtsman at the Royal Navy Dockyard in Devonport.

473. MOBBS, Edgar Robert DSO
Wing 7 caps (12-4t)
Born: Northampton, Northamptonshire, 29 June 1882
Died: Zillebecke, France, 31 July 1917
Career: Bedford Modern School, Olney, Northampton, East Midlands, Barbarians
Debut: v Australia, Rectory Field, Blackheath, January 1909

Mobbs, dubbed 'The Bedford Greyhound', was one of English rugby's first true stars. He scored a try on his debut as one of 11 new caps against Australia. He also scored 177 tries for Northampton, whom he captained between 1906 and 1913 and led England against France in his final appearance. Edgar, a chartered accountant and then the manager of a motor garage, was refused a commission at the start of the First World War because he was 32. Mobbs raised his own company, 'D' Company 7th Northants Regiment, and within 48 hours had recruited 250 athletes, many well-known and rose to become lieutenant Colonel of the regiment.

474. MORRIS, Alfred Drummond CB CMG OBE
Forward 3 caps 1909
Born: Richmond 18 December 1883
Died: Chelsea, London 24 March 1962
Career: Alverstoke School, United Services Portsmouth, Royal Navy, Barbarians, RAF Flowerdown
Debut: v Australia, Rectory Field, Blackheath, January 1909

Morris won all three of his England caps in 1909, but he was a founder member of the RAF Rugby Union in 1920, becoming sole selector and honorary treasurer. He was to remain on the committee until his death 42 years later. Joined the Royal Navy as a midshipman in 1899, serving the Royal Naval Air Service, Royal Flying Corps, RAF retiring in 1944 as deputy director of the Air Training Corps. On the day of his death, against doctors' orders, Morris went to Twickenham and watched the RAF beat the Army 19-14, only to collapse and die on the way home.

475. PENNY, Sidney Herbert
Forward 1 cap 1909
Born: Finchley, London 7 October 1875
Died: Leicester, Leicestershire 23 May 1965
Career: Leicester, Midland Counties
Debut: v Australia, Rectory Field, Blackheath, January 1909

North London-born Penny was a front-row forward who made over 500 appearances, including 246 consecutively for Leicester between 1895 and 1910. He also played for the club against New Zealand on their first-ever tour in 1905. Penny was at the back end of his career when he won his only test cap against Australia in January 1909. He spent the whole of his working life in the shoe trade and only retired in 1960. He was once sacked from a job just an hour after getting married after staying away from the factory for two days because of a rugby injury.

476. TARR, Francis Nathaniel
Centre 4 caps (6-2t) 1909-1913
Born: Belper, Derbyshire, 14 August 1887
Died: Ypres, Belgium, 18 July 1915
Career: Stoneygate School Leicester, Uppingham School, Oxford University, Leicester, Headingley, Midland Counties.
Debut: v Australia, Rectory Field, Blackheath, January 1909

Tarr first won his rugby colours at Uppingham School before completing his education at Oxford University, where he won his blue partnering Percy Lawrie, who would later be his Leicester captain. He made his international debut against Australia in January 1909 and scored both of his tries against France on familiar ground at Welford Road three weeks later. He was articled to solicitors Owston, Dickinson, Simpson and Bigg and was about to take his final exam when he was called on the First Day of the First World War and was killed by a shell serving in the Leicestershire Territorial Regiment.

477. ARCHER, Herbert
No 8 3 caps 1908-1909
Born: Bridgwater, Somerset, 6 August 1883
Died: West Penrith, Cornwall, 26 December 1946
Career: Guy's Hospital, Bridgwater and Albion
Debut: v Wales, Arms Park, Cardiff January 1909

Uncapped Archer was playing for Guy's Hospital when he was selected to be a member of the 1908 British Isles team touring Australia and New Zealand and played in three tests against New Zealand. But it wasn't until the following January that he won the first of his three caps. Archer was the honorary surgeon at Bristol Royal Infirmary before becoming one of the best-known doctors in Bridgewater, working in the District General Hospital for many years before practising in Nether Stoney. Archer retired just two weeks before his Boxing Day death, collapsing while out snipe shooting visiting his daughter in Cornwall.

478. HANDFORD, Frank Gordon
Flanker 4 caps 1909
Born: Eccles, Lancashire 28 January 1884
Died: Marlow, Buckinghamshire, 14 October 1953
Career: The Leys School, Kersal, Manchester, Barbarians, Lancashire
Debut: v Wales, Arms Park, Cardiff, January 1909

Handford won all four of his England caps in 1909, but his international career appeared to have ended when he emigrated to South Africa at the start of the 1909-1910 season. But he was selected to be part of the 1910 British Isles tour to South Africa, playing in all three test matches. He returned to Lancashire soon afterwards and continued to play for Manchester and Lancashire until the outbreak of the First World War, when he saw service in the Machine Gun Corps. When peacetime returned, he took up farming until his retirement.

479. IBBITSON, Ernest Denison
Lock 4 caps 1909
Born: Leeds, Yorkshire, 1 February 1882
Died: Bolton, Ontario (Canada) 11 May 1942
Career: Wesley College Sheffield, Headingley, Yorkshire
Debut: v Wales Arms Park, Cardiff January 1909

Ibbitson started his rugby career at Headingley alongside his younger brother Herbert, who played for Yorkshire together. Ibbitson made his England debut in January 1909 after impressing the selectors in the North vs South trial match a month earlier. He retained his place for the next three matches of that campaign. During the First World War, he served as a gunner and then a Sgt-farrier. in the Honourable Artillery Company. Ibbitson was a woollen merchant with the family firm Thomas Ibbotson and Co. in Leeds until 1915 and then became a textile agent emigrating to Canada to work as a produce broker.

480. JOHNS, William
Forward 7 caps (3-1t) 1909-1910
Born: Gloucester, Gloucestershire, 1 February 1882
Died: Weston-super-Mare, Somerset, 10 March 1965
Career: Sir Thomas Rich's School, Rich's Old Boys, St Catherine's, Gloucester, Gloucestershire
Debut: v Wales, Arms Park, Cardiff, January 1909

Johns started his career as a half-back and captained his school team before playing for Rich's Old Boys and St Catherine's before joining Gloucester, making his senior debut in 1902. He succeeded George Romans as captain but had to wait until January 1909 to win his first England caps. Johns would help Gloucester win their two County Championship titles. A commercial clerk, he became a second lieutenant in the Corps of Royal Engineers and then was a hotelier in the Gloucester area, running the Wellington Hotel, the Amberley Hotel, and Prince of Wales in Berkeley Road, Gloucester.

481. BOLTON, Charles Arthur CBE
Flanker 1 cap 1909
Born: Kensington, London, 3 January 1882
Died: Eastbourne, Sussex, 23 November 1963
Career: Marlborough College, Oxford University, United Services Portsmouth, Barbarians, Surrey
Debut: v France, Welford Road, Leicester, January 1909

Bolton was educated at Marlborough College and Oxford University but never won his university colours. He joined the Manchester Regiment in 1902 and won his only international cap against France at Welford Road, Leicester, seven years later while playing for United Services Portsmouth after impressing in a trial. He served in the Manchester's during the First World War, was mentioned in dispatches four times, and was awarded a CBE in 1919. Four years later, he joined the Royal Tank Corps, rising to the rank of brigadier. In World War Two, Bolton was a member of the British Expeditionary Force in France and the Middle East Forces.

482. HUTCHINSON, Frank MC
Fly-half 3 caps (3-1t)
Born: Wakefield, West Yorkshire, 20 October 1885
Died: Leeds, West Yorkshire, 5 March 1960
Career: Leeds Grammar School, Old Leodiensians, Headingley, Barbarians, Yorkshire
Debut: v France Welford Road, Leicester January 1909

Hutchinson, the son of Herbert Hutchinson, who played for Wakefield Trinity and Yorkshire, started his rugby career at

Leeds Grammar School and then Old Leodiensians before joining Headingley. He would go one step further than his father and win an international cap, scoring a try on his debut against France at Welford Road, Leicester, in January 1909. He would retain his place for the following two matches but got dropped when Adrian Stoop was named captain. Hutchinson, a Hotel proprietor, played cricket for Yorkshire seconds, served as a Second lieutenant in the Royal Garrison Artillery during the First World War and picked up a Military Cross.

483. POULTON-PALMER, Ronald William
Centre 17 caps (28-8t, 1d) 1909-1914
Born: Headington, Oxford, 12 September 1889
Died: Ploegsteert Wood, Belgium, 5 May 1915
Career: Oxford University, Harlequins, Liverpool
Debut: v France, Welford Road, Leicester January 1909

Born Ronald Poulton, he changed his name to Palmer by Royal Licence as a condition of inheriting a fortune from his uncle George Palmer of the Huntley and Palmer biscuit company. He scored a record five tries in the 1909 Varsity match, which still stands today. He captained England to the Home Championship in 1914, scoring four times against France in the last international before the First World War. This would make him one of 26 England internationals to make the ultimate sacrifice. After being commissioned into the Royal Berkshire Regiment, a sniper bullet killed Poulton-Palmer during the Second Battle of Ypres.

484. MORTON, Harold James Storrs
Prop 4 caps 1909-1910
Born: Sheffield, Yorkshire, 31 January 1886,
Died: Whitechapel, London, 3 January 1955
Career: Uppingham School, Cambridge University, The London Hospital, United Hospitals, Blackheath, Barbarians
Debut: v Ireland, Lansdowne Road, Dublin, February 1909

Morton won a Cambridge University blue in 1908, and the first of his four England caps arrived against Ireland in Dublin the following year. Also, in 1909, he captained a Cambridge side during trials even though he couldn't play in the Varsity match because he was in his fifth year. After leaving Cambridge, he joined Blackheath, where, in 1910, he won his final two caps against Wales and Ireland. During the First World War, Morton was a captain in the Royal Army Medical Corps and went on to practice medicine from his home in Hampstead, London and then much later in life in Cambridgeshire.

485. PALMER, Alexander Croydon
Wing 2 caps (10 -2t, 2c)
Born: Dunedin, New Zealand, 2 July 1887
Died: Walton Heath, Surrey 16 October 1963
Career: Waitaki Boys High School, Otago University, The London Hospital, Royal Army Medical Corps, Harlequins, Barbarians, Eastern Counties
Debut: v Ireland, Lansdowne Road, Dublin, February 1909

New Zealand-born Palmer came to England to gain his medical qualifications at the London Hospital, where he was a house surgeon, receiving room officer, and obstetric tutor and registrar. Palmer made an instant impact on his England debut, scoring two tries and kicking one conversion. Strangely, he played the following game against Scotland but was never selected afterwards. During the First World War, he was a major in the RAMC, becoming a consultant gynaecologist to King's College and the Samaritan Hospitals and was a consultant to Epsom and Ewell and Sutton and Cheam Hospitals while in later life was President of the United Hospitals Rugby Club.

486. WILSON, Arthur James
Forward 1 cap 1909
Born: Newcastle-upon-Tyne, Northumberland, 29 December 1886
Died: Flanders, 31 July 1917
Career: Northern, Camborne, Camborne School of Mines, Camborne Students, Cornwall.
Debut: v Ireland, Lansdowne Road, Dublin, February 1909

Newcastle-born Wilson moved from one end of the country to another after deciding he wanted a career in mine engineering. He was soon snapped up by Cornwall, helping them win the 1908 County Championship, and later the same year, he was a member of the Great Britain rugby union team, which won Olympic silver. Far greater reward followed in February 1909 when he won his only England cap. Wilson would mine in West Africa and then became a coffee planter in India but was a private in the Royal Fusiliers when he was killed in action.

487. WRIGHT, Cyril Carne Glenton
Centre 2 caps 1909
Born: Bombay, India, 7 March 1887
Died: Hampstead, London, 15 September 1960
Career: Tonbridge School, Cambridge University, Blackheath, Barbarians, Kent
Debut: v Ireland, Lansdowne Road, Dublin, February 1909

Wright was educated at Tonbridge School and became a double-blue in cricket and rugby at Cambridge. He was still at university when he won his only two international caps in 1909 against Ireland and retained his place for a defeat to Scotland at Richmond. During the First World War, Wright played cricket for Kent seconds and served as a captain and adjutant in The Durham Light Infantry. He became a schoolmaster, returning to Tonbridge as a games master between 1919 to 1929 and then at Dulwich College. Later in life, he left teaching and became a solicitor's clerk.

488. HARRISON, Harold Cecil
Forward 4 caps
Born: Solihull, West Midlands, 26 February 1889
Died: Marylebone, Middlesex, 26 March 1940
Career: King Edward School Birmingham, RMA Woolwich, United Services Portsmouth, Royal Marines, The Army, Royal Navy, Barbarians, Midlands, Kent
Debut: v Scotland, Athletic Ground, Richmond, March 1909

Harrison, known in the Army as 'Tiny' for whom he played in 1910, 1911, and 1914 and between 1909 and 1912 while playing for the Navy 'Dreadnought'. It was while he was serving in the Royal Marines in 1909 that he won his first cap. Military service meant it wasn't until 1914 that he won his final three caps, helping England win the Home Championship. Harris later refereed an international between France and Scotland and continued to serve his country until his retirement in 1939, just a year before he died when he was Commander of the 4th Infantry Brigade.

489. BARRINGTON-WARD, Sir Lancelot Edward KCVO
No 8 4 caps 1910
Born: Worcester, Worcestershire, 4 July 1884
Died: Bury St Edmunds, Suffolk, 17 November 1953
Career: Westminster School, Bromsgrove School, Oxford University, Edinburgh University
Debut: v Wales Twickenham, January 1910

Barrington-Ward was the first rugby player born in Worcester to play for England when he debuted aged 26 against Wales in January 1910 in the first-ever match at Twickenham. He played all four games, helping England win the Home Championship. He was appointed house surgeon at the Great Ormond Street Hospital and an abdominal surgeon at the Royal Northern Hospital, where he became a senior surgeon. He was a consulting surgeon at Wood Green and Southgate Hospital and then Sutton Hospital. Barrington-Ward served as a surgeon to King George VI between 1935 and 1952 and was an extra surgeon to Queen Elizabeth II.

490. BERRY, Henry
Forward 4 caps (6-2t) 1910
Born: Gloucester, Gloucestershire, 31 January 1883
Died: Festubert, France, 9 May 1915
Career: Gloucester, Gloucestershire
Debut: v Wales, Twickenham, January 1910

Berry first took up rugby, serving in the 4th Militia Volunteers while guarding Boer War prisoners on St Helena. After leaving the Army in 1909 after contracting malaria, he started to play for his hometown club, and within a year, the national team won all of his international caps, helping England to their first Home Championship in 18 years, but strangely, he was never selected again. Publican Berry ran the Red Lion and then the Stag's Head. He was recalled to Colours at the outbreak of the First World War and was killed in the Battle of Aubers Ridge.

491. CHAPMAN, Frederick Ernest
Wing 7 caps (20-1t, 7c, 1p)
Born: South Shields, Tyne and Wear 11 July 1887
Died: Hartlepool, County Durham 8 May 1938
Career: South Shields High School, Durham University, Westoe, Hartlepool Rovers, Durham Counties
Debut: v Wales, Twickenham, January 1910

Chapman's part in Twickenham history is now largely unknown, but he scored the first try, the first penalty goal and the first conversion at the stadium on his international debut. He was a member of the British Team tour to Australia and New Zealand in 1908 before making his England debut. He was one of six brothers and won the first four of his caps while playing for Westoe before switching to Hartlepool Rovers after he was appointed house surgeon at Hartlepool Hospital. During the First World War, he served the Royal Army Medical Corp and later went into private medical practice.

492. HAIGH, Leonard
Prop 7 caps 1910-1911
Born: Prestwich, Lancashire, 19 October 1880
Died: Woolwich, Kent, 6 August 1916
Career: Manchester, Lancashire, The Barbarians
Debut: v Wales Twickenham, Greater London January 1910

Haigh didn't play rugby during his education at Sandringham House School in Southport, only association football and cricket. It wasn't until he joined Manchester Rugby Club later in life that he started to do so. But his rise to international fame was rapid. He was nearly 30 when he won his first cap in the first international at Twickenham and then helped win their first Home Championship in 18 years. Haigh, a cotton spinner, became an officer cadet but died of pneumonia after suffering sunstroke while training with the Army Service Corps during the First World War.

493. JOHNSTON, William R
Full-back 16 Caps 1910-1914
Born: Horfield, Gloucestershire, 25 November 1885
Died: Bristol, 29 November 1939
Career: Colston's School Bristol, Horfield, Bristol, Gloucestershire
Debut: v Wales, Twickenham Greater London, January 1910

Johnston started his rugby career at his local club in his native Horfield before joining Bristol in 1908, playing three-quarter back, then half back before settling in at full-back, the position that made him famous. He broke into England's set-up, making his international debut in 1910 and was an ever-present in the England side that won back-to-back Grand Slams in 1913 and 1914. It helped him to become England's most capped full-back. Johnston was a Commercial Traveller for Roy Dick Ltd and captained Bristol for two seasons before ending his career after the First World War.

494. PILLMAN, Charles Henry
Flanker 18 caps (26-8t 1c) 1910-1914
Born: Bromley, Kent, 8 January 1890
Died: Bromley-by-Bow, London, 13 November 1955
Career: Tonbridge School, Blackheath, Barbarians, Kent
Debut: v Wales, Twickenham, January 1910

Flour importer and member of the London Corn Exchange Pillman was the brother of Robert Pillman, another England international. He debuted in the first-ever game at Twickenham in January 1910 and helped England win their first Home Championship in 18 years. He became the star of the 1910 British Team tour to South Africa, the leading scorer with 67 points. Pillman later helped England win Grand Slams in 1913 and 1914. During the First World War, he served with the Dragoon Guards. Then, during the Second World War, he was Area Flour Officer for South East Division.

495. SMITH, Dyne Fenton
Lock 2 caps 1910
Born: Hove, Sussex, 21 July 1890
Died: Lambeth, London, 28 August 1969
Career: Sherborne School, Richmond, Royal Fusiliers, Barbarians, Surrey
Debut: v Wales, Twickenham, January 1910

Smith made his England debut in the first-ever international to be played at Twickenham against Wales in January 1910. He then retained his place for the following game, a 0-0 draw against Ireland, also played at Twickenham. But when England rang the changes for their third game in Paris, he was dropped and never selected again. Smith was then selected as a member of Tommy Smyth's 1910 British Isles to South Africa and played in all three tests. During the First World War, he served as a major in the Royal Fusiliers and was a stockjobber helping run Fenton Smith Bros.

496. SOLOMON, John Charles
Centre 1 cap 1910
Born: Redruth, Cornwall, 8 March 1885
Died: Redruth, Cornwall, 30 June 1961
Career: Redruth, Cornwall
Debut: v Wales, Twickenham, January 1910

Solomon was among Cornwall's most gifted players. He began playing for Treleigh and went straight into the Redruth first XV and was the star of their three-quarter line for the next seven seasons. Solomon made his only England appearance in the first match played at Twickenham against Wales in January 1910. It was said that he was invited to play for England several times afterwards but always declined. He was captain of the British team that won silver in the 1908 Olympics. Solomon was a butcher at the Redruth factory of Cornish Meat and Provision company, and his son Alfred played for Devon and Cornwall in 1947.

497. HAYWARD, Leslie William
Centre 1 cap 1910
Born: Cheltenham, Gloucestershire, 17 May 1885
Died: Birmingham, Warwickshire, 5 July 1937
Career: Cheltenham Grammar School, Cheltenham, Tarbes, T.O.E.C, Gloucestershire
Debut: v Ireland, Twickenham, February 1910

Hayward played association football at Cheltenham Grammar School but would become Cheltenham captain. Hayward, who was initially an accountant, won his only international cap against Ireland in February 1910. Selected in place of John Solomon, he became the first Cheltonian to be capped by England. But in September 1911, he left Cheltenham to work in the South of France, where he would play for Tarbes and later T.O.E.C. After returning to live in the United Kingdom, Hayward settled in Kings Heath, Birmingham, where he would earn a living as a commercial traveller in the rubber trade.

498. ADAMS, Alan Augustus
Centre 1 cap 1910
Born: Greymouth, New Zealand, 8 May 1880
Died: Greymouth, New Zealand, 28 July 1963
Career: Auckland Grammar School, Auckland University, South Island, The London Hospital, London University, Eastern Counties, Barbarians
Debut: v France, Parc des Princes, Paris, March 1910

New Zealander Adams moved to London to complete his medical studies and, at the time, was one of six Kiwis who played for London Hospitals. He caught the eye of England selectors and was picked to play against France in Paris in March 2010. A talented cricketer who made two first-class appearances for Otago. Alan returned to England to serve as a captain in The Prince of Wales's Own, West Yorkshire Regiment in the First World War and was later a New Zealand selector between 1927 and 1928, then from 1934 and 1937. He was also President of the NZRFU in 1929.

499. COVERDALE, Harry
Fly-half 4 caps (4-1d) 1910-1920
Born: Hartlepool, Durham 22 March 1889
Died: South Africa 29 October 1965
Career: Rossall School, Hartlepool Rovers, Blackheath, Barbarians, Durham Counties, Surrey
Debut: v France, Parc des Princes, Paris March 1910

Coverdale played association football during his school days at Rossall but was only 20 when he made his England debut against France in March 1910 after replacing Adrian Stoop in a trial match. It would be another two years before he was recalled to the side. Coverdale served in the Army during the First World War and then played in the first test following the Armistice against Wales in Cardiff. A ship owner and shipping agent before emigrating to South Africa in 1949, he was an England selector between 1931 and 1948, who served in the RAF during the Second World War.

500. HANDS, Reginald Harry Myburgh
Forward 2 caps 1910
Born: Claremont, Cape Town, 26 July 1888
Died: Eppeville, France, 20 April 1918
Career: Oxford University, Blackheath, Middlesex, Barbarians, Western Province
Debut: v France, Parc des Princes, Paris, March 1910

Hands won a Rhodes Scholarship to study law at Oxford and followed his two brothers to win a blue. England v the South, as well as the Rest v England. It led to him playing against France in Paris. He kept his place for the last game against Scotland and helped England claim their first Championship since 1892. He was called to the bar in 1911 before returning home to South Africa, where he became a test cricketer in 1914, but his first-class career lasted just 15 months. He was killed in action while serving as a captain in the Royal Garrison Artillery Brigades during the First World War.

501. HENNIKER-GOTLEY, Anthony Lefroy
Scrum-half 6 caps
Born: Tysoe, Warwickshire, 2 March 1887
Died: Torbay, Devon, 4 May 1972
Career: Tonbridge School, Oxford University, Blackheath, Surrey, Kent, Barbarians
Debut: v France, Parc des Princes, Paris, March 1910

Tonbridge School-educated Henniker-Gotley won an Oxford University blue in 1909 and toured Argentina with the British team playing in the only test. He made his last four appearances before moving to Rhodesia in 1911. He was a political officer in Tanganyika before he was called to the bar, then served as District Commissioner in Tanganyika. After going into business in Durban, Henniker-Gotley became Bursar and assistant master at St Columba's College, Dublin, then a temporary education officer for the RAF, having seen service during the First World War in the North Rhodesia Police and The Army in East Africa.

502. RITSON, Professor John Anthony Sidney DSO MC OBE TD
Forward 7 caps (6-2t) 1910-1913
Born: Chester-le-Street, Durham, 18 August 1887
Died: Guildford, Surrey, 16 October 1957
Career: Uppingham School, Durham University, Edinburgh University, Northern, Barbarians, Northumberland
Debut: v France, Parc des Princes, Paris, March 1910

Ritson had to wait almost two years after being capped by the British Team in New Zealand in 1908 to win his first England cap. He was a member of England's Grand Slam-winning squad in 1913, the last time he played for his country. During the First World War, he was a major in the Durham Light Infantry and twice mentioned in dispatches, winning a Military Cross and Distinguished Service Order in 1917. Ritson became HM Inspector of Mines in Scotland and Wales before becoming a professor of Mining at Leeds University and the Royal School of Mines and was a member of the Board of Mining Examinations.

503. SCORFIELD, Edward Scafe
Lock 1 cap 1910
Born: Preston, Northumberland, 21 April 1882
Died: Mosman, Australia, 11 December 1965
Career: RGS Newcastle, Percy Park, Northumberland
Debut: v France, Parc des Princes, Paris, March 1910

Marine architect Scorfield won his only cap against France in Paris in March 1910 as one of four changes in the pack, and despite playing for England against The Rest the following year, he was never selected again. Scorfield captained Percy Park between 1910 and 1912 and was a member of the Tyneside Rowing Club from 1906 to 1925. He was a member of the Royal Engineers during the First World War, serving in Gallipoli, Salonika and Palestine. Scorfield began drawing cartoons for the Newcastle Weekly Chronicle while working in a Tyneside shipyard before moving to Australia to work for the Bulletin as a cartoonist and illustrator.

504. WILLIAMS, Cyril Stoate
Full-back 1 cap 1910
Born: Stroud, Gloucestershire, 17 November 1887
Died: Victoria, BC, 18 November 1978
Career: Truro College, Mill Hill School, Manchester University, Manchester, Lancashire
Debut: v France, Parc des Princes, Paris March 1910

The son of a Wesleyan Minister, Williams, despite playing in three trial games during the 1909-1910 season, made his only England appearance against France in Paris in March 1910 in the only game that Bill Johnston, originally selected, missed that season. Cyril later became a US Citizen, but during the First World War, after moving to Canada, he served in the 180th Battalion and then the Fourth Battalion Canadian Overseas Expeditionary Force and was wounded in 1918. Williams worked for the Associated Portland Cement Manufacturers in British Columbia as an analytical chemist, becoming a works manager and plant superintendent before his retirement.

505. WODEHOUSE, Vice Admiral Norman Atherton CB
Forward 14 caps (6-2t) 1910-1914
Born: Basford, Nottinghamshire, 18 May 1887
Died: Killed at Sea, West Africa, 4 July 1941
Career: United Services, Royal Navy, Barbarians, Hampshire
Debut: v France, Parc des Princes, Paris, March 1910

During his career, Wodehouse was rated as the best captain England had since John Daniell and rounded off his international career by leading England to the Grand Slam in 1913. By the start of the following season, he was replaced by Ronnie Poulton-Palmer and was never selected again. Wodehouse served in the Royal Navy throughout his working life and was also Aide-de-Camp to HM King George VI, head of the British Military Mission to Portugal and Admiral Superintendent of the Gibraltar Dockyard. Recalled from the retained list to serve in World War Two, he was in charge of an Atlantic convoy when he was announced missing at sea.

506. HIND, Guy Reginald MB BS
Prop 2 caps 1910-1911
Born: Stoke-on-Trent, Staffordshire, 4 April 1887,
Died: Newcastle-under-Lyne, Staffordshire, 8 November 1970
Career: Haileybury & ISC, Guy's Hospital, Blackheath, Barbarians, Kent
Debut: v Scotland, Inverleith, Edinburgh, March 1910

Hind was one of four members of the Guy's Hospital side to make the British Isles 1908 tour to Australia and New Zealand, playing in two test matches. He had to wait until 1910 to make his England debut and clinch the Home Championship title. He followed his father Wheelton into medicine and was Hon. Surgeon Longton Cottage Hospital. Hind returned to his native Stoke-on-Trent during the First World War and was a surgeon at the War Hospital. He would later become a medical officer at a Blind and Deaf School in Stoke and then at the North Stafford Railway.

507. LAWRIE, Percy William
Wing 2 caps (3-1t) 1910-1911
Born: Lutterworth, Leicestershire, 26 September 1888
Died: Leicester, Leicestershire, 27 December 1956
Career: Wyggeston School, Stoneygate, Leicester, Midlands, Barbarians, Leicestershire
Debut: v Scotland, Inverleith, Edinburgh, March 1910

Lutterworth-born Lawrie made his Leicester bow on the wing as a 19-year-old, later moving to the centre. He would have won more caps but lost the best years of his career to the First World War. After the War, he took over the captaincy for what was seen as the first golden period for Leicester Tigers. Cartilage problems curtailed his Leicester career after 206 tries in 318 games, he returned to Stoneygate, where he first played aged 17. An incorporated accountant, Lawrie was a lieutenant in the Royal Artillery in the First World War and served in the Home Guard during the Second World War.

508. STOOP, Frederick MacFarlane
Centre 4 caps 1910-1913
Born: Kensington, London, 17 September 1888
Died: Hindhead Surrey, 24 November 1972
Career: Rugby School, Harlequins, Royal Armoured Corps, Barbarians, Surrey
Debut: v Scotland, Inverleith Edinburgh, March 1910

Rugby School-educated Stoop was the younger brother of Adrian and won three of his four caps playing alongside him. Stoop joined Harlequins in 1907 and three years later won the first of his caps after his friend from school, Ronnie Poulton-Palmer, declined an invitation to play in Scotland. His caps were spread out over three years but wasn't considered a first choice. Stoop served in the First World War as a lieutenant in The Buffs (East Kent Regiment) and then the Machine Gun Corps. He was a stockbroker with Stoop & Co, a firm founded by his father.

509. BROWN, Leonard Graham MC
Prop 18 caps (12-4t) 1911-1922
Born: Brisbane, Queensland, 6 September 1888
Died: Charing Cross, London, 23 May 1950
Career: Brisbane Grammar School, Oxford University, The London Hospital, Blackheath, Barbarians, Surrey
Debut: v Wales, St Helen's, Swansea, January 1911

Rhodes Scholar 'Bruno' Brown attended Oxford University and won his blues between 1910 and 1912 when he was captain. He made his test debut against Wales in January 1911 and was captain for his last against the same opposition 11 years later. Brown's career was interrupted by the First World War when he served as a captain and later a lieutenant colonel in the Royal Army Medical Corps, winning a Military Cross in 1917. He was the NSW rep on the RFU board and RFU President, responsible for Australia, New Zealand and South Africa joining the international board. The ENT specialist also had a large and successful private practice.

510. KING, John Abbott
Hooker/Flanker 12 caps 1911-1913
Born: Leeds, Yorkshire, 21 August 1883
Died: Guillemont, France, 9 August 1916
Career: Giggleswick School, Durbanville, Somerset West (SA), Headingley, Barbarians, Yorkshire
Debut: v Wales, St Helen's, Swansea, January 1911

King played his first club rugby in South Africa but joined Headingley after returning to England in 1906. A farmer in Ben Rydding, who stood only five feet five, he was one of the smallest English forwards ever. He only missed one international in three seasons after breaking ribs against Scotland in March 1912, helping win a Grand Slam a year later. King was one of the first Headingley players to enlist in the Yorkshire Hussars before transferring to The King's Liverpool Regiment and died on the same day as a friend and fellow international Lancelot Slocock. His brother Arthur had an England trial.

511. MANN, Major William Edgar DSO
Forward 3 caps (3-1t) 1911
Born: Edmonton, London, 19 January 1885
Died: Blyth, Northumberland, 14 February 1969
Career: Marlborough College, RMA Woolwich, United Services Portsmouth, The Army, Surrey
Debut: v Wales, St Helen's, Swansea, January 1911

Mann, the son of Sir Edward Mann, High Sheriff of Norfolk, was educated at Marlborough College and spent the early part of his life in the Army, becoming a major in the Royal Field Artillery. He won all three of his caps in 1911, scoring a try against France, the only one of the matches England won. He then transferred to Ireland, losing his place to Roland Lagden and was never selected again. Mann was mentioned in dispatches during the First World War and twice wounded before being awarded the Distinguished Service Order in 1917 and later becoming a dairy farmer.

512. ROBERTS, Alan Dixon MC
Wing 8 caps (15-5t) 1911-1914
Born: Newcastle-upon-Tyne, Tyne & Wear 5 December 1887
Died: Bull Bay, Anglesey, 1 September 1940
Career: Durham School, Cambridge University, Northern, Barbarians, Northumberland
Debut: v Wales, St Helen's, Swansea, January 1911

Durham School-educated Roberts went to Cambridge University but didn't win his university colours. A powerful winger who was a 'brute' to tackle, he was selected for international trials in December 1910, playing for The North and then The Rest against on England occasions. He was called up for his debut a month later in place of Frederick Stoop and scored a try against Wales at St Helen's. Roberts was a solicitor during the First World War. He served as a private in the Royal Fusiliers and then as a captain in the Welsh Regiment and was awarded a Military Cross after being wounded.

513. SCHOLFIELD, John Arthur
Centre 1 cap (3-1t) 1911
Born: Fylde, Lancashire, 6 April 1888
Died: Barnstaple, Devon, 14 September 1967
Career: Sedbergh School, Cambridge University, Manchester, Preston Grasshoppers, Harlequins, Barbarians, Lancashire
Debut: v Wales, St Helen's, Swansea, January 1911

Scholfield represented Sedburgh School before winning his Cambridge University blue in 1909 and 1910 and then won his only cap against Wales in Swansea the following year. Despite scoring one of England's three tries, it wasn't enough to save him from Tim Stoop reclaiming his place for the win over France just a week later. During the First World War, Scholfield, an Insurance broker, served as a captain and adjutant in the Manchester Regiment. He was also wounded and taken POW. Scholfield also played Second XI cricket for Lancashire CCC and later in life was captain of Royal Birkdale Golf Club.

514. WILLIAMS, Stanley Horatio DSO
Full-back 4 caps
Born: Rogerstone, Gwent, 2 November 1886
Died: At Sea South Atlantic, 30 April 1936
Career: Newport Intermediate School, Newport, Monmouth
Debut: v Wales, St Helen's, Swansea, January 1911

Association footballer Williams switched to rugby, joining Newport RFC and was Welsh reserve but never capped and was a member of the British Isle's 1910 tour to South Africa. Then controversial, the RFU invoked Newport's Union membership, and he was capped for England against Wales in January 1911. During the First World War, Williams served as a major in the Royal Field Artillery and then became a manager for the Ebbw Vale Steel and Iron Company's Northamptonshire Branch. He was lost overboard while travelling home on a health cruise to the West Indies and South America.

515. LAGDEN, Ronald Owen
No 8 1 cap (4-2c) 1911
Born: Maseru, Basutoland, 21 November 1889
Died: St Eloi, Belgium, 1 March 1915
Career: Marlborough College, Oxford University, Richmond
Debut: v Scotland, Twickenham, March 1911

Lagden first excelled as a sportsman during his education at Marlborough, playing rugby, cricket, hockey and rackets, and as a Rhodes Scholar, he represented Oxford in all four disciplines. He, however, only won a single England cap, replacing William Mann against Scotland at Twickenham, converting two of three tries. The following year, he took a post at Harrow School as a mathematics master and later became vice-captain of Richmond. Lagden enlisted in the King's Royal Rifle Corps and was attached to the 4th Battalion. But after only a few days in France, he led his company in an assault on the German trenches and was killed.

516. BROUGHAM, Henry
Wing 4 caps (9-3t) 1912
Born: Wellington College, Berkshire, 8 July 1888
Died: La Croix, France, 18 February 1923
Career: Harlequins, London
Debut: v Wales, Twickenham, January 1912

Brougham was never considered good enough to play rugby for either Wellington College or Oxford University, where he won a blue in cricket and rackets, the sport he won an Olympic bronze in 1908, a year after winning the Public Schools Rackets Championships. He made all his international appearances in 1912 and scored a try in three of his four games. Brougham was commissioned into the Royal Artillery at the outbreak of war but was invalided out in 1917 following a German gas attack. Then, in 1918, he contracted tuberculosis whilst commanding a battery in Northern Ireland, his lungs were badly affected, and he never recovered.

517. EDDISON, John Horncastle MC
Forward 4 caps (3-1t) 1912
Born: Edinburgh, Scotland, 25 August 1888
Died: Edinburgh, Scotland, 18 November 1982
Career: Ilkley GS, Bromsgrove School, Headingley, Barbarians, Yorkshire
Debut: v Wales, Twickenham, January 1912

Eddison was born in Scotland but was educated in England, where his father worked for the North British and Mercantile Insurance Company. He would spend the whole of his working life working for the firm, joining in 1908 and retiring in 1951 as manager for Scotland. Eddison won his England caps in 1912, scoring on his last appearance against France in Paris. During the First World War, he was a lieutenant, later a major in the Royal Field Artillery mentioned in dispatches before being awarded the Military Cross in 1916. His son John also played for Headingley.

518. HOLLAND, David
Forward 3 caps (3-1t)
Born: Gloucester, Gloucestershire, 1 September 1887,
Died: Gloucester, Gloucestershire, 7 March 1945
Career: Gloucester, Devon Albion, Devonport Services, Gloucestershire
Debut: v Wales, Twickenham, January 1912

Holland was a hard-working forward who spent four seasons with Gloucester and won a County Championship with Gloucestershire in 1910 before moving to Plymouth after securing employment at Devonport Dockyard and played for Devon Albion until 1913, when he switched codes and joined Oldham Rugby League on the same day as former Gloucester club-mate Billy Hall. Holland played on until 1921, when he returned to his native City to work for timber merchants Price, Walker and Co. During the First World War, he served on HMS Colossus, stationed at Scapa Flow, the crew of which won the Navy Rugby Championship.

519. MACILWAINE, Alfred Herbert MC, DSO
Prop 5 caps 1912-1920
Born: Sculcoates, East Riding of Yorkshire, 27 March 1889
Died: Rhodesia 6 April 1983
Career: Clifton College, Hull and East Riding, The Army, United Services Portsmouth, Harlequins, Yorkshire
Debut: v Wales, Twickenham, January 1912

MacIlwaine was an ever-present for England during the 1912 campaign when he was the first player from Hull since Gilbert Harrison to win a cap. But the First World War would ensure it would be eight years before he won his fifth and final cap against Ireland in February 1920. He served with the Royal Artillery and was awarded a Military Cross, Distinguished Service Order and Croix de Guerre with Palm. After leaving The Army, MacIlwaine farmed in the mountains of Rhodesia and founded the Troutbeck Inn resort. The MacIlwaine Cup was competed for annually by Royal Artillery teams.

520. PYM, John Alfred MC
Scrum-half 4 caps (3-1t)
Born: Kingston upon Thames, Surrey, 25 March 1891
Died: Auckland, New Zealand, 9 February 1969
Career: Cheltenham College, Royal Military Academy Woolwich, The Army, Blackheath, Barbarians, Kent
Debut: v Wales, Twickenham, January 1912

Pym burst onto the international scene with a try on his debut against Wales and made all three of his England appearances in 1912. He only ended up on the losing side once against Scotland. Pym, who represented Blackheath when selected for his country, served in The Army in India as a captain and then major in the Royal Engineers during the First World War. He was wounded and twice mentioned in dispatches and reported dead after his name was confused with someone else. Pym later emigrated to New Zealand to take up farming.

521. STAFFORD, Richard Calvert
Prop 4 caps 1912
Born: Bedford, Bedfordshire, 23 July 1893
Died: Bedford, Bedfordshire, 1 December 1912
Career: Bedford Modern School, Bedford, Midland Counties
Debut: v Wales, Twickenham, January 1912

Stafford was captain of his club Bedford when he was 17 and was picked to play for the South against England in a trial in December 1910, but he had to wait until January 1912 to win the first of his four caps against Wales at Twickenham. An ever-present in the side in that first season, he looked set for a long and successful international career until he was sidelined with a muscle strain in October 1912. When he failed to recover, a specialist was sent for and diagnosed with spine cancer. He died just three weeks later.

522. GREENWOOD, John Eric
Forward 13 caps (30-12c, 2p) 1912-1920
Born: Lewisham, Kent, 23 July 1891
Died: Poole, Dorset, 23 July 1975
Career: Dulwich College, Old Alleynians, Cambridge University, Leicester, Harlequins, Barbarians, Surrey
Debut: v France, Parc des Princes, Paris, April 1912

Cambridge University captain 'Jenny' Greenwood was a member of England's Grand Slam-winning sides of 1913 and 1914. Initially, he intended to retire in 1919 but was dissuaded by Major Stanley and captained England in 1920. During the First World War, he served the Artists Regiment, the East Surrey Regiment, and the Grenadier Guards. A chartered accountant and company director of Boots Chemists, he was also the university rep on the RFU council between 1919 and 1937. Greenwood was also an International Board member, RFU trustee and RFU President and justice for the peace for Nottingham between 1947 and 1953.

523. HYNES, William Baynard
Lock 1 cap 1912
Born: Portsea, Hampshire, 6 April 1889
Died: Chichester, Sussex, 2 March 1968
Career: United Services Portsmouth, Royal Navy
Debut: v France, Parc des Princes, Paris, April 1912

Hynes entered the Royal Navy in 1904, and it would be eight years later that he would win his only England cap, helping secure a share of the Championship with a win over France in Paris. In November 1933, he took command of HMS Ceres, succeeding his captain at the Parc des Princes, Norman Wodehouse. Hynes then studied law and was called to the bar in 1938 but was recalled to the Navy a year later after the outbreak of World War Two, serving until retiring in 1945. He was the secretary of the Parochial Church Council of St John the Baptist Westbourne before his death.

524. NEALE, Maurice Edward
Lock 1 cap 1912
Born: Berkeley, Gloucestershire, 16 February 1886
Died: Bristol, 9 July 1967
Career: Bristol, Blackheath, Abingdon, Barbarians, Gloucestershire
Debut: v France, Parc des Princes, Paris, April 1912

Neale first joined Bristol in 1905, helping Gloucestershire to win the 1910 County Championship, and later the same year, while uncapped, he was selected for the British Team tour to South Africa and played four tests. Neale, a one-time commercial traveller, won his only England cap in France in April 1912 and made 123 appearances for Bristol between 1904 and 1912 before signing for Blackheath. During the First World War, Neale served as a lieutenant in the ASC and was killed after being hit by a car crossing the A38 at Woodford Stone near Berkeley after retiring to Stinchcombe from Stroud.

525. CHEESMAN, William Inkersole
Scrum-half 4 caps 1913
Born: Highgate, Middlesex, 20 June 1889
Died: Swindon, Wiltshire, 20 November 1969
Career: Merchant Taylor's School, Oxford University, Old Merchant Taylors
Debut: v South Africa, Twickenham, January 1913

'Jap' Cheesman was an all-round sportsman who played rugby, cricket, football, hockey and lawn tennis. He won his Oxford University blue in 1910 and 1911, winning the first of his four England caps against South Africa in January 1913. He played in England's next three games, partnering Dave Davies until being replaced by Francis Oakeley. Cheesman continued to play for the OMTs into his late 30s at either centre or full-back. A schoolmaster who taught at Marlborough College, Pembroke House School and in Kenya. He was also a member of the Sudan Civil Service.

526. COATES, Vincent Hope Middleton
Wing 5 caps (18-6t) 1913-1914
Born: Edinburgh, Scotland, 18 May 1889
Died: Maidenhead, Berkshire, 14 November 1934
Career: Monkton Combe Junior School, Haileybury & ISC, Cambridge University, Bridgwater, Bath, Leicester, Richmond, Barbarians, Somerset
Debut: v South Africa, Twickenham, January 1913

Coates first displayed rugby talent at Monkton Combe Junior School, then Haileybury, before attending Oxford University, where he won a blue in 1907. He made all five England appearances in 1913 and scored a hat-trick against France. After completing his medical studies, he was a consulting physician at Trowbridge and District Hospital, the Freshfield Cottage Hospital and the Bath Mineral Water Hospital. He was also a cardiac specialist for Wiltshire County Council and worked in private practice. Coates sadly died in a fall from an express train on his way home to Bath from Paddington.

527. DAVIES, William John Abbott OBE
Fly-half 22 caps (24-4t) 1913-1923
Born: Pembroke, Wales, 21 June 1890
Died: Richmond, Middlesex, 26 April 1967
Career: RNEC Keyham, RNC Greenwich, United Services Portsmouth, Royal Navy, Hampshire
Debut: v South Africa, Twickenham, January 1913

Davies was born in Pembroke, Wales, but was touted as one of England's best players of all time after becoming the most capped fly half with 22 appearances until Rob Andrews broke his record. He also captained his country 11 times, winning Grand Slams in 1921 and 1923 and was a member of the pre-Great War Grand Slam winning sides in 1913 and 1914. The First World War interrupted his career, and he served as a Royal Navy officer. Davies was also offered the chance to play tennis at Wimbledon but declined the offer to focus on his rugby. An admiralty shipwright who authored books on the sport.

528. LOWE, Cyril Nelson
Wing 25 caps (54-18t, 1d) 1913-1923
Born: Holbeach, Lincolnshire, 7 October 1891
Died: Reigate, Surrey, 6 February 1983
Career: Dulwich College, Cambridge University, Old Alleynians, Richmond, Blackheath, Surrey, West of Scotland, RAF
Debut: v South Africa, Twickenham, January 1913

'Kit' Lowe was supposedly the inspiration for W.E Johns's character, Biggles. He attended Cambridge University, where he won rugby blues in 1911, 1912 and 1913. He was ever-present in the 1913 and 1914 Grand Slam campaigns, scoring back-to-back hat tricks against Scotland and France before the First World War. The war checked his career when he served as a fighter pilot, shooting down 30 German aircraft and winning the MC and DFC. Lowe left the RAF in 1919 only to return less than two years later and continued to serve until October 1944 and served as RAF rep on RFU Council.

529. SMART, Sidney Edward John
No 8 12 caps 1913-1920
Born: Kingsholm, Gloucestershire, 20 February 1888
Died: Gloucester, Gloucestershire 25 January 1969
Career: Deacon's School Gloucester, Gloucester, Gloucestershire.
Debut: v South Africa, Twickenham, January 1913

Smart was acknowledged as one of the fittest players of his time to have played for England. He made his Gloucester debut in 1911 and two years later helped England to the first of back-to-back Grand Slam's, but the First World War interrupted his career. He was wounded in action twice, serving in the Gloucestershire Regiment and then the Royal Munster Fusiliers. Smart helped Gloucestershire to county championship glory in 1920 and retired six years later. A railway driller at Gloucester Waggon Works and then a roadman, his son Sidney also played for Gloucester. Smart died while acting as a grandstand steward at Kingsholm.

530. STEINTHAL, Francis Eric
Centre 2 caps 1913
Born: Bradford 21 November 1886
Died: Cuckfield, Sussex, 23 May 1974
Career: Bradford Grammar School, Oxford University, Ilkley, Yorkshire
Debut: v Wales, Arms Park, Cardiff, January 1913

Steinthal would become known as Francis Petrie at the outbreak of the First World War because Steinthal was a German name. Steinthal won an Oxford University blue in 1906 and made his two England appearances against Wales and France in their 1913 Grand Slam winning campaign before losing his place to Arthur Dingle, who had been unavailable for both games. Francis was a captain in the Royal Fusiliers during the First World War. Steinthal was a schoolmaster at Durham School, then St Lawrence College, Ramsgate, before emigrating to the United States, where he was an assistant professor of German and French at the University of California.

531. WARD, Joseph Alfred George
No 8 6 caps 1913-1914
Born: Bottesford, Leicester 19 March 1885
Died: Leicester, Leicestershire Q3 1962
Career: Belgrave, Leicester, Midland Counties, Leicestershire
Debut: v Wales, Arms Park, Cardiff, January 1913

Ward's England career appeared to be over after just two matches in 1913 when he indicated that he would rather play in club matches for Leicester than internationals. But a change of mind saw him return to the side for the narrow win over Scotland as England claimed the Grand Slam. He made another three appearances the following season as they retained the last Grand Slam before the First World War. Ward, who joined Leicester from local side Belgrave, was a member of two Midland Counties Cup-winning sides. He was a bailer rivetter and later worked for Thorneloe & Clarkson, clothing manufacturers in Leicester.

532. DINGLE, Arthur James
Centre 3 caps 1913-1914
Born: Hetton le Hole, County Durham, 16 October 1891
Died: Gallipoli, Turkey, 22 August 1915
Career: Bow School Durham, Durham School, Oxford University, Hartlepool Rovers, Richmond, Barbarians, Durham County, Surrey
Debut: v Ireland, Lansdowne Road, Dublin, February 1913

'Mud' Dingle won an Oxford University blue in 1911 and was still a student when he made his belated England debut against Ireland in February 1913. He had been due to play in two earlier games but was injured. He played a bit-part in two Grand Slam campaigns, and after graduating, he returned to Durham School as a master and also captained Hartlepool Rovers. In the First World War, Dingle was commissioned into the East Yorkshire Regiment and promoted to captain before being shipped to Gallipoli. He died three weeks after landing in Suvla Bay, and his body was never recovered.

533. KITCHING, Alfred Everley
Lock 1 cap 1913
Born: Scarborough, Yorkshire, 6 May 1889
Died: Tollerton, Yorkshire, 17 March 1945
Career: Oundle School, Cambridge University, Blackheath, Barbarians
Debut: v Ireland, Lansdowne Road, Dublin, February 1913

Kitching won his Cambridge University blue in 1910 and 1911 when he was appointed captain. But he needed a touch of good fortune to win his only England cap against Ireland in February 1913. Leicester's George Ward indicated that he would rather play for his club than his country, and Kitching was called up. But despite an England victory, Ward was recalled to face Scotland as England completed the Grand Slam. Kitching made his career in colonial service and became the Provincial Commissioner of Tanganyika Territory in Africa, while, in the First World War, he served in the East African Field Force.

534. OAKELEY, Francis Eckley
Scrum-half 4 caps
Born: Hereford, Herefordshire, 5 February 1891
Died: at sea 1 December 1914
Career: Hereford School, Eastman's School, RNC Osborne, RNC Dartmouth, United Services Portsmouth, Royal Navy
Debut: v Scotland, Twickenham, March 1913

Oakeley was born on the Welsh borders but, at 13, went to Royal Naval College at Osborne on the Isle of Wight and then Dartmouth before entering the service as a midshipman in 1908. Oakeley helped the Navy to beat The Army in March 1913, and he impressed the selectors sufficiently to win his first England cap at the expense of Jap Cheesman to partner his Navy team-mate Dave Davies at half-back. Oakeley was killed during the First World War when the submarine HMS D2 he was serving aboard disappeared.

535. BRUNTON, Joseph DSO MC
Lock 3 caps 1914
Born: Tynemouth, County Durham, 21 August 1888
Died: Hammersmith, London 18 September 1971
Career: North Durham, Rockliff, The Army, Northumberland
Debut: v Wales, Twickenham, January 1914

Brunton was one of three new caps when he made his international debut against Wales in January 1914 as England started the defence of their Grand Slam crown. He then retained his place for the next two games against Ireland and Scotland. But lost his place for the Grand Slam clinching match in France and was never picked again. Brunton, the chairman and managing director of an engineering company, served as a lieutenant in the Seaforth Highlanders and then lieutenant colonel in the Northumberland Fusiliers in the First World War. He represented Northumberland on the Rugby Football Union and was RFU President.

536. BULL, Arthur Gilbert MRCS LRCP
Prop 1 cap 1914
Born: Newport Pagnell, Buckinghamshire, 31 May 1890
Died: Chandlers Ford, Hampshire, 15 March 1963
Career: Bedford Modern School, Olney, Old Bedford Modernians, Northampton, Kings Hospital, Barbarians
Debut: v Wales, Twickenham, January 1914

'Doc' Bull learnt his rugby in Olney as a teenager, joining Northampton four years later, and was selected for an England trial in 1911-12, but it wasn't until January 1914 that he won his only England cap against Wales at Twickenham. Bull was elected Northampton captain, but the First World War broke out, and he served as a lieutenant in the Royal Garrison Artillery between 1914 and 1922. He eventually retired in 1924 but continued to serve on the committee and the East Midlands RU. After studying medicine at Kings Hospital, Bull practised in Kingsthorpe, Northamptonshire, until retiring in November 1949.

537. MAYNARD, Alfred Frederic
Hooker 3 caps 1914
Born: Anerly, Kent, 23 March 1894
Died: Beaumont Hamel, France, 13 November 1916
Career: Seaford School, Durham School, Cambridge University, Harlequins, Durham City, Durham Counties
Debut: v Wales, Twickenham, January 1914

Cambridge University-educated Maynard won his blue in 1912 and 1913 and became the second member of his family to win international honours. His father, William, was the probate registrar for Durham and played for England in their first-ever association football match against Scotland in 1872. Maynard made all three of his England appearances in 1914, helping secure the Triple Crown, but just over six months later, he joined the Royal Navy after the outbreak of the First World War. After being sent to the Somme, Maynard was a lieutenant commanding A Division of the Royal Naval Division and was killed during the Battle of Ancre.

538. TAYLOR, Frederick Mark
Fly-half 1 cap 1914
Born: Leicester, Leicestershire, 18 March 1888
Died: Evington, Leicestershire, 2 March 1966
Career: Medway Street School Leicester, Medway Old Boys, Medway Athletic, Leicester, Midland Counties, Leicestershire
Debut: v Wales, Twickenham, January 1914

Contrary to popular belief, Taylor wasn't the eldest of two brothers to play for Leicester and England on either side of the First World War and is no relation to Sos Taylor despite attending the same school and playing for Leicester. He made his sole appearance against Wales at Twickenham in January alongside George Wood, but they both lost their places to the Royal Navy pairing of Dave Davies and Francis Oakley. Taylor, who stopped playing for Leicester in 1923, was the managing clerk with a firm of Leicester Solicitors Evan Barton, a job he did all his working life.

539. WATSON, James Henry Digby
Wing 3 caps 1914
Born: Southsea, Hampshire, 31 August 1890
Died: at sea, 15 October 1914
Career: King's School Canterbury, Edinburgh Academy, Edinburgh University, Edinburgh Academicals, Blackheath, The London Hospital, Barbarians
Debut: v Wales, Twickenham, January 1914

'Bungy' Watson was the son of James Donald Watson, a New Zealand non-test player who learnt the game at King's School, Canterbury, Edinburgh Academy and then Edinburgh University. An all-round sportsman, he was the University Middleweight Boxing Champion and represented Scotland against Ireland at the long jump. After moving back to London to complete his medical studies, and won the first of his caps against Wales in January 1914 and helped secure a second successive Triple Crown. Months later, Watson was appointed a surgeon in the Royal Navy and was killed when HMS Hawke was torpedoed and sunk by U-9, a German U-boat.

540. WOOD, George William
Scrum-half 1 cap 1914
Born: Leicester, Leicestershire, 5 February 1886
Died: Leicester, Leicestershire, 12 June 1969
Career: Melbourne Road Old Boys, Leicester, Nuneaton, Midland Counties, Leicestershire
Debut: v Wales Twickenham, January 1914

'Pedler' Wood served Leicester at scrum-half for 20 years on either side of the First World War and then played on at Nuneaton for a further ten years until finally retiring from the game in 1934. He won his only England cap alongside his Leicester team-mate Tim Taylor, but they were both replaced by Royal Navy duo David Davies and Francis Oakeley and didn't win another cap after the First World War broke out just months later. He was a keen cricketer who umpired for many years at Victoria Park and was an inspector for the British Union Shoe Machine company until well into his 70s.

541. HARRISON, Arthur Leyland VC
Forward 2 caps 1914
Born: Torquay, Devon, 3 February 1886
Died: Zeebrugge, Belgium, 23 April 1918
Career: Dover College, RNC Dartmouth, United Services Portsmouth, Rosslyn Park, Hampshire
Debut: v Ireland, Twickenham, February 1914

Harrison is the only England rugby union international to be awarded the Victoria Cross. He started playing rugby at Dover College and maintained his interest after entering the Navy in 1901. He was the only new cap when he made his international debut against Ireland in February 1914, replacing Jenny Greenwood. Then, after missing the win over Scotland, he was recalled for the Grand Slam-clinching victory in France. He was serving on HMS Vindictive when he became a national hero during the blocking of Zeebrugge for leading an attack party. His body was never recovered.

542. PILLMAN, Robert Laurence
Flanker 1 cap 1914
Born: Sidcup, Kent, 9 February 1893
Died: Armentieres, France, 9 July 1916
Career: Merton Court School Sidcup, Rugby School, Blackheath, London Counties, Kent
Debut: v France, Stade Colombes, Paris, April 1914

Pillman was the brother of 'Cherry', and he had already had an unsuccessful trial when his elder sibling broke his leg in the Annual Calcutta Cup match against Scotland. The selectors didn't have to look too far. They called upon Pillman to win his only cap as England claimed back-to-back Grand Slams in the last international before the First World War, which would claim his life. Pillman, a solicitor with White and Leonard of Ludgate Circus, played for Blackheath and Kent. A scratch golfer, he was gazetted as a second lieutenant in the Royal West Kent Regiment and died of wounds during the Battle of the Somme.

543. STONE, Francis Le Strange MC
No 8 1 cap 1914
Born: Lewisham, London 14 June 1886
Died: Westminster, London 7 October 1938
Career: Harrow School, Blackheath, Barbarians, London Counties
Debut: v France Stade Colombes, Paris April 1914

Stone was educated at Harrow School and captained Blackheath in 1910 and 1911, but it wasn't until December 1912 that he had his first England trial. He was a solicitor like his father, Edward and later in life, he became a noted golfer. Stone's only England appearance came as they clinched the

1914 Grand Slam by winning away in Paris, and just months later, war was declared, ending any hopes of further caps. During the First World War, he served as a lieutenant and was awarded the Military Cross in 1917, while his brother Walter was awarded the Victoria Cross for most conspicuous bravery a year later.

544. SYKES, Alexander Richard V DSO MC
Forward 1 cap 1914
Born: Birkenhead, Cheshire, 29 May 1891
Died: Odiham, Hampshire, 4 May 1977
Career: Birkenhead School, Liverpool University, Blackheath, Barbarians
Debut: v France, Stade Colombes, Paris April 1914

Sykes came to London in 1912 after completing university on his native Merseyside and joined Blackheath, playing at Rectory Field for two seasons. He was a reserve for England against Scotland in March 1914 and won his only cap a month later in the side that clinched the Grand Slam in Paris as a replacement for Alfred Maynard. Sykes was an architect like his father and worked under Stanley Adshead. During the First World War, he served as a second lieutenant in the Inns of Court, Officers Training Corps, then during World War Two, as a major in the Liverpool Regiment, and was awarded a Military Cross.

545. CUMBERLEGE, Barry Stephenson OBE
Full-back 8 caps 1920-1922
Born: Jesmond, Northumberland, 5 June 1891
Died: Sandgate, Kent, England 22 September 1970
Career: Durham School, Cambridge University, Blackheath, Barbarians, Northumberland
Debut: v Wales, St Helen's, Swansea, January 1920

Cumberlege declined an invitation to tour South Africa with the British Isles in 1910 because he was still at Durham School, but he went to Cambridge University later the same year and won a double blue in rugby and cricket. During the First World War, he served in the Army Service Corps and was awarded an OBE in 1918. A Lloyd's underwriter who helped England to the 1921 Grand Slam. Like his Father Charles, who played first-class cricket for Surrey, Cumberlege, who later refereed 16 internationals, played for Kent, while brother Rutland played rugby for Cambridge University, Barbarians, Northern, and Harlequins.

546. DAY, Harold Lindsay Vernon
Wing 4 caps (16 2t, 2c, 2p) 1920-1926
Born: Darjeeling, India 12 August 1898
Died: Hadley Wood, Hertfordshire 15 June 1972
Career: Bedford Modern School, Leicester, The Army, Royal Artillery, Midlands, Hampshire, Leicestershire
Debut: v Wales, St Helen's, Swansea, January 1920

Day played for Leicester between 1919 and 1929 and was the first Tiger to pass the 1,000-point mark. He made his international debut against Wales under controversial circumstances. Wilfred Lowry was initially selected, but just before kick-off, selectors thought that wet conditions would better suit Day, who scored and converted England's only try of the game. A schoolmaster at Felsted School, he served in the Royal Artillery and later played first-class cricket for Hampshire, The Army and Bedfordshire. Day refereed an international between Scotland and Wales in 1934 and wrote about rugby for several newspapers.

547. HALFORD, Jonathan George
Lock 2 caps 1920
Born: Gloucester, Gloucestershire, 27 April 1886
Died: Stroud, Gloucestershire, 30 May 1960
Career: Linden School, Gloucester, Gloucestershire
Debut: v Wales, St Helen's, Swansea, January 1920

'Biddy' Halford joined the Gloucestershire Regiment in 1903, then worked in a local jam factory and returned to working as a blacksmith's striker, joined his home town club in 1907. His career was stalled by the First World War when he rejoined the Gloucestershire Regiment. He participated in three England trials and was 34 when he debuted against Wales in January 1920 and retained his place for their next game against Scotland. He helped Gloucestershire to a hat trick of County Championships. He was later an omnibus driver and served Gloucester as a selector and then committee man.

548. HAMMETT, Ernest Dyer Galbraith
Centre 8 caps (12-6c) 1920-1922
Born: Radstock, Somerset, 15 October 1891
Died: Hove, Sussex, 23 June 1947
Career: Newport Intermediate School, Newport High School, Newport, Cardiff, Blackheath, Barbarians, Surrey, Somerset
Debut: v Wales, St Helen's, Swansea, January 1920

Hammett was born in Somerset but was educated in Newport, Gwent and played amateur football and lawn tennis for Wales. He declined an invitation for a Welsh trial after joining Newport. Instead, he decided to play for the country of his birth. Ironically the stylish centre started and ended his international with defeats against Wales but in-between as an ever-present in the 1921 Grand Slam campaign. Hammett became a sports master at Brighton College and was the leading scorer for the British Isles on their unofficial 1927 tour of Argentina, with 40 points, playing in the first three test matches.

549. KERSHAW, Cecil Ashworth
Scrum-half 16 caps (6-2t) 1920-1923
Born: Dacca, Bangladesh, 3 February 1895
Died: Worthing, Sussex, 1 November 1972
Career: Wharfedale School Ilkley, Royal Naval College Osborne, Royal Naval College Dartmouth, United Services Portsmouth, Blackheath, Royal Navy, Barbarians
Debut: v Wales, St Helen's Swansea, January 1920

"K" Kershaw was a special all-round sportsman who represented the Royal Navy in cricket, hockey and squash but excelled as a rugby footballer. England went unbeaten in 14 games during his half-back partnership with Dave Davies, and they won Grand Slams in 1921 and 1923. Kershaw fenced for Great Britain at two Olympic Games. The son of Sir Lewis Kershaw, he served the Royal Navy on both land and sea during the First World War, was in submarines in the Baltic and was on the staff for the D-Day Landings in World War Two. Kershaw was later a commercial manager with Richard Costain Ltd.

550. KRIGE, Johannes Albertus
Centre 1 cap 1920
Born: Caledon, Western Cape, 6 June 1891
Died: Caledon, Western Cape, 27 September 1946
Career: Victoria College Stellenbosch (SA), Guy's Hospital, United Hospitals Barbarians, Surrey
Debut: v Wales, St Helen's, Swansea, January 1920

Kringe was one of a strong contingent of South Africans studying medicine at Guy's Hospital, making him eligible to play international rugby for England. He was said to be the best centre in England. After impressing playing for the South in a trial against England at Twickenham in December 1919, he won his only cap. He played inside Cyril Lowe, but despite being a fine athlete, he wasn't considered good enough for international rugby. Krige returned to South Africa in October 1921 and continued to practice as a doctor in his hometown, Caledon, Western Cape, until his death.

The English Rugby Who's Who

Robert Dibble

Roland Lagden

Dave Holland

Biddy Halford

551. MELLISH, Frank Whitmore MC JP
Flanker 6 caps 1920-1921
Born: Rondebosch, South Africa, 26 March 1897
Died: Cape Town, South Africa, 21 August 1965
Career: Wynberg Boys High School, Rondebosch Boys High School, South African College School, Cape Town Highlanders, Villagers, Blackheath, Barbarians, Western Province
Debut: v Wales, St Helen's, Swansea, January 1920

Mellish came to Europe during the First World War and was awarded the Military Cross for action at Ypres in 1916. He stayed on and played for Blackheath, Barbarians and England. He played the opening two games of England's 1921 Grand Slam campaign before returning to South Africa and was immediately selected for their first tour of New Zealand, winning a further six caps. Mellish was an executive with United Tobacco and a flower farmer. He was a colonel in the South African Armoured Division in World War Two and then manager of the 1951 Springbok tour of the British Isles and France.

552. MERRIAM, Sir Laurence Pierce Brooke MC JP
Lock 2 caps 1920
Born: Islington, London, 28 January 1894
Died: St Bart's Hospital, London, 27 July 1966
Career: St Paul's School, Oxford University, Blackheath, Barbarians
Debut: v Wales, St Helen's, Swansea, January 1920

Merriam was an all-round sportsman winning a triple blue in rugby, swimming and water polo at Oxford University. During the First World War, he served in the Rifle Brigade and was wounded twice before being awarded the Military Cross in 1916. His England caps came in 1920, and he also captained Blackheath. Merriam was chairman of British Xylonite and B.X. Plastics, and in the Second World War, was plastics controller. He was knighted in 1949, chairman of the Furniture Industry and Furniture Research Association, and a justice of the peace for Essex and County councillor.

553. MORGAN, James Rydiard
Hooker 1 cap 1920
Born: Cockermouth, Cumbria Q1 1887
Died: Hawick, Roxburghshire, 29 April 1961
Career: Hawick, South of Scotland, Cumberland
Debut: v Wales, St Helen's, Swansea, January 1920

Morgan became the first international born outside Scotland to play for The Greens, joining in 1910 after moving to Hawick to become a manager with Elliott, McTaggert and Co Skinners and Wool Merchants. Teddy was "a hard-working scrummager", but selection for his only England cap was later said to be a case of mistaken identity. It was claimed selectors confused him with Cornwall winger Rodda, who wore the same colour jersey. Unluckily, a broken leg ended his prospects of further recognition. Teddy served Hawick as president and was a director of McTaggert brothers until his death.

554. WAKEFIELD, Sir William Wavell
Flanker 31 caps (18-6t) 1920-1927
Born: Beckenham, Kent, 10 March 1898
Died: Kendal, Cumbria, 12 August 1983
Career: Craig Preparatory School, Sedburgh School, Cambridge University, Royal Air Force, Leicester, Harlequins, Middlesex
Debut: v Wales, St Helen's Swansea, January 1920

The poster boy of 1920s rugby, Wakefield, was the captain of Cambridge University and a Harlequins stalwart for a decade, as well as a member of the Quins side to win the first Middlesex Sevens. He won three Grand Slams and led the 1924 success. Before founding the Rediffusion Group, he served in the RAF and was chairman of Relay Broadcast Services. Wakefield became a Conservative MP, being knighted in 1944, and, on his retirement from Parliament in 1963, became the first Baron Wakefield of Kendal. In 1999, he was inducted as the first English member of the International Rugby Hall of Fame.

555. WRIGHT, William Henry George ISM
Prop 2 caps 1920
Born: Plymouth, Devon, 6 June 1889
Died: Plymouth, Devon, 2 June 1973
Career: Plymouth Albion, Devon
Debut: v Wales, St Helen's, Swansea, January 1920

Jock Wright joined his hometown club Plymouth Albion in 1912 and almost immediately was capped by the county side. But it wasn't until the first Home Championship game after the First World War that he was handed his debut against Wales as one of six new caps in the pack. But after retaining his place for the following match against France, he was never selected again and hung up his boots in 1924. Wright was a boiler maker who worked in HM Dockyard, Bermuda, and the Devonport Dockyard. He was awarded an Imperial Service Medal on his retirement in August 1949.

556. CONWAY, Geoffrey Seymour
Lock 20 caps 1920-1927
Born: Cardiff 15 November 1897
Died: France 3 September 1984
Career: Fettes College, Cambridge University, Rugby, Harlequins, Hartlepool Rovers, Manchester, Blackheath, Barbarians, Lancashire, Durham
Debut: v France, Twickenham, January 1920

Conway was still in the second of three years at Cambridge University when he was called up to make his England debut. He became known as the 'Prince of Dribblers' for his technique of shin-dribbling. Conway was ever-present in the 1923 and 1924 Grand Slam-winning campaigns while he served in both the First World War and the Second World War when he was promoted to lieutenant colonel. A science professor who taught at Rugby School later became a school inspector. He retired to France, where he died after working as an archaeologist in Greece between 1961 and 1969.

557. LOWRY, Wilfrid Malbon
Wing 1 cap 1920
Born: Birkenhead, Cheshire, 14 July 1900,
Died: Heswall, Cheshire, 4 July 1974
Career: The Leys School, Old Lesions, Birkenhead Park, Waterloo, Cheshire
Debut: v France, Twickenham, January 1920

Lowry was unlucky to only win a single cap. He was due to play against Wales two weeks earlier, changed and photographed on the pitch, but after returning to the pavilion, the England selectors decided at the last minute to play Harold Day, whom it felt was better suited to wet conditions. Wilfred served in both World Wars in the Royal Naval Volunteer Reserve in the First World War, then as a lieutenant in the Royal Artillery. Lowry was a cotton broker and was a director of A. J. Buston and Co. in Liverpool until his retirement, while his brother Malcolm was a celebrated poet and novelist.

558. MILLETT, Harry
Full-back 1 cap 1920
Born: Islington, London 2 April 1892
Died: Wandsworth, London 26 May 1974
Career: University College Hampstead, Guy's Hospital, Richmond, Harlequins, Barbarians, London Counties, Middlesex
Debut: v France, Twickenham, January 1920

Millett first caught the attention in 1912 when he played for London against Springboks at both Blackheath and Twickenham but found his way into the national team blocked by Bill Johnston. Then, like so many players, he found his career checked by the First World War when he served as a first lieutenant in the Royal Marines in 1915 and was mentioned in dispatches. He then became a house surgeon at Guy's Hospital and as a surgeon lieutenant in the Royal Navy before returning to Guys as registrar of practical dentistry. Millett had to wait until January 1920 to win his only international cap.

559. SMALLWOOD, Alastair McNaughton
Centre 14 caps (25 -7t, 1d) 1920-1925
Born: Alloa, Scotland, 18 November 1892
Died: Uppingham, Rutland, 9 June 1985
Career: Royal Grammar School Newcastle, Cambridge University, Gosforth Nomads, Northumberland, Leicester, Leicestershire
Debut: v France, Twickenham, January 1920

Scotland-born Smallwood was educated in the North-East and, like his grandson Jerry Macklin, won a blue for Cambridge University. During the First World War, he served in the Northumberland Fusiliers. Smallwood was a member of the 1921 and 1923 Grand Slam-winning sides, but he had to wait until 1925 for his last two caps and was only on the losing side once, in his last game against the country of his birth. He was a schoolmaster and was master in charge of rugby at Uppingham School for 33 years between 1919 and 1952. And was also a bassoonist with Stamford Orchestra.

560. TAYLOR, Frank
Prop 2 caps 1920
Born: Leicester, Leicestershire, 4 May 1890
Died: Leicester, Leicestershire, 22 September 1956
Career: Medway Street School Leicester, Medway Old Boys, Medway Athletic, Leicester, Midland Counties, Leicestershire
Debut: v France, Twickenham, January 1920

While at Medway Street School Leicester, 'Sos' Taylor played in the first England schoolboy international in 1904. He joined Leicester in 1911 after spells with Medway Old Boys and Medway Athletic and helped them win back-to-back Midland Counties Cups in 1912 and 1913. He served during the First World War in the Leicestershire Regiment but, after being badly wounded, was told that he would never play again. Taylor went on to win two England caps against France and Ireland, continuing to play for The Tigers until 1924. He earned a living as a clerk in a local boot factory.

561. HARRIS, Stanley Wakefield CBE
Wing 2 caps (3-1t) 1920
Born: Somerset East, South Africa, 13 December 1894
Died: Kenilworth, Wiltshire, 3 October 1973
Career: Bedford Grammar School, Blackheath, East Midlands, Pirates (SA), Transvaal
Debut: v Ireland, Lansdowne Road Dublin, February 1920

Harris fought at the Battle of the Somme, Flanders and North Russia in the First World War, and while convalescing from wounds, he took to ballroom dancing and won the waltz section of the World Championships. He won two England caps in 1920 and turned down the chance to represent Great Britain in the 1920 Olympic modern pentathlon to concentrate on rugby. Stan represented South Africa in boxing and tennis, winning Queen's and Roehampton titles. A company director, he made two appearances for the British Isles in 1924 after being called up because of an injury crisis and, during World War Two, was a PoW at the hands of the Japanese.

562. MYERS, Edward MC
Centre/Fly half 18 caps (13 - 3t,1d) 1920-1925
Born: New York, United States, 23 September 1895
Died: Bradford, West Yorkshire, 29 March 1956
Career: Dollar Academy, Leeds University, Headingley, Leicester, Bradford, Yorkshire
Debut: v Ireland, Lansdowne Road Dublin, February 1920

Myers was born in New York, but his parents hailed from Yorkshire, where he settled after his education at the Dollar Academy in Dollar, Clackmannanshire. During the First World War, he served in the Yorkshire Regiment and was wounded three times. After joining Bradford in 1919, he became the greatest Individual force in northern rugby, an attraction wherever he played and captained club and county and was a member of the 1921, 1923 and 1924 Grand Slam winning sides. Myers was the director of a textile company. He remained in Bradford until his death and was president of Bradford Rugby Union Club between 1937 and 1939.

563. VOYCE, Anthony Thomas OBE
Flanker 27 caps (15-5t) 1920-1926
Born: Gloucester, Gloucestershire, 18 May 1897
Died: Gloucester, Gloucestershire, 22 January 1980
Career: Gloucester, Cheltenham, Richmond, Blackheath, The Army, Barbarians, Gloucestershire
Debut: v Ireland, Lansdowne Road, Dublin, February 1920

Voyce joined Gloucester as a winger, but Tart Hall's injury saw him switch to the forwards, playing for both county and country in his first season. Tom captained Gloucester for three seasons and played flanker, wing and full-back on the 1924 British Isles' tour to South Africa. During the First World War, as a captain in the Buffs, injuries saw his sight affected for the rest of his life. Voyce was a district manager for the Royal Exchange Group, a director of the Lowndes Lambert Group and a member of the Gloucester City Council. An RFU President, his great nephew Tom Voyce, played for England.

564. BLAKISTON, Sir Arthur Frederick MC
Lock 17 caps (6-2t) 1920-1925
Born: West Derby, Cheshire 16 June 1892
Died: Salisbury, Wiltshire, 31 January 1974
Career: Bedford Modern School, Trent College, Cambridge University, Northampton, Liverpool, Blackheath, Barbarians, East Midlands, Lancashire, Surrey
Debut: v Scotland, Twickenham, March 1920

Like many other players of his generation, Blakiston had his career interrupted by the First World War, during which he served as a trooper in King Edward's Horse and, later, as a Captain in the Royal Field Artillery and was awarded the Military Cross in 1918. In honour of this achievement, the Blakiston Challenge was created. A gruelling pre-season test of strength held at Castle Ashby, Northampton since 2018. Blakiston was a member of the England squad, which won the Grand Slam in 1921 and 1924, which earned him a place on the British Isles' Tour to South Africa, playing four tests. A farmer in Shropshire and Wiltshire, he became the 7th Baronet Blakiston of London on his father's death in August 1941.

565. WOODS, Thomas
Forward 5 caps (3-1t) 1920-1921
Born: Pontypool, Monmouthshire, 30 January 1890
Died: Bridgend, Glamorganshire, November 1959
Career: Newbridge, Pontypool, Devonport Services, United Services Portsmouth, Royal Navy, Devon
Debut: v Scotland, Twickenham, March 1920

Woods was a collier in his native South Wales and parts of Pontypool's famed 'Terrible Eight' before starting a 12-year term in the Royal Navy in March 1909. After joining the services, his rugby career took off and saw him winning the first of his five caps in March 1920. A year later, he helped England to a Grand Slam, scoring his only try against Scotland at Murrayfield. After leaving the Navy that summer, he became one of seven players from the Pontypool area to switch codes in months, joining Wigan and winning a Lancashire Cup and international honours for Wales. Woods ran a boarding house in Bridgend for many years.

566. EDWARDS, Edmund Reginald
Prop 11 caps (3-1t) 1921-1925
Born: Pontypool, Wales 15 August 1893,
Died: Montreal, Canada, 9 May 1951
Career: Presswell School, Newport, Somerset
Debut: v Wales, Twickenham, January 1921

Edwards joined Newport in 1909 but was overlooked by Wales following a trial. He was then invited to play for England, winning his first cap against the country of his birth. An ever-present in England's 1921 Grand Slam winning campaign, Reg played three games in the 1924 Grand Slam success, but his international career was ended after New Zealand's Cyril Brownlie was sent off for seemingly kicking Edwards on the floor, but later denied. The referee subsequently reported Edwards to the RFU for misconduct, and he never played for England again. A Master Butcher, he retired from playing in 1925 and later emigrated to Canada.

567. GARDNER, Ernest Robert
Hooker 10 caps (6-2t) 1921-1923
Born: Cardiff, Wales, 6 October 1886
Died: Plymouth, Devon, 26 January 1952
Career: Devonport Albion, Devonport Services, Royal Navy, Devon
Debut: v Wales, Twickenham, January 1921

Welsh-born servant farm labourer Gardner enlisted in the Royal Marines Light Infantry in 1904. He joined Devon Albion in 1914 and quickly made his mark, but the outbreak of the First World War checked his career. And it wasn't until 1921, when he was 34, that he won the first of his England 10 caps that saw him only on the losing side once. Ernie played in the 1921 and 1923 Grand Slam success and eventually left the Marines in 1925. He was later the head groundsman at the RNE College at Keyham, where he lived until his death.

568. COVE-SMITH, Ronald
Lock 29 caps (3-1t) 1921-1929
Born: Edmonton, Middlesex, 26 November 1899
Died: Brighton, Sussex, 9 March 1988
Career: Merchant Taylors' School, Old Merchant Taylors, Cambridge University, King's College Hospital, London University, United Hospitals, Middlesex
Debut: v Scotland, Inverleith, Edinburgh, March 1921

Cove-Smith was a brilliant all-round sportsman representing Cambridge University in rugby, swimming and water polo, while he also rowed for his college at Henley. He captained his school, club, university, county, and country to the 1928 Grand Slam and the British Isles on their 1924 tour to South Africa. During the First World War, Cove-Smith was commissioned into the Grenadier Guards before holding various eminent medical appointments between 1919 and his retirement in 1965. He became vice-president of the British Medical Association, among numerous other medical societies, hospital groups, and the YMCA.

569. KING, Quentin Eric Moffitt Ayres
Wing 1 cap 1921
Born: Bedford, Bedfordshire, 8 July 1895,
Died: Birmingham, Warwickshire, 30 October 1954
Career: St Edward's School Oxford, Blackheath, The Army, Barbarians
Debut: v Scotland, Inverleith, Edinburgh, March 1921

'Quemma' King was a well-known all-round sportsman in the Army when he served as a major in the Royal Field Artillery during the First World War. He was a heavyweight boxing champion and athletic champion of the Army and also captained the rugby team. He won his only international cap against Scotland in March 1921 after Leicester's Alastair Smallwood moved to centre. But Smallwood wasn't a success and returned to the wing for the Grand Slam-clinching victory in France, and King was never selected for another international game. After leaving the Army in 1925, he became a games master at Worksop College.

570. CORBETT, Leonard James OBE
Centre 16 caps (15,3t,1gm,1p) 1921-1927
Born: Bristol, 12 May 1897
Died: Taunton, Somerset, 26 January 1983
Career: Fairfield School, Saracens (Bristol), Cotham Park, Bristol, Gloucestershire
Debut: v France, Stade Colombes, Paris, March 1921

Corbett served with the British Army Service Corps during the First World War and made his debut in the game against France that clinched the 1921 Grand Slam. He took part in the 1923 Grand Slam, and a year later, he was an ever-present in the third Grand Slam-winning side in four seasons. Corbett captained Bristol, Gloucester, and England. He worked for J.S. Fry & Co and was Superintendent of the Royal Ordinance Factory, Bridgend. Corbett then became a director of Welsh Industrial Estates and wrote about rugby and cricket (he played first-class cricket for Gloucestershire) for the Sunday Times.

571. DAVIES, Vivian Gordon
Fly-half 2 caps 1921-1925
Born: Bromley, Kent, 22 January 1899
Died: Wandsworth, Surrey, 23 December 1941
Career: Marlborough College, Harlequins, Barbarian, Surrey
Debut: v Wales, Arms Park, Cardiff, January 1922

Davies was educated at Bow School, Durham and Marlborough College, where he captained the rugby team in 1916, a year before he served in the Duke of Cornwall's Light Infantry during the First World War. He won his first England cap against Wales at The Arms Park, Cardiff, when Dave Davies was injured but had to wait three years until 1925 to win his final cap against The All Blacks. A master at Bow School, he was twice a member of the Harlequins side that won the Middlesex Sevens. He was Harlequins skipper for four years and a captain in the Royal Artillery until his death.

572. TUCKER, Samuel
Hooker 27 caps (6-2t) 1922-1931
Born: Bristol, 1 June 1895
Died: Bristol, 4 January 1973
Career: St Nicholas Old Boys, The Army, Bristol, Gloucestershire, Barbarians
Debut: v Wales, Arms Park, Cardiff, January 1922

Tucker played for his first club St Nicholas Old Boys, in the centres, but lacking speed, Bristol moved him to hooker. He became Bristol's most-capped player and captained England for two seasons. He helped Gloucester win the County Championship five times, twice as captain. He was famous enough to have a brand of Oranges named after him. Tucker answered an SOS to play for England in Wales in 1930 despite being in a Bristol restaurant having lunch travelling in an open bi-plane and lorry, arriving eight minutes before kick-off and was a member of Tucker Brothers stevedores.

573. BRADBY, Matthew Seymour MBE
Centre 2 caps 1922
Born: Rugby, Warwickshire 25 March 1899
Died: Shatterbury, Wiltshire, 11 June 1963
Career: Rugby School, RNEC Keyham, Cambridge University, United Services Portsmouth, Royal Navy, Barbarians, Hampshire
Debut: v Ireland, Landsdowne Road, Dublin, February 1922

Bradby attended Cambridge University but failed to win a blue and was one of five new caps introduced into the England side for the 1922 trip to Dublin after a heavy defeat to Wales. He retained his place for the following game against France but was then replaced by Alistair Smallwood and was never selected again. He enrolled in the Royal Navy in 1917 and became a tea grower with Shaw Wallace and Co. in Calcutta but was recalled to the Navy in 1939. He served as a lieutenant commander. Bradby later became captain of the nautical school, Heswell, and the training ship Mercury on the Hamble River.

574. DUNCAN, Robert Francis Hugh
Prop 3 caps 1922
Born: Wenvoe, Glamorgan, 10 June 1896
Died: Henley-on-Thames, Oxfordshire, 19 October 1981
Career: Cardiff University, Guy's Hospital, Barbarians, Middlesex
Debut: v Ireland, Landsdowne Road Dublin, February 1922

Duncan, whose father, Thomas, played for Cardiff and the Barbarians, was selected to play for England against Ireland in February 1922 while he was a medical student at Guy's Hospital. Duncan was one of five new caps following a heavy defeat to Wales after initially missing out following a trial match playing for The South against England in December 1921. He served in the First World War as a captain in the Welsh Regiment and then as a lieutenant colonel in the Royal Welsh Fusiliers in World War Two. Duncan was a sales rep for a dental supply company and sales director for the Refrigeration Company (Canada).

575. MAXWELL-HYSLOP, John Edgar
Flanker 3 caps 1922
Born: Bristol, 31 March 1899
Died: Sherborne, Dorset, 10 December 1990
Career: Wellington College, Bristol College, Oxford University, Richmond, Sussex
Debut: v Ireland, Landsdowne Road, Dublin, February 1922

Maxwell-Hyslop was elected captain of Cambridge University in January 1922, and a month later, he was one of five new caps in the England side for a trip to Ireland after a heavy defeat to Wales. He retained his place for the following two games, but after being appointed headmaster of Rottingdean School, Brighton, in 1923, he was never selected again. Maxwell-Hyslop held the position until his retirement in 1961. During the First World War, he was a second lieutenant Royal Field Artillery, while in the Second World War, he served with the RAF as a fitter and then as a flight lieutenant in Intelligence.

576. PICKLES, Reginald Clarence Werrett MC
Full-back 2 caps 1922
Born: Bristol, 11 December 1895
Died: Weston-super-Mare, Somerset, 6 November 1978
Career: Bristol Grammar School, Bristol, The Army, Gloucestershire, Weston-super-Mare, Somerset
Debut: v Ireland, Landsdowne Road, Dublin, February 1922

Pickles captained Bristol Grammar School Rugby, then joined Bristol United while still a schoolboy. He played in 244 games, scoring 70 tries, and was their first post-World War One captain, and played in Gloucestershire's hat-trick of County Championship Final wins in the early 1920s. He was one of five new caps after a heavy defeat to Wales to win the first of his two caps against Ireland and France. Pickles served in the Royal Engineers during the First World War and was awarded the Military Cross in 1917. He worked as a wholesale grocer and provision merchant and then as a manager for Cornhill Insurance.

577. PRICE, Herbert Leo MC
Flanker 4 caps 1922-1923
Born: Sutton, Surrey, 21 June 1899
Died: Victoria Park, Manchester, 18 July 1943
Career: Bishop's Stortford College, Oxford University, Leicester, Harlequins, Barbarians, Surrey
Debut: v Ireland, Landsdowne Road, Dublin, February 1922

Price was a dual England international in rugby union and hockey. A water polo blue at Oxford University, he was also secretary of the rugby team. One of five new caps against Ireland in February 1922, he chose rugby to win his second cap a month later after being selected to play hockey and rugby against Scotland on the same day. Awarded a Military Cross for serving as a lieutenant in the South Wales Borders in the First World War and was a schoolmaster at Uppingham and Christ's Hospital. Price retired from rugby in 1932 when appointed headmaster of Bishop's Stortford College, a post he held until his death.

578. MIDDLETON, John Alan
Full-back 1 cap 1922
Born: Dublin, 11 January 1894
Died: North East Hampshire, Hampshire Q2 1974
Career: St Andrews College Dublin, Wanderers, Leinster, Richmond, The Army, Hampshire
Debut: v Scotland, Twickenham, March 1922

Middleton won his only England cap in their final 1922 Five Nations Championship game after impressing against The Navy, replacing full-back Reg Pickles, but was disappointing. Middleton, a regular soldier before being commissioned in 1914 and the First World War, served in the Royal Army Service Corps and joined Richmond in August 1921. He qualified for Ireland but decided to throw his lot in with England in the days a player could play for any country of his choosing. He again saw action during the Second World War and was taken POW in Italy but escaped in 1943, reaching the rank of Colonel after 35 years of service.

579. PITMAN, Sir Isaac James
Wing 1 cap 1922
Born: Kensington, London, 14 August 1901
Died: Chelsea, London, 1 September 1985
Career: Eton College, Oxford University, Harlequins
Debut: v Scotland, Twickenham, March 1922

Pitman was the first Old Etonian to play for England when he was selected to play against Scotland at the end of the 1922 Home Championship. It proved to be the only cap he won after being ruled out of the 1923 campaign through injury. Pitman became the chairman and joint managing director of Pitman Press and Pitman Publishing. He was also a director of Boots Pure Drug, Bovril, and the Equity and Law Life Assurance Society. During World War Two, Pitman was a squadron leader in the RAF Volunteer Reserve. A director of the Bank of England, he was also a Conservative MP for Bath.

580. WILLIAM-POWLETT, Vice Admiral Sir Peveril Barton Reiby
Prop 1 cap 1922
Born: Abergavenny, Wales, 5 March 1898
Died: Honiton, Devon, 10 November 1985
Career: RNC Osborne, RNC Dartmouth, United Services Portsmouth, Blackheath, United Services Devonport, Wanderers, Royal Navy, Hampshire
Debut: v Scotland, Twickenham, March 1922

William-Powlett joined the Royal Navy in 1914 as a midshipman and specialised in signals during the First World War. He represented the Navy at rugby, whom he captained in 1928, association football and polo and won his only England cap against Scotland in March 1922. He missed the 1923 campaign as he was abroad with the Navy, working his way through the ranks, commanding the Royal Naval College, Dartmouth and then becoming Naval Secretary in 1948 before retiring in 1954. In retirement, William-Powlett became Governor of Southern Rhodesia for five years and then chairman of Appledore Shipbuilders.

581. GILBERT, Frederick George
Full-back 2 caps 1923
Born: Truro, Cornwall, 30 December 1883
Died: Plymouth, Devon, 11 December 1964
Career: Devonport Services, Royal Navy, Cornwall
Debut: v Wales, Twickenham Greater London January 1923

Gilbert spent his early life playing association football and only played rugby after joining the Royal Navy in 1906. And

The English Rugby Who's Who

Harry Alexander

Henry Weston

John Raphael

Curley Hammond

The English Rugby Who's Who

Dai Gent

Alfred Hind

Bill Nanson

Chicky Wedge

Frank Tarr

Ronnie Poulton-Palmer

Lancelot Barrington-Ward

Jim Pitman

five years later was the captain of the first services side. It appeared that he would never win international recognition, but when he was 39, he was called up for the first two games of the 1923 Grand Slam winning campaign, making him England's oldest-ever player by some distance. After retiring from the game in 1924, Gilbert became the groundsman at The Rectory, the home of Devonport Services, until 1938 and worked as a shipwright in Devonport Dockyard until retirement.

582. LUDDINGTON, William George Ernest
Prop 13 caps (16 -5c,1p) 1923-1926
Born: Farnham, Hampshire, 8 February 1894
Died: at sea Sicily, 10 January 1941
Career: Devonport Services, Royal Navy, Devon
Debut: v Wales, Twickenham, January 1923

Luddington followed his father, Thomas, who was in the Army, into the armed services serving in the Royal Navy for the whole of his adult life. His last kick of the game won the 1923 Calcutta Cup tie with a conversion from the touchline. And was ever-present in the back-to-back Grand Slam-winning campaigns in 1923 and 1924. Luddington continued to play for the Royal Navy until 1930 and was serving as a master-at-arms in the Royal Navy during World War Two and was killed during an air attack on HMS Illustrious in the Mediterranean.

583. SANDERS, Frank Warren
Hooker 3 caps 1923
Born: Newton Abbot, Devon, 24 January 1893
Died: Plymouth, Devon, 22 June 1953
Career: Plymouth Albion, Devon
Debut: v Ireland, Welford Road, Leicester, February 1923

Sanders captained both Plymouth Albion and Devon, including in a game against the All Blacks on the opening game of the 1924-25 Invincibles tour. He made all three of his international appearances in 1923 and wasn't selected again despite playing in the North vs the South trial the following season. After Sanders was President of the Devon Referees Society, he moved to Plymouth to work in Devonport Dockyard and became chargeman of pattern-makers after working for Dartmouth pattern-maker Philip and Sons. At the time of his death, he was secretary of the Plymouth Amateur Rowing Club and had been area secretary of the Civil Service Bowling Club.

584. HOLLIDAY, Thomas Edwin
Full-back 7 caps 1923-1926
Born: Wigton, Cumberland, 13 July 1898
Died: Carlisle, Cumberland, 19 July 1969
Career: Aspatria, Cumberland
Debut: v Scotland, Inverleith, Edinburgh, March 1923

'Toff' Holliday was the youngest of four sporting brothers and won his first two caps during the 1923 Grand Slam-winning campaign two years after he first played in a trial match. He captained Cumberland to County Championship success in 1924 and was later the same year selected for the British Isles tour to South Africa but was injured in the first game and took no further part. In 1926, he switched codes and played rugby league for Oldham and England until his retirement in 1931. Toff then returned to Aspatria to run a shop selling drapery and ironmongery.

585. LOCKE, Harold Meadows
Centre 12 caps (3-1t)
Born: Birkenhead, Cheshire, 20 January 1898
Died: Birmingham, Warwickshire, 23 March 1960
Career: Birkenhead School, Birkenhead Park, Bristol, Gloucestershire, Cheshire
Debut: v Scotland, Inverleith, Edinburgh, March 1923

Locke participated in international trials in 1919 and 1920 alongside his Birkenhead Park teammate Wilfred Lowry. It was said that they were sometimes seen as not playing well against higher-quality opposition but had an understanding that brought them a phenomenal number of tries in club rugby. Locke, who worked for a bank and then as a sales manager for Leaver Brothers, had to wait three years for his debut during the 1923 Grand Slam-winning campaign. He then helped retain their crown the following season. He later finished his career with Bristol and Gloucestershire after moving to the south.

586. CATCHESIDE, Howard Carston OBE
Wing 8 caps (18-6t) 1924-1927
Born: Sunderland, Tyne and Wear, 18 August 1899
Died: Wandsworth, London, 10 May 1987
Career: Oundle School, Percy Park, Northumberland
Debut: v Wales, St Helen's, Swansea, January 1924

'Catchy' Catcheside created history when he scored in all four rounds of England's 1924 Grand Slam success, and it was a feat not equalled until Ben Cohen scored in four of the five 2002 rounds. An injury ended his international career in 1927, and between 1932 and 1940, he was honorary treasurer of the Northumberland Rugby Union and was on the England selection committee from 1936 to 1962. A coal exporter and shipbroker, Catcheside served in the Royal Field Artillery in the First World War and the Regular Army in the Second World War and was awarded a Military OBE in 1945.

587. CHANTRILL, Bevan Stanislaw
Full-back 4 Caps 1924
Born: Barton Regis, Gloucestershire, 11 February 1897
Died: Scottburgh, South Africa, 25 February 1988
Career: Bristol Grammar School, Clifton, Royal Air Force, Durban Rovers (SA), Natal, Weston-Super-Mare, Bristol, Richmond, Manchester, Rosslyn Park, Gloucestershire, Somerset
Debut: v Wales, St Helen's, Swansea, January 1924

Chantrill was educated at Bristol Grammar School and joined the Queen's Own Hussars in August 1914, aged 14, before moving to the Royal Flying Corps and Royal Air Force, where he was commissioned as an observer officer. Chantrill had to wait until 1924 to replace 'Toff' Holliday for the second of England's back-to-back Grand Slam campaigns when he was ever-present. He moved to South Africa in 1929 and became a gold miner until retiring in 1963. During the Second World War, he joined the South African Air Force and then the Royal Air Force in Flying Control.

588. JACOB, Herbert Percy
Wing 5 caps (12-4t) 1924-1930
Born: Elham, Kent, 12 October 1902,
Died: Myaree, Western Australia, 8 July 1996
Career: Harvey Grammar School, Cranleigh School, Oxford University, Blackheath,
Debut: v Wales, St Helen's, Swansea, January 1924

'Jake' Jacob was a student at Oxford University, where he won a blue between 1923 and 1925 and was an ever-present in England's 1924 Grand Slam winning campaign, scoring four tries, including a hat-trick against France in their penultimate game. Surprisingly, he would have to wait almost six years until February 1930, to win his last against France. Jacob became a schoolmaster at Worksop College and Cranleigh School, where he was acting headmaster. He was then secretary to the Royal Blackheath Golf Club and a career consultant at the Vocational Guidance Association. Jacob later lived in Australia until his death.

589. ROBSON, Alan
Hooker 5 caps 1924-1926
Born: Wishaw, Lanark, 3 May 1893
Died: Billericay, Essex, 3 August 1981
Career: Northern, Northumberland
Debut: v Wales, St Helen's, Swansea, January 1924

Robson was born in Scotland but grew up in the north east, where he would go on to captain Northern. An ever-present in England's 1924 Grand Slam winning campaign, he had to wait until 1926 to win his final cap. He was the brother-in-law of Herbert Whitley, who also played for Northern, Northumberland and England. He survived being blown up during the battle of the Somme during the First World War while serving as a second lieutenant in Queens Royal West Surreys. Robson was a commercial clerk, then a coal export officer in Swansea, where he also worked in the Brazilian Consulate until he retired.

590. YOUNG, Arthur Tudor
Scrum-half 18 caps 1924-1929
Born: Darjeeling, India, October 14, 1901
Died: Bareilly, India 26 February 1933
Career: Tonbridge School, Cambridge University, Blackheath, The Army, Kent
Debut: v Wales, St Helen's Swansea, January 1924

Young earned himself the nickname of the 'Mighty Atom' standing just 5ft 4ins and weighing 10 stone 7lb, but was an ever-present in two Grand Slam-winning campaigns in 1924 and then again in 1928. He also toured South Africa with the British Isles in 1924, playing in one test. Young captained both Blackheath and Kent and served in the Army in the Royal Tank Corps but died while serving as aide-de-Camp to Sir Norman McMullen, General Officer Commanding Eastern Command India, after contracting pneumonia following a bout of influenza.

591. FAITHFULL, Charles Kirke Tindall
Prop 3 caps 1924-1926
Born: Fareham, Hampshire, 6 January 1903
Died: Farnham, Surrey 8 August 1979
Career: Wellington College, Royal Military College, Halifax, Harlequins, United Services Portsmouth, Devonport Services, The Army, Combined Services, Barbarians, Surrey, Hampshire, Yorkshire
Debut: v Ireland, Ravenhill Belfast February 1924

'Chubby' Faithfull made his England debut in the 1924 Grand Slam-winning campaign but had to wait until 1926 to win his final two caps. He would have won a fourth against Ireland in 1927 had Ron Cove-Smith not found his lost boots in time to take his place. Faithfull, also known as 'The Bull', was an amateur boxer and refereed up to County Championship standard between 1929 and 1936. He served in The Army all his adult life and reached the rank of lieutenant colonel by the time he retired in 1955.

592. HAMILTON-WICKES, Richard Henry
Wing 10 caps (12-4t) 1924-1927
Born: Uxbridge, Middlesex, 31 December 1901
Died: Surbiton, Surrey, 2 June 1963
Career: Bilton Grange, Wellington College, Cambridge University, Harlequins
Debut: v Ireland, Ravenhill, Belfast, February 1924

Hamilton-Wickes played cricket at Wellington College but excelled at rugby by the time he reached Cambridge University, whom he captained along with his club side Harlequins, where he was a prolific try-scorer. Hamilton-Wickes scored a try on his England debut and followed it up with three more in 1925. He was a member of the Quins side to win the first Middlesex Sevens and was a sales manager for an oil company for many years. Hamilton-Wickes was the owner of the Hamilton Old People's Home and sadly died in a fire in his flat.

593. BROUGH, James Wasdale
Full-back 2 caps 1925
Born: Silloth, Cumberland, 5 November 1903,
Died: Workington, Cumberland, 16 September 1986
Career: Silloth, Cumberland
Debut: v New Zealand, Twickenham, January 1925

Brough joined his hometown, Silloth, as a teenager and helped Cumberland beat Kent to win the 1924 County Championship. He won his two England caps the following season against New Zealand and Wales but then lost his place to 'Toff' Holliday and switched codes to join Leeds at the end of that season. He played for Leeds, England and Great Britain and later coached Workington. Brough, who had a spell working in South Africa in a packing factory, later owned a fishing boat supplying crab and lobster and worked as a yeast merchant's rep.

594. GIBBS, John Clifford JP
Wing 7 caps (6-2t)
Born: Bromley, Kent, 10 March 1902,
Died: Thanet, Kent, 11 January 1998
Career: Queens College Taunton, Harlequins, Kent
Debut: v New Zealand, Twickenham, January 1925

Clifford captained both Harlequins and Kent, playing a big role as a fast winger in his club, dominating the Middlesex's sevens. But it was only in the 1927 season that he held down a regular place in the England side, making four appearances and scoring two tries. He played for Quins until 1934, and between 1932 and 1934 he played football for Bromley in the Athenian League. He was a printer and publisher. His brother William also captained Kent and was President of the RFU, while a son, John D, won a blue for Cambridge University in 1965.

595. HILLARD, Ronald Johnstone CMG
Prop 1 cap 1925
Born: Durham, County Durham, 6 May 1903,
Died: Weymouth, Dorset, 23 March 1971
Career: St Paul's School, Oxford University, Old Paulines, Barbarians, Durham, Middlesex
Debut: v New Zealand, Twickenham, January 1925

Hillard had his first England trial the year he won his first Cambridge University blue in 1923, but it wasn't until a year later that he was selected to win his only cap for the visit of the All Blacks to Twickenham following a second trial when he appeared for The Rest against England. Hillard's decision to go into colonial service with the Sudan political service in 1925 ended his international career. He served until 1946 and held several other positions, including becoming chairman of the East African Cement Company, before his retirement in 1968.

596. KITTERMASTER, Harold James
Fly-half 7 caps (9-3t) 1925-1926
Born: Uppingham, Rutland, 7 January 1902,
Died: Broughton, Lancashire, 28 March 1967
Career: Rugby School, Oxford University, Harlequins, Bath, London
Debut: v New Zealand, Twickenham, January 1925

Kittermaster captained Rugby School at rugby and cricket and even made a century against Marlborough at Lords. He went on to win a blue at Oxford University, where A.T. Newton was moved to full-back to accommodate him. He succeeded Eddie Myers in the England team and scored tries against The All Blacks and Wales in his first two matches. Kittermaster was an assistant master at Sherborne and then a master at Rugby School before becoming Headmaster of Cargilfield School Preparatory School in 1937. He was the brother-in-law of Scotland international George MacPherson and his son Peter was an England schoolboy cap.

597. ARMSTRONG, Reginald OBE
Prop 1 cap 1925
Born: Newcastle-upon-Tyne, Tyne & Wear, 6 December 1897
Died: Morpeth, Northumberland, 17 February 1968
Career: Boatham Public School, Durham Medicals, Durham University, Barbarians, Northumberland
Debut: v Wales, Twickenham, January 1925

Armstrong was the captain of Durham Medicals when they won the Northumberland Cup and was also captain of Durham University. Armstrong won his only international cap against Wales in January 1925, but despite an England victory, he was replaced by Roderick MacLennan for their next game against Ireland and was never selected again. He saw action in the First World War in the Durham Light Infantry and then in World War Two in the Eighth Army fighting in the battle for Alamein. In medical practice in Rothbury, Northumberland, for 44 years, Armstrong died only a few weeks after his retirement.

598. MASSEY, Edward John
Scrum-half 3 Caps 1925
Born: West Derby, Lancashire, 2 July 1900,
Died: Woking, Surrey, 30 April 1977
Career: Ampleforth College, Liverpool, Leicester, Barbarians, Lancashire, Leicestershire
Debut: v Wales, Twickenham, January 1925

Massey gave Liverpool long service but was a Leicester player when picked as a travelling reserve to K Kershaw and Arthur Young. After playing an hour of the Calcutta Cup defeat against Scotland with a fractured collarbone and a partially dislocated shoulder, he was never selected again. A cadet pilot in the RAF during the First World War, he was a partner in a merchant's rubber planter and farmer before World War Two when he served with the Royal Army Service Corps and the Pioneer Corps. Massey later worked for the Ministry of Agriculture and then the GQ parachute company until his retirement in 1965.

599. PERITON, Harold Greaves
Flanker 21 caps (18-6t) 1925-1930
Born: Belfast, Northern Ireland, 8 March 1901
Died: Westminster, London, 12 April 1980
Career: Merchant Taylors' School Crosby, Waterloo, Barbarians, Lancashire
Debut: v Wales, Twickenham, January 1925

Belfast-born Periton was the first player capped from Waterloo and later became the only Irishman to captain England against Ireland in Dublin, one of four times he led the team. The cornerstone of England's pack for five years was ever-present in the 1928 Grand Slam-winning campaign. Also, the captain of Lancashire, in December 1929, withdrew from a trial and retired from international rugby. Periton was a member of the Stock Exchange for nearly 30 years, and during World War Two, he served as a liaison officer in the Royal Air Force.

600. LAWSON, Richard Gordon
No 8 1 cap 1925
Born: Workington, Cumbria, 8 October 1898
Died: Workington, Cumbria, 3 January 1961
Career: St Bees School, Workington, Cumberland
Debut: v Ireland, Twickenham, February 1925

Lawson was the eldest of two Workington brothers to play for England. He made his only international appearance against Ireland in February 1925. It was reported three years later England's selectors meant to call him up for his second cap against Wales but capped brother Tom instead. A member of Cumberland's 1924 County Championship-winning side, he was a PoW during the First World War after being shot down serving in the Royal Flying Corps. The chairman of Ogden & Lawson brass founders, he was a captain in the Coastal Defence Battery in the Second World War.

601. MACLENNAN, Roderick Ross Forrest
Prop 3 caps 1925
Born: Glasgow, Scotland, 23 December 1903
Died: Nairn, Scotland, 2 January 1986
Career: Merchant Taylors' School, Headingley, London Scottish, Middlesex
Debut: v Ireland, Twickenham, February 1925

MacLennan was a Gaelic-speaking Scot qualifying for England after being educated at Merchant Taylors' School, whom he captained between 1921 and 1922 and where he was also crowned public school middleweight boxing champion. One of his three caps was against Scotland, who marked the official opening of Murrayfield Stadium in March 1925 by clinching a first-ever Grand Slam. MacLennan was an insurance broker with Lloyds before joining ICI. Then, during World War Two, he served as a captain with the Intelligence Corps, later becoming a director of Belfast fertiliser firm Richardsons until retiring and serving as a county councillor.

602. CUMMING, Major General Sir Duncan Cameron KBE, CBE, OBE
No 8 2 caps 1925
Born: Blackburn, Lancashire 10 August 1903,
Died: Wandsworth, London 10 December 1979
Career: Cambridge University, Blackheath, Barbarians
Debut: v Scotland, Murrayfield, Edinburgh, March 1925

Cumming made his England debut while still at Cambridge University, whom he represented between 1922 and 1924 when Scotland marked the official opening of Murrayfield Stadium by clinching a first-ever Grand Slam. He kept his place for the final game of the 1925 campaign in France, but after graduating, he joined the Sudan administration. During World War Two, he became a general and was responsible for supervising the post-war union of Eritrea and Ethiopia, for which he was knighted. Cumming later joined British Overseas Airways Corporation as managing director of Associated Companies and then was an adviser on African affairs.

603. CONSIDINE, Stanley George Ulick
Wing 1 cap 1925
Born: Bilaspur, India 11 August 1901,
Died: Bath, Somerset 31 August 1950
Career: Blundell's School, Bath, Somerset
Debut: v France, Stade Colombes, Paris, April 1925

Considine first played the game at Blundell's School in Tiverton and joined Bath in 1918. He had an Irish trial in Dublin in 1921 before being spotted by England the following season and given the first of several trial matches. He made his only international appearance against France in April 1925 but badly injured his knee. His enthusiasm for all sports diminished after that, and he retired almost immediately. He played first cricket for Somerset and was a solicitor in Bath. A squadron leader in the RAF during World War Two, he died of liver failure due to alcoholism. His brother, Harold, played for Bath and Richmond.

604. ASLETT, Brigadier Alfred Rimbault DSO
Centre 6 caps (6-2t) 1926-1929
Born: Calcutta, India, 14 January 1901
Died: Cowfold, Sussex, 15 May 1980
Career: Clifton College, Royal Military College Sandhurst, Blackheath, Richmond, The Army, Barbarians, Lancashire, Surrey
Debut: v Wales, Arms Park, Cardiff, January 1926

Aslett was educated at Clifton College, where he played cricket and rugby. He was ever-present for England during their 1926 campaign, scoring both of his tries in a win over France, but he had to wait until 1929 to win his final two caps. Aslett was commissioned in the King's Own Royal Regiment in 1920 and continued to serve until the end of the Second World War when he was twice mentioned in dispatches and was awarded a DSO. Aslett then became director of the Army Sports Control Board and served the RFU as a board member, vice president and selector.

605. BURTON, Cdr Hyde Clarke
Wing 1 cap 1926
Born: Bishop's Stortford, Hertfordshire, 10 June 1898,
Died: Brighton, Sussex, January 27, 1990
Career: RNEC Keyham, Bishops Stortford, Richmond, Royal Navy, Barbarians, Eastern Counties
Debut: v Wales, Arms Park, Cardiff, January 1926

Burton learnt to play rugby in the Royal Navy, and during the First World War, he served in the Grand Fleet and with destroyers in the Mediterranean until he retired in 1921. He made his only international appearance as a Richmond player against Wales in Cardiff five years later. After leaving the Navy, he became a chartered accountant, secretary, and director of gas companies, including the Malta and Mediterranean Gas Company. He was recalled to the Navy during World War Two and served as a commander. Burton later worked in trade and naval intelligence at the Admiralty and attended the Quebec Conference in 1943.

606. FRANCIS, Thomas Egerton Seymour OBE
Centre 4 caps (8-4c) 1926
Born: Uitenhage, Eastern Cape, 21 November 1902,
Died: Bulawayo, Rhodesia, 24 February 1969
Career: Tonbridge School, Cambridge University, Blackheath, Somerset, Transvaal
Debut: v Wales, Arms Park, Cardiff, January 1926

Francis was a double Cambridge University blue in rugby and cricket, while he also played first class cricket for Somerset and Eastern Province. He was a teammate at Tonbridge, Cambridge and Blackheath of Arthur Young. He was an ever-present for England in 1926 before returning to South Africa and Rhodesia, where he was chairman of Francis and Co. and a director of the Reserve Bank of Rhodesia. During World War Two, he became a lieutenant colonel in the King's Royal Rifle Corps. Francis was awarded an OBE for services to rugby and cricket and was instrumental in forming the Bulawayo Country Club.

607. HANVEY, Robert Jackson
Prop 4 caps
Born: Blennerhasset, Cumbria, 16 August 1899
Died: Carlisle, Cumbria, 17 October 1989
Career: East Lancs Battalion, Blennerhasset, Aspatria, Cumberland and Westmorland
Debut: v Wales, Arms Park, Cardiff, January 1926

Hanvey started to play rugby while serving in the East Lancs Battalion at the end of the First World War and formed a team in his home village, Blennerhasset. After moving to Aspatria, he was a member of the Cumberland side that won the County Championship in 1924 and two seasons later won all four of his England caps. After retiring in 1931, he became a referee and was appointed to the International panel eight years later. Hanvey, a shoe repairer in Blennerhasset, became president of the Cumberland RU and then his former club, Aspatria, until his death.

608. STANBURY, Edward
Flanker 16 caps (13-5c,1p) 1926-1929
Born: Plympton, Devon, 29 August 1897
Died: Plympton, Devon, 1 May 1968
Career: Plymouth Albion, Devon, Barbarians
Debut: v Wales, Arms Park, Cardiff, January 1926

Stanbury was a member of England's 1928 Grand Slam-winning side and also captained Devon and Cornwall against New South Wales and the Springboks in 1931 when he scored the equalising try. He spent his honeymoon in London before playing in an international. After retiring, he became a referee and was on the Devon selection committee. He then served as secretary and the county's rep on the RFU board. Between 1922 and his retirement in 1964, he was the rating officer for Plympton St Mary Rural Council. He was also on committees of Plympton Bowling Club and Plympton Cricket Club.

609. WORTON, Joseph Robert Bute
Scrum-half 2 caps 1926-1927
Born: Fulham, London, 31 March 1901
Died: South Western Surrey, Surrey, 14 January 1991
Career: Haileybury & ISC, Royal Military Academy Sandhurst, Harlequins, The Army, Combined Services, Barbarians, Surrey
Debut: v Wales, Arms Park, Cardiff, January 1926

Worton was the captain of Haileybury College before going to the Royal Military Academy in Sandhurst. He had his first England trial in November 1923, but it wasn't until January 1926 that he won his first cap, against Wales, in the same year he was a member of the Harlequins side that won the first Middlesex Sevens. He won his second and final cap in the return match with Wales at Twickenham in 1927. He joined the Duke of Cornwall's Own Middlesex Regiment in 1921 and retired as a lieutenant colonel in 1954, having served through the Second World War.

610. DEVITT, Sir Thomas Gordon BT
Wing 4 caps
Born: Egham, Surrey, 27 December 1902,
Died: Colchester, Essex, 23 December 1995
Career: Sherborne School, Cambridge University, Blackheath, The Army, Barbarians, Middlesex
Debut: v Ireland, Lansdowne Road, Dublin February 1926

Devitt was a double blue representing Cambridge University in rugby and athletics, specialising in the long jump. He was one of three light blues in the team when he made his debut against Ireland in February 1926. One of the best wing three-quarters of his day, he captained Blackheath for a season in 1930. A lieutenant in the Seaforth Highlanders, he resigned his commission but was recalled in 1940 for the Second World War and was promoted to lieutenant colonel. He became the chairman of Macers Ltd and was also a partner in a shipping brokerage, Devitt and Moore.

611. HASLETT, Leslie Woods
Lock 2 caps (3-1t) 1926
Born: Pontypool, Monmouthshire, 5 June 1900
Died: Montreal, Quebec, 7 July 1992
Career: Cheltenham College, Royal Military Academy Woolwich, Blackheath, Birkenhead Park, Eastern Counties
Debut: v Ireland, Lansdowne Road, Dublin, February 1926

Haslett was born in Pontypool but was educated and lived most of his life in England. He first had a trial for England in November 1922, replacing Ron Cove-Smith, but he had to wait until February 1926 to win his first cap. One of three new caps after a draw in Wales, he scored a try on his debut, but after retaining his place against France, he wasn't picked again. Haslett was a chartered accountant who emigrated to Canada to work for Canadian Industries in the manufactured Explosives and Ammunition Department, who became a chemical manufacturer in Montreal, where he died.

612. TUCKER, William Eldon CVO OBE TD
No 8 3 caps 1926-1930
Born: Hamilton, Bermuda, 6 August 1904
Died: Paget, Bermuda, 4 August 1991
Career: Cambridge University, St George's Hospital, Blackheath, Barbarians, Kent
Debut: v Ireland, Lansdowne Road, Dublin, February 1926

Bill Tucker moved to England in 1919 to attend Sherborne School and Cambridge University before continuing his medical training at St George's Hospital. He won his first cap in 1926, and then his last two followed four years later. He became an orthopaedic surgeon who, during World War Two, was a major in the Royal Army Medical Corps and later commanded the 17th London General Hospital. Tucker set up the London Clinic for Injury and became the first surgeon to specialise in sports medicine, returning to Bermuda in 1980. His father also William played for England.

613. WEBB, James William George
No 8 3 caps (3-1t)
Born: Upton, Northamptonshire, 17 October 1900
Died: Daventry, Northamptonshire, 9 August 1970
Career: Northampton, East Midlands
Debut: v France, Twickenham, February 1926

Webb joined the Saints in 1923, and within three years, he was making his first international appearance as the only new cap against France at Twickenham. He retained his place and scored his only try against Scotland but then had to wait until 1929 to win his third cap, this time at prop. He retired soon afterwards and, during World War Two, he was one of the few civilians to take part in the Normandy Landings as one of a select band of aircraft observers to serve on American ships. He lived all his life in Upton, working as a gardener and maintenance worker.

614. COULSON, Thomas John
No 8 3 caps 1927-1928
Born: Bristol, 30 December 1898
Died: Coventry, Warwickshire, 26 March 1948
Career: Gloucester, Coventry, Warwickshire, Midland Counties
Debut: v Wales, Twickenham, January 1927

Coulson started his career with Gloucester, but it wasn't until he moved to Coventry, where he spent the last 24 years of his life, that he won international recognition. He was an outstanding member of the Coventry pack, captaining the club before retiring in 1934. He was one of five west countrymen picked on his debut but only ended up with three caps to his name. He served in the 4th Hussars during the First World War and was an aircraft fitter with Bristol Siddeley before his death at the Coventry and Warwickshire Hospital following a lengthy illness.

615. HANLEY, Joseph
Forward 7 caps 1927-1928
Born: Queenstown, Cork 14 September 1901,
Died: Peverell, Plymouth, 5 May 1981
Career: St Chads Rugby Club, Plymouth Albion, Civil Service Representative XV, Devon
Debut: v Wales, Twickenham, January 1927

'Jerry' Hanley, born in Cork, Ireland, played association football at Devonport High School, but after starting work at Devonport Dockyard, he was encouraged to join St Chad's Rugby Club. Jack Wright, another England international, soon spotted his potential and invited him to join Plymouth Albion. Hanley and clubmates Bert Sparks and Edward Stanbury helped England win the 1928 Grand Slam under Ron Cove-Smith. A knee injury ended his rugby career, and he became a selector before devoting himself to golf. He was a shipwright and then fitter in Devonport Dockyard until his retirement in June 1965.

616. LAIRD, Henri Colin Campbell
Fly-half 10 caps (15-5t) 1927-1929
Born: Chiswick, London, 3 September 1908
Died: Marylebone, London, 3 October 1971
Career: Nautical College Pangbourne, Harlequins, Barbarians, Middlesex
Debut: v Wales, Twickenham, January 1927

Laird still holds the honour of being England's youngest international, aged 18 years and 134 days, when he made his debut against Wales at Twickenham in 1927. He was ever-present when England won the Grand Slam a year later, but his international career ended with defeat against Ireland in 1929 through a knee injury suffered in the County Championship Final and then the emergence of Roger Spong. He was a stockbroker who later became the director of an advertising and marketing company in London. He also directed a 1939 instructional film called 'Modern Rugger.'

617. SELLAR, Kenneth Anderson DSO DSC
Full-back 7 caps 1927-1928
Born: Lewisham, London, 11 August 1906,
Died: Cape Town, South Africa, 15 May 1989
Career: Royal Navel College Dartmouth, United Services Portsmouth, Royal Navel College Greenwich, Royal Navy, Combined Services, Blackheath, Barbarians, London Counties, Hampshire
Debut: v Wales, Twickenham, January 1927

'Monkey' Sellar joined the Royal Navy in 1920, and seven years later won the first of his England caps. He was described as "easily the best full-back in Britain". He only missed one game in the 1928 Grand Slam campaign against Scotland because of the 'flu. A cricketer of some note, he played for Sussex, the Royal Navy and MCC. He saw action in the D-Day Landings on Normandy Beach and was awarded a DSO after leading the assault on Walcheren Island. He later became a stockbroker at WI Carr Sons and Co before returning to South Africa, where he had grown up, until his death.

618. STARK, Kendrick James
Prop 9 caps (5,1c,1p) 1927-1928
Born: Edmonton, Middlesex, 18 August 1904
Died: Horsham, Sussex, 27 March 1988
Career: Dulwich College, Old Alieynians, Honourable Artillery Company, Territorial Army, London Counties, The Barbarians, Surrey
Debut: v Wales, Twickenham, January 1927

Dulwich College and Old Alieynians captain Stark declined an invitation to have a trial for Scotland in December 1926. Instead, he played in a trial for England on the same day and won his first cap against Wales a month later. He qualified for Scotland by serving in the London Scottish Territorials. An ever-present in his two seasons as an international, he was a member of England's Grand Slam-winning side in 1928. He was an oil company employee who later worked in the insurance industry and served as a captain in the Royal Army Service Corps during the Second World War.

619. DAVIES, Patrick Harry
Flanker 1 cap 1927
Born: Stockport, Cheshire, 17 March 1903,
Died: Ware, Hertfordshire, 21 February 1979
Career: Denstone College, Manchester, Sale, Cheshire
Debut: v Ireland, Twickenham, February 1927

Davies became Sale's first England international when he was selected to become one of five new caps to face Ireland at Twickenham in February 1927. It did, however, prove to be his only cap. A tremendous club man, he captained Sale between 1925 and 1927. He was the club president in their centenary year in 1960. He was also president of the Cheshire Rugby Union between 1958 and 1960. During World War Two, he served in the RAF for the duration of the conflict and worked for Ernest Batley Ltd, a prefabricated garage and building manufacturers business.

620. EYRES, Captain Walter Charles Townsend
No 8 1 cap 1927
Born: Barton Regis, Gloucestershire, 17 February 1895
Died: Hyde Park, London, 16 September 1965
Career: United Services Portsmouth, Royal Navy, Richmond, Barbarians, Hampshire
Debut: v Ireland, Twickenham, February 1927

Eyres joined Richmond as a centre, but by the time he was one of five new boys to play against Ireland at Twickenham in February 1927, he had become a back-row forward. He joined the Royal Navy in 1908 when he was 13 and captained the rugby team in 1924 and 1927. During World War Two, he was a personal aide to another former England international admiral, Bonham Carter. He retired from the Royal Navy when he reached the rank of captain and was then appointed as the manager of the White City Stadium in West London.

621. LAW, Douglas Edward
Prop 1 cap 1927
Born: Huddersfield, Yorkshire, 12 October 1902
Died: Hayling Island, Hampshire, 13 July 1986
Career: Birkenhead School, Birkenhead Park, Cheshire
Debut: v Ireland, Twickenham, February 1927

Law replaced Tom Coulson to win his only cap, but the return to the side of Edward Stanbury and the emergence of Ron Cove-Smith effectively ended his international career even though he was a member of the 1927 British tour to Argentina. He had two spells as captain of his club side Birkenhead Park between 1927 and 1929 and then again in 1930-31 and was also Cheshire skipper between 1928 and 1931 when he retired after getting married. Law ran a corn milling and cattle feed business in Birkenhead while a son, Bill, had a Scotland trial.

622. PRATTEN, William Edgar
Lock 2 caps 1927
Born: Mottingham, Kent, 29 May 1907,
Died: Canterbury, Kent, 25 August 1969
Career: Marlborough College, Blackheath, Sidcup, Barbarians, Kent
Debut: v Scotland, Murrayfield, Edinburgh, March 1927

Pratten was the nephew of Ireland international R d'Arcy Patterson. He won both caps in 1927 against Scotland and France, the same year as helping Kent win the County Championship. Pratton spent eight years working for Shell-Mex, joining Wingham Engineering company in 1933 and was chairman and managing director when he died. During World War Two, he served in the Middle East as a major in the Royal Artillery. A former captain, he was treasurer of the Royal St George's Golf Club, a director of Folkestone Water Company, and a commissioner of taxes.

623. ALEXANDER, William
Winger 1 cap 1927
Born: Newcastle-upon-Tyne 6 October 1905
Died: Unknown
Career: Northern, Barbarians, Northumberland, Northumberland and Durham
Debut: v France, Stade Colombes, Paris, April 1927

Alexander won his only international cap against France in April 1927 when he was brought into the side to fill a vacancy on the right wing ahead of Richard Hamilton-Wickes. Both players were made to travel to Paris, before the full selection committee decided on the morning of the game who was playing. It proved to be the only cap Alexander, a chartered accountant, would win. He worked for Price, Waterhouse and Co in Newcastle-upon-Tyne, then in Montreal, Canada, and later moved to a commercial firm in Ottawa. He spent his retirement in France.

624. BISHOP, Colin Charles
Fly-half 1 cap 1927
Born: Hampstead, London 5 October 1903
Died: Winchester, Hampshire, 4 March 1980
Career: University College School, Combined Universities, Cambridge University, Blackheath, Barbarians, Middlesex
Debut: v France, Stade Colombes Paris, April 1927

Bishop was awarded his university colours in eight different sports and joined Blackheath in 1926 after completing his education. Bishop won his only cap with Colin Laird unavailable because of a wedding. He was partnered with his Blackheath teammate Arthur Young in France's first-ever win over England. In the same month, he helped his club reach the finals of the Middlesex Sevens. Bishop announced his retirement from the game soon after his engagement and became the managing director of a catering company, Gunter and Co., until selling the business in the early 1960s. His son John also played for Blackheath.

625. BUCKINGHAM, Ralph Arthur
Centre 1 cap 1927
Born: Blaby, Leicestershire, 15 January 1907
Died: Stoneygate, Leicestershire, 10 April 1988
Career: Stoneygate, Leicester, Leicestershire, Barbarians
Debut: v France, Stade Colombes, Paris, April 1927

Buckingham started his career with Stoneygate before joining Leicester in 1924 and won his only cap against France three years later. He was a travelling reserve a further ten times without gaining another cap. He scored the last try for the combined Leicestershire-East Midlands XV in their 1931 win over South Africa. Playing at either fly-half or in the centres, he was captain of his club and county. Buckingham retired in 1935 and became a vice president at Welford Road. He was the joint owner of Sowter and Buckingham, shoe merchants, until his retirement in 1970.

626. WALLENS, John Noel Stanley
Full-back 1 cap 1927
Born: Birkenhead, Cheshire, 25 December 1901
Died: Melbourne, Australia, 25 July 1962
Career: Waterloo, Lancashire
Debut: v France, Stade Colombes, Paris, April 1927

Wallens was the second Waterloo player to win International honours and played in the same side as the first, Joe Periton, when he won his only cap in a defeat to France in Paris in April 1927. Jack was given a chance with 'Monkey' Sellar, the first choice for two full seasons, unavailable. Two years later, he appeared for Lancashire in their County Championship final defeat against Middlesex. Wallens, who worked in the shipping industry, became a representative of a steamship company in New Zealand. But he later moved to Australia, settling in Melbourne and working as an advertising consultant until his death.

627. AARVOLD, Sir Carl Douglas
Centre 16 caps (21-7t) 1928-1933
Born: Hartlepool, County Durham, 7 June 1907
Died: West Humble, Surrey, 17 March 1991
Career: Durham School, Cambridge University, West Hartlepool, Headingley, Blackheath, Barbarians, Durham
Debut: v Australia, Twickenham, January 1928

Aarvold, educated at Durham School, played for Cambridge University in The Varsity Match four times and was never on the losing side. He was a Grand Slam winner in 1928, toured with the British Lions in 1927 to Argentina, in 1930 to Australia and New Zealand, and also captained England six times. he was called to the bar in 1932 and became the Recorder of Pontefract, Yorkshire, later serving as a circuit judge and Recorder of London until his retirement in 1975. He was president of the Lawn Tennis Association and was knighted in 1968.

628. KIRWAN-TAYLOR, William John OBE
Wing 5 caps (6-2t) 1928
Born: Sutton, Surrey, 29 June 1905,
Died: Lausanne, Switzerland, 28 August 1994
Career: Epsom College, Cambridge University, Blackheath, Barbarians, Surrey
Debut: v Australia, Twickenham, January 1928

Kirwan-Taylor won his blue at Cambridge University while reading law before becoming a surveyor. He was one of five new caps on his debut against Australia in January 1928. He went on to help England win the Grand Slam, and it would be their last for 29 years. He then retired to focus on his business career, which saw him hold several directorships, including Cow & Gate and Unigate. During World War Two, he was a lieutenant colonel in the Rifle Brigade and a general staff officer with the American 1st Airborne Division and was a playing member of the MCC.

629. LAWSON, Thomas Mattocks
No 8 2 caps 1928
Born: Cockermouth, Cumbria, 1 September 1900
Died: Cockermouth, Cumbria, 21 October 1951
Career: St Bee's School, Workington, Cumberland
Debut: v Australia, Twickenham, January 1928

Lawson was the younger of two Workington brothers who played for England. He learnt to play the game at St Bee's School, played in the greatest of Workington sides, and helped Cumberland win the 1924 County Championship. It was believed that he won his first cap by mistake when the selectors intended to call up his brother Richard. After leaving school, he went to work for Ogden and Lawson Brass Founders, a firm founded by his father and became sales director and later co-chairman. During the First World War, he was the welterweight champion of the Western Command.

630. RICHARDSON, James Vere
Centre 5 caps (23,1t,8c,1dg) 1928
Born: Prenton, Cheshire, 16 December 1903
Died: Padstowe, Surrey, 1 May 1995
Career: Uppinghm School, Oxford University, Birkenhead Park, Richmond, Barbarians, Cheshire
Debut: v Australia, Twickenham, January 1928

Richardson was a double Oxford University blue in 1925, winning his colours in Rugby and Hockey, but he also played county cricket for Essex between 1924 and 1926. But he was best known for being an ever-present in England's 1928 Grand Slam-winning campaign representing Birkenhead Park. A partner of stockbrokers Reiss Brothers, he served during World War Two as a major in the Royal Artillery. he was later managing director of H. B Legge & Sons paper merchants, then managing director and deputy chairman of the Jeyes Group and was the oldest surviving Essex player at the time of his death.

631. TURQUAND-YOUNG, David
Lock 5 caps 1928-1929
Born: London, 13 January 1904
Died: Blantyre, Malawi, 14 September 1980
Career: Richmond, the Army, Hampshire, Barbarians
Debut: v Australia, Twickenham, January 1928

'Turkey' Turquand-Young entered the Royal Military Academy Sandhurst as a cadet in 1922 and joined the Royal Tank Corps as a second lieutenant. He made his England debut against Australia and retained his place for the first match in the 1928 Grand Slam against Wales but had to wait until the following season to win his remaining three caps. Turquand-Young later became a chartered accountant and served in the Royal Navy Reserve in World War Two. A fine all-round sportsman, he played football for Wellington Town and represented Great Britain in the modern pentathlon at the 1924 and 1928 Olympic Games.

632. PALMER, Brigadier Godfrey Vaughan CBE TD
Wing 3 caps (6-2t) 1928
Born: Steyning, Sussex, 21 February 1900
Died: Chatham, Kent, 28 April 1972
Career: Royal Military Academy Sandhurst, the Army, North of Ireland RFC, Cross Keys, Harlequins, Richmond, Combined Services, Barbarians, Monmouthshire, Hampshire
Debut: v Ireland, Lansdowne Road, Ireland, February 1928

Palmer won all three of his England caps during their 1928 Grand Slam success after Sir Thomas Devitt reported ill. His biggest contribution came against France at Twickenham when he scored two tries. Guy Wilson then replaced him the following season. Palmer served in the Queens Royal Regiment between 1918 and 1928 before leaving to become a Lloyds underwriter. Recalled to the Army for World War Two, he was promoted to brigadier. Palmer was sales director of Winget Ltd, later chairman of the Institute of Export and then chairman of Celluchem Limited until his retirement.

633. PRENTICE, Frank Douglas
No 8 3 caps 1928-1930
Born: Leicester, Leicestershire, 21 September 1898
Died: Paddington, London, 3 October 1962
Career: Westleigh, Leicester, Leicestershire, Barbarians
Debut: v Ireland, Lansdowne Road, Ireland, February 1928

Prentice feared he would never play rugby again after being badly wounded in the Royal Artillery in the First World War. As captain of Leicester, he helped Leicestershire win the 1925 County Championship. England capped Prentice three times between 1928 and 1930, but he is best remembered as the captain of the 1930 British Lions side that toured Australia and New Zealand and was tour manager in Argentina six years later. During the Second World War, he was taken prisoner of war while serving in the Royal Army Service Corps. He was secretary of the Rugby Football Union from 1947 until before his death.

634. SPARKS, Robert Henry Ware
Prop 9 caps 1928-1931
Born: East Stonehouse, Plymouth 19 February 1899
Died: Cheltenham, Gloucestershire, 15 August 1984
Career: Plymouth Albion, Civil Service, Devon
Debut: v Ireland, Lansdowne Road, Ireland, February 1928

'Bert' Sparks, Jock Wright, Frank Sanders, Jerry Hanley, and Charles Gummer were among five England internationals to work in Devonport Dockyard between the First World War and World War Two. He captained Plymouth Albion, Civil Service and Devon and made three appearances in England's 1928 Grand Slam-winning campaign. At the same time, his Albion and Devon teammates Jerry Hanley, the best man at his wedding, and Edward Stanbury were ever-present. His international career ended in 1931 after England failed to win a game for the first time in 26 years. Sparks continued to work as a charge hand in the dockyard until retirement.

635. BROWN, Thomas William
Full-back 9 caps 1928-1933
Born: Bristol, 14 June 1907
Died: Bristol, 14 May 1961
Career: Colston's School, Bristol, Bristol University, Barbarians, Gloucestershire
Debut: v Scotland, Twickenham, March 1928

Brown first caught the eye at Colston School and developed into one of the finest full-backs of his day. He was capped by England aged 19 and helped Gloucestershire win three successive County Championships. His career was cut short in 1934 when he was banned for life (including entering a ground) by the RFU, following an inquiry, after he was reported going into a rugby league ground. He gained a science degree from Bristol University before opening a garage business in Pilning, Gloucestershire and then became the licensee of the White Hart in Olveston. Gloucestershire.

636. FOULDS, Robert Thompson
Second Row 2 caps 1929
Born: West Derby, Lancashire, 27 April 1906
Died: East Grinstead, Sussex, 28 February 1987
Career: King William's College Isle of Man, Furness, Waterloo, Birmingham, Moseley, Barbarians, North Midlands, Lancashire
Debut: v Wales, Twickenham, January 1929

Foulds was the second XV scrum half at King William's College on the Isle of Man, and it wasn't until he moved to

Waterloo in 1924 that he was converted into a forward. He won both international caps in 1929 but continued to play for another six years. A meat market salesman for Swift and Co., he was later appointed to the board of directors. He was also a director at the Ministry of Food, then managing director and chairman of Stockbreeders Meat Company. His brother-in-law Jackie Carruthers captained Carlisle and Cumberland, and his son David played for Rosslyn Park and Kent.

637. SLADEN, Captain Geoffrey Mainwaring DSO DSC
Centre 3 caps 1929
Born: Reigate, Surrey, 3 August 1904
Died: Thornhill, Dumfrieshire, 4 October 1985
Career: RNC Dartmouth, United Services Portsmouth, Royal Navy, Hampshire
Debut: v Wales, Twickenham, January 1929

Sladen was a fine all-round sportsman representing the Royal Navy in hockey, athletics and rugby, a sport he did not take up until just before leaving Dartmouth. But he flourished after moving from a posting in Hong Kong to RNC Greenwich, where former England international 'K' Kershaw was coaching. He made all three international appearances in 1929 but continued to play for the Royal Navy for another six years. In World War Two, he made his name when he developed the rubber suit (Sladen Suit) used by British frogmen (Chariot Riders) who rode the human torpedoes.

638. SMEDDLE, Robert William
Wing 4 caps (6-2t) 1929-1931
Born: Leeds, Yorkshire, 14 July 1908
Died: Gosforth, Northumberland, 15 December 1987
Career: Blackheath, Moseley, Cambridge University, Durham City, Durham County
Debut: v Wales, Twickenham, January 1929

Smeddle went to Cambridge University and played four times in the Varsity Match, and he was elected secretary in 1931. He had two England trials before winning the first of his caps. A member of the Durham side that lost the 1932 County Championship final to Gloucester, he scored a try on his last international appearance against France. His rugby career was ended by an injury suffered in a club game. Smeddle was a captain in the Army during World War Two and enjoyed a successful business career that saw him trade stocks and shares and own higher purchase and travel businesses.

639. SWAYNE, John Walter Rocke MC TD
No 8 1 cap 1929
Born: Mussoorie, India 27 May 1906,
Died: Burnham-on-Sea, Somerset, 24 June 1987
Career: Bromsgrove School, Bridgwater Albion, Harlequins, Territorial Army, Somerset
Debut: v Wales, Twickenham, January 1929

Swayne first showed potential as a top class rugby player when he captained Bromsgrove School. He would also go on to skipper his club Bridgwater Albion and county Somerset. He won his only cap after replacing Doug Prentice in a trial match. A fine all-round sportsman, he also represented Somerset at golf and squash. He was awarded the Military Cross for his actions in the Middle East during World War Two and retired from the North Somerset Yeomanry as a major. Swayne was a solicitor with Gould and Swayne of Glastonbury from 1931 until his retirement. His younger brother Deneys was capped in 1931.

640. WHITLEY, Herbert
Scrum-half 1 cap 1929
Born: Morpeth, Northumberland, 26 August 1903
Died: Stockton, Yorkshire, 20 March 1975
Career: Durham School, Northern, Northumberland
Debut: v Wales, Twickenham, January 1929

Durham School-educated Whitley was yet to win international honours when he was selected for the 1924 British Lions tour of South Africa. But he went on to win three test caps and scored a try in the first test. He was one of four scrum-halves used in England's 1929 campaign, winning his only cap against Wales. The brother-in-law of fellow England international Alan Robson, who also played for Northern and Northumberland, he worked for Martin's Bank from 1921 until his retirement in 1963. Whitley saw active service with the Royal Marines during the Second World War.

641. WILKINSON, Harry
Flanker 4 caps (6-2t) 1929-1930
Born: Halifax, Yorkshire, 22 March 1903,
Died: Hastings, Sussex, 1 October 1988
Career: Fattenhall College, Halifax, Yorkshire
Debut: v Wales, Twickenham Greater London January 1929

'Wilkie' Wilkinson followed in the footsteps of his father, also named Harry, who won one cap in 1898. He scored two tries against Wales on his debut and then retained his place for the next two games. He captained Halifax and Yorkshire and scored 14 tries on the British Isles tour of Australia and New Zealand but didn't win a test cap. A manager and then company director of Bradford-based wool combers, TH Shaw later served Halifax as fixture secretary and coach, retiring to Malta before returning to live in Hastings until his death.

642. WILSON, Guy Sumerfield
Wing 2 caps 1929
Born: Leigh, Lancashire, 30 August 1907
Died: Lancaster, Lancashire, 8 July 1979
Career: Tyldesley, Manchester, Birkenhead Park, Barbarians, Lancashire
Debut: v Wales, Twickenham, January 1929

Wilson won two caps for the British Isles on their 1927 tour of Argentina, two years before he broke into the England side. He replaced Godfrey Palmer to win the first of his two England caps. He suffered a leg injury playing in a County Championship game against Middlesex at Twickenham, missing their next game against Scotland a week later and was not selected again even though he was a reserve for trial games. Wilson was an insurance broker away from rugby, firstly with Associated Insurance Brokers and then with Guy S Wilson Ltd.

643. HARRIS, Thomas William
No 8 2 caps 1929-1932
Born: Northampton, Northamptonshire Q4 1907
Died: Northampton, Northamptonshire, 11 September 1958
Career: Barry Road School, Alexandra Park, Northampton, East Midlands
Debut: v Scotland, Murrayfield, Edinburgh, March 1929

Harris learnt the game at Barry Road School as a three-quarter but was moved into the pack after joining Alexandra Park. He played his first game for Northampton against Coventry in December 1923, and when he retired in 1937 had played 426 games. He was captain between 1932 and 1936. An Injury against Ireland ended his international career after just two caps. Harris was a member of the Leicestershire and East Midlands side that beat the Springboks in 1932. He collapsed and died in the yard of H Coulter and Son, wholesale fruiters, where he worked as a salesman.

644. MEIKLE, Stephen Spencer Churchill
Fly-half 1 cap (3-1t) 1929
Born: West Derby, Lancashire, 6 July 1905
Died: Liverpool, Lancashire, 4 June 1960
Career: St Bee's School, Waterloo, Barbarians, Lancashire
Debut: v Scotland, Murrayfield Edinburgh March 1929

Meikle was born just a few hundred yards from Waterloo Rugby Club in Blundellsands and learnt the game at St Bee's School. A knee injury to Colin Laird handed him his only international cap, and like brother Graham, five years later, he scored a try on his England debut. He captained Waterloo and Lancashire, becoming an international panel referee. He later served club and county as president and sat on Lancashire's selection committee. He was a commercial chandler with his father and was a director of W H Wheatley and Co in Liverpool when he committed suicide.

645. NOVIS, Anthony Leslie MC
Wing 7 caps (12-4t) 1929-1933
Born: Bombay, India 22 September 1906
Died: Cheltenham, Gloucestershire, 2 November 1997
Career: Oxford University, Headingley, Blackheath, the Army, Yorkshire, the Combined Services, the Barbarians
Debut: v Scotland, Murrayfield, Edinburgh, March 1929

Oxford University blue Novis marked his international debut against Scotland in March 1929 with a try but was never a regular. His caps spread out over four years because of army duties. He was commissioned into the Leicestershire Regiment a month before winning his first cap. He toured Australia with the British Isles in 1930 and captained a Combined Services side against New Zealand five years later. Novis was wounded twice in World War Two and was awarded a Military Cross for his actions in Egypt. He continued to serve his country until his retirement in October 1954.

646. REW, Major Henry
Prop 10 caps 1929-1934
Born: Exeter, Devon, 11 November 1906
Died: El Alamein, North Africa, 11 December 1940
Career: Exeter School, Exeter, Blackheath, the Army, Barbarians, Devon
Debut: v Scotland, Murrayfield, Edinburgh, March 1929

Rew was educated at Exeter School, joining the Royal Tank Regiment in 1928, and only played when his duties allowed. He played four test matches for the British Isles on their 1930 tour to Australia and New Zealand and was a key member of a combined Devon and Cornwall side that drew with South Africa at Devonport in 1931. Before World War Two, he served in India and only returned to active duty from wounds he suffered in France when he laid down his life in the Middle East. His younger brother, Major Robert Rew, captained Exeter.

647. RICHARDS, Edward Ernest
Scrum-half 2 caps 1929
Born: East Stonehouse, Devon 11 March 1905
Died: Plymouth, Devon, 9 June 1982
Career: Penryn, Plymouth Albion, Devon, Devon and Cornwall
Debut: v Scotland, Murrayfield Edinburgh March 1929

Richards came from a Cornish rugby family who played for Penryn. His father, Harry Richards, played for the club, as did his brother, Harry. Indeed, the Richards boys lined up opposite each other at scrum-half, Eddie for Devon and Harry for Cornwall in the County Championship. He played for Devon and Cornwall against South Africa, Australia and the All Blacks. He served in the Royal Navy and had an International trial in December 1932, but when he could not find regular employment as a bricklayer in August 1933, he accepted £400 to join the London Highfield Rugby League Club.

648. COLEY, Eric OBE
No 8 2 caps (3-1t) 1929-1932
Born: Northampton, Northamptonshire, 23 July 1903
Died: Northampton, Northamptonshire, 3 May 1957
Career: Northampton, Barbarians, East Midlands
Debut: v France, Stade Colombes Paris April 1929

Coley played association football at school but switched codes and was blooded in the Saints' first team when he was 18. He went on to captain Northampton and East Midlands and was a member of the first touring side to visit Argentina in 1928. Eric was Honorary Secretary of the East Midlands RU and of Northamptonshire CCC. An England selector who served as a brigadier in the 21 Army Group during World War Two. Later he became a welfare officer at Kodak in Wealdstone before returning to Franklins Gardens to run the hotel and grounds. He was fixture secretary for Saints and East Midlands. His eldest son David played for Northampton and East Midlands.

649. GUMMER, Charles Henry Alexander
No 8 1 cap (3-1t) 1929
Born: Croydon, Surrey, 20 November 1905
Died: Bishop's Waltham, Hampshire, 4 February 1974
Career: Plymouth Albion, Plymouth City Police, Moseley, British Police, Devon
Debut: v France, Stade Colombes, Paris, April 1929

Gummer was one of three Plymouth Albion players in the England team when he scored a try on his only international appearance at the end of the 1929 season. Peter Howard kept him out of the side, and he never played again. He was an apprentice shipwright in Devonport Dockyard, joining Plymouth City Police in 1927 until 1944. He became a major in the British Army for two years, staying in Germany until 1952 on the supervisory police staff. After five years with the RAF, he joined the Ministry of Defence until retirement.

650. MARTINDALE, Samuel Airey
Lock 1 cap 1929
Born: Kendal, Cumbria, 5 May 1905,
Died: Kendal, Cumbria, 19 January 1986
Career: Kendal, Cumberland and Westmorland
Debut: v France, Stade Colombes, Paris, April 1929

In his own words, Martindale started playing rugby "by accident and was never coached by anyone." A natural at the game, he had two spells as captain of his hometown club in 1927 and 1928, between 1932 and 1934. He also captained his county for six seasons. He won his only test cap as one of three newcomers in the pack against France and a year later won one cap on the British Isles tour of Australia and New Zealand. Martindale was a trade joiner and director of his family firm, G.F Martindale and Son.

651. REEVE, James Stanley Roope
Wing 8 caps (15- 5t) 1929-1931
Born: Kensington, London 12 September 1908
Died: East Harling, Norfolk, 6 November 1936
Career: Pembroke College, Cambridge University, Harlequins, Barbarians
Debut: v France, Stade Colombes, Paris, April 1929

Reeve was educated at Cambridge University but did not win a blue. However, he was a player who knew his way to the try line. Two of his five tries came on his final international appearance against Scotland in 1931. A member of the British Isles side that toured Australia and New Zealand in 1930, he scored a try in the first test win over Australia. He followed his father, Judge Raymond Roope Reeve, into the law and was called to the bar but was tragically killed in a car crash in Norfolk when aged just 28.

652. SPONG, Roger Spencer
Fly-half 8 caps 1929-1932
Born: Barnet, Hertfordshire, 23 October 1906
Died: Guildford, Surrey, 27 March 1980
Career: Mill Hill School, Old Millhillians, East Midlands Wanderers, Barbarians, Middlesex
Debut: v France, Stade Colombes, Paris, April 1929

Spong played rugby on the wing at Belmont Prep School because he could run. Making the switch to fly-half, he replaced Stephen Meikle to win his first test cap and played three of four games the following season alongside his Old Millhillians half-back partner Wilf Sobey. He also toured Argentina in 1927 and Australia and New Zealand in 1930 with the British Isles. After leaving school, he joined the family hardware manufacturing business Spong and Co. and was later appointed a director of aircraft engineers at Henshall & Sons. He captained Old Millhillians in 1930 and 1931 and was chairman between 1967 and 1971.

653. ASKEW, John Garbutt
Full-back 3 caps 1930
Born: Gateshead, Tyne & Wear 2 September 1908
Died: Stannington Morpeth 31 August 1942
Career: Durham City, Cambridge University, Durham County, Barbarians
Debut: v Wales, Arms Park Cardiff, January 1930

Askew was educated at Durham School and Cambridge University, where he won three blues. He also played minor counties cricket for Durham in 1927 and made all of his England appearances in 1930. He stopped playing sport upon leaving Cambridge in 1931 to enter colonial service in Nyasaland but was invalided home a year later. In 1933, he went into business with his father and four years later spent 12 months farming in South Africa. After returning to England, he was in business in Newcastle but died after a long illness at just 33.

654. BATESON, Alfred Hardy
Prop 4 caps 1930
Born: Otley, Yorkshire, 10 August 1901
Died: Scarborough, Yorkshire, 21 February 1982
Career: Bramley Old Boys, Otley, Yorkshire
Debut: v Wales, Arms Park Cardiff, January 1930

Bateson played association football for Horsforth in the Wharfedale League until the age of 23 but then, encouraged by a workmate, switched codes to rugby and joined Bramley Old Boys despite only ever watching one game of rugby. In a rapid rise to fame, he won his county cap within a year and, within three years, his four England caps. Bateson stopped playing in 1931 because of work pressure after helping Otley win the Yorkshire Cup for a fourth year running. An apprentice millwright, he worked for 30 years in heating and ventilating, mostly with Leeds City Corporation.

655. BLACK, Brian Henry
Lock 10 caps (30- 2t, 6c, 4p) 1930-1933
Born: South Africa, 27 May 1907
Died: Chilmark, Wiltshire, 29 July 1940
Career: St Andrews South Africa, Oxford University, Blackheath, Barbarians
Debut: v Wales, Arms Park Cardiff, January 1930

Black was born in South Africa but studied at Oxford, where he won his blue in 1929. The following year, he won the first of his ten England caps and was also included in the British Lions party that toured Australia and New Zealand, playing in five tests. He captained Blackheath and, with just a fortnight's practice, represented England in the Bobsleigh World Championships. He had a solicitors practice in London and was the director of a firm of travel agents but was killed serving as a pilot officer in the RAF during the Second World War.

656. FORREST, John William OBE
Lock 10 caps (2-1c) 1930-1934
Born: Barnet, Middlesex Q2 1903
Died: Bath, Somerset, 18 March 1963
Career: United Services Portsmouth, Royal Navy, Combined Services, Hampshire
Debut: v Wales, Arms Park, Cardiff, January 1930

Forrest spent a decade playing for the Royal Navy in the inter-services tournament and captained the Royal Navy between 1932 and 1935. He first had a trial in 1929, was an England regular for almost three seasons and only missed one game of the 1934 Triple Crown-winning campaign. He was also captain and secretary of the United Services Portsmouth. He served in the Royal Navy during World War Two and moved to Bath following his retirement in 1951. In later life, he was the founder and chairman of the Bath Christian Aid Week committee.

657. HOWARD, Peter Dunsmore
No 8 8 caps 1930-1931
Born: Maidenhead, Berkshire, 20 December 1908
Died: Lima, Peru, 25 February 1965
Career: Mill Hill School, Old Millhillians, Oxford University
Debut: v Wales, Arms Park, Cardiff, January 1930

Howard won his university colours and was still at Oxford when he made his England debut in January 1930. He was ever-present in 1930 and 1931 and captained the side against Ireland in 1931. Howard left Oxford with a degree to work for Oswald Mosley's Blackshirts but left and joined the Conservative Party, became a political correspondent of the Daily Express, and later wrote for the Evening Standard. Howard married Wimbledon ladies doubles champion Doris Metaxa and was the head of the spiritual movement Moral Re-Armament from 1961 to 1965, when he died of viral pneumonia in Lima, Peru.

658. KENDREW, Major General Sir Douglas Anthony KCMG CB OBE DSO
Forward 10 caps 1930-1936
Born: Barnstaple, Devon 22 July 1910,
Died: Nottingham, Nottinghamshire, 28 February 1989
Career: Uppingham School, Woodford, Leicester, the Army, Ulster, Combined Services, Barbarians, Eastern Counties
Debut: v Wales, Arms Park, Cardiff, January 1930

Kendrew won ten caps for England between 1930 and 1936. He toured Australia and New Zealand with the British Lions but failed to force his way into the test reckoning. He was also a member of the first England side to beat the All Blacks in 1936. He was commissioned into the Royal Leicestershire Regime as a lieutenant in 1931, and during World War Two, served in North Africa and Italy and then acted as a brigade commander in Italy, Greece and the Middle East. He was later appointed Governor of Western Australia and extended his term twice until 1974.

659. MALIR, Frank William Stewart
Centre 3 caps 1930
Born: Bombay, India, 4 August 1905
Died: Claro, Yorkshire, 22 January 1974
Career: Abberley Bridge, Otley, Barbarians, Yorkshire
Debut: v Wales, Arms Park, Cardiff, January 1930

Malir was born in India, where his father was captain of Bombay Medicals and, along with brother Herbert, who later played for Otley and Yorkshire, was sent to England to school. He learnt his rugby at Amberley Bridge before moving to Otley in 1923. He captained both Otley and Yorkshire, leading them to County Championship success. Along with Alf Bateson, they were the first Otley players to be capped by England after Malir initially trialled in 1928. A member of the Yorkshire committee and secretary of the selection committee, he was the head of the dying department of Springhead Mills, Guiseley.

660. ROBSON, Matthew
Centre 4 caps (3-1t) 1930
Born: Bellingham, Northumberland, 16 December 1908
Died: Edinburgh, Scotland, 30 November 1983
Career: Heriots School, Heriots FP, Oxford University, Blackheath, Barbarians, Northumberland
Debut: v Wales, Arms Park, Cardiff, January 1930

Robson was an ever-present for England in their 1930 Five Nations campaign while still at Cambridge University. International honours came a year after he won his university

The English Rugby Who's Who

Arthur Blakiston

Tom Woods

Reg Edwards

Ronald Cove-Smith

The English Rugby Who's Who

Sam Tucker

Reginald Pickles

Toff Holliday

Alan Robson

Richard Hamilton-Wickes

David Turquand-Young

Tony Novis

colours. As soon as he left in 1930, he went into the Colonial Forest Service in Nigeria, and when he retired in 1956 was the Chief Conservator of Forest, Western Region, Nigeria. During the Second World War Two, he became a captain in the West African Frontier Force. Robson later opened the Edinburgh office of the Nigerian High Commission and was then a senior administrative officer at the University of Edinburgh, where he settled after retiring.

661. SOBEY, Wilfred Henry
Scrum-half 5 caps 1930-1932
Born: Pachuca de Soto, Mexico, 1 April 1905
Died: Wandsworth, London, 27 February 1988
Career: Mill Hill School, Old Millhillians, Cambridge University, Barbarians, London Counties, Hampshire
Debut: v Wales, Arms Park, Cardiff, January 1930

Sobey won his university colours in 1925 and 1926. A year later, he toured Argentina with the British Isles, playing in three of the four test matches. Sobey won his first England cap alongside Old Millhillians half-back partner Roger Spong. In 1930, he was selected as vice-captain of the British Lions for their tour of Australia and New Zealand but injured his knee in the first match, could play no further part, and missed the whole of the 1930-31 season. Sobey was a master at Belmont Preparatory School before becoming headmaster of Kingsfield Preparatory near Watford.

662. KEY, Lt. Col Alan OBE TD
Scrum-half 2 caps 1930-1933
Born: Gerrards Cross, Buckinghamshire, 4 June 1908,
Died: Ploughley, Oxfordshire, 2 July 1989
Career: Cranleigh School, Blackheath, Old Cranleighans, Honourable Artillery Company, Barbarians, London Counties, Middlesex
Debut: v Ireland, Lansdowne Road, Dublin, February 1930

Key was an English Schools hockey international, but he would go on and make his name in rugby as captain of Old Cranleighans and winning two caps for England. He won his first cap after replacing Wilf Sobey, but then he had to wait three years for his second and final cap, standing in for Bernard Gadney. Key worked for Grindlay's Bank and then on the London Stock Exchange. He served in the Army during World War Two and was then the general manager of the Army Kinema Corporation for 22 years between 1947 and 1969, when he retired.

663. BROOK, Peter Watts Pitt
Flanker 3 caps 1930-1936
Born: Thornton Heath, Surrey, 21 September 1906
Died: Bristol, 6 August 1992
Career: Westminster Bank, United Banks, Cambridge University, Harlequins, Bristol, Barbarians, Wiltshire, Eastern Counties, Sussex
Debut: v Scotland, Twickenham, March 1930

Brook won his university colours four years running between 1928 and 1931 and was still at Oxford when he almost crowned his England debut with a match-winning try against Scotland. He won his second cap at Harlequins, where he played alongside war hero Douglas Bader, but had to wait until 1936 to win his final cap. He was ordained chaplain to Canford School, Dorset and then was a housemaster and chaplain at Clifton College. He was an Army chaplain during World War Two. He was also a Conservative on Bristol City Council and Avon County Council.

664. HUBBARD, John
Full-back 1 cap 1930
Born: Woolwich, London 27 June 1902
Died: North Surrey 29 August 1997
Career: Tonbridge School, Blackheath, Harlequins, Barbarians, Kent
Debut: v Scotland, Twickenham, March 1930

Cairns followed his father 'Scatter' in playing for Tonbridge School, Blackheath, Kent, the Barbarians and England. He played for Blackheath between 1919 and 1925, when he moved on to Harlequins. He was a late replacement for the injured John Askew to win his only England cap against Scotland in March 1930. Despite playing in a trial in December 1930, his opposite number, Leslie Bedford, was preferred. Like his father, he was a member of the London Stock Exchange for over 50 years. During World War Two, he was commissioned into the Royal Army Ordnance Corps.

665. TANNER, Rev Christopher Champain AM
Wing 5 caps (3-1t) 1930-1932
Born: Cheltenham, Gloucestershire, 24 June 1908
Died: Crete, Greece, 23 May 1941
Career: Cheltenham College, Pembroke College, Cambridge University, Richmond, Barbarians, Gloucestershire.
Debut: v Scotland, Twickenham, March 1930

Tanner won his university colours in 1930, the same year he made his England debut against Scotland, but he had to wait until 1932 to play his last four games, scoring his only try in his final international also against Scotland. He was ordained into the church in 1935 and served in Farnham, Gloucester and Haslemere. He was the Royal Naval Volunteer Reserve chaplain during the Second World War. He won the rarely awarded Albert Medal for saving wounded men from a sinking HMS Fiji. He died within minutes of dragging a wounded man aboard a rescue ship.

666. BARRINGTON, Thomas James Mountstevens
Fly-half 2 caps 1931
Born: Bridgwater, Somerset, 8 July 1908
Died: Taunton, Somerset, 6 September 1973
Career: Wrekin College, Bridgwater & Albion, Harlequins, Richmond, Bristol, Somerset
Debut: v Wales, Twickenham, January 1931

Barrington captained Wrekin College for three seasons before being capped by Somerset when he was 19. He spent four seasons with Bridgwater and Albion, joining Bristol in 1929, scoring two tries against Cardiff on his debut. Barrington won both of his England caps two years later and joined his father's law firm, Lovibond Son and Barrington, then started Barrington & Sons. He served in the Royal Air Force during World War Two, transferring to the RAF Regiment to be commissioned as a flight lieutenant. Later clerk to Bridgwater County Justices, Somerset River Board, and the Commissioners of Taxes.

667. BEDFORD, Lawrence Leslie
Full-back 2 caps 1931
Born: Headingley, West Yorkshire, 11 February 1903,
Died: Harewood, West Yorkshire, 25 November 1963
Career: Leeds Yarnbury, Headingley, Barbarians, Yorkshire
Debut: v Wales, Twickenham, January 1931

Bedford started his club career with Leeds Yarnbury but joined Headingley in 1924 as a full-back. His career took off after he was moved to centre two seasons later. He became the third Headingley player selected by England and the first in the inter-war years. When he retired he was a member of the Yorkshire committee from 1938 until his death and served as the county president and selector. A notable club cricketer in Yorkshire, he was a dye-stuff chemist and director of a Yorkshire dye-ware and chemical company.

668. BONAVENTURA, Maurice Sydney
Prop 1 cap 1931
Born: Rochford, Essex, 28 April 1902
Died: Lewes, Sussex, 14 July 1992
Career: Cranleigh School, Honourable Artillery Company, Lansbury, Blackheath, Barbarians, Surrey, Singapore Cricket and Sports Club, Royal Bannock Sports Club
Debut: v Wales, Twickenham, January 1931

Bonaventura was born Maurice Sneezum but changed his name by deed pole in July 1923 after his mother remarried. He was educated at Cranleigh School, where he learnt to play rugby and captained the first XV. Bonaventura started working at London Guarantee and Accident Company before joining Asiatic Petroleum, working in the Far East. After returning home, he won his only cap against Wales in January 1931. Bonaventura stayed in the petroleum industry for the rest of his working life, joining Shell-Max B.P after the Second World War in 1945 until he retired in 1962.

669. BURLAND, Donald William
Centre 8 caps (23 -3t, 4c 2p) 1931-1933
Born: Bristol, Gloucestershire 22 January 1908
Died: St Austell, Cornwall, 26 January 1976
Career: Bristol, Barbarians, Gloucestershire
Debut: v Wales, Twickenham, January 1931

Burland scored a try and a conversion on his test debut against Wales in January 1931, but after missing the return match a year later, he was recalled against Ireland in February 1932 and scored all 11 points. His international career ended with a knee injury he suffered in a trial match in December 1933. A major in the Royal Army Service Corps during World War Two, he spent 13 years with Shell-Mex and MP, then became a publican running the Horseshoe Inn, Downed, Bristol, between 1938 and 1964 when he ran a gift shop in Cornwall.

670. DAVEY, Richard Frank
Flanker 1 cap 1931
Born: Paddington, Middlesex, 22 September 1905
Died: Bexhill-on-Sea, Sussex, 24 May 1983
Career: Wellington School, Wellington, Teignmouth, Wanstead, Leytonstone, Exeter, London Counties, Devon, Eastern Counties
Debut: v Wales, Twickenham, January 1931

Davey captained Teignmouth before moving to London, where he had secured a job as a chartered surveyor in a private practice. Even though he played for one of London's less fashionable clubs, Leytonstone, his performances for the Eastern Counties secured him an England trial. After winning his only cap, he was replaced by 'Pop' Dunkley and was never selected again. A talented oarsman, he stroked the crew who won the Eyot Challenge Cup at Hammersmith Amateur Regatta. Then, following World War Two, he moved to Sussex, where he was the Superintending valuer for the valuation office of the Inland Revenue.

671. McCANLIS, Maurice Alfred
Centre 2 caps
Born: Quetta, India, 17 June 1906,
Died: Pershore, Worcestershire, 27 September 1991
Career: Cranleigh School, Oxford University, Old Cranleighans, Gloucester, Northampton, Territorial Army, Barbarians, Gloucestershire
Debut: v Wales, Twickenham, January 1931

McCanlis was a superb all-round sportsman who won a double Oxford University blue in rugby and captained them at cricket. He joined Gloucester in 1928 and retired eight years later, scoring a try in the final England trial to win the first of his two international caps, but was dropped after retaining his place once. A schoolmaster, he taught at Cheltenham and Mayo College, Aimer, India, between 1928 and his retirement in 1966. McCanlis also farmed part-time from 1952 to leaving Cheltenham. Maurice played first-class cricket for Surrey and Gloucestershire and was Secretary of the North Cotswold Hunt.

672. POPE, Edward Brian
Scrum-half 3 caps 1931
Born: Barnet, Hertfordshire, 29 June 1911
Died: Sandwich, Kent, 19 August 2011
Career: Uppingham School, Oxford University, Blackheath, Barbarians
Debut: v Wales, Twickenham, January 1931

Pope captained his school at rugby and hockey and was already an England international when he went to Oxford University, where he won his rugby blue in 1932. He had won all his international caps a year earlier against Wales, Scotland and France. Pope, who served during World War Two in the RAF, was the director of an underwriting agency and brokerage business working on the Lloyds Insurance market, and later, he was also a director of M.A. Shipping and Trading. He died 51 days after celebrating his 100th birthday.

673. SWAYNE, Deneys Harald
Flanker 1 cap 1931
Born: Roorkee, Bengal, 23 November 1909
Died: Mendip, Somerset, 9 September 1990
Career: Bromsgrove School, Worcester College, Oxford University, Harlequins, St George's Hospital, London Counties, Herefordshire and Worcestershire, North Midlands, Gloucestershire, Middlesex
Debut: v Wales, Twickenham, January 1931

Swayne followed in the footsteps of his elder brother John and captained Bromsgrove School. He won his Oxford University colours in 1930 and 1931, as his brother did in 1929. He won his only international cap against Wales at Twickenham. He also played cricket for his school, United Hospitals and West Kent. After gaining his medical qualifications from St George's Hospital, he served as a captain in the Royal Army Medical Corps during World War Two and was wounded in the Normandy Landings. He then set up a general medical practice in Stevenage, Hertfordshire.

674. DEAN, Geoffrey John MC
Scrum-half 1 cap 1931
Born: Lewisham, London 12 November 1909
Died: Poole, Dorset, 12 December 1995
Career: Rugby School, Cambridge University, The Army, LC Club, Harlequins, Barbarians, Sussex
Debut: v Ireland, Twickenham, February 1931

'Tinny' Dean was educated at Rugby School and went to Cambridge University, where he failed to win his university colours despite being good enough to play for his country. He represented Harlequins and won his only England cap when Edward Pope was unavailable to play against Ireland in February 1931, the year he joined the Royal Tank Regiment. He captained the Army for two years before his retirement in 1938. He lost a leg after being wounded and taken prisoner of war. After repatriation, he was promoted to lieutenant colonel and then brigade major in the 9th Armoured Brigade.

675. DUNKLEY, Philip Edward
No 8 6 caps 1931-1936
Born: Daventry, Northamptonshire, 9 August 1904
Died: Doncaster, Yorkshire, 17 June 1985
Career: Old Laurentians, Leicester, Harlequins, Warwickshire
Debut: v Ireland, Twickenham, February 1931

'Pop' Dunkley first had an international trial as a Leicester player in 1928, but it wasn't until he moved to London and started to play for Harlequins that, three years later, he won international recognition with the first two of his six caps. In 1933, Dunkley was appointed Quins captain, a position he held until 1936 when he won his last four caps. It was also in 1936 that he was selected to tour Argentina with the British Lions. Dunkley, who was Warwickshire captain for several seasons, was later secretary of their selection committee and worked in banking with the National Provincial Bank.

676. GREGORY, Gordon George
Hooker 13 caps (4-2c) 1931-1934
Born: Taunton, Somerset, 8 December 1907
Died: Newton Abbot, Devon, 4 December 1963
Career: Huish's School Taunton, Taunton, Bath, Bristol, Somerset
Debut: v Ireland, Twickenham, February 1931

Gregory's selection for his first cap against Ireland in February 1931, in place of the ill Sam Tucker, soon after joining Bath effectively ended the international career of the England captain. It began a run which saw him make 13 consecutive appearances, remarkable in an era of frequent selection changes. He was a member of England's 1934 Triple Crown-winning side and captain of Bristol and Somerset. He was with the Millers Mutual Association, becoming the vice-principal of the Somerset Farm Institute and was an advisor on trade until buying the Fordgate Farm, North Petherton, Somerset.

677. HARDING, Ernest Harold
No 8 1 cap 1931
Born: Mile End, London, 22 May 1899
Died: Liskeard, Cornwall, 25 December 1980
Career: Devonport Services, Royal Navy, Devon
Debut: v Ireland, Twickenham, February 1931

'Jumbo' Harding must have impressed in his international trial in December 1930. Even though he initially missed out on selection for their next game against Wales in January 1931, he became one of six new caps to face Ireland a month later. It proved, however, to be the only time that his country called upon him after Peter Hordern was moved into the back row for their next game against Scotland. Ernest had a career in the Royal Navy, and during World War Two, he was a lieutenant in the Royal Navy Volunteer Reserve and later worked for AD Cable Service.

678. HARRISON, Arthur Clifford
Wing 2 caps 1931
Born: Hartlepool, Durham, 10 May 1911
Died: Hartlepool, Durham, 29 June 2003
Career: Hartlepool Rovers, Barbarians, Durham, Mombasa Sports Club, Selangor Sports Club
Debut: v Ireland, Twickenham, February 1931

Harrison started to play for Hartlepool Rovers aged 15 and, within four years, was selected to make his England debut against Ireland at Twickenham after being a reserve for their first game of the season against Wales. He retained his place, but an injury in a club match ended his international career. He joined Price Waterhouse and Co. in 1933 but left in 1946. During World War Two, he served in the H.A.A. Harrison, became a treasury accountant in Malaya for 14 years, worked as an accountant at Durham Brewers J Nimmo and Son, and later took over as company secretary.

679. HORDERN, Peter Cotton AFC
Flanker 4 caps 1931-1934
Born: Berkhampstead, Hertfordshire, 13 May 1907
Died: Peterborough, Cambridgeshire, 22 June 1988
Career: Brighton College, Oxford University, Newport, Gloucester, Blackheath, Barbarians, Devon, North Midlands, Hampshire
Debut: v Ireland, Twickenham, February 1931

Hordern was the elder brother of the actor Sir Michael Hordern and was coached at Brighton College by former international Ernie Hammett. He won his university colours in 1928 and made his first three England appearances in 1931 but then had to wait until 1934 to win his final cap. He helped Hampshire win the County Championship in 1935, and the British Lions selected him to tour Argentina in 1936. During World War Two, he was a flying instructor in the RAF. An assistant master at Monmouth School and Bromsgrove School, he later became warden of Chancellor's Hall at Birmingham University.

680. KNOWLES, Thomas Caldwell
Fly-half 1 cap 1931
Born: West Bromwich, West Midlands, 6 May 1908,
Died: Birkenhead, Cheshire, 12 September 1985
Career: Ampleforth College, Birkenhead, Barbarians, Cheshire
Debut: v Scotland, Murrayfield, Edinburgh, March 1931

Knowles had his first international trial in 1929 but was selected for the British Lions' tour of Australia and New Zealand a year later despite being uncapped. In 1931, it appeared an injury would rob him of an England cap after he was forced to withdraw from another trial. He won his only cap against Scotland. He captained Birkenhead in 1932 and 1935 and toured Argentina with the British Lions in 1936. During World War Two, he served in the RAF and was chairman of Caldwell's family manufacturing business in Warrington. He was also president of Birkenhead and vice-president of Cheshire.

681. TALLENT, John Arthur CBE
Centre 5 caps (9-3t) 1931-1935
Born: Bromley, Kent, 8 March 1911
Died: Basingstoke, Hampshire, 14 April 2004
Career: Sherborne School, Cambridge University, Blackheath, Barbarians, Kent, East Midlands
Debut: v Scotland, Murrayfield, Edinburgh, March 1931

Tallent captained Sherborne School and then won his university colours in three of his four years at Cambridge. He was never a regular in the England side. His five caps were spread out over four years despite scoring three tries in his first two internationals. John was master in charge of rugby at Stowe School between 1932 and 1936 when he joined the London Stock Exchange. During the Second World War, he became a lieutenant colonel in the Honourable Artillery Company and the Royal Artillery. He then returned to the Stock Exchange until retiring in 1969 and was president of the RFU in Twickenham's Jubilee and president of Basingstoke RFC.

682. WHITELEY, Eric Cyprian Perry
Full-back 2 caps 1931
Born: Croydon, Surrey, 20 July 1904
Died: Epsom, Surrey, 16 March 1973
Career: Dulwich College, Old Alleynians, Honourable Artillery Company, Territorial Army, Barbarians, Surrey
Debut: v Scotland, Murrayfield, Edinburgh, March 1931

Whiteley followed in the footsteps of his father, Cyprian Whiteley, who played for Streatham and took up the game at Dulwich College. After leaving, he continued to play for Old Alleynians and had an international trial in December 1929. But it wasn't until Laurie Bedford turned in two poor displays that he won his international caps. Whiteley became an articled chartered surveyor before becoming a produce broker in Fenchurch Street. He joined the Honourable Artillery Company in World War Two and was promoted to major in 1951. Whiteley then went back to becoming a produce merchant importer until retirement.

683. BARR, Robert John MC TD
Full-back 3 caps (2-1c) 1932
Born: Blisworth, Northamptonshire, 26 May 1907
Died: Great Oxendon, Northamptonshire, 22 September 1975
Career: Stamford School, Leicester, Barbarians, Leicestershire
Debut: v South Africa, Twickenham, January 1932

Barr helped Leicestershire and East Midlands beat the Springboks in 1931 to earn himself a call-up to the England team the following season. But, after three caps, he was unluckily dropped in favour of Tom Brown and was never picked again. Barr was trained in textile engineering, founding the hosiery brand label manufacturing firm Barr, Radcliffe & Co. In World War Two, he served as a second lieutenant in the Army and was reported missing in France in 1940 but was found to be a prisoner of war and, after escaping, got within four kilometres of the Swiss border.

684. CARPENTER, Alfred Denzel
Prop 1 cap 1932
Born: Mitcheldean, Gloucestershire, 23 July 1900
Died: Gloucester, Gloucestershire, 17 April 1974
Career: Cinderford, Gloucester, Barbarians
Debut: v South Africa, Twickenham, January 1932

'Bumps' Carpenter was educated in Swansea but started his career at Cinderford, where he lived for most of his adult life before moving to Gloucester in 1928, where he spent the rest of his senior career until the outbreak of World War Two. 'Bumps' won his only England cap against South Africa in January 1932 but was a reserve 20 times, including as a 38-year-old. He won the County Cup four times with Gloucestershire and worked as a miner, mainly in the Forest of Dean and as a road builder. Later, he played on the same side as his sons George and Denzel.

685. GERRARD, Ronald Anderson DSO
Centre 14 caps 1932-1936
Born: Hong Kong 26 January 1912
Died: Nr Tripoli, Libya, 22 January 1943
Career: Taunton School, Bath, Territorial Army, Barbarians, Somerset
Debut: v South Africa, Twickenham, January 1932

Anderson was sent to England aged 15 to be educated at Taunton School and was first capped by Somerset while still a schoolboy. A talented sportsman, he also played cricket for his adopted county. But he excelled at rugby, captaining Bath between 1934 and 1938 when he retired. A civil engineer with Coles Brothers and then the Surveyor's Department of the City of Bath Corporation before being commissioned into the 43rd Wessex Divisional Engineers and later promoted to major. Anderson was awarded a DSO for minefield clearing but was killed three months later in action fighting in North Africa.

686. HOBBS, Major General Reginald Geoffrey Stirling CB DSO OBE
Lock 4 caps 1932
Born: Eltham, Kent, 8 August 1908
Died: Bromley, Kent, 7 November 1977
Career: Wellington College, Royal Military Academy Woolwich, Richmond, the Army, Barbarians, Kent
Debut: v South Africa, Twickenham, January 1932

'Pooh' Hobbs was the eldest son of Brigadier General Reginald Hobbs, another England international, and he followed in his father's footsteps with a career in the military when he was commissioned into the Royal Artillery in 1928. Four years later, he won all four of his international caps before serving in India, ending his England career. He fought in the Second World War at the Battle of El Alamein and North West Europe. When peace returned, he became Commandant of the Royal Military Academy, Sandhurst and was General Commanding Officer of the 1st Infantry Division. He was the 54th president of the RFU from 1961-62.

687. HODGSON, John McDonald
Forward 7 caps 1932-1936
Born: Gosforth, Northumberland, 13 February 1909
Died: St Pancras, London, 21 April 1970
Career: Northern, Leicester, Northumberland
Debut: v South Africa, Twickenham, January 1932

Hodgson must have thought his chance to play for England would never come after being a reserve throughout their 1930 campaign. He had to wait until January 1932 to win the first of his seven international caps. By then, he had toured Australia and New Zealand with the British Lions in 1930, winning two caps. He was the captain and later president of Northern and was the brother-in-law of another England international, Tom Berry. He was in business with G A Parsons and was loaned to the Ministry of Supply. Then, during World War Two, he fought in Turkey.

688. NORMAN, Douglas James
Hooker 2 caps 1932
Born: Leicester, Leicestershire, 12 June 1897
Died: Oadby, Leicestershire, 27 December 1971
Career: Medway School, Medway Athletic, Leicester, Barbarians, Leicestershire
Debut: v South Africa, Twickenham, January 1932

Norman started playing at Medway School and was soon chosen to captain Leicester Boys. In 1911, he played for England schoolboys, and his Tigers career started in 1914 but was soon interrupted by the First World War when he served in Mesopotamia. He returned to Tigers in 1919 and played through until 1934 and was a member of the Leicestershire side that won the County Championship in 1925. He won his England caps against Wales and South Africa in 1932. He was the monotype keyboard operator for Blackfriars Press and was president of Leicester Schools Rugby Union.

689. ROWLEY, Arthur James
No 8 1 cap 1932
Born: Coventry, Warwickshire, 18 November 1908
Died: Solihull, West Midlands, 11 April 1995
Career: Stoke Park School, Stoke School Old Boys, Coventry, Warwickshire
Debut: v South Africa, Twickenham, January 1932

Rowley learnt to play the game at Stoke Park School in Coventry and was an England Schoolboy international in 1923. He then played in the Warwickshire side, which was defeated by Gloucestershire in the 1931 County Championship Final and was a surprise inclusion for the opening test of 1932 against the Springboks when he was one of seven new caps among the forwards in what was largely an experimental decision by the England selectors. Rowley was a quality engineer who was dropped for the next game against Wales following a 7-0 defeat and was never selected again.

690. SAXBY, Leslie Eric
Flanker 2 caps 1932
Born: Bradfield, Berkshire, May 19, 1900
Died: High Flats, Natal, 26 August 1956
Career: Reading School, Hereford, Gloucester, Barbarians, North Midlands, Gloucestershire
Debut: v South Africa, Twickenham, January 1932

Saxby started playing rugby in the centres for Hereford before moving into the back row, where he made his name. During his eight-year career at Gloucester's Kingsholm, he played 169 games and was captain for four of the eight. He was approaching his 32nd birthday when he won both England caps. He won the County Championship three times with Gloucestershire and was captain of the 1932 success. He joined the RAF at the start of the Second World War and became a squadron leader while stationed in South Africa, where he eventually settled.

691. WEBB, Charles Samuel Henry
Lock 12 caps 1932-1936
Born: Plymouth, Devon, 4 November 1902
Died: Plymouth, Devon, 28 October 1961
Career: Devonport Services, Royal Navy, Royal Marines, Combined Services, Devon
Debut: v South Africa, Twickenham, January 1932

Webb started his career in the Plymouth Division of the Royal Marines and then joined Devonport Services. His performances for Devonport Services brought him to the notice of the Royal Navy and the Royal Marines selectors. The England selectors spotted him playing for the combined Devon and Cornwall side against South Africa in 1931 and capped him against the same opposition soon afterwards. He spent 29 years in the Royal Marines and survived the sinking of HMS Prince of Wales in 1941. After leaving the service, he became a policeman in Devonport Dockyard until retirement.

692. EVANS, Lieut. Cdr Neville Lloyd
Prop 5 caps 1932-1933
Born: Lewisham, Kent, 16 December 1908
Died: St Austell, Cornwall, 27 May 1994
Career: Eltham College, Royal Engineering College, Plymouth Albion, Devonport Services, Combined Services, United Services Portsmouth, Royal Navy, Barbarians, Hampshire, Devon
Debut: v Wales, St Helen's, Swansea, January 1932

'Barney' Evans made five successive test appearances for England but then lost his place in the side through injury after being selected to win a sixth cap against Scotland. Despite never being capped again, he continued to captain Devonport Services, Royal Navy and Devon. He spent 28 years serving the Royal Navy as an engineering officer between 1926 and 1954, including during World War Two. After leaving the Navy, he went to work for Gloucestershire-based engine manufacturers R A Lister and Co until 1963 when he became the secretary of St Enodoc Golf Club in Cornwall, where he lived until his death.

693. ELLIOT, Captain Walter DSC MP
Fly-half 7 caps (3-1t)
Born: Birkenhead, Cheshire, 17 February 1910
Died: Poole, Dorset, 8 September 1988
Career: HMS Conway, Royal Naval College, Royal Naval Aviation Portsmouth, Royal Navy
Debut: v Ireland, Lansdowne Road Dublin, February 1932

Elliot succeeded Roger Spong as England's fly-half, making his debut alongside Bernard Gadney in a new, untried half-back pairing following a heavy defeat against Wales. He made seven successive appearances until Charles Slow replaced him. He joined the Royal Navy after leaving school and was to serve throughout the Second World War before eventually retiring in 1958 to go into business. Two years later, he was elected as the Conservative MP for Carshalton and appointed Comptroller of the Household in 1970 before standing down from Parliament four years later after defending his seat three times.

694. GADNEY, Bernard Cecil
Scrum-half 14 caps (3-1t) 1932-1938
Born: Oxford, Oxfordshire, 16 July 1909
Died: Ipswich, Suffolk, 14 November 2000
Career: Oxford, Stowe, Richmond, Leicester, Headingley, HMS Ganges, HMS King Alfred, Barbarians, Leicestershire, East Midlands, Oxfordshire, Yorkshire
Debut: v Ireland, Lansdowne Road, Dublin, February 1932

Gadney was born in Oxford, and his family were friends with T E Lawrence, better known as Lawrence of Arabia. While at Stowe School, he shared a room with actor David Niven. He captained England eight times and led them to the Triple Crown in 1934. He began the move that led to Prince Obolensky's great try against the All Blacks in 1936, the year he captained the British Lions tour of Argentina. Gadney became a schoolmaster at Winchester House, Northamptonshire, then headmaster of Malsis, a prep school in North Yorkshire; he also took part in the D-Day landings during the Second World War.

695. ROBERTS, Reginald Sidney
Hooker 1 cap 1932
Born: Coventry, Warwickshire, 4 December 1911
Died: Coventry, Warwickshire, Q2 1992
Career: Coventry, Warwickshire
Debut: v Ireland, Lansdowne Road Dublin, February 1932

Roberts first made his name as a Sshoolboy international in 1926. He joined Coventry, debuting in November 1929, appearing 125 times for the club and another 20 for Warwickshire. An England reserve five times, he won his only cap against Ireland in Dublin in February 1932, but a season later, the 21-year-old electrician switched codes for the largest paid by any northern union club for a forward joining Huddersfield, who were captained by another former Coventry player Len Bowkett. Then after a serious injury force forced him to quit, Roberts worked for Rolls Royce until retirement.

696. VAUGHAN-JONES, Arthur
Flanker 3 caps 1932-1933
Born: Pontarddulais, Wales, 25 September 1909
Died: Cape Town, South Africa, 4 December 1987
Career: United Services Portsmouth, Royal Artillery, The Army
Debut: v Ireland, Lansdowne Road, Dublin, February 1932

Vaughan-Jones was born in Pontarddulais near Swansea but was eligible to play for England as he was serving in the Army and played for the service as well as United Services Portsmouth. His inclusion in the England side to travel across the Irish Sea surprised many observers, coming three months after he played in a Welsh trial match in Newport. Vaughan-Jones, an officer in the Royal Artillery, retained his place for their next game, and after playing against his native Wales in January 1933, he suffered a serious injury and was never selected again.

697. LONGLAND, Raymond John
Prop 19 caps 1932-1938
Born: Lavendon, Buckinghamshire, 29 December 1908
Died: Aylesbury, Buckinghamshire, 21 September 1975
Career: Olney, Buckingham, Bedford, Northampton, RAF, Combined Services, Barbarians, East Midlands
Debut: v Scotland, Twickenham, March 1932

Longland enjoyed a 21-year career in the front row at Franklins Gardens. He spent two seasons as captain of the Barbarians in 1936 and 1947 as well as leading the East Midlands. He won his first cap despite missing a trial through injury after playing a prominent role in the Leicestershire and East Midlands win over the Springboks. He helped England win the Triple Crown in 1934 and beat the All Blacks in 1936. A licensee, a carpenter and a joiner, he was a PT Instructor in the RAF during the Second World War and later became a woodwork and PE teacher at Akeley Wood Prep School before his death from leukaemia.

698. BOLTON, Dr Reginald MBE
Flanker 5 caps (6-2t) 1933-1938
Born: Prescot, Lancashire 20 November 1909
Died: Chichester, Sussex, 21 September 2006
Career: Queen Elizabeth Grammar School Wakefield, Wakefield, University College Hospital, Harlequins, Barbarians Yorkshire
Debut: v Wales, Twickenham, January 1933

Bolton captained both University College Hospital and Yorkshire, but he could never secure a regular place in the England set-up. His five caps were spread out over five years. He was regularly picked for trial matches during that period and never quite made the final cut with the selectors, but was called up regularly when a replacement was needed. He represented London University College Hospital at swimming and held several medical appointments before the outbreak of the Second World War when he served in the Royal Army Medical Corps. He became a consulting physician at Epsom District Hospital from 1948 until retirement.

699. BOOTH, Lewis Alfred
Wing 7 caps (9-3t) 1933-1935
Born: Horsforth, Leeds, 26 September 1909
Died: Waddenzee, Holland 25 June 1942
Career: Giggleswick, Headingley, Bohemians, RAF, Barbarians, Yorkshire
Debut: v Wales, Twickenham, January 1933

Booth was an ever-present in his first season in England colours but was taken ill on the morning of the opening match of the 1934 Triple Crown-winning campaign against Wales. He returned to score a try in the victory over Scotland that secured a third win of the campaign. A director of woollen manufacturers L.J Booth & Sons and Park Mills, he had two spells as captain of Headingley in 1935 and 1938. The Second World War ended any further international ambitions, and he signed up as a pilot officer in the RAF but was tragically killed on active service.

700. RONCORONI, Anthony Dominic Sebastian
Lock 3 caps 1933
Born: Hendon, Middlesex, 16 March 1909
Died: Middleton-on-Sea, Sussex, 20 July 1953
Career: Rossall School, West Herts, Richmond, East Midlands, Midland Counties, Surrey
Debut: v Wales, Twickenham, January 1933

Roncoroni started his rugby career with West Herts, winning county honours, but within months of moving to Richmond in 1932, his career took off, taking the place of 'flu victim George Vallance to win the first of his three international caps. In the Second World War, he served in the Royal Artillery and was taken as a prisoner of war, only to escape, walking 400 miles in 35 days to British lines, which earned him a Military Cross. He also participated in the D-Day Landings in Normandy and was immediately wounded. He was a senior executive in the Advertising Department of the Financial Times before his death, aged 44.

701. SADLER, Edward Harry
Flanker 2 caps (3-1t) 1933
Born: Colchester, Essex, 8 May 1910
Died: Surbiton, Surrey, 26 December 1992
Career: Royal Signals, The Army, Hampshire
Debut: v Ireland, Twickenham, February 1933

Sadler played in the same Army team as fellow internationals Doug Kendrew, Carlton Troop, Henry Rew, 'Pooh' Hobbs and Tony Novis. He was also a member of the Hampshire squad which won their first County Championship in 1933, after scoring a try on his international debut against Ireland. Soon afterwards, as a lance corporal, he left the Army to join Oldham Rugby League Club. He was also capped for England and later played for Castleford and Wigan. During the Second World War, he played in Middlesex sevens for the RAF and an England services international against Scotland. He then became a driver and traffic examiner until retirement.

702. TROOP, Group Captain Carlton Lang OBE
No 8 2 caps 1933
Born: Malton, Yorkshire 10 June 1910
Died: Rye, Sussex, 2 June 1992
Career: St Peter's School, Harrogate Old Boys, Royal Military Academy Sandhurst, Richmond, Devonport Services, Aldershot Services, United Services Portsmouth, Duke of Wellington's Regiment, the Army, Barbarians, Hampshire
Debut: v Ireland, Twickenham, February 1933

Troop made his England debut alongside Army team-mate Ted Sadler in a side skippered by another forces player Tony Novis. He was also a member of the Army side that won the Inter-Services Championship with Sadler, Novis and Doug Kerdrew, and they also helped Hampshire win the County Championship. Carlton was commissioned into the Duke of Wellington's Regiment after leaving Sandhurst, and Troop was seconded to the RAF during World War Two and held various military posts, including Director of Sports at the Air Ministry until retiring to South Africa in 1967 but returned to live in Sussex until his death.

703. WESTON, William Henry
Flanker 16 caps
Born: Potterspury, Northamptonshire, 21 December 1904
Died: Towcester, Northampton, 5 January 1987
Career: Oakham School, Northampton, Barbarians, East Midlands
Debut: v Ireland, Twickenham, London, February 1933

The son of Henry Weston, also a Northampton and East Midlands stalwart, Weston was a bruising forward who captained Northampton in five seasons between 1929 and his retirement at the end of the 1937-38 season, aged 35, and also led the East Midlands. In 1931, he was a member of the East Midlands and Leicestershire side that beat the Springboks for the first time. Weston helped England win the Triple Crown in 1934 and toured Argentina with the British Lions two years later. He went into the family business of farming like this father in Yardley Gobion.

704. CRANMER, Peter
Centre 16 caps (14 -1t,1p,2d) 1934-1938
Born: Birmingham, Warwickshire 10 September 1914
Died: Peacehaven Sussex 29 May 1994
Career: St Edwards Oxford, Oxford University, Richmond, Moseley, Barbarians
Debut: v Wales, Arms Park Cardiff, January 1934

Cranmer won his university colours in rugby but surprisingly not in cricket, as he served Warwickshire between 1934 and 1954. He was an England ever-present for four seasons, helping win a Triple Crown in 1934 and 1937, and helped set up Prince Obolensky's second try in the famous win over the All Blacks. He declined an invitation to participate in the 1938 British Lions tour to South Africa because he was Warwickshire captain. A stockbroker and army major in World War Two who later became a journalist for the BBC and Sunday Times until retiring in 1976 after both legs were amputated through illness.

705. DICKS, John
Lock 8 caps 1934-1937
Born: Mears Ashby, Northamptonshire, 12 September 1912
Died: Northampton, Northamptonshire, 7 May 1981
Career: Northampton Grammar School, Old Northamptonians, Wellingborough, Northampton, Barbarians, East Midlands.
Debut: v Wales, Arms Park Cardiff, January 1934

Dicks was educated at Northampton Grammar School but spent the early part of his rugby career at Wellingborough, joining Northampton in 1931, and over the next six years, he made 124 appearances scoring 17 tries. He helped East Midlands win the County Championship in 1934, just months after winning the first of his eight England caps. His career ended abruptly soon after getting married when he discovered that his new bride hated rugby, and he was never seen at Franklins Gardens again. A farmer for most of his adult life in Great Doddington, he was fond of horse racing.

706. FRY, Henry Arthur TD
Flanker 3 caps (6-2t) 1934
Born: West Derby, Lancashire 22 December 1910
Died: Formby, Lancashire, 3 November 1977
Career: Liverpool College, Liverpool, Waterloo, Fylde, Rosslyn Park, The Army, Barbarians, Lancashire
Debut: v Wales, Arms Park Cardiff, January 1934

Fry was an ever-present for England in their 1934 Triple Crown-winning side, scoring two tries against Ireland. He was the captain of his club side, Liverpool, between 1934 and 1936 and was elected to the Lancashire committee in 1934. A solicitor, joined the Territorial Army (Royal Army Service Corps) in 1938 and was commissioned at the outbreak of World War Two when he served in France, Belgium, War

Office, India, Burma, and Ceylon. He was promoted to lieutenant colonel and continued to serve in the TA until 1952 and was then cadet colonel commander in West Lancs until 1957.

707. MEIKLE, Graham William Churchill
Wing 3 caps (12-4t) 1934
Born: Waterloo, Lancashire, 14 October 1911,
Died: St Bees, Whitehaven, 18 June 1981
Career: St Bees, Cambridge University, Waterloo, Leicester, Harlequins, Barbarians, Lancashire
Debut: v Wales, Arms Park Cardiff, January 1934

Graham Meikle was the younger brother of Stephen and won a place to study at Cambridge University but failed to win his university colours. He was given his international call-up following a series of prominent displays for Lancashire and went one better than his brother, scoring two tries on his debut and having two more disallowed. He scored twice more to help England win the Triple Crown, but erratic form ended his international career. A knee injury forced him to retire in 1938, a year after he became an assistant master King Edwards Birmingham. He then taught at Wellington College for 30 years.

708. OWEN-SMITH, Harold Geoffrey Owen
Full-back 10 caps 1934-1937
Born: Rondebosch, Cape Town, 18 February 1909
Died: Rondebosch, Cape Town, 27 February 1990
Career: Diocesan College, Rondebosch, University of Cape Town, Oxford University, St Mary's Hospital, Barbarians
Debut: v Wales, Arms Park, Cardiff, January 1934

'Tuppy' Owen-Smith was already a South African test cricketer and Wisden Cricketer of the Year in 1930 when he won a Rhodes Scholarship to study medicine at Magdalen College, Oxford. He won his university colours in rugby, boxing and cricket, helping England win the Triple Crown in 1934 and beat New Zealand for the first time two years later. He captained St Mary's Hospital and England in 1937 before returning to Rondebosch, where he was a house surgeon at Rondebosch Mowbray Hospital before going into general practice. He served in the South African Army Medical Corps during the Second World War.

709. WARR, Antony Lawley
Wing 2 caps (3-1t) 1934
Born: Selly Oak, Birmingham, 15 May 1913
Died: Taunton, Somerset, 29 January 1995
Career: Bromsgrove School, Moseley, Harlequins, Oxford University, Wakefield, Gloucester, Yorkshire, Richmond, Weston-super-Mare, Sandhurst O.C.TU, Barbarians, Middlesex
Debut: v Wales, Arms Park Cardiff, January 1934

Warr captained Bromsgrove School and won his university colours. Along with his Oxford University team-mate, 'Tuppy' Owen-Smith, he made his England debut against Wales, scoring a try. He then retained his place in Ireland but was dropped for the Triple Crown-winning game against Scotland. A wicket-keeper, he played for Oxford University, The Army and MCC and during World War Two, he oversaw PT at Sandhurst. A school teacher by profession, he taught at Leeds Grammar School, Mill Hill, Bromsgrove and for 29 years at Harrow School from 1946 until his retirement in 1975.

710. WRIGHT, John Cecil
Lock 1 cap 1934
Born: Whitchurch, Shropshire, 6 August 1910
Died: Newport, Gwent, 4 August 2003
Career: Sedbergh School, Crewe & Nantwich, Metropolitan Police, British Police, Newport, Monmouthshire, Middlesex
Debut: v Wales, Arms Park Cardiff, Cardiff, January 1934

Wright was serving in the Metropolitan Police when, after playing three trial games, he displaced Doug Kendrew to win his only England cap against Wales, who fielded 13 new caps. Despite England winning, Wright lost his place to John Forrest and was never selected again. Jack joined the Met in December 1930 and left in October to join the Newport Borough Police. During the Second World War, he served in the 1st battalion of King's Shropshire Light Infantry. He then farmed in Lincolnshire between 1946 and 1957 and in Cardiganshire for many years, returning to Newport and dying two days short of his 93rd birthday.

711. SLOW, Charles Frederick
Fly-half 1 cap 1934
Born: Northampton, Northamptonshire Q2 1911
Died: Stony Stratford, Buckinghamshire, 15 April 1939
Career: Kettering Road School, Northampton Unitarians, Manchester Toc H, Ashton-under-Lyne, Northampton, Leicester, East Midlands
Debut: v Scotland, Twickenham, March 1934

Slow played his first game at Kettering Road School aged 12 and debuted for Northampton in December 1930, scoring ten points in the Leicestershire-East Midlands win over the Springboks the following November. Slow was discarded by Saints in early 1933, joining Leicester, where he formed a partnership with Bernard Gadney, who captained England when he won his only cap. Initially, he worked for the British Dye Stuffs Corporation, then as a commercial traveller for shoe findings manufacturer EC Cook & Co, but was killed in a car crash while he was travelling home after playing for Stony Stratford at Bicester RAF Station.

712. BOUGHTON, Harold John
Full-back 3 caps (14, 1c, 4p) 1935
Born: Gloucester, Gloucestershire, 7 September 1910
Died: Bristol, July 1986
Career: Gloucester, Gloucestershire
Debut: v Wales, Twickenham, January 1935

Boughton was only 16 when he made his first appearance for Gloucester's A team and went on to gain a reputation as a highly effective goal-kicker. But he had to wait eight seasons before international recognition came his way, winning his first cap against Wales in January 1935 and he kicked his country to victory on his second test appearance with three penalties and a conversion. He played in three county finals for Gloucester, making 337 appearances, and was captain immediately after the Second World War. His uncle Fred Ford played for Coventry and had an England trial. He worked as a bus driver for Bristol Tramways and Carriage Co.

713. CANDLER, Peter Laurence
Fly-half 10 caps (6-2t) 1935-1938
Born: Exeter, Devon, 28 January 1914
Died: Natal, South Africa, 27 November 1991
Career: Sherborne School, Richmond, Cambridge University, Exeter, St Bartholomew's Hospital, Barbarians Middlesex
Debut: v Wales, Twickenham, January 1935

Candler was an Oxford University blue when he made his England debut against Wales in January 1935, but it wasn't until the famous 1936 win over the All Blacks that saw him became a regular in the side. Peter helped England secure a Grand Slam crown in 1937, but his international career ended a year later. During World War Two, he served as a lieutenant colonel in the Royal Army Medical Corps. He held several medical appointments at St Bart's but, in 1946, became an obstetric and gynaecological specialist with the Kenya Medical Service and lived in Africa until his death.

714. CLARKE, Allan James
Lock 6 caps 1935-1936
Born: Coventry, Warwickshire, 21 February 1913
Died: Coventry, Warwickshire, 25 September 1975
Career: South Street School, Coventry, Warwickshire
Debut: v Wales, Twickenham, January 1935

Clarke was an England schoolboy international, having learnt to play the game under the tutorage of former

Pop Dunkley

Ray Longland

Ted Sadler

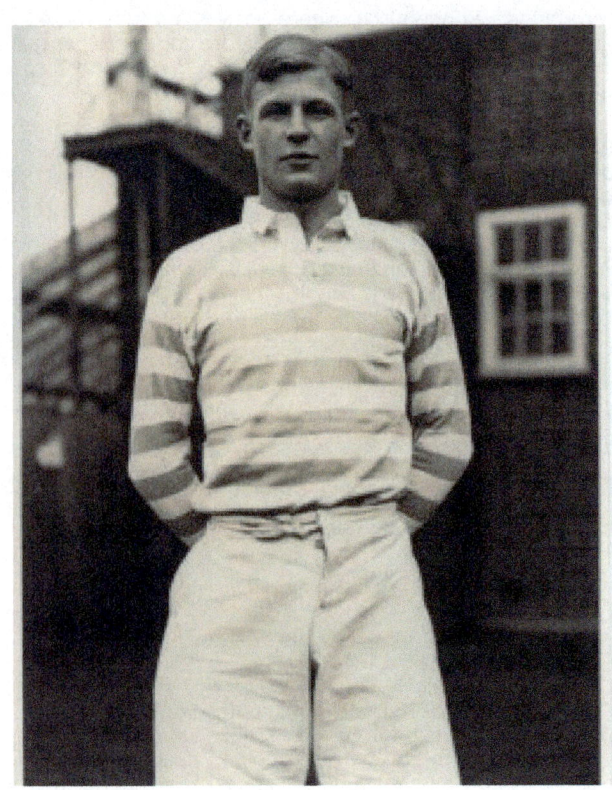

Peter Candler

Coventry player Arthur Dusson at South Street School, where he was a master. He debuted on the same day against Wales in January 1935 as Jimmy Giles, who attended the same school. A gentle giant of England's second row, he was a member of the side that claimed England's first-ever win over Jack Manchester's All Blacks. After retiring from the game, Clarke became the landlord of the Maudsley Hotel, Allesley Old Street in Coventry, until his death in September 1975 following a long illness.

715. CRIDLAN, Arthur Gordon
Flanker 3 caps 1935
Born: Ealing, Middlesex, 9 July 1909
Died: Exeter, Devon, 17 January 1993
Career: Uppingham School, Worcester College, Oxford University, Blackheath, Barbarians, Middlesex
Debut: v Wales, Twickenham Greater London, January 1935
Cridlan captained Uppingham School and won his university colours at Oxford. He was once selected to run cross country for Oxford on the same day as the rugby but chose the latter. Blackheath's captain in 1933 and 1934 won all three caps in 1935. In World War Two, he served in the Royal Engineers in charge of handling shipping movements at Swansea and Antwerp and was awarded the Crown Order of Belgium in 1946. He went to work for the Joined the family food manufacturers and importers business V. Benoist Ltd and was appointed managing director in 1967.

716. GILES, James Leonard
Scrum-half 6 caps (6-2t)
Born: Coventry, Warwickshire, 5 January 1910
Died: Coventry, Warwickshire, 28 March 1967
Career: South Street School, Coventry, Warwickshire
Debut: v Wales, Twickenham Greater London, January 1935
Giles started his rugby career at South Street School, Coventry, making successive appearances for England Schoolboys, which was an unusual occurrence. He joined Coventry in 1928 and was a regular until 1934. He won two caps on the 1938 British Lions tour to South Africa. He led Warwickshire to the 1939 County Championship and later became a Midland Counties selector. He was a supervisor at Dunlop in the engineering spares department for 27 years, collapsing and dying while working in the garden of his home in Finham.

717. HEATON, John
Centre 9 caps (17- 4c, 3p) 1935-1947
Born: St Helens, Lancashire, 30 August 1912
Died: Pwllheli, Wales, 25 October 1998
Career: Cowley School, St Helens, Liverpool University, Notts, Waterloo, Lancashire
Debut: v Wales, Twickenham, January 1935
Heaton was, along with his cousin Dicky Guest, one of the few players whose international career spanned either side of World War Two. An ever-present in 1935, he had to wait again until 1939 to win his next three caps. He played alongside Guest in 1947, captaining his country on his last two test appearances, in an international career that spanned 12 years. He was an architect and was a JP in the City of Liverpool. He captained both Waterloo and Lancashire on either side of the war and was president of club and county.

718. KEMP, Dudley Thomas
No 8 1 cap 1935
Born: Isle of Wight, Hampshire, 18 January 1910
Died: Torridge, Devon January 2003
Career: King Edwards School Southampton, Trojans, Blackheath, Bournemouth, Barbarians, Hampshire
Debut: v Wales, Twickenham, January 1935
Kemp, the 62nd President of the RFU, made his England debut alongside his Blackheath team-mate Arthur Cridlan and was one of four new caps in the pack against Wales in January 1935. But surprisingly, as he didn't appear to have any rivals, he was dropped after just one game and was never selected again. He declined an invitation to tour South Africa with the 1938 British Lions. He served in the Army during World War Two and rose to the rank of lieutenant colonel. He worked for Southern Railway between 1927 and 1960, when he became a rep for Twyford's until retirement.

719. LEYLAND, Roy OBE
Wing 3 caps 1935
Born: Astley, Lancashire, 6 March 1912
Died: Pewsey, Wiltshire, 4 January 1984
Career: Wigan Grammar School, Wigan Old Boys, Liverpool University, Waterloo, Leicester, Richmond, Aldershot Services, the Army, Combined Services, Barbarians, Lancashire, Hampshire
Debut: v Wales, Twickenham, January 1935
'Bus' Leyland won all three of his England caps in 1935 and then toured South Africa with the British Lions three years later despite not winning another test cap. He was a schoolmaster in Litchfield until he was commissioned into the Army Educational Corps. During World War Two, he served in the British Expeditionary Force and as a lieutenant colonel in the Parachute Regiment. Leyland represented the Army on the RFU committee and was a selector and treasurer of both the Army and Combined Services. He continued in various army posts, including as senior instructor at RMA Sandhurst, until he retired.

720. NICHOLSON, Edward Sealy MBE
Hooker 5 caps 1935-1936
Born: Long Ashton, Somerset, 10 June 1912
Died: Beccles, Suffolk, 16 March 1992
Career: Marlborough College, Oxford University, Guy's Hospital, Leicester, Blackheath, Barbarians, Surrey
Debut: v Wales, Twickenham, January 1935
Nicholson won his university colours before attending Guy's Hospital to complete his medical studies. He was one of four students in the team when he made his debut against Wales in January 1935 and was one of three players studying medicine when he was a member of the side that beat the All Blacks a year later, but surprisingly, his international career ended a month later. He was in the RAF during World War Two, reaching the rank of squadron leader with Training Command. After leaving the services, he became a general practitioner at Beccles, Suffolk, until his retirement.

721. PAYNE, Arthur Thomas
No 8 2 caps 1935
Born: Bristol, 11 November 1907
Died: Bristol, 6 June 1968
Career: Dings Crusaders, Bristol, Weston-super-Mare, Gloucestershire
Debut: v Ireland, Twickenham, February 1935
Payne joined Bristol from Dings Crusaders, a club he was associated with for 40 years and, without playing in a trial match, was selected to win his first international cap as a line-out specialist, but after retaining his place for the next game against Scotland, was discarded almost a quickly as he appeared. He returned to Dings in 1938 and captained them to an unbeaten season in the Bristol Combination and also led the club in the first season following World War Two. He was a selector with the Combination and worked as an aircraft engineer in Filton.

722. AUTY, Joseph Richard
Fly-half 1 cap 1935
Born: Batley, Yorkshire, 19 August 1910
Died: Leeds, Yorkshire, 7 June 1995
Career: Mill Hill School, Old Millhillians, Yorkshire Wanderers, Batley, Headingley, Leicester, Barbarians, Yorkshire
Debut: v Scotland, Murrayfield, Edinburgh, March 1935
Auty, who started his career with Batley before joining Headingley, had an international trial in 1933 but then

suffered a serious leg injury which at one stage looked like it would threaten his career. He won his only international cap against Scotland at Murrayfield in March 1935 after playing alongside Bernard Gadney for Leicester against Richmond at the request of England selectors and had more trials in 1937-38 but wasn't selected. He was a woollen manufacturer with Joseph Auty and Co., and even though he had interests in a London theatrical agency, remained in the textile trade until retiring.

723. HAMILTON-HILL, Edward Alfred
Forward 3 caps 1936
Born: Peterborough, Cambridgeshire, 22 November 1908
Died: North Surrey 23 October 1979
Career: HMS Conway, Harlequins, Royal Navy, Surrey
Debut: v New Zealand, Twickenham, January 1936

Hamilton-Hill captained HMS Conway almost immediately after joining the Royal Navy Reserve in 1925, and four years later, while in the Merchant Navy, he started to play for Harlequins and did so for the next ten years. He also spent eight seasons playing for Surrey and made his England debut in the famous 1936 win over The All Blacks. Hamilton-Hill was in business until returning to the Royal Navy for the duration of World War Two. He then moved to Malta in 1946 and became the managing director of Radio and Television Services. His daughter Deirdre was a model in the 1960s.

724. OBOLENSKY, Alexander Sergeevich
Wing 4 caps (6-2t)
Born: Petrograd, Russia, 17 February 1916
Died: Martlesham Heath, Suffolk, 29 March 1940
Career: Trent College, Oxford University, Rosslyn Park, Leicester, Barbarians, Middlesex
Debut: v New Zealand, Twickenham, January 1936

Prince Alexander Obolensky fled Russia with his family in 1917 and grew up in London. It was only after going to Trent College that he took up rugby, scoring over 200 points in two years before heading up to Oxford University, where he won his blue. He became a star overnight after scoring one of England's greatest-ever tries on his debut against New Zealand and touring South America with the RFU later the same year. He was the first international to be killed in World War Two when his Hurricane crashed on landing after a training exercise, and he broke his neck.

725. SEVER, Harry Sedgwick
Wing 10 caps (19-5t,1d) 1936-1938
Born: Bucklow, Cheshire, 3 March 1910
Died: Kingston-upon-Thames, Surrey, 2 June 2005
Career: Shrewsbury School, Sale, Barbarians, Cheshire, Lancashire and Cheshire
Debut: v New Zealand, Twickenham, January 1936

Sever surprisingly never played rugby when he was being educated at Shrewsbury School but instead was vice-captain of the school soccer and cricket teams and played in the fives team. It wasn't until he left school in 1928 that he started to play the game. He announced his international debut with a try in the first ever defeat of the All Blacks and, a year later, helped secure the Triple Crown. He was an actuary by profession and later became a general manager of Refuge Assurance. He was the oldest surviving English rugby international at his death in June 2005.

726. WHEATLEY, Harold Frederick
Prop 7 caps 1936-1939
Born: Coventry, Warwickshire, 26 December 1912
Died: Coventry, Warwickshire, 10 April 2003
Career: Coventry, Kenilworth, Warwickshire
Debut: v Ireland, Lansdowne Road Dublin, February 1936

Wheatley was the youngest of five brothers who played for Coventry, whom he captained for ten years after joining as a 16-year-old. He is the only player to date to represent England in all three rows of the scrum. He appeared three times for his country with brother Arthur and the pair helped Warwickshire win the 1939 County Championship. However, he missed out on a cap after the Second World War when he pulled out of a game in Ireland. He spent all his adult life working for the family haulage business A. Wheatley and Sons.

727. TOFT, Herbert
Hooker 10 caps 1936-1939
Born: Salford, Lancashire, 2 October 1909
Died: Chichester, Sussex, 7 July 1987
Career: Manchester Grammar School, Manchester University, Waterloo, Royal Air Force, Combined Services, Barbarians, Lancashire
Debut: v Scotland, Twickenham, March 1936

Toft was ever-present between making his debut against Scotland in March and the outbreak of World War Two when he served in the RAF. He helped England win a Triple Crown in 1937 and captained them and every other senior side he represented. He was due to become an England selector in 1939 but had to wait until 1945 and served until 1952. He was a schoolmaster and then headmaster from 1933 until he retired, except for six years as sales manager of A Gallenkamp and Co. He was also the rugby correspondent of The Observer.

728. BUTLER, Arthur Geoffrey
Wing (3-1t) 2 caps 1937
Born: Oxford, Oxfordshire, 30 September 1914,
Died: Henley-on-Thames, Oxfordshire, 21 March 2007
Career: Royal Henley Grammar School, Henley, Harlequins, Barbarians, Oxfordshire, East Midlands
Debut: v Wales, Twickenham, January 1937

Butler made two international appearances during England's march to the 1937 Triple Crown, the last before the outbreak of World War Two. But despite scoring a try against Ireland, he lost his place for the season's decider against Scotland and was never selected again. He won the Southern Counties 100 and 220-yard titles and represented Great Britain at an international athletics meeting in Antwerp in 1937. He was a builder and farmer in Crowsley, Oxfordshire. He represented the county on the RFU board and was elected RFU's 56th president in 1963-1964.

729. CAMPBELL, David Watt Ian
Flanker 2 caps 1937
Born: Adelong, New South Wales, 16 July 1915,
Died: Canberra, Australia 29 July 1979
Career: The King's School, Parramatta, Cambridge University
Debut: v Wales, Twickenham, January 1937

Campbell had already captained The King's School, Parramatta, when he came to Cambridge University from Australia to study English literature and excelled at rugby union, winning his blue in 1936. He made two appearances as England won their last Triple Crown in 1937 before the outbreak of World War Two. After returning to Australia in 1938, he joined the Royal Australian Air Force and trained as a pilot. After the war, he became a grazier at the family property of Wells Station, near Canberra. He later became a celebrated poet with several works published in Australia and abroad.

730. HUSKISSON, Thomas Frederick MBE MC
Lock 8 caps 1937-1939
Born: Richmond, Middlesex, 1 July 1914
Died: Stroud, Gloucestershire, 25 April 2004
Career: Merchant Taylors' School, Old Merchant Taylors', the Army, Barbarians, London Counties, Eastern Counties, Lancashire
Debut: v Wales, Twickenham, January 1937

Huskisson started his rugby career at Merchant Taylors' School as a full-back before being moved into the second row. He was selected for a British Lions 1936 tour of

Argentina and helped England win the Triple Crown a year later. He only missed one game before the outbreak of World War Two when he joined the Duke of Wellington's regiment, winning two Military Crosses in Italy. Huskisson joined Swift and Co meat importers as an office boy in 1932 and was made managing director in 1976 before retiring three years later to a village in Pembrokeshire.

731. KEMP, Thomas Arthur
Fly-half 5 caps 1937-1948
Born: Bolton, Greater Manchester, 12 August 1915
Died: Hillingdon, London, 26 November 2004
Career: Denstone College, Cambridge University, St Mary's Hospital, Manchester, Richmond, the Army, Barbarians, London Counties, Lancashire, Middlesex
Debut: v Wales, Twickenham, January 1937

Kemp won his university colours in 1936 and then made his England debut against Wales the following season. He captained England in a war-time international against Wales and, in 1948, was recalled to the international side for games against Australia and Wales. The 11-year gap between appearances against Wales remains a record. He joined the Royal Army Medical Corps in World War Two and served in the Middle East. Kemp also worked at St Mary's Hospital and the now-defunct Paddington General Hospital until his retirement in 1975. He was president of the RFU from 1971 to 1972.

732. MILMAN, Sir Dermot Lionel Kennedy BT
No 8 4 caps 1937-1938
Born: Eltham, Kent, 24 October 1912
Died: Warlingham, Surrey, 13 January 1990
Career: Uppingham School, Cambridge University, Bedford, Edinburgh Wanderers, Barbarians, East Midlands
Debut: v Wales, Twickenham, January 1937

Milman was Uppingham School's captain before going to Cambridge University, where he had varsity trials but missed out on his blue. He was a master at Epsom College when he played the first match in England's 1937 Triple Crown-winning campaign and made three appearances the following season before moving on to teach at Fettes College. During World War Two, he was a major in the Royal Army Service Corps and became a Hostel Development British Council Liaison Officer. In 1962, he succeeded to the title of 8th Baronet Milman of Levaton-in-Woodland, Devon.

733. PRESCOTT, Robert Edward
Prop 6 caps (3-1t) 1937-1939
Born: Paddington, Middlesex, 5 April 1913
Died: Dartmouth, Devon, 18 May 1975
Career: Marlborough College, Oxford University, Harlequins, the Army, Combined Services, Guildford, Middlesex
Debut: v Wales, Twickenham, January 1937

Marlborough College-educated Prescott captained his school team before going to Cambridge University, winning a blue in 1932 as his brother Antony had done four years earlier. He toured Argentina with the British Lions in 1936 and won the first of his six England caps the following January, playing in the first two of England's Grand Slam-winning games. He was the captain of Harlequins and Middlesex when World War Two broke out, serving in the Royal Artillery. He was a solicitor who, in January 1963, became secretary of the RFU for a decade until his retirement. His father, Ernest, was the 23rd president of the RFU.

734. WHEATLEY, Arthur
Lock 5 caps
Born: Coventry, Warwickshire, 6 December 1908
Died: Weston-Super-Mare, Somerset, 4 February 1993
Career: South Street School Hillfields, Coventry, Warwickshire
Debut: v Wales, Twickenham, January 1937

Wheatley captained both Coventry and Warwickshire and played in all three games in England's 1937 Triple Crown-winning campaign, but only after recovering from an injury. He played with younger brother Harold three times for England. They were also part of the Warwickshire side that won the County Championship in 1939, beating Somerset 8-3 at Weston-Super-Mare, where he later died. He also participated in England trials in December 1938 but won no further caps. He was a partner in A Wheatley and Sons, hauliers, and during World War Two, he served in the Home Guard.

735. COOK, John Gilbert
Flanker 1 cap 1937
Born: Houghton Regis, Bedfordshire, 16 May 1911
Died: Overstrand, Norfolk, 10 September 1979
Career: Bedford, North of Ireland, Barbarians, East Midlands
Debut: v Scotland, Murrayfield, Edinburgh, March 1937

Cook represented Bedford School in rugby and cricket but was a surprise inclusion for a trial in December 1935 after an East Midlands selector saw him play for the North of Ireland and used his influence to get him a chance. He was a reserve against Wales for the opening game of the 1937 campaign before winning his only cap against Scotland at Murrayfield. He was Bedford captain between 1936 and 1939 and articled with real property expert J R Eve and Son before working in Ireland. He then became an HM Treasury valuer between 1950 until retirement in 1969. John also played cricket for Bedfordshire CCC and Ireland.

736. REYNOLDS, Frank Jeffrey
Fly-half 3 caps (7-1t,1d) 1937-1938
Born: Canton, South China, 2 January 1916
Died: Somerset West, South Africa, 29 July 1996
Career: Cranleigh School, Old Cranleighans, Royal Military Academy Sandhurst, Blackheath, the Army, Barbarians, Kent
Debut: v Scotland, Murrayfield, Edinburgh, March 1937

Reynolds captained Cranleigh School and then Royal Military Academy Sandhurst in 1936, where he attended as a cadet. He debuted as England clinched the 1937 Grand Slam, replacing Tom Kemp. He won two further caps the following season and was a member of the 1938 British Lions tour to South Africa when he played in two tests. He was commissioned into the Duke of Wellington's regiment and resigned in 1947 with the rank of major. He then trained in the hotel industry at The Dorchester, London and Switzerland. After a spell in New York, he emigrated to South Africa, where he worked until retirement.

737. UNWIN, Ernest James
Wing 4 caps (9-3t) 1937-1938
Born: Birdbrook, Essex, 18 September 1912
Died: Perth, Scotland, 23 November 2003
Career: Haileybury College, Royal Military Academy Sandhurst, Rosslyn Park, the Army, Barbarians, Eastern Counties
Debut: v Scotland, Murrayfield Edinburgh, March 1937

Unwin was the first player from Rosslyn Park to be capped when he burst onto the England scene, scoring a try on his debut to help England claim the 1937 Triple Crown. He scored three tries in his four test match appearances. He toured Argentina with the British Lions in 1936 and South Africa two years later. He played cricket for Essex with his brother Frederick and was also a capable hockey player. He was commissioned into the Middlesex Regiment in 1933 and retired as lieutenant colonel 15 years later to join the family business of corn and seed merchants and farmers.

738. FREAKES, Hubert Dainton
Full-back 3 caps (2-1c) 1938-1939
Born: Durban, South Africa, 2 February 1914,
Died: Honeybourne, Worcestershire, 10 March 1942
Career: Martitzberg College, Rhodes University College, Eastern Province, Oxford University, Harlequins, Barbarians
Debut: v Wales, Arms Park Cardiff, January 1938

'Trilby' Freakes had already played rugby and cricket for Eastern Province before he arrived in England in 1936 as a

Rhodes Scholar to study at Oxford University. He won his colours in athletics and rugby and captained them in the 1938 Varsity Match. Freakes won his first cap in 1938 and his last two the following season before returning to Johannesburg to go into business. At the start of World War Two, he joined the Royal Air Force Volunteer Reserve and became a flying officer in the Royal Air Forces Ferry Command but was killed when his bomber crashed into the ground.

739. NICHOLSON, Basil Ellard
Centre 2 caps (3-1t) 1938
Born: Lewisham, Kent, 1 January 1913
Died: Oxted Surrey, 20 August 1985
Career: Whitgift School, Old Whitgiftians, Harlequins, Barbarians, Surrey
Debut: v Wales, Arms Park Cardiff, January 1938

Nicholson first had an England trial in November 1936 but then suffered 'flu to rob him of a third cap against Scotland in March 1938, when he toured South Africa with the British Lions, winning one cap. At the outbreak of World War Two, he was commissioned into the Royal Engineers, where he served as a lieutenant colonel and a group commander and was involved in planning some parts of the Normandy invasion. After the war, he returned to Neuchatel and Co., whom he joined in the 1930s and was appointed managing director in 1964 until retirement.

740. MARSHALL, Robert Mackenzie DSO
No 8 5 caps (3-1t) 1938-1939
Born: Pontefract, Yorkshire, 18 May 1917
Died: at sea Skagerrak, 12 May 1945
Career: Giggleswick School, Oxford University, Scarborough, Harlequins, Barbarians
Debut: v Ireland, Lansdowne Road, Dublin, February 1938

Marshall won his university colours and became secretary and captain-elect in 1939. He made his international debut in 1938 and was hailed as the new Wavell Wakefield, the poster boy of the 1920s. He scored a try on his debut against Ireland at Lansdowne Road. He retained his place for the last four games before the outbreak of World War Two, serving as a lieutenant commander in the Royal Navy Volunteer Reserve and was awarded a DSO for ramming and sinking a U-Boat but was killed in action towards the end of the year just six days before his 28th birthday.

741. PARKER, Grahame Wilshaw MBE OBE TD
Full-back 2 caps (24 -6c, 4p) 1938
Born: Gloucester, Gloucestershire, 11 February 1912
Died: Sidmouth, Devon, 11 November 1995
Career: The Crypt School, Cambridge University, Gloucester, Blackheath, Barbarians, Gloucestershire
Debut: v Ireland Lansdowne Road, Dublin, February 1938

Parker won his university colours in rugby and cricket, a sport in which he captained Cambridge. He was an opening batsman for Gloucestershire throughout the 1930s. He kicked 15 points on his international debut for England against Ireland, converting six of seven tries and a penalty. But his international career ended with a defeat to Scotland when he landed three penalties. A major in the Royal Army Service Corps during World War Two, he was a master at Dulwich College and then for 22 years at Blundell's School. He was also secretary of Gloucestershire CCC for over a decade.

742. BROWN, Alan Arthur
Flanker 1 cap 1938
Born: St Helens Lancashire, 28 August 1911
Died: Honiton, Devon, 12 August 1987
Career: Cowley School, St Helens, Carnegie College, Headingley, St Luke's College Exeter, Exeter, Aldershot Services, Barbarians, Lancashire, Devon
Debut: v Scotland, Twickenham, March 1938

Brown had a pedigree in the game, captaining both St Helens and Devon, but he played in an era when it was hard to gain a lasting foothold in the England side and only won a single cap, against Scotland at Twickenham in March 1938. He was a lecturer in physical education at St Luke's College Exeter, and then, during World War Two, he served in the 4th Devonshire Regiment in Gibraltar for three years and was seconded to the Army School of Physical Education. He then worked as a senior physical education adviser for the Devon Education Department.

743. BERRY, Joseph Thomas Wade
Flanker 3 caps 1939
Born: Market Harborough, Leicestershire 17 July 1911
Died: Kettering, Northamptonshire, 1 July 1993
Career: Eastbourne College, Market Harborough, Leicester, Barbarians, Leicestershire
Debut: v Wales, Twickenham, January 1939

Berry captained Leicester on either side of a Second World War that wrecked his international career after being an ever-present in England's 1939 campaign. Even though he continued to play for his club, he was too old to be considered for international selection. He farmed a thousand acres in Leicestershire and Northamptonshire. He was the brother-in-law of another England international, John Hodgson, while his wife Margaret was an England international golfer. He represented Leicestershire on the RFU committee for 15 years, was also on the RFU selection committee, and was the RFU's 61st President.

744. CARR, Robert Stanley Leonard
Wing 3 caps 1939
Born: Backlow, Cheshire, 11 July 1917,
Died: Macclesfield, Cheshire, 7 September 1979
Career: Cranleigh School, Old Cranleighans, Manchester, Moseley
Debut: v Wales, Twickenham, January 1939

Carr was a speedy winger who captained his school, Cranleigh, and English Public Schoolboys against Scotland in 1936. He won his three England caps with World War Two looming large. After subduing the great Prince Obolensky in a trial match, he became one of eight new caps to make his debut against Wales. After war was declared, he was commissioned into the Manchester Regiment and the King's African Rifles and was awarded a Military Cross in 1941. Carr played against Scotland in March 1946, but no caps were awarded, and he was a director of James Carr & Sons.

745. COOKE, Paul
Scrum-half 2 caps 1939
Born: Marylebone, Middlesex, 18 December 1916,
Died: Flanders 28 May 1940
Career: St Edward's Oxford, Oxford University, Richmond, Barbarians, East Midlands
Debut: v Wales, Twickenham, January 1939

Cooke started to play for Richmond in 1933 as a three-quarter but would become one of the best scrum halves in the country. An all-round sportsman, he played rugby, cricket, boxing and athletics at school and then college. He won his university colours in 1936 and 1937 and was an uncapped member of the British Isles tour to Argentina in 1936. He joined Barclays Bank after leaving Oxford and won two international caps against Wales and Ireland. Cooke joined the Oxford & Bucks Light Infantry as a 2nd lieutenant early in the Second World War and was killed during the fall of France.

746. GUEST, Richard Heaton
Wing 13 caps (15 -5t) 1939-1949
Born: Prescot, Lancashire 12 March 1918
Career: Cowley School, St Helens, Liverpool University, Waterloo, British Army of the Rhine, Barbarians, Lancashire
Debut: v Wales, Twickenham, January 1939

'Dickie' Guest was one of only three players to have an international career on either side of World War Two. He made his first three appearances in 1939 and scored a try on his final appearance against Scotland a decade later. Six of his England appearances came alongside his cousin Jack Heaton. He captained his university, club, the Army, and county. He also served Lancashire as president and selector, a position he held with England. A captain in the Royal Artillery, he worked for Foster's Glass in St Helens and Rockware Glass in Middlesex before emigrating to Australia.

747. HANCOCK, George Edward
Centre 3 caps 1939
Born: Wirral Cheshire, 21 March 1912
Died: Pershore, Worcestershire, 2 April 1993
Career: Rock Ferry High School, Old Rockferrians, Birkenhead Park, RAF, Mount Hope Canada, RAF Waterbeach, Cheshire
Debut: v Wales, Twickenham, January 1939

Hancock captained Old Rockferrians for a season before moving to Birkenhead Park, the club where he would go on to make his name in the game. He led Cheshire between 1935 and 1939 and again in 1947-48 before retiring. He toured Argentina with the British Lions in 1936 before he won an England cap which finally arrived in 1939. He was ever-present in the final season before the outbreak of World War Two when he served as a flight lieutenant in the RAF between 1939 and 1947. He was a solicitor who ran a practice in Birkenhead.

748. TEDEN, Derek Edmund
Forward 3 caps (3-1t) 1939
Born: Edmonton, Middlesex 19 July 1916
Died: Frisian Islands 15 October 1940
Career: Taunton School, Old Tauntonians, Richmond, Rosslyn Park, Barbarians, Middlesex
Debut: v Wales, Twickenham, January 1939

Teden was a livewire prop discovered by Richmond playing for Old Tauntonians whom he turned out for after a less than distinguished school playing career. Instead, at school, he was more known for water polo. He was soon picked out as a promising talent, and Middlesex quickly recognised this. He scored the match-winning try against Wales on his international debut. Before the start of World War Two, he was a sales rep for his jewel case manufacture father, joined the Royal Auxiliary Air Force and then served as a pilot officer with the RAF Coastal Command, and disappeared on an anti-invasion patrol with No. 206 Squadron.

749. WALKER, Sir George Augustus GCB CBE DSO DFC AFC
Fly-half 2 caps 1939
Born: Garforth, Yorkshire, 24 August 1912
Died: Kings Lynn, Norfolk 11 December 1986
Career: St. Bees School, Royal Air Force, Blackheath, Cambridge University, Barbarians, Eastern Counties, Yorkshire
Debut: v Wales, Twickenham, January 1939

Walker captained his school, St Bees, in Cumberland and then the RAF after joining the service in 1934. He didn't win a blue after attending Cambridge University. He skippered the RAF to victory over the Army and was called into the England side with the Second World War looming. He lost his place after two appearances. He lost an arm in a bomb explosion but continued his interest in rugby as a referee and president of the Rugby Union from 1965 to 1966. He became an air chief marshal and retired as the highest-ranked England player.

750. WATKINS, Rear Admiral John Kingdon OBE TD
Flanker 3 caps 1939
Born: Taunton, Somerset, 24 February 1913
Died: Attleborough, Norfolk, 13 May 1970
Career: Epsom College, Devonport Services, United Services Portsmouth, Royal Navy, Aldershot, Combined Services, Barbarians, Somerset
Debut: v Wales, Twickenham, January 1939

Watkins joined the Royal Navy in 1930 and three years later was making the first of his 12 appearances for the service. But it wasn't until World War Two was on the horizon that he was picked for his country after catching the eye playing for Somerset. He won all three international caps in 1939, just before the war was declared. He continued to play after the conflict ended but wasn't considered for selection. Watkins went on to hold several senior roles, including one with NATO, before his retirement in 1967, but he became the director of Metal and Steel Associations.

751. ELLIS, Jack
Scrum-half 1 cap 1939
Born: Rothwell Haigh, Leeds, 28 October 1912,
Died: Northampton, Northamptonshire, 27 November 2007
Career: Durham University, Carnegie College, Wakefield, Barbarians, Yorkshire
Debut: v Scotland, Murrayfield, Edinburgh, March 1939

Ellis began his career with Wakefield in 1931 and played over 100 games, scoring 37 tries, but it wasn't until the last game before the outbreak of World War Two that he was given his only chance to impress by the England selectors after being a reserve for an earlier game. Serving as a major in the Royal Army Service Corps, he was amongst the British troops who liberated Belsen in 1945. He was a school teacher who taught classics, Latin and Greek at Fettes College in Edinburgh, Rossall School near Fleetwood, Lancashire, and Scarborough Boys' High.

752. PARSONS, Ernest Ian DFC
Full-back 1 cap 1939
Born: Christchurch, Dorset, 24 October 1912
Died: KIA 14 August 1940
Career: Christchurch High School Boys, Canterbury University, Hull & East Riding, RAF, Yorkshire
Debut: v Scotland, Murrayfield Edinburgh, March 1939

Parsons played for his first XV at school and college in New Zealand and worked for the Public Trust Office before, in 1933, leaving what was supposed to be a short stint with the RAF. He broke into the England side for the final international before World War Two and was the last player to be capped after impressing in the final trial match for The Rest against England. He also played for Yorkshire while stationed in the North, and after war broke out, became a pilot officer at Bomber Command and was awarded a DFC months before dying in action.

753. BENNETT, Norman Osborn
Centre 7 caps (3-1t) 1947-1948
Born: Putney, London, 21 September 1922
Died: Dinckley, Lancashire, 7 July 2005
Career: St Mary's Hospital, Waterloo, US Portsmouth, Royal Navy, Barbarians, London County, Hampshire, Surrey, Lancashire.
Debut: v Wales, Cardiff Arms Park, Cardiff, 18 January 1947

Educated at Epsom College and St Mary's Hospital Medical School, where he played alongside E K Scott and 'Nim' Hall, Bennett made his debut as one of 14 new caps when he was a student against Wales in Cardiff in 1947. His international career extended to the end of the 1948 Five Nations. Bennett was a handy cricketer and played one first-class match for Worcestershire in 1946, scoring just 10 runs in his two innings and representing Free Foresters, Royal Navy and MCC. He served as a surgeon-lieutenant in the RNVR for many years.

754. GRAY, Arthur
Full-back 3 caps (2-1C) 1947
Born: Leeds, Yorkshire, 4 September 1917
Died: Scarborough, Yorkshire, 25 August 1991
Career: Otley, Yorkshire, Wakefield Trinity RL
Debut: v Wales, Cardiff Arms Park, Cardiff, January 1947

After serving in the Second World War, Gray scored a

conversion on his debut in the win over Wales in Cardiff in 1947 and followed up with appearances against Ireland and Scotland. He played six times for Yorkshire, worked as a fruit merchant and, within four months of his debut, had turned professional with Wakefield Trinity for an £800 signing fee. He played full-back, but switching codes was not a huge success, and he played just 15 times for his new club up to 1950. His son Martin followed in his footsteps by playing full-back for Otley.

755. HALL, Norman MacLeod
Fly-half 17 caps (39–8c, 4p, 3dg) 1947-1955
Born: Huddersfield, Yorkshire, 2 August 1925
Died: Paddington, London, 26 June 1972
Career: St Mary's Hospital, The Army, Huddersfield, Combined Services, Barbarians, Richmond, Yorkshire, Middlesex
Debut: v Wales, Cardiff Arms Park, Cardiff, January 1947.

Educated at Workshop College, 'Nim' Hall's international career lasted until 1955, but out of 37 test matches played by England in that period, he only featured in 17. He studied at St Mary's Hospital Medical School alongside Sir Roger Bannister but was expelled for failing his exams, and in 1943, he enlisted with the Duke of Wellington's Regiment. His late drop goal sealed a 9-6 victory over Wales on his debut. He did not play in 1948, 1950, 1951 and 1954 and only played in 1949 and 1952 when The Rest beat England in the final trial, although he captained England 13 times. He died aged just 46 after a battle with throat cancer.

756. HENDERSON, Alan Peter
Hooker 9 caps (3–1t) 1947-1949
Born: Kirkintilloch, Scotland, 26 May 1920
Died: Scarborough, North Yorkshire, 4 April 2003
Career: Cambridge University, Public School Wanderers, Blackheath, Edinburgh Wanderers
Debut: v Wales, Cardiff Arms Park, Cardiff, January 1947.

Henderson scored his only try in the 24-5 win over his native Scotland in his first year as an international. The Scots-born hooker was schooled at Taunton College before moving to Cambridge University, where he won a blue and was a student at Pembroke College when he won his first caps. He moved to Edinburgh after graduating to join the staff at Fettes College, where his Taunton headmaster, Scotland international Crichton Miller, was head. He joined his Cambridge and England teammate Micky Steele-Bodger playing for Edinburgh Wanderers, where he won his final cap and coached Fettes until leaving in 1963.

757. KELLY, Geoffrey Arnold
Prop 4 caps 1947-1948
Born: Royston, Hertfordshire, 9 February 1914
Died: Cambridge, Cambridgeshire, 9 March 1997
Career: Letchworth, Bedford, Barbarians, East Midlands, Eastern Counties
Debut: v Wales, Cardiff Arms Park, Cardiff, January 1947.

Kelly had joined Bedford before the Second World War and was still at the club when he won his first cap. But he was still made an honorary life member of Letchworth, for whom he had played in the 1930s when England called him up for his first cap after he had played in a Victory international against New Zealand. He played three times more for his country, against Ireland and Scotland in 1947 and Wales in 1948. In 1961 he helped set up Royston Rugby Club, his home town, becoming their first president and earned his living working in the fertiliser business.

758. MOORE, William Kenneth Thomas
Scrum-half 7 caps 1947-1950
Born: Leicester, Leicestershire, 24 February 1921
Died: Leicester, Leicestershire, 22 August 2002
Career: Devonport Services, Leicester, Kettering, Barbarians, Royal Navy, Cornwall, Leicestershire.
Debut: v Wales, Cardiff Arms Park, Cardiff, January 1947.

Moore was a Leicester-born scrum-half who played 170 appearances for his local club between 1945 and 1953, captaining the club for two seasons from 1950. After the Second World War, where he served in the Navy and played in two Victory internationals, He played his first two tests in 1947, two in 1949 and three in 1950 in a stop-start career. He was a sales manager for a shoe company, and when he retired from playing for Kettering in 1956, he took up the whistle and became a member of the East Midlands and, later, the Staffordshire Referees' Society.

759. MYCOCK, Joseph
Lock 5 caps 1947-1948
Born: Manchester, Lancashire, 17 January 1914
Died: Llanbedr-y-Cennin, Conwy, 30 May 2004
Career: Vale of Lune, Sale, Harlequins, RAF, Combined Services, Barbarians, Lancashire.
Debut: v Wales, Cardiff Arms Park, Cardiff, January 1947.

Mycock captained England on his debut in their first official post-war test whilst he was playing at Sale, where he was made captain at 22 in 1936. But by the time of his third cap against Scotland, Jack Heaton had taken over as skipper. He served with the RAF Technical Training Command in the Second World War, played his last test against Australia in 1948 and then embarked on a globe-trotting business career. He joined W.R. Grace & Co, a chemicals company, becoming a general manager in Santiago, Chile, then relocating to Lima in Peru. He then joined a textile company and had stints in Manila, Lagos, and the United Kingdom.

760. PERRY, Samuel Victor FRS
Lock 7 caps 1947-1948
Born: East Cowes, Isle of Wight, 16 July 1918
Died: Pembrokeshire, Wales, 17 December 2013
Career: Southport, Cambridge University
Debut: v Wales, Cardiff Arms Park, January 1947

Perry could have won more caps but decided to concentrate on his career as a biochemist, which gained him huge accolades in the scientific world. He studied at Liverpool University and served in the Royal Artillery, spending more than three years in prisoner of war camps before making his England debut in the first full post-war international. As a prisoner, he gave talks on biochemistry to fellow inmates. He became head of biochemistry at Birmingham University in 1959, after a spell in the United States, and researched heart disease and muscular dystrophy. He was made a Fellow of the Royal Society in 1974 and moved to Pembrokeshire, where he indulged his passion for gardening.

761. SCOTT, Edward Keith
Centre 5 caps 1947-1948
Born: Truro, Cornwall, 14 June 1918
Died: Truro, Cornwall, 3 June 1995
Career: Clifton College, Oxford University, St Mary's Hospital, Redruth, Harlequins, London Counties, Cornwall
Debut: v Wales, Cardiff Arms Park, Cardiff, January 1947.

Son of a former international, Frank, Scott captained England three times at rugby and was 12th man for the England cricket team in the first Victory test Match in 1945 and played for Gloucestershire and the Minor Counties. He trained to be a doctor at Lincoln College, Oxford, before heading to the famous rugby nursery St Mary's Hospital, He played for Redruth when he won his fifth and final cap in the 1948 Calcutta Cup match. Scott played most of that game with a fractured jaw and retired from rugby altogether. He took over his father's general practice near Truro and served as President of the Cornish RFU.

762. STEELE-BODGER, Michael Roland CBE
Flanker 9 caps 1947-1948
Born: Tamworth, Staffordshire, 4 September 1925
Died: Tamworth, Staffordshire, 9 May 2019
Career: Cambridge University, Edinburgh University, Harlequins, Moseley, Barbarians
Debut: v Wales, Cardiff Arms Park, January 1947

One of rugby's great characters, Steele-Bodger, a vet, played in England's first Championship match after the Second

World War whilst a student at Gonville & Caius College, Cambridge University and was ever-present until the 15-0 defeat by France in 1948. A knee ligament injury curtailed his playing career, but he became a distinguished administrator serving as an England selector, president of the RFU and of IRB chairman. He was associated with the Barbarians for 73 years and was president of the East India Club, where he conducted much of his rugby business. He was made a CBE in 1990 for services to rugby and inaugurated the Steele-Bodger XV fixture against Cambridge University as a warm-up for the Varsity Match.

763. SWARBRICK, David William
Wing 6 caps 1947-1949
Born: Tynemouth, Tyne & Wear, 17 January 1927
Died: 10 April 2016
Career: Oxford University, Blackheath, Barbarians, Midland Counties, Middlesex
Debut: v Wales, Cardiff Arms Park, January 1947

Swarbrick won three blues while studying at Merton College, Oxford University from 1946 to 1948 and was captain of Blackheath from 1950 to 1952 before a head injury cut short his playing days. His final cap had come in the 14-5 defeat to Ireland at Lansdowne Road in 1949 after he had missed most of the previous year's Championship. The winger went on to have a successful career with the chemical giants ICI working for the company in Europe and South Africa. He later became chairman of Hillingdon District Health Authority and served on the board at Mount Vernon Hospital and the council of Brunel University.

764. TRAVERS, Basil Holmes AM OBE
No.8 6 caps (4-2c) 1947-1949
Born: Sydney, Australia, 7 July 1919
Died: Sydney, Australia, 18 December 1998
Career: Sydney University, Oxford University, Harlequins, Barbarians, North Suburbs, NSW
Debut: v Wales, Cardiff Arms Park, January 1947

Australia-born 'Jika' Travers, a goal-kicking No.8, studied at Oxford University on a Rhodes scholarship when he won his first four caps. He moved to Harlequins for his last two appearances in 1949, when he taught at Wellington College. He returned to Australia, captaining New South Wales against the 1950 Lions and working at Cranbrook School, Sydney, before becoming headmaster of Sydney Church of England Grammar School. He had served with the Australian forces in New Guinea in the Second World War, becoming a brigade major and was awarded an OBE.

765. WALKER, Harry
Prop 9 caps 1947-1948
Born: Aston, Warwickshire, 11 February 1915
Died: Coventry, Warwickshire, 5 June 2018
Career: Coventry, Barbarians, Warwickshire
Debut: v Wales, Cardiff Arms Park, Cardiff, January 1947

Walker was a converted flanker who worked as a machine tool fitter and served in the Army in the Second World War. He attended John Gulson School in Coventry and formed an old boys' rugby club to continue playing. He was 31 when he made his international debut – delayed by the conflict and continued to play club rugby until he was 37. He then coached Coventry 2nd XV and helped bring through talents like David Duckham. He also worked as a licensee and was match secretary, president of Coventry, and secretary of Warwickshire. He was the oldest living English rugby player before his death, aged 103.

766. WHITE, Donald Frederick
Flanker 14 caps (6-2t) 1947-1953
Born: Earls Barton, Northamptonshire, 16 January 1926
Died: Earls Barton, Northamptonshire, 21 April 2007
Career: Northampton, the Army, Combined Services, Barbarians, East Midlands, Midland Counties
Debut: v Wales, Cardiff Arms Park, Cardiff, January 1947

White won 14 caps for England and played 448 times for Northampton before retiring when he was 35, having scored more than 900 points for his club, whom he captained for seven seasons. A forward-thinker, he became the first England coach in 1969, leading them to an 11-8 win against South Africa in his first match, although he only stayed in the role for two seasons. He worked in the family shoe business for his entire professional life, winning the Queen's Award for Export Achievement in 1990. He was president of Northampton during their centenary season in 1979/80 and president of the Northampton Male Voice Choir.

767. DONNELLY, Martin Paterson
Centre 1 cap 1947
Born: Ngaruawahia, New Zealand, 17 October 1917
Died: Sydney, Australia, 22 October 1999
Career: Canterbury University, Canterbury, NZ Universities, Oxford University, Blackheath, Barbarians.
Debut: v Ireland, Lansdowne Road, Dublin, February 1947

Better known as a cricketer who scored a double century for New Zealand against England at Lord's in 1949, 'Squib' Donnelly played a single rugby union international for England. He had served as a major in the 4th Armoured Brigade in the Second World War before getting a bursary to Worcester College, Oxford University, where he read history. He won his only cap as a student in the 22-0 defeat to Ireland in Dublin in 1947. Nicknamed 'Squib' because of his short stature, he also played county cricket for Middlesex and Warwickshire and, at test level, for New Zealand. He worked for Courtaulds, a fabric and chemical manufacturer, who transferred him to Sydney to take up a managerial post.

768. GEORGE, James Thomas
Lock 3 caps 1947-1949
Born: Falmouth, Cornwall, 24 August 1918
Died: Flushing, Cornwall, 12 July 1976
Career: Falmouth, Barbarians, Cornwall
Debut: v Scotland, Twickenham, March 1947

Cornishman George served in the Royal Navy as an engine room artificer from 1939 to 1946 before demobilisation, then worked as a shipyard fitter in Falmouth docks. He won two caps in 1947, and his third and final international was the 14-5 defeat to Ireland in 1949. The lock had originally played football for Flushing Athletic but came to prominence when he was in the services, then played for Falmouth, Cornwall, and England. As a tradesman, he was renowned for rowing to work at the docks from his Flushing home every day before his death, aged 57.

769. HOLMES, Cyril Butler
Wing 3 caps (3-1t) 1947-1948
Born: Bolton, Lancashire, 11 January 1915
Died: Bolton, Greater Manchester, 21 June 1996
Career: Manchester University, Manchester, RMC Sandhurst, the Army, Barbarians, North West Counties, Lancashire
Debut: v Scotland, Twickenham, March 1947

Holmes was an athletics star before he made his England debut on the wing in 1947. The PT instructor, a company sergeant major at Sandhurst Royal Military Academy in the Second World War, ran in the 1936 Olympics, dominated by Jesse Owens, being eliminated in the quarter-finals of the 100 yards. He won gold in the 100 yards at the 1937 AAA Championships and the 1938 Empire Games in Sydney. He was at Manchester when he scored a try on his England debut against Scotland and was later employed as a director of the family oil company. He played 27 times for Lancashire, helping them to the 1947 RFU County Championship.

770. NEWTON-THOMPSON, John Oswald DFC
Scrum-half 2 caps 1947
Born: Paddington, London, 2 December 1920
Died: Nr Lueritz, SW Africa, 3 April 1974
Career: Cape Town University, Oxford University
Debut: v Scotland, Twickenham, March 1947

'Ossie' Newton-Thompson was born in London but raised in Cape Town, where his mother, Joyce, was the first female mayor. He won a Rhodes Scholarship and played for Oxford University in the Varsity matches of 1945 and 1946. As a student, he won two caps for England and played cricket for his university and Western Province. He won a DFC flying Spitfires for SAAF in Italy in the Second World War, became a lawyer and went into politics with the United Party in South Africa. He joined the South African Parliament in 1961 but was killed in an air crash in south west Africa when he was contesting the elections.

771. WEIGHILL, Robert Harold George CBE DFC
No.8 4 caps 1947-1948
Born: Kings Norton, Worcestershire, 9 September 1920
Died: Halton, Cheshire, 27 October 2000
Career: Birkenhead Park, Waterloo, RAF, Harlequins, Leicester, Barbarians, Cheshire, Notts, Lincs & Derbyshire
Debut: v Scotland, Twickenham, March 1947

Weighill was England's number 8 from 1947 to 1948 and captained the side in his final test match against France in Paris, which was lost 15-0. An RAF Officer flying for Fighter Command in the Second World War when he was awarded the DFC, he commanded 138 Fighter after the war and served in Germany, rising to the rank of air commodore and commanding the RAF No.1 School of Technical Training at RAF Halton. He was awarded the CBE in 1970, represented the RAF on the RFU committee and was chairman of Combined Services Rugby Football. He became secretary of the RFU and was honorary secretary of the Five Nations and Home Unions Committee.

772. GIBBS, George Anthony
Prop 2 caps 1947-1948
Born: Carrara, Italy, 31 March 1920
Died: Bristol, 26 February 2001
Career: Bristol, Northern, Barbarians, Gloucestershire, Northumberland
Debut: v France, Twickenham, April 1947

Gibbs, whose brother Nigel also played for England, was a product of Clifton College and made his debut in the 1947 match against France that was delayed until April because of the severe winter. He played once more against Ireland in 1948. Gibbs was employed in the tobacco business by W.D & H.O Wills from 1939, and in the Second World War, he served with several regiments, including the Royal Tank Regiment and the 23 Indian Division. After the war, he returned to work for W.D & H.O Wills and later ran their factory in Newcastle-upon-Tyne.

773. NEWMAN, Sydney Charles
Full-back 3 caps (3-1p) 1947-1948
Born: Pretoria, South Africa, 27 July 1919
Died: Johannesburg, South Africa, 2 June 1990
Career: Pretoria, Witwatersrand University, Oxford University, Moseley, Barbarians
Debut: v France, Twickenham, April 1947

Newman, who could land goal-kicks from a virtually unheard-of for the era 55 yards, won blues with Oxford University in 1946 and 1947 when he was a Rhodes Scholar and used his time in England to win three international caps. During the Second World War, he had served in the SA Engineering Corps and was taken prisoner at Tobruk in 1942. He was awarded the Africa Service Medal and Africa Star. After his stint in England, he returned to South Africa and was one of 114 players invited for Springbok trials in 1949 but did not make the series against the All Blacks. He worked as chairman and managing director of a mining company.

774. ROBERTS, Victor George
Flanker 16 caps (6-2t) 1947-1951
Born: Penryn, Cornwall, 6 August 1924
Died: Horsham, Sussex, 14 March 2004
Career: Penryn, Swansea, Harlequins, Barbarians, Cornwall, British Lions
Debut: v France, Twickenham, April 1947

Roberts was a Cornish flanker and officer for Customs & Excise who won 12 caps captaining the side in the 23-5 defeat to Wales in 1951. Roberts had been a naval cadet working on landing craft for D-Day in the Second World War – ending as a lieutenant - before joining the Waterguard branch of Customs & Excise, then filling posts as Chief Preventive Officer at Heathrow and Assistant Waterguard Superintendent at Hull. He toured Australia and New Zealand with the British Lions in 1950 but did not play a test. He became a vice-president of the Barbarians and was a Lions selector.

775. EVANS, Eric MBE
Hooker 30 caps (15-5t) 1948-1958
Born: Droylsden, Manchester, 1 February 1921
Died: Stockport, Greater Manchester 12 January 1991
Career: Loughborough Colleges, Sale, Old Aldwinians, Barbarians, Lancashire
Debut: v Australia, Twickenham, January 1948

England's Grand Slam-winning captain in 1957, Evans, made his debut as a prop before switching to hooker in an international career that extended to 1958 when he was 37. A fitness fanatic who trained with Manchester United captain Roger Byrne, he led England 13 times and played 105 games for Lancashire. He served Sale as president and was chairman of Old Aldwinians, whom he represented early in his career. He was also a Lancashire and England selector in the 1960s and 1970s and worked as director of PE at Openshaw Technical College in Manchester. He was awarded an MBE in 1982 for services to rugby and charity work for the disabled.

776. KEELING, John Hugh
Hooker 2 caps 1948
Born: Cairo, Egypt, 28 October 1925
Died: Creeting St Mary, Suffolk, 13 February 2009
Career: Guy's Hospital, Rhodesia, Barbarians, The Army, Combined Services
Debut: v Australia, Twickenham, January 1948

Keeling, who studied dentistry at Guy's Hospital, was born in Egypt, where his father Frank worked for Shell and was educated at Grahamstown in South Africa. He was picked to make his debut ahead of Peter Henderson after two impressive performances in trials, but only won two caps. He was probably better known as a swimmer representing Guy's Hospital, the Army, and Great Britain in the 1947 University Games. After qualifying, he joined the Royal Army Dental Corps before entering private practice in Rhodesia and later near Ipswich in Suffolk. He was also a renowned actor in repertory theatre.

777. MADGE, Richard John Palmer
Scrum-half 4 caps 1948
Born: Exeter, Devon, 19 December 1914
Died: Exeter, Devon, 22 November 1996
Career: Exeter, Devon
Debut: v Australia, Twickenham, January 1948

Madge, who played his first test aged 33, had his career cut short when he was forced to retire with ligament damage just 10 minutes into his fourth test for England, the 6-3 defeat to Scotland at Murrayfield in 1948. He was replaced at half-back in the match by flanker Mickey Steele-Bodger. He captained Devon before and after the Second World War, having seen action with the Royal Artillery in the Middle East and Italy during the conflict. A product of Exeter School, he was employed by Totnes Rural Council as a surveyor.

778. VAUGHAN, Douglas Brian
No.8 8 caps 1948-1950
Born: Wrexham, Wales, 15 July 1925
Died: Peel, Isle of Man, 19 April 1977
Career: Cambridge University, Royal Navy, Headingley, Harlequins, Devonport Services, US Portsmouth, Barbarians, Yorkshire, Hampshire, Devon
Debut: v Australia, Twickenham, January 1948

Vaughan won eight caps between 1948 and 1950 and played test cricket for Devon and the Royal Navy. He was involved in commissioning the first nuclear submarines in the service before being invalided out of the Navy in 1964 and going into local government on the Isle of Man. He was the manager of the 1962 Lions tour to Australia, also coaching on the trip because there was noone else to do it. The series was lost 3-0 with one test drawn. He was also an England selector from 1959 to 1962 and from 1965 to 1966. His nephew, Justin Vaughan, played test cricket for New Zealand.

779. LUYA, Humphrey Fleetwood
Lock 5 caps 1948-1949
Born: West Derby, Lancashire, 3 February 1918
Died: Keighley, West Yorkshire, 9 May 2008
Career: Waterloo, Carlisle, Headingley, Lancashire, Barbarians
Debut: v Wales, Twickenham, January 1948

Luya was educated at Merchant Taylor's School in Crosby and played for Waterloo and Headingley at a time when players could turn out for two clubs. He joined the Royal Artillery in 1939. In North Africa, he was one of around 12,000 Allied troops who were imprisoned after the defence of Crete in 1941. He was initially placed in Stalag 18s, near Wolfsburg in Austria, before being sent to a camp for officers in Germany. Certain they would be shot, he and another prisoner, George Kennard, escaped and hid in the woods before being freed by the American liberating force. He later worked in the food trade.

780. PREECE, Ivor
Fly-half 12 caps (3-1t) 1948-1951
Born: Coventry, Warwickshire, 15 December 1920
Died: Coventry, Warwickshire, 14 March 1987
Career: Broadstreet, Coventry, Warwickshire, Midland Counties
Debut: v Ireland, Twickenham, February 1948

Reportedly the last player to kick a four-point drop goal, Preece, educated at Broad Street School in Coventry, toured Australia and New Zealand with the British Lions in 1950. He appeared in the drawn test in Dunedin as a centre, after playing second fiddle to legendary Irishman Jack Kyle at fly-half. But he continued to play for England until 1951, retiring as his country's most-capped post-war player. He served as president of Coventry RFC, Warwickshire RFU, and his first club, Broadstreet, named their new ground after him in 2002. A director of George Wilson Industries, he was a JP, and his son Peter was an England international.

781. UREN, Richard
Full-back 4 caps (7-1p, 2c) 1948-1950
Born: Wirral, Merseyside, 26 February 1926
Died: Wirral, Merseyside, 30 May 2010
Career: Waterloo, Barbarians, Cheshire
Debut: v Ireland, Twickenham, February 1948

Uren kicked two conversions on his debut – the 11-10 loss to Ireland in 1948 – winning three caps that year and one in 1950. He worked on a farm, then joined the Fleet Air Arm as a navigator during the Second World War before studying at Midland Agricultural College, then joined the family food merchants HJ Uren & Sons. Business commitments prevented him from going on the 1950 British Lions tour to Australia and New Zealand, and once he finished playing rugby, he played golf for Cheshire. He also sailed, winning the prestigious team event, the Wilson Trophy, in 1957 and 1959.

782. PRICE, Thomas William
Prop 6 caps 1948-1949
Born: Gloucester, Gloucestershire, 26 July 1914
Died: Gloucester, Gloucestershire, 11 July 1991
Career: Gloucester, Cheltenham, Gloucestershire, Barbarians
Debut: v Scotland, Murrayfield, March 1948

Price played for Gloucester from 1934 to 1948, then moved to Cheltenham, where he played until 1951. He was still at Gloucester when he won his first and second caps, aged 33, winning his last four at Cheltenham. He had played in trials before the Second World War and was picked for an unofficial international against Ireland in 1946 before finally getting his chance two years later. His services to Cheltenham were recognised when a road on the site of their old ground was named after him. He worked in a laundry and then an aircraft factory.

783. TURNER, Martin Frederick
Wing 2 caps 1948
Born: Croydon, Surrey, 1 August 1921
Died: Godstone, Surrey, 7 April 2009
Career: Old Whitgiftian, Cambridge University, Blackheath, Barbarians, London Counties, Surrey
Debut: v Scotland, Murrayfield, Edinburgh, March 1948

Turner, a big winger for the time, won both caps in 1948 after serving for the Fleet Air Arm, which he joined in 1940, during the Second World War. A product of Whitgift School, which produced Elliot Daly and Danny Cipriani, Turner played for his old boys' club and has a bar at Whitgift Sports Club named after him. A company director, he won a blue at Cambridge in 1948, was an RFU selector in 1972, chairman of the Surrey selectors, a county panel referee, secretary of Surrey, London Counties, and was a Surrey County Cricket Club Sub-Committee.

784. CANNELL, Lewis Bernard
Centre 19 caps (6-2t) 1948-1957
Born: Coventry, Warwickshire 10 June 1926
Died: London, 19 March 2003
Career: Oxford University, St Mary's Hospital, Northampton, RAF, Combined Services, East Midlands, London Counties, Middlesex
Debut: v France, Stade Colombes, Paris, March 1948

Cannell would have earned more than his 19 caps, but he twice asked the selectors to excuse him as he was taking medical exams and turned down the Lions in 1950. He was educated at Northampton Grammar School and spent three years in the RAF before attending St Mary's Hospital Medical School and qualified in 1958, ten years after his international debut. He worked at St Mary's and St George's Hospital in Tooting and Moorfields and as a GP in South Africa. He later became a consultant radiologist at Addington Hospital, Durban, and Stoke Mandeville Hospital in Buckinghamshire.

785. SYKES, Patrick William
Scrum-half 7 caps 1948-1953
Born: Vancouver, Canada, 3 March 1925
Died: Tavistock, Devon, 14 January 2014
Career: Cambridge University, Wasps, RAF, Combined Services, London Counties, Barbarians, Eastern Counties, Middlesex
Debut: v France, Stade Colombes, Paris, March 1948

Educated at St John's School, Leatherhead, Sykes, a livewire scrum-half, was the first Wasps player to be capped after the Second World War when he played against France in 1948 but had to wait until 1952 for his second international, and he played his final games in the 1953 Championship-winning side. After service in the RAF, he captained Wasps from 1951 to 1955 and was later a vice-president of the club and worked for an artificial flower company before becoming a branch manager for Burroughs Machines, a company that became Unisys. He served as chairman of Eastern Counties and as a Middlesex selector.

786. TOWELL, Allan Clark
Centre, 2 caps 1948-1951
Born: Middlesbrough, 7 March 1925
Died: Frechen, Koln, 6 March 1997
Career: Bedford, Leicester
Debut: v France, Stade Colombes, Paris, March 1948

Towell played for England twice, with his second and last cap coming three years after his debut. That second game, a 5-3 win over Scotland at Twickenham in 1951, saw six of the side playing their final test. The centre, who played for Bedford as a schoolboy, also captained the club and worked as a sports master at Ashby School and Dunstable School. He played for Leicester at fly-half and centre in the 1947–48 & 1948–49 seasons, playing 60 out of the club's 75 games. He was named Leicester's captain for the 1949–50 season, switching to flanker.

787. BERRIDGE, Michael John
Prop 2 caps 1949
Born: Huntingdon, Cambridgeshire, 28 February 1923
Died: Oundle, Northamptonshire, 2 October 1973
Career: Peterborough, Northampton, Leicester, Barbarians, East Midlands, Combined Counties
Debut: v Wales, Cardiff Arms Park, Cardiff, January 1949

Berridge was educated at King's School in Peterborough and started his career at the local club before joining Northampton Saints after the Second World War when rugby restarted. He made 251 appearances for Saints between 1945 and 1956, showing the way for the likes of Ron Jacobs. He played for the Combined Counties in 1947 before making his debut against Wales in 1949. His second and final cap came against Ireland that year, and he also played for Combined Counties against the Springboks in 1951. He worked as a farmer before his premature death.

788. BRAITHWAITE-EXLEY, Bryan
No.8 1 cap 1949
Born: Wetherby, West Yorkshire, 30 November 1927
Died: Austwick, North Yorkshire, 29 May 2009
Career: RAF, Headingley, North Ribblesdale, Yorkshire
Debut: v Wales, Cardiff, January 1949

Educated at Sedbergh School in Cumbria, Braithwaite-Exley played for 18 seasons at Headingley between 1946 and 1963 while working in his family quarrying firm, XL Granite. He was one of the nine new caps when he made his only international appearance and was given the short shrift by selectors who saw him too lightweight. He served on the Austwick Parish Council, West Riding County Council, the North Yorkshire County Council, and the Yorkshire Dales National Park Committee. He was also a non-executive director of the Skipton Building Society for 23 years and chairman from 1995 to 1998.

789. DANBY, Thompson
Wing 1 cap 1949
Born: Trimdon, County Durham, 10 August 1926
Died: Wadhurst, East Sussex, 26 December 2022
Career: Durham City, Gosport, Harlequins, the Army, Combined Services, Barbarians, Durham County, Hampshire
Debut: v Wales, Cardiff Arms Park, Cardiff, January 1949

Danby, a product of St John's College in York, won a single cap for England in the 9-3 defeat by Wales in 1949 before signing to play rugby league for Salford later that year. He played three times for England in the 13-man code and represented Great Britain on the 1950 tour to Australia and New Zealand, playing in three tests. A move from Salford to Workington fell through. He was a teacher, later becoming the master in charge of rugby at Shebbear College in Devon, where he worked for nearly 30 years from 1959 and scored 187 points in 174 games for Salford.

790. GREGORY, John Arthur
Wing 1 cap 1949
Born: Bristol, 22 June 1923,
Died: Nailsea, Gloucestershire, 16 December 2003
Career: Dublin Wanderers, Clifton, Blackheath, Bristol, The Army, Barbarians, Gloucester
Debut: v Wales, Cardiff Arms Park, Cardiff, January 1949

Gregory was an Olympic sprinter good enough to win a silver medal in the 4x100 yards at London in 1948. Welsh wing Ken Jones was also in the Great Britain team and competed in Melbourne in 1952. He had served in RAMC and went to play rugby league in 1947 for Huddersfield, which resulted in him being banned from playing union, only to have his sentence cut to a year up to April 1948. He worked as a sales rep for Imperial Tobacco and won his only union cap, whilst playing for Blackheath, in a 9-3 defeat to Wales. He later became a sports presenter with HTV and wrote a column for the Bristol Evening Post.

791. HOLMES, William Barry
Full-back 4 caps (4-2c) 1949
Born: Buenos Aires, Argentina, 6 January 1928
Died: Salta, Argentina, 10 November 1949
Career: Buenos Aires, Cambridge University, Richmond, Barbarians, Old Georgians (Argentina), Argentina.
Debut: v Wales, Cardiff Arms Park, Cardiff, January 1949

Capped by England and Argentina as a full-back, Holmes was born in Buenos Aires to British parents and was educated at St George's College in Quilmes before heading to the United Kingdom. He won blues at Cambridge and was capped four times by England in 1949 before returning to Argentina to start a ranch. He represented Argentina twice against France, picked after just two club matches. He played against France three times in a year, who were not amused when he turned up in an Argentinian shirt as they recognised him from his games for England. He died in Salta, a week after getting married, from typhoid fever, aged 21.

792. HORSFALL, Edward Luke
Flanker 1 cap 1949
Born: Huddersfield, Yorkshire, 11 August 1917
Died: Bracknell, Berkshire, June 1983
Career: Huddersfield, Bedford, Gloucester, Headingley, Harlequins, Percy Park, Cardiff, RAF, Combined Services, Yorkshire, Hampshire
Debut: v Wales, Cardiff Arms Park, Cardiff, January 1949

Horsfall paid the price for the lack of effectiveness of the England back row against Wales in 1949 when they were beaten 9-3, as he was one of four players to win their only cap that day. A squadron leader in the RAF during the Second World War, he remained in the services until 1967, retiring as a wing commander, before teaching English, history, and

793. HOSKING, Geoffrey Robert d'Aubrey Hosking
Lock 5 caps (3-1t) 1949-1950
Born: St Thomas, Devon, 11 March 1922
Died: Dover, Kent, 13 January 1991
Career: Devonport Services, Royal Navy
Debut: v Wales, Cardiff Arms Park, Cardiff, January 1949

Hosking was a lock who played all four Championship games in 1949, scoring his only test try in the 19-3 win over Scotland. He lined up against Wales the next year, but it was discovered, thanks to an overdue x-ray, that he had been playing with a broken back, and we underwent surgery. He served in the Royal Marines in the Second World War on HMS Frobisher, before being injured in 1945 and returning to the United Kingdom. He rose to the rank of captain and worked at the Royal Marine Depot, in Deal, and the Royal Marine Training School before leaving the service in 1951 and becoming a farmer in South Australia.

794. RIMMER, Gordon
Scrum-half 12 caps
Born: Southport, Merseyside, 28 February 1925
Died: Sefton North, Lancashire, July 2002
Career: Wigan Old Boys, Waterloo, Lancashire, British Lions
Debut: v Wales, Cardiff Arms Park, Cardiff, January 1949

After serving in the Fleet Air Arm in the Second World War, Rimmer continued in the services as a PE sergeant and, in 1948, at RAF Yatesbury, was instructor to another future international, Phil Davies. A British Lion in 1950 in Australia and New Zealand, Rimmer was injured early in the tour but recovered to play in the Wellington test against the All Blacks, which the tourists lost 6-3. He played his final test in 1954, later worked in the brewing industry and as a sports retailer. He was a good enough golfer to represent Lancashire.

795. VAN RYNEVELD, Clive Berrange
Centre 4 caps, (9-3t) 1949
Born: Cape Town, South Africa, 19 March 1928
Died: Cape Town, South Africa, 29 January 2018
Career: Cape Town, Cape Town University, Oxford University, Barbarians
Debut: v Wales, Cardiff Arms Park, Cardiff, January 1949

One of South Africa's greatest all-round sportsmen, van Ryneveld played four times for England in 1949 and two Varsity matches whilst he was a student at Oxford University. As a cricketer, he played 19 tests for South Africa between 1951 and 1958, scoring 724 runs at nearly 27 and taking 17 wickets. He captained the cricket team for three years despite his professional life as a barrister and had a brief career in South African politics as an MP serving the United Party and the Progressive Party. His father, also Clive, was a Springbok half-back who played against the British Lions in 1910.

796. KENDALL-CARPENTER, John MacGregor CBE
No.8 23 caps (3-1t) 1949-1954
Born: Cardiff, South Glamorgan, 25 September 1925
Died: Wellington, Somerset, 24 May 1990
Career: Oxford University, Bath, Penzance & Newlyn, Barbarians, Cornwall
Debut: v Ireland, Lansdowne Road, Dublin, February 1949

Kendall-Carpenter was a three-time blue at Cambridge University who worked as a schoolteacher. His most significant act in rugby came when he chaired the committee that organised the first Rugby World Cup. Captaining every team he played for, he taught at Cranbrook School in Kent, Wellington College in Somerset and Eastbourne College before becoming Head of Wellington. A former RFU President, his committee got the 1987 event in Australia and New Zealand on, and it has mushroomed into the world's third biggest sporting event. He was inducted into the World Rugby Hall of Fame at the end of the 2011 World Cup in New Zealand.

797. KENNEDY, Robert Day
Wing 3 caps 1949
Born: Bulawayo, Rhodesia, 14 August 1925
Died: Bulawayo, Rhodesia, 8 May 1979
Career: Camborne School of Mines, Cornwall
Debut: v Ireland, Lansdowne Road, Dublin, February 1949

Kennedy attended Plumtree School in the-then Rhodesia before heading to England after his military service to attend the Camborne School of Mines in Cornwall. He played three times for England and Cornwall alongside players such as John Kendall-Carpenter. He returned to Rhodesia to work as a mining engineer but, in that trouble-torn country, was tragically killed in an ambush after being wounded travelling home after looking at a gold deposit near Fort Victoria. He was instrumental in helping to set up an annual Kennedy Match in Cornwall in his memory.

798. MATTHEWS, John Robert Clive
Lock 10 caps 1949-1952
Born: Hastings, East Sussex, 14 June 1920
Died: Kensington & Chelsea, London 2 February 2004
Career: Guy's Hospital, Navy, Combined Services, Harlequins, Middlesex, London Counties, British Empire Services
Debut: v France, Twickenham, February 1949

Matthews, a descendant of Clive of India, studied dentistry at Guy's Hospital and practised all his working life, including a spell with RNVR as a surgeon lieutenant in the Second World War when he was stationed at Murmansk in Russia and the naval mission in Moscow. He played for Harlequins when he was first capped and played his final test against France in 1952. Matthews had the honour of captaining London Counties when they beat the great South African side of 1951-2 at Twickenham and inflicted the only defeat on the Springboks in their mammoth 31-match tour, 11-9.

799. STEEDS, John Harold, MBE
Hooker 5 caps 1949-1950
Born: Edmonton, London, 27 September 1916
Died: Colchester, Essex, 9 May 2009
Career: Cambridge University, Middlesex Hospital, Saracens, Barbarians, Middlesex, Colchester.
Debut: v France, Twickenham, February 1949

Steeds played for Saracens whilst still at St Edward's School in Oxford and became the first Saracen to play for England after the Second World War. He had served as a lieutenant surgeon during the conflict with the Royal Navy. Post-war, he worked at Middlesex Hospital as a registrar in paediatrics from 1946 before moving to Colchester in 1950, where he was a general practitioner until his retirement in 1987. Steeds, awarded an MBE, had warmed up for one England game by playing for Colchester 3rd XV when they were a man short. A Saracen from 1938 to 1950, Steeds is in the club's Hall of Fame.

800. BOOBBYER, Brian
Centre 9 caps (6-2t) 1950-1952
Born: Ealing, Middlesex, 25 February 1928
Died: Hereford, Herefordshire, 17 January 2011
Career: Oxford University, Rosslyn Park, Barbarians, Middlesex, Royal Artillery
Debut: v Wales, Twickenham, January 1950

An outstanding rugby player and cricketer, Boobbyer turned his back on both sports, aged 24, to travel overseas and work with Frank Buchman's Moral Re-Armament movement. With the bat, he once went a whole season at Durston House prep school without being dismissed, won cricket and rugby blues at Oxford University, where he read history at Brasenose College, and could have played for Middlesex, but his Christian ideals sent him elsewhere. His work with MRA took him all over Asia – he stayed on after a rugby tour of Japan -and the United States. In 2005, his family published the best of his talks and writings in a book, Like a Cork out of a Bottle.

801. BOTTING, Ian James
Wing 2 caps 1950
Born: Dunedin, New Zealand, 18 May 1922
Died: Christchurch, New Zealand, 9 July 1980
Career: Otago University, Otago, New Zealand Universities, Cambridge University, RAF, Notts, Lincs & Derby, Blackheath, Leicester, Barbarians, New Zealand.
Debut: v Wales, Twickenham, January 1950

Botting was a wing born in New Zealand and toured with the All Blacks to South Africa in 1949, where they were routed, without playing a test. He travelled to Britain to study at Cambridge University. The English press derided his selection to play for England in 1950 so soon after representing New Zealand. A schoolmaster, he played twice for England and later became a minister in the Anglican Church. He was working as a chaplain at St Margaret's College in Christchurch, in his native New Zealand, when he was knocked off his bike and killed.

802. CAIN, John Joseph
Flanker 1 cap 1950
Born: West Derby, Lancashire, 12 June 1920
Died: Sefton, Merseyside, 18 November 1994
Career: Waterloo, Lancashire
Debut: v Wales, Twickenham, January 1950

Educated at St Mary's College in Crosby, Cain was awarded the Military Medal in 1944 for his bravery when serving with the Irish Guards in the Second World War. In one action, Operation Veritable in France, he volunteered to drive to the front, over ground not cleared of mines and under fire, to collect wounded soldiers. His citation added: "During the advance from the Rhine, Sergeant Cain has done excellent work as platoon sergeant of the Carrier Platoon, where his organising ability, devotion to duty and disregard of his own safety, have been the greatest inspiration to this platoon." One of the hardest working forwards of his era, worked in banking and the business machine industry.

803 HOFMEYR, Murray Bernard
Full-back 3 caps (7-2c,1d) 1950
Born: Pretoria, South Africa, 9 December 1925
Died: Knysna, South Africa 17 May 2018
Career: Rhodes University, Grahamstown, Harlequins, Barbarians, Oxford University
Debut: v Wales, Twickenham, January 1950

Educated at Pretoria High School in South Africa, Hofmeyr played three games for England in 1950 when he was at Oxford University as a Rhodes Scholar at Worcester College. The full-back was also a formidable cricketer, carrying his bat in the 1949 Varsity match and averaging over 40 in 44 first-class appearances for his university and North Eastern Transvaal. His best friend in rugby was the England centre Brian Boobbyer with the association leading to Boobbyer joining the Moral Re-Armament Group, which his brother in South Africa championed. He was a senior director of Anglo-American and chairman of SA Breweries, JCI and Argus Holdings.

804. HOLMES, Walter Alan
Prop 16 caps 1950-1953
Born: Nuneaton, Warwickshire, 10 September 1925
Died: Nuneaton, Warwickshire, 6 April 2009
Career: Nuneaton, Midlands Counties, Barbarians, Warwickshire
Debut: v Wales, Twickenham, January 1950

The first Nuneaton player to be capped when he made his debut at 24, Holmes could play in all three rows of the scrum but won all his England caps as a prop. He worked as a Bevin Boy in the Second World War before becoming an engine fitter for Morris Engines in Coventry and Massey Ferguson. He was a Championship winner in 1953 when England were denied the Grand Slam by Ireland in a 9-9 draw, and when he finished as a test player later that year, he was England's most-capped prop. His brothers Bill, Harry and Sam also played for Nuneaton, all four playing together in the 1949/50 season, and his grandson Gary has captained the club.

805. JONES, Herbert Arthur
Lock 3 caps 1950
Born: Barnstaple, Devon, 22 August 1918
Died: Barnstaple, Devon, 5 December 1998
Career: West Buckland School, Barnstaple, Devon, Devon & Cornwall, North Devon
Debut: v Wales, Twickenham, January 1950

Jones was a stalwart of Devon rugby and was regarded as one of the best forwards to come out of the area. He was the third Barnstaple player to win an England cap as one of eight new caps on his debut against Wales. He was picked after his car broke down following a trial match and had to be pushed three miles. He captained a combined Devon & Cornwall side who played the touring Springboks, and admitted he was dropped for having a 'punch-up' with French forwards. He was asked to tour Australia and New Zealand with the Lions in 1950 but rejected the offer because he had to run his Newland Park Farm in Landkey near Barnstaple.

806. SMALL, Harold Dudley
Flanker 4 caps 1950
Born: Durban, South Africa, 7 January 1922
Died: Dundee, South Africa, 3 September 2003
Career: Witwatersrand University, Transvaal, Oxford University, Barbarians
Debut: v Wales, Twickenham, January 1950

South African-born Small was a flanker through the 1950 Championship, having served as an engineer in the Merchant Navy in the Second World War. He was a Rhodes Scholar at Oxford University when he played test rugby and returned to his homeland in 1951, where he worked as a mining engineer and joined the Anglo-American Corporation mining giant in 1968. At Oxford, he won blues in 1949 and 1950, having studied at Witwatersrand University in Johannesburg and played for the mighty Transvaal in South Africa. His one campaign for England ended with a wooden spoon, and he lived in Dundee, Natal, when he died.

807. SMITH, John Vincent
Wing/centre 4 caps (12-4t) 1950
Born: Stroud, Gloucestershire, 23 May 1926
Died: Stroud, Gloucestershire, 17 September 2021
Career: Cambridge University, Stroud, Rosslyn Park, The Army, Barbarians, Gloucestershire.
Debut: v Wales, Twickenham, January 1950

Smith scored four tries from the wing in the 1950 Championship, including two against Scotland in a 13-11 defeat at Murrayfield and never played for England again. A three-time blue at Cambridge University, he worked in the catering industry and as the director of a firm of agricultural merchants. He was President of the RFU, overseeing the development of Twickenham's South Stand. In the 1966 General Election, he stood as the Liberal candidate for Stroud, coming third. He also worked with the United States Rugby Foundation as international director for over 20 years. His book 'Good Morning President' detailed his time at the RFU. He was England's oldest surviving player before his death.

808 ADKINS, Stanley John
No.8/lock 7 caps (3-1t)
Born: Coventry, Warwickshire, 2 June 1922
Died: Coventry, Warwickshire, 2 January 1992
Career: Stoke Old Boys, the Army, Combined Services, Coventry
Debut: v Ireland, Twickenham, February 1950

A championship winner in 1953, 'Akker' Adkins made his debut at No.8 in the 3-0 win over Ireland at Twickenham in 1950, when he replaced DB Vaughan at the back of the scrum. After moving to lock, he was dropped after the Calcutta Cup loss to Scotland that year and was not recalled until the 1953 campaign. He lost his place the next year to Wasps' Peter Yarranton. He worked as an aircraft factory machinist, was a licensee and served as chairman of the Coventry branch of the Licensed House Manager's Association. In the Second World War, he was a lance corporal in the Coldstream Guards, serving in Salerno, Italy, and North Africa.

809. HYDE, John Phillip
Wing 2 caps 1950
Born: Wellingborough, Northamptonshire, 8 June 1930
Died: Bangor, Gwynedd, 28 August 2022
Career: Wellingborough GS, Northampton, The Army, Combined Services, Barbarians, East Midlands
Debut: v France, Stade Colombes, Paris, February 1950

Hyde was selected to play for England whilst still a pupil at Wellingborough Grammar School and playing for Northampton. But between the announcement and the match against France in Paris, he left school to join the Army doing his national service with the Eighth Royal Tank Regiment. England lost that game 6-3, and he played once more in the 13-11 defeat to Scotland. He went to Loughborough College to train as a PT instructor before returning to Wellingborough as a sports and biology teacher, replacing Jeff Butterfield in the sports post. He later lived in Anglesey.

810. BAUME, John Lea
Prop 1 cap 1950
Born: Liversedge, West Yorkshire, 18 July 1920
Died: Gunnislake, Cornwall, 23 September 2005
Career: Northern, Headingley, Harrogate, The Army, Northumberland, Combined Services
Debut: v Scotland, Murrayfield, Edinburgh, March 1950

Baume won one cap, while playing for Northern, in the 13-11 Calcutta Cup defeat of 1950 when he was already nearly 30 years old and was an Adjutant of the Royal Northumberland Fusiliers at Fenham Barracks, Newcastle. He had served in the Second World War with the Royal Northumberland Fusiliers, and the prop saw action in Korea, rising to the rank of major before leaving the Army in 1961. He played six times for the Army and had recovered from several serious injuries, before concentrating on poultry farming in his retirement.

811. BARTLETT, Jasper Twining
Lock 1 cap 1951
Born: Birmingham, Warwickshire, 17 October 1924
Died: Liverpool, Lancashire, 16 January 1969
Career: Liverpool University, Northern Universities, Combined Universities, Waterloo, Royal Engineers, the Army, Combined Services, Barbarians, Cheshire
Debut: v Wales, St Helen's, Swansea, January 1951

Educated at Birkenhead Institute, Bartlett studied civil engineering at Liverpool University and later worked on the Mersey docks. He was a Waterloo player when he made his one and only England appearance in the 23-5 defeat to Wales in Swansea in 1951, and Bruce Neale took his place in the second row for the rest of the Championship. He was reportedly not fully fit for his test debut, but played more than 40 times for Cheshire winning a County Championship in 1949. An engineer who became the general manager of international building maintenance and structural waterproofing firms died when he was 44 after contracting lung cancer.

812. HEWITT, Edwin Newbury
Full-back 3 caps (2-1c) 1951
Born: Coventry, Warwickshire, 22 April 1924
Died: Spain, 18 May 2003
Career: Coventry, Sphinx, Vikings, Warwickshire
Debut: v Wales, St Helen's, Swansea, January 1951

Hewitt, educated at Barkers Butts School and Coventry Technical College, played over 130 games for Coventry between 1946 and 1954 and won his three caps in the 1951 Five Nations Championship. He also played cricket as a batsman in the Coventry Works Cricket League, a high standard at the time and was a member of the MCC. His career ended when he moved to London to work as an engineer and then co-managed locksmiths He was brought up close to the Coundon Road ground he graced later in life. He moved to Spain, where he died in 2003.

813. MOORE, Lord Philip Brian Cecil GCVO KCB CMG PC
No.8 1 cap 1951
Born: Bengal, India, 6 April 1921
Died: East Molesey, Surrey, 7 April 2009
Career: Oxford University, Blackheath, Barbarians, Oxfordshire
Debut: v Wales, St Helen's, Swansea, January 1951

Moore's only cap came in the disastrous defeat to Wales in 1951, but he made a towering contribution to public life away from the rugby pitch. He studied classics at Brasenose College, Oxford, before serving as a navigator in the RAF in the Second World War. He was shot down and became a prisoner of war at the infamous StalagLuft III camp, where he helped in the famous 'Wooden Horse' escape. He became a civil servant in the Ministry of Defence and a private secretary to Queen Elizabeth II. He was awarded a life peerage on retirement, becoming Lord Moore of Wolvercote. His former son-in-law is the rock star Peter Gabriel of Genesis fame.

814. OAKLEY, Lionel Frederick Lightborn
Centre 1 cap 1951
Born: Dacca, India, 24 January 1925
Died: Bedford, November 1981
Career: Bedford, The Army, Barbarians, East Midlands
Debut: v Wales, St Helen's, Swansea, January 1951

Born in a part of India that is now Bangladesh but educated at Bedford School, Oakley had very few equals in public schools rugby and, in modern terms, would have been described as a wonderkid. He made his only test appearance in the shocking 23-5 defeat to Wales in Swansea in 1951. He served in the Second World War with the Royal Artillery and the Indian Airborne Division and in Palestine with the 6th Airborne Division. He left the services in 1948 to work with fertiliser manufacturers A. Nightingale & Sons Ltd, where he was a sales manager.

815. RITTSON-THOMAS, George Christopher
Flanker, 3 caps (3-1t) 1951
Born: Cardiff, Glamorgan, 18 December 1926
Died: Sandford St Martin, Oxfordshire, 21 January 2014
Career: Sherborne School, Oxford University
Debut: v Wales, St Helen's, Swansea, January 1951

Rittson-Thomas scored a try on his debut in the 23-5 defeat to Wales but played just twice more for England and never tasted victory in the white shirt. In his final test, the 11-3 defeat to France, he tore an ankle tendon, leaving England to play with 14 men and French flanker Jean Prat to score eight points. He attended Oxford University, where he won rugby blues and a swimming blue. He was an Olympic trialist in swimming and later had a successful career in banking with Lloyds. He married Silvia Fleming, the daughter of Major Philip Fleming, the uncle of James Bond creator Ian Fleming.

816. SMITH, Trellevyn Harvey
Hooker, 1 cap 1951
Born: Bedford, Bedfordshire, 3 April 1920
Died: Kettering, Northamptonshire, 17 October 2000
Career: Northampton
Debut: v Wales, St Helen's, Swansea, January 1951

Smith was one of 10 new caps for the opening game of the 1951 Championship, a 23-5 defeat by the Welsh, and one of four who never played for England again despite playing in trials. He was unlucky to play at the same time as Eric Evans, who replaced him in the next game against Ireland and was virtually ever-present for the next three seasons. Smith worked as an agricultural engineer and later, whilst living in Kettering, was a director of Woodlands Brigstock Ltd – a company that sold agricultural equipment such as tractors, balers and combine harvesters.

817. STIRLING, Robert Victor OBE
Prop, 18 caps (3-1t) 1951-1954
Born: Lichfield, Staffordshire, 4 September 1919
Died: Halton, Cheshire, 15 January 1991
Career: RAF, Combined Services, Leicester, Wasps, Barbarians, Kent, Notts, Lincs & Derbys
Debut: v Wales, St Helen's, Swansea, January 1951

Stirling, who had started his career at Aylestone St James, was the first Wasps player to captain England when he led the side in 1954, winning a Triple Crown, finishing his test career which started at 31, with 18 successive caps. He served in the RAF during the Second World War, stationed mostly in India, and after the war, was posted to RAF Halton near Aylesbury, then to the Air Ministry in London, hence his move from Leicester to Wasps in 1953. He boxed at heavyweight for the RAF, his service career saw him rise to the rank of wing commander, and he was awarded the OBE in 1970.

818. TINDALL, Victor Ronald CBE
Wing 4 caps 1951
Born: Kingsclere, Hampshire, 1 August 1928
Died: Hale, Cheshire, 11 June 2010
Career: Richmond, New Brighton, Liverpool University, Cheshire, RAF, Combined Services, Barbarians
Debut: v Wales, St Helen's, Swansea, January 1951

Tindall, educated at Wallasey Grammar School, played throughout the 1951 Championship on the wing before a distinguished medical career. An accomplished athlete, he had won a scholarship to Liverpool University and later specialised in obstetrics and gynaecology in Cardiff. He was a senior lecturer at the Welsh National School of Medicine and wrote 12 publications on the subject. He was awarded the CBE in 1992, and his final posting was as chair of his specialist subject at Manchester University. He was often used as a specialist witness at hearings of the General Medical Council, even in retirement, before the onset of Parkinson's Disease.

819. WILKINS, Dennis Thomas
Lock 13 caps 1951-1953
Born: Leeds, West Yorkshire, 26 December 1924
Died: Maidstone, Kent, 30 January 2012
Career: US Portsmouth, Royal Navy, Combined Services, Roundhay, Barbarians, Yorkshire
Debut: v Wales, St Helen's, Swansea, January 1951

'Squire' Wilkins, nicknamed for his love of checked jackets, was the first Roundhay player to be capped whilst at the club. He served as a Fleet Air Arm pilot in the Second World War and with the Royal Australian Navy. He jumped the fence to get into Twickenham to watch England play Wales in 1950 and was arrested. He retired from rugby in 1956, made his last flight in 1957 and joined Kimberley-Clark, the Kleenex producers, as a salesman but was soon on the board. He went on to work for the parent company Reed International, running their European operations.

820. WOODRUFF, Charles Garfield MBE
Wing 4 caps 1951
Born: Newport, Gwent, 30 October 1920
Died: Leicester, Leicestershire, 1 November 2019
Career: Newport, London Civil Service, Civil Service, Harlequins, Cheltenham, Barbarians, London Counties, Kent, Gloucestershire.
Debut: v Wales, St Helen's, Swansea, January 1951

Woodruff, who became the oldest surviving England international just before his death, played all four games of the 1951 Championship. Having served in the Second World War as a flight lieutenant in the RAF, dropping paratroopers into France during the D-Day landings, he was 30 when he won his first cap. He could have played for Wales, being born and schooled in Newport, if he had not been seen by an England scout playing for Cheltenham. He was at Harlequins for 14 years, until he was 42, and played for Stroud 4th XV until the age of 56, being captained by his son, Peter. He worked at the Ministry of Defence and died at Leicester station while preparing to travel to London for the Harlequins' Players' Association lunch.

821. HARDY, Evan Michael Pearce OBE
Fly-half 3 caps 1951
Born: Bareilly, India, 3 November 1927
Died: Taunton, Somerset, 13 January 1994
Career: Blackheath, Combined Services, the Army, Yorkshire
Debut: v Ireland, Lansdowne Road, February 1951

Hardy, a career soldier, nearly made a memorable debut against Ireland in Dublin in 1951, but he hit the post with a drop goal, and England lost the match 3-0. Educated at Ampleforth College in North Yorkshire, he played twice more for England and, in his final game – a 5-3 win over Scotland – he partnered Dennis Shuttleworth, who was also in his army regiment, the Duke of Wellington's. He served in the Korean War and made the rank of colonel. He also served as the Army representative on the RFU and was a fine cricketer representing the Army and the Combined Services in his only first-class match against Warwickshire in 1959. He was an MCC member.

822. NEALE, Bruce Alan
Lock 3 caps 1951
Born: Chelsea, London, 15 September 1923
Died: Ipswich, Suffolk, 28 January 1996
Career: Rosslyn Park, Army, Combined Services, London Counties, Surrey, Billingham, Durham County
Debut: v Ireland, Lansdowne Road, Dublin, February 1951

Educated at Emmanuel School in Battersea, Neale served with the Royal Artillery during the Second World War and played 17 times for the service between 1948 and 1953. All his caps came in 1951 after he replaced 'flu victim Jasper Bartlett in the final trial game. He was selected for England's second game of the campaign against Wales but withdrew after breaking his nose in the last minute of an Army game against Gloucester when he collided with one of his forwards. He captained the Army, Surrey, and Durham and when he left the Army in 1953, went to work for the chemical giant ICI.

823. WILLIAMS, John Michael
Centre 2 caps 1951
Born: Penzance, Cornwall, 24 August 1927
Died: Budock, Cornwall, 6 September 2000
Career: Cambridge University, Penzance & Newlyn, Richmond, Barbarians, Cornwall
Debut: v Ireland, Lansdowne Road, Dublin, February 1951

'Ginger' Williams, a Cambridge blue in 1949, was a hard-running centre who won two caps in 1951 and a stalwart of Cornish rugby, captaining Penzance & Newlyn in 1951/52. A solicitor by profession, he captained Richmond to victory in the 1953 Middlesex Sevens and later held the office of High Sheriff of Cornwall and was President of the Cornwall RFU from 1991 to 1994. He also organised a 'Tankards' side that played against Penzance & Newlyn from 1952 to 1969, in which stars such as British Lion Tony O'Reilly lined up against the locals.

824. HOOK, William Gordon
Full-back 3 caps (2-1c) 1951-1952
Born: Gloucester, Gloucestershire, 21 December 1920
Died: Gloucester, Gloucestershire, 9 May 2013
Career: Gloucester, Gloucestershire
Debut: v Scotland, Twickenham, March 1951

Hook played 129 times for Gloucester between 1938 and 1952, following his brother Bob, who played for the club in the 1930s. Educated at Sir Thomas Rich's School, he was 17 on his club debut but had to wait until he was 30 to win his first international cap. He served as an aircraftman in the Second World War when he was stationed in Ghana and Sierra Leone, and his rugby career took off in the 1946/47 season when he became a Gloucester regular after the retirement of Harold Broughton. A sports shop owner, he represented his county at athletics and Second XI cricket and famously used to eat chocolate at half-time instead of the lemons most were forced to suck.

825. SHUTTLEWORTH, Dennis William OBE
Scrum-half 2 caps 1951-1953
Born: Leeds, West Yorkshire, 22 July 1928
Died: York, North Yorkshire, 2 April 2001
Career: Headingley, Blackheath, RMA Sandhurst, Halifax, Duke of Wellington's Regiment, The Army, Combined Services, Yorkshire, Barbarians
Debut: v Scotland, Twickenham, March 1951

Shuttleworth played twice for England, in games two years apart, and was part of the Championship-winning side in 1953. He had a distinguished military career after joining the Duke of Wellington's Regiment in 1948, serving in Korea and rising to become a brigadier and an Inspector of Army Physical and Adventurous Training before his retirement in 1983. He then served as a schools liaison officer for Yorkshire and Humberside, recruiting new soldiers. The scrum-half served as a Yorkshire selector and had two spells as the Army representative on the RFU board. He was RFU President in 1985/86, a regional director of the 1991 Rugby World Cup and president of the Rugby Football Schools Union.

826. AGAR, Albert Eustace
Centre 7 caps (6-1t, 1d) 1952-1953
Born: Hartlepool, County Durham, 12 November 1923
Died: Bromley, Kent, 4 June 2001
Career: Hartlepool, Durham City, Lloyds Bank, Durham County, London Counties, Harlequins, Middlesex
Debut: v South Africa, Twickenham, January 1952

Agar was playing at Harlequins when he made his test debut in the 8-3 defeat to South Africa in 1952 and played the next six matches before losing his place to Jeff Butterfield in 1953 and never regained it. The centre worked in banking and was a treasurer of Lloyds Bank. He used his financial acumen when he served as treasurer of the Middlesex Rugby Union between 1955 and 1959. He was president of the county, was an England selector from 1962 to 1971, chairman for the last two years, served on the International Board and was RFU President in the 1984-85 season.

827. LEWIS, Alec Ormonde
Flanker 10 caps 1952-1954
Born: Brighton, East Sussex, 20 August 1920
Died: Grahamstown, South Africa, 12 January 2013
Career: Wells, Swindon, Bath, Barbarians, Somerset
Debut: v South Africa, Twickenham, January 1952

Lewis saw action serving in the Second World War with the Eighth Army in North Africa, Sicily, and Italy, where he was wounded after stepping on a mine. He was sent to Palestine to recover, where he started playing football again. He left the Army when he was 27 and played as an amateur for Swindon Town before taking up rugby again. He won his first cap aged 31 against Hennie Muller's great Springbok side in 1952. He worked for Shell and BP, served on the committees of Bath and Somerset and became a national selector and popular tour manager of John Pullin's England side, which beat South Africa away in 1972.

828. WINN, Christopher Elliot
Wing 8 caps (9-3t) 1952-1954
Born: Beckenham, Kent, 13 November 1926
Died: Richmond, Greater London, 27 August 2017
Career: Oxford University, Rosslyn Park, London Counties, Surrey, Sussex, Barbarians
Debut: v South Africa, Twickenham, January 1952

Educated at King's College School, Wimbledon, then Oxford University, Winn scored a try on his debut in the 8-3 defeat to South Africa in 1952. Winn played cricket at Oxford and Sussex CCC, scoring nearly 2,500 runs at an average of 25 in 59 first-class games as a left-handed batsman. He worked as a sales manager with ICI in the paints division. His wedding to Valerie Ball, the athlete and poster girl of the sport in Britain, was covered in 'Tatler'. He died of pancreatic cancer in a nursing home six years before his wife passed away.

829. WOODWARD, John Edward
Wing 15 caps (21-6t,1p) 1952-1956
Born: Wycombe, Buckinghamshire, 17 April 1931
Died: Harefield, 16 January 2017, aged 85
Career: RAF, Wasps, Barbarians, Buckinghamshire, East Midlands, Middlesex
Debut: v South Africa, Twickenham, January 1952

Woodward was a big winger – by the standard of the times - weighing in at 15 stone and 6ft 2in, but his international career was cut short aged 24 after he made his debut four years earlier. An outstanding athlete who ran 100m in 10 seconds, he had attracted attention as a 17-year-old in 1948 when he scored a hat-trick for Wasps in the final of the Middlesex Sevens. He was one of the stars of the 1950s, winning the Championship outright in 1953. Woodward, an RAF PE instructor, took over his family's butchers' shop before running a chain of sports shops and turned down a move to rugby league with Salford.

830. WOODGATE, Elliott Edmund
Prop 1 cap 1952
Born: Dartmouth, Devon, 21 January 1922
Died: Newport, Monmouthshire, 13 January 2000
Career: Kingswear, Paignton, Chepstow, Barbarians, Devon, South West of England
Debut: v Wales, Twickenham, January 1952

Woodgate started his career before the Second World War alongside his twin brother Bill, who was an England trialist, at Kingswear while he was working as an appearance plate layer. He would captain the club and Devon, and became an England reserve in 1950. He got the call-up to win his only cap two years later. He was a reserve for the Wales game when he got home on a Friday night after working on the railways to find a message telling him to get the first train to London because Nuneaton forward Wally Holmes had an eye injury. He later became a steelworks mechanical foreman and was on Chepstow's committee.

831. COLLINS, Philip John
Full-back 3 caps 1952
Born: Redruth, Cornwall, 4 November 1928
Career: Camborne, Cornwall
Debut: v Scotland, Murrayfield, March 1952

Collins made 25 appearances for Cornwall after starting playing for Camborne in 1946 as an attacking full-back and helped England to a 19-3 win over Scotland on his debut when he became his club's first international. His second match was the grim 3-0 win over Ireland in the snow in March 1952, a game that had been postponed from February because of the death of King George VI. A knee injury meant his test career stalled after three caps despite the efforts of Denis Compton's surgeon. An engineering draughtsman by trade, he was still a regular at Camborne matches into his nineties. His father Phil had played centre for Cornwall.

832. BAZLEY, Reginald Charles
Wing 10 caps (6-2t) 1952-1955
Born: Barrow-in-Furness, Lancashire, 15 December 1929
Died: Liverpool, Lancashire 19 November 2009
Career: Furness, Liverpool University, Waterloo, UAU, the Army, Combined Services, Barbarians, Lancashire
Debut: v Ireland, Twickenham, March 1952

Bazley was at Waterloo when he won his 10 caps for England, and his finest moment in the national shirt came when he scored two tries in the 26-8 win over Scotland at Twickenham in 1953. After graduating from Liverpool University in 1951, Bazley worked as a civil engineer and did his national service with the Royal Engineers, playing five times for the Army between 1954 and 1955. A quick attacking wing, he was a noted athlete and had success in the discus, javelin, cross-country running, and playing cricket in the North Lancashire League.

833. LABUSCHAGNE, Nicholas Arthur
Hooker 5 caps 1953-1955
Born: Durban, South Africa, 26 May 1931
Career: Cape Town, Cape Town University, Guy's Hospital, Harlequins, Barbarians, Middlesex, Western Province, Natal
Debut: v Wales, Cardiff Arms Park, Cardiff, 17 January 1953

South African-born Labuschagne's five caps for England came when he was at Harlequins and a dental student at Guy's Hospital. He owned his dental practice for 10 years before moving into retail management. He built up a huge portfolio and became chairman of Storeco, one of the southern hemisphere's largest chains and regional chairman of ABSA Bank. He then managed a chain of hotels in South Africa, including the Champagne Castle Hotel in the mountains of Drakensberg near Durban, and maintained a stable of racehorses. He helped form the South African Barbarians and worked for the South African rugby authorities building up to the 1995 World Cup.

834. REGAN, Martin
Fly-half 12 caps (3-1t) 1953-1956
Born: St Helens, Lancashire, 24 September 1929
Died: Warrington, Cheshire, 29 October 2014
Career: St Helens, Liverpool, Blackheath, Barbarians, Lancashire
Debut: v Wales, Cardiff Arms Park, 17 January 1953

Educated at West Park Grammar School in St Helens, Regan was a Liverpool player throughout his test career, which stretched from 1953, when he was a Championship winner, to 1956. He missed the 1955 tournament when Doug Baker played at fly-half. A PE teacher at St Edward's College in Liverpool, he worked for a food company before returning to teaching at St John's in Warrington when he played for Warrington RL club, which he joined in 1956. He played 64 times for Warrington, scoring 14 tries, staying there until 1961. He eventually became head of PE at St Anselm's College in Birkenhead, Merseyside, where he stayed for 22 years before retiring in 1991.

835. BUTTERFIELD, Jeff
Centre 28 caps (15-5t) 1953-1959
Born: Heckmondwike, 9 August 1929
Died: Wicken, Buckinghamshire, 30 April 2004
Career: Loughborough Colleges, Northampton, Barbarians, Yorkshire, British Lions
Debut: v France, Twickenham, February 1953

One of England's finest centres, Butterfield, played a then-record 28 successive tests in the midfield between 1953 and his last match, against Scotland in 1959. A Lions tourist in 1955, when he played in all four tests against the Springboks, he made 227 appearances for Northampton and captained Yorkshire. He taught at Wellingborough Grammar School in Northamptonshire before becoming a science master at Worksop College. He briefly worked in the paint industry and later opened the Rugby Club in London, which he and his wife, Barbara, ran for 25 years. He was president of Milton Keynes Rugby Club, helped develop rugby union in the Cayman Islands and produced one of the first coaching manuals released by the RFU.

836. WILSON, Dyson Stayt
Flanker 8 caps (12-4t) 1953-1955
Born: Wilderness, South Africa, 7 October 1926
Died: The Lizard, Cornwall, 20 April 2011
Career: Metropolitan Police, Harlequins, London Counties, Middlesex
Debut: v France, Twickenham, February 1953

'Tug' Wilson was a British Lion in 1955 and, at different times, an undercover policeman, fisherman, yachtsman, boxer, farmer and writer. His parents moved to England from South Africa when he was eight. His best year for England came in 1954 when he scored four tries in the Championship, then a record. After rugby, he ran two unsegregated restaurants in Rhodesia, the Curry House and the Bombay Duck and took a fair around the mining towns of Zambia before working on a fishing boat in Cornwall. He crossed the Atlantic twice in yachts before settling on a farm on the Lizard, where he raised cattle.

837. DAVIES, William Philip Cathcart
Centre 11 caps (3-1t) 1953-1958
Born: Abberley, Worcestershire, 6 August 1928
Died: Oxford, Oxfordshire, 25 January 2018
Career: Cambridge University, Cheltenham, Harlequins, Barbarians, Sussex, North Midlands, British Lions
Debut: v Scotland, Twickenham, March 1953

Davies was a strong running centre who excelled on the 1955 British Lions tour to South Africa, playing three tests, including the wins in Johannesburg, on his 27th birthday, and Pretoria. His England career continued until 1958, winning his third Championship, and he scored his only international in his penultimate match against Scotland that year. He continued playing until he was 50 and worked as a teacher, becoming a master at Smallwood Manor, Uttoxeter and Christ's Hospital before acting as head at Cheltenham College Junior School from 1964 to 1986. He was president of Cheltenham Rugby Club and was heavily involved in fundraising for charities for the disabled.

838. HIGGINS, Reginald
Flanker 13 caps (6-2t) 1954-1959
Born: Widnes, Lancashire, 11 July 1930
Died: Frodsham, Cheshire, 29 December 1979
Career: Leeds University, UAU, The Army, Combined Services, Liverpool, Barbarians, Lancashire, British Lions
Debut: v Wales, Twickenham, January 1954

Higgins, whose father Alec and uncle Fred were rugby league internationals, had played league before attending Wade Deacon High School in Widnes. The flanker was a member of England's 1957 Grand Slam-winning squad, but his international career was punctuated by injury. He captained Lancashire, completed his national service in the Royal Signals, representing the Army, and played for the British Lions in the first test against South Africa in 1955 at Ellis Park where he broke a leg. The England and Barbarians selector was a rep for BP and had been suffering from a nervous illness before shooting himself dead.

839. KING, Ian
Full-back 3 caps (5-1c,1p) 1954
Born: Leyburn, North Yorkshire, 5 May 1923
Died: Aylesbury, Buckinghamshire, 9 September 2002
Career: Harrogate, Yorkshire, R.V Stanley's XV
Debut: v Wales, Twickenham, January 1954

A County Championship winner with Yorkshire in 1953, whom he played for 51 times and captained for the 1949/50 season, King won three caps for England, and they came four years after having his first trial, scoring five points in his final test, the 14-3 win over Ireland. It shows the inconsistency of selection in the post-war years that he was the 10th full-back between 1947 and 1954 to win three or four caps. He played for Harrogate for a decade from 1947 to 1957, was educated at Loretto College in Manchester and worked as a salesman and a licensee.

840. QUINN, James Patrick
Centre 5 caps 1954
Born: Widnes, Lancashire, 19 February 1930
Died: Leicester, 18 January 1986, aged 55
Career: The Army, New Brighton, Harrogate, Barbarians, Hampshire, Lancashire, British Lions
Debut: v Wales, Twickenham, 16 January 1954

Quinn was a tough-tackling centre who went on the British Lions tour of South Africa in 1955 without playing a test, then turned to rugby league with Leeds a year later, winning the Challenge Cup in 1957. He had served in the Royal Military Police, representing them in the modern pentathlon before becoming a Liverpool PE teacher at De la Salle Grammar School, Cardinal Allen School, and Bootle College of Further Education. He also coached tennis and swimming and later reported on rugby for The Sunday Express and Radio Merseyside. He was killed in a car crash returning from an England v Wales international.

841. SANDERS, Donald Lewis
Prop 9 caps 1954-1956
Born: Fulham, London, 6 September 1924
Died: Ipswich, Suffolk, 25 October 2011
Career: Ipswich YMCA, Harlequins, Barbarians, London Counties, Eastern Counties
Debut: v Wales, Twickenham, January 1954

Sanders won nine caps in two seasons, but his playing career ended when he was 31, after he was involved in a motorcycle accident that left him in hospital for three months, with 30 fractures to his right leg, and in plaster for 13 months. He became an administrator, managing the England team that beat New Zealand in 1973 in Auckland, was a two-time British Lions selector and served as RFU Treasurer before becoming president. He was chairman of Ipswich YMCA and later president of his first club. Away from rugby, he worked for Shell-Mex and BP Ltd before becoming sales director of Tilcon, a Harrogate aggregate company.

842. YARRANTON, Sir Peter George KBE
Lock 5 caps 1954-1955
Born: Acton, London, 30 September 1924
Died: Teddington, London, 1 June 2003
Career: Wasps, RAF, Combined Services, Barbarians, London Counties, Middlesex
Debut: v Wales, Twickenham, January 1954

Yarranton won his final cap in 1955 before becoming a high-powered rugby and sports administrator. He joined the RAF in 1942, flying bombers in Burma, and took up rugby aged 24 when stationed in Yorkshire and won his first cap aged 29, captained Wasps and came out of retirement to play for the Barbarians in 1963 when nearly 40. He left the RAF to work for Shell Mex, specialising in industrial relations, before moving to the Lensbury Sports Club in Teddington. Yarranton was a PR advisor to the RFU President and worked the tannoy at the Middlesex Sevens. Knighted in 1992, he was the chairman of the Sports Council.

843. YOUNG, Peter Dalton
Lock 9 caps (3-1t) 1954-1955
Born: Bristol, 9 November 1927
Died: Eastbourne, Sussex, 23 May 2002
Career: Cambridge University, Clifton, Rosslyn Park, Dublin Wanderers, Gloucestershire
Debut: v Wales, Twickenham, January 1954

Young was the first player to lead England when based abroad after playing for Dublin Wanderers in Ireland for two games in the 1955 Five Nations Championship. The lock read geography at Pembroke College, Cambridge, played in the 1949 Varsity Match and later worked for Imperial Tobacco in Bristol, although he still turned out for Rosslyn Park. He was sent to Dublin by his employers in 1952, working in tobacco until 1958, moving into shipping with Palgrave Murphy and later founding Galway Ferries. He was chairman of the Irish Pony Club and ran the Dublin International Horse Show before working as chef d'equipe for the Irish three-day event team. In 1990, the Irish President, Mary Robinson, awarded him the Equestrian Federation of Ireland badge.

844. BANCE, John Forsyth
Lock, 1 cap 1954
Born: Kingsclere, Hampshire, 15 January 1925
Died: Ipswich, Suffolk, 19 June 2009
Career: Cambridge University, Bedford, East Midlands, Barbarians
Debut: v Scotland, Murrayfield, March 1954

A product of Radley College and Clare College, Cambridge University, where he read agriculture and was a blue, Bance played for Bedford when he made his only test appearance. The lock was 29 when he was drafted in for the 13-3 win over Scotland for an injured Peter Yarranton. He was a farmer in Wistow in Huntingdonshire for nearly 60 years and helped the East Midlands reach three County Championship finals in four years, winning the title in 1951. He served in World War Two in the Northumberland Fusiliers and later in the Korean War, leaving the army to concentrate on farming.

845. GIBBS, Nigel
Full-back 2 caps (4-2c) 1954
Born: Carrara, Italy, 24 September 1922
Died: Canford, Dorset, 26 May 2014
Career: Oxford University, Guildford & Godalming, Bristol, Harlequins, London Counties, Gloucestershire, Surrey
Debut: v Scotland, Murrayfield, March 1954

Gibbs was a full-back who won an Oxford blue at cricket but not rugby. While at Harlequins and aged 31, he kicked two conversions on his debut against Scotland in 1954, in a game England won 13-6 but he played only once more in the defeat to France that year. Mentioned in dispatches for his actions in the Second World War, when he served as a lieutenant in submarines in the RNVR. After the conflict, he held various teaching jobs, spending 12 years at Charterhouse before becoming the head teacher at Crewkerne School and Colston's School, then deputy head of North Foreland Lodge. His brother George was also an international.

846. LEADBETTER, Victor Hamilton
No.8 2 caps 1954
Born: Kettering, Northamptonshire, Q1 1930
Career: Cambridge University, Royal Signals, Northampton, Gloucester, Newport, Clifton, Edinburgh Wanderers, Edinburgh and Glasgow XV, Barbarians
Debut: v Scotland, Murrayfield, March 1954

Leadbetter was a two-time Cambridge blue and was picked for England while playing for Edinburgh and working for an Iron and steel firm in the west of Scotland. He played twice in the 1954 Championship, including the Calcutta Cup win, when he came in for the injured John Kendall-Carpenter at number 8. He retained his place but was at lock for the defeat against France. A long spell of injuries the following season cost him more caps. He worked for Stewarts and Lloyd, owned an iron and steel company, VHL Ltd and was a director of Avon Gorge Estate Management Ltd based in Bristol.

847. ROBINSON, Ernest Frederick
Hooker 4 caps 1954-1961
Born: Coventry, Warwickshire, 17 January 1926
Died: Coventry, Warwickshire, 2 July 1993
Career: Broadstreet, Coventry, Barbarians
Debut: v Scotland, Murrayfield, March 1954

Robinson made his England debut when Eric Evans was injured in 1954 after he joined Coventry teammates John Gardiner and Stan Adkins for his first trial match. He became England's forgotten man having to wait seven years for his second cap displacing Stan Hodgson for an 11-8 defeat in Ireland. An engineer, he followed his brother Ivor into the middle of Coventry's front row. He went on to serve Coventry as chairman of selectors, playing administrator in the 70s, while his cousin Barry was finance and company secretary at the club. Robinson's wife, Elsie, celebrated her 100th birthday in 2021.

848. WILLIAMS, John Edward
Scrum-half, 9 caps (3-1t) 1954-1965
Born: Leeds, West Yorkshire, 31 January 1932
Died: Sandhurst, Berkshire, 5 October 2009
Career: Old Millhillians, The Army, Headingley, Harlequins, Sale, Barbarians, Middlesex, Cheshire, London Counties, British Lions
Debut: v France, Stade Colombes, Paris, April 1954

Williams won his first eight caps between 1954 and 1956, scoring a try against Scotland in 1956, but mainly because of the emergence of Dickie Jeeps, had to wait until 1965 for his ninth and final appearance. He was a tourist with the British Lions in South Africa in 1955, and although he played eight games, scoring five tries, he did not play a test. Jeeps again kept him out of the side, playing in all four. He had served in the Army before working in the paper trade in London. He became a business agent and died after battling Alzheimer's.

849. BAKER, Douglas George Santley
Fly-half, 4 caps 1955
Born: Las Palmas, Canary Islands, 29 November 1929
Died: Sydney, Australia, 21 December 2022
Career: Oxford University, Old Merchant Taylors, Barbarians, London Counties, East Midlands, Middlesex, British Lions
Debut: v Wales, Cardiff, 22 January 1955

Baker, the only England player born in the Canary Islands, won all four caps as a fly-half in the 1955 championship and played two test matches on the epic 1955 British Lions tour to South Africa, which the tourists drew 2-2. His appearances against the Springboks included the 9-3 third test win in Pretoria, where he operated at full-back. He captained Old Merchant Taylors, and Middlesex, was a schoolmaster at RGS High Wycombe and then Oundle School. He also worked for a fuel company and later emigrated to Australia, where he taught at Scotch College in Adelaide.

850. HANCOCK, William Jack Henry
Lock 2 caps 1955
Born: Newport, Monmouthshire, 26 September 1932
Died: 16 November 2011
Career: The Army, Royal Signals, Cross Keys, Newport
Debut: v Wales, Cardiff Arms Park, Cardiff, January 1955

Hancock was a lock with a boot good enough to kick 53 conversions and 26 penalties in 79 games for Newport and Cross Keys combined and was at the former club when he made his two England appearances in 1955, in a defeat to Wales and a draw with Ireland. Ironically, he rejected an invitation for a Welsh trial to try out for England, but within a year, he went north to rugby league with Salford, where he stayed until 1960, playing 104 games. He had been in the Royal Signals, played union for the Army, and worked for the chemical company ICI.

851. HASTINGS, George William
Prop 12 caps (11-1t, 1c, 2p) 1955-1958
Born: Dursley, 7 November 1924
Died: Lincolnshire, 30 December 2019
Career: Gloucester, Barbarians, Gloucestershire, Western Counties
Debut: v Wales, Cardiff, January 1955

Hastings was educated at Cheltenham Grammar School and spent 13 seasons with Gloucester. He was in the England side that claimed a Grand Slam in 1957 and a year later when his penalty against Scotland helped retain the title. He missed out on the Lions tours of 1950 and 1955 but played more than 20 times for the Barbarians. He captained Gloucestershire and was a County Championship Finalist in 1959. He was an aircraft draughtsman during the Second World War and then worked for the Coal Board in Cardiff before moving to Lincolnshire, where he and his wife, Jean, ran hotels in Horncastle and Boston.

852. HAZELL, David St George
Prop 4 caps (9-3p) 1955
Born: Taunton, Somerset, 23 April 1931
Died: Taunton, Somerset, 26 May 2007
Career: Loughborough Colleges, Leicester, Bristol, Barbarians, Leicestershire, Somerset, Western Counties
Debut: v Wales, Cardiff, January 1955

Educated at Taunton School, Hazell was a goal-kicking prop who scored 265 points in 81 games for Leicester before joining Bristol in 1956 when he returned to his old school to take up a teaching post. He landed a goal in England's 9-6 win over France in the last of his four caps in 1955, and between 1956 and 1964, he made 241 appearances for Bristol and captained Somerset. At Taunton School, he taught PE and maths and was the master in charge of rugby and cricket. He passed away in a Taunton nursing home in 2007.

853. RYAN, Peter Henry
Flanker 2 caps 1955
Born: Bucklow, Cheshire, 1 October 1930
Career: Cambridge University, Richmond, Barbarians, London Counties, Middlesex
Debut: v Wales, Cardiff Arms Park, January 1955

Ryan won both his caps in 1955, a defeat to Wales as one of six England debutants, and a 6-6 draw with Ireland when he played at Richmond. Educated at Harrow School, where he played in the cricket match against Eton in 1949, he went to Cambridge University, attending Gonville & Caius College, winning a blue in 1952 and 1953, before becoming involved in the business. He held several directorships in aviation, where he was chairman of Dan-Air and in recruitment. He also served as the secretary of the Rugby International Golf Society and retired to Switzerland.

854. TAYLOR, Philip Joseph
No.8 6 caps 1955-1962
Born: Wakefield, Yorkshire, 6 June 1931
Died: 23 October 2019
Career: Wakefield, Duke of Wellington's Regiment, The Army, Blackheath, Loughborough Colleges, Northampton, Barbarians, Yorkshire, Hertfordshire
Debut: v Wales, Cardiff Arms Park, January 1955

'Noddy' Taylor, also a keen water polo player, won six caps stretching between 1955 and 1962 with a seven-year gap mainly because Alan Ashcroft was playing at No.8. After playing for Wakefield and doing national service with the Duke of Wellington's Regiment, he played 224 times for Northampton, captaining them from 1961 to 1963, and continued to represent Yorkshire in the County Championship. He taught history and PE at Northampton Grammar School before retiring to Spain, with his wife Irene, where they lived for over 10 years before returning to England to live in Barnard Castle near Durham.

855. BEER, Ian David Stafford CBE
No.8 2 caps (3-1t) 1955
Born: Croydon, London, 28 April 1931
Career: Cambridge University, Harlequins, Bath, Shropshire, Dorset & Wiltshire
Debut: v France, Twickenham, February 1955

Whitgift-educated Beer served in the Royal Fusiliers and played twice for England in the 1955 Championship when his club side was Harlequins. After leaving Cambridge University, he became a teacher and was head of Ellesmere College, aged 29, before working at Lancing College and becoming head at Harrow, retiring in 1991. He was President of the RFU when the game struggled to get to grips with imminent professionalism and chaired an RFU review into promotion and relegation. He was chairman of The Head Masters' Conference, the Physical Education for National Curriculum Committee, and the Independent Schools Council.

856. SCOTT, Harry
Full-back 1 cap 1955
Born: Batley, Yorkshire, 7 November 1926
Died: Dublin, Ireland, 21 January 2012
Career: Eccles, US Portsmouth, US Chatham, Manchester, Lancashire, North-West Counties
Debut: v France, Twickenham, February 1955

A stalwart of Eccles, Manchester and Lancashire, Scott won his only cap in the 16-9 defeat to France at Twickenham in 1955, where he took the place of 'Nim' Hall after his only trial. He played for Manchester for 13 seasons and a decade for Lancashire, for whom he made 46 appearances. He recovered from a cracked fibula to become a County Championship finalist in 1954 and was a winner a season later. He was an engineering draughtsman by trade and worked as a forge and machine shop manager. His father Bobby was a member of Swinton's best-ever rugby league sides.

857. SYKES, Frank Douglas
Wing, 4 caps (3-1t) 1955-1963
Born: Batley, Yorkshire, 9 December 1927
Died: Seattle, USA, 17 May 2017
Career: Huddersfield, Northampton, Boston (US), Yorkshire, British Lions
Debut: v France, Twickenham, February 1955

Sykes had an international career for two halves, winning two caps for England in 1955 and two more on England's tour of Australia and New Zealand in 1963. He was also a British Lion on the epic tour of South Africa in 1955, playing 14 games but no test matches. The wing taught geography and sport at Northampton Grammar School before heading to the United States to teach at Cambridge High School in Boston. He then worked at Cate School in Southern California, playing and coaching at Santa Barbara RFC for 30 years. He settled in Seattle but was a regular at Franklin's Gardens on trips home into his mid-80s.

858. ESTCOURT, Noel Sidney Dudley
Full-back 1 cap 1955
Born: Ralolia, Rhodesia, 7 January 1929
Died: Exeter, Devon, 7 January 2018
Career: Rhodes University, Eastern Province, Cambridge University, Blackheath, Barbarians
Debut: v Scotland, Twickenham, March 1955

Rhodesian-born Estcourt was a Blackheath player when he won his sole England cap in the 9-6 win over the Scots in 1955. Before heading to Cambridge University, he was educated at Plumtree School in Matabeleland, then Rhodes University in Grahamstown, South Africa. He did not win a rugby blue at Cambridge University, despite reportedly practising his kicking for 90 minutes before every match, but he did get two in cricket. A schoolteacher, he returned home shortly after his test debut to teach in Gwelo, becoming principal of Domboshawa Training Centre and then a regional director for the education head office in Mashonaland.

859. ALLISON, Dennis Fenwick
Full-back, 7 caps (15-5p) 1956-1958
Born: Tynemouth, North Tyneside, 20 April 1931
Died: Leeds, West Yorkshire, 13 April 2009
Career: Durham University, Northern, Northumberland, Coventry, Warwickshire, Barbarians
Debut: v Wales, Twickenham, January 1956

Allison, a member of England's Grand Slam-winning side of 1957, played for Northern and Northumberland while studying to be a metallurgist at King's Newcastle. He moved to Coventry to win his seven caps as a left-footed place-kicker. Allison struggled with knee ligament problems throughout his career, but led Warwickshire to a 1958 County Championship final victory at Coundon Road, Coventry. He worked for IMI in Birmingham during his time in the Midlands before moving to Leeds, working for Marston Radiators, where he coached Roundhay. His son-in-law, Ian Metcalfe, was also an England full-back.

860. ASHCROFT, Alan
No.8 16 caps (3-1t) 1956-1959
Born: St Helens, Lancashire, 21 August 1930
Died: St Helens, Lancashire, 26 January 2021
Career: RAF, St Helens, Waterloo, British Lions, Lancashire
Debut: v Wales, Twickenham, January 1956

'Ned' Ashcroft, England's 1957 Grand Slam-winning No.8, started playing rugby at Cowley Grammar School and captained Waterloo's sixth team well into his fifties. England's selectors controversially ended his international career in 1959 when he toured with the British Lions to Australia and New Zealand, playing tests against the Wallabies in Brisbane and the All Blacks in Wellington. An art master at Liverpool College, becoming headmaster, he later ran a garden business with his wife Patsy in Ormskirk, just outside Liverpool. In 2018, when he was 88, he became one of the oldest British Lions to be presented with a ceremonial cap by his friend Ray French.

The English Rugby Who's Who

Lewis Cannell

Jeff Butterfield

Dickie Jeeps

Frank Sykes

861. CURRIE, John David
Lock 25 caps (16-2c,4p) 1956-1962
Born: Clifton, Bristol, 3 May 1932
Died: Leicester, Leicestershire, 8 December 1990
Career: Oxford University, Harlequins, Bristol, Gosforth, Northumberland, Somerset, Barbarians
Debut: v Wales, Twickenham, January 1956

A goal-kicking lock who partnered David Marques in 22 consecutive internationals, Currie, nicknamed 'Muscles', played for Clifton while still at Bristol Grammar School in 1950-51. He won four blues at Oxford when studying at Wadham College and collected his first eight caps as a student. He played one first-class cricket match for Somerset, turned out for Gloucestershire seconds, was an England selector and Harlequins chairman. He worked for WD and HO Wills, then went into business in Maidenhead running employment and recruitment agency MKA Search International, died of a heart attack while driving up the M1 to Loughborough in a blizzard to pick up his son.

862. JACKSON, Peter
Wing 20 caps (18-6t) 1956-1963
Born: Birmingham, 22 September 1930
Died: Solihull, 22 March 2004
Career: Old Edwardians, The army, Aldershot Services, North Midlands, Coventry, British Lions
Debut: v Wales, Twickenham, January 1956

Peter Jackson was a key member of England's 1957 Grand Slam-winning squad, scoring three tries, but it wasn't until scoring a brilliant 30-yard match-winning try against Australia at Twickenham in February 1958 when England were down to 14 men that he achieved legendary status. It helped earn him a place on the Lions tour to Australia and New Zealand a year later when he scored a record 19 tries. Jackson lost his England place to Olympic sprinter John Young in 1960, and it took him three years to win it back, helping them win another Five Nations Championship. He ran an export packing business and served Coventry as fixture secretary, club secretary and president.

863. JACOBS, Charles Ronald
Prop 29 caps 1956-1964
Born: Whittlesey, Cambridgeshire, 28 October 1928
Died: Whittlesey, Cambridgeshire, November 2002
Career: Nottingham University, Peterborough, Northampton, East Midlands, Barbarians
Debut: v Wales, Twickenham, January 1956

Jacobs was a front-row legend of England and Northampton, spending 17 years at Franklin's Gardens, playing 470 games for the club and winning 29 England caps, a Grand Slam in 1957 and the Championship a year later. Known as 'The Badger' because of his scrummaging technique, he studied agriculture at Nottingham University and ran his family farm, selling milk from a churn even when he was a famous international. Business commitments meant he missed out on three British Lions' tours. He was RFU President, a selector and manager of the controversial tour to South Africa in 1984.

864. JEEPS, Richard Eric Gautrey CBE
Scrum-half 24 caps 1956-1962
Born: Chesterton, Staffordshire, 25 November 1931
Died: Newmarket, Suffolk, 8 October 2016
Career: Cambridge University, Northampton, London Counties, Eastern Counties, British Lions
Debut: v Wales, Twickenham, January 1956

Dickie Jeeps was a huge figure in English rugby, from his debut in 1956 to his term as RFU President, aged 44 and as Chairman of the Sports Council. He toured South Africa with the British Lions in 1955, playing four tests, before being capped by England and playing 13 tests for the Lions, a record for an Englishman. His first Lions tour came after he impressed Cliff Morgan in a club match, and the Welsh fly-half lobbied for his inclusion. A Grand Slam winner in 1957, he also played football for Cambridge City, ran a fruit farm in Cambridge, and had interests in a restaurant, Stock's.

865. MARQUES, Reginald William David Marques
Lock 23 caps (3-1t) 1956-1961
Born: Ware, Hertfordshire, 9 December 1932
Died: Ware, Hertfordshire, 29 September 2010
Career: Cambridge University, Royal Engineers, Barbarians, Harlequins, British Lions, Army, Combined Services, Hertfordshire, Surrey
Debut: v Wales, Twickenham, January 1956

At 6ft 5in, Marques was big for his era and played a then-record 22 consecutive times with his fellow Harlequin John Currie between 1956 and 1961. The pair helped England to the 1957 Grand Slam and 1958 Championship, but only Marques made the British Lions trip to Australia and New Zealand in 1959, where he played two tests against the Wallabies and All Blacks at No.8. He went to Tonbridge School alongside the future England cricket captain Colin Cowdrey and worked in his family business making streetlights. He was a member of the 1964 America's Cup challenger team aboard the Sovereign and served as a magistrate and churchwarden.

866. ROBBINS, Peter George Derek
Flanker 19 caps 1956-1962
Born: Coventry, Warwickshire, 21 September 1933
Died: Edgbaston, Birmingham, 25 March 1987
Career: Oxford University, Moseley, Coventry, Barbarians, Warwickshire
Debut: v Wales, Twickenham, January 1956

Robbins taught French and Latin at King Edward's School in Birmingham after leaving St Edmund Hall, Oxford, where he won rugby blues between 1954 and 1957. He served his national service in the RAF and later set up his own cleaning company. A flanker, he won his first 12 caps as a student and was picked for the British Lions tour to Australia and New Zealand in 1959 but missed the trip with a broken leg. He was chairman of the Belfry Sporting Club and wrote about rugby for The Financial Times and The Observer before his premature death from a brain haemorrhage.

867. SMITH, Michael John Knight OBE
Fly-half 1 cap 1956
Born: Broughton Abbey, Leicestershire, 30 June 1933
Career: Oxford University, Hinkley, Leicester, Leicestershire, Barbarians
Debut: v Wales, Twickenham, January 1956

Smith played once for England as a fly-half in the 8-3 defeat against Wales in 1956 and got most of the blame as he never won another cap. He had a highly successful cricket career for Leicestershire, Warwickshire and England, playing 50 tests, captaining England 25 times and scoring over 2,000 test runs and 69 first-class centuries. He was a cricket administrator, the general manager of a ground staff company, the chairman of Warwickshire and a match referee. He was awarded the OBE for services to cricket and England's last double international. His son Neil played seven one-day internationals for England, and his daughter Carole married Sebastian Coe.

868. THOMPSON, Peter Humphrey
Wing 17 caps (15-5t) 1956-1959
Born: Scarborough, Yorkshire, 18 January 1929
Career: Headingley, Waterloo, Barbarians, Yorkshire
Debut: v Wales, Twickenham, January 1956

Thompson played all four games in the 1957 Grand Slam-winning campaign, scoring a try in the final match against Scotland at Twickenham after warming up by scoring five tries for the Barbarians in the 1956 Christmas clash with Leicester. He captained Headingley in 1956-57, the campaign when he was a County championship finalist with Yorkshire. He helped England retain their Championship in 1958 and skippered the side in 1959. He was a sales manager working for Nestle, living in Sussex, and is one of the last surviving members of the 1957 Grand Slam-winning side.

869. BARTLETT, Richard Michael
Fly-half, 7 caps 1957-1958
Born: Kingston, London, 13 February 1929
Died: Liss, Hampshire, 6 March 1984
Career: Cambridge University, Harlequins, Barbarians, Surrey
Debut: v Wales, Twickenham, January 1957

Bartlett was a running fly-half who played near the gain line, setting up try-scoring opportunities for the backs outside him, and played for Harlequins when he was still at school. He captained the club for five seasons between 1954 and 1959, and in 2004 was elected to the Harlequin FC Hall of Fame. Never on the losing side for England, he worked in insurance, as a pig farmer and was a master at Millfield School. After finishing top-class rugby, he continued to captain the Quins A XV, was the president of Surrey RFC in 1981 and served as a Quins and England selector.

870. CHALLIS, Robert
Full-back 3 caps (10-2c,2p)
Born: Long Ashton, Somerset, 9 March 1932
Died: Weston-super-Mare, North Somerset, 12 May 2000
Career: Bristol Cathedralians, Bristol, Somerset, Western Counties
Debut: v Ireland, Lansdowne Road, Dublin, February 1957

Challis, a 1957 Grand Slam-winning side member, was a Bristol full-back who caused a stir on his debut in Dublin when he elected to use place-kicks to find touch from penalties. He is thought to be the first player to do that. It worked as England won 6-0, thanks to a Challis penalty and a Peter Jackson try. He won his first cap after Fenwick Allison broke his arm and managed to oversleep before his debut. A good enough cricketer to play for Somerset Second XI, he worked as a sales representative for a builders merchant and an industrial doors manufacturer.

871. HORROCKS-TAYLOR, John Philip
Fly-half 9 caps (3-1p) 1958-1964
Born: Halifax, West Yorkshire, 27 October 1934
Died: Middlesbrough, North Yorkshire, 11 February 2021
Career: Cambridge University, Halifax, Wasps, Leicester, Middlesbrough, Barbarians, Yorkshire, British Lions
Debut: v Wales, Twickenham, January 1958

Horrocks-Taylor toured with the Lions to New Zealand in 1959, playing in one test in Christchurch the year after his England debut. An elusive fly-half, he was a student at Cambridge University, at St John's College, after national service with the Royal Signals, where he won two blues before his first international cap. The presence of Bev Risman, then Richard Sharp, limited his opportunities to just nine tests for England in six years, although he toured New Zealand and Australia with England in 1963. He was a director of building products and brick manufacturing firms.

872. SYRETT, Ronald Edward
Flanker 11 caps (3-1t) 1958-1962
Born: Amersham, Buckinghamshire, 5 January 1931
Died: Beaconsfield, Buckinghamshire, 20 May 2018
Career: Wasps, RAF, London Counties, Barbarians, Middlesex
Debut: v Wales, Twickenham, January 1958

Wasps flanker Syrett scored a try in the 21-12 win over Scotland that sealed the Triple Crown in 1960. He missed the 1961 season but was recalled to win his final three caps in 1962 when England were disappointing. The brother-in-law of another England player and fellow product of High Wycombe RFC, Ted Woodward, he started his working life away from rugby in the family's butchering business after attending RGS High Wycombe. He then went into sports retailing, became a director at Hawkinsport Ltd, and served as president of the Buckinghamshire Referees Society.

873. HETHERINGTON, James Gilbert George
Full-back 6 caps (9-3p) 1958-1959
Born: Brighton, East Sussex, 3 March 1932
Career: Trojans, Cambridge University, Northampton, Territorial Army, R V. STANLEY'S XV, Saracens, Rosslyn Park, Hampshire, East Midlands
Debut: v Australia, Twickenham, February 1958

Hetherington, educated at Churcher's College in Hampshire and Greenock Academy, played football when invited to make up the numbers in Don White's end-of-season charity match in Kettering. Within months he was in Northampton's first team and played for Hampshire in the County Championship and the following year, in 1955, won a Cambridge blue. He worked for a Northampton engineering company when he replaced Fenwick Allison to win his first cap, but concussions in his first two appearances forced him into retirement within two years. He attempted a comeback at a junior-level Saracens, and Rosslyn Park, later became a management consultant and executive search consultant with Boyden International Ltd.

874. PHILLIPS, Malcolm Stanley
Centre 25 caps (16-5t) 1958-1964
Born: Prestbury, Cheshire, 3 March 1936
Career: Oxford University, Blackpool, Fylde, Barbarians, Lancashire
Debut: v Australia, Twickenham, February 1958

Phillips, whose father Joe was a stalwart of Oldham rugby league club in the 1920s, won 23 of his 25 caps in the centre and two on the wing and was a blue for Oxford University. A student on his try-scoring international debut, he was the record cap holder for England. He worked for a paint company, became involved in rugby administration in the north of England, served as a test selector and on the committee of the Barbarians. The RFU President in 2004/05 spent much of his year in the office putting out political fires and was also a member of the IRB.

875. YOUNG, John Robert Chester CBE
Wing 9 caps (6-2t) 1958-1961
Born: Upton, Chester, 6 September 1937
Died: Dorking, Surrey, 19 March 2020
Career: Oxford University, Harlequins, Barbarians, London Counties, Warwickshire, Surrey, British Lions
Debut: v Ireland, Twickenham, February 1958

Young, who played one test on the 1959 British Lions tour to Australia and New Zealand, was a two-time blue at Oxford and ran 100 metres in 9.6 seconds, although injury stopped him from competing in the 1956 Olympics. A Championship winner in 1958, he qualified as a barrister in 1961 but switched from the law to join Simon Coates, the London stock brokerage. A member of the London Stock Exchange, he was an England selector and rose to become chief executive of the Security and Futures Authority and worked on numerous financial bodies.

876. HERBERT, Albert John
Flanker 6 caps 1958-1959
Born: Stroud, Gloucestershire, 1 January 1933
Career: Marling School, Cheltenham, Cambridge University, RAF, Wasps, East Midlands
Debut: v France, Stade Colombes, March 1958

Herbert won international schoolboy honours during his education at Marling School and played for the RAF during his national service. He won three blues at Cambridge between 1954 and 1956 and joined Wasps before working for ICI and then teaching at Fettes College. Herbert had been a reserve for two games before getting his first cap as a replacement for Peter Robbins for a 14-0 win over France, their biggest win over Les Bleus since 1914. After helping England retain their Championship crown, his career stalled with almost two years on the sidelines with a knee injury he suffered against Cardiff in November 1959. He moved to Australia, where he taught at Geelong Grammar School in Victoria.

877. SCOTT, John Stanley Marshall
Full-back 1 cap 1958
Born: Birkenhead, Wirral, 23 January 1935
Died: Kensington, London, 13 January 2020
Career: Birkenhead Park, Oxford University, Harlequins, London Counties, Cheshire
Debut: v France, Stade Colombes, March 1958

Scott, a solicitor, won his only cap in 1958 but played an international for Malaya against Thailand while serving with the 10th Gurkha Rifles on national service. He was also a member of the America's Cup challenger Sovereign crew in 1964 alongside several Quins teammates. A product of Radley College, he played for England as a student at Oxford University, winning two blues in 1957 and 1958. A vehement anti-European Union campaigner, he was the director of a property consultancy, Brathew Ltd. He was often found at Speakers' Corner and founded the Notting Hill Gate Improvement Trust to co-ordinate conservation in the area.

878. BENDON, Gordon John
Prop 4 caps
Born: Lambeth, London, 9 April 1929
Died: Kingston-upon-Thames, **** January 2001
Career: Esher, Wasps, RAF, London Counties, Eastern Counties, Middlesex, Surrey
Debut: v Wales, Cardiff, January 1959

One of six new caps on his debut against Wales, prop Bendon, educated at King's College, Wimbledon, was ever-present during the 1959 Championship, representing his entire international career. Bendon also played for the combined England-Scotland team against Wales-Ireland in the 1959 Jubilee match at Twickenham. A Wasps stalwart, he played for the club for over 20 years and was later a Middlesex selector. He worked as a sales rep and joined the board of sherry shippers Williams & Humbert International as marketing director, a post he also held with Campari. He married actress Adrienne Scott, with novelist Jackie Collins a bridesmaid.

879. RISMAN, Augustus Beverley Walter
Fly-half 8 caps (8-1c,2p) 1959-1961
Born: Salford, 23 November 1937
Died: 22 June 2023
Career: Loughborough Colleges, Manchester University, UAU, Cumberland, Lancashire, British Lions
Debut: v Wales, Cardiff Arms Park, Cardiff, January 1959

Risman was born in Salford but raised in Cumbria, and later returned north to serve as chairman at Carlisle. Son of Gus Risman, the famous Wales and Salford rugby league player, he played two seasons of international union before following in his father's footsteps and signing for Leigh in March 1961. He later played league for Leeds and won five caps for Great Britain. A schoolmaster, he won six of eight caps at fly-half and toured Australia and New Zealand with the British Lions in 1959, playing three tests before injuring his ankle ahead of the second against the All Blacks. He recovered to play the final international of the trip. He was RFL President in 2010, helped establish student rugby league, managed Fulham and became a director at London Broncos.

880. SMITH, Stephen Rider
Scrum-half 5 caps 1959-1964
Born: Madras, India, 21 October 1934
Died: Oxford, Oxfordshire, 9 August 2010
Career: Cambridge University, Aldershot Services, Richmond, Hampshire, Barbarians
Debut: v Wales, Cardiff Arms Park, Cardiff, January 1959

Smith was born to missionary parents in India before moving to England after the Second World War, studying at Eltham College, then Cambridge University, where he read geography and was captain in the 1959 Varsity Match. After winning five caps he taught at Harrow for five years before returning to India to work as a missionary, playing for the Indian rugby team against Ceylon in 1968. Returning to England he briefly became a housemaster at Birkenhead School before taking up the headship at Caterham School, eventually retiring from teaching. In later life, he organised his local United Reform Church in Sussex and then in Marlow.

881. WACKETT, John Arthur Sibley
Hooker 2 caps 1959
Born: Hatfield, Hertfordshire, 27 September 1930
Career: Welwyn, Rosslyn Park, Hertfordshire, Southern Counties
Debut: v Wales, Cardiff Arms Park, Cardiff, January 1959

Wackett was at Rosslyn Park when he won his two caps in 1959, packing down next to prop Larry Webb, with whom he formed an investment business and radio production company and was later a director of Sealine Business Products in Hertford. He was replaced at hooker by Herbert Godwin after the 3-0 win over Ireland and never played another test but continued his career with Rosslyn Park. The hooker was shocked on his debut when the RFU told him that he could have a blazer badge or a cap, so he took the cap. He regularly visited Old Albanians into his eighties when he lived in Wheathampstead.

882. WEBB, St Lawrence Hugh
Prop 4 caps 1959
Born: Melbourne, Australia, 7 March 1931
Died: At sea, 30 May 1978
Career: Bedford, Aldershot Services, Blackheath, Royal Engineers, Barbarians, Hertfordshire
Debut: v Wales, Cardiff Arms Park, Cardiff, January 1959

Webb, ever-present in the 1959 Championship and the business partner of hooker John Wackett, saw his test career end when he was a late withdrawal against Wales in 1960 to let in Ron Jacobs for a long run in the team. The loosehead originally played in the back row and played 309 games for Bedford, who named the Larry Webb Room at Bedford RFC in his honour. A millionaire who sold his plant hire firm to Bovis and became the chairman of Goldington Investments, died when the helicopter he was piloting went missing over the English Channel. His grandson is former England and Harlequins prop Will Collier.

883. WIGHTMAN, Brian John
No. 8 5 caps 1959-1963
Born: Birmingham, 23 September 1936
Died: Auckland, New Zealand, 29 November 1999
Career: Loughborough Collages, UAU, Moseley, Coventry, Rosslyn Park, North Midlands, British Lions
Debut: v Wales, Cardiff Arms Park, Cardiff, January 1959

'Yeti' Wightman won his first cap while at Moseley and then four more after moving on to Coventry. The No.8, who worked as a schoolteacher, emigrated to Canada in 1964, where he was a player/coach at Wisconsin RFC and the University of British Columbia. He moved to Fiji to take a post with the education department working in sports development. Wightman was honorary secretary general of the Fiji Association of Sports and National Olympic Committee, then president. He worked as chef de mission for various Fijian teams. On retirement, he moved to New Zealand and he was posthumously awarded the Fiji Olympic Order.

884. CLEMENTS, Jeffrey E Woodward
Flanker 3 caps 1959
Born: Wincanton, Somerset, 18 August 1932
Died: Bramley, Surrey, 4 October 1986
Career: Old Cranleighans, Cambridge University, Royal Navy, Devonport Services, US Portsmouth, Barbarians, Hampshire
Debut: v Ireland, Lansdowne Road, Dublin, February 1959

A Cambridge blue for three years from 1953, captaining the side in 1955, after going to the university from Cranleigh

School, Clements was playing for his old boys' side when he won his three caps in 1959. The flanker had been warned that his loyalty to Old Cranleighans would hamper his international aspirations but stayed at the club. He was the only Old Cranleighan to win a blue from the Second World War until Harry Lamont achieved the feat in 2012. He was also a schoolmaster at Cranleigh, then went into business in South East Asia, where he played cricket for Singapore and Malaysia.

885. GODWIN, Herbert
Hooker 11 caps 1959-1967
Born: Abergavenny, Wales, 21 December 1935
Died: Teignbridge, Devon, 7 January 2006
Career: Coventry, the Army, Combined Services, Barbarians, Warwickshire, British Lions
Debut: v France, Twickenham, February 1959

Godwin was part of a feared Coventry front-row, along with Phil Judd and Mike McLean, in the late 1950s and early 1960s but won just 11 caps over eight years. He originally turned down the chance to tour with the British Lions in 1962 because he could not afford to lose his salary as a toolmaker at Massey Ferguson. However, when Stan Hodgson broke a leg in the first game of the trip, he was summoned to South Africa, where he made nine appearances without playing a test. He estimated the tour had cost him £400. He later ran a guest house in Devon.

886. HODGSON, Stanley Arthur Murray MBE
Hooker 11 caps 1960-1964
Born: Durham, County Durham, 14 May 1928
Died: Durham, County Durham, 25 March 2015
Career: Durham City, Durham County, Barbarians, British Lions
Debut: v Wales, Twickenham, January 1960

Hooker Hodgson was a legend in Durham who played competitively until he was nearly 60 and was 31 when he made his England debut in 1960. With the Lions in South Africa two years later, he broke his leg in the first game of the trip, against Rhodesia in Bulawayo, but was asked to stay on for the remainder of the tour because he was such an influential squad member. He was a maintenance fitter at Mackay's carpet factory in Durham for his entire working life, and a fitness fanatic, and even a broken leg in his 50s did not stop him from playing.

887. MORGAN, William George Derek
No.8 9 caps 1960-1961
Born: Newport, Wales, 30 November 1935
Career: Newbridge, Medicals, Percy Park, Monmouthshire, Northumberland, Barbarians
Debut: v Wales, Twickenham, January 1960

Born in Wales but with an English father, Morgan attended Pengam Grammar School, which produced Wales and British Lions captain John Dawes, before studying dentistry at Durham University. He had played for Welsh Secondary Schools, then captained Durham and English Universities whilst starring for Northumberland. He made his debut, ironically against Wales, in 1960, but a knee injury ultimately ended his career. He was chairman of UAU rugby for 26 years, an England selector and a tour manager to Argentina, South Africa and New Zealand. He became a Student RFU rep on the RFU council and was president of the RFU in 2002.

888. ROBERTS, James
Wing, 18 caps (18-6t) 1960-1964
Born: Liverpool, Lancashire, 25 June 1932
Died: Thaxted, Essex, 1 November 2020
Career: Cambridge University, Old Millhillians, Sale, Middlesex, Barbarians
Debut: v Wales, Twickenham, January 1960

Roberts studied engineering at Christ's College, Cambridge, winning blues at centre and on the wing. He scored two tries on his international bow against Wales after his wife had told him to give up dreaming of playing for England as he was 28, but he turned on the radio and heard he had been picked for his debut. Roberts played in the County Championship finals of 1955 and 1956 when he scored a try on the win over Devon. Roberts won a Triple Crown in 1960 and a Championship outright in 1963 and was sales director at vending machine manufacturers Weston Evans before becoming managing director of Booth Dispensers.

889. RUTHERFORD, Donald OBE
Full-back 14 caps (36-6c, 8p) 1960-1967
Born: Tynemouth, Tyne & Wear, 22 September 1937
Died: Penzance, Cornwall, 12 November 2016
Career: St Luke's College, RAF, Combined Services, Percy Park, Wasps, Gloucester, Northumberland. Gloucestershire, British Lions
Debut: v Wales, Twickenham, January 1960

Rutherford trained as a PE teacher at the famous St Luke's College, Exeter, and had an England trial in 1958 but had to wait two years for his debut. He was ever-present in the 1965 and 1966 Championships and went on the 1966 British Lions tour to Australia and New Zealand, playing in the Sydney test against the Wallabies. He taught at Wycliffe College in Stonehouse, but a second broken arm forced him to retire in 1968, and a year later, he was appointed technical director of the Rugby Union, the RFU's first professional appointment. He stayed at Twickenham until 1999. He was awarded the OBE in 2000.

890. SHARP, Richard Adrian William OBE
Fly-half, 14 caps (26–2t,4c,1p,3d)
Born: Mysore, India, 9 September 1938
Career: Oxford University, Redruth, Wasps, Bristol, Cornwall, Royal Navy, British Lions
Debut: v Wales, Twickenham, January 1960

A glamourous fly-half, Sharp, inspired the dashing character Sharpe in the Bernard Cornwell novels. He was educated at Blundell's School and Balliol College, at Oxford University, and during his national service years, he served in the Royal Marines. He led England to their Championships win in 1963, scoring one of Twickenham's greatest tries, a 50-yard effort against Scotland. A British Lion in South Africa in 1962, where he played two tests and suffered a broken jaw, he retired when he was 27. He taught geography at Sherborne School in Dorset, wrote on rugby for The Sunday Telegraph and worked in the china clay industry.

891. WESTON, Michael Philip
Centre/fly-half 29 caps (6-1t,1d) 1960-1968
Born: Durham, County Durham, 21 August 1938
Died: 24 December 2024
Career: Durham City, Richmond, Durham County, Barbarians, British Lions
Debut: v Wales, Twickenham, January 1960

Weston was a two-time British Lion playing six tests in 1962 and 1966 and played centre and fly-half for England, captaining his country on the 1963 tour to Australia and New Zealand. The 29 caps he won was a record for an England back at the time. He was England's team manager at the 1987 World Cup and became chairman of selectors serving on the 1989 British Lions selection committee. He was a chartered surveyor who established an estate agency and managed a property portfolio in his native Durham. A JP, he had a spell as High Sheriff of Durham and played minor counties cricket for his county. His sons Phil and Robin played first-class cricket.

892. WRIGHT, Thomas Peter
Prop 13 caps 1960-1962
Born: Glanford Brigg, Lincolnshire, 28 February 1931
Died: Devizes, Wiltshire, 22 April 2002
Career: Tonbridge, Blackheath, Penarth, Cowbridge, Devizes, Kent, Barbarians
Debut: v Wales, Twickenham, January 1960

Wright grew up in Tonbridge, started playing rugby at Judd School and toured South Africa with the Lions in 1962, playing eight games but no tests as a back injury hampered his trip. He played his final international for England that year. A captain of Blackheath, he had to wait four years from his trial test debut, and he continued to play at a lower level with Devizes when his work in the brewery trade took him to the area. A one-time agricultural contractor who organised deliveries of cider apples, he later worked for Wadworth Brewery as a free-trade manager and died of a heart attack aged 71.

893. PATTERSON, William Michael
Centre 2 caps 1961
Born: Newcastle-upon-Tyne, Northumberland, 11 April 1936
Died: Sale, Cheshire, December 1998
Career: Cambridge University, Gloucester, Sale, Wasps, Chiltern, Barbarians, Cheshire, North Western Counties, British Lions
Debut: v South Africa, Twickenham, January 1961

Patterson toured with the British Lions in 1959, making one test appearance against the All Blacks in Wellington after being called up as a replacement before he had played for England. He won his England caps against South Africa and Scotland, although he went on the non-capped tour to Canada in 1967. A product of Sale Grammar School, he captained Cheshire, winning the County Championship with them in 1961 and skippered two tours of East Africa by the Anti-Assassins, an invitation team drawn from players from the north of England. He worked as a technical sales engineer for Hopkinson's Ltd.

894. RIMMER, Laurance Ivor
Flanker 5 caps 1961
Born: Liverpool, Lancashire, 31 May 1935
Died: Aldeburgh, Suffolk, 31 May 2012
Career: Oxford University, Old Birkonians, Bath, Cheshire, Dorset, Wiltshire, North-West Counties
Debut: v South Africa, Twickenham, January 1961

Rimmer, an Oxford blue in 1958, won all his five caps in 1961 after being awarded a commission in the Intelligence Corps during his national service in Cyprus. At Corpus Christi College, Oxford, he studied geography, then entered teaching at Dauntsey's School in Dorset, moving to the Lancaster Royal Grammar School five years later and at the age of 36 was made headmaster of Framlingham College in Suffolk. He turned Framlingham into a fully independent school before leaving in 1989 and travelled to Malaysia, where he created a new school before returning to England. He died on his 77th birthday.

895. FRENCH, Raymond James MBE
Lock 4 caps 1961
Born: St Helens, Lancashire, 23 December 1939
Career: Leeds University, St Helens
Debut: v Wales, Cardiff Arms Park, January 1961

French played all four games at lock in the 1961 Championship as a 21-year-old before switching codes to rugby league for St Helens, where he played for seven years before four years at Widnes. He studied English and Latin at Leeds University, won four caps for Great Britain, was vice-captain at the 1968 Rugby League World Cup, and taught English at Cowley School in St Helens. He became a commentator on the league for the BBC, describing every Challenge Cup final from 1982 to 2008 and eventually retired in 2013, having been made an MBE.

896. GAVINS, Michael Neil
Full-back, 1 cap
Born: Leeds, 14 October 1934
Career: Old Roundhegians, Loughborough College, Leicester, Moseley, Middlesbrough, Leeds University
Debut: v Wales, Cardiff Arms Park, January 1961

Gavins won his only cap when the England selectors dropped Don Rutherford after the 5-0 defeat to South Africa in 1961. His test against Wales ended in a 6-3 defeat. He studied economics at Loughborough, gaining his BA in 1956, played 121 games for Leicester between 1957 and 1970 after making his debut against the RAF. He left the club when Scottish international Ken Scotland joined and took possession of the full-back's jersey. He set a Middlesbrough club record of 229 points in 1967/68, was an economics teacher and housemaster at Uppingham School in Rutland, working there from 1968 to 1994.

897. PRICE, John
Lock 1 cap 1961
Born: Coventry, Warwickshire, 14 July 1928
Died: Sutherland, New South Wales, 17 July 2016
Career: Coventry Tech Old Boys, Coventry, Warwickshire
Debut: v Ireland, Lansdowne Road, Dublin, February 1961

Price was King Henry VIII's scrum half before a growth spurt. He played football as a centre-half for Herberts in the Coventry and North Warwickshire League, having trials for Coventry City. After leaving Birmingham University, he joined Coventry Tech Old Boys and, after a season, joined Coventry after impressing in a representative match. A member of the Warwickshire side that won County Championship titles in 1958 and 1959, he extended his rugby career by a year after winning his only England cap after eight successive trial games. Business commitments forced him to retire at his peak in 1961 and three years later, he moved to Australia after taking a technical government post.

898. ROGERS, Derek Prior
Flanker, 34 caps (9 -3t)
Born: Bedford, Bedfordshire, 20 June 1939
Career: City University, Bedford, East Midlands, Barbarians, British Lions
Debut: v Ireland, Lansdowne Road, Dublin, February 1961

Rogers was a relentless flanker who was England's record cap holder when his test career finished in 1969, surpassing Wavell Wakefield's mark of 31 appearances. He played two tests on the 1962 British Lions tour of South Africa and was England's captain in 1966. He retired after captaining Bedford to victory over Rosslyn Park in the final of the English knock-out cup at Twickenham. A commercial insurance broker, he later managed the England Under-23 squad, managed the senior side and was RFU President in 2000/01. He was awarded an OBE in 1969.

899. WILLCOX, John Graham
Full-back, 16 caps (17-3p, 4c) 1961-1964
Born: Sutton Coldfield, West Midlands, 16 February 1937
Career: Oxford University, Fylde, The Army, Harlequins, Paris University Club, Headingley, Malton
Debut: v Ireland, Lansdowne Road, Dublin, 11 February 1961

Willcox was a goal-kicking full-back who played for England in all four games in the 1963 Championship-winning campaign. He also played three tests on the 1966 British Lions tour to South Africa and was a talented all-round sportsman, winning four blues for rugby at Oxford and one for boxing at heavyweight. Willcox spent four years in the Army before taking up a teaching post at Ampleforth College in North Yorkshire, where he coached rugby with one of his pupils being former England captain Lawrence Dallaglio. He was also a director of Old Coach Yard Management, a property company.

900. HARDING, Victor Sydney James
Lock, 6 caps (3-1t)
Born: Southwark, London, 18 June 1932
Career: Cambridge University, the Army, Saracens, Sale, Harlequins, Edinburgh Wanderers, Middlesex, Barbarians, London Counties
Debut: v France, Twickenham, February 1961

Harding joined Saracens in 1951, captaining the side in 1956/57, but had to wait until the 1958/59 season to get an England trial. He was at Cambridge University by then, where he studied land management and won three blues, and finally won his first cap aged 28 in 1961. He had a spell at Sale, then returned to Saracens before joining Harlequins in 1964. He had won his last cap against Scotland in 1962 and scored his only international try against France on his debut. He worked as a sales manager for Thames Gas Board, then joined the National Coal Board.

901. JUDD, Philip Edward
Prop, 22 caps 1962-1967
Born: Coventry, Warwickshire, 8 April 1934
Died: Coventry, Warwickshire, 14 June 2015
Career: Coventry, RAF, Barbarians, Warwickshire
Debut: v Wales, Twickenham, January 1962

Judd played 442 times for Coventry, a record at the time. He retired in 1968, immediately after Warwickshire's 9-6 defeat to Middlesex in the County Championship final. He played international rugby until 1967, captaining England in his last five matches, although he had had to play in ten trials before he got his first taste of test rugby. Judd started his rugby career at Broadstreet RFC before beginning his long Coventry career at a club where he is still revered. The Judd Project, which he was involved in the setting up, is a scheme to develop rugby in the area named after the prop. He also founded an engineering company.

902. UNDERWOOD, Adrian Martin
Wing, 5 caps 1962-1964
Born: Kidderminster, Worcestershire, 19 July 1940
Died: Cardiff, Wales, 9 June 2017
Career: Northampton, Exeter, East Midlands, Devon
Debut: v Wales, Twickenham, January 1962

Underwood was the first winger to throw the ball in at a line-out with a torpedo style. A PE teacher, he was the last Exeter player to represent England until Tom Johnson made his debut in 2012. He worked at Northampton Grammar School and was a senior lecturer at St Luke's College, Exeter, where he had studied. In his 17 years at St Luke's, he helped develop 35 full internationals and seven British Lions. He completed a PhD in the teaching of physical education. His book 'Better Rugby' was published in 1973 and reprinted six times as 'Even Better Rugby'. He died after a battle with dementia.

903. WADE, Michael Richard
Centre 3 caps (3-1t) 1962
Born: Leicester, Leicestershire, 13 September 1937
Career: Cambridge University, RAF, Leicester, Barbarians, Stade Bordelais UC, Combined Services,
Debut: v Wales, Twickenham, January 1962

Wade broke into the Leicester side as a schoolboy and made his England appearances in 1962, four years after first being a trial reserve, and spent that summer in France working as a waiter to learn the language. He studied at Emmanuel College, Cambridge, where he played in the undefeated team of 1961 alongside Ian Balding, who would train the 1971 Derby winner Mill Reef. A serious knee injury in 1965 effectively finished his career, as he played only three games in the next two years. He moved to America, where he was a management consultant in Marblehead, Massachusetts.

904. DEE, John MacKenzie
Centre/wing 2 caps 1962-1963
Born: Hartlepool, County Durham, 22 October 1938
Career: Hartlepool, British Lions, Barbarians, Durham Counties
Debut: v Scotland, Murrayfield, Edinburgh, March 1962

Dee won his second and last cap against the All Blacks on England's tour of Australia and New Zealand on the wing, having made his debut as a centre. He played 90 times for Durham Counties and toured South Africa with the British Lions in 1962, playing 12 games without appearing in a test and worked as a PE teacher at Henry Smith Grammar School in Hartlepool. He was part of the Durham Counties' side that contested the remarkable 1967 County Championship final against Surrey. The Twickenham final finished 14-14, and the replay, in Hartlepool two weeks later, ended in a 0-0 draw.

905. HURST, Andrew Charles Brunel
Wing, 1 cap 1962
Born: Cairo, Egypt, 1 October 1935
Died: Reading, 14 March 2011
Career: Oxford University, Wasps, London Counties, Middlesex, Oxfordshire, Barbarians
Debut: v Scotland, Murrayfield, Edinburgh, March 1962

Hurst, the great-great nephew of the famous engineer Isambard Kingdom Brunel, was born in Cairo. His family moved to England when he was a youngster, and he was educated at Dragon School, Oxford, Abbotsholme, Staffordshire and Oxford University. After serving in the Royal Navy, mainly in Malta, he became a solicitor, founding ACB Hurst and Co in Henley in 1971, where he worked until he was 73. He was Wasps' skipper when he won his only cap in a 3-3 draw with Scotland at Murrayfield and met his wife Bernadita when he led a Bosuns RFC tour to seven countries, including Chile, in 1969.

906. PARGETTER, Thomas Alfred
Lock 3 caps 1962-1963
Born: Stratford-upon-Avon, Warwickshire, 21 July 1932
Died: Chipping Campden, Gloucestershire, 28 April 2009
Career: Cambridge University, Stratford-upon-Avon, Moseley, Coventry, Warwickshire, Midland Counties
Debut: v Scotland, Murrayfield, Edinburgh, March 1962

Pargetter, Stratford-upon-Avon's first full international, was the cornerstone in a powerful Warwickshire pack that won five County Championship finals between 1958 and 1963. He retired from senior rugby in February 1961 but changed his mind and returned with Coventry eight months later. Before the end of the season had won his first test cap as one of three men brought into a pack mauled by Ireland despite not having played for nine weeks. He worked in the family bakery business his great-grandfather opened in the 1850s, running it himself until July 1984. A younger brother, Tony, also played for Moseley and Warwickshire.

907. PURDY, Stanley John
Flanker 1 cap 1962
Born: Rugby, Warwickshire, 6 February 1936
Career: Rugby, the Army, Combined Services, Fylde, Warwickshire, Barbarians
Debut: v Scotland, Murrayfield, Edinburgh, March 1962

Purdy was the first player born in rugby to win an international cap for England whilst playing for his hometown club. The flanker played in the seven County Championship finals Warwickshire won between 1958 and

1965 and was considered by the Lions for the 1959 tour to New Zealand before being capped by England. He continued to play for rugby for another decade after winning his only test cap in 1962. He later became chairman of the Midlands selectors and worked for Massey-Ferguson before joining PA Management Consultants. A director of a plumbing equipment distributor and bathroom design, he now lives in Saffron Walden, Essex.

908. CLARKE, Simon John Scott
Scrum-half 13 caps (3-1t) 1963-1965
Born: Westcliff-on-Sea, Essex, 2 April 1938
Died: Wimbledon, London, 12 October 2017
Career: Cambridge University, Royal Navy, Bath, Yokohama, Blackheath, Kent, Devon, Sussex, Barbarians
Debut: v Wales, Cardiff Arms Park, Cardiff, January 1963

A two-time blue and Championship winner in 1963, who also played cricket for Cambridge University and Kent seconds, Clarke won his first 10 caps as a student and his last three out of Blackheath. He attended Dowling College Cambridge after leaving Wellington College school, where he earned a BA in history. He worked as a sales manager for Thomas Potterton Ltd, had a spell working in Yokohama, Japan, and was employed by De La Rue, the banknote maker. He also served in the Royal Marines as a second lieutenant, was an adviser with the careers organisation Inspiring Futures and a mentor at King's College School, Wimbledon.

909. DAVIS, Alec Michael
Lock 16 caps
Born: Lichfield, Staffordshire, 23 January 1942
Died: Sherborne, Dorset, 10 May 2022
Career: Torquay Athletic, Royal Navy, Devonport Services, United Services, Harlequins, Barbarians, Devon, Staffordshire
Debut: v Wales, Cardiff Arms Park, Cardiff, January 1963

Davis played for England from 1963, when he won the Championship, until 1970 before becoming coach of the national side for the 1979/80 season when he was a teacher at Sherborne School. He could not afford proper boots for his test debut, so he bought a pair of football boots and dyed them black. He coached England for three seasons, and the side, captained by Bill Beaumont, won the Grand Slam in 1980 in his first campaign in charge. He taught at Haileybury and St Paul's before moving to Sherborne and had previously coached England's under-16s and under-19s and ran the rugby at Sherborne for 39 years until 2013.

910. DOVEY, Beverley Alfred
Prop 2 caps 1963
Born: Lydney, Gloucestershire, 24 October 1938
Career: Cambridge University, Lydney, Bristol, Rosslyn Park, Roundhay, Gloucestershire, Somerset, Yorkshire, Southern Counties, Barbarians
Debut: v Wales, Cardiff Arms Park, Cardiff, January 1963

Dovey was educated at Lydney Grammar School and Leeds and Cambridge Universities, playing in both the UAU final for Leeds and the 1960 Varsity Match for Cambridge. He became one of seven new caps on his debut, but after retaining his place, was dropped in favour of Nick Drake-Lee following a 0-0 draw in Ireland. Dovey, who served Gloucestershire for a decade, was recalled for a trial in November 1969 after six years out of the side. A master at Merchant Taylor's School in Northwood, he had two stints at Millfield sandwiched between becoming headmaster of Sir William Romney's School, Tetbury.

911. DRAKE-LEE, Nicholas James
Prop 8 caps (3-1t) 1964-1965
Born: Kettering, Northamptonshire, 7 April 1942
Died: 22 January 2021
Career: Cambridge University, Rosslyn Park, Leicester, Manchester, Waterloo, East Midlands, Lancashire
Debut: v Wales, Cardiff Arms Park, Cardiff, January 1963

A blue at Cambridge, where he attended Downing College, from 1961 to 1963, Drake-Lee was reputed to weigh only 12 stone, which was light for a prop, even in those days. He won eight caps when he was the youngest player on the pitch against Wales, aged 22, playing for Leicester, after which his international career ended. He won the Five Nations title in 1963, taught at Stonyhurst College, a famous rugby-playing school in the Ribble Valley before he retrained and became a chartered surveyor specialising in the licensed trade. He had two rugby-playing brothers, while his son Bill played for Leicester.

912. MANLEY, Donald Charles
Flanker 4 caps 1963
Born: Exeter, Devon, 17 February 1932
Died: Exeter, Devon, 9 June 2021
Career: Exeter, The Royal Signals, Devon, Barbarians
Debut: v Wales, Cardiff Arms Park, Cardiff, January 1963

Manley was a cabinet maker who played for Exeter for 15 seasons, captaining the club and making more than 450 appearances, but he had to wait until he was nearly 31 and play in seven trials before his international debut. He was ever-present in the 1963 Championship-winning side. He played for Devon until 1967 and captained the Barbarians before he had even played for England. He worked for Brooks in Exeter, run by former Devon player Arthur Brook, who gave him time off for rugby before becoming self-employed and later coaching Exeter Colts. He was Exeter president from 1994 to 2004.

913. OWEN, John Ernest
Lock 14 caps (3-1t) 1963-1967
Born: Sutton Coldfield, 21 September 1939
Career: Cambridge University, Blackheath, Moseley, Coventry, Barbarians
Debut: v Wales, Cardiff Arms Park, Cardiff, January 1963

Owen was a big presence in the England line-out from the Championship-winning year of 1963, scoring his only try on his debut in the 13-6 win over Wales. He toured Australia and New Zealand with England in 1963, but injury scuppered his trip, and he was only available to play in one test, the 18-9 defeat to the Wallabies in Sydney. A blue at Cambridge, he worked for Jaguar in the market research department in Coventry before holding several directorships, notably in a family engineering business, Rubery Owen Holdings. The company has made stands for grounds such as Old Trafford and Twickenham and served the motor industry.

914. THORNE, John David
Hooker 3 caps 1963
Born: Bristol, 1 January 1934
Died: Bristol, 25 October 2008
Career: Bristol, Gloucestershire, Western Clubs, Western Counties
Debut: v Wales, Cardiff Arms Park, Cardiff, January 1963

Thorne was 29 when he made his debut in 1963 and toured Australia and New Zealand with England the same summer. He represented Western Clubs against Canada in 1962 and Western Counties against New Zealand a year later. He played 287 games for Bristol between 1955 and 1971, although he did return to Cleve in 1965 when John Pullin became first-choice hooker. He returned to Bristol to help out when Pullin was with the British Lions in New Zealand in 1971. He was the public address announcer at Bristol's Memorial Ground, worked for a shoe manufacturer in the city, and then ran an off-license.

915. PERRY, David Gordon
No.8 15 caps (6-2t) 1963-1966
Born: Woolwich, London, 26 December 1937
Died: Leeds, West Yorkshire, 8 April 2017
Career: Cambridge University, Harlequins, Bedford
Debut: v France, Twickenham, February 1963

A Championship winner in 1963 and captain in the tournament in 1965, Perry was forced to quit the game when he was just 27 because of injury but forged a highly successful business career. A graduate of Christ's College, Cambridge, winning a blue in 1957, he worked for British Printing Corporation before joining John Waddington PLC, the makers of Monopoly. He became chairman and chief executive of the company and fought off two takeover bids from the disgraced media tycoon Robert Maxwell before retiring in 1997. He later held numerous non-executive directorships, including posts with the Dewhirst Group and the National and Provincial Building Society.

916. WILSON, Kenneth James
Prop 1 cap 1963
Born: Newark, Nottinghamshire, 25 November 1938
Died: Oldham, Lancashire, 1 December 1993
Career: Cheltenham, Gloucester, RAF, Combined Services, Gloucestershire
Debut: v France, Twickenham, February 1963

'Tug' Wilson won his only cap against France in 1963 before turning professional with Oldham RL later that year. He cost the Roughyeds £2,000 and spent 12 years at Watersheddings. He had been the RAF heavyweight boxing champion, beating the golden boy of the era, Billy Walker on points, and fought Bob Foster, the future light-heavyweight world champion. He was hugely popular at Oldham, and his last two games were against Australia. A bus controller who later coached at Oldham, he died after a long battle with Parkinson's disease aged 55.

917. HOSEN, Roger Wills
Full-back 10 caps (63-6c,17c) 1963-1967
Born: Habe, Cornwall, 12 June 1933
Died: Truro, Cornwall, 9 April 2005
Career: Loughborough College, Plymouth Albion, Wasps, Cheltenham, Northampton, Bristol, Cornwall, Midlands Counties, Barbarians
Debut: v New Zealand, Eden Park, Auckland, May 1963

Hosen had to wait until he was 30 for international recognition and, even then, found his chances limited because of John Willcox and Don Rutherford. Despite scoring a record 38 points in the 1967 Five Nations Championship, he was never picked again. He scored 1,463 points for Northampton and played cricket for Cornwall and the Minor Counties. Born overlooking the Penryn rugby ground, he was a schoolteacher who taught PE and geography at Northampton Grammar School, Rugby School and Cheltenham College. He later ran the Seven Stars Inn, Stithians, Cornwall, before his death from a heart attack.

918. MARRIOTT, Victor Robert
Flanker 4 caps 1963-1964
Born: Battersea, London, 29 January 1938
Career: Harlequins, Army, Combined Services, London Counties, Surrey
Debut: v New Zealand, Eden Park, Auckland, May 1963

Marriott won all his caps against southern hemisphere opposition, three on the 1962-63 tour of Australia and New Zealand and his last against the All Blacks in 1964. He was dropped after a heavy defeat, and tore knee ligaments playing in a club game against Blackheath and the subsequent breakdown cost him further caps. Educated at Balham Grammar School in south London, he played for Harlequins when he was capped, having served his national service in the Royal Army Educational Corps. He worked as a salesman with British Olivetti Accounting Machines, then joined National Cash Registers Ltd as a sales team leader and systems analyst.

919. RANSON, John Matthew
Wing 7 caps (6-2t) 1963-1964
Born: Durham, County Durham, 26 July 1938
Career: Birmingham University, Durham City, Rosslyn Park, Headingley, Selby, North Midlands, Middlesex, Barbarians
Debut: v New Zealand, Eden Park, Auckland, May 1963

Ranson scored a try on his debut against the All Blacks in 1963 in Auckland. The wing, then at Rosslyn Park, played the entire 1964 Championship when England shared third place with France. The son of a professional footballer, Jack, he taught at Durham School, where he was educated, and Birmingham University and was also a brewer, previously having joined Arthur Guinness & Son Ltd as an under-brewer. An all-round athlete, he was Victor Lodurum of the London Breweries Championships and, in cricket, took a hat-trick for Northwood v MCC. He moved to Malta and, in 2016, made the news when he fought off three burglars from his house there.

920. SANGWIN, Roger Dennis
Centre 2 caps 1964
Born: Holderness, East Riding of Yorkshire, 2 December 1937
Died: Hull, East Riding of Yorkshire, 20 March 2022
Career: Hull & East Riding, Yorkshire, North Eastern Counties, Barbarians
Debut: v New Zealand, Twickenham, January 1964

Sangwin won both his caps in 1964, his last in the 6-6 draw with Wales before Malcolm Phillips returned to the side, Mike Weston reverted to inside centre, and his international career ended. A product of Sedbergh School, he missed the 1963 county championship final with a leg injury. He studied architecture at Hull University, becoming a partner in the architectural practice Lazenby, Needler and Sangwin in his home city, designing many projects in Yorkshire. He was instrumental in the formation of Hull Ionians RFC, was the founding director of rugby, and used his architectural skills to design the clubhouse.

921. FORD, Peter John Ford
Flanker 4 caps 1964
Born: Gloucester, Gloucestershire, 2 May 1932
Career: RAF, Gloucester, Gloucestershire, Barbarians
Debut: v Wales, Twickenham, January 1964

Ford played 506 games for Gloucester, scoring 146 tries, between 1951 and 1965, but had to wait until he was 31 for his test debut in 1964. He played all four games in the Championship that year, but that was all the international action he saw. He made 46 appearances for Gloucestershire before serving on the club committee, although he still turned out for the second team occasionally if they were short. He was made captain of Gloucester in 1955 at the age of 23. He ran a transport company in Cheltenham, was president of Gloucester RFC, served on the RFU committee and was an England selector at the club.

922. ROWELL, Robert Errington
Lock, 2 caps 1964-1965
Born: Corbridge, Northumberland, 29 August 1939
Career: Hull University, Loughborough College, Leicester, Fylde, Waterloo, Lancashire, Midland Counties
Debut: v Wales, Twickenham, January 1964

Rowell won two caps against Wales in 1964 and 1965 and played 355 games in the second row for Leicester between 1962 and 1978, a mark passed by Martin Johnson. He captained the Tigers in his penultimate season at the club and was a schoolteacher at Fosse School, and later a director of a haulage company, RE Rowell Transport, while remaining heavily involved with the Leicester club. He served on sub-committees looking at the club's future and was chairman of selectors until moving to Derbyshire. However, he kept in touch with events in Leicester and, in 2003, succeeded David Matthews as president.

923. BROPHY, Thomas John
Fly-half 8 caps 1964-1966
Born: Liverpool, Lancashire, 8 July 1942
Career: Liverpool, Loughborough Colleges, Lancashire, Barbarians
Debut: v Ireland, Twickenham, February 1964

Brophy, the Liverpudlian fly-half with the Beatles haircut, turned to rugby league with Barrow the week before the England rugby union trial after winning eight caps. He stood just 5ft 6in but helped Barrow to the 1967 Challenge Cup Final when they were beaten 17-12 by Featherstone Rovers. He worked as a chemistry teacher at Rossall School after studying at Liverpool University and Loughborough. He also played for Rochdale Hornets and Salford, but he continued to coach union at school after getting permission from the RFU. He later became headmaster of St Gregory's Catholic High School in Warrington for 19 years.

924. PAYNE, Colin Martin
Lock 10 caps (3-1t) 1964-1966
Born: Edmonton, London, 19 May 1937
Died: Bedford, Bedfordshire, 7 March 2005
Career: Oxford University, Harlequins, West of Scotland, Barbarians, Surrey, Warwickshire
Debut: v Ireland, Twickenham, February 1964

Payne was educated at Sherborne School before winning an Oxford University blue in 1960. Despite being a member of the Warwickshire side that won the County Championship in 1962, 1964 and 1965, he had to wait until 1964 to win his first England cap. He was dropped for the County final in 1960 while a student the year he had his first England. While he was captain of Harlequins, he ordered a rugby league scout to leave the players' bar at The Stoop after offering Tony Todman £4,000 to turn professional. A television engineer for Rediffusion Ltd, he was later involved in developing cable television in Scotland.

925. PEART, Thomas George Anthony Hunter
No.8 2 caps 1964
Born: Hartlepool, County Durham, 10 September 1936
Died: Darlington, County Durham, 3 August 1988
Career: Blackheath, The Army, Hartlepool Rovers, Barbarians, Durham County
Debut: v France, Stade Colombes, Paris, February 1964

Peart, who had captained Sedbergh School and won England schoolboy honours, broke into Hartlepool's side in 1954 when the more experienced Bill Corkin wasn't available regularly. His father, Fred, was the Rovers chairman, and he had his first international trial in 1958. During the Suez crisis, he served as a second lieutenant in the Parachute Regiment on national service. He was at Hartlepool in 1964, the year he made his England debut but was one of 11 caps axed the following season. His brother-in-law Douglas Elliott captained Scotland, and he worked in the family fuel and timber merchants before his death from cancer aged 51.

926. WRENCH, Frederick David Bryan
Prop 2 caps 1964
Born: Northwich, Cheshire, 27 November 1936
Died: Durston, Somerset, 18 June 2018
Career: Wilmslow, Leeds University, UAU, Cambridge University, Harlequins, Northampton, Wolfhounds, Cheshire, Barbarians
Debut: v France, Stade Colombes, Paris, 22 February 1964

Educated at Sandbach School in Cheshire, Wrench read chemistry at Leeds University before taking an MA in education at Cambridge, where he won a blue in 1960. He won his caps in the 1964 Five Nations against France, helping his side win 6-3 in Paris on his debut before losing 15-6 to Scotland. The tighthead prop worked for Proctor & Gamble before teaching chemistry at Haberdashers' Aske's School in Hertfordshire, convenient for playing for Harlequins, whom he captained for a season. Later, he took a teaching post at Taunton School in 1970, living in Wellington and Bradford-on-Tone.

927. FRANKCOM, Geoffrey Peter
Centre 4 caps 1965
Born: Bathavon, Somerset, 5 April 1942
Career: Cambridge University, Bedford, Headingley, Bath, RAF, La teste (France), Somerset, Barbarians
Debut: v Wales, Cardiff Arms Park, January 1965

Frankcom won his caps out of Cambridge University, where he studied modern languages before becoming a master at Bedford School but played more than 100 times for Bath. He joined the RAF in 1967, serving as a flight lieutenant in Strike Command, flying Phantom F4s and serving in Germany. He was also an instructor with the French Air Force, playing for La teste before finishing his flying career as a squadron leader in 1983. His debut against Wales was marred when, at the post-game dinner, he accused Welsh forward Brian Thomas of biting him during the match. He was not picked for the rest of the season.

928. HORTON, Anthony Lawrence
Prop 7 caps 1965-1967
Born: Brentford, London, 13 July 1938
Died: Cranbrook, Kent, 9 March 2020
Career: Royal Marines, Blackheath, Van der Stel (SA), London Counties, Barbarians, British Lions, Surrey
Debut: v Wales, Cardiff Arms Park, Cardiff, January 1965

'Pinky' Horton, a destructive scrummager of a tighthead prop, did his national service with the Royal Marines before making his debut when he was 26. He played in three tests on the 1968 British Lions tour to South Africa, a year after playing his final match for England. He was employed in a family business of wine merchants until 1964, then lived for a short while in South Africa, where he worked for Stellenbosch Farmer Wineries before returning to England and winning his caps. He then worked for JR Phillips & Co Ltd before entering the insurance world.

929. RICHARDS, Stephen Brookhouse
Hooker 9 caps 1965-1967
Born: West Kirby, Wirral, 28 August 1941
Career: Oxford University, Richmond, Bristol, Sheffield, Middlesex, Yorkshire
Debut: v Wales, Cardiff Arms Park, Cardiff, 16 January 1965

An Oxford blue in 1962, Richards won his nine caps between 1965 and 1967 and trained as a solicitor. Educated at Clifton College in Bristol, he toured Canada with England in 1967 after a quick rise to prominence for Middlesex and England from Richmond's second XV. Later he moved to Sheffield to work whilst playing for the local club and Yorkshire, and in retirement, lived in Oxfordshire. His last match for England, in 1967 against Wales in Cardiff, saw him on the wrong end of the teenage Keith Jarrett, who scored 19 points in a 34-21 win for the Welsh.

930. ROSSER, David William Albert
Centre 5 caps 1965-1966
Born: Portsmouth, Hampshire, 27 March 1938
Career: Cambridge University, the Army, Manchester, Wasps, London Welsh, Hampshire, Barbarians
Debut: v Wales, Cardiff Arms Park, January 1965

Rosser was a student at Cambridge University when he won his first four caps in 1964 and at Wasps when he won his last in the Wales match of 1966. Along with Geoff Franckcom, who he had been at Cambridge with, they continued their university link-up when they made their test debuts in the same game. A three-time blue, he taught English at Dulwich College before moving to Sherborne School in Dorset. He was at Sherborne for three years, then moved to a post at Millfield School. He was later director of the charity Old Millfieldians Development Academy of Youth Rugby.

931. RUDD, Edward Lawrence
Wing 6 caps 1965-1966
Born: Aigburth, Liverpool, 28 September 1944
Career: Oxford University, Liverpool, Lancashire, North West Counties, Barbarians
Debut: v Wales, Cardiff Arms Park, Cardiff, January 1965

Rudd was educated at St Edward's College in Liverpool, which helped produce Mike Slemen and Kyran Bracken, where he had a final England schools trial. He was an Oxford blue in 1962 and 1963, scoring two tries. Two months earlier, he had scored a memorable try for his University against the All Blacks. His efforts secured him a trial, but he never won a test in his six appearances for England, with four defeats and two draws. He worked in banking, joining Martin's Bank in December 1967 and later played hockey before returning to playing for Liverpool's fifth team in the mid-1980s.

932. SILK, Nicholas
Flanker 4 caps 1965
Born: Lewes, Sussex, 26 May 1941
Career: Oxford University, Harlequins, St Thomas' Hospital, British Universities, Sussex
Debut: v Wales, Cardiff Arms Park, Cardiff, January 1965

Silk captained Oxford University in 1963 while studying at Merton College, two years before making his test debut in the 1965 Championship, in which he played all four matches. The former England schools captain, he led Sussex and Oxford University and was earmarked as a future leader of his country. He skippered an England XV in a final trial but then was dropped. His playing career ended with a knee injury he suffered playing for British universities against Bristol in 1966 at 24. He studied medicine and coached St Thomas' Hospital, qualifying as a doctor. He was based in Petersfield, worked as a midwifery consultant and has acted as an Expert Witness for court cases.

933. SIMPSON, Colin Peter
Wing 1 cap 1965
Born: Ipswich, Suffolk, 21 September 1942
Career: Ipswich, the Army, Combined Services, Harlequins, Wolfhounds, Eastern Counties, Barbarians
Debut: v Wales, Cardiff Arms Park, Cardiff, January 1965

Simpson made his only test appearance after scoring in the final trial match at Twickenham in 1965 when playing for the Rest. He was dropped after the 14-3 defeat by Wales, with Peter Cook taking his place. A decent cricketer who played for Suffolk, he was in the Army, serving in the Royal Anglian Regiment before resigning his commission. He then worked at Wellington College in Berkshire as adjutant and quartermaster of the Combined Cadet Force before becoming a golf club secretary. His last job before his retirement was at West Sussex Golf Club in Pulborough, Sussex.

934. COOK, Peter William
Wing 2 caps 1965
Born: High Wycombe, Buckinghamshire, 8 January 1943
Career: Richmond, Surrey, London Counties, Barbarians
Debut: v Ireland, Lansdowne Road, Dublin, February 1965

Cook was educated at Dulwich College, joined Richmond after leaving school in 1962, and broke into the first team in February 1963. In his first full season with the seniors, he became a prolific try scorer with 28 and won county honours with Surrey. A civil engineering student with British Rail, he had already been a reserve against Scotland when he replaced Colin Simpson in preference to Andy Hancock, but after only two tests lost his place. He made a career in construction company and was sales and marketing director of a sub of tarmac construction before becoming Esher's full-time commercial manager and club secretary.

935. HANCOCK, Andrew William
Wing 3 caps (3-1t) 1965-1966
Born: Dartford, Kent, 19 June 1939
Died: St Ives, Cambridgeshire, 9 February 2020
Career: London University, Sidcup, Cambridge, Northampton, Wasps, Barbarians, Staffordshire
Debut: v France, Twickenham, February 1965

Hancock scored one of the finest tries seen at Twickenham when, in the dying minutes against Scotland in 1965, he ran the length of the field to touch down and secure a 3-3 draw. The try was featured in the opening sequence of the sports programme *Grandstand*. He played against France again in 1966, when he injured a hamstring in England's 13-0 defeat and missed out on the Lions tour that summer. He stepped down a few levels, playing for Stafford and the Chelmsford Undertakers, a veterans' team, before retiring aged nearly 40. He worked in town and country planning for Staffordshire County Council.

936. ARTHUR, Terence Gordon
Centre, 2 caps 1966
Born: Hartlepool, County Durham, 5 September 1940
Died: February 2022
Career: West Hartlepool, Manchester University, Cambridge University, Wasps, Moseley, Waterloo, Barbarians, Durham, Buckinghamshire, North Midlands
Debut: v Wales, Twickenham, January 1966

Arthur won a Cambridge blue cap alongside his future Wasps and England centre partner David Rosser. He scored 50 tries in 100 appearances for Wasps before moving on to Moseley. He won his caps in 1966 and qualified as an actuary. He set up his own firm in 1976 before holding non-executive positions with companies such as Axa Rosenberg Investment Management Ltd and Whittingdale Holdings Ltd and has written extensively on pension and economics issues. In 2007 Arthur's book 'Crap: A Guide to Politics' was published as a follow-up to his 1975 book '95 Per Cent Crap' which was also a book about the ludicrousness of politics.

937. POWELL, David Lewes
Prop 11 caps 1966-1971
Born: Rugby, *Warwickshire*, 17 May 1942
Career: Long Buckby, Rugby, Northampton, East Midlands, British Lions, Barbarians
Debut: v Wales, Twickenham, January 1966

'Piggy' Powell is a legend of Northampton rugby, where he made 370 appearances, captained and coached the

Jim Roberts

Disk Manley

Ken Wilson

Andy Hancock

club and later maintained one of the best pitches in the Premiership as the groundsman at Franklin's Gardens. A farmer, his England debut came in 1966, and he was the only forward from the country to make the 1966 Lions tour to Australia and New Zealand. He played 14 times on the trip without making the test side and picked up his nickname after rooming with Denzil 'Porky' Williams. His last test came in 1971, although he played club rugby until 1978 before a stint as coach of Northampton in the 1980s.

938. PULLIN, John Vivian
Hooker 42 caps (3-1t) 1966-1976
Born: Aust, Gloucestershire, 1 November 1941
Died: Aust, Gloucestershire, 4 February 2021
Career: Bristol Saracens, Bristol, Barbarians, Gloucestershire, British Lions
Debut: v Wales, Twickenham, January 1966

Pullin was one of the big characters in English rugby, winning 42 caps and playing in seven tests for the Lions, including all four on the triumphant tour of New Zealand in 1971. He captained England to defeat in Dublin in 1973 when other teams refused to travel because of terrorist threats, sparking his 'we may not be any good, but at least we turned up' comment. He also captained England to wins over South Africa in Johannesburg in 1972, New Zealand in Auckland and Australia at Twickenham in 1973 when English rugby was otherwise at a low point. He was a farmer in Aust, Gloucestershire, until his death from cancer.

939. SAVAGE, Keith Frederick
Wing 13 caps (3-1t) 1966-1968
Born: Warwick, Warwickshire, 24 August 1940
Career: Loughborough Colleges, Northampton, Harlequins, East Midlands, British Lions
Debut: v Wales, Twickenham, January 1966

Savage was an England winger between 1966 and 1968 and a two-time Lion who played all four tests for the tourists in South Africa in 1968. He qualified as a physical education teacher in 1961, working at schools in Warwickshire, Northampton and Watford and resigned from his post at the latter so he could go on the Lions tour to take on the Springboks. He worked with Automative Products in Leamington, which supplied clutches and brake equipment until 1969, before moving to Johannesburg in South Africa, where he worked as an English teacher.

940. SPENCER, Jeremy
Scrum-half 1 cap 1966
Born: London 27 June 1939
Career: Harlequins, St Jean-de-Luz (France)
Debut: v France, Twickenham, January 1966

Spencer was educated at RGS Guildford, where he was offered a trial with Spurs and wasn't a Quins regular until Roger Lewis dislocated a shoulder. He was heading to Laren, Holland, to exhibit handloom weaving when news of his unexpected selection broke after the elastic in his shorts snapped in the final trial and was replaced. A brilliant artist, he travelled to Europe in his Volkswagen Combie, working in education, and was a painter who once had an exhibition of his work with the Spanish artist Juan Benito. He lived in an air shelter home as a technical advisor to the French Rugby Federation and did his national service in the army under protest as a conscientious objector.

941. TAYLOR, Robert Bainbridge
Flanker 16 caps (16-2t) 1966-1971
Born: Northampton, Northamptonshire, 30 April 1942
Career: Northampton, East Midlands, Hampshire, Barbarians
Debut: v Wales, Twickenham, January 1966

Flanker Taylor played 313 times for Northampton, scoring 280 points, and played all four tests on the Lions tour of South Africa in 1968, and 14 games in all on the trip. Taylor, who captained England against Wales in 1970, taught maths and PE at Wellingborough Grammar School from 1965 before moving to Lings Upper School, Northampton, a decade later. He was Northampton coach, secretary, and president, served on the East Midlands Rugby Union committee, including a stint as chairman and was also fixtures secretary for Old Northamptonians RFC. He was RFU President in 2007/08 and played for Hampshire whilst at college in Winchester.

942. ASHBY, Roland Clive
Scrum-half 3 caps (3-1t) 1966-1967
Born: Lorenzo Marques, Mozambique, 24 January 1937
Died: Oxford, Oxfordshire, 21 May 2015
Career: Wasps, Shropshire, Barbarians, Buckinghamshire, East Midlands
Debut: v Ireland, Twickenham, January 1967

Ashby was born to South African parents in Portuguese Mozambique before his family moved to England when he was 14, finishing his schooling at RGS High Wycombe. He served his national service in the Royal Navy, and when selected for England for his second cap in France, he had to be smuggled back from the match through passport control. He did get a British passport, having previously declared himself South African, but was posted as a deserter in the Portuguese army for not completing national service with them. He had studied agriculture at Harper Adams Agricultural College in Newport before joining the family business.

943. GREENWOOD, John Richard Heaton
Flanker 5 caps (3-1t) 1966-1969
Born: Macclesfield, Cheshire, 11 September 1940
Career: Cambridge University, Waterloo, Coventry, Barbarians, Lancashire
Debut: v Ireland, Twickenham, February 1966

Greenwood made a try-scoring debut for England against Ireland but was dropped in 1967 and did not play again until he returned in 1969 for one game as captain against Ireland. He had the team in early for unofficial weekly training, and they won 17-15. Before the next game, against France, training was snowed off, he injured his eye playing squash, and his test career was over. He continued to play for Lancashire and then played in Italy for Rugby Roma, did some coaching and was in charge of England from 1983 to 1985. He taught at Stoneyhurst College, and his son Will was a 2003 World Cup winner.

944. McFADYEAN, Colin William
Centre, 11 (15-4t, 1d) 1966-1968
Born: Tavistock, Devon, 11 March 1943
Career: Loughborough Colleges, Bristol, UAU, Moseley, Somerset, British Lions
Debut: v Ireland, Twickenham, February 1966

McFadyean played 11 successive internationals for England, captaining them in his last two and four tests for the British Lions against the All Blacks in 1966. A physical education teacher, McFadyean, taught at the Central Grammar School in Birmingham from 1965 to 1967 before becoming a lecturer at Alsager College in Cheshire. In 1989, McFadyean was appointed director of rugby at Bristol, but his tenure did not last long, with the board worried about having finances for a paid coach. He later worked at the National Sports Centre at Lilleshall before returning to teaching at Ilminster Avenue Primary School in Bristol.

945. TREADWELL, William Thomas
Hooker 3 caps 1966
Born: Brentford, London, 13 March 1939
Career: Guy's Hospital, Wasps, London Counties, Surrey, Barbarians
Debut: v Ireland, Twickenham, February 1966

Treadwell studied dentistry at Guy's Hospital and played his three tests in the 1966 Championship when he replaced John Pullin at hooker after the 11-6 defeat by Wales. He played for Wasps from 1956 to 1969 and was the club's president. He ran a dental practice in Oxfordshire and was the official dentist for the England team from 1987 to 2018, and the Lions. Dudley Wood, then secretary of the RFU, appointed him to examine the players before they went on tour in the mid-1980s, and he continued patching players up at Twickenham during matches. He was involved with the England Rugby Internationals Club for over 30 years.

946. HEARN, Robert Daniel
Centre 6 caps 1966-1967
Born: Cheltenham, Gloucestershire, 12 August 1940
Career: Oxford University, Bedford, Barbarians
Debut: v France, Stade Colombes, Paris, February 1966

Hearn had turned down a trial with Ireland and won six caps before tragedy struck in October 1967. Playing for the Midlands, London & Home Counties against the touring All Blacks, he attempted to tackle New Zealand three-quarter Ian MacRae and broke his neck. He was paralysed and spent nine months in Stoke Mandeville Hospital before returning home and amazingly continued to coach rugby at Haileybury School, where he also taught economics, from a wheelchair, but was given just £3,500 in compensation. He became lifelong friends with MacRae and coached England flanker David Cooke at Haileybury. He wrote a 1972 autobiography titled 'Crash Tackle'.

947. SHERRIFF, George Albert
No.8, 3 caps 1966-1967
Born: Stepney, London, 29 May 1937
Career: Saracens, London Counties, Middlesex, Barbarians
Debut: v Scotland, Murrayfield, Edinburgh, 19 March 1966

Sherriff, a Saracens Hall of Fame member, was a latecomer to the sport, starting at 24 after a club official saw him handling timber in a London dock and he made his first team debut after two years in 1963. Three years later, he played for England following a move from lock to No.8. His final cap came in 1967 against New Zealand, but he continued at Saracens until 1973, winning the Middlesex Cup in 1972. He runs a successful Essex-based wholesale business selling wood and building materials, has several other directorships and served as president of Saracens from 1989 to 1991.

948. WINTLE, Trevor Clifford
Scrum-half 5 caps 1966-1969
Born: Forest of Dean, Gloucestershire, 10 January 1940
Career: Lydney, Cambridge University, Rosslyn Park, St Mary's Hospital, Northampton, Barbarians, Gloucestershire, Middlesex, East Midlands
Debut: v Scotland, Murrayfield, Edinburgh, March 1966

Wintle attended two rugby nurseries in Lydney Grammar School and St Mary's Hospital Medical School before playing once for England in 1966 and four times in 1969. His international career was another one finished with the 30-9 defeat by Wales in Cardiff in 1969. He won blues at Cambridge in 1960 and 1961, played for England under-15 and under-19 and represented England Schools at cricket. At Cambridge University he was a member of the team including Geoff Frankcom, which won all 14 games in 1961 - most against senior sides. He worked as a general practitioner in Wallingford.

949. COULMAN, Michael John
Prop 9 caps (3-1t) 1967-1968
Born: Stafford, Staffordshire, 6 May 1944
Died: Rochdale, Greater Manchester, 21 April 2023
Career: Stafford, Moseley, British Police, Staffordshire, North Midlands, British Lions
Debut: v Australia, Twickenham, 7 January 1967

Staffordshire policeman Coulman was an athletics and boxing champion for the service and played for England through the 1967 and 1968 Championships. He was a British Lion in 1968, being picked for the third test against South Africa, but an ankle injury after five minutes finished his tour. Later, he left the police to join Salford Rugby League, making 441 appearances and scoring 135 tries. He also played in the 1975 Rugby League World Cup for England and won three Great Britain caps. After coaching Salford, he worked for Stanneylands catering group and had managerial roles with Wilson's Brewery and Whitbread. He died after a battle with Alzheimer's.

950. GLOVER, Peter Bernard
Wing 3 caps 1967-1971
Born: York, Yorkshire, 25 September 1945
Career: RAF, Bedford, Bath, Combined Services, Barbarians, Macclesfield
Debut: v Australia, Twickenham, January 1967

Glover would have fitted into the modern game as he was 6ft 2in and 16 stones - massive for a winger in the 1960s. His three caps came between 1967 and 1971 after David Duckham switched to centre to cover for John Spencer. He went on an uncapped tour of Japan and played for Bath, for whom he made 41 appearances before finishing his career with Macclesfield after moving into the local area. He was an RAF instructor-pilot, spent some time at the Pakistan Air Force Academy in Risalpur and then became a civil airline pilot operating out of Manchester.

951. JENNINS, Christopher Robert
Centre 3 caps 1967
Born: Runcorn, Cheshire, 5 February 1942
Career: Waterloo, New Brighton, Lancashire, North West Counties
Debut: v Australia, Twickenham, January 1967

Jennins won his three caps in seven weeks in 1967, with his last coming in the 16-12 defeat at the hands of France. He was part of the North West Counties' side that beat Australia in December 1966, earning him his first cap against the Wallabies. He played 34 times for Lancashire, tasting defeat in the 1964 and 1966 County Championship finals but was a winner in 1969, kicking a match-winning penalty. He was educated at Rydal Penrhos School in Colwyn Bay, then attended Liverpool University, studying for a Bachelor of Commerce before working as a chartered accountant on the Wirral.

952. LARTER, Peter John
Lock, 24 caps (6-1t,1p) 1967-1973
Born: Totnes, Devon, 7 September 1944
Career: Northampton, Weston-super-Mare, RAF, Combined Services, Leicestershire, British Lions, Barbarians
Debut: v Australia, Twickenham, January 1967

Larter, a good enough basketball player to represent the RAF, was a regular in England's second row for six years and played one test for the British Lions in South Africa in 1968. He was an officer in the RAF, playing for Northampton when he was stationed at RAF North Luffenham, and was in the force for 35 years. He later became a regional administrator of BIGGA, the golf green keepers' association. He also worked as a citing officer for the RFU and on the disciplinary panels at the 2007 and 2011 Rugby World Cups. With Don White, he was one of the founders of the William Webb Ellis Lodge.

953. BARTON, John
Lock, 4 caps (6-2t) 1967-1972
Born: Meriden, West Midlands, 19 March 1943
Died: Coventry, Warwickshire, 12 January 2021
Career: Coventry, Nuneaton, Barbarians, Warwickshire
Debut: v Ireland, Lansdowne Road, Dublin, 11 February 1967

A product of Caludon Castle School, Coventry, Barton played 265 times for his local club, first as lock, then No.8, but was capped for England in 1967 in the second row. A knee injury hampered his career, and he won his fourth and final cap in 1972 against France. He toured South Africa with England in 1972 and won the English Cup with Coventry in 1973. He was also in the Midland Counties West side that beat the All Blacks in December 1972. He worked in insurance as a financial advisor and was a long-time fixtures secretary at Coventry.

954. FINLAN, John Frank
Fly-half, 13 caps (9-3d) 1967-1973
Born: Warwick, Warwickshire, 9 September 1941
Career: Coventry, Moseley, North Midlands, Barbarians
Debut: v Ireland, Lansdowne Road, Dublin, February 1967

Finlan won 13 caps, partnering six different scrum halves and had three years between his 12th and his final appearance. A product of Saltley Grammar School in Birmingham, he dropped goals in his second and third tests against France and Scotland, and at the end of his playing career, he served as an England selector. In 1986, as part of the IRB Centenary, he helped select the British Lions team that played a Rest of the World XV. Finlan worked as a systems analyst for the buying department of the Midlands Electricity Board and as a management accountant and consultant with the National Health Service.

955. PALLANT, John Noel
Lock/No.8 3 caps 1967
Born: Nottingham, Nottinghamshire, 24 December 1944
Career: Loughborough Colleges, UAU, Nottingham, The North, Midland Counties, Barbarians
Debut: v Ireland, Lansdowne Road, Dublin, February 1967

Pallant, an All-England Schools hammer champion, won two caps at No.8 and one at lock whilst playing for Nottingham in the 1967 Championship, becoming the club's second England international. He also played basketball and left Loughborough College in 1968 for a teaching post in Nottingham. Shortly afterwards, he was made head of physical education at Merchant Taylor's School in Northwood, Hertfordshire, having been interviewed on the same day as British Lions John Taylor and Gerald Davies. He stayed at the school from 1968 to 1997, although he returned briefly in 2005 to coach the Colts' team.

956. PICKERING, Roger David Austin
Scrum-half 6 caps 1967-1968
Born: Birmingham, Warwickshire, 15 June 1943
Career: Cleckheaton, Hull University, Bradford, Dax (Fra), Barbarians, Yorkshire
Debut: v Ireland, Lansdowne Road, Dublin, February 1967

Pickering, educated at Whitecliffe Mount School and Hull University, was a six-time capped scrum half who had to turn down the chance to tour with the Lions in 1968 because of employment commitments. He played for Bradford before taking a teaching job in France, where he played for Dax. He went into business and was an operations director in the holiday industry. He was appointed the first full-time chief executive of the Five Nations in 1996, helping in the genesis of the European Cup, and helped organise the Lions trip to Australia in 2001, the first real-money spinner for the tourists.

957. ROLLITT, David Malcolm
No. 8/flanker 11 caps (3-1t) 1967-1975
Born: Barnsley, Yorkshire, 24 March 1943
Died: Hammersmith, London, 17 December 2022
Career: Loughborough Colleges, UAU, Bristol, Wakefield, Richmond, Gloucestershire, South of England, Barbarians
Debut: v Ireland, Lansdowne Road, Dublin, February 1967

Rollitt won 11 caps spread out over eight years. He did not help his cause when he told a few of his teammates what he felt about their attitude after a 30-9 defeat in Cardiff in April 1969, and it was six years before he was capped again. He played 415 times for Bristol, scoring 101 tries whilst working as a schoolmaster who taught physics, maths and PE at Colston's School in Bristol, then moving to St Paul's School in London. He had several coaching posts in the capital with Harlequins, Richmond, London Division, Imperial Medics and Rosslyn Park in 2005, where he worked for a year.

958. WATT, David Edward James
Lock 4 caps 1967
Born: Bristol, 5 July 1938
Career: Harlequins, Bristol, Gloucestershire, Barbarians
Debut: v Ireland, Lansdowne Road, Dublin, February 1967

Watt could have played for Wales through his father but turned down an invitation to a Welsh trial in 1961. He had to wait until 1967 for his England cap, although he had had a trial in 1962 and on the trip to Dublin. He retired from top-level rugby in 1975 because of a leg injury, appearing in over 500 games for Bristol despite playing football until his 19th birthday. He captained Gloucestershire's 1972 County Championship-winning side and was an RFU Knockout Cup finalist in 1973. A Gloucestershire and Bristol selector, he worked as a sales promotion executive for a tobacco company.

959. WEBB, Rodney Edward
Wing 12 caps (6-2t) 1967-1972
Born: Newbold-on-Avon, Warwickshire, 18 August 1943
Career: Coventry, Midlands, Warwickshire, Barbarians
Debut: v Scotland, Twickenham, 18 March 1967

Webb won a dozen caps whilst a member of the powerful Coventry side, one of the dominant forces in English rugby at the time. He scored a try on his debut, with his other touchdown coming against France in 1969. The winger, a former Warwickshire javelin champion, had qualified as a planning engineer but went into the sports goods business and ended up rescuing the Gilbert brand, famous for their rugby balls. In the early 1980s, he bought the ailing business, re-generated it and set up the Gilbert Rugby Football Museum in St Matthew Street, Rugby. He sold James Gilbert to a management buy-out in 2000.

960. GITTINGS, William John
Scrum-half 1 cap 1967
Born: Coventry, 5 October 1938
Died: Newton, *New Hampshire*, USA, 6 February 2019
Career: Barkers' Butts, Coventry, Warwickshire, Midlands Counties
Debut: v New Zealand, Twickenham, November 1967

Gittings, the first player from the famous Barkers' Butts club to play for England, won his only cap in the 23-11 defeat to the All Blacks in 1967, although he sat on the bench 14 times when there were no replacements. He was an English Cup winner twice with Coventry, for whom he played 337 times up to 1977. A sheet metal worker and later sales manager with Motor Panels in Coventry, who worked in the aviation industry, he also worked for J S Chin & Co, the Coventry company that helped construct the bluebird car used by Donald Campbell to break the world land-speed record in 1964.

961. LLOYD, Robert Hoskins
Centre 5 caps (6-2t) 1967-1968
Born: Plympton, Devon, 3 March 1943
Career: Clifton, Harlequins, Surrey, Barbarians
Debut: v New Zealand, Twickenham, November 1967

Lloyd scored two tries on his test debut, a 23-11 defeat to the All Blacks in 1967, but missed out on the 1968 British Lions tour to South Africa because he was taking exams to become a civil engineer. He studied at Hatfield College of Technology, and, after captaining Harlequins for two seasons up to 1972, moved to the Far East to work for the Hong Kong government in 1973, a job he held for 30 years before moving to Chun Wo Construction for three years and finally retiring in 2007. He played 46 times for Surrey, where only Bob Hiller played more.

962. BELL, Peter Joseph
Flanker 4 caps 1968
Born: Wandsworth, London, 28 April 1937
Career: Cranbrook, Ashford, Maori, Blackheath, Barbarians, Kent, Bay of Plenty (New Zealand)
Debut: v Wales, Twickenham, January 1968

Bell first made his name with Ashford in Kent before spending nine months in New Zealand, working as a Forrester, playing for Maori on the North Island, and then Australia before returning home. He joined Blackheath and had six England trials before making his debut aged 30 after being tipped to replace David Perry but lost out to George Sherriff who impressed selectors playing for Barbarians in March 1966. He captained the Rest on his way to his first cap and was a farmer in Kent, where his father had a 240-acre dairy farm in Stede Quarter, Biddenden.

963. GAY, David John
No.8 4 caps
Born: Bath, Somerset, 10 March 1948
Career: Bath, Harlequins, Somerset, Barbarians
Debut: v Wales, Twickenham, January 1968

Gay was 19 years old when he won the first of his four caps in 1968. He is still a regular at the Rec, where he played for Bath, making 237 appearances for the club. As a solicitor, he is a partner in the law firm Burningham & Brown, which he joined in 1968, and is based in the town. He was a senior partner there with Brendan Perry, father of Matt, whom he met on the rugby pitch. He played for Harlequins while studying at Guildford Law School, and his brother, Allen and father, Bill, played for Bath.

964. HILLER, Robert
Full-back 19 caps (138–3t,12c,33p,2d) 1968-1972
Born: Woking, Surrey, 14 October 1942
Career: Oxford University, Harlequins, Surrey, Barbarians
Debut: v Wales, Twickenham, January 1968

Hiller was England's premier full-back for four years but one of the unluckiest not to wear a British Lions shirt. Hiller went on two tours with the Lions to South Africa in 1968 and New Zealand in 1971 but did not play a test. He captained England seven times, scored a-then England record 138 points, and was also Quins's record points scorer with 1504, which stood from 1976 to 2013 until beaten by Nick Evans. He taught maths at Bec Grammar School in Tooting, then King's College School in Wimbledon and has served as president of Harlequins.

965. KEEN, Brian Warwick
Prop 4 caps 1968
Born: Bury St Edmunds, Suffolk, 1 June 1944
Career: Dorchester, Newcastle University, Northern, Moseley, Bedford, Northumberland, Northern Counties, Barbarians, Brazil
Debut: v Wales, Twickenham, January 1968

Old Hardyean Keen was a Newcastle University agriculture student who forced his way into the Northumberland County team, where the selectors spotted him. He won his four caps in the 1968 Championship while playing for Doncaster, the first player from the club to win international honours. He joined ICI as a fertiliser rep in 1968 before moving to South America, where three years later, he played for Brazil four times. He scored a try in Bedford's 1975 RFU Club Final win, becoming a farm manager, remaining in the industry as an agricultural consultant, and lived in Shipton-under-Wychwood, Oxfordshire.

966. PARSONS, Michael James
Lock 4 caps 1968
Born: Chipping Norton, Oxfordshire, 13 March 1943
Career: Oxford, Northampton, Oxfordshire
Debut: v Wales, Twickenham, January 1968

Parsons was one of eight debutants when England played Wales in 1968, earning an 11-11 draw against a side containing Gareth Edwards and Barry John. By then, he was a Northampton player, having made his name at Oxford RFC. A farmer, he won all four caps in 1968 but had to retire from rugby later that year when he injured his knee in the preliminary rounds for the Middlesex Sevens, although he attempted a comeback several times with Oxford's junior sides. He has farmed near Woodstock in Oxfordshire and has been the director of a property company.

967. PROUT, Derek Henry
Wing, 2 caps 1968
Born: Launceston, Cornwall, 10 November 1962
Died: Southampton, Hampshire, 27 July 2005
Career: Launceston, Redruth, Loughborough College, Northampton, Harlequins, Cornwall, Barbarians, Trojans
Debut: v Wales, Twickenham, January 1968

Cornishman Prout was a schoolboy international and talented sprinter at Cornwall Technical College who won two caps, while playing on the wing for Northampton, in the 1968 Championship. He played for Cornwall 41 times between 1960 and 1969 and made 61 appearances, scoring 32 tries in four years at Franklins Gardens. After a season at Harlequins, he joined the Trojans, who he later coached until 1981. A PE teacher and lecturer, he also coached Hampshire, was a vice-president of the club and a member of the Student RFU committee, where he acted as a selector for student national teams.

968. REDWOOD, Brian William
Scrum-half 2 caps 1968
Born: Bristol, 6 February 1939
Career: Bristol, Central Sports (Lusaka), Gloucestershire
Debut: v Wales, Twickenham, 20 January 1968

A product of Bristol Grammar School and Exeter University, Redwood followed in the footsteps of his father, Percy and brother, Bob, in playing for his hometown club. He made 243 appearances, scored 56 tries, and kicked a club record 17 drop goals in 1967-68. Despite only having one good eye, he won his caps in 1968, seven years after his first trial, but was harshly dropped by selectors after suffering concussion against Ireland. He moved to Zambia soon afterwards to work for tobacco giants Rothmans and was a personnel officer with Rolls Royce. He served Bristol as fixtures secretary and chairman.

969. WEST, Bryan Ronald
Flanker 8 caps 1968-1970
Born: Northampton, Northamptonshire, 7 June 1948
Career: Loughborough Colleges, Northampton, East Midlands, Barbarians
Debut: v Wales, Twickenham, January 1968

West was a British Lion in 1968, without playing a test in South Africa, although he looked set to miss the trip with ankle trouble before being called out as a replacement.

He won eight caps before turning to rugby league with Wakefield Trinity for an £8,000 signing-on fee but only stayed there for a year. An international aged 19 and a student at Loughborough, he taught physical education at Trinity School in Northampton before becoming games master at St Olave's Grammar School in Orpington, Kent. He also had a spell teaching at the British International School of Jeddah.

970. BROOKE, Terence John
Centre 2 caps 1968
Born: Berrylands, Surrey, 8 October 1940
Died: Redhill, Surrey, 1 April 2020
Career: Warlingham, Richmond, Surrey, Barbarians, London Counties
Debut: v France, Stade Colombes, Paris, February 1968

Brooke learnt to play rugby at school in Leicester before moving to Purley Grammar School. He first won Surrey honours playing for Warlingham, becoming their first former player to represent England. Chris Robshaw was the second. He was 26 when he moved into senior rugby with Richmond, winning his first cap, replacing Colin McFadyean, for whom he was initially overlooked. He helped Surrey share the County Championship in 1967 after drawing a replay with County Durham 0-0. His brother Ray played for Rosslyn Park and Hampshire, and he worked as a chartered structural engineer for 40 years, spending 33 with the same firm.

971. DUCKHAM, David John MBE
Wing/centre 36 caps (36-10t) 1969-1976
Born: Coventry, Warwickshire, 28 June 1946
Died: Lambeth, London, 9 January 2023
Career: Coventry, Warwickshire, Barbarians
Debut: v Ireland, Lansdowne Road, Dublin, February 1969

Duckham was one of the most exciting talents in Europe in a seven-year test career, which included three tests for the British Lions on the victorious tour of New Zealand in 1971. He was the only English back in the Barbarians side that beat the All Blacks 23-11 in 1973. A star of a powerful Coventry side, he worked for Barclays Bank and then moved into a marketing and PR role in the building industry. He later became the marketing director at Bloxham School in Oxfordshire and ran a sports after-dinner speaking business, The Southern Sporting Clubs, before his death.

972. FAIRBROTHER, Keith Eli
Prop 12 caps 1969-1971
Born: Coventry, Warwickshire, 6 May 1944
Career: Nuneaton, Coventry, Warwickshire, Barbarians
Debut: v Ireland, Lansdowne Road, Dublin, February 1969

Fairbrother joined Coventry as a 17-year-old prop before helping England beat the Springboks in just his fifth test. He played in Coventry's back-to-back RFU Knockout Cup Final wins in 1973 and 1974 before turning professional with Leigh RL. He worked at Jaguar as a tinsmith when he left Couldon Castle School, then became a large-scale fruit and vegetable merchant, a shoe salesman in Russia and a property developer in the leisure industry. His intervention as chairman and owner of Coventry in the 1990s prevented the once powerful club from going to the wall.

973. FIELDING, Keith John
Wing 10 caps (10-3t) 1969-1972
Born: Birmingham, Warwickshire, 8 July 1949
Career: Moseley, Loughborough Colleges, North Midlands
Debut: v Ireland, Lansdowne Road, Dublin, February 1969

Fielding was a student at Loughborough when he won the first of ten caps and taught in Leicester. Selectors overlooked him during the 1972-73 season, but then he scored nine tries, helping England win the Scottish Centenary Sevens at Murrayfield. It earned him an £8,500 move to rugby league with Salford in 1973. He scored a record 46 tries in his first season and won caps for England and Great Britain, retiring in 1983 with 253 Salford tries. He earned fame as a contestant in BBC TV's Superstars in 1981, winning the British final and the Challenge of the Champions. He taught PE at Marple Hall School and Bramhall High School in Stockport.

974. HORTON, Nigel Edgar
Lock 20 caps (4-1t) 1969-1980
Born: Birmingham, Warwickshire, 13 April 1948
Career: Birmingham Police, Moseley, Wasps, Toulouse (France), North Midlands
Debut: v Ireland, Lansdowne Road, Dublin, February 1969

Horton, an athletic lock, was the first man to play for England in three separate decades. He joined Birmingham City Police when he left school and was in the force when he won his first cap. He moved to Toulouse to run a bar, playing for the local club and occasionally turning out for Wasps on visits to England and played his last international, against Ireland, in the 1980 Grand Slam campaign. A British Lion in 1977, he formed Rugby Football Consultants, then joined Richter Engineering to promote Predator training equipment. He helped the Midland Counties West side beat the All Blacks in December 1972.

975. SPENCER, John Southern
Centre 14 caps (6-2t) 1969-1971
Born: Staincliffe, West Riding of Yorkshire, 10 August 1947
Career: Cambridge University, Headingley, Wharfedale, Barbarians
Debut: v Ireland, Lansdowne Road, Dublin, February 1969

Spencer, a solicitor in Yorkshire, toured New Zealand with the victorious 1971 British Lions without playing a test, having gained three blues at Cambridge University. He also captained England four times in his last four appearances, finishing with the game against the President's XV in 1971, and since finishing playing, he has been heavily involved in the administrative side of the game. He has served on the RFU Council and management board, been chairman of the Barbarians, worked on the IRB board and was a director of the British Lions. He has been Wharfedale's president, and was manager of the 2017 Lions tour to New Zealand and RFU President.

976. DALTON, Timothy Joseph
Fly-half 1 cap 1969
Born: Warwick, Warwickshire, 2 September 1940
Died: Tauranga, New Zealand, 7 February 2014
Career: Coventry, Rugby, Warwickshire, Tauranga Cadet OB, Bay of Plenty
Debut: v Scotland, Twickenham, March 1969

Dalton was a Coventry fly-half who made history when he became England's first replacement, coming on as a winger for Keith Fielding in the 1969 game against Scotland at Twickenham. He made 249 appearances for Coventry from 1960 to 1970, mostly in partnership with George Cole at half-back, and played 48 times for Warwickshire, winning five county titles. He finished his playing career with Rugby Lions before emigrating to New Zealand, where he played for Tauranga Cadet OB and Bay of Plenty, successfully setting himself up as an antique dealer and running an auction house before his retirement.

977. PLUMMER, Keith Clive
Wing 4 caps 1969-1976
Born: Falmouth, Cornwall, 17 January 1947
Career: Penryn, Bristol, Newport, Cornwall, Barbarians
Debut: v Wales, Cardiff Arms Park, Cardiff, April 1969

Plummer played 53 times for Cornwall, making his England debut in 1969, but was forced to wait seven years to play three games in the 1976 Championship, a disaster for England when Peter Squires was injured. He played for

Penryn, making his debut aged 16 in 1963, and Bristol and even guested for Newport on their 1973 tour to South Africa. He worked as a car mechanic, later becoming a director of several motor dealerships in Cornwall and the west of England. The former wing also served as president of Cornwall Rugby Union and was involved when Graham Dawe was made coach in 2013.

978. BUCKNALL, Anthony Launce
Flanker 10 caps 1969-1971
Born: Torquay, Devon, 7 June 1945
Career: Oxford University, Richmond, Middlesex, London Counties, Eastern Counties
Debut: v South Africa, Twickenham, December 1969

A boxing and rugby blue in 1965 and 1966 at Oxford University, stockbroker Bucknall was an inexperienced and surprising choice who had the unenviable task of captaining England against Wales in 1971 when they lost 22-6. He played a key role in Richmond's 1974 Middlesex Sevens' success. A Gilts salesman for the various incarnations of W. Greenwell and Co., Midland Bank and HSBC for 33 years. Now retired and living in Putney, south west London, his wife, Brenda, is the sister of former England cricketer Allan Lamb. He also had a stint as an England selector while captaining Richmond.

979. HALE, Peter Martin
Wing 3 caps 1969-1970
Born: Hall Green, Warwickshire, 12 August 1943
Died: Kingsbridge, South Devon, November 2022
Career: Solihull, Moseley, Midland Counties, North Midlands
Debut: v South Africa, Twickenham, December 1969

Hale, a product of Solihull School, played for his local club before joining Moseley and was the club's leading scorer with 44 tries in the 1967-68 season. He made his debut in England's first-ever win over South Africa when Rod Webb was injured. He turned down a move to Swinton RL, telling them he wanted to continue playing for England, but was immediately axed after becoming a scapegoat for a defeat to Wales. He also played tennis for Warwickshire and was a clerk with chartered accountants William J. Jennings, Warner & Co. before becoming a sales representative for Saville Tractors and a director of Sportbuild.

980. SHACKLETON, Ian Roger
Fly-half 4 caps (3-1t) 1969-1970
Born: Shipley, Yorkshire, 17 June 1948
Career: Cambridge University, Harrogate, Bradford, Richmond, Yorkshire, Lavelanet (France)
Debut: v South Africa, Twickenham, December 1969

Shackleton won his last cap when he was 21 before three years in France put paid to his international aspirations in the days before cheap travel. Educated at Bradford Grammar School, he studied land economy and economics at Cambridge University before moving to Carcassonne, taking up a research post at Montpelier University playing for Lavelanet, and even though he returned, and played for Yorkshire until his mid-30s, he was never picked again. He set up a company, latterly known as Roger Shackleton Group International Ltd, to help bring sponsors into rugby. He has also been involved in a property company and coached at Harrogate.

981. STARMER-SMITH, Nigel Christopher
Scrum-half 7 caps 1969-1971
Born: Cheltenham, Gloucestershire, 25 December 1944
Career: Oxford University, Harlequins, Oxfordshire, Surrey, Barbarians
Debut: v South Africa, Twickenham, December 1969

Starmer-Smith toured Canada with England in 1967 but had to wait until the first win over South Africa for his cap. The scrum-half, a double blue at Oxford, taught at Epsom College, became involved with BBC radio before graduating to television, covering rugby and hockey, and hosting Rugby Special. He edited Rugby World magazine and became the official commentator and consultant to the IRB, covering events such as the World Series Sevens. He also covered the 2003 Rugby World Cup for ITV. He has written several books, including an official history of the Barbarians, but is now suffering from dementia.

982. STEVENS, Claude Brian
Prop 25 caps (8-2t) 1969-1975
Born: Godolphin, Cornwall, 2 June 1940
Died: St. Austell, Cornwall, 10 October 2017
Career: Penzance & Newlyn, Harlequins, Barbarians, British Lions
Debut: v South Africa, Twickenham, December 1969

Cornish legend 'Stack' Stevens played over 500 times for Penzance & Newlyn and 83 times for his county. The prop toured with the 1971 British Lions and played in England's wins over South Africa in 1972 at Ellis Park and the All Blacks in Auckland a year later, where he scored a try. A farmer, he also had a spell at Harlequins when he used to deliver vegetables to Covent Garden market on a Friday before heading home to Cornwall after a match. He was part of Campaign Kernow, lobbying for a team from Cornwall to be allowed to compete independently in the Commonwealth Games. His son John plays for the Cornish Pirates.

983. WARDLOW, Christopher Story
Centre 6 caps 1969-1971
Born: Carlisle, Cumberland, 12 July 1942
Career: Carlisle, Northampton, Cumberland & Westmorland, North West Counties, Barbarians
Debut: v South Africa, Twickenham, December 1969

Wardlow was a strong running centre who missed the 1971 British Lions tour to New Zealand after breaking his jaw in a practice game at Coventry. He gained revenge when he was part of the North West Counties' side that beat the All Blacks at Workington 16-14 in 1972. He was England's second-ever replacement when he came on for Bob Hiller to make his debut, but he started the entire 1971 Championship. He helped Coventry win an RFU Knock-Out Cup in 1973 and worked in the road haulage industry and as a transport manager for London County Buses.

984. NOVAK, Michael John
Wing 3 caps (3-1t) 1970
Born: Stratford-upon-Avon, Warwickshire, 27 September 1947
Career: Eastbourne, Harlequins, Surrey, Sussex
Debut: v Wales, Twickenham, February 1970

Novak scored on his test debut but was powerless to stop a Welsh win, and he was one of four players who played their last international in a 35-13 defeat by France in 1970. After leaving Eastbourne Grammar School, he was a dental student at Guy's Hospital. He was rated as a highly talented winger but determined to further his medical career. He went to work in New York in the early 1980s then took a professorship in Kentucky. His last post was in the Department of Periodontics at the University of Texas Health Science Centre in San Antonio, Texas.

985. BULPITT, Michael Philip
Wing 1 cap 1970
Born: Richmond, Yorkshire, 12 April 1944
Career: Blackheath, Eastern Counties, Rosslyn Park, London Counties, Barbarians
Debut: v Scotland, Murrayfield, March 1970

Bulpitt was in the London Counties side that played the Springboks in 1969, a match disrupted by anti-apartheid demonstrations led by Peter Hain and Jack Straw. He won his only cap in the 14-5 defeat to Scotland in 1970 as a replacement for Martin Hale but lost his place when John Novak moved to the left wing for the final game of the Championship against France and was never picked again. He worked for Coleman Prentice & Varley before joining Lloyds Bank as Assistant Advertising Manager, where he developed the bank's famous 'Black Horse' campaign and was chief manager of marketing communications when he retired.

986. JACKSON, Barry K
Prop 2 caps 1970
Born: St Helens, Lancashire, 9 August 1937
Died: Warrington, Lancashire, 7 October 2019
Career: Broughton Park, Barbarians, North West Counties
Debut: v Scotland, Murrayfield, Edinburgh, March 1970

Jackson was the first player from Broughton Park to be capped. He started playing rugby union while working as an apprentice at David Brown Engineering, where he met Roland Miller, the ex-Lancashire wing who persuaded him to change from soccer. He won his first cap off the bench, coming on at flanker for Bryan West against Scotland in 1970 and started his second at his preferred loosehead. He also played at lock for North West Counties against the All Blacks in January 1964. He worked as a machine tool design engineer and battled Alzheimer's in his later life.

987. JORDEN, Anthony Mervyn
Full-back 7 caps (22-5c,4p) 1970-1975
Born: Radlett, Hertfordshire, 28 January 1947
Died: 20 October 2023
Career: Cambridge University, Blackheath, Upper Clapton, Harlequins, Bedford, Barbarians, Eastern Counties
Debut: v France, Stade Colombes, Paris, April 1970

A product of Monmouth School, Jorden was an accomplished cricketer for Cambridge University, Bedfordshire and Essex and once dismissed five of the top six Sussex batsmen when playing for his university. He made his England debut against France in 1970, coming in for Bob Hiller and kicking two conversions and a penalty. He did not play again until 1973 and appeareand in his last test in 1975. He had a brief spell coaching at Wasps in the early 1990s when the club was in turmoil and also coached London. He was a chartered surveyor and joint senior partner at Jorden Salata and was the founder of the National Administration Receivers Association.

988. LEADBETTER, Michael Morris
Lock 1 cap 1970
Born: Southport, Merseyside, 25 July 1946
Died: Colchester, Essex, 17 April 2009
Career: Broughton Park, Lancashire, North West Counties, Barbarians
Debut: v France, Stade Colombes, Paris, April 1970

Leadbetter won one cap in 1970, in the 35-13 defeat to France, when he was playing at Broughton Park before going on to forge a career in social services. He had studied print technology at Manchester College of Art and Design but became a social worker after taking an MA in psychoanalysis at Manchester University. Part of the North West Counties team that beat the All Blacks in 1972, he also played rugby league for Rochdale Hornets. He was a director of social services in Tameside and then Essex before becoming interim executive director of social services in Ealing, then Kensington and Chelsea.

989. REDMOND, Gerald Francis
No.8 1 cap 1970
Born: Weston-super-Mare, Somerset, 23 March 1943
Career: Cambridge University, Bedford, Bristol, Weston-super-Mare, Somerset
Debut: v France, Stade Colombes, Paris, April 1970

Redmond won his only cap as a student at Cambridge University in the 35-13 defeat to France that rounded off England's dismal season in 1970. He won three blues at Cambridge, captaining them in 1971 after Phil Keith-Roach contracted hepatitis, and toured Argentina and Brazil with the combined Oxford & Cambridge side that year. A tough No.8, he had stints at Bedford and Bristol and taught at Cranleigh School in Surrey before running the New Ocean Hotel in his native Weston-super-Mare, where he also did some coaching in the late 1980s after retiring from playing.

990. HANNAFORD, Ronald Charles
No.8 3 caps (3-1t) 1971
Born: Gloucester, Gloucestershire, 19 October 1944
Career: Durham University, Cambridge University, Rosslyn Park, Bristol, Barbarians, Gloucestershire
Debut: v Wales, Cardiff Arms Park, Cardiff, January 1971

Hannaford was educated at the Crypt School in Gloucester, Durham University and Churchill College, Cambridge, winning a blue in 1967. He scored a try on his 1971 debut against Wales. He was a biology master at Sherborne School before heading to Clifton College and Millfield, then heading to New Zealand in 1975, where he was a player-coach at Naenae Old Boys in the Wellington League. He returned to take up a post at Rendcomb College, where he and his wife, Jane, ran Park House before moving to Seaford College. He retired to Brittany and was president of the Old Cryptians Club.

991. JANION, Jeremy Paul Aubrey George
Wing/centre, 12 caps 1971-1975
Born: Bishop's Stortford, Hertfordshire, 25 September 1946
Career: Bedford, Richmond, Barbarians, London Counties, Eastern Counties
Debut: v Wales, Cardiff Arms Park, Cardiff, January 1971

Janion's test career as a wing and centre ran from the 1971 Championship to the 1975 tour of Australia, when he was a replacement and ended up playing both internationals in midfield. The trained accountant was a tough tackler, and his partnership with Peter Preece helped keep the South Africans quiet in England's unexpected 18-9 win over the Springboks at Ellis Park in 1972. He worked with companies such as Marconi and Guinness and was a finance director in Kuwait before returning to the United Kingdom to expand the company Connaught Commercial Services. In later life, he became a highly successful property developer.

992. NEARY, Anthony
Flanker 43 caps (19-5t) 1971-1980
Born: Manchester, Lancashire, 25 November 1948
Career: British Universities, Broughton Park, Barbarians, Lancashire, British Lions
Debut: v Wales, Cardiff Arms Park, Cardiff, January 1971

Neary was a stalwart of the England back row for nearly a decade and played his last game for his country in the Grand Slam-deciding win over Scotland in 1980. He toured with the British Lions in 1974 and 1977, playing one test on the second trip, and scored a try for England when they beat the All Blacks at Eden Park, Auckland, in 1973. A solicitor, he missed the 1980 trip to South Africa and retired as England's most-capped player. A member of the North team that beat the All Blacks in 1978, he was jailed for theft in 1998 and has since worked in commercial property.

993. NINNES, Barry Francis
Lock 1 cap 1971
Born: St Ives, Cornwall, 23 March 1948
Career: St Ives, Coventry, Cornwall, Warwickshire
Debut: v Wales, Cardiff Arms Park, Cardiff, January 1971

Ninnes, a member of the powerful Coventry side of the 1970s, won his only cap in the 22-6 loss to Wales in 1971 and was one of two players dropped for the next game. Peter Rossborough was the other, and although Rossborough played again, it was the end of Ninnes' international career.

The lock won the English Cup with Coventry in 1973 when he was working as a factory manager. A Christian, he later became a director of Kings Foundation based in Sheffield. He believes in using sport to help people develop, and the foundation provides activity camps and employment opportunities and trains volunteers.

994. PAGE, John Jackson
Scrum-half 5 caps 1971-1975
Born: Brighton, West Sussex, 16 April 1947
Career: Cambridge University, Bedford, Northampton, Barbarians
Debut: v Wales, Cardiff Arms Park, Cardiff, January 1967

'Jacko' Page, a three-time blue at Cambridge, played throughout the 1971 Championship at scrum-half, then had to wait four years for his final cap when he was picked for the 7-6 win over Scotland at Twickenham after England had lost their first three matches. He was a member of the Northampton side that won a Daily Mail Pennant in 1976. He studied mechanical sciences at Queens' College, Cambridge, but moved into banking and was with Lloyds for 28 years, rising to become a senior manager in Wolverhampton, running a group of branches. He became managing director of energy performance certificate provider Premier Home Movers.

995. ROSSBOROUGH, Peter Alec
Full-back 7 caps (34-1t,3c,7p,1d) 1971-1975
Born: Coventry, Warwickshire, 30 June 1948
Career: Durham University, Coventry, UAU, British Universities, Durham County, Warwickshire, Barbarians
Debut: v Wales, Cardiff Arms Park, Cardiff, January 1971

Rossborough won his seven caps as a goal-kicking full-back when he was a member of a mighty Coventry side with whom he won the English Cup in 1973 and 1974. He was part of the England team that beat New Zealand in Auckland in 1973 and managed the England squad that won the World Cup Sevens in 1993 with Lawrence Dallaglio and Matt Dawson in the side. The full-back worked as a teacher and was headmaster of Ashlawn School in Rugby for 24 years before retiring in 2008. He acted as a coaching consultant at Coventry, where he is president and was chairman when the club were rescued from financial problems.

996. WRIGHT, Ian Douglas
Fly-half 4 caps 1971
Born: Croydon, London, 24 December 1945
Died: Cheltenham, Gloucestershire, 18 February 2000
Career: Rosslyn Park, Northampton, Sussex, London Counties, Surrey, Devon, Oxfordshire
Debut: v Wales, Cardiff Arms Park, Cardiff, January 1971

Wright was 18 and still at Worthing High School when, as a last-minute stand-in, he scored a try for Sussex in a County Championship game against Kent. He captained St Luke's College and won his caps in 1971, two years after having his first trial after impressing for England under-25s against Fiji. He played cricket for Sussex CCC and captained Northampton when they were Daily Mail Pennant winners in 1976 but fell out with the club soon afterwards and returned to Rosslyn Park. A teacher in Bishops Stortford and Oxford, he was just 54 when he died.

997. COTTON, Frances Edward
Prop 31 caps (4-1t) 1971-1981
Born: Wigan, Lancashire, 3 January 1947
Career: Liverpool, Loughborough College, Coventry, Sale, Barbarians, Lancashire, British Lions
Debut: v Scotland, Twickenham, March 1971

A prop who could play both sides, Cotton was a member of the 1974 invincible Lions in South Africa and won a Grand Slam with England in 1980. He had to leave the Lions tour of South Africa that year after suffering chest pains playing against the South African Federation in Stellenbosch and was diagnosed with pericarditis. He played one more test but was forced to retire with hamstring trouble. In 1997, he was the victorious Lions tour manager and was part of the RFU hierarchy that appointed Clive Woodward as England coach before leaving to concentrate on his business interests after forming Cotton Traders with former England scrum-half Steve Smith.

998. COWMAN, Alan Richard
Fly-half 5 caps (6-2d) 1971-1973
Born: Workington, Cumbria, 18 March 1949
Career: Newcastle University, Loughborough Colleges, UAU, Coventry, Cumberland and Westmoreland, North West Counties
Debut: v Scotland, Twickenham, March 1971

Cowman was at Loughborough with Fran Cotton and Steve Smith and was a member of the North West Counties team, which beat the All Blacks in 1972, the first time an English side. After seeing an advert on a college notice board, he taught chemistry and PE at King Henry VIII Grammar School in Coventry. He joined Coventry after taking schoolboys to tournaments at Coundon Road and played in the back-to-back RFU Knockout Cup winning sides in 1973-74. After becoming head of a school in Dorset, he now lives in retirement in Exeter, Devon.

999. RALSTON, Christopher Wayne
Lock 22 caps (4-1t) 1971-1975
Born: Hendon, London, 25 May 1944
Career: Richmond, Middlesex, London Counties, Barbarians
Debut: v Scotland, Murrayfield, Edinburgh, March 1971

Ralston, a rugged lock for Richmond and England, was a member of the invincible Lions squad who toured South Africa in 1974 and played in the final test in Johannesburg. A veteran of the away wins over South Africa and New Zealand in 1972 and 1973, respectively, he was the victim of a raking incident in 1978 when playing for Richmond against Llanelli, which left him needing 32 stitches and caused the cancellation of fixtures between the clubs. He worked in advertising, and his company, Ralston Holding Company Ltd, which his father started, published in-flight and cruise-ship magazines.

1000. CREED, Roger Norman
Flanker 1 cap 1971
Born: Solihull, Warwickshire, 19 November 1945
Career: Moseley, Old Silhillians, Coventry, Warwickshire, Barbarians
Debut: v President's XV, Twickenham, April 1971

Solihull School-educated Creed broke into the Moseley side when he was 17 but dislocated his shoulder after four games and lost his place. After joining Old Silhillians, Alf Wyman recruited him to play for Coventry's Nighthawks midweek side and, within a week, he forced his way into the senior team. A member of the One Cap Club after playing against a President's Overseas XV, he played in Coventry's 1973 RFU Knockout Cup winning side in 1973. His brother Graham also played for Coventry. He worked in the family power tools business Power Tools Specialists and then in real estate management.

1001. DIXON, Peter John
Flanker/No.8, 22 caps (16-4t) 1971-1978
Born: Keighley, Yorkshire, 30 April 1944
Died: Setmurthy, Cumbria, 2 August 2023
Career: Oxford University, Harlequins, Gosforth, Barbarians, British Lions
Debut: v President's XV, Twickenham, April 1971

Dixon, a four-time Oxford blue between 1967 and 1970 when he was studying social anthropology, only won his first cap in April 1971 but shortly afterwards was on tour with the legendary British Lions in New Zealand. He played three tests on that trip, played international rugby until 1978 and officially retired a year later when he was not picked to play the All Blacks despite starring in the North's defeat of the Kiwis earlier that season. He worked at Durham University, where he was a lecturer in anthropology, and had a spell at the University of Botswana and died after a battle with brain cancer.

1002. BEESE, Michael Christopher
Centre 3 caps (4-1t) 1972
Born: Bristol, 8 October 1948
Career: Bath, Liverpool, Barbarians, Western Counties, Somerset
Debut: v Wales, Twickenham, January 1972

Beese was a centre for Bath in the 1970s, making 316 appearances for the club, but won his three caps playing for Liverpool while studying in the town. He coached at Bath in the late 1980s under Jack Rowell. He scored his only test try in his final international against France in 1972 and worked in town planning as planning director of GL Hearn in the property consultants' Bath office. Before that, he worked in the Avon County Council Planning Department. He served as a vice-president of Bath for several years before being made club president in 2013.

1003. BRINN, Alan
Lock 3 caps 1972
Born: Ystrad, Rhondda, Wales, 21 July 1940
Died: Gloucester, Gloucestershire, 9 February 2022
Career: Gloucester
Debut: v Wales, Twickenham, 15 January 1972

Brinn was a long-serving Gloucester lock who played a record 574 games for the club from 1960 to 1979 but had to wait until he was 31 for his England debut. Part of the Gloucester side that won the inaugural English Cup in 1972, he won his three caps in 1972. He started working in banking but soon opened a sports outfitters in Eastgate Street, Gloucester. He took over as chairman of Gloucester when Peter Ford stepped aside in 1993 and was in the job as the game went professional. He also served as an associate national selector for England.

1004. BURTON, Michael Alan
Prop 17 caps 1972-1978
Born: Maidenhead, Berkshire, 18 December 1945
Career: Gloucester, Barbarians, Gloucestershire, British Lions
Debut: v Wales, Twickenham, January 1972

Burton was a tough Gloucester prop who became the first Englishman to be sent off in a test match when he was dismissed during the violent clash with Australia in Brisbane in 1975. That match had started with a fight that he carried on, and local referee Bob Burnett ordered him off, although a disciplinary hearing found he needed more punishment. A tourist with the invincible Lions in South Africa in 1974 without playing a test, he played 360 times for Gloucester between 1964 and 1978 and won two English Cups plus four County Championships with Gloucestershire. He runs a successful sports travel, corporate hospitality and event management company.

1005. OLD, Alan Gerard Bernard
Fly-half 16 caps (98-1t,8c,23p,3d) 1972-1978
Born: Middlesbrough, North Yorkshire, 23 September 1945
Career: Durham University, Middlesbrough, Leicester, Yorkshire, the North, Barbarians, British Lions
Debut: v Wales, Twickenham, January 1972

Old toured South Africa with the 1974 Lions. He had to settle for being stand-by for Phil Bennett at fly-half but did score a record 37 points in the game against South West Districts, although his tour was ended by injury. His England career ran from 1972 to 1978 and included the away wins against South Africa and New Zealand in 1972 and 1973, respectively. He worked as a technical administrator for the Northern Division and had a successful career in education. He taught at Worksop College when he was playing and later became principal of Redcar & Cleveland College. His brother Chris was an England test cricketer.

1006. RIPLEY, Andrew George OBE
No.8 24 caps (8-2t) 1972-1976
Born: South Liverpool, Lancashire, 1 December 1947
Died: East Grinstead, Sussex, 17 June 2010
Career: Rosslyn Park, Brescia (Ita), Barbarians, British Lions
Debut: v Wales, Twickenham, January 1972

Ripley toured with the 1974 Lions, won the BBC Superstars series in 1980 and reached the semi-finals of the 400 metres in the AAA Championship in 1978. He also became a world indoor veteran rowing champion and almost made the Cambridge University Boat Race crew at the age of 50. He was an anti-establishment figure who would become president of Rosslyn Park. He would have played test matches for any Lions team that did not have Mervyn Davies in it at No. 8. An accountant, he had played for Rosslyn Park until he was 41. In 2005, he was diagnosed with prostate cancer and became an ambassador for the Prostate Cancer Society.

1007. WEBSTER, Jan Godfrey
Scrum-half, 11 caps
Born: Southport, Lancashire, 24 August 1946
Died: Walsall, Staffordshire, 6 February 2019
Career: Walsall, Moseley, Staffordshire, Barbarians
Debut: v Wales, Twickenham, January 1972

Scrum-half Webster starred in the away wins over South Africa in 1972 and New Zealand in 1973 after taking five years from his first England trial to make the full side. He captained Moseley from 1971 to 1974, when the club enjoyed some of its most successful times, including reaching the first-ever RFU Knockout Cup Final. He finished his playing career with Walsall but returned to Moseley to serve as president from 2002 to 2006. He ran a sports-outfitting company in the Midlands, specialising in footwear. He worked as a sports consultant and has been involved with youth sports, especially cricket and athletics, in the Caribbean.

1008. KNIGHT, Peter Michael
Full-back/wing 3 caps 1972
Born: Bristol, 7 October 1947
Died: Aylesbury, Buckinghamshire, 4 October 2015
Career: Bristol, Gloucestershire
Debut: v France, Stade Colombes, Paris, February 1972

Knight saved the best till last when he won his third and final cap in England's epic 18-9 win over the Springboks at Ellis Park in 1972. He won the County Championship with Gloucestershire in 1972 and was an RFU Knock Out Finalist. He taught at Sherborne in Dorset, Clifton College and the British School in Brussels. He began training in theology at Trinity Theological College in Bristol and was ordained as an Anglican minister. He was a minister at All Saints' Church in Lydiard Millicent, Wiltshire and a curate at Christ the Servant Church, Stockwood, before carrying on his ministry in Swindon and Buckinghamshire.

1009. WESTON, Lionel Edward
Scrum-half 2 caps 1972
Born: Wenlock, Shropshire, 22 February 1947
Career: Loughborough College, West of Scotland, East Midlands, Rosslyn Park, Barbarians
Debut: v France, Stade Colombes, Paris, February 1972

Weston won both of his caps playing for West of Scotland while working as a teacher at Kelvinside Academy in

Glasgow. The scrum-half toured South Africa with England in 1972 without playing in the test and was replaced by Steve Smith during the last week of the trip ahead of England's historic win at Ellis Park. He worked as a special educational needs coordinator at Stowe School in Buckinghamshire, where he was Walpole House's housemaster from 1987 to 2000. He retired from teaching at Stowe in 2009 after 30 years at the school.

1010. MARTIN, Nicholas Owen
Lock 1 cap 1972
Born: Cambridge, Cambridgeshire, 26 June 1946
Career: Cambridge University, Bedford, Harlequins, Barbarians, South-East, London Counties
Debut: v France, Stade Colombes, Paris, February 1972

Martin captained Cambridge when Martin Green was injured and won his only cap coming off the bench in the 37-12 defeat to France in 1972. Despite impressing, playing for the South-East in Divisional games, he wasn't given another chance. Educated at Perse School in Cambridge, he worked in local government firstly with Haverhill Urban District Council and later was assistant borough secretary of Bury St Edmunds. He was director of the Mid-East Anglian Enterprise Agency and town centre manager in Haverhill before leaving the post in 2007. He later became chairman of the Eastern Counties selectors and was president of Newmarket RFC.

1011. EVANS, Geoffrey Williams
Centre 9 caps (7-1t,1d) 1972-1974
Born: Coventry, 10 December 1950
Career: Coventry, Barbarians, British Lions
Debut: v Scotland, Murrayfield, Edinburgh, March 1972

Evans, former All-England Schools long jump champion, was a member of the fabled Coventry team of the 1970s. He was a member of the Midland Counties West side that beat the All Blacks in December 1972 and won the RFU Knockout Cup in 1973. That summer, he recorded a second win over the All Blacks when England won in Auckland. A tourist with the British Lions to South Africa in 1974, where he scored a hat-trick against South Western Districts, He was a banker with Midland Bank and then HSBC before starting his own finance company and now lives in retirement in Claverdon, South Warwickshire.

1012. DOBLE, Samuel Arthur
Full-back 3 caps (20-2c,6p) 1972-1973
Born: Wolverhampton, Staffordshire, 9 March 1944
Died: Birmingham, Warwickshire, 17 September 1977
Career: Moseley, Staffordshire,
Debut: v South Africa, Ellis Park, Johannesburg, June 1972

Wolverhampton PE teacher Doble was one of the best kickers of any era but only won three caps because of the mismanagement of the England side at the time. He scored 581 points for Moseley in 1971/72 and nearly 4000 in his 11 years at the club. He helped Staffordshire win the County Championship, and the Midland Counties West beat the All Blacks. His International career ended when he declined to play in Ireland. He was dropped by Moseley in 1976 due to loss of form and retired shortly afterwards with a rib injury given as the reason. However, it became clear that he had a rare lymphatic cancer and died aged 33.

1013. MORLEY, Alan John MBE
Wing 7 caps (8-2t) 1972-1975
Born: Bristol, 25 June 1950
Career: Bristol, Barbarians, Gloucestershire, British Lions
Debut: v South Africa, Ellis Park, Johannesburg, June 1972

Morley scored a try on his debut in England's shock 18-9 win over the Springboks at Ellis Park in 1972 and toured South Africa with the Lions in 1974 without playing a test match. The wing represented Bristol 519 times between 1968 and 1986, scoring 384 tries and a total of 1,547 points for the club and in first-class games, he scored an incredible 479 tries. He qualified as a building surveyor, working for Hartnell Taylor Cook as a financial advisor at Octagon Consultancy in his hometown. He was awarded an MBE for services to rugby in 1984 and was on the board at Bristol.

1014. PREECE, Peter Stuart
Centre 12 caps 1972-1976
Born: Meriden, Warwickshire, 15 November 1949
Career: Coventry, Leamington, Warwickshire, Barbarians
Debut: v South Africa, Ellis Park, Johannesburg, June 1972

The son of another Coventry stalwart, Ivor, Preece won 12 caps for England, the same number as his father. He went to school with fellow Coventry stars David Duckham and Peter Rossborough at Henry VIII School. He made his debut in the historic 18-9 win over the Springboks in 1972. He scored four tries against New South Wales on the 1975 tour of Australia and also played in the 16-10 win over the All Blacks at Eden Park in 1973. A building-society employee when he was playing, he later worked as a pension consultant in Leamington with Harrison Beale & Owen Financial Services.

1015. WATKINS, John Arthur
Flanker 7 caps 1972-1975
Born: Gloucester, Gloucestershire, 28 November 1945
Career: Gloucester, Gloucestershire, Barbarians
Debut: v South Africa, Ellis Park, Johannesburg, June 1972

Watkins was an under-rated flanker who did a shift at prop on his debut when 'Stack' Stevens was taken off against South Africa at Ellis Park in 1972. He moved to the front row while Stevens was being treated, and history records England won 16-10, and he played in the 1973 win over the All Blacks in Auckland. He played 386 times for Gloucester, winning the English Cup in 1972 and winning successive County Championships with Gloucestershire from 1974 to 1976. He worked as a tool engineer for Priestley's in Gloucester, then Service Aluminium, and was a referee.

1016. ANDERSON, William Francis
Prop 1 cap 1973
Born: Burscough, Lancashire, 4 May 1940
Career: Orrell, Liverpool, Southport, West Park, Barbarians, Lancashire
Debut: v New Zealand, Twickenham, January 1973

Anderson was educated at Hutton Grammar School and began his senior career with Southport before moving to Orrell. Being part of the of the North West Counties side which beat the All Blacks in November 1972 earned him his only cap against the same opposition in January 1973, replacing Fran Cotton, the year he won a County Championship with Lancashire and was a finalist 12 months later. He was the first player capped by England direct from Orrell and coached Southport, West Park, New Brighton. He worked as a draughtsman with mining engineers Gullick & Dobson in Wigan and now lives in Bootle, Cumbria, in retirement.

1017. WARFIELD, Peter John
Centre 6 caps 1973-1975
Born: Waddington, Lincolnshire, 1 April 1951
Career: Durham University, Cambridge University, Rosslyn Park, Barbarians
Debut: v New Zealand, Twickenham, January 1973

Warfield won six caps at the centre after attending Durham University. He spent a year in the United States, studying art, and took a post-graduate degree at Cambridge University when he won his last three caps. He played in England's defeat in Dublin in 1973 when other nations refused to travel because of the terrorist threat and was briefly in the

Army Education Corps. He had taught at Christ's Hospital in Horsham before arriving at Harrow School in 1984, where he coached rugby and cricket and taught Latin as well as religious studies, history, English and history of art. He retired from teaching in 2013.

1018. SMITH, Stephen James
Scrum-half 28 caps (8-2t) 1973-1983
Born: Stockport, Greater Manchester, 22 July 1951
Career: Loughborough College, Sale, Northern Division, Barbarians, British Lions
Debut: v Ireland, Lansdowne Road, Dublin, February 1973

Smith was the scrum-half when England won the Grand Slam in 1980 and a replacement for the British Lions in South Africa later that year. A five-time England captain in 1982 after Bill Beaumont was forced to retire, he was also whistled up as a replacement on the 1983 Lions trip to New Zealand. He worked as a teacher and, in retirement, worked as a television commentator for ITV Sport. He was in the hot seat, alongside John Taylor when Jonny Wilkinson dropped his goal in the 2003 Rugby World Cup final. In 1987, Smith co-founded the leisure wear business Cotton Traders with his 1980 teammate Fran Cotton.

1019. UTTLEY, Roger Miles OBE
Lock/flanker/number 8 23 caps (8-2T) 1973-1980
Born: Blackpool, Lancashire, 11 September 1949
Career: Gosforth, Wasps, Barbarians, British Lions
Debut: v Ireland, Lansdowne Road, Dublin, February 1973

Uttley made his name on the 1974 British Lions tour to South Africa when he was taken as a lock and played all four tests in the winning series as a flanker. He helped beat the All Blacks in Auckland in 1973 and, in 1980, won the Grand Slam under Bill Beaumont. The Slam-clinching game against Scotland was his last test. A schoolmaster at Harrow School, he retired after 26 years as director of physical education, he was assistant coach to Ian McGeechan on the victorious Lions tour of 1989 in Australia and helped Geoff Cooke take England to the 1991 Rugby World Cup final. He managed England from 1997 to 1999.

1020. COOPER, Martin John
Fly-half 11 caps (4-1t) 1973-1977
Born: Burton-upon-Trent, Staffordshire, 23 April 1948
Career: Wolverhampton, Moseley, Barbarians, Staffordshire
Debut: v France, Twickenham, February 1973

Cooper came on as a replacement when England beat the All Blacks in New Zealand for the first time. But his other 10 caps came as a starting fly-half. He could play anywhere from fly-half outwards, and scored the only try in England's 4-0 win over Ireland at Lansdowne Road in 1977. He retired in 1982 after helping Moseley share the English Cup when they drew 12-12 with Gloucester but already had his off-field career mapped out. He had done articles with a firm of chartered accountants after leaving grammar school before working with a building society and started Martin Cooper Wealth Management in Worcester.

1021. SQUIRES, Peter John
Wing 29 caps (24-6t) 1973-1979
Born: Ripon, 4 August 1951
Career: Harrogate, Yorkshire, Barbarians, British Lions
Debut: v France, Twickenham, February 1973

Squires was a try scorer in the win over the All Blacks in Auckland in 1973. He also toured New Zealand with the 1977 British Lions, playing in one test match, but a hamstring injury hampered his trip. He also played county cricket for Yorkshire from 1972 to 1976. He had played scrum-half and fly-half originally, and when he was picked for his England debut had only been playing on the wing for 18 months. He had worked as a PE teacher at Harrogate College, teaching rugby and cricket, but latterly was employed as a territorial manager by several breweries, including Wharfe Bank, Theakston and Caledonian, working in the north east of England.

1022. ROUGHLEY, David
Centre 3 caps 1973-1974
Born: Warrington, Cheshire, 10 December 1946
Career: Warrington, Liverpool, Lancashire
Debut: v Australia, Twickenham, November 1973

Educated at Beaumont School in Warrington, Roughley joined his local club as a 16-year-old before moving to Liverpool. He was a reserve at England trials in 1969 and went on the non-capped tour of the Far East in 1971, but a thigh injury forced him home after one game. Part of the North West Counties side that beat the All Blacks in 1972 made his test debut the following season. He coached Warrington, where he was club president and worked as a mechanical engineer with McKechnie Chemicals, Widnes, a draughtsman for a Warrington-based engineering company and the Highways Agency.

1023. SMITH, Keith
Centre 4 caps 1974-1975
Born: Leeds, West Yorkshire, 19 November 1952
Died: Leeds, West Yorkshire, 2 June 2006
Career: Roundhay, Yorkshire, Barbarians
Debut: v France, Parc des Princes, Paris, March 1974

Smith was a talented centre who made his test debut against France in 1972. He played once more that year, then twice in 1975, but turned to rugby league after 85 games and 672 points for Roundhay. He signed for Wakefield Trinity in 1976 and played for them in the 1979 Challenge Cup final, which Trinity lost 12-3 to Widnes. The centre also represented England in league, and once his professional career was over, he became a postman and coached at East Leeds Amateur RFLC. He fought a long battle against cancer and died in a Leeds hospice in 2006, aged 53.

1024. HARE, William Henry MBE
Full-back 25 caps (240-2t,14c,67p,1d) 1974-1984
Born: Newark, Nottinghamshire, 29 November 1962
Career: Newark, Nottingham, Leicester, Barbarians, British Lions
Debut: v Wales, Twickenham, March 1974

'Dusty' Hare was a goal-kicking full-back who won a Grand Slam in 1980 and memorably kicked the penalty that gave England a 9-8 win over Wales at Twickenham. His career took off at Leicester, where he played 394 games, and on retirement in 1989, he had scored a first-class rugby record of 7,337 points. A British Lion in New Zealand in 1983, he played first-class cricket for Nottinghamshire and was a farmer. He worked at the Leicester academy and then as head scout before moving to Northampton as academy recruitment and development manager in 2010 but returned to Leicester seven years later. He was also Nottingham's director of rugby.

1025. BEAUMONT, Sir William Blackledge Beaumont CBE, DL
Lock 34 caps 1975-1982
Born: Preston, Lancashire, 9 March 1952
Career: Fylde, Lancashire, Barbarians
Debut: v Ireland, Lansdowne Road, Dublin, January 1975

Beaumont captained England to the Grand Slam in 1980 and led the British Lions to South Africa later that year. He captained England 21 times and helped the North of England beat the All Blacks in 1979 but was forced to retire with a head injury. He became a captain on *A Question of*

Sport and a formidable rugby administrator. He managed the 2005 Lions tour to New Zealand, brokered the deal that saved the Five Nations in 1999 and represented the RFU on the IRB. He was Chairman of the RFU and World Rugby and was knighted in 2019. He also ran a textiles business in Lancashire, and the County Championship trophy is named after him.

1026. WHEELER, Peter John
Hooker 41 caps 1975-1984
Born: South Norwood, Surrey, 26 November 1948
Career: Leicester, Barbarians, British Lions
Debut: v France, Twickenham, February 1975

Wheeler was a Grand Slam winner in 1980, captained Leicester to three English Cup wins from 1979 to 1981 and played 349 times for Leicester and seven tests for the Lions. He worked in insurance but was made chief executive of Leicester just as the game went professional and was at the helm in the boardroom when they became the best side in Europe. He also represented Leicester on the board of Premiership Rugby, worked on the Professional Game Board, which runs elite rugby in England and worked on the RFU's Legacy Group of the 2015 Rugby World Cup. He became rugby director and was made a life member of the Tigers.

1027. BENNETT, William Neil
Fly-half 7 caps (23-2t,5p) 1975-1979
Born: Ramsey, Isle of Man, 20 April 1951
Career: Bedford, Colwyn Bay, London Welsh, Barbarians, Surrey
Debut: v Scotland, Twickenham, March 1975

A product of Tiffin School in Surrey, fly-half Bennett won three caps in 1975 and 1976 and his final four in the Championship in 1979. An Englishman playing for London Welsh by then, he scored all of England's points in the 12-7 defeat to Ireland in Dublin and the 7-6 win over France at Twickenham. On the 1975 tour to Australia, he played one test match in Sydney and scored a record 36 points in the 64-12 win over Western Australia in Perth. A schoolteacher and English Cup winner with Bedford in 1975, he taught maths and was head of sport at Cranleigh School in Surrey.

1028. BUTLER, Peter Edward
Full-back 2 caps (10-2c,2p) 1975-1976
Born: Gloucester, Gloucestershire, 23 June 1951
Career: Gloucester, Gloucestershire
Debut: v Australia, Sydney Cricket Ground, Sydney, May 1975

At Gloucester, where Butler scored 2,961 points for the club, they still cannot believe the full-back only got two caps for England – one in 1975 and one against France in 1976. He was a prodigious goal kicker, once scoring over 500 points in a season, and also scored 367 points for Gloucestershire. He toured Australia, winning his first cap in Sydney, but was replaced by Alastair Hignell for the second test and in his final cap, England claimed the Wooden Spoon after four losses. An English Cup winner in 1978, he was involved in a chemical company and wrote a column in the Gloucester Citizen called 'What the Butler saw.'

1029. KINGSTON, Peter
Scrum-half 5 caps 1975-1979
Born: Lydney, Gloucestershire, 24 July 1951
Career: Moseley, Gloucester, Pontypool, Gloucestershire, North Midlands, South West Counties
Debut: v Australia, Sydney Cricket Ground, Sydney, May 1975

Kingston won two caps on the 1975 tour to Australia and his last three in 1979. He played 178 times for Gloucester between 1974 and 1981, was a PE teacher and went into coaching as soon as he finished playing. He coached the Gloucester under-21s, second team, academy and the first-team backs and was assistant England Schools coach from 1996 to 1999 when Jonny Wilkinson and Mike Tindall came through. He taught at Pate's Grammar School in Cheltenham for 33 years, until retiring in 2009 but carried on coaching at Newent RFC in Gloucestershire, where he served as president.

1030. MANTELL, Neil Dennington
Lock 1 cap 1975
Born: Reigate, Surrey, 13 October 1953
Career: Rosslyn Park, Nottingham, Surrey, South East Counties, Midlands, Barbarians
Debut: v Australia, Sydney Cricket Ground, Sydney, May 1975

Mantell joined Rosslyn Park when he left Reigate Grammar School and played for England Under-19s and 23s before his full debut against Australia on the 1975 summer tour after making an appearance in the English Cup Final. That was his only cap, but he also played for Nottingham, making 120 appearances and captaining the side before his retirement in 1987. He captained Midlands before retirement, also coaching them from 1991. He worked as an accountant and lives in Bakewell, Derbyshire, where he has a holiday letting interest in the Castle Cliffe guest house.

1031. MAXWELL, Andrew William
Centre 7 caps (4-1t) 1975-1978
Born: West Kirby, Cheshire, 3 March 1951
Died: 19 January 2013, aged 61
Career: Caldy, New Brighton, Headingley, Cheshire, Yorkshire
Debut: v Australia, Sydney Cricket Ground, Sydney May 1975

Maxwell started his playing career at Old Caldeians in the late 1960s, and even though he moved on as a player, he remained a member of the club and was eventually made a life member. The attacking centre made his test debut on the summer tour to Australia in 1975, when he was at Headingley, and played his last international against France in Paris in 1978 when a knee injury ended his career. He worked in sales for breweries, including the Hartlepool-based Camerons known in the north east of England for its Castle Eden Ale. He died in his sleep in 2013, aged 61.

1032. NELMES, Barry George
Prop 6 caps (4-1t) 1975-1978
Born: Bristol, 17 April 1948
Died, Cardiff, Wales, 1 December 2006
Career: Bristol, Cardiff, Gloucestershire, Western Counties, South of England, Barbarians
Debut: v Australia, Sydney Cricket Ground, Sydney, May 1975

Nelmes was a prop who achieved the rare distinction of being a popular Englishman in Wales. He won all his six caps whilst playing for Cardiff, turning out 166 times and forming a formidable front row with Alan Phillips and Mike Knill. He captained the club and would have had more England caps but for the presence of Fran Cotton. His attended Portway Secondary School in Bristol, playing for his local club aged 16, and represented England Under-15s years before becoming the first Cardiff player to be capped by the old enemy. Before his sudden death, he was the landlord of The Retreat Pub in Llanedeyrn, Cardiff.

1033. WORDSWORTH, Alan John
Fly-half 1 cap 1975
Born: Thornton Heath, Surrey, 9 November 1953
Career: Cambridge University, Harlequins, Old Whitgiftians
Debut: v Australia, Sydney Cricket Ground, Sydney, May 1975

Wordsworth, educated at Whitgift School, came off the bench to replace Neil Bennett after a quarter of an hour to win his only cap in the 16-9 defeat to Australia in Sydney. He had won a blue in 1973 at Cambridge, where he read economics, but missed the 1974 Varsity Match and the final England trial after injuring a calf playing football. Also winning England under-23s honours, he was from a family of doctors hailed as the new Richard Sharp but suffered a collapsed hip and turned his back on the senior game, preferring to play for Old Whitgiftians and was a director of B & L Realisations.

1034. HIGNELL, Alastair James CBE
Full-back 14 caps (48-3c,14p) 1975-1979
Born: Ely, Cambridgeshire, 4 September 1955
Career: Cambridge University, Bristol, Barbarians
Debut: v Australia, Ballymore Stadium, Brisbane, May 1975

Hignell was a hugely talented all-round sportsman who won the first of his 14 caps in the brutal Brisbane test of 1975, captained Cambridge University at rugby and cricket, and scored 11 first-class centuries, including a knock of 119 against the West Indies at Bristol in 1976. He combined playing rugby with playing county cricket for Gloucestershire and teaching. He moved into journalism and broadcasting, becoming a respected commentator with BBC Radio and continued working until 2008 despite being diagnosed with multiple sclerosis. The man-of-the-match at the Varsity Match receives the Alastair Hignell Medal, and his autobiography *Higgy* was Rugby Book of the Year in 2012.

1035. WILKINSON, Robert Michael
Lock 6 caps 1975-1976
Born: Luton, Bedfordshire, 25 July 1951
Died: Haynes, Bedfordshire, 1 February 2021
Career: Cambridge University, Bedford, Barbarians
Debut: v Australia, Ballymore, Brisbane, May 1975

Wilkinson was one of the uncapped members of the Barbarians team who beat the All Blacks in 1973. Tom David was the other but earned full international honours two years later on England's tour to Australia. The second row, who won three blues from 1971 to 1973, had studied geography at Emmanuel College, Cambridge, and made his international debut in the infamous Brisbane test of 1975 and won a John Player Cup. He had already toured New Zealand in 1973 when he was a student. He ran a fruit business, importing bananas, is a past president of Hawks Club and served as treasurer at Bedford.

1036. CORLESS, Barrie James
Centre 10 caps (4-1t) 1976-1978
Born: Booton, Norfolk, 7 November 1945
Career: Coventry, Moseley, Barbarians
Debut: v Australia, Twickenham, January 1976

Corless was a schoolmaster in Solihull when he marked his international debut with a try against Australia in 1976 in a 23-6 win. He was a Coventry player but played the 1977 and 1978 Championships as a Moseley player after moving clubs. He became the first full-time director of rugby in England at Northampton. He was at Franklin's Gardens for five years, overseeing a turnaround in the club's fortunes before moving to Gloucester in 1995. After 20 months in charge at Kingsholm, he left and moved back to Moseley and later Nottingham. He coached at Solihull College.

1037. KEYWORTH, Mark
Flanker 4 caps 1976
Born: Bridgnorth, Shropshire, 19 February 1948
Died: Llanon, Wales, 24 November 2014
Career: Swansea, Aberystwyth, North Midlands, Shropshire
Debut: v Australia, Twickenham, January 1976

Keyworth was one of a select band capped for England when he was playing in Wales. He was at Swansea when he won his four caps in 1976. He played 259 times in the Swansea back row, scoring 37 tries, between 1972 and 1981 and won a Welsh Cup in 1978, the first time they had won the competition. He was a regular at All Whites Former Players' Association functions until his death. He had played rugby for Cirencester Agricultural College while studying at the faculty in preparation for taking over the family farm in Cardiganshire. He died suddenly on the farm, aged 66.

1038. LAMPKOWSKI, Michael Stanislav
Scrum-half 4 caps (4-1t) 1976
Born: Scunthorpe, Lincolnshire, 4 January 1953
Career: Scunthorpe, Headingley, Notts, Lincs & Derbyshire, Midlands and North
Debut: v Australia, Twickenham, January 1976

Lampkowski, the son of a Polish soldier, played football at school and didn't take up rugby until leaving. He was the seventh scrum-half used by England in a year when he won the first of his four caps. He won England under-23 honours before switching codes to Wakefield Trinity for a £10,000 fee, where he was a Challenge Cup finalist in 1979. He made 162 appearances, scored 46 tries, and was one of the first players to have a knee ligament replaced by dacron-fibre. An electrician, whose brother Steve played for Lincolnshire, he became a director of Harrison Electrical Ltd in Leeds.

1039. COOKE, David Alexander
Centre 4 caps 1976
Born: Malta, 10 February 1949
Career: Harlequins, Northampton, Bletchley
Debut: v Wales, Twickenham, January 1976

Cooke, an ex-pupil of Gravesend Grammar School, played most of his club career at Harlequins, captaining them to the Middlesex Sevens title in 1978. Towards the end of his career, he moved to Northampton, then to Bletchley, whom he helped reach their first Buckinghamshire Cup Final in 1982. He was picked for the England tour to Argentina in 1973, but that was called off, and he was injured for the New Zealand tour that replaced it. He worked as a schoolteacher and was capped in 1976.

1040. WYATT, Derek Murray
Wing 1 cap 1976
Born: Woolwich, London, 4 December 1949
Career: Oxford University, Bedford, Bath, Barbarians
Debut: v Scotland, Murrayfield, Edinburgh, February 1976

Wyatt, whom Saracens rejected, won his only cap off the bench against Scotland in 1976 when he came on for David Duckham, but he had already toured Australia with England in 1975. An RFU Knockout Cup winner in 1975, he scored 145 tries in 152 games for Bedford before moving on to Bath, equalling their try-scoring record in his first two seasons. He won his Oxford University blue when he was 32 and worked in publishing before becoming the Labour Member of Parliament for Sittingbourne and Sheppey from 1997 to 2010, previously serving on Haringey Council and was on the culture, media & sport select committee.

1041. ADEY, Garry John
No.8 2 caps 1976
Born: Loughborough, Leicestershire, 13 June 1945
Career: Loughborough Town, Leicester, Leicestershire, Midlands, Barbarians
Debut: v Ireland, Twickenham, November 1976

Adey played 381 times for Leicester between 1965 and 1981 and was 31 when he won two caps for England, replacing Andy Ripley in the back row. An engineer, he continued to be involved with Leicester when he finished playing, having been involved in three English Cup wins, as he served as a director of Tigers until 2014. He is chairman of the Adey Group, a successful family business based in Loughborough and established in 1925 that is involved in steel fabrication and processing. The company were involved in the re-development of Leicester's Welford Road ground and the building of the North Caterpillar Stand.

1042. SLEMEN, Michael Anthony Charles
Wing 31 caps (32-8t) 1976-1984
Born: Liverpool, Lancashire, 11 May 1951
Died: Liverpool, Lancashire, 20 July 2020
Career: Liverpool, Lancashire, Devon, the North, British Lions, Barbarians
Debut: v Ireland, Twickenham, March 1976

Wing Slemen won the Grand Slam with England in 1980 and toured with the Lions to South Africa that year. He studied pharmacy at Aston University and St Luke's College, Exeter, where he played rugby for Devon, and taught PE at Merchant Taylors' in Crosby, where he also ran the Duke of Edinburgh scheme. He was a member of the Northern Division team who beat the All Blacks in 1979 and found out about his England call-up in 1976 when a journalist phoned the staffroom to tell him he was in the side to play Ireland. An assistant England coach, his son David played for Harlequins and Esher.

1043. WILLIAMS, Christopher Gareth
Fly-half 1 cap 1976
Born: Pontypridd, Wales, 21 February 1950
Career: Gloucester, RAF, Lydney, Headingley, Gloucestershire, Western Counties
Debut: v France, Parc des Princes, March 1976

Williams played 101 times for Gloucester, from 1975 to 1979, scoring 27 tries as well as playing 20 games for Gloucestershire. Born in Wales, he was educated at Lydney Grammar School and Magdalen College School in Oxford, playing for Lydney and then Headingley when he was stationed at Catterick with the RAF between 1974 and 1976. He helped Gloucester win the 1978 John Player and Gloucestershire two County Championship Finals. He served in the RAF, which saw him turn out for various clubs around the country, then became a businessman with varied interests, including a classic car restoration business.

1044. COWLING, Robin James
Prop 8 caps 1977-1979
Born: Ipswich, Suffolk, 24 March 1944
Career: Gloucester, Leicester, Barbarians, Gloucestershire
Debut: v Scotland, Twickenham, January 1977

Cowling played 320 times for Gloucester, winning the National Knock Out Cup in 1972, before joining Leicester in 1974 and working as a farm manager in the area. He played 184 times for the Tigers, helping them to three Cup wins and getting capped by England. He moved to Cornwall in 1987 to take over a farm near Helston before going into coaching. He joined Exeter Chiefs in 1997 and stayed for 21 years, barring two at Cornish Pirates, until stepping down as academy manager in 2018. Jack Nowell, Luke Cowan-Dickie and Henry Slade all came through on his watch at Sandy Park.

1045. KENT, Charles Philip
Centre 5 caps (4-1t) 1977-1978
Born: Bridgwater, Somerset, 4 August 1953
Died: Dartmoor, Devon, 23 March 2005
Career: Oxford University, Rosslyn Park, Barbarians
Debut: v Scotland, Twickenham, January 1977

A try scorer on his test debut, Kent was a dashing centre for Rosslyn Park and won his five caps for England between 1977 and 1978. He won four blues at Oxford University as he was studying medicine at Worcester College, and his career meant he had to take a step back from representative rugby. He started playing at Bridgwater & Albion RFC, where he was a member until his death and played for Rosslyn Park in the 23-14 English Cup final defeat to Gosforth in 1976. He worked as a general practitioner in Crediton in Devon. He passed away when he collapsed after riding over Dartmoor.

1046. RAFTER, Michael
Flanker 17 caps 1977-1981
Born: Bristol, 31 March 1952
Career: Bristol, Gloucestershire, Barbarians
Debut: v Scotland, Twickenham, January 1977

Rafter helped win a Grand Slam in 1980 when he came off the bench in the win over Wales at Twickenham and captained Gloucestershire in back-to-back County titles and Bristol to the 1983 English Cup. He was a PE teacher at Filton High in Bristol after training at St Luke's in Exeter alongside Mike Slemen and John Scott. A talented footballer who had trials with Bristol City, he later coached Bedford and Gloucestershire. He worked as an RFU citing commissioner and as a director of a leisurewear company called Monsoon Ruggur and is the nephew of former England hooker Sam Tucker.

1047. YOUNG, Malcolm
Scrum-half 10 caps (1t,4c,1p) 1977-1979
Born: Mickley, Northumberland, 4 January 1946
Career: Cambridge University, Gosforth, Northumberland
Debut: v Scotland, Twickenham, January 1977

Educated at Queen Elizabeth Grammar School in Hexham and Downing College, Cambridge, Young won a blue at university but for football, as an outside left, at Wembley, in 1967. He was understudy to Nigel Starmer-Smith through the 1969-70 season but was not capped until he was 31, in 1977, in the 26-5 win over Scotland. He was a goal-kicking scrum-half who played in Gosforth's John Player Cup final wins of 1976 and 1977 when they were amongst the best teams in England. A County Championship winner in 1981, he worked for British Steel in Consett and Redcar.

1048. SCOTT, John Philip
Lock/No.8 34 caps (4-1t) 1978-1984
Born: Exeter, Devon, 28 September 1954
Career: Exeter, Rosslyn Park, Cardiff, Barbarians
Debut: v France, Parc des Princes, Paris, January 1978

Scott was No.8 when England won the Grand Slam in 1980 and won 30 of his 34 caps while playing at Cardiff, where he is still a folk hero. He led England on a tour to South Africa in 1984, where they were demolished in both tests, and he never played international rugby again. He joined Cardiff in 1978, making 268 appearances for the club, leading them from 1980 to 1984 and winning five Welsh Cups. A director of an embroidery company and an outdoor-wear business in Cardiff, he had a column in the South Wales Echo and was inducted into Cardiff's Hall of Fame in 1999.

1049. DODGE, Paul William
Centre 32 caps (15-1t,1c,3p) 1978-1985
Born: Leicester, Leicestershire, 26 February 1958
Career: Leicester, Barbarians, British Lions
Debut: v Wales, Twickenham February 1978

Dodge was 19 when he made his England debut in the centre, was a Grand Slam winner under Bill Beaumont in 1980 and a two-test British Lion in South Africa in 1980. He captained his country eight times, played 437 times for Leicester, winning three consecutive English Cups between 1979 and 1981, and when he played his last test, he was England's most-capped centre. In retirement, he worked at the Leicester academy. His sons Alex and Ollie came through the Tigers system and continued working in the family bookbinding company Syston Bindery. He was made Club President of Leicester in 2013.

1050. HORTON, John Philip
Fly-half 13 caps (12-4d) 1977-1984
Born: St Helens, Lancashire, 11 April 1951
Career: St Helens, Sale, Bath, Bristol, Barbarians
Debut: v Wales, Twickenham, February 1978

Fly-half Horton was the victim of a late tackle that saw Welsh flanker Paul Ringer sent off in England's stormy 9-8 win at

Twickenham in their 1980 Grand Slam campaign. He had dropped two goals in the previous game against France, and was at Bath from 1973 to 1985, scoring 125 drop goals in 380 first-team games before Stuart Barnes came along. He played a few games for Bath as a guest in 1988 after a spell at Bristol. He was educated at Cowley School and Didsbury College, worked as a PE teacher at Bath Technical College and was director of rugby at Bloxham School in Oxfordshire.

1051. MORDELL, Robert John
Flanker 1 cap 1978
Born: Twickenham, London, 2 July 1950
Career: Wasps, Rosslyn Park, Middlesex, London Division
Debut: v Wales, Twickenham, February 1978

Mordell was a tough flanker who grew up in the shadow of England's stadium. He was sent off for punching in the 1976 English Cup final when playing for Rosslyn Park. He played rugby league for Oldham from 1980 to 1983 and had his jaw broken by Welshman Paul Woods in one match against Hull. He returned to rugby union after being reinstated by the IRB in 1991. The back-rower played at Thamesians, where he is a vice president and lived in Feltham near Twickenham. He taught PE and maths at Whitton School before joining rugby league. He later switched to a career in finance and was a financial manager for BMW.

1052. CAPLAN, David William Nigel
Full-back 2 caps 1978
Born: Leeds, West Yorkshire, 5 April 1954
Career: Oxford University, Headingley, Stamford, Barbarians, Yorkshire
Debut: v Scotland, Murrayfield, March 1978

Educated at Leeds Grammar School, Caplan was unlucky to play in the same era as Alastair Hignell and Dusty Hare, two outstanding full-backs, otherwise he may have won more caps. He played twice in 1978, a year after he had finished his dentistry studies at Newcastle University, where he won the year prize from the British Dental Association. He spent two years practicing in York before moving to Stamford in Lincolnshire, where he worked for more than 30 years and where he is currently employed at the Oasis Dental Care practice. He played for Stamford RFC and still takes a keen interest in rugby.

1053. COLCLOUGH, Maurice John
Lock 25 caps (4-1t) 1978-1986
Born: Oxford, Oxfordshire, 2 September 1953
Died: Pembrokeshire, *Dyfed*, 27 January 2006
Career: Angouleme (Fra), Wasps, Poitiers (Fra), Swansea, Liverpool, Barbarians
Debut: v Scotland, Murrayfield, Edinburgh, 4 March 1978

Colclough won a Grand Slam in 1980 and eight caps for the British Lions on tours of South Africa and New Zealand. He had many business ventures, including a leisure centre in France, a floating bar in Swansea and interests in South Africa. He is well-known for getting prop Colin Smart to drink aftershave at a 1982 post-match dinner in Paris. He scored the decisive try against the All Blacks when England beat them in 1983. He was diagnosed with a brain tumour and returned from South Africa to live in Wales before his premature death.

1054. BOND, Anthony Matthew
Centre 6 caps 1978-1982
Born: Urmston, Manchester, 3 August 1953
Career: Broughton Park, Sale, Barbarians
Debut: v New Zealand, Twickenham, November 1978

Bond broke his leg in England's 24-9 win over Ireland in their 1980 Grand Slam-winning campaign. He was replaced by Clive Woodward and played once more for England against Ireland two years later. He scored two tries when the North beat the All Blacks 21-9 at Otley in 1979 and worked in advertising as Northern Sales Manager on Building Magazine, then for nearly 20 years for United Business Media, where he worked on an occupational health and safety magazine. He was a director of a Tonbridge, Kent-based PR and marketing company, TB2B Media.

1055. PEARCE, Gary Stephen
Prop 36 caps 1979-1991
Born: Dinton, Buckinghamshire, 2 March 1956
Career: Northampton, Nottingham, Buckinghamshire, Midlands, Barbarians
Debut: v Scotland, Twickenham, February 1979

Pearce spent the best part of two decades at Northampton from 1978, played 411 games, won all his 36 caps while at the club and at the time was England's most-capped prop. His England career stretched from 1979 to the 1991 Rugby World Cup, where he made one appearance and was on the bench in the final. He had also played in the 1987 tournament, and finally left Northampton in 1996 to move to Nottingham. The Saints Supporters Club paid for a portrait of their front-row giant to be painted by Geoff Stalker and displayed at Franklin's Gardens. He was a surveyor for Sir Robert McAlpine Ltd in Hemel Hempstead.

1056. CARDUS, Richard Michael
Centre 2 caps 1979
Born: Leeds, West Yorkshire, 23 May 1956
Career: Roundhay, Wasps, Cardiff, Barbarians
Debut: v France, Twickenham, May 1979

Cardus, virtually unknown outside his native, Yorkshire, won his two caps in the 1979 Five Nations Championship and toured Japan, Fiji and Tonga that summer with England under Bill Beaumont whilst at Roundhay. He later played for Wasps, skippering them in the 1986 John Player Cup final defeat to Bath before joining Cardiff, for whom he made 58 appearances between 1986 and 1990. He worked for Scottish & Newcastle Brewery until 1988, then for ANC Express Parcel Services. He later ran Miko Coffee in Glamorgan before taking a job as a works manager at an engineering company in Barry, Wales.

1057. SMART, Colin Edward
Prop 17 caps 1979-1983
Born: Highbury, London, 5 March 1950
Career: Newport, Kent, Barbarians
Debut: v France, Twickenham, March 1979

Smart propped for England between 1979 and 1983, winning his last 14 caps in a row once Fran Cotton was forced to retire. After attending Cardiff College of Education, he joined Newport in 1973 and rejected the chance of a Wales squad place in 1974. He was another Englishman popular in Wales as he played 306 games for Newport, becoming the third man from England to captain the club. Famous for being fooled into drinking aftershave at the post-match dinner in Paris in 1982 by lock Maurice Colclough, he credited the RFU medical officer Leo Walkden with saving his life. The prop was inducted into the Newport Hall of Fame in 2013 and taught at Hartridge High School in Newport.

1058. CARLETON, John
Wing 26 caps (28-7t) 1979-1984
Born: Orrell, Lancashire, 24 November 1955
Career: Orrell, Cheshire, Lancashire, North, Barbarians
Debut: v New Zealand, Twickenham, November 1979

Carleton scored a hat-trick when England sealed the Grand Slam over Scotland at Murrayfield in 1980. That helped earn him a summer trip with the British Lions to South Africa, playing three tests, and he played another three on the Lions

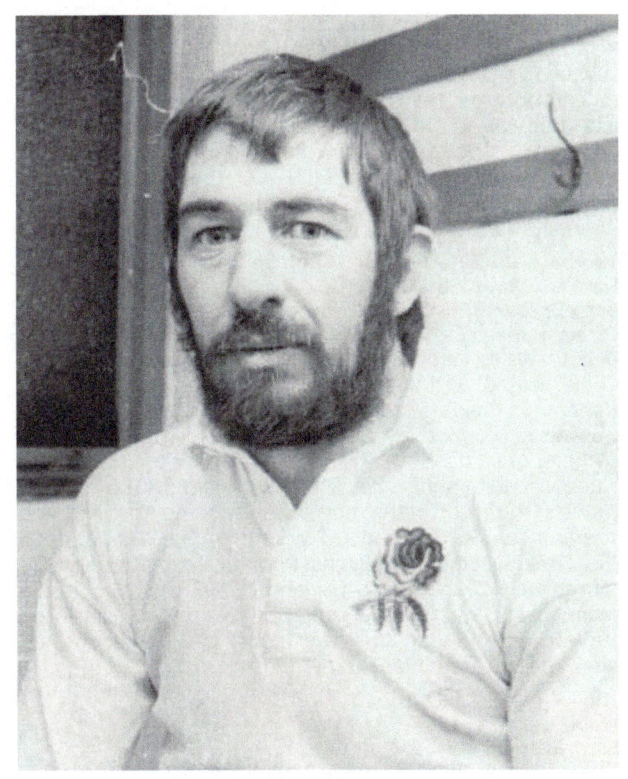

Frank Anderson

Bob Mordell

Gary Pearce

John Carleton

trip to New Zealand in 1983. He worked as a schoolteacher but resigned from his post at Park High School, Hindley, to go on his first Lions tour. He later worked as a banker specialising in real estate with Bank of Ireland Healthcare, then as executive director of the Housing Corporation in the North of England. He then worked as chief executive officer of the housing association Genesis Homes.

1059. CUSWORTH, Leslie
Fly-half 12 caps (12-4d) 1979-1988
Born: Normanton, West Yorkshire, 3 July 1954
Career: Wakefield, UAU, Moseley, Leicester, Yorkshire, North East Counties, North Midlands, Barbarians
Debut: v New Zealand, Twickenham, November 1979

A three-time English Cup winner with Leicester between 1979 and 1981, Cusworth was a clever fly-half whose international career was curtailed by the emergence of Rob Andrew. He played 365 times for Leicester, scoring 947 points. The former PE teacher, who worked at Dartmouth High School, turned his hand to coaching. He was the brains behind England's win in the 1993 World Cup Sevens, an assistant coach with England under Jack Rowell and worked as director of rugby at Worcester. He moved to Argentina full time in 2006 to work for the IRB, developing rugby in the country and was later director of rugby of the Argentinian union.

1060. PRESTON, Nicholas John
Centre 3 caps (4-1t) 1979-1980
Born: Prestwich, Greater Manchester, 5 April 1958
Career: Richmond, Surrey, London, Barbarians
Debut: v New Zealand, Twickenham, November 1979

Preston was a try-scorer in the 17-13 win over France in 1980, forming part of England's Grand Slam-winning team. A stalwart of Richmond, he starred in back-to-back Middlesex Sevens wins in 1979 and 1980 and was also capped by England under-23s. A County Championship semi-finalist with Surrey, he worked in sales for Xerox. He joined the data-processing company Wang Laboratories before moving to Sequent Computer Systems, which IBM took over. He is co-owner and managing director of Cerno Professional Systems. He was elected president of Richmond in 2012 and was chairman of Richmond Rugby Ltd.

1061. BLAKEWAY, Philip John
Prop 19 caps 1980-1985
Born: Cheltenham, Gloucestershire, 31 December 1950
Career: Cheltenham, Gloucester, Moseley, Barbarians
Debut: v Ireland, Twickenham, January 1980

Blakeway was odds-against to play any international rugby when he broke his neck playing for Gloucester against South Wales Police in 1978, but two years later, he made his England debut and was a cunning tighthead prop for the side that won the Grand Slam in 1980. Picked for the British Lions tour to South Africa later that year, he had his trip shortened by a rib injury, but another neck injury forced his retirement in 1985. He made a brief comeback, aged 41, for Moseley in 1992. He is a director of a firm dealing in fruit and vegetable farming in Tewkesbury and has been a financial advisor.

1062. WOODWARD, Sir Clive Ronald
Centre 21 caps (16-4t) 1980-1984
Born: Ely, Cambridgeshire, 6 January 1956
Career: Loughborough College, Harlequins, Leicester, Manly (Aus), Barbarians
Debut: v Ireland, Twickenham, January 1980

Woodward was a mercurial centre who won the Grand Slam with England in 1980 and then coached them to World Cup glory. He worked for Xerox and played for Manly in Sydney before returning to England. He coached at Henley, London Irish and Bath before getting the England job in 1997. He survived England's quarter-final exit in the 1999 World Cup to lead his great team to rugby's ultimate prize four years later but walked out in 2004, overseeing a disastrous tour in charge of the Lions in New Zealand in 2005. He worked for Southampton Football Club and the British Olympic Association. He is a television pundit and a columnist for the Daily Mail.

1063. COOKE, David Howard
Flanker 12 caps 1981-1985
Born: Brisbane, Australia, 19 November 1955
Career: Harlequins, Barbarians, Indonesia
Debut: v Wales, Cardiff Arms Park, Cardiff, January 1981

Cooke was a dashing flanker who played 258 times for Harlequins, helping them to the English Cup in 1988, but was once dropped by club coach Earle Kirton for going surfing. Australia-born, he played for Indonesia in the inaugural Hong Kong Sevens in 1976. In 1985, he played for Quins at the Stoop in the morning against the Army but was summoned over the road to Twickenham by England coach Dick Greenwood to play against Romania that afternoon. He toured New Zealand with England in 1985, captaining the team against Southland and playing two tests. A chartered surveyor, he founded an estate agency and worked for Red Kite Property Asset Management.

1064. SHEPPARD, Austin
Prop 2 caps 1981-1985
Born: Bristol, 1 May 1950
Career: Bristol, Gloucestershire, Barbarians
Debut: v Wales, Cardiff Arms Park, Cardiff, January 1981

Sheppard made his debut as a replacement for Fran Cotton during the 1981 match against Wales and played his second and last test at the same venue four years later. He toured New Zealand with England in 1985 and played over 400 games for Bristol, winning the English Cup in 1983, and 26 times for Gloucestershire, for whom he appeared in three County Championship finals before his last full season in 1985/86. He was part of a fearsome front row when Bristol were a power in English rugby, coached youngsters at the club and ran the family undertaking business in the Bristol area.

1065. DAVIES, Geoffrey Huw
Full-back/centre/fly-half 21 caps (16-4t) 1981-1986
Born: Eastbourne, Sussex, 18 February 1959
Career: Cambridge University, Wasps, Coventry, Cardiff, Barbarians
Debut: v Scotland, Twickenham, February 1981

Davies, a two-time blue at Cambridge, was a versatile back who scored a brilliant try against Scotland on his debut, toured South Africa in 1984, New Zealand in 1985 and played his last test match in 1986. His athleticism and footballing skill meant he could play fly-half, centre or full-back, where he ended his international career. He attended King Edward VI Grammar School in Stourbridge before Cambridge, where he read land economy. A qualified chartered surveyor, he worked as Head of Asset Management at Harbert Management Corporation, a real estate company in London, and as director of Pedmore Properties.

1066. JEAVONS, Nicholas Clive
Flanker 14 caps (4-1t) 1981-1983
Born: Calcutta, India, 12 November 1957
Career: Moseley, Midlands, Barbarians, British Lions
Debut: v Scotland, Twickenham, February 1981

Jeavons was converted from a No.8 to flanker shortly before his international debut and scored his only test try in the

15-11 win over Australia at Twickenham in 1982. Nicknamed 'The Body Beautiful' by novelist Jilly Cooper, he toured New Zealand – as a replacement - with the Lions in 1983, playing six non-international games but did not play for England again after that year. A product of Wolverhampton Grammar School and Wolverhampton Polytechnic, he worked as a director of Thorne International Boiler Services in Wolverhampton from 1991. The family business won a Queen's Award for Enterprise in 2001.

1067. HESFORD, Robert
No. 8 10 caps 1981-1985
Born: Blackpool, Lancashire, 26 March 1951
Died: 3 August 2023
Career: Durham University, Bristol, Wasps, Barbarians, Durham, Gloucestershire, East Midlands
Debut: v Scotland, Twickenham, February 1981

Hesford, who came from a family of soccer goalkeepers, made his England debut as a replacement for Nick Jeavons in the 1981 game against Scotland but had his international chances initially limited by John Scott's presence. He played more than 300 times for Bristol, winning the English Cup in 1983, before coaching the first team. He taught young offenders, played for Whitehall as a 40-year-old and had other coaching posts with clubs such as Barton Hill, Dings Crusaders and Broad Plain. His father, Bob, was Huddersfield Town's goalkeeper in the 1938 FA Cup final, and his brother Iain kept goal for Blackpool.

1068. ROSE, William Marcus Henderson
Full-back, 10 caps (82-2t,4c,22p) 1981-1987
Born: Loughborough, Leicestershire, 12 January 1957
Career: Cambridge University, Leicester, Coventry, Harlequins, Barbarians
Debut: v Ireland, Lansdowne Road, Dublin, March 1981

Rose burst on the international scene as a student at Cambridge University in 1981, winning five caps in two seasons, then had to wait five years to win another five. On his recall in 1987, he scored 41 of England's 48 points in the Championship, but concussion early in the first game of that year's inaugural Rugby World Cup ended his test career. He had studied land economy at Cambridge University and worked at DTZ Debenham Thorpe, running the firm's West End investment agency and then property developers Development Securities. He was then a director of the Mayfair-based investment and asset-management company Deerbrook Group and JP Clayton Estate Co.

1069. SARGENT, Gordon Alan Frank
Prop 1 cap 1981
Born: Gloucester, Gloucestershire, 18 October 1949
Died: Bristol, 25 June 2013
Career: Lydney, Gloucester, Gloucestershire, Barbarians
Debut: v Ireland, Lansdowne Road, Dublin, March 1981

Sargent won his only cap when he came off the bench as a replacement for Phil Blakeway against Ireland in 1981. Sargent started his career at Lydney but made an impact on a bigger stage at Gloucester, playing 200 times between 1976 and 1987 and starting every round of that side's domestic cup win in 1978. He was made captain of Gloucester and led an inexperienced Gloucestershire side to the County Championship semi-finals in 1987. He worked in construction and served on the Lydney committee, where he had two spells as a player until his death, whilst his wife Ann was the club's accountant.

1070. FIDLER, John Howard
Lock 4 caps 1981-1984
Born: Cheltenham, Gloucestershire, 16 September 1948
Career: Gloucester, Barbarians, Gloucestershire
Debut: v Argentina, Ferro Carril Oeste, Buenos Aires, May 1981

Fidler was a stalwart Gloucester second row who played 281 times for the club, won five County Championships with Gloucestershire and toured Argentina and South Africa with England in 1981 and 1984. A policeman, he played both tests against the Pumas and, three years later, both against the Springboks on a dispiriting trip for England when they were ripped apart by the brilliant centre Danie Gerber. He later served as Gloucester team secretary and then as team manager as the game went on and made the transition to professionalism. He ran a construction business, and his son, Rob, also played in the second row for Gloucester and England.

1071. MILLS, Stephen Graham Ford Mills
Hooker 5 caps 1981-1984
Born: Cirencester, Gloucestershire, 24 February 1951
Career: Gloucester, Gloucestershire, South & South West, Barbarians
Debut: v Argentina, Ferro Carril Oeste, Buenos Aires, May 1981

Mills, who suffered from being Peter Wheeler's hooking understudy, was on the bench 16 times for England without coming on and won just five caps when he was worth nearer 40. He played 300 times for Gloucester in one of their most successful eras, winning the John Player Cup in 1978. A County Championship finalist in 1980 and a winner four years later, he led Gloucester to the Daily Mail Anglo-Welsh pennant in 1982, becoming the first English side to win it in five years. He worked as a computer programmer for Eagle Star Insurance while playing and later for GCHQ.

1072. SWIFT, Anthony Hugh
Wing 6 caps 1981-1984
Born: Preston, Lancashire, 24 May 1959
Career: Swansea, Fylde, Bath, Barbarians
Debut: v Argentina, Ferro Carril Oeste, Buenos Aires, May 1981

Swift was a prolific wing who won his six caps at Swansea before moving to Bath and helping them become England's dominant side. He studied accountancy and economics in Cardiff and scored 126 tries for Swansea before his switch to the Recreation Ground, where he played nearly 400 matches and touched down 161 times. His England career lasted until the tour of South Africa in 1984, but he continued playing for Bath as they racked up domestic honours. An accountant, he worked as an auditor for Deloitte before becoming a partner with Robson Taylor financial advisors. Juggling jobs, he was Bath's first chairman during the professioanl era and managing director of healthcare firm Apodi Limited.

1073. WINTERBOTTOM, Peter James MBE
Flanker 58 caps (13-3t) 1982-1993
Born: Horsforth, West Yorkshire, 31 May 1960
Career: Exeter, Headingley, Hawke's Bay (NZ), Transvaal (SA), Harlequins, Barbarians, Yorkshire
Debut: v Australia, Twickenham, January 1982

Winterbottom was the first forward to win 50 caps in the white jersey. He toured New Zealand with the British Lions in 1983 and 1993 and, on the first trip, was named one of New Zealand's Players of the Year despite the Lions's defeat. A World Cup finalist in 1991, he also played in 1987 and won two Grand Slams. He worked on his uncle's farm in the north of England when playing for Headingley before moving to London to play for Harlequins and taking up a job in the City as a Eurobond dealer for BGC Partners and Creditex before leaving finance. He now runs Full Contact Ltd and Peter Winterbottom Management.

1074. STRINGER, Nicholas Courtenay
Full-back 5 caps 1982-1985
Born: Stanmore, London, 4 October 1960
Career: Wasps, Barbarians
Debut: v Australia, Twickenham, January 1982

Stringer was a decent enough cricketer to be on the ground staff at Lord's and might have wished he had stuck to cricket when a hamstring injury denied him his first start against

France in 1982. He had won his first cap off the bench against Australia but did not make a full start for another two years, again against the Wallabies. His last cap came against Romania in 1985, and he was forced to retire from rugby in 1988 after repeated concussions. He worked in insurance and, not long after retiring, he emigrated to Perth, Australia, coached at a junior club, Southern Lions and was an analyst at his son's club, Cottesloe.

1075. SYDDALL, James Paul
Lock 2 caps 1982-1984
Born: Barton, Greater Manchester, 7 March 1956
Career: Waterloo, Northern Division, Lancashire, Barbarians
Debut: v Ireland, Twickenham, February 1982

Despite being born into a rugby league family Syddall was one of the heroes of the North when they beat the All Blacks at Otley in 1979, but it took three years to win his first cap. The Waterloo man won three County Championships with Lancashire and toured North America with England in 1982. His last cap came against the all-conquering Australian side of 1984. A qualified surveyor, the former second row worked for Network Rail as a route managing director based in Warrington and was involved in the electrification programme of lines in the northwest of England.

1076. BAINBRIDGE, Stephen
Lock 18 caps 1982-1987
Born: Newcastle-upon-Tyne, Northumberland, 7 October 1956
Career: Gosforth, Fylde, Orrell, Northumberland, Barbarians
Debut: v France, Parc des Princes, Paris, February 1982

A two-test Lion in New Zealand in 1983, Bainbridge, who qualified as a teacher at Alsager College in Cheshire, was an athletic second-row who served bans in 1984 and 1985 after being sent off in domestic matches. He played his last international during the 1987 Rugby World Cup. A teacher in Gateshead, he had played in two County Championship finals with Northumberland. He worked in the motor industry, then moved to Philadelphia to take a post with Reynolds and Reynolds, an American automotive consultancy. He returned to the United Kingdom as a sales and development officer for Benfield Motor Group, which Lookers took over.

1077. BOYLE, Stephen Brent
Lock 3 caps 1983
Born: Warrington, Cheshire, 9 August 1953
Career: Gloucester, Moseley, Barbarians
Debut: v Wales, Cardiff Arms Park, Cardiff, February 1983

Boyle, a former schoolboy footballer for Herefordshire, won his three caps in 1983, earning a place on the Lions tour to New Zealand, playing six games but none of the test matches. He played 312 games for Gloucester from 1972, scoring 77 tries from the second and back rows, before joining Moseley in 1984. Revered as a true hard man by the Kingsholm faithful and most of his opponents, he worked in banking, insurance and the car industry but then went into the hotel business, running the Pilgrim House Country Hotel in Hereford. He also owned the Three Salmons Hotel in Usk before retiring to live in France and buying a farm near Agen.

1078. TRICK, David Mark
Wing 2 caps 1983-1984
Born: Dartford, Kent, 26 October 1960
Career: Plymouth Albion, Tavistock, Bath, Somerset, Barbarians
Debut: v Ireland, Lansdowne Road, Dublin, March 1983

Trick was a lethal finisher who was unfortunate to be playing at the same time as Rory Underwood but played 247 games for Bath and scored 171 tries for the club. He toured Argentina with England in 1981 and South Africa in 1984, where he won his second and final cap, and was in the Bath side that won a third successive English Cup in 1986. A former school's sprint champion, he clocked 10.4 seconds for the 100 metres. He was a stockbroker and worked for an ad agency and sports sponsorship firm. He is a sought-after after-dinner speaker and has co-authored books with Lawrence Dallaglio. He also served as president of Bath.

1079. YOUNGS, Nicholas Gerald
Scrum-half 6 caps 1983-1984
Born: West Runton, Norfolk, 15 December 1959
Career: Bedford, Leicester
Debut: v Ireland, Lansdowne Road, Dublin, March 1983

Youngs' rugby career was eclipsed by the exploits of his sons Ben and Tom, but he was a robust scrum-half who helped beat the All Blacks in 1983 and toured South Africa with England in 1984. He played his last test match against Wales in 1984, but that was a strong time for England number nines with Richard Hill and Nigel Melville about to come onto the international scene. He was a prolific try scorer for Leicester with 71 tries and did his bit for England's future, teaching Ben the rudiments of scrum-half play when he was looking to switch position. He ran the family farm in Norfolk.

1080. SIMPSON, Paul Donald
Flanker/No.8 3 caps 1983-1987
Born: Leeds, 7 June 1958
Career: Gosforth, Bath, Northern Division, Barbarians
Debut: v New Zealand, Twickenham, November 1983

Simpson made a memorable start to his test career as part of the England side that beat the All Blacks 15-9 in 1983. Having spent five years at Gosforth, he got his international break as a member of the powerful Bath team he represented until 1991. The flanker won one cap in 1984, then was played out of position in his third and last, in 1987 against Ireland when England were thumped. A rugby league player at school, he worked as a salesman for Allied Dunbar in his playing days. He was a division manager for Acuma shortly but is an independent financial advisor and a director of Angell Mallinder.

1081. WHITE, Colin
Prop 4 caps 1983-1984
Born: Newcastle-upon-Tyne, Northumberland, 31 March 1947
Died: Tynedale, Northumberland, 19 January 2011
Career: Gosforth, Northern Division, Barbarians
Debut: v New Zealand, Twickenham, November 1983

Prop White was 36 when England beat the All Blacks on his debut, and he also did it five years after chopping off three of his fingers in an accident at work as a tree surgeon. Two fingers were rescued after he had put them in ice before heading to the hospital. He was part of the powerful Gosforth side of the 1970s, twice winning the English Cup, beating the All Blacks with the North in 1979 and captaining his club in the 1981 Cup final against Leicester. He had studied physical education before going into the tree surgery business. He suffered from colon cancer and had two strokes before his death.

1082. HALL, Jonathan Peter
Flanker/No.8 21 caps (8-2t) 1984-1994
Born: Bath, Somerset, 15 March 1962
Career: Bath, Somerset, South West Counties, Barbarians
Debut: v Scotland, Murrayfield, Edinburgh, February 1984

Hall, a feared back-rower in the brilliant Bath team of the 1980s and 1990s, made 277 appearances for the club and toured South Africa with England in 1984 and New Zealand in 1985. The flanker was also a member of the 1987 World Cup squad, although he did not play a match. A former sportswear salesman, he was Bath's first director of rugby after the game went professional but was sacked in 1998 and moved to Ireland, where he coached Garryowen. He formed PGIR Ltd, a Wiltshire-based performance and analysis company that has worked providing real-time data for the RFU, World Rugby, Bath Rugby and FIFA.

1083. BARLEY, Bryan
Centre 7 caps (4-1t) 1984-1988
Born: Wakefield, West Yorkshire, 4 January 1960
Career: Wakefield, Sandal, Barbarians
Debut: v Ireland, Twickenham, February 1984

Barley was a tough tackler with good hands, and there is a suspicion he would have earned more caps if he had played for a more fashionable club than Wakefield. Indeed, when he made his debut against Ireland, he was the first player capped directly from the club for 45 years. He played for Wakefield from 1978 to 1993, won four caps in 1984, toured New Zealand in 1985 without playing a test and won three more caps on the 1988 tour to Australia and Fiji. A Leeds University graduate, he studied maths and economics and worked in insurance later for the company RP Hodson, based in Wakefield.

1084. UNDERWOOD, Rory MBE
Wing 85 caps (210-49t) 1896-1996
Born: Middlesbrough, North Yorkshire, 19 June 1963
Career: Leicester, RAF, Bedford, Barbarians
Debut: v Ireland, Twickenham, February 1984

A trained RAF fighter pilot, Underwood was the first England player to win 50 caps, played in the 1991 Rugby World Cup final and was a Lion in 1989 and 1993. Returning to England from Malaysia when he was 14, he won three Grand Slams and did not miss a Five Nations match for 10 years up to 1995. He left the RAF and had trained as a commercial pilot but went into management consultancy. He set up Wingman Ltd, a performance consultancy, with another former RAF man, Dave Moss. He scored 134 tries in 236 games for Leicester and served on the Tigers' board.

1085. REDFERN, Stephen Paul
Prop 1 cap 1984
Born: Leicester, Leicestershire, 26 October 1957
Career: Leicester
Debut: v Ireland, Twickenham, February 1984

Redfern, who won his only cap off the bench, had a decade at Leicester before moving to rugby league with Sheffield Eagles in 1985, although his career at the top level was cut short by injury in 1987. He has had a varied career in coaching since finishing playing with stints in Sweden, Italy and Germany, as well as a spell with the England women's team. He has also coached Nuneaton and the Leicestershire Under-18s and has helped out at Bridgnorth. He is a director of Redfox Sports, a Leicester-based sports management company, and Majorca Beach Rugby. His brother Stuart also propped for Tigers

1086. DUN, Andrew Frederick
Flanker 1 cap 1984
Born: Bristol, 26 November 1960
Died: 23 July 2023
Career: Bristol, Gloucester, London Scottish, Wasps, Gloucestershire, Middlesex
Debut: v Wales, Twickenham, March 1984

Dun was a 6ft 3in blond flanker studying at St Bartholomew's Hospital in London and playing for Wasps when he made his England debut in 1984, having toured Japan with the student side a year earlier. He worked as a general practitioner in the south-west of England and played for Bristol, whom he captained, and coached Old Bristolians and Clifton. He worked as deputy managing director of the medical imaging service Alliance Medical Ltd, and then he was appointed chief executive of Enara Group Ltd in Woking. He became the chief operating officer at InHealth in High Wycombe and chairman of Beaufort Care Group.

1087. RENDALL, Paul Anthony George
Prop 28 caps 1984-1991
Born: London, 18 February 1954
Died: Cippenham, Berkshire, 13 June 2023
Career: Slough, Wasps, Askeans, London Division, Middlesex, Buckinghamshire, South-West, Barbarians
Debut: v Wales, Twickenham, March 1984

Rendall, nicknamed 'The Judge', played in the 1987 and 1991 World Cups, winning his last international cap when he was 37 in the pool match against Italy. He was injured on the 1981 tour of Argentina and educated at St Joseph's School in Slough. He worked in engineering and was an English Cup finalist with Wasps in 1986 before founding the Front Row Union Club with Jeff Probyn and Brian Moore. He had coached at Slough and Bracknell Rugby Club, leading them to six promotions in seven years. Rendall, a director of the Atlas Foundation, died after a battle with motor neurone disease.

1088. BAILEY, Mark David
Wing 7 (4-1t) 1984-1990
Born: Castleford, West Yorkshire, 21 November 1960
Career: Durham University, Cambridge University, Ipswich, Bedford, Wasps, Barbarians
Debut: v South Africa, Boet Erasmus Stadium, Port Elizabeth, June 1984

A four-time blue at Cambridge University, Bailey read economic history at Durham University before studying for a PhD in history. He won seven caps, and was a member of the 1987 Rugby World Cup squad, played cricket for Suffolk and won the English League with Wasps in 1990. A schoolteacher by profession, he worked as head at Leeds Grammar School before becoming Professor of Late Medieval History at The University of East Anglia. In 2011, he was appointed as a high master of St Paul's School in London and stayed in the post until 2020 before moving back to the University of East Anglia.

1089. BUTCHER, Christopher John Simon
No.8 3 caps 1984
Born: Karachi, India, 19 August 1960
Career: Harlequins, Middlesex, London Division
Debut: v South Africa, Boet Erasmus Stadium, Port Elizabeth, June 1984

Chris Butcher played his final Test against Australia, in 1984, having toured South Africa with England that summer. Struggling with a knee injury he worked as a debt collector in the Middle East, sold advertising for travel magazine, in the West Indies, played club rugby in South Africa and for Natal, and returned to the UK in the early 1990s to take a job in the City. Butcher was on his travels again backpacking in Botswana and East Africa shortly afterwards, before working in foreign exchange in Japan and then in Hong Kong and Singapore, for 11-and-a-half years. Butcher returned to England, settling in Norfolk, and in 2023 was in training for that year's Round the World Clipper Race

1090. HILL, Richard John
Scrum-half 29 caps (8-2t) 1984-1991
Born: Birmingham, Warwickshire, 4 May 1961
Career: Salisbury, Bath, Barbarians
Debut: v South Africa, Boet Erasmus Stadium, Port Elizabeth, June 1984

One of the fulcrums of Bath's great side of the 1980s, Hill had a great half-back partnership with Stuart Barnes, and captained England three times. The last occasion was against Wales in 1987, when he was banned for his part in that violent match but made the Rugby World Cup squad later that year. He was a Grand Slam winner and World

Cup finalist in 1991. He became an assistant coach at Bath and has since taken in spells at Harlequins, Gloucester, and Bristol (who he led to the Premiership in 2005) then Newport, Newport, Chalon-sur-Saône, Worcester, Rouen and Perigueux Dordogne Athletic Club.

1091. PALMER, John Anthony
Centre 3 caps 1984-1986
Born: Malta, 13 February 1957
Career: Bath, Somerset, Barbarians
Debut: v South Africa, Boet Erasmus Stadium, Port Elizabeth, June 1984

Educated at Prior Park College in Bath and St Mary's College, Twickenham, Palmer, who made his debut when he was 17, scored 1,343 points in 14 seasons at Bath, making 335 first-team appearances for the club and was captain when they beat Wasps to win the John Player Cup. He retired after beating Leicester in the 1989 final and was shamefully overlooked by England's selectors when he was in his prime, winning two caps on the 1984 tour to South Africa. A school teacher whilst he was playing, he worked at the Bath Academy until 2012 and then returned to teaching at Prior Park.

1092. PREEDY, Malcolm
Prop 1 cap 1984
Born: Gloucester, Gloucestershire, 15 September 1960
Career: Gloucester, Gloucestershire, South & South West, Barbarians
Debut: v South Africa, Boet Erasmus Stadium, Port Elizabeth, June 1984

Preedy was part of an all-Gloucester front row, along with Steve Mills and Phil Blakeway, when he won his only cap on England's 1984 tour to South Africa. A product of Hucclecote Secondary School, he had joined Gloucester aged 19 from Longlevens RFC, shared the John Player Cup when Gloucester drew with Moseley in 1982 and captained the club in 1986-87. He won the County Championship with Gloucestershire in 1983 and 1984 and once won a club game against Bristol with a drop goal. His last game for Gloucester was in 1991, and Preedy moved to Cheltenham and worked as an engineer for AGA Rangemaster.

1093. BRAIN, Stephen Edward
Hooker 13 caps 1984-1986
Born: Moseley, West Midlands, 11 November 1954
Career: Solihull, Moseley, Coventry, Rugby, Midlands
Debut: v South Africa, Ellis Park, Johannesburg, June 1984

Brain played for England through all levels, from schools to Under-23s, before finally making his international debut against the Springboks in 1984. He had been earmarked for selection in October 1983 but blotted his copybook when he was sent off for fighting with Brian Moore, delaying his international bow. A builder who coached in Boston in the USA, he left Coventry after being offered a job as a builders merchants rep then later ran the Raglan Arms in Rugby, helping the local team climb from Division Four to Division One in four seasons.

1094. REES, Gary William
Flanker 23 caps (8-2t) 1984-1991
Born: Long Eaton, Derbyshire, 2 May 1960
Career: Nottingham, Midlands, Barbarians
Debut: v South Africa, Ellis Park, Johannesburg, June 1984

Flanker Rees was a one-club man playing 307 games for Nottingham from 1977 to 1994 and then joining the club's coaching staff, extending his stay to more than 30 years. He played four times at the 1987 Rugby World Cup and once at the 1991 tournament against the United States in his final test. In 2021, he joined specialist insurance broking firm Miller as part of their sports team. He has also helped former England coach Stuart Lancaster by analysing back-row players. Neil Back has credited Rees with helping him develop as a flanker when he had a spell at Nottingham in the late 1980s.

1095. BARNES, Stuart
Fly-half 10 caps (34–5c,7p,1d) 1984-1993
Born: Grays, Essex, 22 November 1962
Clubs: Oxford University, Newport, Bristol, Bath, Barbarians, British Lions
Debut: v Australia, Twickenham, November 1984

Barnes played in an era when the selectors distrusted his cavalier instincts and preferred Rob Andrew. He was educated at Bassaleg School, turned down a chance to play for Wales in 1981, but played for Newport before joining Bristol, losing a Cup final to Bath. He switched to The Rec in 1985 and was part of an era of unparalleled success at the club, winning six English Cups and scoring 1,604 points. After winning his first England cap in 1984, he took nine years to get to double figures but toured New Zealand with the Lions in 1993. He retired to embark on his successful media career with Sky Sports, The Times, and Sunday Times.

1096. CHILCOTT, Gareth James
Prop 14 caps 1984-1989
Born: Bristol, 20 November 1956
Career: Bath, Somerset, South West, Bristol Lions
Debut: v Australia, Twickenham, November 1984

Chilcott was a popular prop who played for Bath 373 times between 1977 and 1993, winning five league winners' medals and seven cup winners' medals and touring Australia with the Lions in 1989. He was one of four England players suspended for the brawl with Wales at Cardiff Arms Park in 1987 but still made the World Cup squad that year. His final test came against Romania in 1989, but he rumbled on four years for Bath. Since then, he has been a radio pundit and is involved in a music venue in Bristol, The Tunnels, and Venatour, a sports travel company and bounced back from a liver transplant in 2016.

1097. LOZOWSKI, Robert Andrew Peter
Centre 1 cap 1984
Born: Ealing, London, 18 November 1960
Career: Wasps, Barbarians, Middlesex,
Debut: v Australia, Twickenham, November 1984

Educated at Gunnersbury School in West London, Lozowski, who had a Polish father and Italian mother, played for his local senior club, Wasps, 263 times and was club captain in the 1988/89 season. He played his only test against the brilliant Wallabies of Mark Ella in 1984 when England were outplayed 19-3 by the Australians. He helped Richmond win the Courage League National Division Two in 1997. He works as an event director for Emap and has organised huge conferences such as Civils 2009. His son Alex, a promising footballer with Chelsea, played for Wasps before a successful move to Saracens.

1098. MELVILLE, Nigel David
Scrum-half 13 caps 1984-1988
Born: Leeds, Yorkshire, 6 January 1961
Career: Otley, Wakefield, Wasps, Barbarians, British Lions
Debut: v Australia, Twickenham, November 1984

Melville captained England on his debut and six more times before quitting rugby in 1988, aged 27, after having five knee operations, a neck injury and a chipped ankle. He had worked for Nike as a player and coached Wasps to the Premiership title in 1996 and two English Cup wins before moving to Gloucester in 2002. At Kingsholm, he won another English Cup, a Premiership Championship final, and

Gloucester topped the league by 15 points in 2002. He was CEO and president of rugby operations for USA Rugby. He then moved to the RFU as Director of Professional Rugby and in 2020 was appointed executive chairman of the investor board at Premiership Rugby.

1099. REDMAN, Nigel Charles
Lock 20 caps (4-1t)
Born: Cardiff, Wales, 16 August 1964
Career: Bath, Barbarians, British Lions
Debut: v Australia, Twickenham, November 1984

Redman was first capped as a 19-year-old and had a glorious 16-season career at Bath, winning 10 English Cups, six English league titles and a European Cup. A trained electrical engineer, he played in the 1987 and 1991 Rugby World Cups. In 1997, then aged 33, he was called up by the Lions in South Africa as an injury replacement for Doddie Weir and captained them against Free State. He coached at Worcester, Basingstoke and Weston before joining the RFU as an academy coach. He later returned to Worcester, worked for British Swimming as Head of Performance Team Development, and is now the RFU's team performance director.

1100. ANDREW, Christopher Robert MBE
Fly-half 71 caps, (396–2t,33c,86p,21d) 1985-1997
Born: Richmond, Yorkshire, 18 February 1963
Career: Cambridge University, Middlesbrough, Nottingham, Gordon (Aus), Wasps, Toulouse (Fra), Newcastle, Barbarians, British Lions
Debut: v Romania, Twickenham, January 1985

Andrew won three Grand Slams with England in 1991, 1992 and 1995. He appeared in the 1991 World Cup final and was a winning British Lion in Australia in 1989 and played all three tests for the tourists in New Zealand in 1993. He was part of the Newcastle Revolution, which led to them winning the Premiership in 1998, before retiring a year later due to injury. He remained at Newcastle as director of rugby, then joined the RFU as its director of elite rugby, and then as Professional Rugby Director. He scored a first-class century for Cambridge University against Nottinghamshire in 1984 and he worked as chief executive of Sussex CCC, then in 2023 moved to the ECB as managing director of the professional game.

1101. DOOLEY, Wade Anthony
Lock 55 caps (12-3t) 1985-1993
Born: Warrington, 2 October 1957
Career: Preston Grasshoppers, Fylde, Barbarians, British Lions
Debut: v Romania, Twickenham, January 1985

Dooley, a winning British Lion in 1989, World Cup finalist in 1991, and Grand Slam winner in 1991 and 1992, was a 6ft 8in policeman known as 'The Blackpool Tower'. One of four players banned for the brawl in Wales in 1987 when he broke Phil Davies' cheekbone, he formed a tough second-row partnership with Paul Ackford for the Lions and England. In 1993, he was a Lion again in New Zealand but returned home after his father's death and was not allowed to rejoin the tour. He retired from the police in 2007 and ran a tea room - Dizzy Ducks, Wrea Green, Lancashire and is an RFU citing officer.

1102. HARDING, Richard Mark
Scrum-half 12 caps (4-1t) 1985-1988
Born: Bristol, 29 August 1953
Career: Cambridge University, Bristol, Barbarians, South & South West
Debut: v Romania, Twickenham, January 1985

Harding did an MA in land economy at Cambridge, and his presence at scrum-half forced Alastair Hignell to play full-back. He was a member of the England squad at the 1987 Rugby World Cup, playing three games, but he captained England against Fiji in Suva, and Dewi Morris was preferred for the 1989 Championship. He won the English Cup with Bristol in 1983, and his name is still well known to Bristol residents with the successful estate agents he runs in the area. Harding, a qualified chartered surveyor, sold the company for over £2 million but bought it back a year later.

1103. ORWIN, John
Lock 14 caps 1985-1988
Born: Bradford, West Yorkshire, 20 March 1954
Career: Gloucester, RAF, Bedford, Barbarians
Debut: v Romania, Twickenham, January 1985

Orwin did not play rugby union until he joined the RAF as a mechanic aged 17 but ended up with 14 caps, three as captain against Ireland in the Dublin Millennium Challenge in 1988 and on the tour to Australia that summer. Aged 35 at the time, he was dropped after that trip, and Will Carling took over. He had moved from Gloucester to Bedford when he left the RAF to take over a pub before working for a water company in his native Yorkshire. The lock coached at Morley, Wibsey, Altrincham and Datchworth and ran a garage. He later worked as an engineer and played for Biggleswade into his 50s.

1104. SIMMS, Kevin Gerard
Centre 15 caps (4-1t) 1985-1988
Born: Prescot, Merseyside, 25 December 1964
Career: Cambridge University, Wasps, Liverpool St Helens, Barbarians
Debut: v Romania, Twickenham, January 1985

Simms studied medicine at Cambridge University, where he played Varsity rugby alongside Rob Andrew, before completing his clinical training at that famous rugby hotbed St Mary's Hospital Medical School in Paddington. Simms played in the 1987 Rugby World Cup, scoring a try against Japan, and was Will Carling's first international centre partner a year later against France in Paris. The skilful centre played one more international before being replaced by Simon Halliday but continued to play for Wasps and Liverpool St Helens, whom he captained. He is now a general practitioner on Merseyside and has served as the medical officer for Liverpool St Helens.

1105. SMITH, Simon Anthony
Wing 9 caps (12-3t) 1985-1986
Born: Baldock, Hertfordshire, 29 April 1960
Career: Cambridge University, Lichfield, Fylde, Wasps, Rosslyn Park, Barbarians
Debut: v Romania, Twickenham, January 1985

Smith, educated in Wales at Gowerton School, won his nine caps as a Wasp in 1985 and 1986 after studying land economy at Cambridge University, where he won blues in rugby and athletics. He scored a try on his debut against Romania and toured New Zealand in 1985, and at club level was a losing finalist in the English Cup a year later. He has worked as a business development officer for rugby-jobs.com and Sport2Business, has been a male model for many years and works as a personal trainer after teaching economics and rugby at Cranleigh School. His son Sam has played for Harlequins and Worcester.

1106. MARTIN, Christopher Ronald
Full-back 4 caps 1985
Born: Truro, 27 June 1961
Career: Penryn, Bath, Cornwall
Debut: v France, Twickenham, February 1985

Martin, who won England under-23, England B and England Student honours, made 163 appearances for Bath between 1980 and 1988, winning his four caps for England in the 1985 Five Nations Championship. The full-back was the 51st player used by England in 12 months and also played 20 times for Cornwall. He has a maths degree from Bath

University, has worked in computers before moving to New Zealand in 1989, where he worked in telecommunications and IT around Wellington, most recently for Vodafone and One New Zealand. He also coaches cricket running summer camps and individual sessions.

1107. TEAGUE, Michael Clive
Flanker/No.8, 27 caps (12-3t) 1985-1993
Born: Gloucester, Gloucestershire, 8 October 1959
Career: Gloucester, Cardiff, Moseley, Barbarians, British Lions
Debut: v France, Twickenham, February 1985

Teague was a hard-as-nails back row forward who played in the 1991 Rugby World Cup final, won the Grand Slam that year, and toured Australia with the British Lions in 1989 when he was man of the series, and in 1993 in New Zealand. He is a revered figure at Gloucester, where he was team manager, making 291 appearances whilst working in the building trade and winning the English Cup in 1982. He was involved in two pubs – one in Gloucester opposite Kingsholm and one in Cheltenham - and is still a director of a building and property development company in the West Country.

1108. HARRISON, Michael Edward
Wing 15 caps (28-7t) 1985-1988
Born: Barnsley, Yorkshire, 19 April 1956
Career: Loughborough College, Wakefield, Yorkshire, Barbarians
Debut: v Wales, Twickenham, June 1985

Harrison, nicknamed 'Burglar Bill' by All Black fans after scoring two breakaway tries on the 1985 tour of New Zealand, was made England captain when scrum-half Richard Hill was suspended after the 1987 punch-up game against Wales. He had two years out of the game after a car crash in 1975, and led England to the 1987 Rugby World Cup, scoring a hat-trick against Japan. The winger, a converted scrum-half, captained England in two games in the 1988 Championship but never played international rugby after the 11-3 defeat to Wales at Twickenham. He worked for a building society and still works in the financial sector.

1109. HUNTSMAN, Robert Paul
Prop 2 caps 1985
Born: Beverley, East Riding of Yorkshire, 5 May 1957
Career: Hull, Headingley, Wasps, Northern Division
Debut: v New Zealand, Lancaster Park, Christchurch, June 1985

Huntsman won his two caps on England's tour to New Zealand in 1985 but retired aged 31 after a string of injuries proved too much to take in what was then an amateur game. A County Championship finalist in 1983, he played at Wasps when he was at teacher training college in Reading, taught PE at Ermysted's Grammar School in Skipton, Yorkshire, and when he finished playing with Headingley, lectured in sports science and opened the River View gym in Beverley. He lives in Cherry Burton near Beverley, has coached at Hull RUFC and was head of rugby union at Hymers College in Hull.

1110. SALMON, James Lionel Broome
Centre 12 caps (4-1t) 1985-1987
Born: Hong Kong, 16 October 1959
Career: Blackheath, Wellington (NZ), Harlequins, Barbarians, Kent
Debut: v New Zealand, Lancaster Park, Christchurch, June 1985

Salmon won three caps for New Zealand in 1981 while playing for Wellington and qualified for the All Blacks on residency. On returning to England, he had to serve another three-year eligibility period to qualify for his home country and made his England debut, ironically against New Zealand. A strong-running centre, he was in the 1987 Rugby World Cup squad, where he played his last test match. He has been a television pundit for Sky Sports and was on the board at Harlequins. He has worked in sports PR and marketing as a player agent and has his own company, JS13.

1111. HALLIDAY, Simon John
Wing/centre, 23 caps (8-2t) 1986-1992
Born: Haverfordwest, Wales, 13 July 1960
Career: Oxford University, Bath, Harlequins, Barbarians
Debut: v Wales, Twickenham, January 1986

Halliday could play centre or wing, was in Bath's all-conquering side of the 1980s and 1990s and scored a first-class century for Oxford University against Kent in 1982. A three-time rugby blue and 1991 World Cup finalist, he was part of the Grand Slam-winning England side of 1992 and has had an eventful career out of rugby. He worked in the City, holding several posts in investment banking, and was at Lehman Brothers when the bank collapsed in 2008. A former RFU Council member and on the board at Esher, he was chairman of EPCR, the organisation that runs the European club competitions until 2021. Halliday then worked with Ealing Trailfinders and subsequently became chairman of Championship Rugby.

1112. ROBBINS, Graham Leslie
No.8 2 caps 1986
Born: Sutton Coldfield, Warwickshire, 24 September 1956
Career: Sutton Coldfield, Coventry, Midlands, Warwickshire
Debut: v Wales, Twickenham, January 1986

Robbins scored 118 tries in 271 games for Coventry before retiring in 1990 and later served the club as a coach, general manager and joint director of rugby. While in 2006, he and Ian Carvell withdrew a bid to buy the club. An aviation fireman at Birmingham Airport, he won two caps in the 1986 Five Nations, but his injury opened the way for Dean Richards to make the place his own. He was spotted by Harry Walker playing for Sutton Coldfield in the Warwickshire Cup, scored against the All Blacks and beat the Wallabies while playing for the Midlands. He now lives in Cwn Penmachno, North Wales.

1113. CLOUGH, Francis John
Centre 4 caps 1986-1987
Born: Wigan, Greater Manchester, 1 November 1962
Career: Cambridge University, Orrell, Wasps, Bedford, Barbarians
Debut: v Ireland, Twickenham, March 1986

Clough was the first schoolboy rugby league international to win a full union cap after turning down the chance to turn professional to attend university. He played in the 1987 World Cup after captaining Cambridge University, where he played alongside Rob Andrew and Gavin Hastings. He followed a well-worn path trodden by Cambridge graduates, headed to Wasps and won the English League with the club in 1989-90. He went into teaching and was director of science at Uppingham School in Rutland before heading to Wellingborough School. He moved to the prestigious Millfield in Somerset, first as a second deputy and physics teacher, and is now surmaster at St Paul's School, London.

1114. RICHARDS, Dean MBE
48 caps (24-6t) 1986-1996
Born: Nuneaton, Warwickshire, 11 July 1963
Career: Roanne (Fra), Leicester, Leicestershire, Midlands, Barbarians
Debut: v Ireland, Twickenham, March 1986

Policeman Richards played six tests for the Lions on the 1989 and 1993 tours but was not always the first choice for his country in a career that stretched from 1986 to 1996. After retiring as a player in 1998, he took over as manager at Leicester when Bob Dwyer left the club, winning four Premierships and European Cups in 2001 and 2002. He had a spell at Grenoble before taking over at Harlequins, who had just been relegated. He immediately won promotion back to the Premiership but lost his job after the Bloodgate scandal and was banned for three years. He was Newcastle Falcons' director of rugby until 2022.

1115. CUSANI, David Anthony
Lock 1 cap 1987
Born: Wigan, Greater Manchester, 16 July 1959
Career: Wigan, Liverpool St Helens, Orrell, Lancashire, Barbarians
Debut: v Ireland, Lansdowne Road, Dublin, February 1987

Cusani won his only cap as part of a makeshift second row, alongside Nigel Redman, in the 17-0 defeat to Ireland in Dublin in 1987. Wade Dooley and Steve Bainbridge were both injured and although the new boy Cusani fronted up, he was replaced for the next game and did not play another test. He had won England B and Under-23 caps and toured South Africa in 1984, but he retired at just 31 in June 1991 after more than ten years at Orrell. He ran a sporting travel company, DAC Travel, based in Wigan and was involved with another, Relax Solutions.

1116. DAWE, Richard Graham Reed
Hooker 5 caps 1987-1995
Born: Tavistock, Devon, 4 September 1959
Career: Launceston, Bath, Sale, Plymouth, Cornwall, South West, Barbarians
Debut: v Ireland, Lansdowne Road, February 1987

Dawe sat on the bench 33 times for England in the era of Brian Moore and no tactical substitutions. He won his third cap against Wales in 1987 and was banned for his part in the infamous brawl which handed Moore his first cap in the next game against Scotland. He won eight English Cups and six League titles at Bath before becoming a player-coach at Sale. A farmer, he turned out for Plymouth Albion, where he was director of rugby past his 50th birthday and worked at Saracens as a scrum coach. He also coached Cornwall, worked as a coaching consultant and helped out England briefly under Eddie Jones.

1117. MOORE, Brian Christopher
Hooker 64 caps (4-1t) 1987-1995
Born: Birmingham, Warwickshire, 11 January 1962
Career: Nottingham, Harlequins, Richmond, Barbarians, British Lions
Debut: v Scotland, Twickenham, April 1987

Moore made his debut for England when Graham Dawe was suspended in 1987 and hardly missed an international for the next eight years. A World Cup finalist in 1991 and three-time Grand Slam winner, he helped Richmond win a Courage League National Division Two title in 1997, is a qualified lawyer and worked in the City for Edward Lewis LLP and Memery Crystal LLP but has not practised since 2003. Known as 'Pit Bull', he is a trained manicurist and has worked in the media for BBC TV, TalkSport and The Daily Telegraph. A vociferous critic of poor referees, he qualified as a match official in 2010.

1118. WILLIAMS, Peter Nicholas
Fly-half 4 caps 1987
Born: Wigan, Greater Manchester, 14 December 1958
Career: Orrell, Lancashire
Debut: v Scotland, Twickenham, April 1987

Williams was England's first-choice fly-half at the 1987 Rugby World Cup, ahead of Rob Andrew, but turned professional with Salford for £15,000 a year later. His father Roy was a prop for Llanelli before switching codes. He was capped by Wales at the 13-man game in 1992, becoming the first player to do the England union/Wales league double, and he also won two caps for Great Britain plus three for the Welsh. He was originally a PE and history teacher, but when he signed for Salford, he re-trained as a physiotherapist and then worked for the NHS, Wigan Warriors and a clinic in Tunbridge Wells.

1119. WEBB, Jonathan Mark
Full-back 33 caps (296–4t,41c,66p) 1987-1993
Born: Ealing, London, 24 August 1963
Career: Bristol, Bath, Northern, Barbarians
Debut: v Australia, Concord Oval, Sydney, May 1987

Webb appeared at the 1987 and 1991 Rugby World Cups, scoring all of England's points in the 12-6 loss to Australia in the latter's final. He was a medical student at Bristol University and played for Bristol in the 1988 English Cup Final, winning the competition with Bath in 1992. He won three successive Courage League titles at The Rec before retiring in 1993. Now a Bristol-based surgeon specialising in knee surgery and sports medicine, he was the Rothmans Rugby Player of the Year in 1992. He joined the RFU council in 2016 and, in 2021, was elected to World Rugby's Executive Committee.

1120. CARLING, William David Charles OBE
Centre 72 caps (54-12t) 1988-1997
Born: Bradford-on-Avon, Wiltshire, 12 December 1965
Career: Harlequins, Army, Barbarians, British Lions
Debut: v France, Parc des Princes, Paris, January 1988

England's first high-profile captain, Carling, was also the youngest at 22 when he was made skipper by Geoff Cooke in 1988. He captained England 59 times, won Grand Slams in 1991, 1992 and 1995, took England to the World Cup final in 1991 and toured New Zealand with the British Lions in 1993. A former army officer, he temporarily lost the captaincy when he described the RFU committee as '57 old farts' ahead of the 1995 World Cup. He was part of the Harlequins side that won two English Cup Finals in 1988 and 1991 and his business interests include motivational speaking, corporate hospitality, media and a cycling club. He was also a leadership advisor for England under Eddie Jones'

1121. PROBYN, Jeffrey Alan
Prop 37 caps (12-3t) 1988-1993
Born: Bethnal Green, London, 27 April 1956
Career: Richmond, Wasps, Askeans, Bedford, Barking, Blackheath, Barbarians
Debut: v France, Parc des Princes, Paris, January 1988

Probyn was a brilliant scrummager who won Grand Slams in 1991 and 1992 and appeared in the 1991 Rugby World Cup final. The tighthead prop had had to wait until he was 31 for his first cap, although he had been part of the England squad at the 1987 tournament without playing a game. He retired from international rugby in 1993 but continued to play for various clubs and, aged 44, was a backup front rower for Saracens. He worked in the family furniture business in Shoreditch, served on the RFU Council and the Barbarians committee and managed the England under-21 squad. He writes a column for The Rugby Paper.

1122. SKINNER, Michael Gordon
Flanker 21 caps (12-3T) 1988-1992
Born: Newcastle-upon-Tyne, Northumberland, 26 November 1958
Career: Blaydon, Rosslyn Park, Harlequins, Barbarians
Debut: v France, Parc des Princes, Paris, January 1988

Skinner was a flanker with a powerful personality and a tackle to match as Marc Cecillon, the French back-rower, found out in the 1991 Rugby World Cup quarter-final. He was uncapped when he was called up as a replacement for the 1987 tournament, but the selectors did not know where he was, and it was left to Des Lynam to issue a plea on the television programme *Grandstand* for the flanker to get in touch. Skinner won an English Cup with Harlequins in 1988, worked as a freelance computer consultant, including for the Metropolitan Police and had jobs as a poppular media pundit and after-dinner speaker.

1123. OTI, Christopher
Wing 13 caps (32-8t) 1988-1991
Born: Paddington, London, 16 June 1965
Career: Cambridge University, Nottingham, Wasps, Barbarians, British Lions
Debut: v Scotland, Murrayfield, Edinburgh, March 1988

Oti was a student at Cambridge when he scored a hat-trick in the 35-3 win over Ireland in 1988 at Twickenham. That was the day 'Swing Low, Sweet Chariot, was sung by the crowd for the first time, but who started it and who it was directed at is the subject of conjecture. England's first black player for over 80 years, he toured Australia with the British Lions in 1989 but had to return home early with an injury. He played twice in the 1991 Rugby World Cup but injuries forced his retirement in 1994. A qualified surveyor, he coached at London Nigerian and lives in Lagos, Nigeria.

1124. BENTLEY, John
Wing 4 caps (4-1t) 1988-1997
Born: Dewsbury, Yorkshire, 5 September 1966
Career: Otley, Sale, Rotherham, Yorkshire, Newcastle, British and Irish Lions
Debut: v Ireland, Lansdowne Road, Dublin, April 1988

Bentley had a nine-year gap between his second and third England caps because he played rugby league with Leeds, Halifax and Great Britain. A former policeman, he returned to rugby union in 1996 with Newcastle and starred on the British Lions tour of South Africa in 1997, playing two tests in the winning series and having a memorable battle with Springbok wing James Small. He switched codes again, joining Huddersfield. He has hosted rugby camps for youngsters, worked on Leeds Tykes community programmes and was employed as a business development manager at the club. He is an after-dinner speaker.

1125. EGERTON, David William
Flanker/No.8, 7 caps (4-1t)
Born: Pinner, Middlesex, 19 October 1961
Died: Bristol, 8 February 2021
Career: Loughborough College, Salisbury, Wasps, Bath, Barbarians
Debut: v Ireland, Lansdowne Road, Dublin, April 1988

Egerton won all his caps whilst playing for Bath and toured Australia with England in 1988 and Argentina in 1990. A former shot put champion, he worked as a financial advisor and won five league titles and five English Cups during his time at The Rec. He coached at Bridgwater & Albion before moving to Bristol, where he worked under the Australian Bob Dwyer as a forwards coach. He was part of a consortium that tried to buy Bristol in 1999 and worked for Commercial Union, a precursor of Aviva, and various other investment companies, including a stint in Hong Kong. He also commentated for BBC Bristol until his death.

1126. EVANS, Barry John
Wing 2 caps 1988
Born: Hinckley, Leicestershire, 10 October 1962
Career: Hinckley, Leicester, Coventry, Worcester, Midlands, Barbarians
Debut: v Australia, Concord Oval, Sydney, June 1988

Evans, educated at John Cleveland College, scored 156 tries for Leicester but managed just two caps for England on the 1988 summer tour to Australia and Fiji after being called into the squad at the 11th hour, after helping win a Courage National League One title. He turned down a place on England's tour of North America in 1982 after Nottingham University said he would lose his place if he didn't take examinations while away. An England under-16, under-18 student and B cap, he trained as a PE and maths teacher but worked for Rank Xerox and became a telecom industry executive with Vodafone until retiring.

1127. ROBINSON, Richard Andrew OBE
Flanker 8 caps (4-1t) 1988-1995
Born: Taunton, Somerset, 3 April 1964
Career: Loughborough College, Taunton, Bath, South-West, Barbarians
Debut: v Australia, Concord Oval, Sydney, June 1988

Robinson was a competitive flanker in the glory days of Bath. The European Player of the Year in 1989 also won England B caps and captained the club to league and cup double success in 1992, then a Courage League Championship. A tourist with the 1989 British Lions, he would be an assistant coach on the 2001 and 2005 tours. The former schoolteacher led Bath to the European Cup in 1998 and was a key member of Sir Clive Woodward's set-up in the 2003 Rugby World Cup win. He took over the main job in 2004 when Woodward resigned and has also coached Edinburgh, Scotland, Bristol and Romania. In 2023 he returned to Bath, for whom he played 249 matches, to head up the academy.

1128. ACKFORD, Paul John
Lock 22 caps (4-1t) 1988-1991
Born: Hanover, Germany, 26 February 1958
Career: Cambridge University, Plymouth Albion, Rosslyn Park, Metropolitan Police, Harlequins, Barbarians
Debut: v Australia, Twickenham, November 1988

Police inspector Ackford had a 10-year gap between playing for England B and making his full debut, aged 30. An abrasive lock, he played all three tests for the Lions in the winning series in Australia in 1989 and played his final game for England in the 1991 World Cup final. A Grand Slam winner in 1991, he came out of retirement to play for injury-hit Harlequins in the 1992 English Cup Final and put in a massive performance as they went down to Bath. He left the police to become the rugby union correspondent for The Sunday Telegraph, having written for The Observer as a player, before retiring in 2013.

1129. HARRIMAN, Andrew Tuoyo
Wing 1 cap 1988
Born: Lagos, Nigeria, 13 July 1964
Career: Cambridge University, Harlequins, Barbarians
Debut: v Australia, Twickenham, November 1988

From a wealthy Nigerian background, Harriman, known as the 'Prince of Pace', could run 200 metres in 20.9 seconds and captained the England team that won the World Cup Sevens in 1993. Educated at Radley College and Cambridge University, he won the 1988 English Cup with Harlequins, coached the England Sevens side in the 1990s and has been involved in the Nigerian Development & Construction Company for over 30 years. A chartered surveyor, he has also worked for an oil exploration business in Nigeria, been on the board of Crown Energy and is a director of Irene Hope Ltd, a property company.

1130. MORRIS, Colin Dewi
Scrum-half, 26 caps (21-5t) 1988-1995
Born: Crickhowell, Wales, 9 February 1964
Career: Liverpool St Helens, Orrell, Sale, Barbarians, British Lions
Debut: v Australia, Twickenham, November 1988

Born to a Welsh father and an English mother, Morris was a tough scrum-half who played as a ninth forward. He started all three tests on the 1993 Lions tour to New Zealand and played in the 1995 Rugby World Cup as England's first-choice number nine. His rivalry with Richard Hill restricted his test

Steve Bainbridge

Dave Cusani

Peter Williams

John Bentley

appearances, as no tactical replacements existed. He took a break after the 1995 World Cup but returned to play for Sale, helping them to the 1997 English Cup final. He worked as a columnist for the News of the World, as a commentator and an analyst with Sky, and as an after-dinner speaker.

1131. BUCKTON, John
Centre 3 caps 1988-1990
Born: Hull, East Riding of Yorkshire, 22 December 1961
Career: Hull & East Riding, Marist Old Boys (NZ), Saracens, Yorkshire
Debut: v Australia, Twickenham, November 1988

Saracens legend Buckton played 319 games for the club between 1984 and 1996 and won the English Cup in 1998. He toured Australia and Fiji with England in 1988 but had to return home early with an injury, then won his first cap as a replacement for Will Carling against the Wallabies in 1988. He won two more caps on the tour to Argentina in 1990 but played in an era when England had some outstanding centres. He captained Saracens from 1990 to 1992 and remains active at the club, serving as president and organising an occasional Saracens Legends XV. He is based in Waltham Forest and is a support consultant for Anite Business Systems.

1132. BATES, Stephen Michael
Scrum-half 1 cap 1989
Born: Merthyr Tydfil, Wales, 4 March 1963
Career: Wasps, Newcastle, Barbarians
Debut: v Romania, Stadionul National 2, Bucharest, May 1989

Bates played his one test in the 58-3 win over Romania and toured South Africa in 1994. He played in combination with Rob Andrew for Wasps and then Newcastle working as head coach and helping the side to the Premiership title in 1998 and an English Cup win in 2001. A schoolteacher working at Lord Wandsworth College in Hampshire, he later coached Border Reivers and Scotland A before re-joining Newcastle and coaching England Saxons. In 2011 he became director of sport at the prestigious Fettes College in Edinburgh, leaving to coach England Under-20s. He departed Twickenham to join the staff at Abingdon School.

1133. GUSCOTT, Jeremy Clayton MBE
Centre 65 caps (143-30t, 2d) 1989-1999
Born: Bath, Somerset, 7 July 1965
Career: Bath, Barbarians, British & Irish Lions
Debut: v Romania, Stadionul National 2, Bucharest, May 1989

Three Grand Slams, one World Cup final, and eight Lions tests are testament to the qualities of Guscott, one of England's finest players. He scored a hat-trick on debut in Bucharest, followed that up with a test-winning try for the Lions in his second international appearance in Brisbane shortly afterwards and dropped the series-winning goal for the Lions in South Africa in 1997. He won six League titles, six English Cups and the European Cup, in 1998, with Bath. He worked for British Gas and is now a BBC analyst, a columnist for The Rugby Paper, was a director of a cosmetics company and has a property rental firm.

1134. HODGKINSON, Simon David
Full-back 14 caps (203-1t,35c,43p) 1989-1991
Born: Thornbury, Gloucestershire,15 December 1962
Career: Nottingham, Moseley, Barbarians
Debut: v Romania, Stadionul National 2, Bucharest, May 1989

A prolific goal-kicker, Hodgkinson nailed a then-world record seven penalties in the 25-6 win over Wales in 1991 and was in the squad that reached the Rugby World Cup final that year. He lost his starting spot to Jonathan Webb and suffered a run of injuries that briefly forced him to quit rugby in 1993 before a comeback with Moseley, then re-joining Nottingham. A business studies graduate from Trent College, he co-founded a sports brokerage, Marquesman, which later became Samurai International Sportswear. He coaches rugby at Oundle School alongside fellow former international John Olver and has been a director of Nottingham-based Owen & Owen Retirement Development Ltd.

1135. LINNETT, Mark Stuart
Prop 1 cap (4-1t) 1989
Born: Rugby, Warwickshire, 17 February 1963
Career: Rugby, Moseley, Worcester, Birmingham & Solihull, Midlands, British Police, Barbarians
Debut: v Fiji, Twickenham, November 1989

Linnett's only cap came when he scored a try in the 58-23 win over Fiji in 1989, although he was on the bench four times for his country. He ended his senior career at Pertemps Bees but was tempted out of retirement, aged 44 in 2007, to play in a National Trophy tie. The prop joined the police in 1979, later working as a detective at Kings Heath Station and playing rugby for the force, helping win the British Police Cup in his last game, he retired from service in 2014. He played for England's veteran team, is a qualified physical training instructor and has coached Birmingham & Solihull Colts.

1136. MULLINS, Andrew Richard
Prop 1 cap 1989
Born: Eltham, 12 December 1964
Career: Durham University, Harlequins, London, Barbarians
Debut: v Fiji, Twickenham, November 1989

Mullins won his sole cap in 1989 in the 10-try win over Fiji after he had studied for a degree in maths at Durham University and an MBA at City University in London. He helped Quins win an English Cup in 1988 and won England B honours against the Soviet Union. The prop retired from rugby in 1997 but had already been working for Mitsubishi UJF Securities, one of the world's biggest financial institutions, since the amateur days of 1992. A trained accountant, he then worked at Resolve Gets Results LLP before becoming managing director of Muldare Ltd in Bradford and has been on the Quins board.

1137. HESLOP, Nigel John Heslop
Wing 10 caps 1990-1992
Born: West Hartlepool, County Durham, 4 December 1963
Career: Waterloo, Liverpool St Helens, Orrell, British Police, Combined Services, The North, Barbarians
Debut: v Argentina, Estadio Jose Amalfitani, Buenos Aires, July 1990

A Grand Slam winner in 1991, Heslop was famously floored by a punch from Serge Blanco, who was helped out by French flanker Eric Champ in the violent Rugby World Cup quarter-final in Paris later that year. He missed the semi-final and final, forcing England to play Simon Halliday on the wing. He was an officer with the Merseyside Police and joined Oldham RL in 1992 after becoming an outcast in England's plans. He suffered injuries and returned to Orrell after three years but didn't add to his caps before retiring in 1998. His son Danny also played for Liverpool St Helens.

1138. LEONARD, Jason
Prop 114 caps (5-1t) 1990-2004
Born: Barking, Essex, 14 August 1968
Career: Saracens, Harlequins, Essex, Eastern Counties, London Counties, British & Irish Lions
Debut: v Argentina, Estadio Jose Amalfitani, Buenos Aires, July 1990

A carpenter by trade, Leonard, kept the good things of the amateur game at heart even when the game went professional in 1995. He made his debut in 1990, won 114 England caps, played in two World Cup finals, took part in three British & Irish Lions tours, won four Grand Slams and had one serious neck operation. Known as the 'Fun Bus', he started his club career at Saracens via Barking but moved to Harlequins after England's tour to Argentina in 1990. He is involved in the construction industry, has served on the RFU Council and was President of the Union during the 2015 World Cup. He was chairman of the British & Irish Lions on the 2021 tour to South Africa.

1139. PEARS, David
Fly-half/full-back 4 caps 1990-1994
Born: Workington, Cumbria, 6 December 1967
Career: Sale, Harlequins, Worcester, Wharfedale, The North, Barbarians
Debut: v Argentina, Velez Sarsfield, Buenos Aires, July 1990

Pears played four times for England but would have had many more caps but for a series of badly-timed injuries. The England B international helped Harlequins win the English Cup in 1991 and was a finalist the following season. Later in his career he played for Bracknell and Worcester before spending three seasons at Wharfedale. He never fell out of love with the game despite the blows it dealt him, including a suspected broken neck, knee, back and pelvic injuries. He worked for Cantor Fitzgerald, the investment bank, and as an equities trader with Mint Equities in Canary Wharf in London.

1140. RYAN, Dean
Flanker/No.8 4 caps (4-1t) 1990-1998
Born: Tuxford, Nottinghamshire, 22 June 1966
Career: Saracens, Wasps, Newcastle, Bristol, Barbarians
Debut: v Argentina, Velez Sarsfield, Buenos Aires, July 1990

Ryan won the Premiership with Wasps in 1997, captained Newcastle to victory in 1998 and won his four caps between 1990 and 1998 before embarking on a career in coaching. A former corporal in the Army, he started coaching at Bristol before moving to Gloucester and was analysis for Sky Sports. Scotland coach Andy Robinson snapped up Ryan to help him in the 2012-13 international season. He became director of rugby at Worcester, guiding them back to the Premiership after a Championship play-off win. He was England's Head of International Player Development, then the Dragons as director of rugby. He left the Dragons in 2023.

1141. OLVER, Christopher John
Hooker 3 caps 1990-1992
Born: Manchester, Lancashire, 23 April 1961
Career: Harlequins, Northampton, Barbarians
Debut: v Argentina, Twickenham, November 1990

Olver won three caps for England but had the unwanted distinction of being on the bench another 31 times, without getting on, in the days before tactical replacements. The hooker captained England on the 1993 tour to Canada when caps were not awarded in the two-test series. He skippered the Harlequins English Cup win in 1988. He taught at Northampton School and was in charge of rugby at Oundle School, near Peterborough, until retiring in 2017, working with former England full-back Simon Hodgkinson. His son, Sam, was a Junior World Cup winner in 2014 and he is the uncle of the Curry twins, Tom and Ben.

1142. BAYFIELD, Martin Christopher
Lock 31 caps 1991-1996
Born: Bedford, Bedfordshire, 21 December 1966
Career: Bedford, Northampton, Metropolitan Police, Barbarians, British Lions
Debut: v Fiji, National Stadium, Suva, July 1991

A massive lock who stands at 6ft 10, Bayfield won Grand Slams with England in 1992 and 1995 and played all three tests for the Lions in New Zealand in 1993. He was an officer with the Metropolitan Police, and then Bedfordshire Police before rugby went professional but was forced to retire from playing because of a neck injury in 1998. A varied post-rugby career has seen him act in Harry Potter films as Robbie Coltrane's body double for the character Hagrid. He is one of rugby's best after-dinner speakers and also co-presents the rugby coverage on TNT Sport.

1143. RODBER, Timothy Andrew Keith
Lock/flanker/No 8 44 caps (25-5t) 1992-1999
Born: Richmond, Yorkshire, 2 July 1969
Career: The Army, Northampton, Barbarians, British & Irish Lions
Debut: v Scotland, Murrayfield, Edinburgh, January 1992

Rodber was a hero of the 1997 Lions tour to South Africa. A World Cup Sevens-winner in 1993, he was sent off playing for England against Eastern Province in South Africa a year later but returned to play in the 1995 and 1999 Rugby World Cups. He served as an officer in the Green Howards, where he stayed until he retired from playing in 2001. He had started an events and sponsorship company with former Northampton colleague Harvey Thorneycroft in 1998, which he eventually sold, and spent a decade at outsourcing firm Williams Lea, latterly as chief executive in the United States before joining commercial property company The Instant Group in which former teammate Matt Dawson is also involved.

1144. HUNTER, Ian
Wing/full-back 7 caps (15-3t) 1992-1995
Born: Harrow, London, 15 February 1969
Career: Nottingham, Northampton, Barbarians, British Lions
Debut: v Canada, Wembley Stadium, October 1992

When he was playing, Hunter set up the company Jellyfish Creative, a strategic marketing consultancy in Northampton. A trained designer, he was forced to retire in 1999 with a persistent shoulder injury, but he was in a better position than many players. Rugby league club Wigan pursued him, and he won his seven England caps between 1992 and 1995, scoring twice on his debut against Canada at Wembley. His 1993 Lions tour to New Zealand was cut short by a dislocated shoulder suffered in the opening game against North Auckland. He is a regular summariser at Northampton games for BBC Radio.

1145. UBOGU, Victor Eriakpo
Prop 24 caps (5-2t) 1992-1999
Born: Lagos, Nigeria, 8 September 1964
Career: Oxford University, Richmond, Moseley, Bath
Debut: v Canada, Wembley Stadium, October 1992

Ubogu's career took off when he joined Bath, and he forced his way into the England team in 1992, playing at the 1995 Rugby World Cup. A European Cup winner with Bath in 1998, he had arrived in England from Nigeria as a 13-year-old to attend West Buckland School in Devon and, after Oxford University, set himself the target of getting in the national squad by 1993. He made it, being picked for the tour of Argentina in 1990. A larger-than-life character, he owned a sports bar, Shoeless Joe's, on London's King's Road and launched VU Ltd, a sporting travel and hospitality business based in Twickenham.

1146. UNDERWOOD, Tony
Wing 27 caps (65-13t) 1992-1998
Born: Ipoh, Malaysia, 17 February 1969
Career: Cambridge University, Leicester, Newcastle, Barbarians, British & Irish Lions
Debut: v Canada, Wembley Stadium, 17 October 1992

Underwood is the younger brother of Rory, and the pair became the first siblings to represent England in the same game when they lined up against South Africa in 1992. He was part of the 1995 Grand Slam team and went to the

Rugby World Cup that year. A Lion in South Africa in 1997, where he played one test, he won the Premiership with Newcastle in 1998 to go with the English Cup he won with Leicester. He qualified as a pilot and worked for EasyJet and Virgin Atlantic Airways and later was based in Dubai, working for Emirates. He is an ambassador for Achilles Information.

1147. CLARKE, Benjamin Bevan
Flanker/No.8 40 caps (15-3t) 1992-1999
Born: Bishop's Stortford, Hertfordshire, 15 April 1968
Career: Saracens, Bath, Richmond, Worcester, Barbarians, British Lions
Debut: v South Africa, Twickenham, November 1992

Clarke made his England debut in 1992 but announced himself on the world stage with jaw-dropping performances playing for the British Lions in New Zealand in 1993 and gaining the grudging respect of the Kiwi public. He played all three tests, becoming rugby hot property, and he left Bath in 1996 for a big-money deal with Richmond, where he won a Courage League National Division Two title. He returned to Bath in 1999 and joined Worcester as a player/coach. A Grand Slam winner in 1995, he became a money broker in the City of London and is the director of a property company.

1148. DE GLANVILLE, Philip Ranulph
Centre 40 caps (40-8t) 1992-1999
Born: Loughborough, Leicestershire, 1 October 1968
Career: Oxford University, Bath, Barbarians
Debut: v South Africa, Twickenham, November 1992

de Glanville played 189 times for Bath during their successful period from 1989 to 2001. When Will Carling stepped down as captain, Jack Rowell handed him the England captaincy for the Five Nations of 1997 and tours of Argentina and Australia. But Clive Woodward preferred Lawrence Dallaglio as captain when he took over, although de Glanville remained in the squad until the 1999 Rugby World Cup. He worked in marketing and communications for the technology firm Xansa before joining Sport England. He was Director of Elite Sport at Hartpury College in Gloucester and is now co-owner of an executive recruitment firm, Hanover Fox, and serving on the RFU council. In 2023 he was made president of the Students' Rugby Football Union.

1149. JOHNSON, Martin Osborne CBE
Lock, 84 caps (10-2t) 1993-2003
Born: Solihull, Warwickshire, 9 March 1970
Career: Leicester, King Country (NZ), Barbarians, British & Irish Lions
Debut: v France, Twickenham, January 1993

New Zealand tried to get Johnson after he had played for their under-21 side whilst spending time down under, but the Englishman went on to become arguably his country's greatest player. A World Cup-winning captain, two-time British Lions skipper, double European Cup-winning captain and the skipper of four successive Premiership titles from 1999-2002, he was made England manager in 2008 and guided them to the Six Nations title in 2011 but left following the Rugby World Cup in New Zealand. He is an ambassador for several companies, including Mastercard, supports Help for Heroes, has been involved with Prudential RideLondon, and works for the BBC during the Six Nations.

1150. BRACKEN, Kyran Paul Patrick Bracken MBE
Scrum-half 51 caps, (15-3t) 1993-2003
Born: Dublin, Ireland, 22 November 1971
Career: Waterloo, Bristol, Saracens, Barbarians, British & Irish Lions
Debut: v New Zealand, Twickenham, November 1993

Bracken duelled with Matt Dawson for the England number 9 jersey for much of his career, having beaten the All Blacks in his first test. He was out for three months after that game after being stamped on the ankle by New Zealand's Jamie Joseph. A trained solicitor, who played for Bristol whilst at the city's university, he was a replacement on the 1997 British Lions tour of South Africa, captained England in North America in 2001 and was part of England's World Cup-winning squad in 2003. He won ITV's Dancing on Ice, launched his Ice Party and worked as a corporate speaker. Sons Charlie and Jack have played age-grade rugby for England.

1151. CALLARD, Jonathan Edward Brooks
Full-back 5 caps (69-3c,21p) 1993-1995
Born: Leicester, Leicestershire, 1 January 1966
Career: Newport, Bath, Barbarians
Debut: v New Zealand, Twickenham, November 1993

Callard, a former PE and biology teacher, joined Bath from Newport in 1989, winning five league titles and five English Cups, before spells as an assistant and head coach. He kicked all 15 points when England beat Scotland at Murrayfield in 1994 and the penalty that won the European Cup for Bath against Brive in 1998. He coached Leeds and worked with England Under-21s. He joined the RFU's National Academy, coached the kickers at the 2007 Rugby World Cup, and before being appointed National Academy Performance Manager, coached England Under-20s and the Saxons. He has worked as a sports consultant at JC16 and at Leeds as head coach. In 2022 he returned to Bath to work as a kicking coach.

1152. BACK, Neil Anthony MBE
Flanker 66 caps (83-16t,1d) 1994-2005
Born: Coventry, Warwickshire, 16 January 1969
Career: Barkers Butts, Nottingham, Leicester, Barbarians, British & Irish Lions
Debut: v Scotland, Murrayfield, Edinburgh, February 1994

Back overcame prejudice against his height of 5ft 10 to become part of England's greatest back row, win the 2003 World Cup, and be picked for three British Lions tours. He also won two Heineken Cups with Leicester and six league titles. He was banned for six months for pushing referee Steve Lander after the 1996 English Cup final against Bath. He worked on the Leicester coaching staff before moving to Leeds as head coach, then joined National 3 Midlands outfit Rugby Lions. After a spell with Edinburgh, he worked in financial services and is the business development director at TPS Visual Communications. His son Fin plays for Nottingham Forest.

1153. OJOMOH, Stephen Oziegbe
Flanker/No.8 12 caps 1994-1998
Born: Benin City, Nigeria, 25 May 1970
Career: Rosslyn Park, Bath, Gloucester, Parma (Ita), Newport, Moseley, Barbarians
Debut: v Ireland, Twickenham, February 1994

Nigerian-born back rower Ojomoh played for many clubs but won all his 12 caps at Bath in the 1990s. He forced his way into the England squad for the 1995 Rugby World Cup, playing four games and coming off the bench in the epic quarter-final win over Australia in Cape Town. His last test was on the 1998 'Tour of Hell' in New Zealand. He became involved in childcare, opening the Babyface Nursery in Bath before opening the Little Willows Day Nursery, also in Bath. He also coached Trowbridge to promotion to South West One East in 2014 and the RFU Intermediate Cup. His son Max plays for Bath.

1154. CATT, Michael John OBE
Full-back/wing/centre/full-back 75 caps (142–7t,16c,22p,3d) 1994-2007
Born: Port Elizabeth, South Africa, 17 September 1971
Career: Eastern Province (SA), Bath, London Irish, Barbarians, British & Irish Lions
Debut: v Wales, Twickenham, March 1994

Catt arrived in England from South Africa and joined Bath as the backup to Stuart Barnes. He won 75 caps, a World Cup, and a Grand Slam in 1995 and became the oldest man to play in a World Cup final in 2007, although New Zealand's Brad Thorn eclipsed that four years later and eventually joined the coaching staff. His kick to touch clinched the World Cup in 2003. He became a coach at London Irish, toured as an assistant coach with England to South Africa in 2012 and was officially appointed attacking skills coach for the senior national set-up. He coached Italy's attack before joining Andy Farrell's Ireland set-up.

1155. HULL, Paul Anthony
Full-back 4 caps 1994
Born: Lambeth, London, 17 May 1968
Career: Bristol, RAF, Barbarians
Debut: v South Africa, Loftus Versfeld, Pretoria, June 1994

RAF PT instructor Hull played 289 first-team games in 12 years at Bristol and then served as academy manager, assistant coach, head coach and chief scout. His England debut came in the memorable 32-15 win over South Africa at Loftus Versfeld in 1994, and he attracted the interest of two rugby league clubs, Warrington and Castleford, before being forced to retire because of an Achilles injury. He assisted the Saxons with Stuart Lancaster, was director of rugby at Dean Close School in Cheltenham and a talent spotter for Worcester. After running the rugby at Bath's Prior Park College, he became the RFU's head of professional match day officials.

1156. ROWNTREE, Christopher Graham
Prop 54 caps 1995-2006
Born: Stockton-on-Tees, County Durham, 18 April 1971
Career: Nuneaton, Leicester, Barbarians, British & Irish Lions
Debut: v Scotland, Twickenham, March 1995

Rowntree went on two British Lions tours in 1997 and 2005 as a player and won two European Cups with Leicester and four Premierships in 398 games for the club. The prop joined the Leicester staff before working at the RFU Academy, becoming an assistant coach with the senior side under Martin Johnson. Also a scrum coach on the 2009, 2013 and 2017 Lions tours, he was retained by Stuart Lancaster but left after the 2015 World Cup. He coached with Georgia, then joined Munster, becoming head coach in 2022 and leading them to the 2023 United Rugby Championship title.

1157. WEST, Richard John
Lock 1 cap 1995
Born: Hereford, Herefordshire, 20 March 1971
Career: Richmond, Gloucester, Midlands and South West Division, Barbarians
Debut: v Samoa, King's Park Stadium, Durban, June 1995

West went to the 1995 Rugby World Cup as an uncapped player and played his only test in the pool game against Samoa. The second row, who played more than 100 times for Gloucester, was one of the first players to turn professional when he joined Richmond in 1996, but his career was cut short in 1997 by a neck injury that needed two bone grafts. He studied at the University of the West of England in Bristol and worked in surveying. He is currently managing director of 5 Consulting Ltd, a construction development consultancy specialising in hotel chains, breweries and industrial buildings based in Gloucestershire.

1158. HOPLEY, Damian Paul MBE
Wing/centre 3 caps 1995
Born: Lambeth, London, 12 April 1970
Career: Cambridge University, Wasps, Barbarians
Debut: v Samoa, King's Park Stadium, Durban, South Africa, June 1995

Hopley, who studied theology at Cambridge, won the World Cup Sevens with England in 1993 and earned three caps in 1995. After six operations, he was forced to retire with cruciate ligament damage incurred on England Sevens duty in Hong Kong. He made a comeback but was forced to concede to his knee in 1998, aged 27. Driven by the lack of support for injured players, he founded the Professional Rugby Players' Association (now The RPA) that year and was chief executive until 2022, becoming one of the most influential people in the game.

1159. MALLETT, John Anthony
Pos: Prop, 1 cap
Born: Lincoln, 28 May 1970
Career: Bath, South West Counties
Debut: v Samoa, King's Park Stadium, Durban, South Africa, 4 June 1995

Mallett, educated at St Hugh's School, Woodhall Spa, and then Millfield won three league titles with Bath between 1993 and 1996 and three Anglo-Welsh Cups in one of the club's most golden periods. The prop was also a replacement when Bath won the-then Heineken Cup in 1998, beating Brive 19-18 in the final in Bordeaux. Mallett, who had studied at Borough Road College whilst playing for Bath United, toured South Africa with England in 1994, made his debut at the World Cup the next year and was also on the 1997 trip to Argentina. On retiring in 2003 he took a job as director of rugby at Brighton College, where he stayed for a year, before moving to Millfield where his pupils included Mako Vunipola.

REGAN, Mark Peter MBE
Hooker 46 caps (15-3t) 1995-2008
Born: Bristol, 28 January 1972
Career: Bristol, Bath, Leeds, Barbarians, British & Irish Lions
Debut: v South Africa, Twickenham, November 1995

Regan, a tourist with the 1997 Lions and a 1998 European Cup winner with Bath, was part of the World Cup-winning squad in 2003 but announced his international retirement in 2004 after being left out by new coach Andy Robinson. He continued to play club rugby for Leeds and Bristol and came out of test retirement for England's summer tour to South Africa in 2007. Impressive displays led him to the 2007 Rugby World Cup, where he started the final against South Africa. He coached at Clifton and Chew Valley, is involved in a crane repair company, runs coaching courses, and is an after-dinner speaker and analyst for BBC Radio Bristol.

1161. DALLAGLIO, Lawrence Bruno Nero OBE
Flanker/No. 8 85 caps (85-15t) 1995-2007
Born: Shepherd's Bush, London, 10 August 1972
Career: Wasps, Barbarians, British & Irish Lions
Debut: v South Africa, Twickenham, November 1995

Dallaglio, a World Cup winner in sevens and 15s, was a one-club man who captained Wasps to European Cup wins in 2004 and 2007 and played all three tests for the winning British Lions in South Africa in 1997. He was made England captain by Clive Woodward in 1997 before becoming a trusted lieutenant of Martin Johnson in England's 2003 World Cup victory. Regaining the captaincy when Johnson retired, he quit tests after the 2007 World Cup final but led Wasps to another Premiership title in 2008. He is an analyst for TNT Sport, has a column in The Sunday Times, and has set up the Dallaglio Foundation and Dallaglio RugbyWorks.

1162. DAWSON, Matthew James Sutherland MBE
Scrum-half, 77 caps (101-16t, 6c,3p) 1995-2006
Born: Birkenhead, Cheshire 31 October 1972
Career: Northampton, Wasps, Barbarians, British & Irish Lions
Debut: v Samoa, Twickenham, December 1995

Dawson was a World Cup winner in 2003 when his break set up Jonny Wilkinson's drop goal in the final and a three-time British Lion who scored a spectacular try against South Africa in 1997. He won the World Cup Sevens with England in 1993 and made his Northampton debut as a teenager but missed the 2000 European Cup win through injury. A schoolboy county cricketer and Chelsea footballer, he moved to Wasps in 2004 and won the Premiership in his first season. He was a captain on BBC TV's A Question of Sport for 17 years and works as an analyst for BBC Radio Five Live. He has also won Celebrity MasterChef. He works at Instant Group with Tim Rodber and in 2021 co-founded Lemon and Lime Associates, a management consultancy

1163. GRAYSON, Paul James
Fly-half, 32 caps (400-2t,78c,72p,6d) 1995-2004
Born: Chorley, Lancashire, 30 May 1971
Career: Waterloo, Northampton, British & Irish Lions
Debut: v Samoa, Twickenham, December 1995

Grayson scored 400 points for England, appeared at two World Cups in 1999 and 2003, and kicked Northampton to victory in the 2000 European Cup final against Munster. A Lion in South Africa in 1997, he moved into coaching while still playing at Northampton, where he scored 2,784 points in 259 games, helping Budge Pountney engineer a last-day escape from relegation in 2004. He then returned to coaching the backs before working as an assistant to Jim Mallinder. He left the club in November 2012 after 19 years. He is an analyst on BBC Radio Five Live and director of Tackle Line Rugby Ltd while his sons James and Ethan have played for the Saints.

1164. SLEIGHTHOLME, Jonathan Mark
Wing 12 caps (20-4t) 1996-1997
Born: Malton, Yorkshire, 5 August 1972
Career: Wakefield, Bath, Northampton, Barbarians
Debut: v France, Parc des Princes, Paris, January 1996

Sleightholme won 12 caps in less than 18 months when he was at Bath, but in 1997, after being left out of the British Lions squad, he was transfer-listed by the club and joined Northampton. A qualified PE teacher, he helped them win the European Cup in 2000, although the winger was injured for the semi-final and final, and he had two good seasons with Wayne Smith before retiring in 2004. He founded Sport2Business and was Group Director of HR and Talent Management at the Mark Group, the energy efficiency company, before joining the Curve Group. Sons Ollie and Frankie are in the Northampton set-up.

1165. ARCHER, Garath Stuart
Lock 21 caps 1996-2000
Born: Durham, County Durham 15 December 1974
Career: Durham City, Bristol, Newcastle
Debut: v Scotland, Murrayfield, Edinburgh, March 1996

Archer was a tough second row who won the Premiership with Newcastle in 1998 and played for England against Tonga and Fiji during the 1999 Rugby World Cup. He was ever-present in the 2000 Six Nations, but his international career finished that season, and he was forced to retire from rugby because of a back injury in 2004. He took up rowing and won the men's open title at the 2009 British Indoor Rowing Championships, beating the Great Britain rowers. He was a tanker broker in the North East before working in shipping insurance and now works for OLTCO in the North East, a firm supplying resin driveways.

1166. ADEBAYO, Adedayo Adeyemi
Wing 6 caps (10-2t) 1996-1998
Born: Idaban, Nigeria, 30 November 1970
Career: Bath, Parma (Italy), Southlands (NZ), Barbarians
Debut: v Italy, Twickenham, November 1996

Adebayo was part of the dominant Bath team of the 1990s, winning six caps for England, including two on the 1997 tour to Argentina when the British Lions were in South Africa. He was part of the training squad for the 1991 World Cup but missed out and then had a year out of rugby with a knee injury, which stalled his career. A World Cup Sevens winner with England in 1993 and a Heineken Cup winner with Bath in 1998, he had a stint in Italy with Parma and coached the Scottish sevens side Bone Steelers. He runs Premier Lifestyle, a Nigerian-based corporate hospitality business.

1167. GOMARSALL, Andrew Charles Thomas MBE
Scrum-half 35 caps (37-6t,2c,1d) 1996-2008
Born: Durham, County Durham, 24 July 1974
Career: Wasps, Bath, Bedford, Gloucester, Worcester, Harlequins, Leeds, Barbarians
Debut: v Italy, Twickenham, November 1996

Gomarsall was a much-travelled scrum half involved in the 2003 Rugby World Cup-winning campaign and started the final in 2007. His progress to the 2007 Final was remarkable. Before that year, he had not played for England since 2004, had been released by Worcester in 2006 and was on a pay-as-you-play deal at Harlequins. After touring South Africa in the summer, he forced his way into the squad and ended up number one number nine in France. He has worked for ESPN and ITV as a rugby analyst, runs a corporate and speaking firm and is a director of N2S Ltd, an IT lifecycle management company.

1168. SHAW, Simon Dalton MBE
Lock 71 caps (10-2t) 1996-2011
Born: Nairobi, Kenya, 1 September 1973
Career: Pirates (NZ), Bristol, Wasps, Toulon (Fra), Barbarians, British & Irish Lions
Debut: v Italy, Twickenham, November 1996

The first man to play 200 Premiership games, Shaw played for England for 13 years and went to three Rugby World Cups. He did not play a game in the 2003 World Cup when he was flown out to replace Danny Grewcock. The 6ft 9in lock was sent off in Auckland against the All Blacks in 2004 and won four Premiership titles with Wasps, two Heineken Cups, a Challenge Cup and an English Cup after moving to Toulon. He played in two Top 14 finals and a Heineken Cup final. He is involved in a hospitality company, a pub, a bar in Twickenham and lives in Toulon.

1169. SHEASBY, Christopher Mark Andrew
No.8 7 caps (5-1t) 1996-1997
Born: Windsor, Berkshire, 30 November 1966
Career: Cambridge University, Harlequins, Wasps, London Irish, Barbarians
Debut: v Italy, Twickenham, November 1996

Sheasby won the World Cup Sevens with England in 1993, three years before making a try-scoring debut for the full team against Italy. The No.8 started against Argentina later in 1996 and won the rest of his caps off the bench in 1997. He continued to play club rugby until well into his mid-30s and landed the English Cup with London Irish in 2002, aged 35. A maths graduate, he has coached at Staines, Bracknell and Marlow, worked on the radio and is an after-dinner speaker. He was married to Kate Staples, Zodiac from the TV programme *Gladiators*.

1170. STIMPSON, Tim Richard George
Full-back/wing 19 caps (35-2t,5c,5p) 1996-2002
Born: Liverpool, Lancashire, 10 September 1973
Career: West Hartlepool, Newcastle, Leicester, Perpignan (Fra), Leeds, Nuneaton, Nottingham, Barbarians, British & Irish Lions
Debut: v Italy, Twickenham, November 1996

A Lions tourist in 1997, when he was the top points scorer on the trip to South Africa, Stimpson won two European Cups with Leicester and also won five Premierships in a row with Newcastle Falcons and Leicester Tigers between 1998-2002. After retiring in January 2006, he was a director of Sporting Partnerships, which saves money for sports clubs and donates some of its fees to charity. He completed the Arctic Rugby Challenge in 2015 as a member of a group that trekked to the North Pole and had a game of rugby. He is head of rugby at Headkayse, who have developed a hi-tec rugby head guard.

1171. GREENING, Phil Bradley Thomas
Hooker 24 caps (30-6t) 1996-2001
Born: Gloucester, Gloucestershire, 3 October 1975
Career: Gloucester, Sale, Wasps, British & Irish Lions
Debut: v Italy, Twickenham, November 1996

Greening was a mobile hooker selected for the 2001 British & Irish Lions, although injury stopped him from playing a game. He hooked for England from 1996 to 2001 and captained England Sevens. He was a Premiership and European Cup winner with Wasps but had to retire in 2005 because of a persistent toe injury. On retirement, he coached the England Sevens, side worked in banking in Singapore and coached at London Welsh. He is an ambassador for England Rugby Travel and co-founded the Athlete Factory UK, which has a performance centre in Chester. After a brief stint with the Sri Lankan Rugby Union, he works with USA Rugby.

1172. HARDWICK, Robin John Kieren
Prop 1 cap 1996
Born: Kenilworth, Warwickshire, 29 March 1969
Career: Coventry, La Rochelle (Fra), London Irish, Birmingham, Barbarians
Debut: v Italy, Twickenham, November 1996

Hardwick played just once for England and toured Argentina with the national side while playing at Coventry with Danny Grewcock as a clubmate. The prop had a spell in France with La Rochelle before joining London Irish, where he played 167 times and won the English Cup in 2002. He was director of rugby and sports academy manager at Bedford Modern School and lead rugby coach at Queen Ethelburga's College in York. Hardwick, who turned out for Richmond in his post-professional days, has also coached at Luton RFC. His son Tom was on the books at Leicester Tigers.

1173. BEAL, Nicholas David
Full-back/wing/centre 15 caps (15-3t) 1996-1999
Born: Howden, Yorkshire, 2 December 1970
Career: Northampton, Barbarians
Debut: v Argentina, Twickenham, December 1996

The versatile Beal played 264 games for Northampton between 1992 and 2004, won the World Cup Sevens with England in 1993 and toured South Africa with the British Lions in 1997. On that tour he scored a hat-trick against the Junior Springboks but did not play a test. He missed Northampton's European Cup win in 2000 with injury, played his last test in the 1999 World Cup and retired from the game in 2004 to concentrate on his career. He has been a director of David Williams Independent Financial Advisers in Northampton since 2000 and has also worked with AXA.

1174. HILL, Richard Anthony MBE
Flanker/No.8, 71 caps (60-12t) 1997-2004
Born: Dormansland, Surrey, 23 May 1973
Career: Saracens, Barbarians, British & Irish Lions
Debut: v Scotland, Twickenham, February 1997

Hill, a three-time British Lion and World Cup winner, is the only player Clive Woodward never dropped during his reign as England coach. He could play six, seven or eight, wearing the number six shirt in England's fabled back row with Neil Back and Lawrence Dallaglio. He was forced out of the Lions tour in 2001 after a blatant smash in the face from Australian centre Nathan Grey in the second test. Rated one of England's best forwards, he mentored academy players at Saracens and worked as a pathway player-manager at the RFU and on the RFU Council. He has been England's men's team manager since 2016.

1175. HEALEY, Austin Sean
Full-back/wing/fly-half/scrum-half, 51 caps (75-15t) 1997-2003
Born: Wallasey, Merseyside, 26 October 1973
Career: Waterloo, Orrell, Leicester, Barbarians, British & Irish Lions
Debut: v Ireland, Lansdowne Road, Dublin, February 1977

Healey was a victim of his own versatility but was good enough to play wing, scrum-half and full-back at test level and once, in Pretoria, in the 2000 test against South Africa, fly-half. He played in the 1999 Rugby World Cup but failed to make the cut four years later. He won back-to-back European Cup finals for Leicester in 2001 and 2002 and toured with the Lions in 1997. He is an analyst for TNT Sport and has worked in banking for Credit Suisse. He is a director of MAP Environmental and is the founder of Super Skills Travel.

1176. GARFORTH, Darren James
Prop 25 caps 1997-2000
Born: Coventry, Warwickshire, 9 April 1966
Career: Coventry, Saracens, Leicester, Nuneaton, Barbarians
Debut: v Wales, Cardiff Arms Park, Cardiff, March 1997

Garforth, who still runs a scaffolding business in the Midlands, was a member of Leicester's ABC club and won four Premiership titles and two European Cups with the Tigers between 1991 and 2003. His work on building sites aided his strength and he gained 25 caps crammed into three years up to 2000 with England before Phil Vickery established himself as the number one tighthead prop. He opted out of England's tour of North America in 2001, saying at 35, he was better off having a rest, and coach Clive Woodward agreed but did not give the prop another cap. He left Leicester to join Nuneaton as a player/coach.

1177. CORRY, Martin Edward MBE
Lock/flanker, No.8 64 caps (30-6t) 1997-2008
Born: Birmingham, Warwickshire, 12 October 1973
Career: Newcastle, Bristol, Leicester, Barbarians, British & Irish Lions
Debut: v Argentina, Ferrocaril Oeste, Buenos Aires, May 1997

Corry was called up as a replacement for the 2001 Lions tour to Australia, forced his way into the test team, and was ever-present in the internationals in 2005 in New Zealand. A 2003 World Cup winner, he played his last international in the 2007 World Cup final, retired from test rugby officially a year later, and retired altogether in 2009. He had five Premiership titles and two European Cups to add to his World Cup. He worked as a sales director for Oracle, a computer company, and a technology firm. He works for the software development company Alteryx and has worked as a radio pundit and motivational speaker.

1178. DIPROSE, Anthony James
No.8 10 caps (5-1t) 1997-1998
Born: Orsett, Essex, 22 September 1972
Career: Loughborough University, Saracens, Harlequins, Barbarians, British & Irish Lions
Debut: v Argentina, Ferrocaril Oeste, Buenos Aires, May 1997

Diprose was called up as a replacement by the 1997 Lions in South Africa shortly after making his England debut in Argentina. He won the English Cup with Saracens, but the strength of the back row limited his England chances, although he won caps on the 'Tour of Hell', captaining the side in the 76-0 defeat by Australia in Brisbane in 1998. He returned after helping Harlequins return to the Premiership at the first attempt following their 2005 relegation. He remained at the Stoop as assistant academy manager, running the academy and acting as first-team defence coach. He left to become director of sports at Canford School in Dorset.

1179. GREENSTOCK, Nicholas James Jeremy
Centre 4 caps (10-2t) 1997
Born: Dubai, UAE, 3 November 1973
Career: Wasps, Harlequins, London Irish
Debut: v Argentina, Ferrocaril Oeste, Buenos Aires, May 1997

Greenstock, who is assistant secretary of the England Rugby Internationals Club, gained entrance to that elite group when he played four times for England in 1997 on tour in Argentina, in Sydney and against the Springboks in the autumn internationals. Son of Sir Jeremy Greenstock, a high-ranking diplomat, the centre won the European Challenge Cup with Harlequins in 2001 but retired from full-time rugby a year later. He worked for the Royal Bank of Scotland, playing part-time for Quins and then London Irish before leaving the bank to set up Gatehouse Advisory Partners with his father and Sir David Manning, another diplomat. The company advises organisations on geopolitics.

1180. HAAG, Stephen Martin
Lock 2 caps 1997
Born: Chelmsford, Essex, 28 July 1965
Career: Bath, Bristol, Barbarians
Debut: v Argentina, Ferrocaril Oeste, Buenos Aires, May 1997

Haag won two caps on England's tour of Argentina in 1997 and a European Cup in 1998 with Bath, for whom he made 315 appearances, winning Five League titles and two English cups. Haag joined Bristol as a coach in 2003, helping win promotion to the Premiership in 2005 before returning to Bath as an academy coach. Haag joined the RFU working with the Under-20s when they reached the final of the 2009 Junior World Championships before becoming the first-team coach at Bath and Nottingham. He returned to England Under-20s as they won the 2016 Junior World Cup, coached at Rouen in France and is performance director of Transition 15.

1181. MALLINDER, David James
Full-back 2 caps 1997
Born: Halifax, Yorkshire, 16 March 1966
Career: Sale, Barbarians
Debut: v Argentina, Ferrocaril Oeste, Buenos Aires, May 1997

Mallinder has had a highly successful coaching career but had been a strong full-back for Sale, playing nearly 400 games between 1989 and 2001 before joining the coaching staff. He guided them to the European Shield before taking a post at the RFU Academy and coaching the Saxons. He headed to newly-relegated Northampton and got them straight back into the Premiership before taking them to the 2011 European Cup final. Northampton won the 2014 European Challenge Cup and followed that up a week later by landing the Premiership. He left Franklin's Gardens to work for the RFU on young player development and was Performance Director of the Scottish Rugby Union from 2019 but announced he would leave in 2024.

1182. YATES, Kevin Peter
Prop 4 caps 1997-2007
Born: Medicine Hat, Canada, 6 November 1972
Career: Chippenham, Bath, Wellington (NZ), Hurricanes (NZ), Sale, Saracens, Nice (Fra), Barbarians
Debut: v Argentina, Ferrocaril Oeste, Buenos Aires, May 1997

Canadian-born prop Yates won two caps on the 1997 tour to Argentina and had to wait a record nine years and 353 days for his next, in Bloemfontein against South Africa in 2007. He moved to New Zealand, where he became the first British player to gain a Super Rugby contract in Wellington. He returned to England with Sale before moving to Saracens, then finally to Nice, in the French third division. He worked as a sales trader for Churchill Capital in Monaco before returning to England to work for a medical assistance company. He now works at Bendac Group, an LED solutions company.

1183. COCKERILL, Richard
Hooker 27 caps (15-3t) 1997-199
Born: Rugby, Warwickshire, 16 December 1970
Career: Coventry, Leicester, Clermont (Fra), Barbarians
Debut: v Argentina, Ferrocaril Oeste, Buenos Aires, May 1997

Cockerill, who joined Leicester in 1992, was a combative hooker and then director of rugby at Welford Road. He famously stared out All Black's hooker Norm Hewitt during the haka at Old Trafford in 1997, and his test career lasted until the 1999 Rugby World Cup. As a player, he won five league titles, two English Cups and two European Cups before spending two years in France with Clermont. He returned to Leicester's staff in 2004 and coached the academy before stepping into the top job, winning the Premiership three times. He coached briefly in Toulon, and then Edinburgh was England's forwards' coach, leaving to take up a contract with Montpellier. He was sacked by the French club in 2023.

1184. GREWCOCK, Daniel Jonathan MBE
Lock 69 caps (10-2t) 1997-2007
Born: Coventry, Warwickshire, 7 November 1972
Career: Coventry, Saracens, Bath, Barbarians, British & Irish Lions
Debut: v Argentina, Ferrocaril Oeste, Buenos Aires, June 1997

Grewcock went on the 2001 and 2005 British & Irish Lions tours and was sent off playing for England against the All Blacks in Dunedin in 1998. A hand injury limited him to one appearance at the 2003 Rugby World Cup, but he flew home early and did not even get his medal for a year. The second row was in line for a spot in the 2007 World Cup but was banned for punching and missed the tournament. He retired after 229 games for Bath and became director of the academy at the club until becoming Director of Sport at Oundle School. He then took a dual role with Bristol's Academy and Clifton College.

1185. MAPLETOFT, Mark Sterland
Fly-half 1 cap (3-1p) 1997
Born: Mansfield, Nottinghamshire 25 December 1971
Career: Rugby, Gloucester, Saracens, Harlequins, London Irish, Barbarians
Debut: v Argentina, Ferrocaril Oeste, Buenos Aires, June 1997

Mapletoft, appointed England Under-20s coach in 2023, played 110 games for Gloucester between 1994 and 1999 before moving to Saracens and retiring in 2005 when he was at London Irish via Harlequins. A sports science graduate from Loughborough University, he also studied leisure and tourism management at the University of Gloucestershire while playing at Kingsholm. He was assistant academy manager at Saracens before joining the RFU National Academy. He then moved to Harlequins as backs coach in 2010, where he stayed for over a decade. He returned to Twickenham as an assistant coach with the Under-18s before taking the head coach role with the Under-20s.

1186. KING, Alexander David
Fly-half 5 caps (23-1t,3c,3p,2d) 1997-2003
Born: Brighton, Sussex, 17 January 1975
Career: Rosslyn Park, Wasps, Clermont (Fra), Barbarians
Debut: v Argentina, Ferrocaril Oeste, Buenos Aires, June 1997

King was fly-half in the Wasps side that rampaged through England and Europe, winning two European Cups and three straight Premierships. He was involved in the 2003 Rugby World Cup build-up, playing in the warm-up win over Wales in Cardiff. That would prove to be his last international. He ended his career in France before joining the Clermont coaching staff and helping them to their first Top 14 title. He was Northampton's backs coach under Jim Mallinder, winning the Premiership in his first season at the club. He had a spell with Wales, then coached the Montpellier before moving to Gloucester. Warren Gatland took him back to Wales in 2023.

1187. GREEN, William Robert
Prop 4 caps 1997-2003
Born: Littlehampton, Sussex, 25 October 1973
Career: Villagers (SA), Wasps, Leinster
Debut: v Australia, Twickenham, November 1997

Green was part of a golden era for Wasps, winning the European Cup and the three Premiership titles. The prop's only start for England came on his debut in 1997, but he won three more caps off the bench, including one against New Zealand in Dunedin on the 1998 'Tour of Hell'. He moved to

Leinster in Ireland in 2005 before retiring from the game two years later. He was a business studies graduate from Oxford Brookes University. He attended Cirencester Agricultural College while still playing and worked for Edge Renewables Ltd, an energy company when he moved to be managing director of Green Forest Renewables Ltd in Somerset.

1188. GREENWOOD, William John Heaton MBE
Centre 55 caps (155-31t) 1997-2004
Born: Blackburn, Lancashire, 20 October 1972
Career: Waterloo, Leicester, Harlequins, Barbarians
Debut: v Australia, Twickenham, November 1997

England have never replaced Will Greenwood, a three-time British & Irish Lion and World Cup winner, since he played his last test in midfield in 2004. During the 2003 Rugby World Cup, he returned home after the pool match against South Africa because his wife Caroline was experiencing difficulties with her pregnancy. He worked as a banker in his first stint at Harlequins and moved to Leicester before returning to the Stoop. He was an analyst for Sky Television, a columnist for The Daily Telegraph and a coach at Maidenhead RFC. He works with Afiniti, a tech company, as chief customer officer. He is also a director of Legends Holidays.

1189. LONG, Andrew Edward
Hooker 2 caps 1997-2001
Born: Poole, Dorset, 2 September 1977
Career: Bath, Munster, Rotherham, Newcastle, Cetransa El Salvador (Spa), Northampton, Barbarians
Debut: v Australia, Twickenham, November 1997

Hooker Long had the misfortune to be replaced at half-time in his international debut, with Clive Woodward hauling him off in favour of Richard Cockerill, and gained only one more cap, on the 2001 tour to North America. Much-travelled, he played most of his 201 Premiership games at Bath and Newcastle, and he had just signed for Gloucester from Northampton when he was forced to retire because of neck trouble in 2012. After rugby, he worked in the City for Monitise, a mobile money business, and owns Impact2, a coaching provider helping businesses. He was head coach at Bishop's Stortford RFC and worked with Worcester as a throwing coach.

1190. PERRY, Matthew Brendan
Full-back/centre 36 caps (50-10t) 1997-2001
Born: Bath, Somerset, 27 January 1977
Career: Bath, Barbarians, British & Irish Lions
Debut: v Australia, Twickenham, November 1997

Perry was a fearless full-back, but his international career was finished by the time he was 24. A European Cup winner with Bath in 1998, although he was left out of the final, he had won his first cap in 1997 and by 2001 was England's most-capped full-back. However, that year, Clive Woodward preferred Iain Balshaw at number 15, and although Perry played all three tests on the Lions tour to Australia, he never played for England again and was forced to retire with disc problems in 2007. He worked for the mobile financial services company Monitise until he co-founded Transition 15. He has also appeared as a pundit on Sky Sports and TNT Sport.

1191. REES, David Llewellyn
Wing 11 caps (15-3t) 1997-1999
Born: Kingston-upon-Thames, Surrey, 15 October 1974
Career: Sale, Bristol, Leeds, Newbury
Debut: v Australia, Twickenham, November 1997

Wing Rees scored one of the great tries at Twickenham in December 1997, gathering his own chip to out-pace the All-Blacks' defence for his first test score. He scored two against Wales in the next season's Five Nations but played his last international in 1999 while at Sale. He then moved to Bristol, and in 2003 signed for Leeds when Bristol went down. He later played for Newbury and Clifton down the leagues. He studied graphic design at Manchester Metropolitan University and is a coach for Oakfields Personal Training in Bristol. His' father, Peter, played flanker for Saracens in the 1960s.

1192. WEST, Dorian Edward MBE
Hooker 21 caps (15-3t) 1998-2003
Born: Wrexham, Wales, 5 October 1967
Career: Nottingham, Leicester, Barbarians, British & Irish Lions
Debut: v France, Stade de France, Paris, February 1998

Originally a flanker, West converted to hooking during a spell at Nottingham in the early 1990s and never looked back. Rejecting a trial with Wales, he was a policeman with Leicestershire Constabulary's armed response unit before the game went professional and was in England's 2003 World Cup-winning squad. He went into coaching at the RFU academy, taking the under-19s, before joining Jim Mallinder as the pair led the under-21s to a Grand Slam and the Saxons to the Churchill Cup. He went to Northampton with Mallinder and helped to win a Premiership crown, a Championship title, and a European Cup Final. He is now the Sale Sharks forwards' coach.

1193. VICKERY, Philip John MBE
Prop 73 caps (10-2t) 1998-2009
Born: Barnstaple, Devon, 14 March 1976
Career: Bude, Redruth, Gloucester, Wasps, British & Irish Lions
Debut: v Wales, Twickenham, February 1998

Vickery made an indelible mark on English rugby by winning the 2003 Rugby World Cup and captaining England in the 2007 tournament. The Cornishman, a British & Irish Lion in 2001 and 2009, he led England on their successful tour of Argentina in 2002. The farmer's son had 11 years at Gloucester, then joined Wasps, where he won domestic and European titles before being forced to retire with neck trouble. He coached at Worcester briefly but has fingers in several pies outside rugby. He runs a leisure wear label 'Raging Bull', and has business interests in the food industry. He won Celebrity MasterChef and worked as a media pundit and occasional columnist.

1194. WILKINSON, Jonathan Peter CBE
Fly-half/centre 91 caps (1179-6t, 162c, 239p, 36d) 1998-2011
Born: Frimley, Surrey, 25 May 1979
Career: Newcastle, Toulon (Fra), British & Irish Lions
Debut: v Ireland, Twickenham, April 1998

Wilkinson made his test debut in 1998 as a teenager and retired in glory with Toulon in 2014 after leading them to a second European Cup. The fly-half, responsible for English rugby's most iconic moment in 2003, played in four World Cups, two Lions tours, two World Cup finals, and won two European Cups, a French Top 14 title, four Six Nations wins (including a Grand Slam), an English Premiership with Newcastle, and two domestic Cups. He coached part-time at Toulon, was the 2003 International Player of the Year, and made CBE in the Queen's Birthday honours in 2015. He still helps out England players with their kicking.

1195. BENTON, Scott
Scrum-half 1 cap 1998
Born: Bradford, Yorkshire, 8 September 1974
Career: Gloucester, Leeds, Sale, Orrell, Barbarians
Debut: v Australia, Lang Park, Brisbane, June 1998

Scrum-half Benton won his only cap in the 76-0 defeat to Australia in Brisbane in 1998 when Matt Dawson was injured on the 'Tour of Hell'. He was an unused replacement five times in tests but had his international ambitions thwarted by the presence of Dawson, Kyran Bracken and Andy

Gomarsall. He toured South Africa with England in 2000, but his opportunities were limited by injury. He has coached at Morley RUFC and has coached the first team at Silcoates School in Wakefield, Yorkshire. He is now a rugby coach and PE teacher at the Rodillian Multi Academy Trust in Yorkshire.

1196. BROWN, Spencer Peter
Wing 2 caps 1998
Born: Eton, Berkshire, 11 June 1973
Career: Richmond, Bristol, Bedford, Rugby, Nottingham, Royal Navy, Combined Services
Debut: Australia, Lang Park, Brisbane, June 1998

Brown was another player to get his only taste of test rugby on the 1998 'Tour of Hell' but was around the squad until 2001. A former Royal Marine who served for 13 years, he played sevens for England and represented England A. He retired and trained to become a strength-and-conditioning coach with Northampton, later working at Bedford. He earned a first-class honours degree in sport & exercise science at Northampton University, studied for a PhD at the University of Warwick, and has worked as a personal trainer in Bermuda at his gym, Island Rehab Hut, after first going to the island for the Classics tournament.

1197. POOL-JONES, Richard John
Flanker 1 cap 1998
Born: London, 22 October 1969
Career: Cambridge University, Biarritz (Fra), Wasps, Stade Francais (Fra), Barbarians
Debut: v Australia, Lang Park, Brisbane, June 1998

Pool-Jones won his only cap in the 76-0 defeat to Australia in 1998, having started playing senior rugby at Wasps but spent most of his career playing in France. The flanker played at Stade Francais and represented the club in their 2001 European Cup final defeat by Leicester. He owns a printing business in Paris, as well as other business interests, worked in French television and radio and, in 2011, became a vice president of Stade after helping to rescue them from financial oblivion. He had a spell as sporting director of the club before returning to his vice-chairman's post.

1198. RAVENSCROFT, Stephen Charles Wood
Centre 2 caps 1998
Born: Bradford, West Yorkshire, 2 November 1970
Career: Saracens, London Welsh, Barbarians
Debut: v Australia, Lang Park, Brisbane, June 1998

Ravenscroft was another player whose only taste of international rugby came on the infamous 'Tour of Hell' in 1998, playing against Australia and coming off the bench against New Zealand in Auckland. The centre played for Saracens, winning the English Cup in 1998, before having five seasons at London Welsh. A solicitor, he was a partner specialising in employment law with White & Case LLP and is now a partner at Memery Crystal, a law firm in the City of London. He turned out for the Spoon AAs, formerly the Anti-Assassins, who are the rugby charity Wooden Spoon team. He was president of Saracens.

1199. STURNHAM, Ben
Flanker 3 caps 1998
Born: St Albans, Hertfordshire, 6 March 1974
Career: Saracens, Bath, Bristol
Debut: v Australia, Lang Park, Brisbane, June 1998

Sturnham was at Saracens during the 1998 trip to Australia when he won his three caps, then moved to Bath and had two years at Bristol before retiring with a serious knee injury. He was director of rugby at Newbury, has worked as a head-hunter and was employed by Carmichael Fisher in London as an executive search consultant specialising in property. He was also an ambassador for Klas International Ltd, a company which helps sports stars and others move into roles in business. He has worked for Korn Ferry as a real estate management consultant.

1200. CHAPMAN, Dominic Edward
Wing 1 cap 1998
Born: Kingston-upon-Thames, Surrey, 7 March 1976
Career: Harlequins, Richmond, Bracknell
Debut: v Australia, Lang Park, Brisbane, June 1998

Ireland wanted to cap Chapman, who was eligible through his paternal grandparents and won one cap for England as a replacement in the 76-0 thrashing by the Wallabies in Brisbane in 1998. He scored a then-record 17 tries for Richmond in the 1998/99 Premiership season and was one of the fastest wingers around after employing Margot Wells as his sprint coach. Tom Hudson, who worked as director of sports at Surrey University, said he could turn him into an Olympic athlete, but he chose rugby and moved to Richmond as the game was turning professional. Chapman now works as a marketing director.

1201. POTTER, Stuart
Centre 1 cap 1998
Born: Lichfield, Staffordshire, 11 November 1967
Career: Nottingham, Leicester, Rugby, Barbarians
Debut: v Australia, Lang Park, Brisbane, June 1998

Potter, a European Cup finalist with Leicester in 1997, came off the bench to win his only cap in England's 76-0 defeat to Australia in Brisbane in 1998. He had missed that year's Five Nations with an injury after being called up to the squad by Clive Woodward. The centre won two English Cups and three Premiership titles with The Tigers, where he stayed until 2000 whilst continuing various business interests. He played 103 times for the Tigers and 18 times for England A before joining Rugby in 2001. He took over the family insurance business and is also a director of a sports agency, Agent Rugby Ltd.

1202. LEWSEY, Owen Joshua MBE
Full-back/wing/fly-half 55 caps (110-22t) 1998-2007
Born: Bromley, Kent, 30 November 1976
Career: Bristol, Wasps, Barbarians, British & Irish Lions
Debut: v New Zealand, Carisbrook, Dunedin, June 1998

Lewsey made a late run for a starting berth in the 2003 Rugby World Cup, having not won a cap for two years, scoring five tries in a pool match against Uruguay. He toured with the British & Irish Lions in 2005 and won every club honour with the great Wasps sides of the 2000s. He served in the Royal Artillery, was the Welsh Rugby Union's Head of Rugby, having worked in finance, and is based in Hong Kong as the CEO of Teneo Financial Advisory. He is also a visiting professor of leadership at The University of Law Business School.

1203. SANDERSON, Patrick Harold
Flanker/No.8 16 caps (5-1t) 1998-2007
Born: Chester, Cheshire, 6 September 1977
Career: Sale, Harlequins, Worcester
Debut: v New Zealand, Carisbrook, Dunedin, June 1998

Sanderson, elder brother of Alex, captained England on their 2006 tour to Australia, having led them in the 2005 Churchill Cup, and was skipper of Worcester for six years, playing 156 games and scoring 24 tries after being an English Cup finalist at Harlequins. He was forced to retire with a shoulder injury in 2011. He ran a chocolate fountain business with his wife, Nicky, worked for Deutsche Bank in the City in the global transactions department, then moved to JP Morgan and the Royal Bank of Canada. Most recently, he was employed by Ninety-One Asset Management.

1204. BEIM, Thomas David
Wing 2 caps (5-1t) 1998
Born: Frimley, Surrey, 11 December 1975
Career: Gloucester, Hamiltons (SA), Sale, Birmingham, Viadana (Ita), Pertemps Bees, Barbarians
Debut: v New Zealand, Carisbrook, Dunedin, June 1998

Beim won his two caps in 1998 when England took a depleted side to the southern hemisphere and toured Argentina in 2002. A winger, he scored five tries for Gloucester in a Heineken Cup match against Roma in 2000 before leaving three years later to play in Italy. He has carved out a successful career in international polo. He had played the game before rugby took over and had rejected an offer to play polo in Dubai, splitting his time between teams in England, Australia and Argentina and representing his country in a second sport. He is now a builder in Cirencester, Gloucestershire.

1205. SIMS, David
Lock 3 caps 1998
Born: Gloucester, Gloucestershire, 22 November 1969
Died: Bristol, 19 March 2022
Career: Sunnybank (Aus), Gloucester, Worcester, Bedford, Exeter, Taunton, Launceston, Barbarians
Debut: v New Zealand, Carisbrook, Dunedin, June 1998

Sims won all three caps in 1998 and played in Gloucester's second row. After a spell at Worcester, he was talked out of retirement to play for Exeter, who were then in National Division One and was still playing and coaching at Withycombe RFC into his mid-40s. Whilst playing there, he was stamped on and had six blood clots in his leg and lung, which left him on warfarin. He ran a shop with his wife Jill in the West Country. Jilly, Tilly and Boo is an Annie Sloan chalk paint stockist that also runs workshops. He died of a heart attack aged 52.

1206. BAXENDELL, Joshua John Neill
Centre 2 caps 1998
Born: Manchester, 3 December 1972
Career: Sheffield, Sale
Debut: v New Zealand, Eden Park, Auckland, June 1998

Baxendell played for Sale from 1993 to 2005, winning his two England caps on the infamous 'Tour of Hell' in 1998 during the 40-10 defeat to New Zealand in Auckland and the 18-0 loss to the Springboks in Cape Town. A one-club man, he coached the backs at Sale, where he won a Courage League Two title in 1994, helped out the Russian Rugby Union and then returned to Sale as a skills coach. Since leaving the game, he has had fingers in many pies, working as an asset manager and property consultant. The qualified surveyor is now a property consultant at BE Group.

1207. FIDLER, Robert John
Lock 2 caps 1998
Born: Cheltenham, Gloucestershire, 21 September 1974
Career: Gloucester, Bath
Debut: v New Zealand, Eden Park, Auckland, June 1998

Fidler, son of Gloucester legend John, was at Kingsholm for nine seasons, playing 217 games before leaving for Bath in 2003. Knee problems hampered his time at the Rec. He managed 80 games and left the club in 2007. A 2002 Premiership Finalist with Gloucester before winning an English Cup a year later and was a finalist with Bath in 2005. He then joined Cinderford for a year before coaching at Old Patesians. He spent two years at college studying construction and carpentry before joining the family building firm JHF Construction, which he has run since his father retired to Cornwall.

1208. SAMPSON, Paul Christian
Wing 3 caps 1998-2001
Born: Wakefield, Yorkshire, 12 July 1977
Career: Blackheath, Wasps, Bath, Worcester, London Welsh, Barbarians
Debut: v South Africa, Newlands, Cape Town, July 1998

Sampson was a quick enough sprinter to beat Dwain Chambers in the English Schools' 100m final but was snapped up by rugby when he was called into the England squad while still at Woodhouse Grove in 1996. He had spells in league with Wakefield and London Broncos, played over 100 times for Wasps and retired in 2011 after five seasons at London Welsh. He was married to TV presenter Kirsty Gallacher and is a director of the International Training Club. He works on a project to provide housing for people suffering from brain damage from sport. He is part-owner of a café in Windsor.

1209. LUGER, Daniel Darko MBE
Wing 38 caps (120-24t) 1998-2003
Born: Chiswick, London, 11 January 1975
Career: Richmond, Orrell, Saracens, Harlequins, Perpignan (Fra), Toulon (Fra), RK Nada (Cro), Nice Cote d'Azur (Fra), Barbarians, British & Irish Lions
Debut: v Netherlands, McAlpine Stadium, Huddersfield, November 1998

A member of the 2003 World Cup-winning squad when he played four games, Luger's international career finished with a quarter-final win against Wales in Brisbane. His 2001 British & Irish Lions tour to Australia was wrecked by a fractured cheek before a test was played, opening the way for Jason Robinson to take over. He had two stints with Harlequins and one with Saracens before playing for several teams in France and coaching on the Cote d'Azur. The winger - who has a Croation father - lives in Monaco, works in financial trading with Tavira Securities, and has dabbled in bobsleighing.

1210. McCARTHY, Neil
Hooker 3 caps 1999-2000
Born: Slough, Berkshire, 29 November 1974
Career: Bath, Bedford, Gloucester, Bristol, Orrell, Barbarians
Debut: v Ireland, Lansdowne Road, Dublin, March 1999

McCarthy won all three of his England caps off the bench while playing for Gloucester and represented his country at every level from under-16 to senior. A hooker who could prop as well, he was a squad member in the 1999 Rugby World Cup, playing one game against the United States before a knee injury ended his playing career. He managed the Leicester Academy, overseeing the development of players such as Dan Cole, Manu Tuilagi and Tom and Ben Youngs before moving to a similar role at Gloucester in 2015. He began working for the British Bobsleigh and Skeleton Association, then GB Pentathlon and became head of player development at Premiership Rugby.

1211. HANLEY, Steven Melvyn
Wing 1 cap (5-1t) 1999
Born: Whitehaven, Cumbria, 11 June 1979
Career: Sale, Barbarians
Debut: v Wales, Wembley Stadium, April 1999

Hanley scored a try in his only test for England and was involved in the training squad ahead of the 1999 Rugby World Cup, but then he dislocated his shoulder. He was out with a broken leg when his Sale side won the European Challenge Cup. He won the Premiership with the club in 2006 but missed the final, and back trouble forced his retirement, and he went out with 75 Premiership tries in 135 appearances. He stayed at the club, working as a business development manager. He then worked for First & Last in hospitality and now works in business development for Sedulo in Manchester, appearing on the after-dinner circuit.

1212. MATHER, Barrie-Jon
Centre 1 cap 1999
Born: Wigan, Greater Manchester, 12 January 1973
Career: Sale, Kubota Spears (Jap), Coventry
Debut: v Wales, Wembley Stadium, London, April 1999

Mather, a former Great Britain rugby league international, won his only cap in the 1999 defeat to Wales at Wembley. The huge centre at 6ft 6in tall had spells in league with Castleford, Wigan and Western Reds before moving to Sale, returning to Castleford then spending two more years in union at Coventry and Kubota Spears in Japan. He then coached in Japan, Blackpool RFC and the London Irish Academy. He switched codes again, becoming the head of player development and England team manager at the RFL before working for the New South Wales Rugby League and was high performance director at the New South Wales Institute of Sport. In 2023 he joined the Fiji Rugby Union as general manager of high performance.

1213. WOODMAN, Trevor James
Prop 22 caps 1999-2004
Born: Plymouth, Devon, 4 August 1976
Career: Bath, Plymouth Albion, Gloucester, Sale
Debut: v United States, Twickenham, August 1999

Woodman was England's starting loosehead prop in the 2003 Rugby World Cup final while at Gloucester and looked set for a mountain of caps before he was forced to retire with a back injury when he was at Sale. After finishing playing, he moved to Australia, where he coached at Sydney University for three years and had a brief stint as national scrum coach for the Australian Rugby Union. He returned to England to work as a forwards' coach at Wasps and scrum coach at Gloucester, which he still regards as his home club. He also coached at Cheltenham College, where he is an ambassador.

1214. WORSLEY, Joseph Paul Richard MBE
Flanker/No. 8 78 caps (50-10t) 1999-2011
Born: Redbridge, Essex, 14 June 1977
Career: Wasps, Barbarians, British & Irish Lions
Debut: v Tonga, Twickenham, 15 October 1999

Worsley was a destructive tackler and prolific ball-carrying back row who was part of the great Wasps teams of the 2000s and a member of England's Rugby World Cup-winning squad in 2003. Having joined Wasps as a 16-year-old, he won a Grand Slam with England under-18s and won his first cap in the 1999 World Cup. The flanker toured South Africa with the Lions in 2009, playing one test match. Former Wasps team-mate Raphael Ibanez recruited him as defence coach at Bordeaux-Begles in the French Top 14. He then coached at Clermont and Castres, with the Georgian national team and was a consultant at Ampthill.

1215. COHEN, Ben Christopher MBE
Wing 57 caps (155-31t) 2000-2006
Born: Northampton, Northamptonshire, 14 September 1978
Career: Northampton, Brive (Fra), Sale, Barbarians, British & Irish Lions
Debut: v Ireland, Twickenham, February 2000

A World Cup winner in 2003, Cohen was one of the best wingers in the world in his day, becoming a major pillar in Clive Woodward's all-conquering side. He won the European Cup with Northampton at club level, moved to Brive in France, and then returned to England with Sale. He retired in 2011, is involved in an anti-bullying group, the Ben Cohen StandUp Foundation, and has appeared in Strictly Come Dancing on BBC Television. He has been the face of High & Mighty, the fashion chain. His uncle George was a member of England's 1996 World Cup-winning side. His father, Peter, was murdered in 2000.

1216. TINDALL, Michael James MBE
Centre, 75 caps (74-14t,2c) 2000-2011
Born: Otley, Yorkshire, 18 October 1978
Career: Bath, Gloucester, Barbarians
Debut: v Ireland, Twickenham, February 2000

Tindall was a key member of the all-conquering side of 2003, missed the 2007 Rugby World Cup but was back for the 2011 campaign where he was fined £25,000 for his off-the-field conduct. He had an 11-year test career and spells at Bath, joining straight from Queen Elizabeth Grammar School, Wakefield, and Gloucester to his retirement in 2014 following a year as player/coach. He has coached and played and coached at Minchinhampton RFC. He married King Charles III's niece, Zara Phillips, whom he met at the 2003 World Cup in 2011. He co-hosts The Good, Bad and Rugby podcast and is a partner at FXD Capital.

1217. BALSHAW, Iain Robert MBE
Full-back/wing 35 caps (65-13t) 2000-2008
Born: Blackburn, Lancashire, 14 April 1979
Career: Bath, Leeds, Gloucester, Biarritz (Fra), Barbarians, British & Irish Lions
Debut: v Ireland, Twickenham, February 2000

Balshaw burst on the international scene in 2000 and was part of an England side that ran riot in the 2001 Six Nations before foot-and-mouth caused the postponement of the final match against Ireland. He played three tests for the British Lions in 2001 off the bench and came off the bench in the 2003 Rugby World Cup final. He moved from Bath, where he played 127 games, to Leeds, Gloucester, and Biarritz in France. He retired from the game after failing to recover from a knee injury. He is a partner at Alpha Group PLC, a foreign exchange firm in London.

1218. WHITE, Julian Martin MBE
Prop 51 caps 2000-2009
Born: Plymouth, Devon, 14 May 1973
Career: Plymouth Albion, Crusaders (NZ), Bridgend, Saracens, Bristol, Leicester, British & Irish Lions
Debut: v South Africa, Loftus Versfeld Stadium, Pretoria, June 2000

White was a powerful scrummager who played all four tests for the British & Irish Lions in 2005 and was a member of England's 2003 Rugby World Cup-winning squad. He had played in New Zealand before returning to the United Kingdom with Bristol and Leicester. A revered hard man who had several brushes with the disciplinary officer, he retired from international rugby before the 2007 World Cup when he made himself unavailable but was coaxed back by Martin Johnson for seven more caps, including England's trip to Argentina. He combined rugby with farming and his Crabtree Farm, where he raises cattle for the beef industry in Leicestershire and hosts holidaymakers.

1219. FLATMAN, David Luke
Prop 8 caps 2000-2002
Born: Maidstone, Kent, 21 January 1980
Career: Saracens, Bath
Debut: v South Africa, Loftus Versfeld, Pretoria, June 2000

Flatman won his first two caps off the bench when he was a Saracens player on the 2000 tour of South Africa and toured the United States and Canada in 2001. His final test came on the 2002 trip to Argentina when he was only 22, although he forced his way into the reckoning on England's 2010 visit to Australia. He played for England Schools with Jonny Wilkinson and made 161 appearances for Bath before he was forced to quit. He wrote several newspaper columns and became Bath's communications director. He now works as an ITV Sport and TNT Sport analyst, has a column in the Evening Standard, and hosts corporate events.

1220. LLOYD, Leon David
Wing/centre 5 caps (10-2t) 2000-2001
Born: Coventry, Warwickshire, 22 September 1977
Career: Leicester, Gloucester, Barbarians
Debut: v South Africa, Loftus Versfeld Stadium, Pretoria, June 2000

Lloyd scored two tries in Leicester's 2001 European Cup final win over Stade Francais from the wing. He won six Premiership titles, two Domestic Cups and another European Cup trophy after playing in a losing final four years earlier. He moved to Gloucester in 2007 but played just six games, scoring five tries before a knee injury hastened his retirement in 2008. Since then, he has worked as a foundation director at Oakham School in Leicestershire, advised the Cabinet Office on care for veterans and co-founded Bespoke Speaker Training. He co-founded Centrum Solutions and sits on the RFU disciplinary committee.

1221. ROBINSON, Jason Thorpe OBE
Full-back/wing/centre 51 caps (140-28t) 2001-2007
Born: Leeds, Yorkshire, 30 July 1974
Career: Bath, Sale, Fylde, Barbarians, British & Irish Lions
Debut: v Italy, Twickenham, February 2001

Robinson did the lot with Wigan at club level in rugby league between 1991 and 2000 and everything in rugby union with Sale and England. A try-scorer in the 2003 World Cup final, he dazzled on the Lions tour of Australia in 2001, won the Premiership with Sale in 2006, captained England and played in a second World Cup final in 2007. He coached Sale, but that lasted only one season. He has held a variety of ambassadorial roles with the likes of HSBC, Vodafone and O2 and is a director of JR Sports Stars. He is a non-executive director at Sale.

1222. BORTHWICK, Stephen William
Lock 57 caps (10-2t) 2001-2010
Born: Carlisle, Cumbria, 12 October 1979
Career: Preston Grasshoppers, Bath, Saracens
Debut: v France, Twickenham, April 2001

Borthwick made his England debut in 2001 but missed out on the World Cup in 2003 and played only the pool stages in 2007. He was made England captain by Martin Johnson, having captained Bath, but lost his place after being injured in 2010 and missing the summer tour to Australia. The lock skippered Saracens to the Premiership title in 2011 when they beat Leicester in the final at Twickenham. He worked with Eddie Jones, who signed him for Sarries in 2008, as a forwards coach with the Japan national side and with England before joining Leicester, leading them to the 2022 Premiership title. He was appointed head coach when the RFU sacked Eddie Jones in 2022 and led England to the bronze medal at the 2023 Rugby World Cup.

1223. KAY, Benedict James MBE
Lock 62 caps (10-2t) 2001-2009
Born: Liverpool, Lancashire, 14 December 1975
Career: Waterloo, Leicester, Barbarians, British & Irish Lions
Debut: v Canada, Fletcher's Field, Markham, June 2001

Kay, a Rugby World Cup winner in 2003 and double European champion with Leicester, was the only English player to play every minute of the 2007 World Cup, which led to an unlikely second appearance in the final. The son of Sir John Kay, a member of the Privy Council, he toured New Zealand with the British & Irish Lions in 2005. He retired from rugby in 2010 after winning six Premiership titles with the Tigers to take up a commentating job with ESPN. He works for TNT Sport, ITV and TalkSport as an analyst, has written a column for The Times and is a non-executive director of Leicester as well as being a partner at Pablo London, an advertising agency.

1224. MOODY, Lewis Milton MBE
Flanker 71 caps (45-9t) 2001-2011
Born: Ascot, Surrey, 12 June 1978
Career: Leicester, Bath, British & Irish Lions
Debut: v Canada, Fletcher's Field, Markham, June 2001

A World Cup winner in 2003, Moody also played in the 2007 and 2011 tournaments and was England's captain in the last in New Zealand. He won two European Cups, six Premierships with Leicester, and two Six Nations titles with England. In 2005, he became the first Englishman to be sent off in a test match at Twickenham when he was dismissed for fighting with his Leicester teammate Alex Tuilagi in a win over Samoa. He has trekked to the North Pole for charity, is an ambassador for several rugby sponsors, has been director of rugby at Bradford on Avon RFC, runs coaching courses and is a performance coach at KBM Inspired.

1225. NOON, Jamie Darren
Centre 38 caps (35-7t) 2001-2009
Born: Goole, East Riding of Yorkshire, 9 May 1979
Career: Newcastle, Brive (Fra), Barbarians
Debut: v Canada, Fletcher's Fields, Markham June 2001

Noon scored a hat-trick against Scotland at Twickenham in England's 43-22 win and was the first choice for the Six Nations a season later. The centre made the squad for the 2007 Rugby World Cup, but a knee injury wrecked his tournament after two games. But he did tour New Zealand the following year. His last test was against Italy in 2009, and he signed for Brive in France that year after a decade at Newcastle, where he won English Cups in 2001 and 2004 and played with Jonny Wilkinson and Toby Flood. He stayed in France after retiring, working as a rugby agent with World in Motion.

1226 STEPHENSON, Michael Edward
Wing 3 caps 2001
Born: Tynemouth, Tyne and Wear, 28 September 1980
Career: Newcastle, Bath, Leeds, Percy Park
Debut: v Canada, Fletcher's Field, Markham, June 2001

Stephenson reached two National Cup semi-finals at Durham School and won English Cups with Newcastle in 2001 and 2004 and three caps for England on the summer tour of North America in 2001. The wing had six seasons at Newcastle, scoring 32 tries in 84 Premiership appearances, before moving to Bath and then Leeds. He coached the backs at Wharfedale and was a player/coach at Percy Park. He now works in sports medicine as a sales consultant for DuPuy Synthes Trauma in the North East of England, and he is also chairman of the Durham committee of Wooden Spoon, the rugby charity.

1227. WALDER, David John Hume
Fly-half 4 caps (41-2t, 11c, 3p) 2001-2003
Born: Newcastle, Northumberland, 7 May 1978
Career: Newcastle, Wasps, Mitsubishi Dynaboars (Jap)
Debut: v Canada, Fletcher's Field, Markham, June 2001

One of the fledgling Falcons who starred for Newcastle in the early 2000s, Walder lived in the shadow of Jonny Wilkinson but won two English Cups and scored the winning try in the 2001 final against Harlequins. A move to Wasps in 2006 brought more trophies, and he finished his playing career in Japan with two years at Mitsubishi Dynaboars. He had worked with Rosslyn Park and Richmond Ladies, returning to Newcastle under Dean Richards to work with the kickers. He was appointed Newcastle's full-time attack coach, head coach, and then director of rugby up to 2023, moving to Bristol as an assistant coach.

1228. WHITE-COOPER, William Robert Steven
Flanker 2 caps 2001
Born: Cape Town, South Africa, 15 July 1974
Career: Harlequins, Barbarians
Debut: v Canada, Sports Complex, Burnaby Lake, June 2001

White-Cooper played in the back row at Harlequins for nine years, winning a European Challenge Cup, and was an English Cup finalist. He toured North America with England in 2001, where he won both his caps. The flanker, a business studies graduate, retired when he was 27, halfway through a two-year contract to start a new career in insurance with MIS in Cranleigh. He then entered the recruitment industry. He worked as a director at Execuzen before founding Apertus Consultancy, which works in the banking sector. He then founded add-victor, a corporate recruitment agency.

1229. WOOD, Martyn Benjamin
Scrum-half 2 caps (5-1t) 2001
Born: Harrogate, North Yorkshire, 25 April 1977
Career: Wasps, Bath
Debut: v Canada, Sports Complex, Burnaby Lake, June 2001

Wood won his caps off the bench on England's 2001 tour to North America and won two Premierships with Wasps before moving to Bath. The scrum-half flew to Australia during the 2003 Rugby World Cup as cover when Kyran Bracken, Matt Dawson and Andy Gomarsall were struggling with injury but never joined the squad as the casualties recovered and he had to return home. He was forced to retire with a neck injury sustained in a trampolining accident. He had a brief spell as director of rugby at Yorkshire Carnegie and then joined Harrogate. He has been involved in the property business.

1230. WATERS, Fraser Henry Hamilton
Centre 3 caps 2001-2004
Born: Cape Town, South Africa, 31 March 1976
Career: Bath, Bristol, Wasps, Treviso (Ita), Barbarians
Debut: v United States, Boxer Stadium, San Francisco, June 2001

Waters might only have won three England caps, but he was one of the most important figures in Wasps' dominance of England and Europe between 2003 and 2008, winning four Premiership titles and two European Cup crowns, in 2004 and 2007, and the 2003 Challenge Cup. He was man of the match in the 2007 European Cup final and toured North America with England in 2001 and Australia in 2004. Formerly at Bath and Bristol, he left Wasps to take up a contract with Treviso in Italy. He studied accountancy and economics at Bristol University and has worked at Talbot Underwriting as a broker relationship manager and accident and health underwriter.

1231. BARKLEY, Oliver John
Fly-half/centre 23 caps (82-2t,9c,18p) 2001-2008
Born: Hammersmith, London, 28 November 1981
Career: Bath, Gloucester, Racing Metro (Fra), Grenoble (Fra), Scarlets, London Welsh
Debut: v United States, Boxer Stadium, San Francisco, June 2001

Barkley was 19 when he made his England debut in 2001 but managed only 23 caps in the next seven years, although he did play in the 2007 Rugby World Cup. He had two stints at Bath, the second finished by a broken leg in 2011, and one at Gloucester before heading to France. The fly-half returned to the United Kingdom with Scarlets in Wales before joining London Welsh after they were promoted to the Premiership. He ran a rugby academy for youngsters and has written for men's style magazine Blokely. He is involved in property development, coached in Kowloon and founded Vapoura Rum in 2022.

1232. PALMER, Thomas Phillip
Lock 42 caps 2001-2012
Born: Harringay, London, 27 March 1979
Career: Leeds, Wasps, Stade Francais (Fra), Gloucester, Bordeaux-Begles, Benetton Treviso, Barbarians
Debut: v United States, Boxer Stadium, San Francisco, June 2001

Palmer had a five-year gap between his first and second caps but was a regular presence in the England side in sex seasons and played in the 2011 Rugby World Cup. The athletic lock has had a varied club career, starting at Leeds, including two stints at Wasps, where he won Premiership and European titles. Like Martin Johnson and Tom Wood, he played in New Zealand as a youngster. He attended Otago Boys' High School before returning to England and a place at Leeds University, where he studied physics. He was a player-coach at Bordeaux-Begles. He then joined Vannes as forwards' coach after a spell at Rouen.

1233. VOYCE, Thomas Michael Dunstan
Full-back/wing 9 caps (15-3t) 2001-2006
Born: Truro, Cornwall, 5 January 1981
Career: Bath, Wasps, Gloucester, London Welsh, Barbarians
Debut: v United States, Boxer Stadium, San Francisco, June 2001

A two-time European Cup winner and triple English Premiership champion with Wasps, Voyce toured North America in 2001 and Australia and New Zealand in 2004 but got his only decent run with England in 2006. That season, he played four games in the Six Nations and toured Australia again before his test career stalled. A move to Gloucester brought an Anglo-Welsh Cup in 2011. The great nephew of another Tom Voyce, an England and Gloucester legend of the 1920s, the wing finished with 66 tries in 220 Premiership appearances. On retirement, he joined foreign currency specialists Baydonhill FX, then worked for Investec.

1234. HODGSON, Charles Christopher
Fly-half/centre 38 caps (269-8t,44c,44p,3d) 2001-2012
Born: Halifax, West Yorkshire, 12 November 1980
Career: Sale, Saracens, British & Irish Lions
Debut: v Romania, Twickenham, November 2001

Hodgson opened his test account with a bang by scoring 44 points on his debut in the 134-0 win over Romania, but injury robbed him of the chance of places in the 2003 and 2007 Rugby World Cups. A Premiership winner with Sale in 2006, the fly-half moved to Saracens in 2011, continuing to rack up points, and retired with 2,469 to his name and another title. He attended Durham University and planned to coach Oxford University's backs, working as Saracens's head of recruitment when he joined London Irish as a kicking coach. He now works for the medical tech company Smith & Nephew.

1235. SANDERSON, Alexander
Flanker/No.8 5 caps (5-1t) 2001-2003
Born: Chester, Cheshire, 7 October 1979
Career: Sale, Saracens
Debut: v Romania, Twickenham, November 2001

Sanderson scored on his test debut, coming off the bench in the 134-0 win over Romania, toured Argentina in 2002 and won three more caps in 2003 when he was involved in the World Cup training squad. The back-rower was forced to retire with a back injury in 2005, aged 26. He worked briefly with the Saracens forwards after retirement before coaching stints with the Queensland Reds and England under-18s. He joined Eddie Jones' back-room team at Saracens, where he was an assistant, helping the club win five Premiership titles and three Champions Cups. He is now Sale's director of rugby, taking them to the Premiership final in 2023.

1236. THOMPSON, Stephen Geoffrey MBE
Hooker 73 caps (20-4t) 2002-2011
Born: Hemel Hempstead, Hertfordshire, 15 July 1978
Career: Northampton, Brive (Fra), Leeds, Wasps, British & Irish Lions
Debut: v Scotland, Murrayfield, Edinburgh, February 2002

Thompson was converted from flanker to hooker by his boss at Northampton, Ian McGeechan, and proceeded to win a World Cup in 2003 and tour with the Lions in 2005. Thompson looked set for a second World Cup in 2007 but retired with neck problems. He had signed for Brive in France and took a role as an advisor with the French club, got a second opinion on his neck, and – returned to playing after repaying a £500,000 insurance pay-out. He played at the 2011 World Cup before moving to Dubai, working with the UAE Rugby Federation before being diagnosed with early-onset dementia and he reported he could not remember winning the World Cup.

1237. DUNCOMBE, Nicholas Steven
Scrum-half 2 caps 2002-2003
Born: Taplow, Buckinghamshire, 21 January 1982
Died: Lanzarote, Canary Islands, 14 February 2003
Career: Harlequins
Debut: v Scotland, Murrayfield, Edinburgh, February 2002

Duncombe had a glittering career in front of him but tragically died less than a year after his test debut, aged just 21. He was tipped for the top, and a place at the 2007 Rugby World Cup and beyond was his for the taking, if not the 2003 edition. He won two caps as a replacement in the 2002 Championship and represented England at sevens in the 2002 Commonwealth Games. He was in Lanzarote on a holiday and training break with Harlequins teammate Nathan Williams when he was taken ill. He died of cardiac and respiratory failure due to blood poisoning. There is a statue of Duncombe at the Stoop, home of Harlequins, close to the North Stand.

1238. PAUL, Henry Rangi
Centre 6 caps (6-3c) 2002-2004
Born: Tokoroa, New Zealand, 10 February 1974
Career: Ponsonby (NZ), Bath, Gloucester, Leeds, Rotherham
Debut: v France, Stade de France, Paris, March 2002

Paul had his first taste of rugby union in England during a short stint with Bath in 1996 which punctuated a highly successful career in Rugby League that took in spells with the all-conquering Wigan side and Bradford Bulls. He won 23 league caps for New Zealand before signing union forms with Gloucester, but his union test career never really took off in the 15-man game. He has helped coach Russia and, was on the staff at the 2011 Rugby World Cup, and was director of rugby at Bradford & Bingley. He worked as a rugby programme manager at Queen Ethelburga's Collegiate in Yorkshire and coached with Canada 15s and 7s.

1239. APPLEFORD, Geoff
Centre 1 cap 2002
Born: Dundee, South Africa, 26 September 1977
Career: Natal (SA), Pumas (SA), London Irish, Northampton
Debut: v Argentina, Velez Sarsfield, Buenos Aires, June 2002

Appleford, who qualified for England through his grandparents, headed to England in 2000 from his native South Africa when he was recruited by the-then London Irish coach Dick Best. He played in Irish's 2002 English Cup final win over Northampton, scoring two tries, and toured Argentina with England later that summer winning his only cap in the 28-16 win over the Pumas. He signed for Northampton but suffered a horrific shoulder injury on England Sevens duty that year and was forced to retire in 2007 without ever playing a game for the Saints. He entered the computer industry and has worked for the RFU as a software developer.

1240. CHRISTOPHERS, Philip Derek
Wing 3 caps (5–1T) 2002-2003
Born: Heidelberg, Germany, 16 June 1980
Career: Leicester, Brive (Fra), Bristol, Leeds, Castres (Fra), Pays d'Aix (Fra)
Debut: v Argentina, Velez Sarsfield, Buenos Aires, June 2002

German-born Christophers was at the Leicester Academy before heading to Brive in France, then returning to the United Kingdom with Bristol. After two years at Leeds, he signed for Castres and returned to the England squad's fringes ahead of the 2007 Rugby World Cup. After ankle and knee injuries, he was released by Castres but played two seasons with Pays d'Aix in the French ProD2. He studied for an MBA in Toulouse and worked as an export manager for Euromair and Mixer SRL, a firm that supplies paint-spraying equipment in the Marseille area, and now works for the Wagner Group in Voiron, France.

1241. CODLING, Alexander John
Lock 1 cap 2002
Born: Lewisham, London 25 September 1973
Career: Wasps, Blackheath, Richmond, Bedford, Neath, Harlequins, Saracens, Northampton, Montpellier (Fra), London Welsh, Cardiff, Barbarians
Debut: v Argentina, Velez Sarsfield, Buenos Aires, June 2002

Codling has had a varied coaching career since retiring from playing in 2004 with back trouble, winning one cap, against Argentina. He pursued a career in teaching as head of sport at Trinity School in Surrey and had coaching posts at Ebbw Vale, saving them from relegation, before joining London Welsh as forwards' coach. He moved to Barking, leading them to the top of National One, then London Scottish and Rotherham Titans. He took Rosslyn Park to the brink of promotion to the Championship before becoming Ulster forwards' coach. He then helped Eddie Jones' England and Oyonnax before being named head coach of Newcastle in 2023.

1242. HORAK, Michael John
Full-back 1 cap 2002
Born: Johannesburg, South Africa, 3 June 1977
Career: Free State (SA), Bristol, Leicester, London Irish, Treviso (Ita), Saracens
Debut: v Argentina, Velez Sarsfield, Buenos Aires, June 2002

South African-born Horak, English-qualified through his mother, won his only cap in Argentina while at London Irish, having served stints at Leicester and Bristol after moving to England. He played rugby league back home before being spotted by Bob Dwyer and signing for the Tigers in 1997. His best spell in England came at Irish, where he won the English Cup in 2002. He retired in 2010 and returned to South Africa, where he worked as a defensive coach with the Free State Cheetahs and at their academy. A season at Eastern Province Kings ended when he signed as defence coach of the Sharks.

1243. JOHNSTON, John Benedict
Centre 2 caps 2002
Born: Clatterbridge, Merseyside, 8 November 1978
Career: Waterloo, Saracens, Brive (Fra)
Debut: v Argentina, Velez Sarsfield, Buenos Aires, June 2002

Johnston toured South Africa with England in 2000 and made his test debut in Argentina in 2002. Despite featuring for the Saxons in the Churchill Cup, he won just one more cap when he came on as a replacement for Will Greenwood in the 31-28 win over the All Blacks at Twickenham in 2002. He

The English Rugby Who's Who

Nigel Heslop

Barrie-Jon Mather

Jason Robinson

Henry Paul

joined Brive in France in 2007, then signed as a player-coach with Nottingham in English rugby's second tier in 2009. He coached the backs at Nottingham, who narrowly missed the Championship play-offs in 2015, under head coach Martin Haag. In September 2016, he took over as head of rugby at St George's College, Weybridge.

1244. SIMPSON-DANIEL, James David
Wing/centre 10 caps (15-3t) 2002-2007
Born: Stockton-on-Tees, County Durham, 30 May 1982
Career: Gloucester
Debut: v New Zealand, Twickenham, November 2002

Simpson-Daniel's 10 caps were spread over five years after he shone against a Barbarians side containing Jonah Lomu. He played 272 times for Gloucester, scoring 118 tries. The 2008 Premiership Player of the Season retired in September 2014 with an ankle problem at 32 but had already started Kings Biltong with his brothers Charlie and Mark. A horse racing fan, he worked in PR with bookmakers Fitzdares and part-owned Monbeg Dude with former Gloucester team-mates Mike Tindall and Nicky Robinson. The horse finished third in the 2015 Grand National at Aintree, and he now works in foreign exchange and has various business interests in the food and drinks industry.

1245. MORRIS, Robert Jonathan S
Prop 2 caps 2003
Born: Hertford, Hertfordshire, 20 February 1982
Career: Northampton, Newcastle, Connacht (Ire)
Debut: v Wales, Millennium Stadium, Cardiff, February 2003

Morris was on Northampton's books when he played two games in the 2003 Six Nations but could not nail down a regular spot. The prop, who won a Commonwealth Youth Games silver medal in the discus, could have had a full-time career in athletics but chose rugby when Saints came calling and signed him from Hertford when he was 18. He later made 35 appearances for Newcastle Falcons before signing for Connacht in Ireland. The powerful scrummager was forced to retire in 2010, aged 28, after several back injuries. He has coached with Galwegians Under-21s and the Connacht A team and is a personal trainer in Hertfordshire.

1246. SMITH, Oliver James
Centre 5 caps 2003-2005
Born: Leicester, Leicestershire, 14 August 1982
Career: Leicester, Montpellier (Fra), Harlequins, Barbarians, British & Irish Lions
Debut: v Italy, Twickenham, March 2003

Smith, who could play centre or wing, narrowly missed out on a spot in the 2003 Rugby World Cup squad after making his debut earlier that year and featuring in warm-up games against Wales and France. The Leicester player was, however, picked for the 2005 British and Irish Lions and played in the warm-up test against Argentina in Cardiff and four midweek games on the trip. He was tempted by rugby league and trained with NRL giants Brisbane Broncos. He was forced to retire in December 2010 and coached at Esher, London Welsh and Bury St Edmunds.

1247. WORSLEY, Michael Anthony
Prop 3 caps 2003-2005
Born: Warrington, Cheshire, 1 December 1976
Career: West Park, Orrell, Bristol, London Irish, Harlequins
Debut: v Italy, Twickenham, March 2003

Worsley timed his run for the 2003 Rugby World Cup slightly wrong, and his appearance off the bench against Italy that year was not enough to put him in the mix for the squad. The prop won his caps while with London Irish and then after moving to Harlequins. He studied law at Bristol University, but when he was forced to retire, he went into banking, working for the private bank Insinger de Beaufort and then Credit Suisse. He teaches economics and business studies at Cranleigh School having doen a similar job at at Marlborough College and is involved in holiday cottage lettings in the Cotswolds.

1248. ABBOTT, Stuart Richard MBE
Centre 9 caps (10-2t) 2003-2006
Born: Cape Town, South Africa, 3 June 1978
Career: Griffons (SA), Western Province (SA), Leicester, Stormers (SA), Wasps, Harlequins
Debut: v Wales, Millennium Stadium, Cardiff, August 2003

A product of Stellenbosch University, Abbott played for South Africa Under-23 before heading to England in 1999 to play for Leicester and then Wasps. His mother is English, and he rejected the chance to play for South Africa. He was picked by Clive Woodward for England and forced his way into the 2003 World Cup-winning squad. A Premiership and European champion at Wasps, he moved to Harlequins but played only 17 times before retiring, aged 29, because of a shoulder injury. He is the managing director of a fuel business in Cape Town and works part-time with VUSA Rugby and Learning Academy.

1249. SCARBROUGH, Daniel Graham
Full-back/wing 2 caps (5-1t) 2003-2007
Born: Bingley, West Yorkshire, 16 February 1978
Career: Wakefield, Leeds, Saracens, Racing Metro (Fra), Lille (Fra)
Debut: v Wales, Millennium Stadium, Cardiff, August 2003

Scarbrough won both his caps in the Rugby World Cup years against Wales in 2003 and South Africa in 2007 without ever appearing in the tournament. Comfortable at wing or full-back, he moved to Saracens from Leeds, but injuries plagued him, and he went to France with a spell at Racing Metro from 2008 to 2011. He finished rugby with a year at Lille, where he also did some coaching and helped with player development. He is the rugby coach at Bradford Grammar School but was diagnosed with early-onset dementia in 2020. He has joined the legal case against governing bodies.

1250. JONES, Christopher Michael
Lock/flanker 12 caps (5-1t) 2004-2007
Born: Manchester, Lancashire, 24 June 1980
Career: Sale, Worcester, Yorkshire Carnegie, Barbarians
Debut: v Italy, Stadio Flaminio, Rome, February 2004

Jones, a good line-out forward, won 12 caps between 2004 and England's tour of South Africa ahead of the 2007 Rugby World Cup. He studied business at Sheffield Hallam University, where Sale spotted him, and won the Premiership in 2006 and touring Australia with England the same year. A double Player of The Year at Sale, he later joined Worcester, who were relegated in his final season at the club. He joined Yorkshire Carnegie but retired two years later, in 2016, after concussion struggles. He is a financial advisor for St James Place Wealth Management in Knutsford, Cheshire.

1251. STEVENS, Matthew John Hamilton
Prop 44 caps 2004-2012
Born: Durban, South Africa, 1 October 1982
Career: Bath, Saracens, Sharks (SA), Barbarians, British & Irish Lions
Debut: v New Zealand, Carisbrook, Dunedin, June 2004

Stevens bounced back from a two-year drug ban to claim a place in the squad for the 2011 Rugby World Cup and a spot on the 2013 Lions tour to Australia. Stevens was at Bath, having played in the 2007 World Cup when he was admitted to taking cocaine and was banished from the sport. He opened a coffee shop, Jika Jika, in Bath with team-mate Lee Mears before winning the 2011 Premiership with Saracens and playing in the 2012 Six Nations. He reached the final of ITV's *The X Factor: Battle of the Stars*. He lives in Cape Town, working in hospitality at Boschendal Wine Farm and is now in property development.

1252. LIPMAN, Michael Ross
Flanker 10 caps 2004-2008
Born: London, 17 February 1980
Career: New South Wales Waratahs (Aus), Bristol, Bath, Melbourne Rebels (Aus)
Debut: v New Zealand, Eden Park, Auckland, June 2004

London-born to an English father and an Australian mother, Lipman was raised in Sydney, where he started his career, before arriving in England to play for Bristol. The start of the flanker's international career was hampered by injury, and he wasn't a regular in the England side until 2008. A year later, while at Bath, he was banned for nine months after refusing to take a drug test linked to an end-of-season party. A series of concussions forced him to retire in June 2012, and he works as a real estate salesman for Doyle Spillane in Sydney and has business interests in Singapore. He is also battling early-onset dementia.

1253. TITTERRELL, Andrew James
Hooker 5 caps 2004-2007
Born: Dartford, Kent, 10 January 1981
Career: Saracens, Waterloo, Sale, Gloucester, Leeds, Edinburgh, London Welsh, British & Irish Lions
Debut: v New Zealand, Eden Park, Auckland, June 2004

Titterrell, a much-travelled hooker, won the Premiership with Sale in 2006 and was a 2003 Churchill Cup winner. He was a shock selection for the 2005 British & Irish Lions tour to New Zealand, although he did not play a test. A varied career ended in 2014 when he was forced to retire from the game, aged 33, having signed for London Welsh but did not play a game. He has strength and conditioning qualifications and has worked with the Spanish and Canadian rugby sides, as well as Leeds. He joined the staff at Wasps as a part-time conditioner, then forwards coach, before heading to the England Under-20s as a pathway coach and then forwards' coach.

1254. PAYNE, Timothy Adam North
Prop 22 caps 2004-2010
Born: Swindon, Wiltshire, 29 April 1979
Career: Coventry, Bristol, Cardiff, Wasps, British & Irish Lions
Debut: v Australia, Lang Park, Brisbane, June 2004

Payne spent a decade at Wasps from 2003, winning three Premierships and two European Cups, and featured on five England tours between 2004 and 2010 and was called up as an injury replacement for the British & Irish Lions in South Africa in 2009. He retired from playing in 2013 with neck problems and coached at the London Irish academy and with former England team-mate Nick Easter at Wimbledon. He joined London Scottish in 2015 and that year was named forwards' coach of the side, working alongside another former England international, Peter Richards. He works as a player management & marketing consultant at Aurum Professional Management Group.

1255. CUETO, Mark John MBE
Wing 55 caps (100-2t) 2004-2011
Born: Workington, Cumbria, 26 December 1979
Career: Sale, British & Irish Lions
Debut: v Canada, Twickenham, November 2004

Cueto is best known for scoring the try that never was in the 2007 Rugby World Cup final against South Africa when the video referee chalked off his effort. He toured New Zealand with the 2005 British & Irish Lions and won the Premiership with Sale in 2006, playing nearly 300 games for the club, and was involved in a second World Cup in 2011. Fast, strong and a deadly finisher, he finished his domestic career in 2015 as the Premiership's leading try scorer with 90 touchdowns. The wing worked in Sharks' commercial department, and on radio and television. He is now sales director at 4thUtility, in Hale in Cheshire, a high-speed broadband supplier.

1256. HAZELL, Andrew Robert
Flanker 7 caps (5-1t) 2004-2007
Born: Gloucester, Gloucestershire, 25 April 1978
Career: Gloucester
Debut: v Canada, Twickenham, November 2004

Hazell played 266 times for Gloucester in nearly 17 years at the club before being forced to retire after failing to recover from a concussion in 2014. He was on the fringes of England's 2003 Rugby World squad. He toured Australia and New Zealand that summer without making the tournament but was capped a year later. The flanker played four times in the 2005 Six Nations and won the European Challenge Cup in 2006, scoring a try in the final against London Irish. He runs his own companies, Inside Out Technology and Smart Home Sounds, which install automated technology and sound systems in homes.

1257. SHERIDAN, Andrew John
Prop 40 caps 2004-2011
Born: Bromley, Kent, 1 November 1979
Career: Richmond, Bristol, Sale, Toulon (Fra), British & Irish Lions
Debut: v Canada, Twickenham, November 2004

Sheridan, a converted back row forward and lock strong enough to be a powerlifter, was the scourge of Australia when he destroyed their scrum in 2005 and in the 2007 Rugby World Cup quarter-final in Marseille. Bristol's New Zealander boss Peter Thorburn turned him into a prop and toured twice with the British & Irish Lions. He helped Sale to the Premiership in 2006 and won a European Cup at Toulon in 2013 before being forced to retire with a neck injury. He passed wine-tasting exams in France and is now in the trade, living in Carqueiranne. He is the managing director of Varvarians, a travel firm.

1258. VYVYAN, Hugh Donnithorne
No.8 1 cap (5-1t) 2004
Born: Guildford, Surrey, 8 September 1976
Career: Villagers (SA), Newcastle, Saracens, Barbarians
Debut: v Canada, Twickenham, November 2004

Vyvyan won his only cap in the back row as a replacement for Steve Borthwick, scoring a try in the 70-0 win over Canada in 2004. He had played in South Africa during his gap year, won English Cups with Newcastle in 2001 and 2004 and toured Argentina with England in 2002. He captained England on two Churchill Cup tours and joined Saracens, helping them win the Premiership in 2011. He made his 238 Premiership appearances, then a record. He retired, worked at Saracens as commercial director, then for Pitch International on rugby and cricket broadcasting deals, and is now at Gallagher as business development director in London.

1259. ELLIS, Harry Alistair
Scrum-half 27 caps (25-5t) 2004-2009
Born: Wigston, Leicestershire, 17 May 1982
Career: Leicester, British & Irish Lions
Debut: v South Africa, Twickenham, November 2004

A sports science graduate from Loughborough University, Ellis was a Leicester scrum-half who toured with the 2009 British & Irish Lions to South Africa that year. He missed the European Cup final and 2007 Rugby World Cup with a ruptured ACL and admitted later that he could not even watch England play in the final. He announced his retirement in 2010, aged 28, when his knee went again and made just

24 of his 173 appearances for Leicester in his last three years at the club. Educated at Leicester Grammar School, he returned there as a PE teacher when he was forced out of rugby and worked with The RPA.

1260. TAIT, Mathew James Murray
Full-back/wing/centre 8 caps (25-5t) 2005-2010
Born: Shotley Bridge, County Durham, 6 February 1986
Career: Newcastle, Sale, Leicester
Debut: v Wales, Millennium Stadium, Cardiff, February 2005

Tait made his debut as an 18-year-old in Cardiff when he was dumped on his backside by Gavin Henson and harshly dropped by England coach Andy Robinson immediately afterwards. He recovered by winning a silver medal in the 2006 Commonwealth Games sevens and regaining his place in the full set-up. He played in the 2007 Rugby World Cup final against South Africa. Stuart Lancaster picked him for a Saxons squad, but he did not make the 2015 World Cup training squad. He studied biomechanics at Newcastle University, retired in 2018, and is now based in the Middle East, working as general manager of the Dubai Sevens.

1261. FORRESTER, James
No.8 2 caps 2005
Born: Oxford, Oxfordshire, 9 February 1981
Career: Gloucester
Debut: v Wales, Millennium Stadium, Cardiff, February 2005

Forrester was a hyper-talented back rower with Gloucester and made his full international debut off the bench against Wales after winning England Under-21, Saxons and Sevens honours, but elbow and shoulder injuries disrupted his progress. He scored an extra-time try to clinch the European Challenge Cup for Gloucester in the final against London Irish, but a knee injury forced his retirement in October 2008, aged 27. After retirement, he worked in Singapore as an investment broker, coached locally and coached the Singapore National team. He now part-owns UFIT Urban Fitness, based in a gym in Singapore, and is involved with the Gloucester-Hartpury women's team on the commercial side.

1262. BELL, Duncan Stuart Crampton
Prop 5 caps 2005-2009
Born: King's Lynn, Norfolk, 1 October 1974
Career: Ebbw Vale, Sale, Pontypridd, Bath, Newport Gwent Dragons, Barbarians
Debut: v Italy, Twickenham, March 2005

Bell started his professional career in Wales and went on England's summer tour in 1998 without playing a test before trying to play for Wales. The IRB blocked that move, and he made his England debut in 2002, a year before he moved to Bath, where he won the Challenge Cup in 2008. Three more caps followed in 2009 before the prop retired in 2012, announcing he had been a victim of depression throughout his career. He came out of retirement in 2014 to play for the Dragons and then Lydney, where he also worked as a coach. He works as a mortgage and protection consultant with Chartwell Funding Ltd.

1263. GOODE, Andrew James
Fly-half 17 caps (107-1t,15c,20p,4d) 2005-2009
Born: Coventry, Warwickshire, 3 April 1980
Career: Leicester, Saracens, Brive (Fra), Sharks (SA), Worcester, Wasps, Newcastle
Debut: v Italy, Twickenham, March 2005

Goode was part of two winning European Cup campaigns with Leicester in 2001 and 2002 and helped the Tigers to four Premierships. he had a spell in Super Rugby with the Sharks in South Africa and broke the Premiership record by scoring 33 points against London Irish in Wasps' first game since their permanent move to the Ricoh Arena in December 2014. He answered an SOS call from Newcastle in December 2015, coming out of retirement to help them avoid relegation. He has a regular podcast, The Rugby Pod, with Jim Hamilton, is a matchday host at Leicester and works for Global Reach PLC in foreign exchange.

1264. VAN GISBERGEN, Mark Cornelius
Full-back 1 cap 2005
Born: Hamilton, New Zealand, 30 June 1977
Career: Waikato (NZ), Wasps, Lyon (Fra)
Debut: v Australia, Twickenham, November 2005

The son of a New Zealand mother and a Dutch father, Van Gisbergen's career was going nowhere when he was working as an electrician for an alarm company in Hamilton and failing to get a contract from Waikato. But Warren Gatland took him to Wasps in 2002, and he stayed for eight years, winning two European Cups and four Premierships. The full-back got on the pitch for England just once in a test match, coming off the bench in a 26-16 win over Australia at Twickenham in 2005. Van Gisbergen is back in New Zealand, living in Mount Maunganui, in the Bay of Plenty, running his distribution business and surfing.

1265. DEACON, Louis Paul
Lock 29 caps 2005-2011
Born: Leicester, Leicestershire, 7 October 1980
Career: Leicester
Debut: v Samoa, Twickenham, November 2005

Deacon signed for Leicester as a professional in the glory days of the club in 2000 but went on to play 274 times for the club and be in three winning Premiership final squads. He made his England debut in 2005, played in the 2011 Rugby World Cup in New Zealand and was Leicester's Players' Player of the Year twice. He was hampered by back trouble, and in February 2015, he officially announced his retirement from the game. He worked in Leicester's community and sponsorship departments and coached Spain part-time in the 2015 European Nations Cup. He then worked with Coventry before becoming England Women's forwards' coach in 2021.

1266. FRESHWATER, Perry Thomas
Prop 10 caps 2005-2007
Born: Wellington, New Zealand, 27 July 1973
Career: Wellington (NZ), Leicester, Coventry, Rugby, Perpignan (Fra), Barbarians
Debut: v Samoa, Twickenham, November 2005

Freshwater played for New Zealand Under-21s before pitching up at Leicester in 1995 and being involved in two European Cup-winning campaigns. He left the Tigers in 2003 and won all his caps, including two at the 2007 Rugby World Cup while playing for the French club Perpignan. He won the Top 14 title with Perpignan in 2009, their first win for over 50 years and eventually retired just before turning 39. He gained cult status in France and was employed as Perpignan team manager after he finished playing, helping English-speaking players settle in the area and is now coaching at the club.

1267. MEARS, Lee Andrew
Hooker 42 caps (5-1t)
Born: Torquay, Devon, 5 March 1979
Career: Bath, British & Irish Lions
Debut: v Samoa, Twickenham, November 2005

Hooker Mears is yet another graduate from England's unbeaten Schools tour to Australia in 1997. The Bath man, schooled at the noted rugby nursery Colston's, played 268 times for his club before retiring in 2013 on medical advice after a routine heart screen. He toured with the British & Irish Lions to South Africa in 2009 and was a member of the 2007 and 2011 England Rugby World Cup squads. He opened the coffee shop Jika Jika with Bath club-mate Matt Stevens and had a part-time role coaching England's hookers. He also works for executive coaching company The Preston Associates and is co-founder of T-Cup, a well-being business.

1268. VARNDELL, Thomas William
Wing 4 caps (15-3t)
Born: Ashford, Kent, 16 September 1985
Career: Bedford, Leicester, Wasps, Bristol, Scarlets, Yorkshire Carnegie
Debut: v Samoa, Twickenham, November 2005

Varndell burst on the scene at Leicester, recording the quickest hat-trick in Premiership history in 13 minutes against Worcester. and toured Australia and New Zealand with England in 2006 and 2008 and came off the bench when Leicester won the 2009 Premiership final before moving to Wasps where he continued to rack up the tries. With 92 tries, he is the second-highest try scorer in Premiership history after Chris Ashton. He also played for England Saxons and England Sevens and co-owned a health and fitness company, Fitness Burners. An RFU agent, he is a director of Elite Athlete Management and does matchday commentary for BBC Radio Leicester.

1269. BROWN, Alexander Thomas
Lock 3 caps 2006-2007
Born: Bristol, 17 May 1979
Career: Bath, Pontypool, Bristol, Gloucester
Debut: v Australia, Olympic Stadium, Sydney, June 2006

Brown played 227 times in the Premiership for Bristol and Gloucester from 2003 before being forced to retire with a shoulder injury in 2012. He made his test debut in 2006 in Australia, having been due to start in the 2005 autumn internationals before a neck injury, and played two tests on the 2007 summer tour to South Africa ahead of that year's World Cup. He won the European Challenge Cup with Gloucester in 2006 and was part of the side that finished top of the Premiership in 2007 and 2008 without winning the play-offs. He is still on the staff at Kingsholm, where he works as chief executive officer.

1270. LUND, Magnus Burnett
Flanker 10 caps (5-1t) 2006-2007
Born: Manchester, Lancashire, 25 June 1983
Career: Sale, Biarritz (Fra)
Debut: v Australia, Stadium Australia, Sydney, June 2006

Lund, the son of a Norwegian basketball player, was a Premiership winner with Sale in 2006. The flanker was called up by Andy Robinson for the summer tour of Australia and played both tests but failed to make the 2007 Rugby World Cup squad after touring South Africa. He moved to Biarritz in 2008, where he played with his brother Erik, before heading back to Sale in 2014. Lund, a Commonwealth Games silver medallist in Sevens in 2006, played in the 2010 European Cup final with Biarritz, but the club were relegated in 2014. He has a personal training business in Biarritz.

1271. RICHARDS, Peter Charles
Scrum-half 13 caps 2006-2008
Born: Portsmouth, Hampshire, 10 March 1978
Career: Treviso (Ita), Bristol, Gloucester, Harlequins, London Irish, Wasps
Debut: v Australia, Olympic Stadium, Sydney, June 2006

Richards was taken on England's 1998 'Tour of Hell' without playing a test and had to wait until 2006 for his full international debut. The scrum-half, a European Cup winner at Wasps, came off the bench six times in the 2007 Rugby World Cup, including the final against South Africa. He was forced to retire with back trouble in 2010 and coached the Israeli national squad, Esher and was London Irish skills coach, then heading up the academy. He was appointed London Scottish director of rugby and then worked at St George's in Weybridge. He spent a year selling Covid tests before joining Return2Play, part of the Meliora Medical Group.

1272. CHUTER, George Scala
Hooker 24 caps (5-1t) 2006-2010
Born: Greenwich, London, 9 July 1976
Career: Saracens, Leicester
Debut: v Australia, Stadium Australia, Sydney, June 2006

After four years at Saracens, Chuter had had enough of rugby and left the club to go travelling in the United States and Australia. He returned after the Sydney Olympics, signed for Leicester, and went on to hook for the Tigers 292 times, play in the 2007 Rugby World Cup final as a replacement, and win six Premiership titles. The front rower retired from the game in 2014, coached at Loughborough University and Hinckley RFC and acted as a match-day host at Welford Road. He went full-time at an events company, Under the Posts, and is an occasional analyst on TalkSport and BBC Radio Leicester.

1273. WALSHE, Nicholas Patrick James
Scrum-half 2 caps 2006
Born: Chiswick, London, 1 November 1974
Career: Rosslyn Park, Harlequins, Bath, Saracens, Sale, Bedford, Barbarians
Debut: v Australia, Stadium Australia, Sydney, June 2006

Walshe won two caps on England's 2006 tour to Australia but became better known as a coach of the England teams that won the U20 World Junior Championships in 2013 and 2014. He cut his coaching teeth at Old Sulians in Bath and Bedford, where he was a player-coach before he joined the RFU Elite Rugby Department as assistant to Rob Hunter. He became head coach of the Under-20s and led the side to the world title in France before joining coaching at Gloucester, Coventry, and then Cokethorpe School as director of sport. He runs PWW Ltd, a company that rents properties in the Cotswolds and London.

1274. ALLEN, Anthony Owen
Centre 2 caps 2006
Born: Southampton, Hampshire, 1 September 1986
Career: Gloucester, Leicester
Debut: v New Zealand, Twickenham, November 2006

Allen was thrown in at the deep end by then-coach Andy Robinson when he made his test debut against the All Blacks in 2006, aged just 20. He won only one more cap against Argentina a week later and retired in 2015 with a knee injury, having previously recovered from a leg injury which could have cost him the limb through gangrene. He had a mobile coffee business in High Wycombe, the 'Flying Bean'. Later he coached England Under-20s and at the Leicester Academy before moving to Coventry. He now coaches at Loughborough and is a rugby consultant at Quantum Sports.

1275. PERRY, Shaun Andrew
Scrum-half 14 caps (10-2t)
Born: Wolverhampton, Staffordshire, 4 May 1978
Career: Coventry, Bristol, Brive (Fra), Worcester
Debut: v New Zealand, Twickenham, November 2006

Former electrician Perry's time in the England side coincided and ended with their unlikely run to the 2007 Rugby World Cup final in Paris, although he did not play after the group match against South Africa. That was the scrum-half's last international as he missed the 2008 Six Nations with a fractured windpipe before heading to France with Brive. A knee injury contributed to his retirement in 2013. He coached at Shrewsbury School and runs his own company, which offers one-on-one sessions for players of all abilities. He moved to Old Swinford Hospital School in Stourbridge in 2018 and helped out scrum-halves at Wasps.

1276. SACKEY, Paul Henry
Wing 22 caps (55-11t) 2006-2009
Born: Westminster, London, 8 November 1979
Career: Bedford, London Irish, Wasps, Toulon (Fra), Stade Francais (Fra), Barbarians
Debut: v New Zealand, Twickenham, November 2006

A try every other game, including four in the 2007 Rugby World Cup, suggests Sackey should have earned more than 22 caps, but his career was hampered by injury when he was at the top of his game. He played for England Sevens and won a European Cup with Wasps in 2007, but after failing to break back into the senior team, he joined Toulon in 2010, then went to Stade Francais before returning to the Premiership with Harlequins in 2013 just when he was thinking of retirement. He was involved in a business sourcing luxury cars, was a Wasps ambassador and founded a company, NetZero, to help businesses reduce their carbon footprint.

1277. FLOOD, Tobias Gerald Albert Lieven
Fly-half/centre 60 caps (301-4t,40c,66p,1d) 2006-2013
Born: Frimley, Surrey, 8 August 1985
Career: Newcastle, Leicester, Toulouse (Fra), Cambridge University
Debut: v Argentina, Twickenham, November 2006

Flood, who hails from a family of actors, competed in two Rugby World Cups, coming on as a replacement in the 2007 final. The fly-half had understudied Jonny Wilkinson at Newcastle before helping Leicester to win the 2010 Premiership final and was captain for the 2013 Final victory when the Tigers beat Northampton. He left Leicester for French Top 14 side Toulouse, ending his England career, but returned to Newcastle, retiring to become kicking coach briefly. He studied for an MBA in business at Cambridge, playing in the Varsity Match, before taking a post as a Commercial Account Executive at Conga, a software development firm.

1278. FARRELL, Andrew David OBE
Fly-half/centre 8 caps (5-1t) 2007
Born: Wigan, Lancashire, 30 May 1975
Career: Saracens
Debut: v Scotland, Twickenham, February 2007

Farrell was a giant of rugby league with Wigan, winning four Challenge Cups and five league titles, scoring over 3,000 points and playing 34 times for Great Britain. He crossed codes when he was nearly 30 but was hampered by injuries, but went to the 2007 Rugby World Cup. He was the Saracens first-team coach when they landed the Premiership in 2011 before joining England full-time and was on two Lions tours as a coach but left after the 2015 World Cup. An assistant to Ireland boss Joe Schmidt before taking the top job landing a Six Nations Grand Slam in 2023, clinching it by beating son Owen's England.

1279. MORGAN, Oliver Charles
Full-back 2 caps 2007
Born: Hammersmith, London, 3 November 1985
Career: Gloucester
Debut: v Scotland, Twickenham, February 2007

Morgan was a fearless full-back but had to retire prematurely in 2013 when he was 27 after a serious knee injury. He played under-16, 18 and 21s for England, won two full caps in the 2007 Six Nations, and he helped Gloucester win the Anglo-Welsh Cup in 2011. He has since turned his hand to coaching, helping Gloucester win the JP Morgan Asset Management Sevens in 2013 and 2014. He became Director of Rugby at Cheltenham College in 2015 and assistant director of sport there in 2021. He studied for a degree in management and leadership at Northumbria University.

1280. REES, Thomas
Flanker 15 caps (5-1t) 2007-2008
Born: London, 11 September 1984
Career: Wasps
Debut: v Scotland, Twickenham, February 2007

Flanker Rees won Premiership, European and Anglo-Welsh Cup titles before the age of 24 and was taken to the 2007 Rugby World Cup. In 2008 he was part of a back row that stood toe-to-toe with the All Blacks in two tests before a crippling run of shoulder and knee injuries took their toll. From a medical background, he then applied to study medicine at Imperial College in London and started his course in October 2012, qualifying in 2018, aiming to become a GP. He was an ambassador at Wasps, helped out the RPA addressing young players on how to prepare for life after rugby and served on RFU disciplinary hearings.

1281. EASTER, Nicholas James
No.8 54 caps (45-9t) 2007-2015
Born: Epsom, Surrey, 15 August 1978
Career: Villagers (SA), Rosslyn Park, Orrell, Harlequins
Debut: v Italy, Twickenham, February 2007

Easter was late to international rugby, but a move to Harlequins, whom he played 281 times, saw his career take off. He had worked as a teacher in South Africa, where his great grandfather, Pieter Le Roux, won Springbok honours. He was a trainee analyst for Sarasin & Partners before getting a professional contract, but after scoring four tries against Wales in 2007, he was an England regular through to the 2011 Rugby World Cup. He coached at Wimbledon, Newcastle and Worcester. The four-time Quins Player of the Year won a Premiership, European Challenge Cup and the English Cup and is the director of rugby at Chinnor RFC and a consultant with CDS Sports.

1282. STRETTLE, David
Wing 14 caps (10-2t) 2007-2013
Born: Warrington, Cheshire, 23 July 1983
Career: Rotherham, Harlequins, Saracens, Clermont (Fra)
Debut: v Ireland, Croke Park, Dublin, February 2007

Strettle made his test debut at Croke Park, scoring England's only try in a dismal 43-13 defeat to Ireland. The wing, a talented footballer as a youngster, played for England Sevens. He toured South Africa in 2007 and New Zealand in 2008 but missed the 2007 Rugby World Cup with an injury. He joined Saracens in 2010, winning the Premiership in 2011 and 2015 and earning a spot in England's World Cup training squad. He was a 2017 Champions Cup finalist with Clermont in their defeat to Saracens and then returned to Saracens, winning the 2019 Premiership and Champions Cup before retiring. A sports science graduate, he is the managing director of PIC Homes.

1283. GERAGHTY, Shane Joseph James
Fly-half/centre 6 caps (5-1c,1p) 2007-2009
Born: Coventry, Warwickshire, 12 August 1986
Career: London Irish, Brive (Fra), Northampton, Bristol, Stade Francais (Fra)
Debut: v France, Twickenham, March 2007

Geraghty lit up Twickenham after coming off the bench against France in 2007 when he was at London Irish, where he broke into the first-team as an 18-year-old while still in the academy. He toured Australia and New Zealand with England in 2010, playing for the midweek team and also won England under-21 and sevens honours. He moved to Northampton before heading to Brive. He returned to Irish, then went to Bristol, where he was educated at Colston's School, before joining Stade Francais, where he won the 2018 Challenge Cup. Geraghty has been involved in several property companies.

1284. HASKELL, James Andrew Welbon
Flanker/No.8 77 caps (20-4t) 2007-2018
Born: Windsor, Berkshire, 2 April 1985
Career: Wasps, Highlanders (NZ), Ricoh Black Rams (Jap), Stade Français (Fra), Northampton, British & Irish Lions
Debut: v Wales, Millennium Stadium, Cardiff March 2007

Haskell missed the 2007 Rugby World Cup but played in the 2011 tournament. The flanker, a European Cup winner at Wasps in 2007 and Premiership winner in 2008, moved to Stade Francais, then played in Japan and New Zealand, when he joined England on their 2012 summer tour of South Africa and re-signed for Wasps. He played every game in the 2015 Six Nations, marked 150 games for Wasps the same year, and retired in 2019 after a year at Northampton. A Lion in 2017, he has his fingers in several business pies. These include a coffee business, a property company, and The Good, The Bad and The Rugby podcast.

1285. TURNER, Stuart Charles
Prop 3 caps 2007
Born: Southport, 22 April 1972
Career: Waterloo, Orrell, Worcester, Rotherham, Sale, Caldy, Barbarians
Debut: v Wales, Millennium Stadium, Cardiff, March 2007

Turner, a test debutant at 35, made his one start for England in Bloemfontein on the 2007 tour to South Africa and won his three caps that season, the year after winning the Premiership with Sale. He got his big break when he signed for Sale and played 147 league games for the Cheshire side. He left Sale in 2009 and played for Caldy, working as their head coach for three years. He was a director of Abtek Biologicals in Liverpool. The company is involved in the development of antibiotic-susceptibility testing products. He coached at Waterloo and was the operations manager for Neogen Corporation.

1286. BROWN, Michael Noel
Full-back/wing 72 caps (65-13t) 2007-2018
Born: Southampton, Hampshire, 4 September 1985
Career: Harlequins, Newcastle, Leicester, Barbarians
Debut: v South Africa, Free State Stadium, Bloemfontein, May 2007

Brown made his debut on the 2007 tour to South Africa but had to wait five years before he finally became an England regular under Stuart Lancaster. The full-back was destined to be a one-club man, playing 351 times for Harlequins in 16 years, but moved to Newcastle in 2021 before being released after a year. He resurrected his career at Leicester and signed a new contract there for the 2023-24 season when he would have passed his 38th birthday. The son-in-law of former England footballer Tony Woodcock, he won two Premiership titles with Quins but missed the 2021 final because he was suspended. In 2024 he extended his stay at Welford Road with a new deal.

1287. SCHOFIELD, Dean Francis
Lock 2 caps 2007
Born: Manchester, Lancashire, 19 January 1979
Career: Sale, Toulon (Fra), Worcester, London Welsh, Barbarians
Debut: v South Africa, Free State Stadium, Bloemfontein, May 2007

Schofield was an abrasive lock who was unlucky not to have more international recognition than two caps on England's summer tour of South Africa in 2007. The second row joined Sale from Wakefield and spent nearly a decade there, winning the Premiership in 2006 and captaining the club in the 2009/10 season. He was in France as Toulon lost both the Top 14 and the European Challenge Cup final in 2012 before he moved to Worcester and London Welsh. He then moved to Yorkshire Carnegie before coaching Sedgley Park Tigers. He did not turn professional until he was 22 and was involved with GB Homes and works for Kerry James Interiors.

1288. CAIRNS, Matthew Ian
Hooker 1 cap 2007
Born: Birkenhead, Cheshire, 31 March 1979
Career: Sale, Northampton, Saracens, Harlequins
Debut: v South Africa, Free State Stadium, Bloemfontein, May 2007

Cairns was another member of the cavalry drafted in when a depleted England side went to South Africa in 2007 and won his only cap off the bench in the 58-10 defeat to the Springboks in Bloemfontein. He played for the Saxons in 2003 and 2004, had two spells at Saracens, bookending a year at Sale before finishing his career at Harlequins. He studied to become a financial advisor and took a job with Willson Grange, a partner of St James' Place Wealth Management. He currently works with PFP Wealth Ltd in Merseyside. He is also a director of a family jam business 'Mammy Jamias', and coaches Caldy.

1289. CROMPTON, Darren Edward
Prop 1 cap 2007
Born: Exeter, 12 September 1972
Career: Bath, Richmond, Cardiff, Bristol, Barbarians
Debut: v South Africa, Free State Stadium, Bloemfontein, May 2007

Crompton was on the 1998 'Tour of Hell' without winning a cap, and it was another nine years before his only test appearance on the 2007 trip to South Africa. He was at Richmond before the club folded, and after a spell at Cardiff, had a second stint at Bristol, teaming up with Dave Hilton and Mark Regan in a veteran front row who helped the club stay in the Premiership in 2006 and got them up to third the season after. Crompton played on into his 40th year and has since coached at London Welsh, Plymouth Albion and Weston-super-Mare and worked in the building industry.

1290. WINTERS, Royston Anthony Maria
Lock 2 caps 2007
Born: Cuckfield, Sussex, 13 December 1975
Career: Loughborough College, Bedford, Harlequins, Bristol, Barbarians
Debut: v South Africa, Free State Stadium, Bloemfontein, May 2007

Winters won his two caps on the 2007 tour of South Africa tour and played for England A in a career that lasted from 1998 to 2013. After Haywards Heath, he graduated to Bedford, Harlequins in 2005 and then Bristol, for whom he made 188 appearances before retirement aged 37. He has since played for Haywards Heath Vets and had been offered another contract by Bristol, but a four-month lay-off with ankle surgery persuaded him to pursue a career as an electrician. He had qualified in the trade whilst a professional player and is a director of Mandol Ltd in his native Sussex.

1291. SKIRVING, Benjamin David
No.8 1 cap 2007
Born: Harlow, Essex, 9 October 1983
Career: Saracens, Bath, Bristol
Debut: v South Africa, Loftus Versfeld Stadium, Pretoria, June 2007

Skirving won his only cap at number 8 on England's tour of South Africa in 2007, having played his first game for the Saxons a year earlier. He had trouble with injuries, which hampered his career at Saracens, although he had 100 appearances in the bag when he was 22 with Bath and Bristol. He had played 171 Premiership games before that move but retired in 2015 aged 31, with Bristol still in the second tier of English rugby. The back-rower took a job as head of rugby at Hymers College in Hull, then Churcher's College in Petersfield, and for the RFU in coach development.

1292. ABENDANON, Nicolas Jan
Full-back 2 caps 2007
Born: Bryanston, South Africa, 27 August 1986
Career: Bath, Clermont (Fra), Vannes (Fra)
Debut: v South Africa, Loftus Versfeld Stadium, Pretoria, June 2007

It took a move to France for people to start talking about Abendanon as an international full-back, but eight years after his second cap, he was still in the wilderness because of England's decision not to pick foreign-based players. He moved to Clermont in 2014 and, in his first season, became a European Cup finalist and was voted European Player of the Year. He has Dutch nationality through his parents. He played over 200 games for Bath in a decade at The Rec and toured South Africa with England in 2007. He retired in 2023, after playing for Vannes, to become a skills coach at Bayonne.

1293. HIPKISS, Daniel James
Centre 13 caps 2007-2010
Born: Ipswich, Suffolk, 4 June 1982
Career: Leicester, Bath
Debut: v Wales, Twickenham, August 2007

Hipkiss was a 2007 World Cup finalist, making a late run for that tournament after winning his first cap in a warm-up match against Wales. Hipkiss came on as a replacement in the final against South Africa. The centre spent 13 years at Leicester, scoring the winning try in the 2010 Premiership final against Saracens, and played in the 2007 and 2009 European Cup finals. He became a chef at The Bertinet Kitchen in Bath, where he ended his career, worked as a project manager for Stonewood Builders in Castle Coombe, and is head of learning & development at the Matt Hampson Foundation.

1294. NARRAWAY, Luke James William
Flanker/No.8 7 caps 2008-2009
Born: Worcester, Worcestershire, 7 September 1983
Career: Gloucester, Perpignan (Fra), London Irish
Debut: v Wales, Twickenham, February 2008

Narraway made his international debut in the Six Nations clash with Wales in 2008 and impressed on England's summer tour to New Zealand. He suffered a neck injury in 2009, and in 2012, he left Gloucester, where he spent nine years and won the Challenge and Anglo-Welsh Cups, to sign for Perpignan in France. Also playing for the Saxons, he spent two seasons with the Catalan side before returning to the Premiership in 2014 with London Irish. He went into coaching with Coventry, where he won a National League 1 title in his first season, and Bordeaux-Begles before joining the Dragons in 2019.

1295. CIPRIANI, Daniel Jerome
Fly-half, 16 caps (64-3t,8c,11p) 2008-2018
Born: Roehampton, London, 2 November 1987
Career: Wasps, Melbourne Rebels (Aus), Bath, Gloucester, Sale, Barbarians
Debut: v Wales, Twickenham, February 2008

Sixteen caps spread over 10 years was a scant reward for Cipriani's talents, and his continued non-selection for England became a cause celebre. On his first England start, against Ireland in 2008 with Jonny Wilkinson on the bench, he had Twickenham rocking with 18 points. He won European Cup and Premiership titles with Wasps, later won the Premiership and RPA Player of the Year awards with Gloucester, and was an English Cup finalist with Sale. Eddie Jones gave him a start for the final test against South Africa in 2018, but that was his final cap. He has worked as an analyst on TV.

1296. VAINIKOLO, Lesley Paea 'I'muli
Wing 5 caps 2008
Born: Nuku'alofa, Tonga, 4 May 1979
Career: Gloucester, La Rochelle (Fra), RAC Angerien (Fra), Barbarians
Debut: v Wales, Twickenham, February 2008

Tongan Vainikolo had a stellar career in rugby league with Canberra Raiders, Bradford Bulls and New Zealand before crossing codes in 2007 when he signed for Gloucester. The wing had scored 149 tries for Bradford in 152 games and made an immediate impact for Gloucester when he touched down five times on his debut against Leeds. He moved to La Rochelle in France and then played at Angerien before taking up a coaching role at the club and settling in France. In 2019 he moved to New Zealand, taking a job as director of rugby at Wesley College in Auckland, Jonah Lomu's old school, and has interests in a sportswear company.

1297. WIGGLESWORTH, Richard Eric Peter
Scrum-half 33 caps (5-1t)
Born: Blackpool, *Lancashire*, 9 June 1983
Career: Sale, Saracens, Leicester
Debut: v Italy, Stadio Flaminio, Rome, February 2008

Wigglesworth retired from playing suddenly in December 2022 when Steve Borthwick was made England coach, and the scrum-half took over as Leicester's interim boss. As a player, he won seven Premiership titles with three different clubs and three Champions Cups with Saracens. He was an England under-21 Grand Slam winner in 2004 before forcing his way into the full side. He played in the 2011 Rugby World Cup and was named in the squad for the tournament four years later. He was involved in a Leeds-based sports recruitment company, Blackbook Sports, with fellow players Chris Ashton and Mark Cueto and is an assistant coach with England.

1298. CROFT, Thomas Richard
Flanker 40 caps (20-4t) 2008-2015
Born: Basingstoke, Hampshire, 7 November 1985
Career: Leicester, British & Irish Lions
Debut: v France, Stade de France, Paris, February 2008

Croft, a five-test Lion in 2009 and 2013, was injury-plagued and retired in 2017 after struggling with a neck injury. He won four Premiership titles with Leicester but came close to being paralysed in 2012 when he misjudged a tackle on Harlequins' Nick Easter and suffered a triple fracture of a vertebra. A cruciate injury followed, and then his neck problems. An athletic back row, he could also play lock. He part-owns a coffee bar at Leicester's Welford Road and works for Davidsons Homes in the Midlands. He was educated at Oakham School, where he was in the same year as England cricketer Stuart Broad.

1299. HODGSON, Paul Kevin
Scrum-half 9 caps 2008-2010
Born: Epsom, Surrey, 25 April 1982
Career: Bristol, London Irish, Worcester
Debut: v Ireland, Twickenham, March 2008

Hodgson was a lively scrum-half who played for England Under-18 and Under-21 before sevens duty and made his full test debut in the 2008 Six Nations. A runner-up in the 2009 Premiership with London Irish, he toured Argentina in 2009 and Australia a year later with England. After retiring, he became the London Irish Academy's backs coach, worked with Surrey, and coached at Sutton & Epsom. He became Director of Sport at Cranmore School in Surrey, where Barry Everitt, another former Irish player, has taught. Hodgson is also the Director of Sport for Effingham Schools Trust.

1300. OJO, Temitope Oluwadamilola
Wing, 2 caps (10-2t) 2008
Born: Tottenham, London, 28 July 1985
Career: London Irish
Debut: v New Zealand, Eden Park, Auckland, June 2008

'Topsy' Ojo scored twice on his test debut in England's 37-20 defeat to New Zealand in Auckland. The winger with a BA in business studies from the Open University, was fined £500 for his part in a late night out in New Zealand, and the second test of the trip marked his last cap. A product of the London Irish Academy, he played more than 300 times for The Exiles, was a 2009 Premiership finalist and was a Churchill Cup winner with the England Saxons, coaches at St John's School in Leatherhead and co-commentates for TNT Sport, Amazon Prime and TalkSport. He is involved with the portable pop-up bar, The 301 Bar.

1301. CARE, Daniel Stuart
Scrum-half 87 caps (79-14t,3c) 2008-
Born: Leeds, Yorkshire, 2 January 1987
Career: Leeds, Harlequins
Debut: v New Zealand, Eden Park, Auckland, June 2008

Care broke the Harlequins appearance record, playing his 352nd game for the club in February 2023 and won the 2012 and 2021 Premierships with the club. The scrum-half was in the England set-up almost continuously from 2008 to 2018, barring injury, before Eddie Jones dropped him following the 2018 fixture against Japan. He got back for the 2022 Australia tour, playing in all three tests, and was part of the 2023 World Cup squad. He was on Sheffield Wednesday's books as a youngster and won silver at the 2006 Commonwealth Games with England Sevens. He co-hosts the BBC's Rugby Union Weekly podcast.

1302. PAICE, David James
Hooker 8 caps 2008-2013
Born: Darwin, Australia, 24 November 1983
Career: London Irish
Debut: v New Zealand, Eden Park, Auckland, June 2008

Paice, a graduate in construction management, played for Souths in Brisbane, Australia, before travelling to England on his gap year and staying when he joined the academy at London Irish in 2003. He won the National Cup with Irish under-19s that year and by 2008, after playing for the Saxons, had forced his way into the full England squad and toured New Zealand. He was banned for seven weeks for his part in a brawl during a club match against Gloucester in 2012 but toured Argentina with England in 2013. He retired in 2018, after 14 years at Irish and returned down under, and now works for the Brisbane Airport Corporation.

1303. HOBSON, Jason Dean
Prop 1 cap 2008
Born: Swansea, Wales, 10 February 1983
Career: Exeter, Bristol, Wasps, Barbarians
Debut: v New Zealand, Lancaster Park, Christchurch, June 2008

Hobson won only one cap, but his post-rugby career is flying. He worked with his father, David, in a company, Gateguards, based in Newquay, which makes replica planes – three of which were used in the Hollywood film Red Tails. Now, he is a director of a virtual flight simulator company. He had two spells at Bristol and was at Wasps for two years before returning to the West Country club. A neck injury ended his career in 2014. He coached at Clifton College and Bristol University and has been head coach at Nailsea & Backwell RFC. He has been diagnosed with early-onset dementia and joined the legal fight against unions.

1304. ARMITAGE, Delon Anthony
Full-back/wing/centre 26 caps (44-7t,2p,1d) 2008-2011
Born: San Fernando, Trinidad, 15 December 1983
Career: London Irish, Toulon (Fra), Lyon (Fra)
Debut: v Pacific Islanders, Twickenham, November 2008

Armitage played for Racing Rugby Club de Nice as a youngster and represented France Under-16s before returning to England and joining the academy at London Irish. England honours followed at Under-19, Under-21, sevens and Saxons levels before he was picked for the full test team in 2008. Relegated to the Saxons in 2012 by Stuart Lancaster, he was dropped from that squad after an incident outside a Torquay nightclub. The full-back back moved to France with Toulon in 2012, winning three European titles and finished his career in 2019, with Lyon. He worked briefly at Chinnor RFC and has a rugby academy based in Staines.

1305. FLUTEY, Riki John
Centre 14 caps (20-4t) 2008-2011
Born: Featherston, New Zealand, 10 February 1980
Career: Hurricanes (NZ), London Irish, Wasps, Brive (Fra), Ricoh Black Rams (Jap), British & Irish Lions
Debut: v Pacific Islanders, Twickenham, November 2008

Flutey qualified for England on residency grounds and has the distinction, like Elliot Daly, of playing for and against the British & Irish Lions. The centre played for New Zealand Maori against the tourists in 2005 and one test for the Lions in South Africa in 2009. He was voted RPA Player of the Year in 2008 and had a brief spell in France with Brive that was ended by injury. He returned to the Premiership with Wasps before heading to Japan with Ricoh Black Rams. He worked on the North Island of New Zealand for a company selling shipping containers but has been an assistant coach at the Highlanders since 2019.

1306. KENNEDY, Nicholas John
Lock 7 caps (5-1t) 2008-2009
Born: Southampton, Hampshire, 19 August 1981
Career: London Irish, Harlequins, Toulon (Fra)
Debut: v Pacific Islanders, Twickenham, November 2008

Kennedy was a line-out specialist called up in 2008 and scored on his test debut against the Pacific Islanders. He spent a decade at London Irish, playing 217 times for the Exiles, and had his last game for England in 2009 after playing every game of the Six Nations. He moved to Toulon in France in 2012, where he won a European Cup, before joining Harlequins in 2013. Studying sports law at De Montfort University, Leicester, he re-joined London Irish as academy director before becoming director of rugby from 2014 to 2016. He has worked in the media and is head of recruitment at Saracens.

1307. MONYE, Ugochukwu Chiedozie Chinye
Wing 14 caps (10-2t) 2008-2012
Born: Islington, London, 13 April 1983
Career: Harlequins, Barbarians
Debut: v Pacific Islanders, Twickenham, November 2008

Monye, a schoolboy sprinter, before turning to rugby, toured South Africa with the British & Irish Lions in 2009, playing two tests, and was a strong, hard-running wing with a distinguished club career with Harlequins. The Londoner played 237 games for Quins, winning the European Challenge Cup in 2004 and 2011 and the Premiership in 2012. He retired in 2015 to work as an analyst with TNT Sport and take a sport and exercise sciences course at Surrey University. He was a member of England's 2011 World Cup training squad and has appeared on *Strictly Come Dancing* and as a captain on *A Question of Sport*.

1308. HARTLEY, Dylan Michael
Hooker 97 caps (20-4t) 2008-2018
Born: Rotorua, New Zealand, 24 March 1986
Career: Worcester, Northampton
Debut: v Pacific Islanders, Twickenham, November 2008

Hartley won his 97th cap, a record for an England hooker, against Australia in 2018 and would have sailed past three figures but for being banned for 60 weeks. An 11-week ban after being sent off in the Premiership final cost him a place on the British & Irish Lions tour in 2013. A Premiership winner with Northampton, he was made England captain by Eddie Jones, leading the side to a Grand Slam in 2016, and helped secure a record 18 wins on the trot. He retired with a knee injury after being left out of the World Cup reckoning. He relocated to Dubai to work for Globe Power, coach Dubai Sharks and has been a TV pundit.

1309. CRANE, Jordan Stephen
No.8 3 caps 2008-2009
Born: Bromsgrove, Worcestershire, 3 June 1986
Career: Leeds, Leicester, Bristol
Debut: v South Africa, Twickenham, November 2008

Crane was a powerful ball-carrying number 8 after joining Leicester, where he played more than 200 games, from Leeds in 2006. The back-rower, an Under-21 international, was picked for the elite squad by Martin Johnson but was back in the Saxons in 2009, the same year he kicked the winning penalty in a shoot-out against Cardiff during the European Cup quarter-final. A former Saxons captain, he joined Bristol in 2016 before retiring in 2019 and going straight onto the Bears coaching staff. He was a useful football goalkeeper as a youngster and was on the books at the West Bromwich Albion Academy.

1310. ARMITAGE, Steffon Elvis
Flanker 5 caps 2009-2010
Born: San Fernando, Trinidad, 20 September 1985
Career: Saracens, London Irish, Toulon (Fra), Pau (Fra), Biarritz (Fra), Nice (Fra), Stade Nicois (Fra), Barbarians
Debut: v Italy, Twickenham, February 2009

Armitage won just five caps between 2009 and 2010, by the time he was 25, and that was it, despite being European Player of the Year in 2014 and winning three Champions Cups with Toulon. He never returned to the Premiership, where he could have been eligible for England, and after leaving Toulon, he played at a succession of clubs in France. He was handed a suspended sentence for sexual assault in France in 2019, which led to a proposed move to San Diego Legion being scrapped. He is still based in the south of France, playing for Nice.

1311. FODEN, Benjamin James
Full-back/wing 34 caps (35-7t) 2009-2013
Born: Chester, Cheshire, 22 July 1985
Career: Sale, Northampton, Rugby United New York (USA)
Debut: v Italy, Twickenham, February 2009

Foden, educated at Bromsgrove School, signed for Sale in 2004 but left in 2008 to join Northampton, where he hoped to play scrum-half. He established himself instead as a full-back, playing 250 times for the Saints whilst winning his England caps under Martin Johnson and Stuart Lancaster. A Premiership winner in 2014, he was a contestant in *The X Factor: Celebrity*, making the semi-finals. He moved to the USA with New York after a decade at Franklin's Gardens and coached at Fordham University. He was married to pop star Una Healy of The Saturdays, works in real estate in New York and coaches at Iona University.

1312. BANAHAN, Matthew Andrew
Wing/centre, 16 caps (20-4t) 2009-2011
Born: St Brelade, Jersey, 30 December 1986
Career: Bath, Gloucester
Debut: v Argentina, Old Trafford, Manchester, June 2009

Banahan was a leading schoolboy hockey player, but at 6ft 7in tall and over 18 stone was at the London Irish Academy as a second row before switching to the wing when he moved to Bath as a 19-year-old. He scored 16 tries in his first full season at the club. England recognition followed in 2009 and at the 2011 Rugby World Cup, where he played his last test. After over 250 games for Bath, he moved to Gloucester and retired in 2021. Inducted into the Premiership Rugby Hall of Fame in 2023, he has coached at Kingswood School in Bath and is a matchday summariser for BBC Radio Somerset.

1313. MAY, Thomas Alexander
Centre 2 caps 2009
Born: Lambeth, London, 5 February 1979
Career: Newcastle, Toulon (Fra), Northampton, London Welsh
Debut: v Argentina, Old Trafford, Manchester, June 2009

May was one of a clutch of Newcastle backs who made the big-time after emerging in the late 1990s. A strong centre, he won his two caps in the summer of 2009 against Argentina and won two English Cups with Newcastle before joining Toulon in 2009, where he stayed for two years before returning to England with Northampton, then London Welsh. He hung up his boots after a 19-year career, making 247 Premiership appearances and has worked in the media on television and radio. He co-founded FutureProof Pro Ltd and is Head of Sport at Evyve Charging Network.

1314. WILSON, David George
Prop 44 caps (5-1t) 2009-2015
Born: South Shields, 9 April 1985
Career: Newcastle, Bath
Debut: v Argentina, Old Trafford, Manchester, June 2009

Wilson spent his early England career as a run-on replacement as Dan Cole made the starting tighthead spot his own. He played 55 Premiership games for Newcastle before moving to Bath, where he was a 2015 Premiership finalist. The prop played for the Saxons in 2008, made his England debut under Martin Johnson and played one game against Romania in the 2011 Rugby World Cup in New Zealand. He missed the 2015 Six Nations with neck trouble but returned in May to stake his claim for a second World Cup spot before finishing his career back at Newcastle. He now works as a physiotherapist in the north east.

1315. VESTY, Samuel Brook
Full-back/centre/fly-half 2 caps 2009
Born: Leicester, Leicestershire, 26 November 1981
Career: Leicester, Bath
Debut: v Argentina, Old Trafford, Manchester, June 2009

Vesty was a versatile back who came through the Leicester academy and made his first-team debut for the Tigers in 2002. He played 157 times for Leicester, winning three Premiership titles and playing in two losing European Cup finals, before leaving for Bath in 2010. The fourth generation of his family to play for Leicester, he also played cricket for Leicestershire Seconds. After retiring from playing, he became transition coach at Worcester before being promoted to backs coach two years later. He toured Argentina as a skills coach, with England in 2017 before joining Northampton as a backs coach under Chris Boyd. He was promoted to head coach.

1316. ROBSHAW, Christopher Denis
Flanker 66 caps (10-2t) 2009-2018
Born: Redhill, Surrey, 4 June 1986
Career: Harlequins, San Diego Legion (USA)
Debut: v Argentina, Estadio Padre Ernesto Martearena, Salta, June 2009

Robshaw won his second England cap in 2012 against Scotland, when he captained the side 966 days after making his debut in Argentina. He continued leading England under Stuart Lancaster until after the disastrous 2015 World Cup campaign. He was part of the 2016 Grand Slam and series win in Australia. He clocked up 300 appearances for Quins, was a two-time Premiership Player of the Year, moved to the USA with San Diego Legion in 2021 and retired in 2022 after shoulder trouble. He is on the Dress 2 Kill Ltd board, owns an events company and coffee shop and is involved in Gallagher's Sports Division.

1317. ERINLE, Ayoola Olasunkanmi
Centre 2 caps 2009
Born: Lagos, Nigeria, 20 February 1980
Career: Leicester, Wasps, Biarritz (Fra), Nottingham, US Carcassonne (Fra), Barbarians
Debut: v Australia, Twickenham, November 2009

Erinle played over 100 times for Wasps and won the European Cup before moving to Leicester. He then moved to Biarritz, from where he won his two caps in 2009, but when the French side did not renew his contract in 2011, he returned to England with Nottingham in the Championship but was back in France with US Carcassonne. He was a double winner on the television programme *Countdown* and studied pharmacy at King's College, London, but put that on hold to concentrate on rugby. When he retired, he got a first in physics and engineering at Loughborough University, securing a job with the Ministry of Defence as a marine engineer.

1318. LAWES, Courtney Linford
Lock/flanker 105 caps (10-2t) 2009-2023
Born: Hackney, London, 23 February 1989
Career: Northampton, British & Irish Lions
Debut: v Australia, Twickenham, November 2009

Lawes, a two-time Lion, remained a force in English rugby despite a string of injuries as he headed towards a fourth World Cup in 2023 after starting the 2019 final against South Africa. Born in Hackney, he moved to Northampton as a youngster, attending Northampton Grammar School for Boys and joining the local club as a professional in 2007. A Premiership winner in 2014 with Saints, he captained England in their 2-1 away win against Australia in 2022 and toured with the Lions, winning five caps, in 2017 and 2021. He played his 250th game for Northampton in January 2022. Lawes announced his retirement from the international game after the 2023 World Cup.

1319. DORAN-JONES, Paul Peter L
Prop 6 caps 2009-2013
Born: Enfield, London, 2 May 1985
Career: Leinster (Ire), London Welsh, Wasps, Gloucester, Northampton, Harlequins, Rosslyn Park
Debut: v Argentina, Twickenham, November 2009

A schoolmate of James Haskell's at Wellington College, Doran-Jones played for Lansdowne in Dublin whilst studying applied science at Trinity College, graduating to the Leinster side. He won an A-League title with Wasps and was called up by England in 2009 after an injury to Dave Wilson, making his debut against Argentina. He moved from club to club, ending up at Wasps again, then having a spell at Rosslyn Park, where his friend Jordan Turner-Hall was coaching. He is involved in property development with Town & Country Property Auctions and Albion Housing Residential Developers, which he founded and is married to TV presenter Zoe Hardman.

1320. COLE, Daniel Richard
Prop 2010-
Born: Leicester, Leicestershire, 9 May 1987
Career: Leicester, British & Irish Lions
Debut: v Wales, Twickenham, February 2010

Cole won his 100th England cap against Ireland in March 2023, three-and-a-half years after he feared he might have been stuck on 95 after the 2019 World Cup final. He kept his head down for Leicester, passing 300 Tigers appearances in 2022 before being recalled by Steve Borthwick for the 2023 Six Nations. He was part of Leicester's Premiership win under Borthwick in 2022, his fourth with the club and won Six Nations titles with England in 2011, 2016 and 2017. On two Lions tours, in 2013 and 2017, he played 14 times, winning three caps and started England's 2023 World Cup semi-final defeat against South Africa.

1321. MULLAN, Matthew James
Prop 17 caps 2010-2017
Born: Brighton, 23 February 1987
Career: Worcester, Wasps
Debut: v Italy, Stadio Flaminio, Rome, 14 February 2010

A product of the Worcester academy after being educated at Bromsgrove School in Worcestershire, Mullan made his England debut off the bench against Italy in 2010, having previously played for the Saxons. He moved to Wasps in 2013 after more than 100 appearances for the Warriors, where he was a European Challenge Cup finalist and also passed a century of games before retiring in 2019 due to a lack of motivation after a long spell out with injury. In between, he had toured New Zealand in 2014, Australia in 2016 and Argentina in 2017 with England. Mullan, a qualified personal trainer, runs Front Row Fitness in Cirencester, Gloucestershire.

1322. YOUNGS, Benjamin Ryder
Scrum-half 127 caps (100 -20t) 2010-2023
Born: Cawston, Norfolk, 5 September 1989
Career: Leicester
Debut: v Scotland, Murrayfield, Edinburgh, March 2010

Youngs became England's most-capped men's player when he passed Jason Leonard's mark of 114 against Wales in 2022. The son of another England scrum-half, Nick, he was Premiership Discovery of the Season in 2010, and that summer scored on his first England start against Australia in Sydney. He made his Leicester debut in 2007, played in the 2011, 2015, 2019 and 2023 Rugby World Cups and won two caps for the Lions on their victorious trip to Australia in 2013. He has won five Premiership titles with Leicester and, with his brother Tom, became the first siblings to start a Lions test since Gavin and Scott Hastings in 1989. He retired from test rugby after the 2023 World Cup.

1323. ASHTON, Christopher John
Wing, 44 caps (100-20t) 2010-2019
Born: Wigan, 29 March 1987
Career: Northampton, Saracens, Toulon (Fra), Sale, Harlequins, Worcester, Leicester, Barbarians
Debut: v France, Stade de France, Paris, March 2010

Ashton retired in 2023 as the Premiership's highest try scorer, with 101 and a record 41 in the Champions Cup. He won five Premierships with four different clubs to add to two Champions Cups with Saracens. He started at Wigan Warriors, scoring 30 tries in 52 games, before switching codes in 2007 with Northampton, scoring 39 tries in 25 Championship games to help Saints to promotion. He scored 24 tries for Toulon, breaking the Top 14 season record. His international career was harmed by two harsh bans. He scored a length of the field effort against Australia in 2010 and finished off with the trademark 'Ash Splash'.

1324. HAPE, Shontayne Edward
Centre 13 caps (10-2t)
Born: Auckland, New Zealand, 30 January 1981
Career: Bath, London Irish, Montpellier (Fra)
Debut: v Australia, Subiaco Oval, Perth, June 2010

Hape starred in rugby league with the Auckland Warriors and Bradford Bulls, winning 14 caps for his native New Zealand before joining Bath in 2008 and qualifying for England on residency. Martin Johnson picked the centre for the England squad for the 2010 Six Nations but had to wait until the summer tour to make his union test debut. Hape played in the 2011 Rugby World Cup and retired in 2013 because of concussion issues. A keen DJ who admitted to playing while concussed, he returned to New Zealand, working in insurance and then for the New Zealand Rugby League in development.

1325. ATTWOOD, David Michael John
Lock 24 caps 2010-2016
Born: Bristol, 5 April 1987
Career: Bath, Bristol, Gloucester, Toulon (Fra)
Debut: v New Zealand, Twickenham, November 2010

Attwood retired in 2023 after two spells at Bristol, two at Bath, one at Gloucester and one at Toulon to pursue a career in law and to swim the Channel for a spinal injury charity. The second row racked up more than 300 senior appearances and had been a decent discus thrower as a youngster who studied for a BSc in philosophy and physics at Bristol University before doing a law conversion course at the end of his on-pitch career at West of England University. He also defended teammates, such as Kyle Sinckler, at RFU disciplinary hearings during his career to help him in the legal profession.

1326. FOURIE, Carel Hendrik
Flanker 8 caps 2010-2011
Born: Burgersdorp, South Africa, 19 September 1979
Career: Cheetahs (SA), Rotherham, Leeds, Sale
Debut: v New Zealand, Twickenham, November 2010

Fourie, born in South Africa's Eastern Cape, qualified for England on residency in 2009 and made his test debut off the bench against the All Blacks a year later. He had taken his time to crack it at the top level with Rotherham, but once the flanker moved to Leeds in 2007, his career took off. Fourie originally missed the cut for the 2011 Rugby World Cup but was recalled for the warm-up game against Ireland, only to get injured himself and was forced to retire in 2013 because of a shoulder injury. He then worked as a community coach at Sale before moving back to South Africa.

1327. WOOD, Thomas Andrew
Flanker/No.8 50 caps 2011-2017
Born: Coventry, Warwickshire, 3 November 1986
Career: North Otago (NZ), Worcester, Northampton, Barbarians
Debut: v Wales, Millennium Stadium, Cardiff, February 2011

Wood came out of the Worcester Academy but furthered his rugby education in New Zealand by playing for North Otago before returning to Sixways before moving to Northampton. He captained England on the successful summer tour to Argentina in 2013 and was a Premiership winner the following season. Named Premiership Player of the Year in 2011, he suffered a health scare in 2020 when he had a pulmonary embolism but recovered to play until his retirement, after persistent shoulder trouble, in 2022. He racked up 240 appearances for Saints and owns a bespoke carpentry business, Waller & Wood Woodworks, with former teammate Alex Waller and sits on the Premiership Rugby Sporting Commission.

1328. CORBISIERO, Alexander Richard
Prop 20 caps 2011-2015
Born: New York, USA, 30 August 1988
Career: London Irish, Northampton, British & Irish Lions
Debut: v Italy, Twickenham, February 2011

Born in New York, with Italian ancestry, Corbisiero immigrated to England before he was five. He was a 2009 Premiership finalist with London Irish and winner with Northampton in 2014. Handed his England debut by Martin Johnson, he played four times in the 2011 World Cup and was called up as a replacement by the Lions in 2013, playing two tests against the Wallabies. He took time out in 2015, suffering from knee trouble, but did not play again after securing work with NBC in the USA covering the Premiership. The prop survived testicular cancer, hosts the Scrum Down podcast and is a director of ASM Sports, sourcing sports scholarships to American universities.

1329. TUILAGI, Etuale Manusamoa
Centre/wing 2011-
Born: Fatausi-Fogapoa, Western Samoa, 18 May 1991
Career: Leicester, Sale, British & Irish Lions
Debut: v Wales, Twickenham, August 2011

Tuilagi, one of six rugby-playing brothers, escaped potential deportation because he was in the UK on a holiday visa to make his England debut a year later in 2011 and be picked for that year's World Cup aged 20. He was fined £4,800 for wearing a sponsored gum shield, arrested for jumping into Auckland harbour from a ferry and fined another £3,000. Injuries have limited his England appearances, and it took him 11 years to reach 50 caps. He was a World Cup finalist in 2019. He won two Premiership titles with Leicester and three Anglo-Welsh/Premiership Rugby Cups and was a Premiership finalist with Sale in 2023.

1330. BOTHA, Mouritz Johannes
Lock 10 caps 2011-2012
Born: Vryheid, South Africa, 29 January 1982
Career: Bedford, Saracens, Sharks (SA),
Debut: v Wales, Twickenham, August 2011

When Botha was washing carpets and playing for Bedford Athletic, a test career would have seemed miles off, but a move to Saracens in 2009 via Bedford blues got him noticed. The second row played in the 2010 Premiership final and won it in 2011 with Saracens before making his international debut in the lead-up to the 2011 Rugby World Cup. He qualified on residency, played 142 times for Saracens and toured South Africa with England in 2012. After concussion forced his retirement, he coached Heidelberger RK, the German national team, Ampthill, and Bishop's Stortford. He is now part-time at Bedford School and Belgium forwards and line-out. Botha is now coaching the Saracens women's team

1331. SHARPLES, Charles David J
Wing 4 caps (10-2t) 2011-2012
Born: Hong Kong, China, 17 August 1989
Career: Gloucester, Moseley,
Debut: v Wales, Twickenham, August 2011

Hong Kong-born Sharples was raised in Stroud, educated at St Peter's School, Gloucester, Wycliffe College in Stonehouse, and played for Dursley Rugby Club. He was at Gloucester from the age of 14 until his retirement, aged 32, because of a shoulder injury barring a period when he was dual registered with Moseley. He scored 91 tries in 275 games for the Cherry and Whites and won four caps, with his two tries coming against Fiji. The wing, a Gloucester country sprinter as a youngster and considered one of the fastest players in the Premiership, helped his club win the Challenge Cup in 2015. He works as a financial advisor in Cheltenham.

1332. SIMPSON, Joseph Paul Mackay
Scrum-half 1 cap 2011
Born: Sydney, Australia, 5 July 1988
Career: Wasps, Blackheath, Gloucester, Saracens, Bath, Sale
Debut: v Georgia, Forsyth Barr Stadium, Dunedin, September 2011

Simpson called time on a 17-year career, which included 230 games for Wasps, in 2023 after a brief stint at Sale. The scrum-half, educated at St Benedict's School in Ealing, who was a handy athlete and cricketer as a youngster, spent two early years on loan at Blackheath, and his speed was one of his biggest weapons in rugby. He won his only cap against Georgia during the 2011 World Cup in New Zealand. He played in two European and Premiership semi-finals and was 2017 Premiership Final at Wasps. He now works in business development at Walker Crips, an investment management company.

1333. BARRITT, Bradley Michael
Centre 26 caps (10-2t) 2012-2015
Born: Durban, South Africa, 7 August 1986
Career: Sharks (SA), Saracens, British & Irish Lions
Debut: v Scotland, Murrayfield, Edinburgh, February 2012

South African-born Barritt retired in 2020, after winning five Premiership titles and three European Cups with Saracens between 2011 and 2019. The centre, who had played for the Emerging Springboks and was a 2007 Super Rugby finalist with Sharks, made his England debut in 2012 after playing in the 2009 Churchill Cup. He was called up as a replacement for the 2013 Lions in Australia and played for England at the 2015 World Cup. Inducted into the Premiership Hall of Fame in 2023, he returned to South Africa and is managing director of a financial services company in Cape Town. He co-founded Tiki Tonga Coffee in 2017.

1334. DOWSON, Philip David Acton
No.8 7 caps 2012
Born: Guildford, Surrey, 1 October 1981
Career: Newcastle, Northampton, Worcester
Debut: v Scotland, Murrayfield, Edinburgh, February 2012

Dowson was one of seven new caps selected by Stuart Lancaster for his first game in charge of England in 2012. The back row had put together an impressive career in the Premiership, which finished with 262 appearances in the league for three different clubs, a Powergen Cup win with Newcastle in 2004, and a league title with Northampton in 2014. He ended his career at Worcester in 2017 and headed back to Franklin's Gardens as an assistant coach with Northampton before, in June 2022, he succeeded Chris Boyd as director of rugby, having been head coach and helping Saints to the playoffs.

1335. FARRELL, Owen Andrew
Fly-half/centre, 2012-
Born: Billinge, Lancashire, 24 September 1991
Career: Saracens, Bedford, British & Irish Lions
Debut: v Scotland, Murrayfield, Edinburgh, February 2012

Farrell spent his early years playing league in Wigan, but his father Andy's move to Saracens prompted a move to St George's School in Harpenden. Quickly recognised as a huge talent and leader, he made his Saracens debut aged 17 years and 11 days, then a record, in 2008 and his England debut four years later, the year after winning the first of six Premierships, to 2023, with Saracens. A three-time Six Nations winner, treble European Cup champion and three-time Lion, he was handed the captaincy of England by Eddie Jones, leading them to the 2019 World Cup final, and he was the third man to win 100 England caps. In 2024 Farrell announced he would be taking a break from Test rugby for mental health reasons

1336. PARLING, Geoffrey Matthew Walter
Lock 29 caps (5-1t) 2012-2015
Born: Stockton-on-Tees, *County Durham*, 28 October 1983
Career: Newcastle, Leicester, Exeter, British & Irish Lions, Munakata Sanix blues (Jap), Melbourne Rebels (Aus), Barbarians
Debut: v Scotland, Murrayfield, Edinburgh, February 2012

Parling was a line-out technician of a lock and was always likely to end up in coaching after a playing career that yielded two Premiership titles with Leicester and one with Exeter. A three-test Lion in 2013, in Australia, he played his last test at the 2015 World Cup. The second-row finished his playing career at the Rebels in Melbourne in 2018 via Japan and immediately joined the coaching staff. In 2020, he worked for the Wallabies as forwards' coach under Dave Rennie for a short period and remained at the Rebels for the 2023 Super Rugby Pacific season on a deal extending to 2025.

1337. DICKSON, Lee Alwyne Walter
Scrum-half, 18 caps
Born: Verden, Germany, 29 March 1985
Career: Newcastle, Northampton, Bedford
Debut: v Scotland, Murrayfield, Edinburgh, February 2012

Born in Germany, Dickson represented Scotland at the Under-19 World Cup in 20-4, courtesy of his Scottish father, before throwing his lot in with the country of his mother. He moved to Northampton from Newcastle in 2008, making more than 250 appearances for the Midlanders and winning the Premiership in 2014 and the Challenge Cup in 2009 and 2014. He left Saints in 2017 to become a player/coach at Bedford in the Championship, leaving there in 2019 to become head of rugby at Barnard Castle School in County Durham, which he and referee brother Karl attended as pupils.

1338. TURNER-HALL, Jordan Turner-Hall
Centre 2 caps 2012
Born: Camden, London, 5 January 1988
Career: Harlequins
Debut: v Scotland, Murrayfield, Edinburgh, February 2012

Turner-Hall won his two England caps in 2012, the year he helped Harlequins lift the Premiership title after beating Leicester 30-23 at Twickenham. A robust midfielder nicknamed 'The Bull', he had won the Challenge Cup the year before and played for England at every level. A hip injury forced his retirement in 2015, after 181 games for Quins, and he stayed at the club working in the youth programme. He coached Wimbledon RFC, Hurstpierpoint College in Sussex, Rosslyn Park and Ipswich School. In 2020, he returned to Harlequins as an academy coach and, in 2022, joined England Under-20s as the defence coach.

1339. MORGAN, Benjamin John
No.8 31 caps (25-5t) 2012-2015
Born: Bristol, 18 February 1989
Career: Scarlets (Wal), Gloucester
Debut: v Scotland, Murrayfield, Edinburgh, February 2012

Morgan started his rugby career at Dursley RFC, then the Scarlets in Wales, before joining Gloucester, his boyhood club, in 2012. Eligible for Wales, under residency, he plumped for England in January 2012 and a month later was making his debut at Murrayfield. A ball-carrying No.8 He won his last cap in the 2015 World Cup, overcoming a fractured ankle to make the tournament, although Eddie Jones did call him into camp in 2018. He toured with England each summer from 2012 to 2014, but later in his career was hampered by injury, and he retired in 2023 after 11 years at Kingsholm. He owns a scaffolding company, No.8 Scaffolding, in Dursley.

1340. WEBBER, Robert William
Hooker 16 caps (5-1t) 2012-2015
Born: York, Yorkshire, 1 August 1986
Career: Leeds, Wasps, Bath, Sale, Barbarians
Debut: v Italy, Stadio Olimpico, Rome, February 2012

Hooker Webber started his international career towards the end of a seven-year stint at Wasps in 2012 ahead of a move to Bath. He had toured Australasia in 2010, playing in the non-cap game against New Zealand Maori, but was handed his senior debut by Stuart Lancaster, who picked him for the 2015 World Cup. He moved to Sale a year later, finishing there in 2020. He had coached at Bath University and Sandbach RFC but, on retirement, took a job with Jersey. In 2021, he was promoted to head coach, helping them to the Championship title in 2023, only for the club to go bust. He then landed a job as forwards' coach at Chicago Hounds.

1341. JOHNSON, Thomas Anthony
Flanker 8 caps (5-1t) 2012-2014
Born: Dusseldorf, Germany, 16 July 1982
Career: Chinnor, Reading, Coventry, Exeter, Barbarians
Debut: v South Africa, Kings Park Stadium, Durban, June 2012

After spells with Chinnor, Reading, and Coventry, Johnson joined Exeter in 2007 and helped them win promotion to the Premiership in 2010. The flanker, a regular with the Saxons, got his breakthrough on the 2012 tour to South Africa, becoming the first Exeter player to be capped by England since 1964. He won his last England cap on the 2014 tour to New Zealand and stayed at Exeter until his retirement in 2017. His firm, Tom Johnson Lifestyle, based in Exmouth, has been running since 2017, and in 2022, he founded Plused Ltd, a well-being company and was a County Shield finalist with Oxfordshire.

1342. MARLER, Joseph William George
Prop 2012-
Born: Eastbourne, Sussex, 7 July 1990
Career: Harlequins, Barbarians, British & Irish Lions
Debut: v South Africa, Kings Park Stadium, Durban, June 2012

Marler joined the Harlequins academy from Haywards Heath RFC in 2008 and, in 2023, was approaching 300 senior games for the club. The loosehead prop won the Premiership with Harlequins that season, adding another in 2021. His career is littered with controversy and suspensions. He also retired from test rugby in 2018 but reversed the decision and was a member of the England squad that reached the 2023 World Cup semi-finals despite missing the Six Nations, his third Rugby World Cup. The 2017 Lions tourist hosts a podcast, The Joe Marler Show.

1343. JOSEPH, Jonathan Byron Alexander
Centre 54 caps (85-17t) 2012-2020
Born: Derby, Derbyshire, 21 May 1991
Career: London Irish, Bath, Biarritz (Fra), British & Irish Lions
Debut: v South Africa, Kings Park Stadium, Durban, 9 June 2012

A product of the London Irish Academy, Joseph, who attended Millfield School, was an international when he left for Bath in 2013. A 2011 Junior World Cup runner-up, he was a fixture in the early years of Eddie Jones' reign, winning a Grand Slam in 2016 and playing all three tests in the series win over Australia that summer. A Lion in 2017, he made the squad for the 2019 World Cup, coming off the bench in the final defeat to South Africa. The centre passed 50 caps in the winning 2020 Six Nations campaign before injury and selection counted against him. England has also capped his younger brother Will. He moved to Biarritz in 2023

1344. WALDROM, Thomas Robert
No.8 5 caps 2012-2013
Born: Lower Hutt, New Zealand, 28 April 1983
Career: Hurricanes (NZ), Crusaders (NZ), New Zealand Maori, Leicester, Exeter, Barbarians
Debut: v South Africa, Ellis Park, Johannesburg, June 2012

Born in New Zealand, Waldrom qualified for England through his grandmother and made his debut on the 2012 tour to South Africa. He had only been in the United Kingdom for two years since joining Leicester in 2010 after playing Super Rugby in New Zealand. The No.8 was involved in the 2013 Six Nations and moved to Exeter in 2014, scoring 16 Premiership tries in his first season. He played for Wellington in the Mitre10 Cup in New Zealand before retiring in 2018. He worked for DB Breweries before moving to Mitre 10 as trade manager in 2022 and took up athletics again, having been a school's discus champion.

1345. GOODE, Alexander David
Full-back 21 caps (8-1t,1p) 2012-2016
Born: Cambridge, Cambridgeshire, 5 May 1988
Career: Saracens, Barbarians, NEC Green Rockets (Jap)
Debut: v South Africa, Ellis Park, Johannesburg, 16 June 2012

Goode was earmarked as Saracens' next fly-half as a youngster, but the rapid progress of Owen Farrell saw him make his mark as a full-back in six Premiership and three Champions Cup wins. He has filled in at 10 over the years for the club, as his lack of opportunities with England perplexed observers. A talented footballer who was part of the Ipswich academy, he passed the 350 appearances mark for Saracens, a record for the club, in 2023, but he won just two caps under Eddie Jones. He was European Player of the Year in 2019 and had a spell in Japan when Saracens were relegated over the salary cap scandal.

1346. YOUNGS, Thomas Nicholas
Hooker 28 caps 2012-2015
Born: Norwich, Norfolk, 28 January 1987
Career: Bedford, Nottingham, Leicester, British & Irish Lions, Barbarians
Debut: v Fiji, Twickenham, November 2012

A converted centre, Youngs followed his father, Nick, and younger brother, Ben, into the England team when he made his debut in 2012. Earlier that year, he had toured South Africa, despite not having started a Premiership game at hooker and played in the midweek side and was a 2013 Lion in Australia, playing in all three tests. He won the Premiership with Leicester in 2013 and became club captain in 2016. In October 2021, he announced he was taking an indefinite leave from the game to look after his seriously ill wife, Tiffany, and retired in April 2022. He works on the family farm in Norfolk.

1347. VUNIPOLA, Makovina Wanangarua I Whanga Nui-Atara
Prop 79 caps (10-2t) 2012-2021
Born: Wellington, New Zealand, 14 January 1991
Career: Bristol, Saracens, British & Irish Lions
Debut: v Fiji, Twickenham, November 2012

Vunipola was born in New Zealand but spent much of his early life in Wales, where his father, Tongan international Fe'ao, played club rugby. He attended Millfield School before joining Bristol in 2010, then champions Saracens a year later and was part of their domination of the domestic and European scene. A three-tour Lion, he played a part in every test on the 2013, 2017 and 2021 trips and started all three knock-out games when England made the final of the 2019 World Cup. The prop has won four Premiership crowns, three European Cups and a Championship title with Saracens.

1348. LAUNCHBURY, Joseph Oliver
Lock 2012-
Born: Exeter, Devon, 12 April 1991
Career: Worthing, Wasps, Rosslyn Park, Toyota Verblitz (Jap), Harlequins
Debut: v Fiji, Twickenham, November 2012

Discarded by the Harlequins academy, Launchbury made his name at Wasps after a stint at Worthing, under ex-Wasps prop Will Green, and a loan spell at Rosslyn Park. The lock was named club captain in 2016, by which time he established himself as an international. Named Premiership Young Player of the Season in 2013, he played at the 2015 and 2019 World Cups but missed the 2023 World Cup after tearing his hamstring the day before going into camp. His

1349. BURNS, Freddie Spencer
Fly-half 5 caps (57-1t,8c,12p) 2012-2014
Born: Bath, Somerset, 13 May 1990
Career: Gloucester, Leicester, Bath, Toyota Industries (Jap), Highlanders (NZ)
Debut: v New Zealand, Twickenham, 1 December 2012

Burns became a Leicester legend when his last-gasp drop goal won the Premiership final for the Tigers against Saracens in 2022. Burns joined Gloucester from the Bath academy and played for England in the 2010 Junior World Cup in Argentina. He nailed down a starting spot at Gloucester and, in December 2001, made his full debut off the bench in the 38-21 win over the All Blacks. He toured Argentina with England in 2013, scoring 31 points in the two tests, and played two tests in New Zealand in 2014. He was released by Leicester in 2023 to take an opportunity in Super Rugby with the Highlanders and in 2024 was back in Japan playing for Shoki Shuttles. career has turned full circle, and he returned to Harlequins after spending time in Japan when Wasps went bust.

1350. TWELVETREES, William Wesley Frederick
Centre 22 caps (15-3t) 2013-2015
Born: Chichester, Sussex, 15 November 1988
Career: Bedford, Leicester, Gloucester, Ealing Trailfinders, British & Irish Lions
Debut: v Scotland, Twickenham, February 2013

Twelvetrees, like Joe Marler, a graduate of Haywards Heath RFC, was spotted by Leicester academy manager Andy Key, playing for Leicester Lions, and joined Tigers in 2008. He had a stunning season at Bedford before returning to Welford Road in 2009 and staying there until 2012, when he moved to Gloucester, making over 250 appearances and winning his England caps. He was called up by the Lions in 2013 because of an injury crisis, playing against the Brumbies and the Rebels, but failed to make England's World Cup squad in 2015. A talented ball player and goal-kicker, he signed a deal to move to Ealing for the 2023-24 season.

1351. KVESIC, Matthew Boris
Flanker 4 caps 2013-2019
Born: Iserlohn, Germany, April 14, 1992
Career: Worcester, Gloucester, Exeter, Zebre Parma (Ita), Coventry
Debut: v Argentina, Ernesto Martearena, Salta, June 2013

Kvesic's second stint at Worcester ended in heartbreak were liquidation in October 2022, and he moved to Zebre Parma, in Italy, before signing for Coventry for the 2023-24 season. He was part of the England Under-20s team that finished runners-up in the 2011 Junior World Championship, but opportunities with the senior team were limited. He toured Argentina in 2013 and New Zealand in 2014 and played against Italy in the 2019 World Cup warm-up game without making the 2015 or 2019 tournaments. Of Croatian and Polish descent with English parents, he was born in Germany, where his father served with the British Army. He won the Challenge Cup at Gloucester in 2015.

1352. WADE, Christian
Wing 1 cap 2013
Born: Slough, Berkshire, 15 May 1991
Career: Wasps, Racing 92 (Fra), British & Irish Lions
Debut: v Argentina, Ernesto Martearena, Salta, June 2013

Wade spent seven years at Wasps, scoring 82 Premiership tries, and played for England at Under-20s, Saxons and Sevens levels. But he only won one senior cap in Argentina in 2013, then was called to Australia by the British & Irish Lions. His size may have counted against him. He is 5ft 9in, but he had devastating speed, scoring six tries against Worcester in one game in 2016. He left Wasps to try out American Football joining the NFL International Player Pathway programme with the Buffalo Bills. He scored one spectacular touchdown in a pre-season game against the Indianapolis Colts but was released in 2022 and joined Racing 92 in the Top 14.

1353. EASTMOND, Kyle Ovid
Centre 6 caps (5-1t) 2013-2014
Born: Oldham, Lancashire, 17 July 1989
Career: Bath, Wasps, Leicester
Debut: v Argentina, Ernesto Martearena, Salta, June 2013

Eastmond crossed to rugby union from league in 2011, joining Bath from St Helens, where he had spent four years and scored all his side's points in the 2009 Grand Final defeat to Leeds. A four-cap England player in rugby league, he completed the league/union double on England's 2013 tour to Argentina after coming off the bench in the uncapped game against the Barbarians and scoring. He missed out on the 2015 World Cup and retired two games after switching back to the Leeds Rhinos. He managed a property portfolio before a short stint in coaching with Jersey Reds.

1354. VUNIPOLA, Viliami
No.8 2013-
Born: Sydney, Australia, 3 November 1992
Career: Wasps, Saracens
Debut: v Argentina, Ernesto Martearena, Salta, June 2013

Vunipola, born in Sydney and educated at Harrow School, was at Wasps via their academy before joining brother Mako at Saracens, where he has won three Premiership, three European Cup crowns and a Championship title. When fit, he was a fixture in the England side until 2020 and in the Saracens run of domestic and European dominance. He pulled out before the 2017 Lions tour with a shoulder injury, then helped England to the 2019 World Cup final. Vunipola was left out by Eddie Jones in March 2020 but returned for the 2022 winning summer tour to Australia, scoring in the second test victory. He was part of England's squad at the 2023 World Cup.

1355. THOMAS, Henry Morgan
Prop 7 caps 2013-2014
Born: Kingston-upon-Thames, Surrey, 30 October 1991
Career: Sale, Bath, Montpellier (Fra)
Debut: v Argentina, Ernesto Martearena, Salta, June 2013

Thomas caused a stir when he switched his international allegiances to Wales ahead of the 2023 World Cup, but he was eligible through his father. Nigel, who hailed from Swansea and hadn't played for England for nearly nine years. Born in London, he was raised in Bath, attending King Edward's School, and joined his hometown club from Sale, in 2014. By then, he was an England player, winning his first two caps against Argentina, and helped Bath get to the Premiership final in 2015. Overlooked by England and with Bath struggling, he moved to France with Montpellier and won the Top 14 in 2021, who handed him an extended short-term deal in November 2023.

1356. MAY, Jonathan James
Wing 78 caps (180-36t) 2013-2023
Born: Swindon, Wiltshire, 1 April 1990
Career: Moseley, Gloucester, Leicester
Debut: v Argentina, Estadio Jose Amalfitani, Buenos Aires, June 2013

A one-time centre for England Under-20s, May made the most of his pace to rack up 35 test tries from the wing at senior level by 2023. A Gloucester academy product, he had a loan spell at Moseley before, in 2012, gaining Saxons recognition and being named Premiership Breakthrough Player of the Season. He toured South Africa with England in 2012 and made his full debut the next summer in Argentina. The wing, who describes himself as a 'student of speed', clocked 10.49 metres per second in a test, comparable with top sprinters. He was not in the original 2023 World Cup squad but called up after Anthony Watson's injury. He retired from international rugby after that tournament in France

1357. YARDE, Marland Xiphus Germain
Wing 13 caps (40-8t) 2013-2017
Born: Castries, St Lucia, 20 April 1992
Career: London Irish, Harlequins, Sale, Bayonne (Fra), Barbarians
Debut: v Argentina, Estadio Jose Amalfitani, Buenos Aires, June 2013

Born in St Lucia, Yarde headed to the UK as a youngster, attending Whitgift School in Croydon and signing for London Irish. Capped 13 times, starting and finishing on tours of Argentina, he had a controversial club career. He joined Harlequins from London Irish in 2014 and was a European Challenge Cup finalist before leaving three years later, under a cloud, after reportedly missing training sessions. He went to Sale, where he won a Premiership Rugby Cup in 2020, but left the club by mutual consent after being arrested. He signed for French club Bayonne for the 2022-23 season.

1358. MYLER, Stephen John
Fly-half 1 cap (2-1c) 2013
Born: Widnes, Cheshire, 21 July 1984
Career: Northampton, London Irish, Ospreys (Wal)
Debut: v Argentina, Estadio Jose Amalfitani, Buenos Aires, June 2013

Myler, from a famous rugby league family, signed for Widnes Vikings from the St Helens academy and played 49 times in Super League before switching to union and Northampton in 2006, and only Paul Grayson has scored more points for the club. He racked up 2,655 points for the Saints in 330 games, winning the Premiership and Challenge Cup in 2014 before heading to Ospreys in 2016. He was capped on England's tour to Argentina in 2013 and retired in 2023 after another 200-plus points for the Welsh region. He helped London Irish win promotion to the Premiership in 2019 and has coached the Wales Women's national side.

1359. TOMKINS, Joel Andrew
Centre 3 caps 2013
Born: Warrington, Cheshire, 21 March 1987
Career: Saracens
Debut: v Australia, Twickenham, November 2013

Tomkins, the older brother of league superstar Sam, won three caps for England at centre in the autumn of 2013 during a three-year stint in rugby union. After making his league debut for Wigan in 2005, aged 18, he scored a length-of-the-field try in Wigan's 28-18 Challenge Cup final win over Leeds in 2011 and switched codes later that year when he joined Saracens. He was named in England's squad for the 2013 tour to Argentina but missed the trip with an ankle injury. He returned to Super League with Wigan, then moved to Hull KR, Catalan Dragons and Leigh Centurions retiring in 2021 and is now a fire officer with Greater Manchester Fire Brigade.

1360. NOWELL, Jack Thomas
Wing 46 caps (70-14t) 2014-2023
Born: Truro, Cornwall, 11 April 1993
Career: Penzance & Newlyn, Exeter, La Rochelle (Fra), British & Irish Lions
Debut: v France, Stade de France, Paris, February 2014

Nowell announced he was leaving Exeter in 2023 for La Rochelle after 11 years at the club, two Premiership titles and a Champions Cup win. The wing scored a try in the final as England beat Wales to win the 2013 IRB Junior World Championship. He played two tests for the Lions in 2017 in New Zealand, and he announced he would not be available for the 2023 World Cup ahead of the tournament because of his move to France. He had more than his fair share of setbacks and played the last stages of the 2020 double-winning season with the Chiefs with a foot injury. He hails from a fishing family in Cornwall and owns the Swordfish Inn in Newlyn.

1361. BURRELL, Luther Davies
Centre 15 caps (20-4t) 2014-2016
Born: Huddersfield, West Yorkshire, 6 December 1987
Career: Leeds, Sale, Northampton, Newcastle, Barbarians
Debut: v France, Stade de France, Paris, February 2014

Burrell moved to Northampton in 2012 after stints with Leeds and Sale and won the Premiership with Saints a few months after his England debut. The centre won 13 caps under Stuart Lancaster but was left out of the 2015 World Cup when Sam Burgess controversially got the nod. Eddie Jones called him back for the summer tour to Australia in 2016 but replaced him after 29 minutes of the first test in Brisbane, and Burrell was never capped again. He had a spell in rugby league with Warrington Wolves and spoke about the racism he had experienced in rugby union, sparking an RFU probe which said he had suffered discrimination at Newcastle.

1362. FORD, George Thomas
Fly-half 2014-
Born: Oldham, Greater Manchester, 16 March 1993
Career: Leicester, Bath, Sale
Debut: v Wales, Twickenham, May 2014

Ford, from a league background thanks to his father Mike, became the first Englishman to win the Junior World Player of the Year award in 2011. In 2009 he became the youngest player to make his professional debut for Leicester, breaking Owen Farrell's record, at 16 years 237 days. He had two stints at Leicester, winning Premierships in 2013 and 2022. He moved to Sale in 2022, helping them to the Premiership final despite missing half the season with an Achilles injury from the previous final with Leicester. He played through the 2016 Grand Slam and in the 2019 World Cup final. He has a coffee shop, with his brother Joe in Oldham.

1363. GRAY, Joe Aidan
Hooker 1 cap 2014
Born: Nottingham, Nottinghamshire, 5 August 1988
Career: Northampton, Harlequins, Saracens
Debut: v New Zealand, Eden Park, Auckland, June 2014

Gray won two Premierships with Harlequins, in 2012 and 2021, in two periods at the club, bookending a spell at Saracens from 2018 to 2020. The hooker, who started his career at Northampton, made his England debut, off the bench, in the 20-15 defeat to the All Blacks in 2014 and retired in 2022. He already had an eye on coaching, having helped out at Northampton School for Boys when injured early in his career, then at KCS Old Boys, Wimbledon RFC and Barnes RFC before becoming head coach at London Scottish in 2022. He worked with England, under Steve Borthwick, as line out throwing coach ahead of the 2023 World Cup.

1364. PENNELL, Christopher James
Full-back/wing 1 cap 2014
Born: Worcester, Worcestershire, 26 April 1987
Career: Worcester
Debut: v New Zealand, Eden Park, Auckland, June 2014

Pennell was nominated for the Premiership Player of the Year award in 2014 for a series of heroic performances for Worcester despite the club being relegated. On that summer's tour to New Zealand, he was given his test debut off the bench, played for England Saxons in 2015 but missed the Rugby World Cup despite helping Worcester regain Premiership status. He is the son of the late England cricketer Graham Dilley and played 253 times for Worcester before leaving in 2021. He runs a rugby academy, is on the board of the Worcester Community Foundation and works as a surveyor in the area.

1365. BROOKES, Kieran
Prop 16 caps 2014-2016
Born: Stoke-on-Trent, Staffordshire, 29 August 1990
Career: Fylde, Newcastle, Leicester, Northampton, Wasps, Toulon (Fra)
Debut: v New Zealand, Forsyth Barr Stadium, Dunedin, June 2014

As a youngster, Brookes spent two years in Australia and also had a six-month exchange at a South African school before attending drama school. He worked as an extra on Coronation Street and Shameless before concentrating on rugby with Fylde, then Newcastle and Leicester. He returned to Newcastle by the time of his England debut. A move to Wasps saw the club make the Premiership final in 2020, but he had to miss the game against Exeter as his housemate tested positive for Covid. He moved to Toulon in 2021 with his England career over, winning the Challenge Cup in 2023.

1366. ROKODUGUNI, Semesa
Wing 4 caps (20-4t) 2014-2017
Born: Nausori, Fiji, August 28, 1987
Career: Bath, US Montauban (Fra)
Debut: v New Zealand, Twickenham, November 2014

Rokoduguni became the first serving soldier to make his England debut since Tim Rodber, in 1999, when he faced the All Blacks in 2014. The wing had played for Lychett Minster RFC, the Army and Bath Utd before signing a senior deal with Bath in 2012, the start of a decade at the club. He scored 10 tries in helping Bath to the Premiership final in 2015 whilst a lance corporal on secondment from the Royal Scots Dragoon Guards. He was the fourth generation of his family to serve in the Army and was a tank driver in Afghanistan. He plays for the French Pro D2 side US Montauban.

1367. KRUIS, George Edward John
Lock 45 caps (15-3t) 2014-2020
Born: Guildford, Surrey, 22 February 1990
Career: Saracens, Bedford, Panasonic Wild Knights (Jap), British & Irish Lions, Barbarians
Debut: v New Zealand, Twickenham, November 2014

Kruis had more in the tank when he headed to Japan in 2020 to win consecutive titles with the Panasonic Wild Knights. He had played in the 2019 World Cup final, had won the 2016 Grand Slam, and been on the 3-0 winning trip to Australia that year. The lock started professional life at Saracens in 2009, winning four Premierships, three Champions Cups and a Lions cap on the 2017 tour. He retired in 2022, but not before back-heeled a conversion for the Barbarians against England. He runs a CBD and supplement supplier, Fourfive, which he set up with Saracens teammate Dom Day and has coached England's line out.

1368. WATSON, Anthony Kenneth Chisom
Wing 2014-
Born: Ashford, Surrey, 26 February 1994
Career: London Irish, Bath, Leicester, British & Irish Lions
Debut: v New Zealand, Twickenham, November 2014

Watson overcame a serious knee injury to add to two previous Achilles ruptures to regain his England spot in 2023 after two years out. However he missed the 2023 World Cup with a calf injury. The wing played in the 2015 World Cup, won five Lions caps on tours in 2017 and 2021 and was ever-present in the 2016 Grand Slam and a subsequent clean sweep in Australia. He moved to Leicester when Bath would not offer him a new deal thanks to salary cap reductions, making the Premiership semi-finals in 2023. A Junior World Cup winner in 2013, he was a European Challenge Cup finalist in 2014 and a Premiership finalist with Bath in 2015.

1369. BURGESS, Samuel
Centre 5 caps 2015
Born: Dewsbury, Yorkshire, 14 September 1988
Career: Bath
Debut: v France, Twickenham, August 2015

Burgess's inclusion in the 2015 World Cup squad was a major talking point after he was parachuted from South Sydney Rabbitohs via Bath to England. Bath and England were at loggerheads on whether to play him in the back row or midfield, but Stuart Lancaster picked him as centre ahead of the likes of Luther Burrell. He returned to rugby league with South Sydney in 2016, picking up a career in that code that landed him the NRL title in 2014 and nearly 100 games for Bradford Bulls. He went into coaching with the Rabbitohs and is now Warrington Wolves head coach.

1370. CLARK, Calum Taylor
Flanker 1 cap 2015
Born: Stockton-on-Tees, County Durham, 10 June 1989
Career: Leeds, Northampton, Saracens
Debut: v France, Twickenham, August 2015

Clark was yellow-carded during his only senior England appearance, a 2015 World Cup warm-up against France. Educated at Barnard Castle School, Clark started at Leeds, went to Northampton and in 2012 was handed a 32-week ban for hyperextending the elbow of Rob Hawkins, the Leicester hooker, who suffered a serious fracture. A Premiership winner with Northampton, he retired from playing in 2021 and studied at the University of East London whilst at Saracens, completing a thesis entitled 'Thematic analysis of rugby players' accounts of resourcing when things get tough'. He now works as head of psychological performance and in player development and well-being at Saracens.

1371. SLADE, Henry James Harvey
Centre 2015-
Born: Plymouth, Devon, 19 March 1993
Career: Plymouth Albion, Exeter
Debut: v France, Twickenham, August 2015

Slade overcame diabetes to reach 50 caps for England in 2022, play in a World Cup final and win two Premierships and a Champions Cup with Exeter. A Junior World Cup winner in 2013, starting at fly-half, the now-centre made a late run to make the 2015 World Cup squad after making his debut in a warm-up game. A broken leg later that year meant he missed the start of the Eddie Jones reign as England coach, but he has been a regular since. He found out he was diabetic as an 18-year-old, has a glucose monitor on his arm and won an Anglo-Welsh Cup in 2014.

1372. COWAN-DICKIE, Luke Anthony
Hooker 2015-
Born: Truro, Cornwall, 20 June 1993
Career: Plymouth Albion, Exeter, Sale, British & Irish Lions
Debut: v France, Twickenham, August 2015

Cowan-Dickie won the Junior World Championship, with Exeter teammates Henry Slade and Jack Nowell, in 2013 and was at a senior World Cup two years later. An integral part of Exeter's Premiership and European success in 2020, the hooker scored tries in three pool matches at the 2019 World Cup, coming off the bench in the final and starting two out of three tests on the Lions tour to South Africa in 2021. He was a prop at Truro College and announced he would leave Exeter in 2023 to head to Montpellier in the Top 14. When the move fell through, the 2014 Anglo-Welsh Cup winner moved to Sale.

1373. GEORGE, Jamie Edward
Hooker 2015-
Born: Welwyn Garden City, Hertfordshire, 20 October 1990
Career: Saracens, British & Irish Lions
Debut: v France, Stade de France, Paris, August 2015

George, the son of former Northampton scrum-half Ian, made the 2015 World Cup squad after being promoted to the training party when Dylan Hartley was suspended. The hooker came under the wing of Schalk Brits and John Smit in his early days and has amassed six Premierships, three Champions Cups, and three tests for the Lions in 2017. George, a World Cup finalist in 2019, attended Haileybury College with England cricketer Sam Billings and joined the Saracens Academy when he was 14. He became the first England hooker to score a hat-trick against Georgia in 2020. He owns a physio and sports rehab practice, Carter & George, in Hertford with his friend Rhys Carter.

1374. CLIFFORD, Jack Anthony
Flanker 10 caps (5-1t) 2016-2017
Born: Brisbane, Australia, 12 February 1993
Career: Harlequins, Ealing Trailfinders
Debut: v Scotland, Murrayfield, Edinburgh, February 2016

Clifford made his debut in Eddie Jones' first game as England's head coach but had already captained the Under-20s to their World Cup win in 2013. He came on in every game of the 2016 Grand Slam and in two tests in Australia that summer, but in 2017, he started having shoulder trouble and missed the tour to Argentina. Another dislocation in 2020, in his 100th game for Harlequins, and an unsuccessful operation forced Clifford to retire aged 27. He worked briefly as a trainee tanker broker but is now employed by Gallagher as a business development executive.

1375. HILL, Paul Oliver
Prop 6 caps 2016-2021
Born: Aschaffenburg, Germany, 2 March 1995
Career: Otley, Darlington Mowden Park, Yorkshire Carnegie, Northampton
Debut: v Italy, Stadio Olimpico, Rome, February 2016

Born in Germany but raised in the North of England, Hill arrived at Northampton via Otley, Darlington Mowden and the-then Yorkshire Carnegie in 2015 and has made more than 150 appearances for Saints. The prop was called up by Eddie Jones in 2016, making his debut against Italy, and toured Australia that summer but then had to wait five years for another cap against Canada in 2021. A 2014 Junior World Cup winner, he signed a new deal to extend his stay at Franklin's Gardens in 2021 and enrolled on a welding course and an electrician's traineeship.

1376. ITOJE, Oghenemaro Miles
Lock/flanker 2016-
Born: Camden, London 28 October 1994
Career: Saracens, British & Irish Lions
Debut: v Italy, Stadio Olimpico, Rome, February 2016

Itoje passed 50 England caps against Australia in 2021, aged 27, by which time he had already played six tests on two Lions tours, in a World Cup final, won three Champions Cups and four Premierships with Saracens and been named European Player of the Year, in 2016. He was co-captain of the Under-20s side that won the 2014 Junior World Cup and led Saracens to their 2015 LV=Cup win. He studied politics at the School of Oriental and African Studies in Bloomsbury, London. He appeared on the cover of Tatler with Lady Amelia Windsor and has been the face of Marks & Spencer.

1377. DALY, Elliot Fitzgerald
Wing/centre/full-back 2016-
Born: Croydon, Surrey, 8 October 1992
Career: Wasps, Saracens, Barbarians, British & Irish Lions
Debut: v Ireland, Twickenham, February 2016

Daly was a good enough cricketer to attract the interest of Surrey CCC. He plumped for rugby and made his Wasps debut in 2010. Good enough to play anywhere in the back three and midfield, he became the second England player to be sent off at Twickenham, after Lewis Moody, when he was red-carded against Argentina in November 2016 for a reckless challenge on Leonardo Senatore, but was consistently in Jones's side until 2020. He moved to Saracens in 2019, doing the Premiership and European double and starting the World Cup final. He has played five tests on two Lions tours and missed the 2023 Six Nations with a hamstring injury, before making the 2023 World Cup.

1378. HARRISON, Teimana
Flanker/No.8 5 caps (5-1t) 2016-2018
Born: Opotiki, New Zealand, 5 September 1992
Career: Northampton, Provence (Fra)
Debut: v Wales, Twickenham, May 2016

Harrison was recommended to Northampton by Dylan Hartley, another New Zealand-born Saint, who spotted him visiting his old school in Rotorua. He stayed at Franklin's Gardens for 11 years, playing over 180 games, and was called up by England in 2016. He toured Australia in 2016 but was replaced by Eddie Jones after 31 minutes of the third test, and his last cap came in December that year. He was an Anglo-Welsh Cup semi-finalist in 2018, then a Premiership Cup winner the following year, and played in a Premiership semi-final. He joined Provence in Pro D2 in France in 2022. He is involved in a clothing brand, Wolfe.

1379. DEVOTO, Oliver Jonathan
Centre 2016-
Born: Yeovil, Somerset, 22 September 1993
Career: Bath, Exeter
Debut: v Wales, Twickenham, May 2016

Devoto joined the Bath academy whilst at Bryanston School, was Premiership Breakthrough Player of the Year in 2014 and played in the 2015 Premiership final. After a move to Exeter, he started in the winning 2016 final for the Chiefs and added another plus a European Cup title in 2020. He toured South Africa with the Saxons in 2016 and Argentina with the full side in 2017 without playing a test. A 2018 Anglo-Welsh Cup winner, he was a Premiership finalist in 2019 and 2021 and was a 2023 Premiership Rugby Cup winner and completed a BSc in building surveying at the University College of Estate Management.

1380. GENGE, Ellis
Prop 2016-
Born: Bristol, 16 February 1995
Career: Bristol, Leicester
Debut: v Wales, Twickenham, May 2016

Genge captained England for the first time against France at Twickenham in 2023. He led Leicester to the Premiership title in 2022 before moving back to Bristol, where he started his career in 2013. He played for Old Redcliffians and Hartpury College, having grown up on the Knowle West Estate, and joined Leicester in 2016. The prop was in the 2019 World Cup squad, coming off the bench twice, but by 2023 had become a senior England player. He revealed he played against Wales in 2023 with severe tonsilitis. He is a Bristol Rovers fan and co-owns Syn, a gym in Leicester, with former Tigers teammate Sam Aspland-Robinson.

1381. TAYLOR, Thomas William James
Hooker 1 cap 2016
Born: Macclesfield, Cheshire, 11 November 1991
Career: Sale, Wasps
Debut: v Wales, Twickenham, May 2016

Taylor, a graduate of the Sale academy, made his first team debut in 2011, following in the footsteps of his father, David, who played for the club in the 1980s. He made 106 appearances, played for England in a non-cap game against the Barbarians in 2014 and 2015, and got capped in 2016 just before leaving for Wasps. His five years there were affected by knee and shoulder injuries, and he returned to Sale in 2021, helping them to second place in the 2023 Premiership table. He coaches at Macclesfield RFC, his hometown club, where three generations of his family have played.

1382. SINCKLER, Kyle Norval Jonathan Sean
Prop 2016-
Born: Wandsworth, London, 30 March 1993
Career: Harlequins, Bristol, British & Irish Lions
Debut: v South Africa, Twickenham, November 2016

Sinckler took up rugby with Battersea Ironsides and was picked up by the Harlequins academy. He has been on two Lions tours, with six test caps, and played in the 2019 World Cup final, only lasting two minutes, before being knocked out. He moved to Bristol in 2020, winning the Challenge Cup in October that year when Covid delayed the tournament. The prop, who learnt his craft under Welsh legend Adam Jones at Harlequins, only missed eight of England's 60 games between March 2018 and March 2023. He was a 2016 European Challenge Cup finalist with Quins and played in the 2020 and 2021 Premiership semi-finals with Bristol.

1383. HUGHES, Nathan William Jeremy
No.8 22 caps (5-1t) 2016-2019
Born: Lautoka, Fiji, 10 June 1991
Career: Auckland (NZ), Wasps, Bristol, Bath, Black Rams Tokyo (Jap)
Debut: v South Africa, Twickenham, November 2016

Hughes turned down the chance to play for his homeland, Fiji, at the 2015 World Cup to throw his lot in with England. He had played hockey in Fiji, attending St Thomas High School in Lautoka, but was scouted by the head of PE at Kelston Boys' High School in New Zealand, which produced Va'aiga Tuigamala and Mils Muliaina when they were on tour in Fiji and offered him a scholarship. After playing for Auckland in 2013, he ended up at Wasps, where he spent six years before another three with Bristol. He plays for Black Rams in Tokyo and stated he wanted to play for Fiji at the 2023 World Cup but that did now happen.

1384. TE'O, Benjamin James
Centre 18 caps (10-2t) 2016-2019
Born: Auckland, New Zealand, 27 January 1987
Career: Leinster (Ire), Worcester, Toulon (Fra), Sunwolves (Jap), British & Irish Lions
Debut: v South Africa, Twickenham, November 2016

Te'o moved from New Zealand to Australia as a teenager and played rugby league for the Brisbane Broncos and the South Sydney Rabbitohs until 2014, when he switched codes with Leinster. A powerful centre, he made the 2017 Lions tour to New Zealand, playing in two tests, having switched to Worcester on a huge contract and played all of the 2018 Six Nations. He did not make the 2019 World Cup after an alleged altercation with Mike Brown at a training camp in Treviso and moved to Toulon. He retired after a season in the NRL with Brisbane Broncos and is now coaching the Redcliffe Dolphins in Queensland.

1385. EWELS, Charles
Lock 2016-
Born: Bournemouth, Dorset, 29 June 1995
Career: Bath, Bulls (SA)
Debut: v Fiji, Twickenham, November 2016

Ewels made history by setting an unwanted record for the fastest red card in Six Nations history when he was sent off after 82 seconds of England's game with Ireland at Twickenham in 2022. The lock, a Junior World Cup winner in 2014, five years after joining the Bath academy, forced his way into Eddie Jones' England squad in 2016. He made it to 30 caps without nailing down a place and was forced home from England's 2022 tour to Australia with a serious ACL injury. He joined the Bulls temporarily, playing in the Currie Cup but missed out on the 2023 World Cup.

1386. CURRY, Thomas Michael
Flanker/No.8 2017-
Born: Hounslow, London, 15 June 1998
Career: Sale, British & Irish Lions
Debut: v Argentina, Estadio San Juan del Bicentenario, San Juan, June 2017

Curry became the youngest England player since Jonny Wilkinson in 1998, when he made his debut against Argentina in San Juan, five days short of his 19th birthday. The twin of Ben has since developed into one of the best flankers in the world, playing in the 2019 World Cup final and all three Lions tests in 2021. He captained England in the first two games of the 2022 Six Nations, the youngest to do so since Will Carling in 1988. He flew home early from the 2022 tour to Australia with a concussion and missed the 2023 Six Nations with a hamstring injury. Curry is involved in property with Ben and his father, David.

1387. LOZOWSKI, Alexander Jozef Patrick
Centre 5 caps (5-1t) 2017-2018
Born: Brent, London, 30 June 1993
Career: Leeds, Wasps, Saracens, Montpellier (Fra)
Debut: v Argentina, Estadio San Juan del Bicentenario, San Juan, June 2017

Lozowski emulated his father, Rob, when he made his debut in the centre for England in Argentina in 2017 but has not amassed as many caps as his talent deserved. Dropped by Eddie Jones after the 2018 game against Japan, he did not feature again under the Australian. A talented footballer who played for the Chelsea academy, he started at Leeds whilst studying and joined Wasps before blooming at Saracens. He had a year in France with Montpellier when Saracens were relegated in 2020. He returned in 2021 and landed his third Premiership title with the Londoners in 2023 to add to two Champions Cups.

1388. WILLIAMS, Harry Anthony Hall
Prop 19 caps 2017-2021
Born: Lambeth, London, 1 October 1991
Career: Wasps, Nottingham, Jersey, Exeter, Montpellier (Fra)
Debut: v Argentina, Estadio San Juan del Bicentenario, San Juan, June 2017

Williams joined the Wasps academy whilst studying sports science and English at Loughborough University, but after spells in the Championship with Nottingham and Jersey, he was spotted by Exeter's Rob Baxter in 2015. He was part of Exeter's good run in the Premiership, playing in five successive finals, winning in 2017. He was part of the Exeter side that won the Premiership and European double in 2020, and three years later, after a season ended by a knee injury, he was set to join Montpellier in the Top 14 following 162 appearances for the Devon club. He attended Whitgift School with fellow England internationals Elliot Daly and Marland Yarde.

1389. WILSON, Mark Edward
Flanker/No.8 23 caps (5-1t) 2017-2021
Born: Kendal, Cumbria, 6 October 1989
Career: Newcastle, Sale
Debut: v Argentina, Estadio San Juan del Bicentenario, San Juan, June 2017

Wilson spent nine years in his spell at Newcastle, going on loan to Blaydon as a youngster, and was a seasoned pro by the time he got capped. He had played for England Students and England Counties, and even his wife being heavily pregnant back in the north east would not stop him from playing in Argentina. He came off the bench in the 2019 World Cup final, moved to Sale that year after Newcastle had been relegated, returning to Kingston Park in 2020. He retired because of knee trouble in 2022, aged 32. Later that year, he started coaching at Falcons, leaving in 2023.

1390. ARMAND, Donovan Wade
Flanker/No.8 2 caps 2017-2018
Born: Harare, Zimbabwe, 23 September 1988
Career: Western Province (SA), Stormers (SA), Exeter
Debut: v Argentina, Estadio San Juan del Bicentenario, San Juan, June 2017

Armand was one of the pillars of Exeter's domestic and European success after arriving from Zimbabwe via the Stormers in South Africa. He got scant reward for his hard-hitting style of play with two caps, both off the bench, against Argentina in 2017 and Ireland a year later. From a farming background in Zimbabwe, he relished playing at Exeter and claimed he had no international aspirations. He retired in 2022 and set up a company called The Gaming Athlete, dealing with the mental and physical health of gamers. He is a director of Sampson Armand Ltd, a firm working with business leaders which has clients including the NHS, Castrol and BP.

1391. COLLIER, William St Lawrence Webb
Prop 2 caps (5-1t) 2017
Born: Hammersmith, London 5 May 1991
Career: Harlequins
Debut: v Argentina, Estadio San Juan del Bicentenario, San Juan, June 2017

Collier played his 200th game for Harlequins in January 2022, the month before extending his stay at the club, which had already lasted 12 years. The prop, with the help of Adam Jones, had turned into a proper scrummaging tighthead by the time he made his England debut off the bench against Argentina in San Juan in 2017. He scored a try in the second test but was not seen again at test level, despite being called up to training in June 2022. He was involved in Pigsty, a Bristol-based restaurant, with former Harlequin Olly Kohn. His grandfather is former England international Larry Webb.

1392. FRANCIS, Piers George
Centre, 9 caps (5-1t) 2017-2019
Born: Gravesend, Kent 20 June 1990
Career: blues (NZ), Waikato (NZ), Counties Manukau (NZ), Edinburgh, Doncaster, Northampton, Bath, Kurita Water Gush Akishima (Jap)
Debut: v Argentina, Estadio San Juan del Bicentenario, San Juan, June 2017

Francis pitched up on England's 2017 tour to Argentina straight from the blues in New Zealand after signing to join Northampton for the 2017-18 season. Eddie Jones gave him his debut at the first opportunity, and he toured South Africa in 2018 and made the 2019 World Cup. Jones said he admired how he had taken himself off to New Zealand to improve himself after being in the Saracens academy for three years in his teens. He struggled with injuries at Northampton, often went to America in the summer to get fit in Arizona and now plays for Japanese club Kurita Water Gush Akishima.

1393. ISIEKWE, Nicholas Akamonye
Lock/flanker 2017-
Born: Hemel Hempstead, Hertfordshire, 20 April 1998
Career: Saracens, Northampton
Debut: v Argentina, Estadio San Juan del Bicentenario, San Juan, June 2017

At 6ft 7in and nearly 19 stone, Isiekwe is a huge physical presence who made his Saracens debut when he was 19. But his test career hit the buffers when Eddie Jones substituted him after 36 minutes of the first test in South Africa in 2018. He was recalled for the 2022 Six Nations and tour to Australia, whilst Steve Borthwick kept him involved in 2023. He won a third Premiership with Saracens in 2023 and was also a member of their 2019 double-winning side. He had open heart surgery in 2022 but returned to play in the 2023 Six Nations.

1394. MAUNDER, Jack Andrew
Scrum-half 1 cap 2017
Born: Exeter, Devon, 5 April 1997
Career: Plymouth Albion, Exeter, Barbarians
Debut: v Argentina, Estadio San Juan del Bicentenario, San Juan, June 2017

Maunder travelled to Argentina for two minutes of action off the bench in the first test, which was his lot on the tour. The Exeter scrum-half, whose father, Andy, also played for Chiefs, was dual-registered with Plymouth Albion when he made his senior debut in 2016, aged 19, a year after playing his first men's match for Redruth. A former pupil at Blundell's School, he was behind Australian Nic White for a while at Sandy Park but started the 2020 winning Premiership and Champions Cup finals when the Wallaby had left. After playing for the Barbarians against a World XV in May 2023, he revealed Exeter had released him.

1395. SOLOMONA, Denny
Wing 5 caps (5-1t) 2017-2018
Born: Auckland, New Zealand, 27 September 1993
Career: Sale, Highlanders (NZ), North Harbour (NZ)
Debut: v Argentina, Estadio San Juan del Bicentenario, San Juan, June 2017

Defensive slips from Solomona gifted Argentina two tries on his debut, but he had the last laugh, scoring in the 79th minute of a 38-34 win. Solomona arrived in England to play league for London Broncos in 2014, then moved to Castleford Tigers, scoring 40 tries in a season, before Sale paid Castleford compensation to bring him to rugby union. He spent five years at Sharks, toured South Africa with England in 2018 but left Sale abruptly mid-season after 47 tries in 98 games. He was sent home from an England camp in 2017 after a night out with Manu Tuilagi. He returned to New Zealand, signing for the Highlanders in 2022.

1396. UNDERHILL, Samuel Gregory
Flanker 2017-
Born: Dayton, Ohio, USA, 22 July 1996
Career: Gloucester, Ospreys (Wal), Bath
Debut: v Argentina, Stadio Estanislao Lopez, Santa Fe, June 2017

Underhill is a destructive flanker who was mentored by Richard Hill in his days at the Ospreys when he was studying at Cardiff University. He made his debut in the second test of the 2017 tour to Argentina and became, with Tom Curry, one of Eddie Jones's 'Kamikaze Kids' at the 2019 World Cup, making the final. He studied politics and economics at Bath when he moved to the West Country, but a string of injuries, including concussions, limited his appearances. He was called up as a replacement for Jack Willis at the 2023 World Cup and was the man of the match in the bronze medal game against Argentina.

1397. SIMMONDS, Samuel David
No.8 18 caps 2017-2021
Born: Torquay, Devon, 10 November 1994
Career: Exeter, Plymouth Albion, Exeter, Montpellier (Fra), British & Irish Lions
Debut: v Argentina, Twickenham, November 2017

Simmonds declared himself unavailable for the 2023 World Cup three months before the tournament ahead of his move to Montpellier. The No.8 European Player of the Year in Exeter's double in 2020 called temporary time on his England career after 18 caps spread over nearly six years. Picked as a Lion in 2021, when he was out of the national team, he played one test off the bench three years after his last appearance for England, but he returned to the squad in the 2022 Six Nations. He is a prolific try scorer, scoring 19 times in 26 games in 2019-20. Brother Joe, a fly-half, captained Chiefs that campaign.

1398. HEPBURN, Alec William
Prop 6 caps 2018
Born: Perth, Australia, 30 March 1993
Career: Henley Hawks, London Welsh, Cottesloe, Exeter
Debut: v Italy, Stadio Olimpico, Rome, February 2018

Australian-raised Hepburn was part of the Wasps academy after being spotted playing for Henley Hawks, then had a spell at London Welsh in 2014, after winning the Junior World Cup in 2013, before returning home. Rob Hunter, the Exeter forwards' coach, knew him from his England Under-20 days, and the prop arrived at Sandy Park in 2015. A major knee injury stalled his progress in 2017, but he rebounded to win his first senior cap. He was part of the double-winning side at Exeter in 2020 and was in the sides that lost the 2016, 2018 and 2021 Premiership finals.

1399. SHIELDS, Bradley David Fenner
Flanker 8 caps (10-2t) 2018-2019
Born: Masterton, New Zealand, 2 April 1991
Career: Wellington (NZ), Hurricanes (NZ), Wasps, Perpignan (Fra), Barbarians
Debut: v South Africa, Ellis Park, Johannesburg, June 2018

Shields captained the Hurricanes in Super Rugby down under before signing for Wasps in 2018, reaching the Premiership and European Challenge Cup semi-finals and making his England debut on the summer tour to Australia. An abrasive flanker, he had won the Junior World Cup with New Zealand in 2011 and had featured in All Blacks squads without winning a cap. Eligible for England through his parents, he suffered a foot injury in the lead-up to the 2019 World Cup and did not feature again at test level. When Wasps went to the wall in 2022, he signed with French outfit Perpignan, helping them win a Top 14 access match.

1400. SPENCER, Benjamin Thomas
Scrum-Half 2018-
Born: Stockport, Cheshire 31 July 1992
Career: Cambridge, Saracens, Bath
Debut: v South Africa, Ellis Park, Johannesburg, June 2018

Spencer started his career with Cambridge in National League One before joining Saracens after impressing in a pre-season trial. He was Saracens top try scorer in the 2018 campaign and won an Anglo-Welsh Cup, three European Cups and four Premiership titles. The former England under-20 and Saxons international was called into England's 2019 World Cup squad as an injury replacement for Willi Heinz a year after making his international debut in South Africa. He attended Ivybridge College near Plymouth, and returned to the West Country in June 2020 when he signed a long-term contract with Bath.

1401. MOON, Benjamin
Prop 8 caps 2018-2019
Born: Tiverton, Devon, 14 July 1989
Career: Exeter Chiefs
Debut: v South Africa, Twickenham, November 2018

Loosehead Moon made the first of over 300 appearances for Exeter Chiefs in an October 2008 National Division One home fixture against Sedgley Park. When he retired in 2023, he was the last remaining player from the club's days in the RFU Championship, having helped them win promotion in 2010. The former England under-16, under-18 and under-20 International won two Premiership titles, a European Champions Cup crown, and an LV= Cup winners' medal during his 15 seasons with the Chiefs. Eddie Jones handed him his chance on the international stage for the opening game of the 2018 autumn international campaign. He is a director of Moon's self-storage.

1402. MERCER, Zach Ivan
No 8/flanker 2018-
Born: Leeds, West Yorkshire 28 June 1997
Career: Bath, Montpellier (Fra), Gloucester
Debut: v South Africa, Twickenham, November 2018

Mercer is the son of former New Zealand rugby league international Gary, who enjoyed a long career in the UK after moving to Bradford Northern in 1987. Born in Yorkshire, he spent much of his childhood in Scotland, where he was an age group international member of Glasgow Warriors academy. He made his Premiership debut after joining Bath before Eddie Jones included him in his training squad as an apprentice. He won his first cap after Ben Morgan pulled out of a clash with South Africa. He joined Gloucester in July 2023 after winning the Top 14 title and Top 14 Player of the Year award with Montpellier.

1403. COKANASIGA, Ratu Josateki Tuivanuavou Waqanivalu
Wing 2018-
Born: Suva, Fiji, 15 November 1997
Career: Old Merchant Taylors' FC, London Irish, Bath
Debut: v Japan, Twickenham, November 2018

Cokanasiga was born in Fiji but moved to England when he was three because his father served in the British Army and was educated at Merchant Taylors' School. He began playing rugby for Old Merchant Taylors' FC in the seventh tier of English rugby in London 2NW before being invited to join the London Irish academy. He helped the Exiles claim a Championship title in 2017 and, in May 2018, moved to Bath. A former England under-20 international was plucked from relative obscurity for the 2017 summer to tour Argentina but had to wait 18 months to make his test debut against Japan, and he made one appearance at the 2019 World Cup, scoring two tries against the USA in Kobe.

1404. HILL, Edward
Back Row/second row 2018-
Born: Worcester, Worcestershire 26 March 1999
Career: Worcester Warriors, Bath
Debut: v Japan, Twickenham, November 2018

Hill started playing at Melvern Rugby Club before being picked up by the academy at his hometown, Worcester Warriors. He made an instant impact in the Premiership after coming off the bench to score a debut brace against Leicester Tigers. He was named club captain in July 2020 but was made redundant and had his contract terminated in October 2022 when the Warriors were liquidated. He joined Bath on loan before the Warriors were kicked out of the Premiership, and the move quickly became permanent. An England under-16, under-18 and under-20 international won his first senior cap as a late replacement against Japan.

1405. ROBSON, Daniel John
Scrum-half 2019-
Born: Stoke-on-Trent, Staffordshire, 14 March 1992
Career: Longton, Gloucester, Wasps, Pau (Fra)
Debut: v France, Twickenham, February 2019

Robson followed in the footsteps of his father, Simon, who played for Moseley and made the bench for England without getting onto the pitch. He played for the Longton senior side before joining Gloucester, where he won the 2015 European Challenge Cup before joining Wasps. He had a loan spell at his father's former club early in his career and was a Premiership finalist in 2017 and 2019. He was still at Wasps in October 2022 when they were kicked out of the Premiership after entering administration. He made his test debut nearly three years after his first call-up and is now playing for Pau in France.

1406. HEINZ, William Alexander
Scrum-Half 13 caps 2019-2020
Born: Christchurch, New Zealand, 24 November 1986
Career: Canterbury, Crusaders, Gloucester, Worcester Warriors
Debut: v Wales, Twickenham, August 2019

Heinz captained his hometown club, Canterbury, in New Zealand's ITM Cup and appeared in Super Rugby for the Crusaders before moving to Gloucester. He qualified for England through his grandmother, who hailed from Bishop's Waltham near Southampton and was first called into an England training squad by Eddie Jones in May 2017. He won his first cap in the build-up to the 2019 World Cup in Japan but was injured coming off the bench in the semi-final win over the All Blacks in Yokohama. His career in England ended in March 2022 when he returned to New Zealand and re-joined Canterbury.

1407. LUDLAM, Lewis Wesley D'fefa
Flanker 2019-
Born: Ipswich, Suffolk, 8 December 1995
Career: Northampton Saints, Old Albanians, Coventry, Birmingham Moseley, Rotherham Titans
Debut: v Wales, Twickenham, August 2019

Ludlam was educated at St Joseph's College in Ipswich and joined Northampton Saints Junior academy before stepping up to the Senior Academy and was a member of the England under-20 side that lost the 2015 Junior World Cup Final. He spent time on dual-registration deals with National League sides early in his career to gain experience and was in the Saints side that beat Saracens in the 2019 Premiership Rugby Cup, the year that he made four appearances at the Rugby World Cup. But he found his chances limited under Eddie Jones over the next four years but played every minute of the 2023 Six Nations under Steve Borthwick.

1408. SINGLETON, Jack Howard
Hooker 2019-
Born: Dacorum, Hertfordshire, 14 May 1996
Career: Worcester Warriors, Saracens, Gloucester, Toulon (Fra)
Debut: v Wales, Twickenham, August 2019

Singleton came through Saracens Academy before leaving to join Worcester Warriors, where he won the club's Young Player of the Season award in 2017 and England under-20 honours. Eddie Jones took him on the 2017 summer tour to Argentina, but he remained on the bench for both games. He won his first cap in the build-up to the 2019 Rugby World Cup before returning to Saracens upon their completion. He left for Gloucester on a season-long loan after Saracens were relegated after breaches of the salary cap, and the move became permanent ahead of the 2021-2022 campaign. He joined Toulon in November 2023 as a medical joker.

1409. MARCHANT, Joseph
Centre 2019-
Born: Winchester, Hampshire, 16 July 1996
Career: Worthing, Harlequins, London Scottish, blues, Stade Francais (Fra)
Debut: v Wales, Twickenham, August 2019

Marchant won youth honours for Hampshire before joining the Harlequins academy in 2014, making his debut against Newcastle Falcons a year later. In November 2019, he took advantage of a clause in his Quins contract that allowed him to take a sabbatical playing Super Rugby for The Blues in Auckland. He was a member of the Quins side that lost the 2020 Premiership Cup Final to Sale Sharks and started their Premiership final victory over Exeter Chiefs. He made his England debut in the 2019 Rugby World Cup build-up but did not make the squad and moved to play for Stade Francais from the 2023-2024 campaign after performing well at the 2023 Word Cup.

1410. McCONNOCHIE, Ruaridh Lawson
Winger 2 caps 2019
Born: Lambeth, London, 23 October 1991
Career: Nuneaton, Hartpury College, Bath
Debut: v Italy, St James Park, Newcastle, September 2019

McConnochie was a member of the Great Britain Olympic Sevens squad that secured a silver medal at the 2016 Rio Olympics. He was included in Eddie Jones 2019 Rugby World Cup scoring his first points against the USA after making his debut in a warm-up game. He was also capped by England Students and England Counties and joined Bath in the summer of 2018 after being a regular on the World Sevens circuit. He was named in Scotland's 2023 Six Nations squad after not being picked by England for three years. His grandfather, James McDonald, played football for Scotland.

1411. FURBANK, George Arthur
Full-Back 2020 -
Born: Hinchingbrooke, Cambridgeshire, 17 October 1996
Career: Northampton Saints, Nottingham
Debut: v France, Stade de France, Paris, February 2020

Furbank began playing rugby with his hometown club, Huntingdon and joined Northampton's junior academy before attending Bedford School, a fertile breeding ground for the club's senior academy. He was the skipper of the Saints side that won the Premiership Rugby U18s League trophy and was on Leicestershire CCC's books until he was 15. He scored a try against Exeter Chiefs on his Saints debut in the Anglo-Welsh Cup in November 2017 and was a member of the side that won the Premiership Rugby Cup final two years later. He was one of eight uncapped players called up for the 2020 Six Nations when Eddie Jones sought to build depth.

1412. STUART, William James
Prop 2020-
Born: Westminster, London 12 July 1996
Career: Wasps, Blackheath, Birmingham Moseley, Nottingham, Bath
Debut: v France, Stade de France, Paris, February 2020

The Red Baron shot down tighthead Stuart's war hero great-grandad Ronald Adam, who later became a Hollywood actor, while his grandfather played in the back row with infamous Ugandan dictator Idi Amin. A member of the England side that won the 2016 World Rugby Under 20 Championship. He made spells in the National Leagues with Blackheath, Birmingham Moseley and Nottingham before being given his Wasps debut. After joining, he was a semi-finalist in the 2020 Premiership, and the 2021 European Challenge Cup was in the England side that won the Autumn Nations Cup in December 2020.

1413. EARL, Benjamin Arthur
Back-Row 2020-
Born: Redhill, Surrey, 7 January 1998
Career: Saracens, Bristol Bears
Debut: v Scotland, Murrayfield, Edinburgh, February 2020

Earl played cricket for Kent until he was 15 and played his rugby for Sevenoaks in Kent before joining the Saracens academy. He was a member of the England Under-20 side that won the Grand Slam in 2017 and reached the World Rugby U20 Championship final later the same year. A Premiership Rugby Cup finalist with Saracens, he was loaned to Bristol Bears when the club were relegated to the Championship, winning the 2020 European Challenge Cup 2020 and reaching a Premiership semi-final. He won a Six Nations title, the Autumn Nations Cup with England, and two Premiership crowns with Sarries in 2019 and 2023. Playing mostly at No.8, he was England's stand-out player at the 2023 World Cup

1414. HILL, Jonathan Paul
Lock 2020-
Born: Ludlow, Shropshire, 8 June 1994
Career: Hartpury College, Gloucester, Exeter Chiefs, Sale Sharks
Debut: v Italy, Stadio Olimipico, Rome, October 2020

From a family of livestock dealers, Hill began his professional career with Hartpury College National League Two South on a dual registration from Gloucester. But it wasn't until June 2015, when he joined Exeter Chiefs, that his career flourished. A nephew of former rugby league international Paul Loughlin, he was a Premiership finalist in 2018 and 2019 and helped the Chiefs win a league and European double a year later. He went on the 2021 Lions tour to South Africa without making the test side, appeared in further Premiership finals with Exeter and Sale Sharks, and won a Six Nations Championship and an Autumn Nations Cup.

1415. THORLEY, Oliver Andrew
Winger 2020-
Born: Camden, London, 11 September 1996
Career: Gloucester
Debut: v Italy, Stadio Olimipico, Rome, October 2020

Thorley, a product of Cheltenham College, became Gloucester's youngest first-team try scorer when he crossed against Ospreys in March 2015 in the LV Cup. A member of the England under-20 side that won the 2016 IRB Junior World Championship. He was named the RPA Young Player of the Year Award for the 2019 campaign and picked up the Premiership Rugby Try of the Season Award. Thorley topped the Premiership try-scoring charts in 2020 with 11, the best return by a Gloucester player. His great uncle Martin Britt played football for West Ham United and made his only England appearance in Rome.

1416. LAWRENCE, Oliver Francis
Centre 2020-
Born: Birmingham 18 September 1999
Career: Worcester Warriors, Bath
Debut: v Italy, Stadio Olimipico, Rome, October 2020

Lawrence's father, Michael, played rugby on the wing for Moseley, and he only turned to rugby after spending time in the academies at Aston Villa and Birmingham City. He burst onto the scene with Worcester with a try on his first-team debut in the Anglo-Welsh Cup and made his England debut against Italy in 2020 and has won a Six Nations title and the Autumn Nations Cup. He won the 2022 Premiership Rugby Cup with Worcester but moved to Bath with the Warriors, suffering dire financial problems, and in May 2023 was named the Premiership's Player of the Season.

1417. DUNN, Thomas George
Hooker 2020-
Born: Bath, Somerset, 12 November 1992
Career: Bath, Chippenham,
Debut: v Italy, Stadio Olimipico, Rome, October 2020

Dunn, a graduate of the University of Bath, spent two years on loan at Chippenham before earning a full-time contract with his home town club. He started his career at loosehead before switching to the middle of the front row. He received England call-ups in 2017, 2018 and 2019 but had to wait until the 2020 Six Nations win over Italy to win his first cap. He was Bath's joint top try-scorer, with Will Muir in the 2020/21 season when he was a European Challenge Cup semi-finalist with seven to his name. He also runs a butchers and events catering business.

1418. WILLIS, Jack Steven
Back-Row 2020-
Born: Reading, Berkshire, 24 December 1996
Career: Wasps, Toulouse (Fra)
Debut: v Georgia, Twickenham, November 2020

Willis is the eldest of two brothers. Tom was a Wasps teammate, and they both played for Reading Abbey before joining Wasps Academy. He was a member of England's side that won the 2016 U20 World Championship, but his senior career, which started with a try-scoring debut against Georgia, has been blighted by knee injuries. In 2020, he helped Wasps reach a Premiership Final, winning the "Players' Player of the Year" award, the Premiership Player of the Season award, and the Discovery of the Season. A European Challenge Cup semi-finalist in 2022, he moved to Toulouse after Wasps were liquidated, reaching a Champions Cup semi-final and Top 14 final.

1419. MALINS, Maxim Hugo
Fly-half 2020-
Born: Cambridge, Cambridgeshire, 7 January 1997
Career: Saracens, Old Albanians, Bristol Bears
Debut: v Georgia, Twickenham, November 2020

Malins played for Bishop's Stortford until he joined Saracens Academy and, in 2016, helped Old Albanians return to the National League One after signing on a dual registration. He was in the Saracens side that lost to Northampton in the 2019 Premiership Rugby Cup final. After Saracens were relegated to the Championship, he spent the season with Bristol Bears, scoring a try in their 2020 European Challenge Cup Final victory. He was also a try scorer in Saracens' 2023 Premiership Final victory over Sale Sharks and helped England win the 2020 Autumn Nations Cup final. He returned to Bristol Bears for the 2023/24 campaign.

1420. OBANO, Ohwobeno Osemudiamen A.M
Prop 2021-
Born: Lambeth, London 25 October 1994
Career: Bath, Coventry,
Debut: v Scotland, Twickenham, February 2021

Obano was educated at the London Oratory School and then Dulwich College, where he was twice a National Schools Cup winner and was a member of Wasps academy but was released after suffering a long-term back injury before joining Bath. The cousin of England lock Maro Itoje, three days younger, he was loaned to Coventry to gain senior experience. He had two unsuccessful trials at Fulham as a youngster, produced a documentary called Everybody's Game, and made his England debut in 2021. Obano, a former barman, was named in England's 2023 World Cup training squad and founded Sinnybaby Media.

1421. MARTIN, George Frederick
Lock 2021-
Born: Nottingham, Nottinghamshire, 18 June 2001
Career: Leicester Tigers
Debut: v Ireland, Lansdowne Road, Dublin, March 2021

Martin was educated at Loughborough Grammar and Melton Brooksby College before joining the Leicester Tigers academy and was a member of the squad that went through two seasons with an unbeaten record. A former England under-18 captain, he recovered from being out of action for a year after seriously damaging his knee in his second Premiership appearance. He had only made seven appearances for the Tigers, scoring one try when Eddie Jones gave him his International debut. He was a European Challenge Cup semi-finalist in 2021 before coming off the bench for the Tigers' 2022 Premiership final victory. Martin came of age in England's semi-final defeat to South Africa at the 2023 World Cup.

1422. CHICK, Callum Jason
Back-Row 2021-
Born: Newcastle-upon-Tyne, Northumberland, 25 November 1996
Career: Newcastle Falcons
Debut: v USA, Twickenham, July 2021

Chick joined the Newcastle Falcons academy when he was 12 and made his way through the ranks to sign his first professional contract with the club at the end of the 2014/2015 campaign. An England under-18 international had already appeared in a first-team friendly against Sale Sharks and would go on and captain the Falcons sevens side. He helped England win the 2016 World Rugby Under-20 Championship and won the Falcons Academy Player of the Year award in 2017. He recovered from a serious knee injury to make his England debut against the USA in July 2021.

1423. HEYES, Joseph Connor Rhys
Prop 2021-
Born: Nottingham, Nottinghamshire, 13 April 1999
Career: Leicester Tigers, Loughborough Students
Debut: v USA, Twickenham, 4 July 2021

Heyes looked set to follow in the footsteps of his father, Darren, and grandfather, George, who was Gordon Banks's understudy at Leicester City when he became a goalkeeper in the Nottingham Forest academy. He started playing rugby at 14 with Nottingham Moderns, then Newark, before joining Leicester Tigers Academy, and Hayes came off the bench in their 2021 European Challenge Cup Final win over Montpellier, making his England debut weeks later. He was also a replacement in the Tigers 2022 Premiership Final win over Saracens, having become the second youngest prop in club history to make 100 appearances in the semi-final win over Northampton Saints.

1424. LANGDON, Curtis John
Hooker 2021-
Born: Weston-super-Mare, Somerset, 3 August 1997
Career: London Irish, Henley Hawks, Sale Sharks, Macclesfield, Doncaster Knights, Fylde, Worcester Warriors, Montpellier (FRA), Northampton Saints
Debut: v USA, Twickenham, 4 July 2021

Former England under-20 international Langdon started his career at London Irish but had to wait until he moved to Sale Sharks via a series of dual-registration loans to National League clubs to get his first taste of the Premiership. A member of the Sale side that won the 2020 Premiership Rugby Cup, scoring a try in the final win over Harlequins. He won his England caps against The USA and Canada the following summer. He and Cameron Neild reunited with former Sale boss Steve Diamond at Worcester Warriors but he headed to France when the club were liquidated three games later and joined Northampton Saints for the 2023/2024 campaign.

1425. LUDLOW, Lewis Wyndham
Back-Row 2021
Born: Bedford, Bedfordshire, 11 September 1994
Career: Gloucester
Debut: v USA, Twickenham, July 2021

Ludlow started playing at Ampthill RFC, where his father Paul was a coach and was offered a place at Hartpury College, joining Gloucester's academy when he was 17. He played for England at Under-18s, Under-19s and Under-20s levels. He was eligible for Wales through his grandfather and trained with Welsh under-18s. He was a member of the Gloucester squad that lost successive European Challenge Cup finals in 2017 and 2018. He became the fifth player in history to captain England on his debut when he made his bow on the international stage against the USA in July 2021 and is planning a future career in the police.

1426. McNALLY, Joshua James
Lock 2021-
Born: Ely, Cambridgeshire, 21 August 1990
Career: Henley Hawks, London Welsh, London Irish, Bath
Debut: v USA, Twickenham, July 2021

McNally joined the Royal Air Force as a weapons technician in 2009 and was allowed to join Henley Hawks as part of the Royal Air Force Rugby Union Centre of Excellence Scheme after being posted to RAF Brize Norton. He gained Premiership experience with London Welsh and then moved to London Irish when they were in the Championship. McNally was named UK Armed Forces Sportsman of the Year in 2018 and overcame a minor stroke caused by having a small hole in his heart to make his England debut in the 2021 summer test against the USA two months after playing for Bath in a European Challenge Cup semi-final.

1427. RANDALL, Harry Alan J
Scrum-half 2021-
Born: Slough, Berkshire 18 December 1997
Career: Hartpury College, Gloucester, Bristol Bears
Debut: v USA, Twickenham, July 2021

Randall was born in Slough, but the family moved to Wales when he was four. He is the younger brother of Jake Randall, the youngest player in the Scarlets history. He played for Wales under-18s before moving across the Seven Bridge to join Hartpury College, where he spent a season before being picked up by Bristol Bears ahead of their return to the Premiership via Gloucester. A 2016 World Rugby Under-20 Championship winner, he was a finalist and a Grand Slam winner a year later. He scored a try after 15 seconds in the Bears' 2020 European Rugby Challenge Cup final success.

1428. SMITH, Marcus Sebastian
Fly-half 2021-
Born: Manila, Philippines, 14 February 1999
Career: Harlequins
Debut: v USA, Twickenham, July 2021

Smith, who has an English father and Filipino mother, moved to England when he was 13 and won a sports scholarship to attend Brighton College. He first caught the eye playing for Harlequins in the 2016 Premiership Rugby Sevens Series and won the 2017 Under-18s Academy Final. He was a key member of the Quins side that secured the 2021 Premiership Final victory over Exeter Chiefs, which helped him earn an injury call into the Lions squad for their South Africa tour. He was first called into the England squad as an apprentice and was the highest points scorer in the 2022 Six Nations Championship.

1429. STEWARD, Frederick Nicholas Overbury
Full-back 2021-
Born: East Dereham, Norfolk, 5 December 2000
Career: Leicester Tigers, Ampthill
Debut: v USA, Twickenham, July 2021

Steward hailed from Leicester's fertile Norfolk breeding grounds and was in the Tigers academy team that won the National Under-18 League title in 2018 and 2019 without losing a game in either season. He soon established himself as one of the best full-backs in the World. In May 2022, He was named RPA Player's Young Player of the Year and England Men's Player of the Season and helped his side win the Premiership final. In November 2022, he was named full-back in world Rugby's Team of the Year before retaining his crown as the RPA's England men's Player of the Season.

1430. BLAMIRE, Jamie
Hooker 2021-
Born: Whitehaven, Cumbria 22 December 1997
Career: Newcastle Falcons, Tynedale
Debut: v USA, Twickenham, July 2021

Blamire started playing rugby league at Seaton Rangers before joining the Falcons as a Gosforth academy student who played for Tynedale before processing at Kingston Park. He was a 2017 under-20 Grand Slam and World Cup finalist who helped the Falcons reach the 2017 Premiership Rugby Cup semi-finals. He made his Premiership debut as a back-row replacement and was part of the squad which helped the Falcons to the 2019 A-League final and won promotion to the Premiership in 2020. He made his England debut against the USA in July 2021 and scored a hat-trick against Canada on his first start a week later.

1431. CURRY, Ben Anthony
Flanker 2021-
Born: Hounslow, Middlesex, 15 June 1998
Career: Sale Sharks,
Debut: v USA, Twickenham, July 2021

Curry, the twin brother of Tom, was educated at Oundle School, where his uncle, former England hooker John Olver taught, and shared the 2017 Sale Sharks Young Player of the Season award with his sibling. A member of the Sale side that lifted the 2020 Premiership Rugby Cup after beating Harlequins, he was also part of the England Under-20 side that won the Grand Slam in 2017 and captained the team that were the 2018 World Rugby Under-20 Championship finalists. He toured Argentina with England in 2017 but had to wait until 2021 to win his first cap, off the bench against the United States, but missed the 2023 Premiership final through injury.

1432. DAVISON, Trevor
Prop 2021-
Born: Newcastle-upon-Tyne, Northumberland, 20 August 1992
Career: Blaydon, Newcastle Falcons, Northampton Saints
Debut: v USA, Twickenham, July 2021

Davison started his career with his hometown club, Blaydon, and won England Counties honours while working as a joiner before signing professional forms with the Falcons. Davison, who can play on either side of the scrum, helped Newcastle reach the 2019 Premiership Rugby Cup semi-finals and promotion to the Premiership a year later. He clocked up over 100 appearances for Newcastle before, in March 2023, leaving to join Northampton Saints, with Oisin Heffernan moving in the opposite direction and appearing in a Premiership semi-final. He made his senior England debut off the bench against the USA and his second cap against Australia.

1433. UMAGA, Jacob Ionatana Falefasa
Fly-half 2021-
Born: Halifax, West Yorkshire, 8 July 1998
Career: Wasps, Hinckley, Yorkshire Carnegie, Auckland, Benetton (Ita)
Debut: v USA, Twickenham, July 2021

Umaga is a member of the famous rugby clan. His father, Mike, was capped by Samoa, and his uncle Tana by the All Blacks. He came through the Leicester Tigers Academy but left for Wasps when he was 18. He played in England's under-20s Grand Slam success and was a Junior World Cup Finalist in 2017, and was then part of the Auckland side that won the 2018 Mitre Cup. He was in the Wasps side that lost the 2020 Premiership Final to Exeter Chiefs before being made redundant when the club were liquidated. He won his England cap against the United States in 2021, a year after his first call-up.

1434. DOMBRANDT, Alex Joseph
No 8 2021 -
Born: South Croydon, Surrey, 29 April 1997
Career: Cardiff Met RFC, Harlequins,
Debut: v Canada, Twickenham, July 2021

Dombrandt was educated at John Fisher School in his native Croydon and started playing rugby at Warlingham when he was six. He spent three years at Cardiff Metropolitan University studying for a sport and physical education degree, playing for the University side. It made him eligible for the Welsh under-20 side, and he signed for his childhood club Harlequins in February 2018. At the end of his first season he scored in Harlequins' Premiership final win over Exeter Chiefs and scored two tries in a non-cap game against the Barbarians but had to wait until July 2021 to make his full-test debut against Canada.

1435. KELLY, Daniel
Centre 2021-
Born: Rochdale, Greater Manchester, 16 June 2001
Career: Loughborough Students, Leicester Tigers
Debut: v Canada, Twickenham, July 2021

Kirkham Grammar School-educated Kelly joined his local club in Rochdale when he was six before becoming part of the Sale Sharks Academy and even dabbled in rugby league with Wigan Warriors. After not being offered professional terms went to Loughborough University to take a degree in marketing and management, playing for the rugby team and soon caught the eye of Leicester Tigers. He joined the Tigers in April 2020 for the end of the delayed 2019-2020 campaign. The former Ireland under-20 international made his England debut against Canada in July 2021.

1436. RADWAN, Adam Belal Abdulmoneim
Winger 2021-
Born: Osmotherley, North Yorkshire, 30 December 1997
Career: Newcastle Falcons, Darlington Mowden Park
Debut: v Canada, Twickenham, July 2021

Radwan, who has an Egyptian father, started playing his junior rugby at Middlesbrough and then Billingham. He almost escaped the Newcastle net after being released from their senior academy after a season but returned after impressing playing sevens for the club. After becoming the top try scorer in the European Challenge Cup, he was named the 2018 Falcons' Academy Player of the Season. He was a key part of the Falcons side that were promoted back to the Premiership in 2020. Eddie Jones gave him his test debut against Canada after his impressive progress at England training and he responded by scoring a hat-trick of tries.

Andy Farrell

Callum Chick

Jamie Blamire

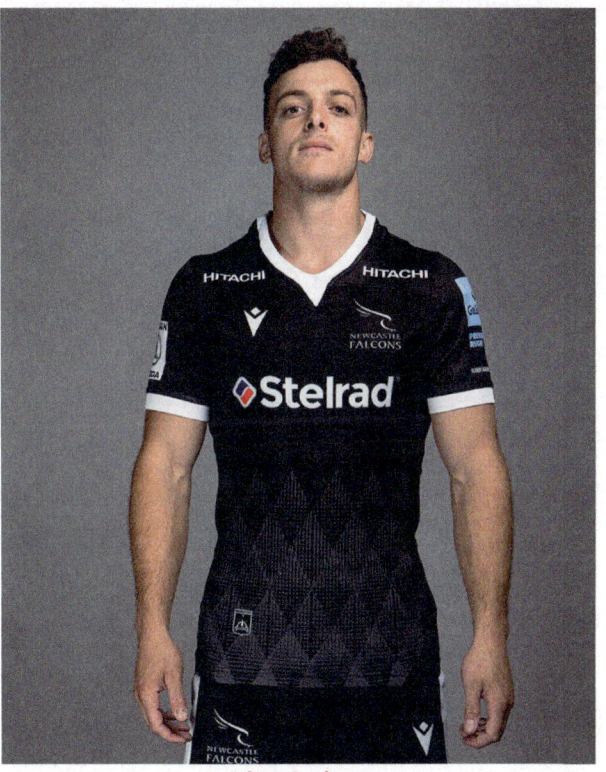

Adam Radwan

1437. WELLS, Harry Ronald
Lock 2021-
Born: Peterborough, Cambridgeshire, 29 September 1993
Career: Leicester Tigers, Nottingham, Bedford blues
Debut: v Canada, Twickenham, July 2021

Wells made his Leicester debut when he was 19 and spent time with Clermont Auvergne academy as part of a club exchange before being allowed to leave Welford Road for Bedford but re-joined two years later after helping the Blues reach the Championship playoffs. An England Under-20 Junior World Cup winner, he was part of the Tigers squad that reached the finals 2013 Premiership Sevens and was ever-present in the successful 2017 Anglo-Welsh Cup campaign. He was a replacement in The 2022 Premiership Final victory and was a semi-finalist in 2023, winning his only cap against Canada in the 2021 summer tests.

1438. ATKINSON, Mark James
Centre 1 cap 2021
Born: Knowsley, Merseyside, 8 March 1990
Career: Sale Sharks, Wasps, Esher, Bedford blues, Gloucester, Barbarians
Debut: v Tonga, Twickenham, November 2021

Atkinson got an overdue first cap, aged 31, and immediately said his time in rugby outside the Premiership, with Esher and Bedford, had made him the player he is. After spells at Sale and Wasps, he played three years in the Championship, the first when Esher got relegated in 2012 before joining Gloucester in 2014, passing 100 appearances for the club in the 2018-19 season. A severe knee injury in October 2022 put him out of the rest of that campaign. He was a member of the Gloucester side that were back-to-back European Challenge Cup finalists in 2017 and 2018 and was a Premiership semi-finalist in 2019.

1439. MITCHELL, Alexander Arthur David
Scrum-half 2021-
Born: Maidstone, Kent, 25 May 1997
Career: Northampton Saints
Debut: v Tonga, Twickenham, November 2021

Mitchell was in the Sale system before switching to the Northampton academy and making his first team debut in 2017. His England debut came in 2021, a season which saw him score 12 tries in 28 games for the Saints when he was named The Players' and Supporters' Player of the Season. He was a Premiership Rugby Cup winner in 2019 and three-times a Premiership semi-finalist and initially missed out on selection for the 2023 World Cup but finished the tournament as Steve Borthwick's first-choice scrum-half.

1440. RODD, Bevan
Prop 2 caps 2021
Born: Dunoon, Argyll and Bute, 26 August 2000
Career: Sale Sharks
Debut: v Australia, Twickenham, November 2021

Rodd, who grew up on the Isle of Man, got his first cap, starting against Australia in 2021 when Joe Marler and Ellis Genge pulled out of the game with Covid and followed up by starting against South Africa a week later. A product of Sedbergh School and the Sale academy, he spent much of his childhood in the Isle of Man and was a regular starter for Sharks by the age of 20. He was eligible for Scotland, where both parents played international volleyball and had ambitions to be a farmer. He played for Sale in their 2023 Premiership final defeat to Saracens.

1441. QUIRKE, Raphael
Scrum-half, 2 caps (5-1t) 2021
Born: Manchester, Lancashire, 18 August 2001
Career: Sale Sharks
Debut: v Australia, Twickenham, November 2021

Quirke was just 20 when he made his debut off the bench against Australia and a week later scored a crucial try in England's 27-26 win against the world champions, South Africa. He slipped down the scrum-half pecking order behind Jack van Poortvliet and Ben Youngs, and a hamstring injury in 2022 put him out of the Australia tour reckoning and much of the next season. He came through youth rugby at Broughton Park RFC, where his father Saul was a coach and was an age-group triathlon champion. A Premiership semi-finalist in 2021 and a finalist two years later.

1442. DOLLY, Nicholas
Hooker 2021-
Born: Sydney, Australia, 11 June 1999
Career: Sale Sharks, Leicester Tigers, Barbarians
Debut: v South Africa, Twickenham, 20 November 2021

Dolly was born in Australia but qualified for England through his mother, making his debut with 20 minutes off the bench against South Africa in 2021. The hooker was at Sale originally and had numerous spells with Championship clubs, the last being Coventry, from whom he joined Leicester in 2021. He marked his Tigers debut against Exeter that year with two tries, becoming the first forward to perform the feat on his league bow for 20 years. In May 2022, he suffered a severe knee injury after being crocodile-rolled by Newcastle's Adam Brocklebank and was out for 11 months, not playing in the entire 2022-23 Premiership season.

1443. CHESSUM, Oliver Andrew
Lock/flanker 2022-
Born: Boston, Lincolnshire, 6 September 2000
Career: Nottingham, Leicester Tigers
Debut: v Italy, Rome, Stadio Olimpico, February 2022

Chessum's dislocated ankle, suffered in England training, derailed his season when he had played the first four games of the 2023 Six Nations. The lock had joined Nottingham straight from Carres Grammar School in Lincolnshire and joined Leicester in 2020 after they had decided not to take him into their senior Academy. A Premiership winner in 2022, he also represented England Counties and had made his England debut in Rome earlier that year as a replacement for Tom Curry. He played in all three games on the victorious summer tour of Australia. His brother, Lewis, is also at Leicester and has played for England Under-20s.

1444. ARUNDELL, Henry
Full-back/wing, 2022-
Born: Dhekelia, Cyprus, 8 November 2002
Career: London Irish, Racing 92
Debut: v Australia, Optus Stadium, Perth, July 2022

Arundell set tongues wagging with a length-of-the-field score against Toulon for London Irish in the Challenge Cup in May 2022 and two months later was capped by England, scoring with his first touch in Perth. A foot injury wrecked his autumn campaign, but he returned for the 2023 Six Nations, starting the final game on the wing against Ireland in Dublin. Educated at Harrow, he starred in the 2022 Under-20 Six Nations and scored five tries in a 71-0 win over Chile at the 2023 World Cup before moving to Racing 92 following the collapse of London Irish. His contract extension in Paris made him ineligible for England until at least 2026.

1445. VAN POORTVLIET, Jack Corstiaan
Scrum-Half 2022-
Born: Norwich, Norfolk, 15 May 2001
Career: Leicester Tigers
Debut: v Australia, Optus Stadium, Perth, July 2022

Van Poortvliet, schooled at Oakham, got over being dropped from Leicester's Premiership final team in 2022 after playing in the semi-final and also in the Premiership Rugby Cup last four by scoring on his test debut in Perth the next month. Originally a fly-half, he switched to No.9 in Leicester academy's league-winning season in 2018. He injured his ankle in a warm-up game against Wales and was ruled out of the 2023 World Cup after being named in the squad. His great-great-grandfather came to England from Holland before World War One, and he has Scottish ancestry on his mother Clare's side.

1446. FREEMAN, Thomas William
Wing 2022-
Born: Oxford, Oxfordshire, 5 March 2001
Career: Northampton Saints
Debut: v Australia, Lang Park, Brisbane, July 2022

Freeman was released by the Leicester academy as a 16-year-old. He joined Northampton's senior academy in 2019 and made his Saints debut at 19 in 2020. He scored 14 tries in 18 games in 2021-22 and toured Australia with England, making his debut in the second test of the summer series. At 6ft 2in and weighing over 16 stone, he can play wing, centre or full-back but did not have the technique for a test player when Leicester rejected him. He went to Moulton College, in Northamptonshire, which has a sports academy and bulked up sufficiently to attract Northampton's interest. He was a fly-half as a youngster and a Harlequins fan.

1447. PORTER, Guy Edward
Centre 2022-
Born: Kensington, London, 23 January 1997
Career: Sydney Stars (Aus), Sydney Rays (Aus), Brumbies (Aus), Leicester
Debut: v Australia, Lang Park, Brisbane, July 2022

Porter played for Rosslyn Park as a young boy before moving to Australia with his parents when he was seven. He studied at Sydney University and got into the Brumbies system, signing for the franchise in 2019. Covid wrecked the 2020 Super Rugby season, so he headed to Leicester and, within two years, was in the England team on tour, back in Australia. He had a thigh injury in 2023 but recovered to be called up to the Six Nations training squad by Steve Borthwick, who had signed him for Leicester, without playing a game.

1448. JOSEPH, William
Centre 2022-
Born: Derby, Derbyshire, 15 July 2002
Career: London Irish
Debut: v Australia, Lang Park, Brisbane, July 2022

Joseph, younger brother of former England centre Jonathan, was taken as one of Eddie Jones' apprentices on the 2022 summer tour and ended up coming off the bench in the second test and being an unused replacement in the third. He joined the London Irish Academy at 13 and made his Premiership debut in 2021 before he was catapulted into the national reckoning. Educated at Millfield, he was involved in the choir and rugby. The school's head of rugby, John Mallett, described him as a replica of his brother on the pitch. Sister Hannah plays netball for England and Loughborough Lightning.

1449. COLES, Alexander Joel C
Lock 2022-
Born: Cambridge, Cambridgeshire, 21 September 1999
Career: Northampton Saints
Debut: v Argentina, Twickenham, November 2022

Coles has won the Blakiston Challenge, a gruelling annual pre-season endurance test at Northampton, twice - the only player to do so - and the first forward to come out on top. The second row, who can also play flanker, made his Saints debut in 2018, a year after touring South Africa with England Under-18s. As a young boy, he played for Cambridge, Newmarket and Shelford and, as a professional player, studied politics, philosophy and history part-time at Birbeck College in London. He started against Argentina in 2022 and came off the bench against Japan but was not involved in the 2023 Six Nations.

1450. RIBBANS, David George
Lock, 4 caps 2022-2023
Born: Somerset West, South Africa, 29 August 1995
Career: Western Province (SA), Stormers (SA), Northampton Saints, Toulon (Fra)
Debut: v Japan, Twickenham, November 2022

Ribbans played for Western Province age-grade sides, the senior team in the Currie Cup, and briefly for the Stormers in Super Rugby. In 2017, the second row headed to Northampton and passed 100 appearances for the Saints in the 2021-22 season. He made his England debut in 2022 but had been in training camp as far back as 2020 when he started against Japan and made two more appearances off the bench. Ollie Chessum's injury in 2023 saw him drafted back into the squad for the final Six Nations game against Ireland. A commerce graduate from the University of Cape Town, he signed for Toulon in 2023.

1451. HASSELL-COLLINS, Oliver John
Wing 2023-
Born: Reading, Berkshire, 17 January 1999
Career: Rosslyn Park, Rams, London Irish, Leicester
Debut: v Scotland, Twickenham, February 2023

Hassell-Collins passed 100 appearances for London Irish in the 2022-23 season. It was announced in March 2023 that he would be joining Leicester for the next campaign, before the Exiles were banished from the Premiership. A big wing, good under the high ball, he played England Under-20s and Sevens before his first senior cap. He played the first two games of the 2023 Six Nations but was injured for the third, against Wales, and Anthony Watson came for the rest of the tournament. He was axed from the second of three World Cup training squads in June 2023.

1452. WALKER, Jack Robert
Hooker 2023-
Born: Steeton, West Yorkshire, 6 May 1996
Career: Yorkshire Carnegie, Bath, Harlequins
Debut: v Italy, Stadio Olimpico, Rome, February 2023

Walker was on the bench for the 2023 Six Nations, coming on three times, which was a reward for perseverance in stints at three clubs. He had captained England Under-20s at the 2016 Junior World Cup, won by England, but missed the final with a concussion. It took another six years for him to get his first call-up from Eddie Jones in 2022, touring Australia, but Luke Cowan-Dickie's injury gave him the opportunity to understudy Jamie George the next year. He had captained Yorkshire Carnegie as a very young player before moving to Bath and then, in 2021, Harlequins.

1453. PEARSON, Tom
Flanker 2023-
Born: Hereford, Herefordshire, 26 October 1999
Career: Cardiff Met, London Irish, Northampton Saints
Debut: v Wales, Principality Stadium, Cardiff, 5 August 2023

A physical flanker, Pearson first caught the attention of Eddie Jones when the Australian named him a training squad in May 2022. He was caught up in the collapse of London Irish and signed for Northampton in 2023, remaining in the England camp before they left for France despite not being named in the squad for the tournament. A product of Cardiff Metropolitan University, like Alex Dombrandt, he was at the Gloucester academy before joining Irish. He was named Premiership Rugby's Breakthrough Player of the Year and the RPA's Young Player of the Year for the 2022-23 season.

1454. DAN, Theodor
Hooker 2023-
Born: London, 26 December 2000
Career: Saracens, Bishops Stortford (loan). Ampthill (loan)
Debut: v Wales, Principality Stadium, Cardiff, 5 August 2023

Dan was England's big bolter for the 2023 World Cup when he was picked for the squad, having been playing in the Championship on loan at Ampthill at the start of the season. Recalled by Saracens because of an injury crisis, he ended up playing 70 minutes of the Premiership final win over Sale when Jamie George went off early. Born in London, of Romanian descent, he played England Under-18s and 20s and was named in the party for France 2023 two days after his test debut. At the World Cup, he made four appearances, scoring against Chile and in the bronze medal match against Argentina.

1455. WILLIS, Thomas Daniel
No.8 2023-
Born: Reading, Berkshire 18 January 1999
Career: Wasps, Bordeaux-Begles (Fra), Saracens
Debut: v Wales, Principality Stadium, Cardiff, 5 August 2023

Willis made his England debut off the bench in the World Cup warm-up game against Wales to cap a tumultuous year which saw him move to Bordeaux-Begles in the French Top 14 when his boyhood club Wasps went to the wall. He played at Reading Abbey as a youngster, following brother Jack, and played at Under-18 and 20 level for England, captaining the latter age group. A Premiership finalist for Wasps in 2020, he moved to Saracens in 2023 from France to keep his England aspirations alive.

PLAYER INDEX

Aarvold, Carl 113
Abbott, Stuart 201
Abendanon, Nick 207
Ackford, Paul 184
Adams, Frank 20
Adams, Alan 93
Adebayo, Adedayo 190
Adey, Garry 172
Adkins, Akker 141
Agar, Albert 143
Alcock, Arnold 85
Alderson, Frederic 49
Alexander, Harry 74
Alexander, William 20
Allen, Anthony 204
Allison, Fenwick 147
Allport, Alfred 50
Anderson, Stanley 67
Anderson, Frank 169
Anderton, Charles 41
Andrew, Rob 181
Appleford, Geoff 199
Archer, Herbert 90
Archer, Garath 190
Armand, Don 219
Armitage, Delon 208
Armitage, Steffon 209
Armstrong, Rex 110
Arthur, Terry 158
Arundell, Henry 226
Ashby, Clive 160
Ashcroft, Alec 89
Ashcroft, Ned 147
Ashford, William 89
Ashton, Chris 210
Ashworth, Abel 51
Askew, John 117
Aslett, Alfred 110
Assinder, Eric 89
Aston, Randolph 48
Atkinson, Mark 226
Attwood, Dave 211
Auty, Dick 129
Back, Neil 188
Bailey, Mark 179
Bainbridge, Steve 178
Baker, Hiatt 40
Baker, Edward 55
Baker, Doug 146
Balshaw, Iain 196
Banahan, Matt 209
Bance, John 145
Barkley, Olly 198
Barley, Bryan 179
Barnes, Stuart 180
Baron, James 62
Barr, Bobby 123
Barrett, Edward 79
Barrington-Ward, Lancelot 91
Barrington, Jimmy 121
Barritt, Brad 212
Bartlett, Jasper 141
Bartlett, Ricky 150
Barton, John 162
Batchelor, Tremlett 85
Bates, Steve 186
Bateson, Harold 31
Bateson, Alfred 117
Batson, Thomas 15
Batten, John 18

Baume, John 141
Baxendell, Jos 195
Baxter, Bim 68
Bayfield, Martin 187
Bazley, Reginald 144
Beal, Nick 191
Beaumont, Bill 170
Bedford, Harry 42
Bedford, Lawrence 121
Beer, Ian 147
Beese, Mike 168
Beim, Tom 195
Bell, John 25
Bell, Henry 37
Bell, Fred 68
Bell, Robert 68
Bell, Peter 163
Bell, Duncan 203
Bendon, Gordon 151
Bennett, Billy 171
Bennett, Neil 133
Bennetts, Barrie 89
Bentley, John Edmund 13
Bentley, John 184
Benton, Scott 193
Berridge, Mike 138
Berry, John 49
Berry, Harry 92
Berry, Tom 132
Beswick, Teddy 34
Biggs, John 24
Birkett, Reginald 13
Birkett, Louis 21
Birkett, John 84
Bishop, Colin 133
Black, Brian 117
Blacklock, Joseph 64
Blakeway, Phil 176
Blakiston, Freddie 103
Blamire, Jamie 224
Blatherwick, Thomas 25
Body, James 15
Bolton, Wilfred 34
Bolton, Charles 90
Bolton, Reggie 125
Bonaventura, Maurice 121
Bond, Tony 174
Bonham-Carter, Edgar 50
Bonson, Fred 39
Boobbyer, Brian 139
Booth, Lewis 125
Borthwick, Steve 197
Botha, Mouritz 211
Botting, Ian 140
Boughton, Harold 127
Boyle, Cecil 17
Boyle, Steve 178
Boylen, Patsy 87
Bracken, Kyran 188
Bradby, Matthew 103
Bradley, Robert 78
Bradshaw, Harry 52
Brain, Steve 180
Braithwaite-Exley, Bryan 138
Braithwaite, Jacky 82
Brettargh, Arthur 68
Brewer, Jeaffreson 21
Briggs, Arthur 50
Brinn, Alan 168
Broadley, Tom 52

Bromet, William 49
Brook, Peter 121
Brooke, Terence 164
Brookes, Kieran 216
Brooks, Marshall 18
Brooks, Freddie 85
Brophy, Tom 157
Brough, Jim 109
Brougham, Henry 95
Brown, Bruno 94
Brown, Tom 114
Brown, Alan 132
Brown, Spencer 194
Brown, Alex 204
Brown, Mike 206
Brunton, Joseph 97
Brutton, Rev 40
Bryden, Henry 18
Bryden, Charles 21
Buckingham, Ralph 113
Bucknall, Tony 165
Buckton, John 186
Budd, Jimmy 26
Budworth, Richard 47
Bull, Arthur 98
Bullough, Ned 51
Bulpitt, Mike 165
Bulteel, Mark 21
Bunting, William 63
Burgess, Sam 216
Burland, Don 122
Burns, Benjamin 13
Burns, Freddie 214
Burrell, Luther 215
Burton, George 26
Burton, Hyde 111
Burton, Mike 168
Bush, James 15
Butcher, Walter 79
Butcher, Chris 179
Butler, Arthur 130
Butler, Peter 171
Butterfield, Jeff 144
Byrne, Fred 54
Byrne, Francis 62
Cain, John 140
Cairns, Matt 206
Callard, Jon 188
Campbell, David 130
Candler, Peter 127
Cannell, Lewis 137
Caplan, David 174
Cardus, Richard 174
Care, Danny 208
Carey, Godfrey 55
Carleton, John 174
Carling, Will 183
Carpenter, Alfred 123
Carr, Robert 132
Cartwright, Vincent 78
Catcheside, Carston 108
Catt, Mike 188
Cattell, Dick 60
Cave, John 42
Cave, William 80
Challis, Bob 150
Chambers, Ernest 87
Chantrill, Bunny 108
Chapman, Charles 37
Chapman, Fred 92

Chapman, Dominic 194
Cheesman, William 96
Chessum, Ollie 226
Cheston, Ernest 17
Chick, Callum 223
Chilcott, Gareth 180
Christophers, Phil 199
Christopherson, Percy 49
Chuter, George 204
Cipriani, Danny 207
Clark, Charles 22
Clark, Calum 216
Clarke, Allan 127
Clarke, Simon 155
Clarke, Ben 188
Clayton, John 13
Clements, Jeff 151
Cleveland, Charles 40
Clibborn, William 39
Clifford, Jack 217
Clough, Fran 182
Coates, Charles 33
Coates, Vincent 96
Cobby, William 68
Cockerham, Arthur 73
Cockerill, Richard 192
Codling, Alex 199
Cohen, Ben 196
Cokanasiga, Joe 220
Colclough, Maurice 174
Cole, Dan 210
Coles, Alex 227
Coley, Eric 116
Collier, Will 219
Collins, William 19
Collins, Philip 144
Considine, Stanley 110
Conway, Geoffrey 101
Cook, John 131
Cook, Peter 158
Cooke, Paul 132
Cooke, David Alexander 172
Cooke, David Howard 176
Coop, Thomas 52
Cooper, John 89
Cooper, Martin 170
Coopper, Sydney 73
Corbett, Len 103
Corbisiero, Alex 211
Corless, Barry 172
Corry, Martin 191
Cotton, Fran 167
Coulman, Mike 161
Coulson, Thomas 112
Court, Edward 38
Cove-Smith, Ron 103
Coverdale, Harry 93
Cowan-Dickie, Luke 216
Cowling, Robin 173
Cowman, Dick 167
Cox, Norman 76
Crane, Jordan 209
Cranmer, Peter 126
Creed, Roger 167
Cridlan, Arthur 129
Croft, Tom 207
Crompton, Charles 13
Crompton, Darren 206
Crosse, Charles 19
Cueto, Mark 202

Cumberlege, Barry..............99
Cumming, Duncan.............110
Cunliffe, Foster....................19
Currey, Fred..........................16
Currie, John........................149
Curry, Tom..........................218
Curry, Ben...........................224
Cusani, David......................183
Cusworth, Les......................176
D'Aguilar, Francis..................16
Dallaglio, Lawrence............189
Dalton, Timothy..................164
Daly, Elliot..........................217
Dan, Theo............................228
Danby, Tom.........................138
Daniell, John.........................66
Darby, Arthur........................67
Davenport, Alfred.................13
Davey, Maffer........................88
Davey, Richard....................122
Davidson, James...................64
Davidson, Joseph..................66
Davies, Dave.........................96
Davies, Harry......................112
Davies, Phil.........................144
Davies, Huw........................176
Davies, Vivian.....................103
Davis, Mike.........................155
Davison, Trevor...................224
Dawe, Graham.....................183
Dawson, Ernest.....................26
Dawson, Matt......................189
Day, Harold...........................99
de Glanville, Phil.................188
de Winton, Robert.................52
Deacon, Louis......................203
Dean, Tinny.........................122
Dee, John.............................154
Devitt, Thomas....................111
Devoto, Ollie.......................217
Dewhurst, John......................40
Dibble, Robert.......................84
Dicks, John..........................126
Dickson, Lee........................212
Dillon, Edward......................79
Dingle, Arthur........................97
Diprose, Tony......................191
Dixon, Peter.........................167
Dobbs, George.......................83
Doble, Sam..........................169
Dobson, Thomas...................61
Dobson, Denys.......................77
Dodge, Paul.........................173
Dolly, Nic.............................226
Dombrandt, Alex.................224
Donnelly, Squib..................135
Dooley, Wade......................181
Doran-Jones, Paul..............210
Dovey, Beverley..................155
Down, Percy..........................89
Dowson, Aubrey....................67
Dowson, Phil.......................212
Drake-Lee, Nick..................155
Duckett, Horace.....................53
Duckham, David.................164
Dudgeon, Herbert..................64
Dugdale, John........................13
Dun, Andy...........................179
Duncan, Robert...................104
Duncombe, Nick.................199
Dunkley, Pop.......................122
Dunn, Tom..........................222
Duthie, James........................78
Dyson, Jack............................48
Earl, Ben..............................222
Easter, Nick.........................205
Eastmond, Kyle...................214
Ebdon, Percy..........................62
Eddison, John........................95
Edgar, Charles.......................76
Edwards, Reg......................103
Egerton, Dave......................184
Elliot, Charles........................39
Elliot, Edgar...........................74
Elliot, Walter........................125
Elliott, Albert..........................55
Ellis, Sidney...........................32
Ellis, Jack.............................133
Ellis, Harry...........................202
Emmott, Charles...................51
Enthoven, Henry....................26
Erinle, Ayoola......................210
Estcourt, Noel......................147
Evans, Barney......................125
Evans, Barry........................184
Evans, Eric...........................136
Evans, Geoff........................169
Evanson, Wyndham..............21
Evanson, Arthur.....................35
Evershed, Frank.....................42
Ewels, Charlie......................218
Eyres, Wallace.....................112
Fagan, Arthur.........................41
Fairbrother, Keith................164
Faithfull, Chubby................109
Fallas, Herbert.......................37
Farrell, Andy........................205
Farrell, Owen.......................212
Fegan, John...........................60
Fernandes, Charles...............33
Fidler, John..........................177
Fidler, Rob...........................195
Field, Edwin...........................52
Fielding, Keith.....................164
Finch, Richard........................33
Finlan, John.........................162
Finlinson, Horace..................60
Finney, Stephen.....................16
Firth, Frederick......................54
Flatman, David....................196
Fletcher, Tom.........................63
Fletcher, Nigel........................74
Fletcher, William....................17
Flood, Toby..........................205
Flutey, Riki...........................208
Foden, Ben...........................209
Fookes, Ernest.......................61
Ford, George........................215
Ford, Peter...........................156
Forrest, Reggie.......................66
Forrest, Jeff..........................117
Forrester, James...................203
Foulds, Roy..........................114
Fourie, Hendre.....................211
Fowler, Frank.........................25
Fowler, Henry........................23
Fowler, Howard.....................25
Fox, Francis...........................47
Francis, Piers........................219
Francis, Tim.........................111
Frankcom, Geoff..................157
Fraser, Edward......................20
Fraser, George.......................77
Freakes, Hubert...................131
Freeman, Harold...................16
Freeman, Tommy................227
French, Ray..........................153
Freshwater, Perry................203
Fry, Henry............................126
Fry, Thomas..........................32
Fuller, Herbert.......................34
Furbank, George..................221
Gadney, Bernard..................125
Gamlin, Herbert.....................67
Gardner, Ernest....................103
Gardner, Herbert...................26
Garforth, Darren..................191
Garnett, Harry.......................24
Gavins, Mike........................153
Gay, David...........................163
Genge, Ellis..........................217
Gent, Dai...............................82
Genth, James.........................19
George, James.....................135
George, Jamie......................217
Geraghty, Shane..................205
Gerrard, Ronald...................124
Gibbs, George......................136
Gibbs, John..........................109
Gibbs, Nigel.........................145
Giblin, Lyndhurst..................61
Gibson, Arthur.......................14
Gibson, Charles.....................74
Gibson, George.....................67
Gibson, Thomas....................80
Gilbert, Dick..........................88
Gilbert, Frederick................104
Giles, Jimmy........................129
Gittings, Bill.........................162
Glover, Peter........................161
Godfray, Reginald.................82
Godwin, Herbert..................152
Gomarsall, Andy..................190
Goode, Alex.........................213
Goode, Andy........................203
Gordon-Smith, Gerald..........73
Graham, David......................75
Graham, Harry.......................20
Graham, John........................23
Gray, Arthur.........................133
Gray, Joe..............................215
Grayson, Paul......................189
Green, John............................81
Green, Joseph........................14
Green, Will...........................192
Greening, Phil......................190
Greenstock, Nick.................191
Greenwell, John.....................53
Greenwood, Dick................160
Greenwood, John...................96
Greenwood, Will.................193
Greg, Walter..........................22
Gregory, Gordon..................122
Gregory, Jack.......................138
Grewcock, Danny................192
Grylls, William.......................81
Guest, Dickie.......................132
Guillemard, Arthur................14
Gummer, Charles................116
Gunner, Charles.....................22
Gurdon, Charles....................32
Gurdon, Temple....................25
Guscott, Jerry.......................186
Haag, Martin........................192
Haigh, Leonard......................92
Hale, Peter...........................165
Halford, George.....................99
Hall, Charley..........................75
Hall, John...............................54
Hall, Jon...............................178
Hall, 'Nim'...........................134
Halliday, Simon....................182
Hamersley, Alfred..................14
Hamilton-Hill, Edward........130
Hamilton-Wickes, Richard....109
Hammett, Ernest...................99
Hammond, 'Curly'.................81
Hancock, Andy.....................151
Hancock, Froude...................39
Hancock, George.................133
Hancock, Patrick...................79
Hancock, William.................146
Handford, Frank....................90
Hands, Reginald....................93
Hanley, Jerry........................112
Hanley, Steve.......................195
Hannaford, Charlie..............166
Hanvey, Bob........................111
Hape, Shontayne..................210
Harding, Ernest....................123
Harding, Richard.................181
Harding, Victor....................154
Hardwick, Peter.....................78
Hardwick, Rob.....................191
Hardy, Evan.........................142
Hare, Dusty..........................170
Harper, Charles.....................67
Harriman, Andy...................184
Harris, Stan..........................102
Harris, Thomas....................115
Harrison, Arthur....................98
Harrison, Cliff......................123
Harrison, Gillie......................24
Harrison, Harold....................91
Harrison, Mike.....................182
Harrison, Teimana...............217
Hartley, Dylan......................209
Hartley, Jock..........................76
Haskell, James......................206
Haslett, Leslie......................111
Hassell-Collins, Ollie...........227
Hastings, George.................146
Havelock, Harry.....................87
Hawcridge, John....................38
Hayward, Leslie.....................92
Hazell, Andy.........................202
Hazell, David........................146
Healey, Austin......................191
Hearn, Bob...........................161
Heath, Arthur.........................23
Heaton, Jack........................129
Heinz, Willi..........................221
Henderson, Alan..................134
Henderson, Robert................35
Henniker-Gotley, Anthony.....93
Hepburn, Alec......................220
Heppel, Walter.......................79
Herbert, Alfred.....................150
Hesford, Bob.......................177
Heslop, Nigel.......................186
Hetherington, Jim................150
Hewitt, Ted............................33
Hewitt, Walter......................141
Heyes, Joe............................233
Hickson, John........................40
Higgins, Reg........................145
Hignell, Alastair...................172
Hill, Basil...............................79
Hill, Jonny............................222
Hill, Paul..............................217
Hill, Richard Anthony.........191
Hill, Richard John................179
Hill, Ted................................220
Hillard, Ronald.....................109
Hiller, Bob...........................163
Hind, Alfred...........................82
Hind, Guy...............................94
Hipkiss, Dan.........................207
Hobbs, Reginald Francis......68
Hobbs, Reginald Geoffrey....124
Hobson, Jason......................208
Hodges, Harold.....................83
Hodgkinson, Simon.............186
Hodgson, Charlie.................198
Hodgson, John.....................124
Hodgson, Paul......................207
Hodgson, Stan.....................152
Hofmeyr, Murray..................140
Hogarth, Thomas...................84
Holland, Dave........................95
Holliday, 'Toff'.....................108
Holmes, Barry......................138
Holmes, Cyril.......................135
Holmes, Edgar.......................48
Holmes, Wally......................140
Hook, William......................143

Hooper, Charles 54
Hopley, Damian....................189
Hopley, John 85
Horak, Michael 199
Hordern, Peter 123
Horley, Charles......................39
Hornby, 'Monkey' 24
Horrocks-Taylor, Phil 150
Horsfall, Edward..................138
Horton, John 173
Horton, Nigel 164
Horton, Tony.........................157
Hosen, Roger 156
Hosking, Geoffrey 139
Houghton, Samuel 51
Howard, Peter 117
Hubbard, George 121
Hubbard, John 51
Hudson, Arthur.......................83
Hughes, George 62
Hughes, Nathan 218
Hull, Paul 189
Hulme, Frankie 78
Hunt, James 34
Hunt, Robert..........................32
Hunt, William 23
Hunter, Ian............................187
Huntsman, Paul...................182
Hurst, Andy..........................154
Huskisson, Thomas.............130
Hutchinson, Frank.................90
Hutchinson, James 83
Hutchinson, William Charles..23
Hutchinson, William Henry....20
Huth, Harry 26
Hyde, John...........................141
Hynes, William 96
Ibbitson, Ernest 90
Imrie, Henry...........................82
Inglis, Rupert..........................39
Irvin, Sam 80
Isherwood, Francis.................16
Isiekwe, Nick 219
Itoje, Maro............................217
Jackett, John 82
Jackson, Allan.........................26
Jackson, Barry......................166
Jackson, Peter......................149
Jackson, Walter......................55
Jacob, Frederick.....................63
Jacob, Jake...........................108
Jacob, Philip 65
Jacobs, Ron..........................149
Jago, Raphael.........................83
Janion, Jeremy.....................166
Jarman, Wallace.....................73
Jeavons, Nick.......................176
Jeeps, Dickie........................149
Jeffery, George......................39
Jennins, Christopher 161
Jewitt, John 77
Johns, William 90
Johnson, Martin...................188
Johnson, Tom......................213
Johnston, Billy.......................92
Johnston, Ben 199
Jones, Chris 201
Jones, Frederic.......................53
Jones, Herbert 140
Jorden, Tony........................166
Joseph, Jonathan 213
Joseph, Will..........................227
Jowett, Donald 42
Judd, Phil 154
Kay, Ben...............................197
Kayll, Henry............................25
Keeling, John 136
Keen, Brian..........................163
Keeton, George 79
Kelly, Dan 224
Kelly, Geoffrey 134
Kelly, Thomas 83
Kemble, Arthur......................38
Kemp, Dudley 129
Kemp, Tommy 131
Kendall-Carpenter, John....139
Kendall, Toggie 76
Kendrew, Joe........................117
Kennedy, Robert 139
Kennedy, Nick......................208
Kent, Charles 173
Kent, Tom...............................49
Kershaw, Cecil 99
Kewley, Edward 19
Kewney, Alf 83
Key, Alan...............................121
Keyworth, Mark 172
Kilner, Barron 32
Kindersley, Richard 36
King, Alex.............................192
King, Ian...............................145
King, John 94
King, Quentin.......................103
Kingston, Peter.....................171
Kirwan-Taylor, William.......113
Kitching, Alfred 97
Kittermaster, Harold...........109
Knight, Frederick 89
Knight, Peter 168
Knowles, Edward...................62
Knowles, Tom 123
Krige, Jannie 99
Kruis, George 216
Kvesic, Matt..........................214
Labuschagne, Nick 144
Lagden, Ronald......................95
Laird, Colin 112
Lambert, Danny.....................85
Lampkowski, Mike..............172
Langdon, Curtis 223
Lapage, Walter.......................87
Larter, Peter.........................161
Launchbury, Joe 213
Law, Archibald 24
Law, Douglas 113
Lawes, Courtney..................210
Lawrence, Henry 17
Lawrence, Ollie 222
Lawrie, Percy..........................94
Lawson, Richard 110
Lawson, Thomas 114
le Fleming, John 41
Leadbetter, Mike 168
Leadbetter, Vic.....................146
Leake, William........................50
Leather, Jumbo......................86
Lee, Frederic 23
Lee, Harry...............................85
Leonard, Jason.....................186
Leslie-Jones, Frederick..........60
Lewis, Alec...........................143
Lewsey, Josh.........................194
Leyland, Roy.........................129
Linnett, Mark 186
Lipman, Michael..................202
Livesay, Robert 66
Lloyd, Bob 163
Lloyd, Leon...........................197
Locke, Harold.......................108
Lockwood, Dicky...................41
Login, Spencer 22
Lohden, Frederick 53
Long, Andy 193
Longland, Ray......................125
Lowe, Cyril.............................96
Lowrie, Fred 42
Lowry, Wilfrid......................101
Lozowski, Rob......................180
Lozowski, Alex 218
Luddington, William...........108
Ludlam, Lewis......................221
Ludlow, Lewis 223
Luger, Dan............................195
Lund, Magnus......................204
Luscombe, Frank...................16
Luscombe, Harry 14
Luxmoore, Arthur 74
Luya, Humphrey..................137
Lyon, Arthur...........................14
Lyon, George 68
MacIlwaine, Alfred 95
Mackie, Osbert 64
Mackinlay, James...................16
MacLaren, William.................14
MacLennan, Roderick 110
Madge, Richard 137
Malins, Max..........................222
Malir, Frank..........................117
Mallett, John........................189
Mallinder, Jim......................192
Mangles, Roland....................63
Manley, Dick 155
Mann, William........................94
Mantell, Neil........................171
Mapletoft, Mark...................192
Marchant, Joe 221
Markendale, Ellis 32
Marler, Joe...........................213
Marques, David 149
Marquis, John 74
Marriott, Charles 37
Marriott, Ernest 22
Marriott, Victor 156
Marsden, George 73
Marsh, Henry.........................17
Marsh, James 52
Marshall, Howard..................53
Marshall, Mike 132
Marshall, Murray....................18
Martin, Chris 181
Martin, George 223
Martin, Nick.........................169
Martindale, Sam 116
Massey, Edward 110
Mather, Barrie-Jon 196
Mathias, John.........................80
Matters, John 68
Matthews, John 139
Maud, Philip...........................53
Maunder, Jack......................219
Maxwell-Hyslop, John 104
Maxwell, Andy 171
May, Jonny 209
May, Tom 214
Maynard, Alfred 98
McCanlis, Maurice 122
McCarthy, Neil 195
McConnochie, Ruaridh 221
McFadyean, Colin 150
McLeod, Norman 31
McNally, Josh 223
Mears, Lee...........................203
Meikle, Graham 127
Meikle, Stephen...................115
Mellish, Frank 101
Melville, Nigel 180
Mercer, Zach........................220
Merriam, Laurence 101
Michell, Arthur.......................20
Middleton, Bernard 35
Middleton, John..................104
Miles, Jack..............................78
Millett, Harry........................101
Mills, Frederick 16
Mills, Steve 177
Mills, William..........................83
Milman, Dermot..................131
Milton, Cecil 84
Milton, Jumbo 79
Milton, William.......................19
Mitchell, Alex 226
Mitchell, Frank 60
Mitchell, Willie 47
Mobbs, Edgar.........................89
Moberly, William 17
Monye, Ugo.........................208
Moody, Lewis.......................197
Moon, Ben...........................220
Moore, Bill...........................134
Moore, Brian........................183
Moore, Edward......................36
Moore, Norman.....................80
Moore, Philip 141
Mordell, Bob 174
Morfitt, Samuel......................54
Morgan, James....................101
Morgan, Ben 212
Morgan, Derek.....................152
Morgan, Olly 205
Morley, Alan.........................169
Morris, Alfred.........................89
Morris, Dewi 184
Morris, Robbie.....................201
Morrison, Dolly......................48
Morse, Sydney.......................18
Mortimer, William 67
Morton, Harold......................91
Moss, Frank...........................38
Mullan, Matt........................210
Mullins, Andy 186
Mycock, Joe 134
Myers, Edward.....................102
Myers, Harry..........................65
Myler, Stephen 215
Nanson, Billy..........................85
Narraway, Luke 207
Nash, Edward 20
Neale, Bruce 142
Neale, Maurice 96
Neame, Stuart 31
Neary, Tony..........................166
Nelmes, Barry.......................171
Newbold, Charles..................80
Newman, Syd.......................136
Newton, Andrew 86
Newton, Philip 35
Newton-Thompson, Ossie....136
Nicholas, Philip 86
Nicholl, William......................35
Nicholson, Basil 132
Nicholson, Elliot.....................73
Nicholson, Ernie 129
Nicholson, Thomas 53
Ninnes, Barry.......................166
Noon, Jamie 197
Norman, Doug.....................124
North, Eustace 50
Northmore, Samuel 64
Novak, John.........................165
Novis, Tony 116
Nowell, Jack.........................215
O'Neill, Arthur........................75
Oakeley, Francis 97
Oakes, Robert........................63
Oakley, Lionel 141
Obano, Beno........................222
Obolensky, Alexander 130
Ojo, Topsy 208
Ojomoh, Steve.....................188
Old, Alan..............................168
Oldham, William....................88
Olver, John 187
Openshaw, William 31
Orwin, John 181
Osborne, Richard 14
Osborne, Sidney....................81

Oti, Chris 184	Purdy, Stanley...................154	Rowell, Bob 157	Slocock, Andrew 85
Oughtred, Bernard 76	Pyke, James 51	Rowley, Arthur.................124	Slow, Charlie 127
Owen, John 155	Pym, John 95	Rowley, Hugh 31	Small, Harry 140
Owen-Smith, Tuppy 127	Quinn, Pat 145	Rowntree, Graham 189	Smallwood, Alastair 102
Page, Jacko 167	Quirke, Raffi 226	Royds, Percy 66	Smart, Colin 174
Paice, David 208	Radwan, Adam 224	Royle, Arty 42	Smart, Sidney...................97
Pallant, John 162	Rafter, Mike 173	Rudd, Ted 158	Smeddle, Robert 115
Palmer, Alick 91	Ralston, Chris 167	Russell, Richard 82	Smith, Fenton 92
Palmer, Francis 80	Ramsden, Harold 65	Rutherford, Don 152	Smith, John 140
Palmer, Godfrey 114	Randall, Harry 223	Ryalls, Henry 38	Smith, Keith 170
Palmer, John 180	Ranson, John 156	Ryan, Dean 187	Smith, Marcus 223
Palmer, Tom 198	Raphael, John 77	Ryan, Peter 146	Smith, Mike 149
Pargetter, Thomas 154	Ravenscroft, John 33	Sackey, Paul 205	Smith, Ollie 201
Parker, Grahame 132	Ravenscroft, Steve 194	Sadler, Ted 126	Smith, Simon 181
Parker, Sidney 19	Rawlinson, William 23	Sagar, John 75	Smith, Stephen 151
Parling, Geoff 212	Redfern, Steve 179	Salmon, Jamie 182	Smith, Steve 170
Parsons, Ernest 133	Redman, Nigel 181	Sample, Charles 37	Smith, Trevor 142
Parsons, Jim 163	Redmond, Gerry 166	Sampson, Paul 195	Smith, Whacker 75
Patterson, Bill 153	Redwood, Bill 163	Sanders, Frank 108	Soane, Buster 54
Pattisson, Richard 36	Rees, David 193	Sanders, Sandy 145	Sobey, Wilf 121
Paul, Henry 199	Rees, Gary 180	Sanderson, Alex 198	Solomon, Bert 92
Paul, Josiah 21	Rees, Tom 205	Sanderson, Pat 194	Solomona, Denny 219
Payne, Arthur 129	Reeve, Jim 116	Sandford, Joseph 84	Sparks, Robert 114
Payne, Colin 157	Regan, Mark 189	Sangwin, Roger 156	Speed, Harry 55
Payne, John 35	Regan, Martin 144	Sargent, Gordon 177	Spence, William 49
Payne, Tim 202	Rendall, Paul 179	Savage, Keith 160	Spencer, Ben 220
Pearce, Gary 174	Rew, Henry 116	Sawyer, Charles 33	Spencer, Jeremy 160
Pears, David 187	Reynolds, Jeff 73	Saxby, Les 124	Spencer, John Southern 164
Pearson, Alec 20	Reynolds, Shirley 131	Scarbrough, Dan 201	Spong, Roger 116
Pearson, Tom 228	Rhodes, John 61	Schofield, Dean 206	Spooner, Reginald 78
Peart, Thomas 157	Ribbans, Dave 227	Schofield, John 32	Springmann, Henry 31
Pease, Frank 41	Richards, Dean 182	Scholfield, John 95	Spurling, Aubrey 35
Pennell, Chris 215	Richards, Edward 116	Schwarz, Reginald 68	Spurling, Norman 40
Penny, Sid 90	Richards, James 50	Scorfield, Edward 93	Squires, Peter 170
Penny, William 26	Richards, Peter 204	Scott, Charles 73	Stafford, Dick 96
Percival, Launcelot 50	Richards, Stephen 157	Scott, Edward 134	Stafford, William 19
Periton, Joe 110	Richardson, James 114	Scott, Frank 86	Stanbury, Edward 111
Perrott, Edward 21	Richardson, Ryder 33	Scott, Harry 147	Standing, Graham 136
Perry, David 156	Rickards, Cyril 18	Scott, John Philip 173	Stanger-Leathes,
Perry, Matt 193	Rimmer, Gordon 139	Scott, John Stanley 151	Christopher....................81
Perry, Sam 134	Rimmer, Laurie 153	Scott, Mason 41	Stark, Kendrick 112
Perry, Shaun 204	Ripley, Andy 168	Scott, William 47	Starks, Anthony 61
Peters, Jimmy 84	Risman, Bev 151	Seddon, Bob 41	Starmer-Smith, Nigel 165
Phillips, Charles 33	Ritson, John 93	Sellar, 'Monkey' 112	Start, Sydney 86
Phillips, Malcolm 150	Rittson-Thomas, George 141	Sever, Hal 130	Steeds, John 139
Pickering, Arthur 86	Robbins, Graham 182	Shackleton, Roger 165	Steele-Bodger, Micky 134
Pickering, Roger 162	Robbins, Peter 149	Sharp, Richard 152	Steinthal, Francis 97
Pickles, Reg 104	Roberts, Alan 94	Sharples, Charlie 211	Stephenson, Michael 197
Pierce, Richard 65	Roberts, Ernest 75	Shaw, Cecil 84	Stevens, Matt 201
Pilkington, William 65	Roberts, Jim 152	Shaw, Fred 65	Stevens, Stack 165
Pillman, Cherry 92	Roberts, Khaki 86	Shaw, James 66	Steward, Freddie 224
Pillman, Robert 98	Roberts, Reginald 125	Shaw, Simon 190	Still, Ernest 18
Pinch, John 61	Roberts, Sam 41	Sheasby, Chris 190	Stimpson, Tim 190
Pinching, Nipper 17	Roberts, Vic 136	Sheppard, Austin 176	Stirling, Bob 142
Pitman, James 104	Robertshaw, Rawson 39	Sheridan, Andrew 202	Stoddart, Drewy 38
Plummer, Ken 164	Robinson, Andy 184	Sherrard, Charles 15	Stoddart, Wilfred 63
Pool-Jones, Richard 194	Robinson, Arthur 42	Sherriff, George 161	Stokes, Frederic 15
Poole, Bob 62	Robinson, Ernie 148	Shewring, Harry 82	Stokes, Lennard 21
Poole, Francis 60	Robinson, Jason 197	Shields, Brad 220	Stone, Francis 98
Pope, Brian 122	Robinson, John 54	Shooter, John 67	Stoop, Adrian 81
Porter, Guy 227	Robinson, Tot 64	Shuttleworth, Dennis 143	Stoop, Tim 94
Portus, Garnet 87	Robshaw, Chris 209	Sibree, Herbert 87	Stout, Frank 63
Potter, Stuart 194	Robson, Alan 109	Silk, Nicholas 158	Stout, Percy 66
Poulton-Palmer, Ronald 91	Robson, Dan 221	Simmonds, Sam 220	Strettle, David 205
Powell, Piggy 158	Robson, Matthew 117	Simms, Kevin 181	Stringer, Nick 177
Pratten, William 113	Rodber, Tim 187	Simpson, Colin 158	Strong, Edmund 37
Preece, Ivor 137	Rodd, Bevan 226	Simpson, Joe 211	Stuart, Will 221
Preece, Peter 169	Rogers, Budge 153	Simpson, Paul 178	Sturnham, Ben 194
Preedy, Malcolm 180	Rogers, John 48	Simpson, Thomas 78	Summerscale, George 82
Prentice, Doug 114	Rogers, Walter 80	Simpson-Daniel, James 201	Sutcliffe, John 47
Prescott, Robin 131	Rokoduguni, Semesa 216	Sims, Dave 195	Swarbrick, David 135
Preston, Nick 176	Rollitt, Dave 162	Sinckler, Kyle 218	Swayne, Deneys 122
Price, John 153	Roncoroni, Anthony 126	Singleton, Jack 221	Swayne, Jack 115
Price, Leo 104	Rose, Marcus 177	Skinner, Mickey 183	Swift, Tony 177
Price, Petley 24	Rossborough, Peter 167	Skirving, Ben 206	Syddall, Jim 178
Price, Tom 137	Rosser, David 158	Slade, Henry 216	Sykes, Alexander 99
Probyn, Jeff 183	Rotherham, Alan 36	Sladen, Geoffrey 115	Sykes, Frank 147
Prout, Derek 163	Rotherham, Arthur 65	Sleightholme, Jon 190	Sykes, Patrick 138
Pullin, John 160	Roughley, David 170	Slemen, Mike 173	Syrett, Ron 150

Tait, Mathew 203	Twynam, Henry 31	Watkins, John 133	Willis, Tom 228
Tallent, John 123	Ubogu, Victor 187	Watkins, John 169	Wilson, Arthur 91
Tanner, Christopher 121	Umaga, Jacob 224	Watson, Anthony 216	Wilson, Charles 34
Tarr, Frank 90	Underhill, Sam 219	Watson, Bungy 98	Wilson, Charles 65
Tatham, William 35	Underwood, Martin 154	Watson, Fischer 88	Wilson, David 209
Taylor, Arthur 36	Underwood, Rory 179	Watt, Dave 162	Wilson, Guy 115
Taylor, Bob 160	Underwood, Tony 187	Webb, Charles 124	Wilson, Mark 219
Taylor, Ernest 52	Unwin, Geoffrey 66	Webb, James 112	Wilson, Roger 50
Taylor, Henry 31	Unwin, Jimmy 131	Webb, Jon 183	Wilson, Tug 144
Taylor, John 64	Uren, Dick 137	Webb, Larry 151	Wilson, Tug 156
Taylor, Noddy 147	Uttley, Roger 170	Webb, Rod 162	Wilson, Walter 86
Taylor, Sos 102	Vainikolo, Lesley 207	Webber, Rob 212	Winn, Chris 143
Taylor, Tim 98	Valentine, Jim 48	Webster, Jan 168	Winterbottom, Peter 177
Taylor, Tommy 218	van Gisbergen, Mark 203	Wedge, Thomas 86	Winters, Roy 206
Te'o, Ben 218	van Poortvliet, Jack 227	Weighill, Bob 136	Wintle, Trevor 161
Teague, Mike 182	van Ryneveld, Clive 139	Wells, Cyril 54	Wodehouse, Norman 94
Teden, Derek 133	Vanderspar, Charles 18	Wells, Harry 226	Wood, Albert 38
Teggin, Alfred 37	Varley, Harry 52	West, Bryan 163	Wood, Alf 87
Tetley, Thomas 23	Varndell, Tom 204	West, Dorian 193	Wood, Bob 55
Thomas, Charles 60	Vassall, Harry 34	West, Richard 189	Wood, Martyn 198
Thomas, Henry 214	Vassall, Jumbo 88	Weston, Henry 76	Wood, Pedlar 98
Thompson, Peter 149	Vaughan-Jones, Arthur 125	Weston, Lionel 168	Wood, Robert 76
Thompson, Steve 199	Vaughan, Douglas 137	Weston, Mike 152	Wood, Tom 211
Thomson, George 25	Verelst, Courteney 22	Weston, William 126	Woodgate, Elliott 143
Thomson, Wardlaw 51	Vernon, George 25	Wheatley, Arthur 131	Woodhead, Ernie 32
Thorley, Ollie 222	Vesty, Sam 209	Wheatley, Harold 130	Woodman, Trevor 196
Thorne, John 155	Vickery, George 81	Wheeler, Peter 171	Woodruff, Peter 142
Tindall, Mike 196	Vickery, Phil 193	White-Cooper, Steve 198	Woods, Samuel 48
Tindall, Vic 142	Vivyan, Elliott 75	White, Colin 178	Woods, Tom 102
Titterrell, Andy 202	Voyce, Tom 102	White, Don 135	Woods, Tommy 88
Tobin, Frank 15	Voyce, Tom 198	White, Julian 196	Woodward, Clive 143
Todd, Alexander 74	Vunipola, Billy 214	Whiteley, Eric 123	Woodward, Ted 176
Todd, Robert 24	Vunipola, Mako 213	Whiteley, Willie 62	Wooldridge, Charles 36
Toft, Herbert 130	Vyvyan, Hugh 202	Whitley, Herbert 115	Wordsworth, Alan 171
Tomkins, Joel 215	Wackett, John 151	Wigglesworth, Henry 38	Worsley, Joe 196
Toothill, Jack 49	Wade, Christian 214	Wigglesworth, Richard 207	Worsley, Mike 201
Tosswill, Leonard 77	Wade, Greg 36	Wightman, Brian 151	Worton, John 111
Touzel, Charles 24	Wade, Mike 154	Wilkins, Squire 142	Wrench, David 157
Towell, Allan 138	Wakefield, Wavell 101	Wilkinson, Bob 172	Wright, Cyril 91
Travers, Jika 135	Walder, Dave 197	Wilkinson, Edgar 40	Wright, Frank 34
Treadwell, Bill 161	Waldrom, Thomas 213	Wilkinson, Harry 47	Wright, Ian 167
Trick, David 178	Walker, Gus 133	Wilkinson, Harry 115	Wright, James 48
Tristram, Henry 37	Walker, Harry 135	Wilkinson, Jonny 193	Wright, Jock 101
Troop, Carlton 126	Walker, Jack 227	Wilkinson, Percy 17	Wright, John 127
Tucker, Bill 111	Walker, Roger 20	Willcocks, Thomas 77	Wright, Peter 153
Tucker, Sam 103	Wallens, Jack 113	Willcox, John 153	Wyatt, Derek 172
Tucker, William 55	Walshe, Nick 204	William-Powlett, Peveril 104	Yarde, Marland 215
Tuilagi, Manu 211	Walton, Katie 75	Williams, Chris 173	Yarranton, Peter 145
Turner-Hall, Jordan 212	Walton, William 55	Williams, Cyril 93	Yates, Kevin 192
Turner, Dawson 15	Ward, George 97	Williams, Harry 218	Yiend, William 47
Turner, Edward 22	Ward, Herbert 61	Williams, John 143	Young, Arthur 109
Turner, George 23	Ward, James 34	Williams, Johnny 146	Young, John 150
Turner, Henry 15	Ward, John 61	Williams, Peter 103	Young, Malcolm 173
Turner, Martin 137	Wardlow, Chris 165	Williams, Samuel 77	Young, Peter 145
Turner, Stuart 206	Warfield, Peter 169	Williams, Stanley 95	Youngs, Ben 210
Turquand-Young, David 114	Warr, Tim 127	Williamson, Rupert 88	Youngs, Nick 178
Twelvetrees, Billy 214	Waters, Fraser 198	Willis, Jack 222	Youngs, Tom 213

Got a book in you?

Victor PUBLISHING

This book is published by Victor Publishing.

Victor Publishing specialises in getting new and independent writers' work published worldwide in both paperback and Kindle format.

We also look to re-publish titles that were previously published but have now gone out of circulation or off-sale.

If you have a manuscript for a book (or have previously published a now off-sale title) of any genre (fiction, non-fiction, autobiographical, biographical or even reference or photographic/illustrative) and would like information on how you can get your work published and on sale in print and digitally, please visit us at:

www.victorpublishing.co.uk

or get in touch at:

enquiries@victorpublishing.co.uk

Printed in Great Britain
by Amazon